TEACHER'S EDITION

JUNTOS

UNO

PRENTICE HALL
Simon & Schuster Education Group
A VIACOM COMPANY

PRENTICE HALL STAFF CREDITS

Director of Foreign Languages: Marina Liapunov

Director of Marketing: Karen Ralston

Project Support: Julie Demori

Advertising and Promotion: Carol Leslie, Alfonso Manosalvas, Rip Odell

Business Office: Emily Heins

Design: Jim O'Shea, AnnMarie Roselli

Editorial: Guillermo Lawton-Alfonso, José A. Peláez, Generosa Gina Protano,
Barbara T. Stone .

Manufacturing and Inventory Planning: Katherine Clarke, Rhett Conklin

Media Resources: Libby Forsyth, Maritza Puello

National Consultants: Camille Wiersgalla, Mary J. Secrest

Permissions: Doris Robinson

Product Development Operations: Laura Sanderson

Production: Janice L. Lalley

Sales Operations: Hans Spengler

Technology Development: Richard Ferrie

ISBN 0-13-415571-8

1 2 3 4 5 6 7 8 9 10 00 99 98 97

PRENTICE HALL
Simon & Schuster Education Group
A VIACOM COMPANY

JUNTOS
THE PHILOSPHY

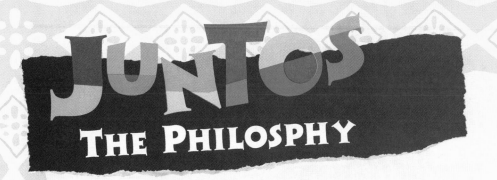

Juntos reflects the vision and philosophy of the **Standards for Foreign Language Learning** developed by the American Council on the Teaching of Foreign Languages and the American Association of Teachers of Spanish, as well as other second-language associations.

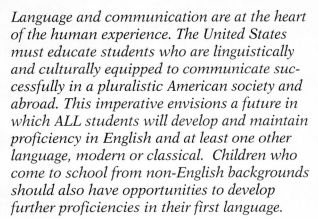

Language and communication are at the heart of the human experience. The United States must educate students who are linguistically and culturally equipped to communicate successfully in a pluralistic American society and abroad. This imperative envisions a future in which ALL students will develop and maintain proficiency in English and at least one other language, modern or classical. Children who come to school from non-English backgrounds should also have opportunities to develop further proficiencies in their first language.

The **Standards** identifies five goals of foreign language education: Communication, Cultures, Connections, Comparisons, and Communities. These principles provide the framework for understanding the goals of **Juntos**.

JUNTOS
THE GOALS

COMMUNICATION

Communication is the central goal, the heart, of second language learning.

The **Juntos** plan encourages students to speak Spanish from the first day! They will understand, talk, read, and write Spanish, immediately taking their first important steps toward developing communicative proficiency and confidence.

CULTURE

Through the study of a second language, students begin to understand and appreciate the diversity of the many cultures of people who speak the language.

In **Juntos**, the Spanish language and cultures are woven together into one tapestry using video segments, literature, photographs, art, and original articles from newspapers and magazines.

CONNECTIONS

Through the study of a second language, students will access new information and explore issues related to many other disciplines.

In ***Juntos***, students investigate content and issues such as the environment, the pyramids and other ancient ruins, hiero-glyphs, animals, plants, poetry, sports, fashion, fitness, music, and art.

COMPARISONS

Studying a second language leads invariably to important comparisons of cultures and language.

In ***Juntos***, students directly compare and contrast cultures, customs, literature, and languages as they begin to reach a better understanding of their own language and cultures.

COMMUNITIES

The concept of "community" is redefined. In the context of second-language study and the reality of world cultures, the focus should be "communities" within our pluralistic society.

Juntos celebrates the diversity of world communities while helping students gain a new

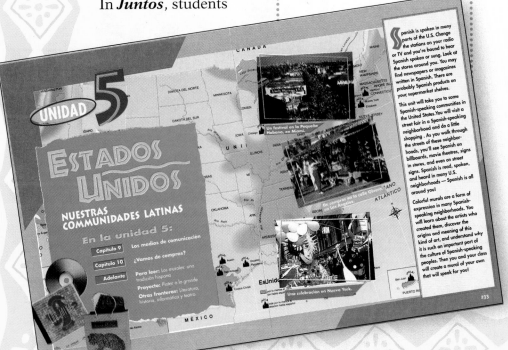

HOW THE PROGRAM WORKS

Juntos is a multi-media three-level Spanish program. The plan for the program is based on surveys, questionnaires, conferences, meetings, and one-on-one discussions with thousands of teachers nationwide.

At levels one and two, the program structure is based on six units, each containing two chapters followed by a special cultural section called *Adelante*.

THE UNIT:
THE CULTURAL SETTING

Each unit is situated in a country or region of the world where Spanish is spoken: Central and South America, the Caribbean, Spain, and the special regions of the United States with a large Hispanic population.

The location is integral to the topics of each of the two chapters in the unit. It forms the basis for the theme, the vocabulary, the activities, readings, and all other authentic material included in the unit.

If you like water sports, you will like Puerto Rico. It has 300 miles of shoreline and just about every water sport from scuba diving to parasailing. And you can enjoy these sports almost every day of the year because Puerto Rico has a tropical climate.

In Puerto Rico you can find colonial-style towns, modern cities, and a tropical rain forest. And there is El Morro, a sixteenth-century fortress that guards San Juan harbor.

The original inhabitants of Puerto Rico were the Tainos, who came to the Caribbean from South America. In 1508 Puerto Rico was colonized by Spain. Today, Puerto Rico is a commonwealth of the United States.

This unit will be your guide to Puerto Rico. You will visit the beaches, explore the rainforest, and get plenty of sun. See you at the beach! Terrific! ¡Qué chévere!

El castillo de El Morro en San Juan, Puerto Rico.

137

CAPÍTULO 5

ARENA, SOL Y MAR

Objetivos

COMUNICACIÓN
To talk about:
• sports and activities you want to do
• sports and activities you know how to do
• the beach and water sports

CULTURA
To learn about:
• leisure activities of Puerto Rican teenagers
• baseball in Puerto Rico
• key locations in Puerto Rico using a map

VOCABULARIO TEMÁTICO
To know the expressions for:
• beach activities
• water sports
• sports equipment
• things to take to the beach

ESTRUCTURA
To talk about:
• what you know how to do: the verb *saber* with the infinitive of another verb
• what you want to do: the verb *querer* with the infinitive of another verb

¿SABES QUE...?

Puerto Rico is part of the U.S., but not a state in the traditional sense. It is called an *Estado Libre Asociado*, or "Free Associated State." Puerto Ricans are American citizens. They elect a governor and a legislature as in any other state, but they do not elect national representatives or senators. Instead, Puerto Ricans choose a Presidential Commissioner who speaks for them, but who may not vote in the U.S. Congress.

Hacer surf es muy popular en Puerto Rico.

138

139

in Puerto Rico; the environment is explored in Costa Rica; fashion is the focus in Madrid, Spain.

ADELANTE:

AN IMMERSION IN CULTURE

The *Adelante* section closes each unit. Its central focus is a high-interest, culturally rich article called *Del mundo hispano*. Within the *Adelante* section, there are reading strategies and comprehension activities, writing suggestions, a hands-on project, and several short informative articles that cross other areas of the curriculum, including history, science, math, art, and literature. *Adelante* is the culmination of the unit and the integration of all of the learning that has occurred.

THE CHAPTER:

THE COMMUNICATIVE CORE OF THE PROGRAM

Within the unit, the two chapters are related to each other by theme: fashion and fitness, beach sports and weather, recent news events and today's technology, planning a foreign exchange trip and then taking it!

The theme fits the location. Beach sports are centered

ADELANTE

ANTES DE LEER

El Yunque es un bosque tropical cerca de San Juan, Puerto Rico. Tiene más de° 28.000 acres y una gran variedad de flora y fauna.
Mira las páginas 174-177. Según las fotos y los títulos,° ¿cuál es el tema principal de este artículo?
a. serpientes y otros reptiles
b. un bosque tropical
c. cómo sacar fotos en un bosque

◄ La cotorra puertorriqueña es un ave en peligro de extinción.

◄ En El Yunque hay flores exóticas, como las orquídeas.

◄ El coquí es una rana muy pequeña.

175

JUNTOS
MANAGING SECOND LANGUAGE LEARNING

Managing second language learning is one of the greatest challenges in high school education. **Juntos** addresses each challenge directly and effectively.

1 The challenge: *The goal of language learning is communication, which means extensive student involvement within the classroom.*

Juntos *responds by getting students motivated.*

• The topics of the chapter themes rank high on the interest survey conducted among high school students. Because students care about the topics, they will make the effort to communicate.

• From the very beginning, students are asked to respond from their own personal experience, to express their own opinions and points of view, and to think critically.

• Every activity is designed specifically to move students towards proficiency.

2 The challenge: *Language learning requires constant grouping and regrouping of students in pairs and small groups, and then back to full class discussions.*

Juntos *responds with activities that are designed to work both in pairs and in small group settings:*

• Directions are simple and clear so that students know how to get started without constant teacher intervention.

• Students reviewed all of the activities in **Juntos** to determine interest level and clarity.

• Activities specifically address the desired grouping.

• There are communicative models on every page that get students started.

• Prompts and hints provide support to students working with each other.

• The Teacher's Edition further identifies the suggested grouping plan for the activities.

The challenge: *The range of ability levels in a second-language classroom is likely to be greater than in any other course.* A typical classroom may include college-bound high achievers and students with limited academic aspirations. There may be students who speak Spanish as their first language and those who have never heard it before. Students too shy to talk comfortably when speaking English are asked to communicate orally in Spanish. Additionally, the range of interests and language-learning abilities may be wide.

Juntos *addresses the individual needs of all students.*

• Every activity is designed to encourage the success of all students.

• For students uncomfortable speaking in a group, the many paired activities offer a protected setting for developing confidence and competence.

• The Tutor Pages provide a structure for more able students or native speakers to help other students develop vocabulary, structure, and communicative competence.

• The Teacher's Edition suggests specific approaches for students having difficulty.

• Strategies for drawing upon the resources of native speakers to help learners who are having difficulty are offered in the Teacher's Edition.

The challenge: *Addressing different learning modalities is critical to language learning.*

Juntos *provides a full range of activities to accommodate visual, auditory, and kinesthetic learners.*

• Within each section, the activities provide variety and balance, including dialogs, surveys, roleplaying, writing, hands-on projects, art projects, and demonstration or TPR activities.

• A regular feature of the Teacher's Edition called **Reaching all students** offers specific guidelines for addressing the auditory, kinesthetic, and visual learners.

• Among the sections of each chapter, the variety of approaches supports all students. For the auditory learner, **Conversemos** explores theme and vocabulary through discussion. **Realidades** and **Palabras en acción** give students who need a visual approach. For students who learn by doing, the **Para resolver** and **Manos a la obra** projects are especially effective.

THE CHAPTER ORGANIZATION

Every chapter in levels one and two has ten sections:

OBJECTIVOS

The objectives provide an overview of the chapter and the basis for evaluating student progress. At a glance, teachers can review how the communicative, cultural, vocabulary, and structure objectives are interrelated.

CONVERSEMOS

Students get involved in the communicative objectives of the chapter, using the vocabulary and structure, and discovering the theme.

REALIDADES

Magazine and newspaper articles, journals, and other authentic informative materials link the host country or region to the chapter objectives. Follow-up group activities, including surveys, diagrams, graphic organizers, and debates, give students further opportunity to put the objectives into practice.

PALABRAS EN ACCIÓN

A lively illustration with labeled vocabulary and dialog in context supports the students' exploration of the chapter objectives. A variety of paired and small group activities

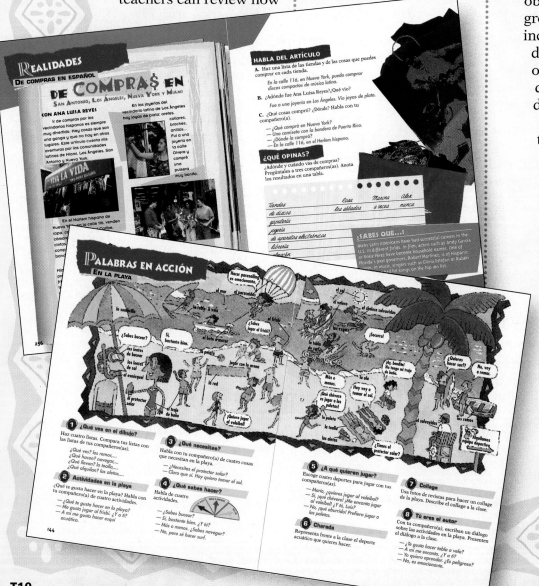

offer auditory, visual, and kinesthetic learning through dialogs, collages, writing, and roleplay situations.

Para Comunicarnos Mejor

The communicative approach to explaining and practicing Spanish structure offers hands-on grammar activities with a personal focus. Students continue to develop their communicative skills, drawing from their own experiences, making choices, and selecting preferred options.

Situaciones

Several authentic realia-based activities develop students' critical thinking skills while integrating the vocabulary and structure topics that they have learned.

Para Resolver

This group problem-solving project offers students a chance to explore the cultures of a region, to expand their knowledge of the country, and to apply the

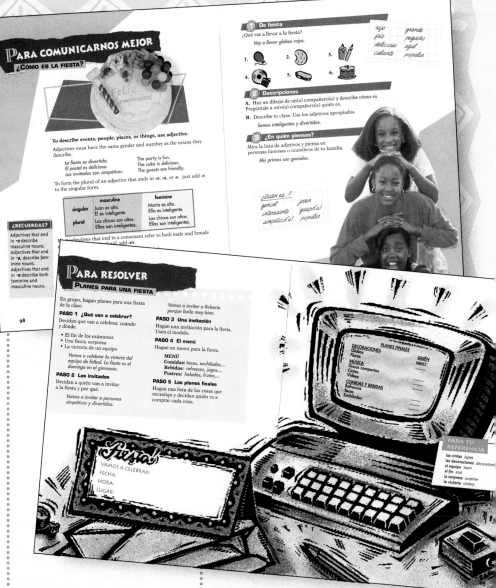

chapter's objectives.

Entérate

This cultural reading extends the topic of the chapter and offers additional vocabulary-building opportunities.

Vocabulario Temático

Organized into natural thematic categories, the active vocabulary of the chapter is summarized for handy reference and additional practice.

La Conexión Inglés-Español

Making comparisons with English words that students already know and the chapter vocabu-

SPECIAL COMPONENTS

- **Activity Magazines**
- **Activity Book**
- **Teaching Resources (Tutor Pages and Activity Support Pages)**
- **Color Transparencies and Teacher's Guide**
  - **Activity Kit**

ACTIVITY MAGAZINES

Twelve engaging and colorful magazines provide a special spotlight on the countries or regions featured in the student textbooks and videos. Designed to extend students' knowledge of customs and cultures while providing additional reading, the magazines have regular features that moti-vate students to communicate in Spanish.

ACTIVITY BOOK

The Activity Book is linked directly to the student textbook, providing opportunities to reinforce the communicative and cultural objectives for the program. Appropriate for either classwork or homework, the activity book provides written practice of topics presented in the student text, as well as special study guides for the articles in the *Adelante* section.

TEACHING RESOURCES: ACTIVITIES—TUTOR PAGES

The Tutor Pages offer practical suggestions to guide more able students or native speakers to help their classmates who need a boost. Students of different abilities are engaged through the Tutor Pages to work together in a focused and productive interaction Tutors assign a writing activity or initiate a conversation and check "their" student's progress using the answers and hints provided. Each Tutor Page ends with an extension activity that allows students to go beyond the initial assignment.

TEACHING RESOURCES: ACTIVITIES

The Teaching Resources Binder includes a section of activities that

Filled with lesson plan and specific ideas for managing the classroom, this guide was designed to save the busy teacher hours of time. In addition, specific suggestions are included for schools using block scheduling for second-language classrooms.

survey forms, worksheets, and additional cultural information. These pages are correlated to the *Actividades* section of the Teacher's Edition.

COLOR TRANSPARENCIES AND TEACHER'S GUIDE

Transparencies include project summaries, fine art, photos, locator maps, dialog trees, language activities, and thematically related discussion starters—all designed for the teacher's use with small groups or the entire class. The accompanying Guide Book offers suggestions for using each type of transparency, as well as specific pages to be reproduced for student use.

THE ACTIVITY KIT

The Activity Kit makes a variety of realia from the program available to students. It includes maps, communication cards, schedules, recipes, and money.

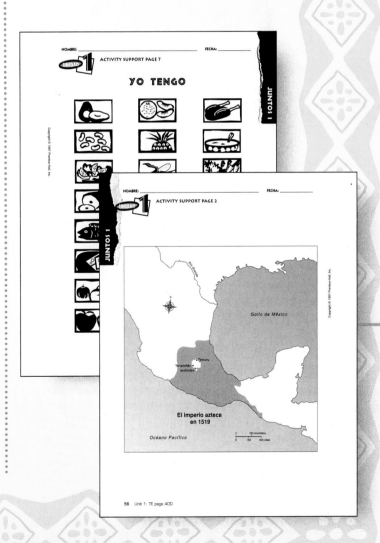

JUNTOS

ASSESSMENT COMPONENTS

- **Teaching Resources**
  Assessment Checklists
  Chapter Tests
  Oral Proficiency Suggestions
  Portfolio Assessment
  Listening Comprehension
- **Audio CDs/Audio Cassettes**
- **Computer Test Bank**
  (software and booklet)

ASSESSMENT CHECKLISTS

Because *Juntos* places self-assessment high on the list of priorities, students take responsibility for evaluating their own progress as they communicate in Spanish.

CHAPTER TESTS

Comprehensive chapter tests thoroughly assess students' understanding of the structure and vocabulary objectives introduced in the chapter.

ORAL PROFICIENCY

Several oral proficiency situations offer teachers a strategy for evaluating student proficiency in an informal activity.

PORTFOLIO ASSESSMENT

Guidelines and suggestions for helping students to select work for their portfolios insures an excellent long-term and qualitative way to evaluate student progress.

LISTENING COMPREHENSION

To assess students' listening comprehension, scripts and activities are included in the Assessment materials. If preferred, teachers can use the audiotape cassette to narrate the comprehension script.

COMPUTER TEST BANK

The computer test bank offers teachers additional options for assessing students' progress in a software format.

JUNTOS

SPECIAL COMPONENTS FOR SPANISH-SPEAKERS

- **Conexiones**
- **Conexiones Teacher's Guide**
- **Cuaderno**
- **Audio cassette/ Audio CDs**

CONEXIONES: LECTURAS PARA HISPANOHABLANTES

This highly illustrated reader is designed both for students who speak Spanish as their first language and for more advanced second-language learners. It is divided into twelve chapters, each with the same theme as the chapters in the student text. The reader includes authentic short stories, poems, legends, and nonfiction articles that reflect and support the cultures of Spanish-speaking people.

CONEXIONES TEACHER'S GUIDE

The Teacher's Guide includes suggestions and activities to introduce, guide, and extend each selection contained in *Conexiones*. Discussion suggestions based on chapter themes are included with graphic organizers that provide tools for student analysis of the works that they read.

CUADERNO PARA HISPANOHABLANTES

This workbook provides additional practice and extends the activities of the student text, but also offers specific suggestions for the student who speaks Spanish as a first language but may need special support to develop writing, structure, and spelling skills. Additionally, every chapter offers activities for improving study skills.

AUDIO CDs/ AUDIO CASSETTES

Selected short stories and poems from *Conexiones* are included on these audio components. They are designed to improve the students' reading fluency and speed and to enhance their appreciation for and pride in the beauty of the spoken language.

JUNTOS TECHNOLOGY COMPONENTS

- Videotapes/Videodiscs
- Video Activity Books
- Audio CDs/Audio cassettes
- Teaching Resources: Audio Scripts and Activities
- CD-ROM

VIDEOTAPES/VIDEODISCS

Filmed on location in Mexico, Central and South America, the Caribbean, Spain, and in the U.S. locations featured in the Student Text, each unit of the video includes "realia" drawn from documentaries, advertisements, news and weather reports, music videos, and sports events. Hosted by high school students in each country, these non-scripted videos support the chapter and unit themes and offer students a direct look at the cultures and lifestyles of young people in each region. The language is natural and the conversation real. Each video contains five different segments:

• the cultural introduction to the host country or region;

• two theme-based segments, one for each of the two chapters of the unit;

• a cultural video magazine based on the *Adelante* section;

• the unit project, *Manos a la obra*.

VIDEO ACTIVITY BOOKS

The Video Activity Books include the transcripts for each of the videos as well as activity pages for students' use while watching the videos.

AUDIO CDs/AUDIO CASSETTES

The audio components of the program support the communicative, vocabulary, and structure objectives of each level. Readings of stories, articles, and poems add to the students' opportunity to hear spoken Spanish.

AUDIO SCRIPTS AND ACTIVITIES

The scripts for the chapter audio tapes are included in the Teaching Resources Book with specific activities to provide listening comprehension practice.

CD-ROM

The interactive CD-ROM includes video, animations, and maps. Designed to encourage further exploration of the chapter concepts, the CD-ROM can be used in individual and small group settings.

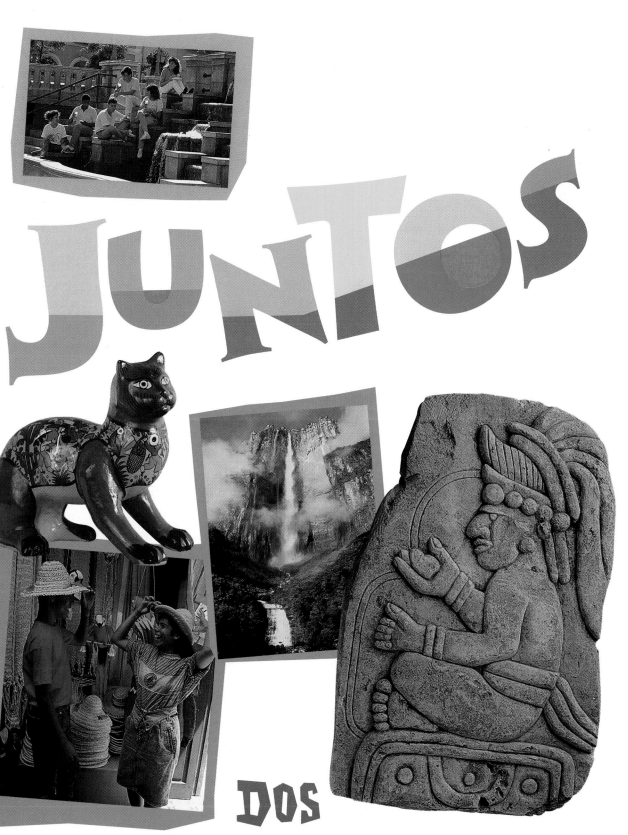

JUNTOS

DOS

PRENTICE HALL
Simon & Schuster Education Group
A VIACOM COMPANY

PRENTICE HALL STAFF CREDITS

Director of Foreign Languages: Marina Liapunov

Director of Marketing: Karen Ralston

Project Support: Julie Demori

Advertising and Promotion: Carol Leslie, Alfonso Manosalvas, Rip Odell

Business Office: Emily Heins

Design: Jim O'Shea, AnnMarie Roselli

Editorial: Guillermo Lawton-Alfonso, José A. Peláez, Generosa Gina Protano,

Barbara T. Stone

Manufacturing and Inventory Planning: Katherine Clarke, Rhett Conklin

Media Resources: Libby Forsyth, Maritza Puello

National Consultants: Camille Wiersgalla, Mary J. Secrest

Permissions: Doris Robinson

Product Development Operations: Laura Sanderson

Production: Janice L. Lalley

Sales Operations: Hans Spengler

Technology Development: Richard Ferrie

ISBN 0-13-415662-5

1 2 3 4 5 6 7 8 9 10 00 99 98 97

PRENTICE HALL
Simon & Schuster Education Group
A VIACOM COMPANY

PROGRAM ADVISORS

Pat Barr-Harrison
Prince George's County Public Schools
Upper Marlboro, MD

Jacqueline Benevento
Rowan College
Glassboro, NJ

Christine Brown
Glastonbury Public Schools
Glastonbury, CT

Celeste Carr
Howard County Public Schools
Ellicott City, MD

Jo Anne Engelbert
Montclair State University
Montclair, NJ

Maria J. Fierro-Treviño
Northside Independent School District
San Antonio, TX

Sol Gaitan
The Dalton School
New York, NY

Charles Hancock
Ohio State University
Columbus, OH

Mary Ann Hansen
Connecticut State Department
of Education
Hartford, CT

William Jassey
Norwalk Public Schools
Norwalk, CT

Dora Kennedy
University of Maryland
College Park, MD

Jacqueline M. Kiraithe-Cordova
California State University
Fullerton, CA

Guillermo Lawton-Alfonso
Universidad de la Habana
Habana, Cuba
Columbia University, NY

Douglas Morgenstern
Massachusetts Institute of Technology
Cambridge, MA

Bert J. Neumaier
Farmington Public High School
Farmington, CT

Edward Powe
The University of Wisconsin
Madison, WI

Ramon Santiago
Lehman College
Bronx, NY

Carol Barnett
Forest Hills High School
Forest Hills, NY

Barbara Bennett
District of Columbia Public Schools
Washington, D.C

Linda Bigler
Thomas Jeffferson High School
Fairfax County, VA

Felix Cortez
The Dalton School
New York, NY

Yolanda Fernandes
Montgomery County Public Schools
Rockville, MD

Cindy Gerstl
Prince George's County Public Schools
Upper Marlboro, MD

Hilda Montemayor Gleason
Fairfax County Public Schools
Alexandria, VA

Leslie Grahn
Prince George's County Public Schools
Upper Marlboro, MD

Mark Grudzien
West Hartford Public Schools
West Hartford, CT

Adriana Montemayor Ivy
Denver Public Schools
Denver, CO

Judith Katzman
West Hartford Public Schools
West Hartford, CT

Delia Garcia Menocal
Emerson High School
Emerson, NJ

Ruth Rivera
Prince George's County Public Schools
Upper Marlboro, MD

Mónica Alpacs
Lima, Peru

Virginia Álvarez
Santo Domingo, Dominican Republic

Lola Aranda
Mexico City, Mexico

Gloria Beretervide
Buenos Aires, Argentina

Andrés Chávez
Los Angeles, CA

Chris Chávez
Chicago, IL

Manuel Coronado
Madrid, Spain

Linda Cuellar
San Antonio, Texas

Eric Delgado
San Juan, Puerto Rico

Carmen Franchi
Miami, FL

José Hernandez
San Jose, Costa Rica

Diana Martínez
Los Angeles, CA

Kurt and Christine Rosenthal
Lima, Peru

Lita Vértiz
Mexico City, Mexico

CONTENIDO

¡BIENVENIDOS!

ENCUENTROS

TELÉFONO

autobús

VIII

UNIDAD **2**

TEXAS: CONSERVANDO LA HERENCIA HISPANA

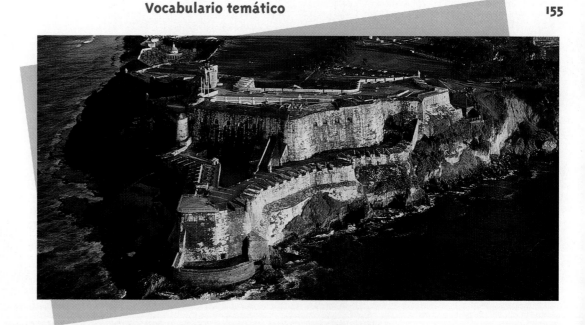

CAPÍTULO 6 ¿CÓMO TE AFECTA EL TIEMPO? 156

ADELANTE   174

UNIDAD 4

ESPAÑA DÍA A DÍA

184

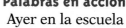

ADELANTE   222

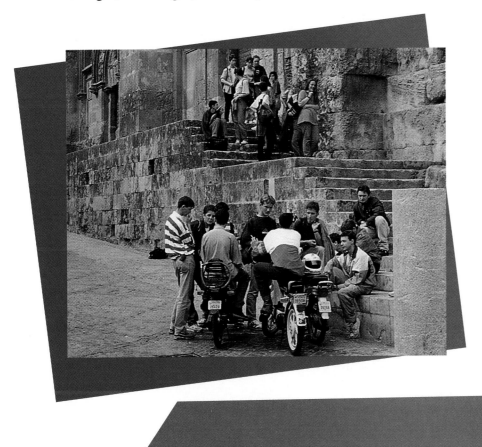

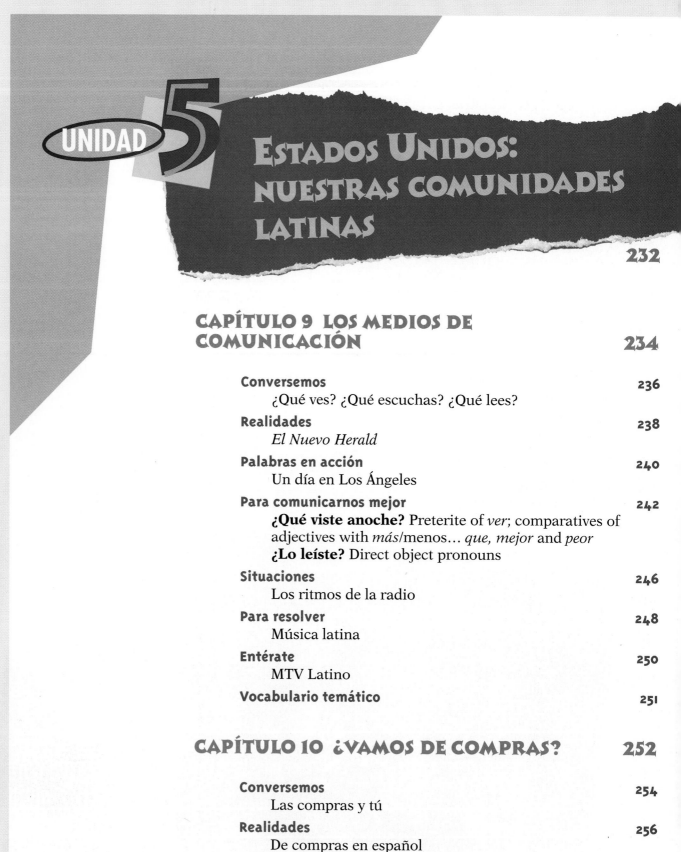

UNIDAD 5

ESTADOS UNIDOS: NUESTRAS COMUNIDADES LATINAS

232

ADELANTE   270

XVIII

XIX

BIENVENIDOS AL MUNDO HISPANO

You are about to begin a great journey into the language and culture of the Spanish-speaking world. As you start to communicate in Spanish, you will get acquainted with many of the countries and cities of the world where people speak Spanish — a world of 300 million people that spans 20 countries, three continents, and numerous islands. The doors that will open to you could very well make your life more exciting and rewarding.

Buen viaje! Have a good trip!

WHERE IN THE WORLD?

In the section that follows, you will find maps that highlight countries of the world where people speak Spanish. The maps will give you information about the countries: the name of the country in Spanish, its location, geographic landforms, and the products and wildlife that you will find there. Enjoy studying the maps as you think about where in the world you would want to visit.

MAPS AND TABLES

• Population Statistics
• Geographic Landforms Use in the Maps
• Symbols Used in the Maps
• Map of Spain
• Map of South America
• Map of Mexico, Central America, and the Caribbean
• Map of the U.S.
• Map of the World

Population Statistics (Countries where Spanish is the Primary Language)

Country	Population	Country	Population
Mexico	86,170,000	Bolivia	7,411,000
Spain	39,200,000	Dominican Republic	7,591,000
Columbia	35,600,000	El Salvador	5,635,000
Argentina	33,900,000	Honduras	5,164,000
Peru	22,900,000	Paraguay	5,003,000
Venezuela	19,085,000	Nicaragua	3,932,000
Chile	14,000,000	Puerto Rico	3,500,000
Cuba	10,900,000	Uruguay	3,200,000
Ecuador	11,055,000	Costa Rica	3,200,000
Guatemala	9,705,000	Panama	2,500,000

GEOGRAPHIC LANDFORMS USED IN THE MAPS

On the pages that follow, you will find maps illustrated with geographic landforms. For reference, the landforms that appear in these maps are illustrated below with the name of each feature in Spanish.

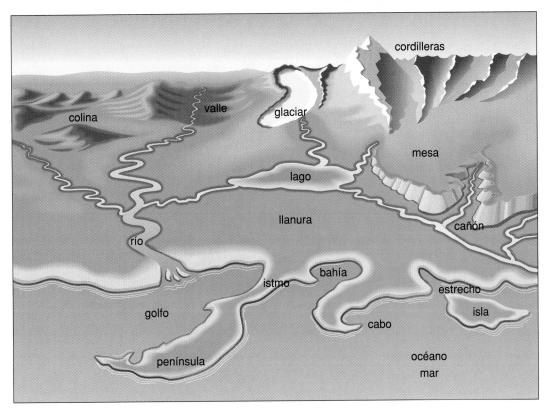

SYMBOLS USED IN THE MAPS

The maps that follow contain symbols that will give you a glimpse of the agricultural products, industries, and animals that you will likely see when you visit the region.

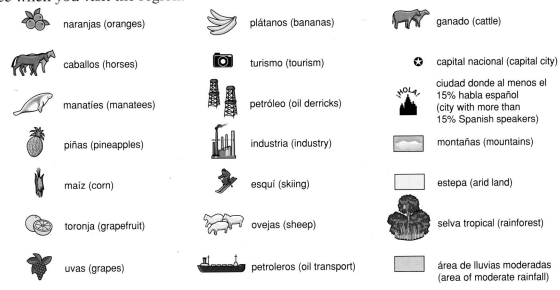

naranjas (oranges)

plátanos (bananas)

ganado (cattle)

caballos (horses)

turismo (tourism)

capital nacional (capital city)

manatíes (manatees)

petróleo (oil derricks)

ciudad donde al menos el 15% habla español (city with more than 15% Spanish speakers)

piñas (pineapples)

industria (industry)

montañas (mountains)

maíz (corn)

esquí (skiing)

estepa (arid land)

toronja (grapefruit)

ovejas (sheep)

selva tropical (rainforest)

uvas (grapes)

petroleros (oil transport)

área de lluvias moderadas (area of moderate rainfall)

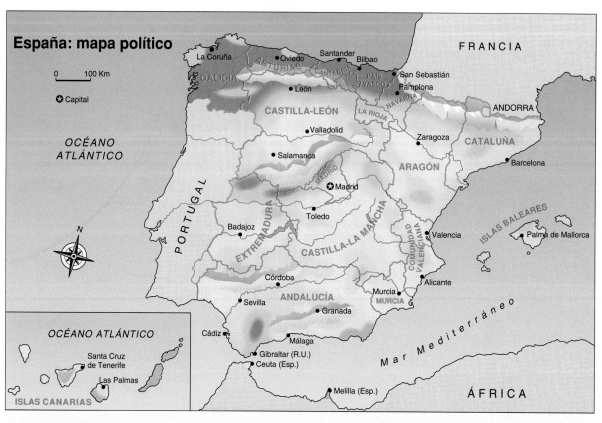

España: mapa político

0   100 Km

⊛ Capital

OCÉANO
ATLÁNTICO

FRANCIA

La Coruña   Oviedo   Santander   Bilbao
GALICIA   ASTURIAS   CANTABRIA   PAÍS VASCO   San Sebastián
León   Pamplona
NAVARRA
ANDORRA
CASTILLA-LEÓN   LA RIOJA
Valladolid   Zaragoza   CATALUÑA
Salamanca   ARAGÓN   Barcelona
MADRID
⊛ Madrid
PORTUGAL
Toledo
EXTREMADURA
Badajoz   CASTILLA-LA MANCHA   COMUNIDAD VALENCIANA   Valencia   ISLAS BALEARES   Palma de Mallorca
Alicante
Córdoba   Murcia
ANDALUCÍA   MURCIA
Sevilla   Granada
Cádiz   Málaga
Gibraltar (R.U.)
Ceuta (Esp.)
Melilla (Esp.)   ÁFRICA

Mar Mediterráneo

N

OCÉANO ATLÁNTICO
Santa Cruz
de Tenerife
Las Palmas
ISLAS CANARIAS

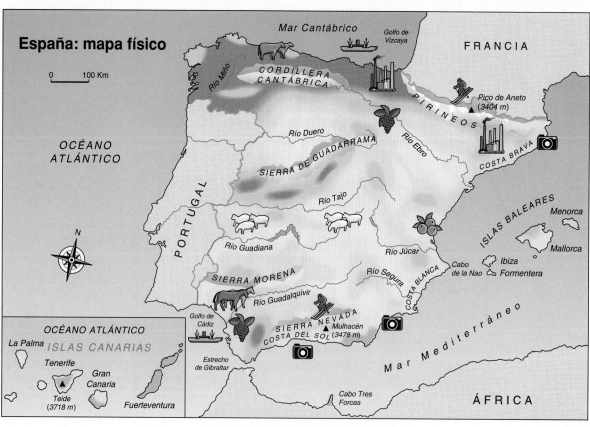

España: mapa físico

0   100 Km

OCÉANO
ATLÁNTICO

Mar Cantábrico   Golfo de Vizcaya
FRANCIA

Río Miño
CORDILLERA CANTÁBRICA
PIRINEOS
Pico de Aneto (3404 m)
Río Duero
SIERRA DE GUADARRAMA
Río Ebro
COSTA BRAVA
Río Tajo
PORTUGAL
ISLAS BALEARES   Menorca
Río Guadiana   Río Júcar
Mallorca
SIERRA MORENA
Río Segura
Cabo de la Nao   Ibiza
COSTA BLANCA   Formentera
Río Guadalquivir
SIERRA NEVADA   Mulhacén (3478 m)
Golfo de Cádiz
COSTA DEL SOL
Estrecho de Gibraltar
Cabo Tres Forcas
ÁFRICA

N

Mar Mediterráneo

OCÉANO ATLÁNTICO
La Palma   ISLAS CANARIAS
Tenerife
Gran Canaria
Teide (3718 m)
Fuerteventura

XXII

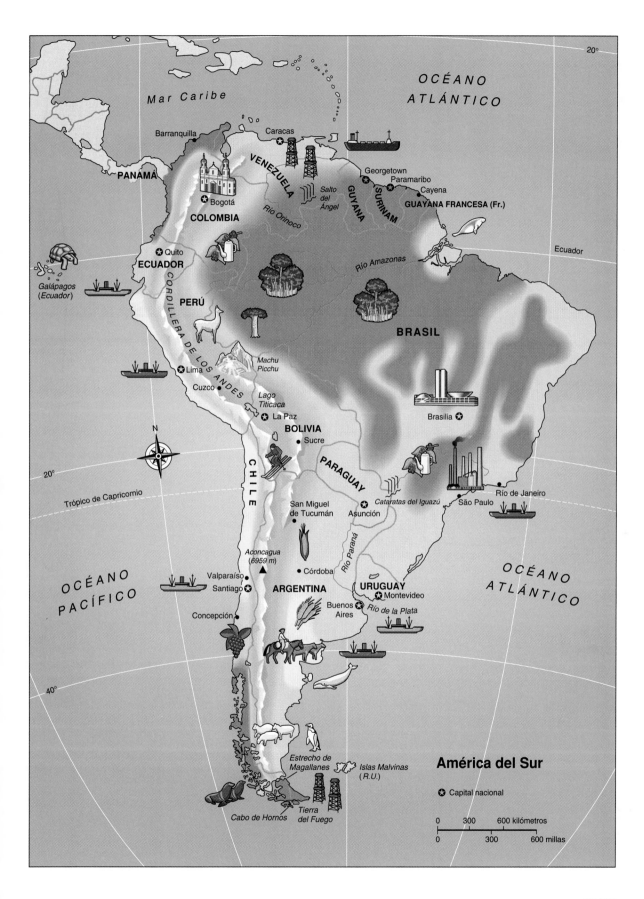

Mar Caribe

OCÉANO ATLÁNTICO

20°

Barranquilla

Caracas

VENEZUELA

PANAMÁ

Bogotá

COLOMBIA

Río Orinoco

Salto del Ángel

GUYANA

SURINAM

Georgetown
Paramaribo
Cayena

GUAYANA FRANCESA (Fr.)

Quito

ECUADOR

Ecuador

PERÚ

Río Amazonas

Galápagos (Ecuador)

CORDILLERA DE LOS ANDES

BRASIL

Machu Picchu

Lima

Cuzco

Lago Titicaca

La Paz

BOLIVIA

Sucre

Brasilia

N

20°

Trópico de Capricornio

CHILE

PARAGUAY

San Miguel de Tucumán

Asunción

Cataratas del Iguazú

São Paulo

Río de Janeiro

OCÉANO ATLÁNTICO

Aconcagua (6959 m)

Córdoba

Río Paraná

Valparaíso

Santiago

ARGENTINA

URUGUAY

Montevideo

OCÉANO PACÍFICO

Concepción

Buenos Aires

Río de la Plata

40°

Estrecho de Magallanes

Islas Malvinas (R.U.)

Cabo de Hornos

Tierra del Fuego

América del Sur

✪ Capital nacional

0   300   600 kilómetros

0   300   600 millas

XXIII

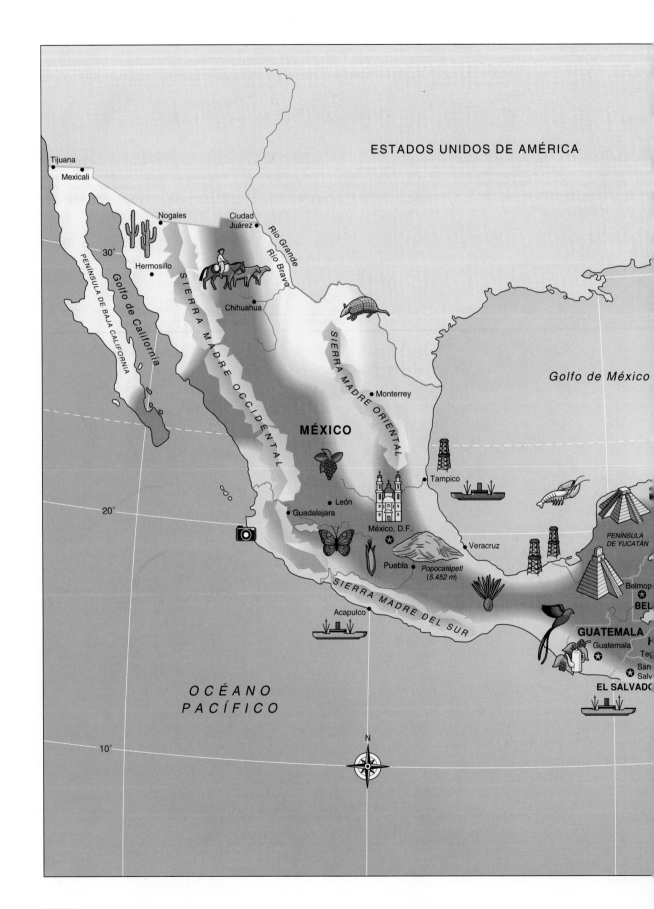

ESTADOS UNIDOS DE AMÉRICA

Tijuana

Mexicali

Nogales

Ciudad Juárez

30°

Hermosillo

Río Grande

Río Bravo

Chihuahua

PENÍNSULA DE BAJA CALIFORNIA

Golfo de California

SIERRA MADRE OCCIDENTAL

SIERRA MADRE ORIENTAL

Monterrey

Golfo de México

MÉXICO

León

Guadalajara

Tampico

México, D.F.

Veracruz

Puebla

Popocatépetl
(5.452 m)

SIERRA MADRE DEL SUR

PENÍNSULA
DE YUCATÁN

Belmop

BEL

Acapulco

GUATEMALA

Guatemala

Teg

San
Salv

EL SALVADO

OCÉANO
PACÍFICO

20°

10°

N

México, América Central y el Caribe

⭐ Capital nacional

| 0 | 300 | 600 | 900 kilómetros |
| 0 | | 300 | 600 millas |

OCÉANO ATLÁNTICO

BAHAMAS

Estrecho de La Florida

Nassau ⭐

La Habana ⭐

CUBA

Camagüey ●

Guantánamo (EE.UU.)

Santiago de Cuba ●

JAMAICA ⭐

Kingston ●

Puerto Príncipe ⭐

HAITÍ

Santo Domingo ⭐

REPÚBLICA DOMINICANA

ISLAS VÍRGENES (EE.UU. y R.U.)

San Juan ⭐

Ponce ●

PUERTO RICO

ANTIGUA Y BARBUDA

SAN CRISTÓBAL Y NEVIS

GUADALUPE (Fr.)

DOMINICA

SANTA LUCÍA

BARBADOS

SAN VICENTE Y GRANADINAS

GRANADA

TRINIDAD Y TABAGO

MAR CARIBE

...AS

...AGUA

...nagua

...ua

San José ⭐

COSTA RICA

Canal de Panamá (EE.UU.)

Colón ●

Panamá ⭐

PANAMÁ

AMÉRICA DEL SUR

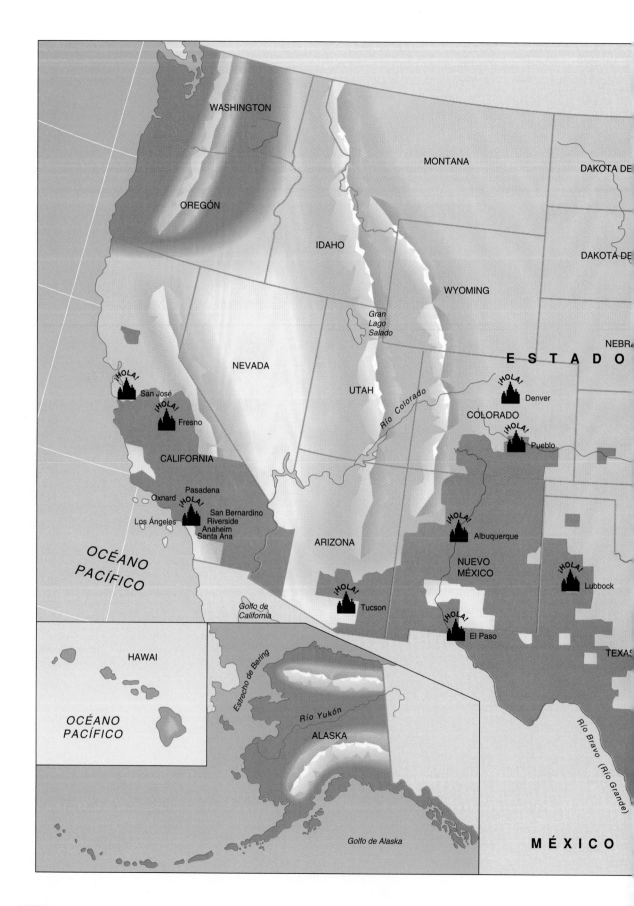

WASHINGTON

OREGÓN

MONTANA

DAKOTA DE

IDAHO

WYOMING

DAKOTA DE

NEBRA

Gran
Lago
Salado

NEVADA

UTAH

Río Colorado

ESTADO

¡HOLA!
San José

¡HOLA!
Denver

¡HOLA!
Fresno

COLORADO

CALIFORNIA

¡HOLA!
Pueblo

Pasadena

Oxnard

¡HOLA!

San Bernardino
Riverside
Anaheim
Santa Ana

Los Ángeles

¡HOLA!
Albuquerque

¡HOLA!
Lubbock

OCÉANO
PACÍFICO

ARIZONA

NUEVO
MÉXICO

¡HOLA!
Tucson

Golfo de
California

¡HOLA!
El Paso

TEXAS

HAWAI

Estrecho de Bering

OCÉANO
PACÍFICO

Río Yukón

ALASKA

Río Bravo (Río Grande)

Golfo de Alaska

MÉXICO

XXVI

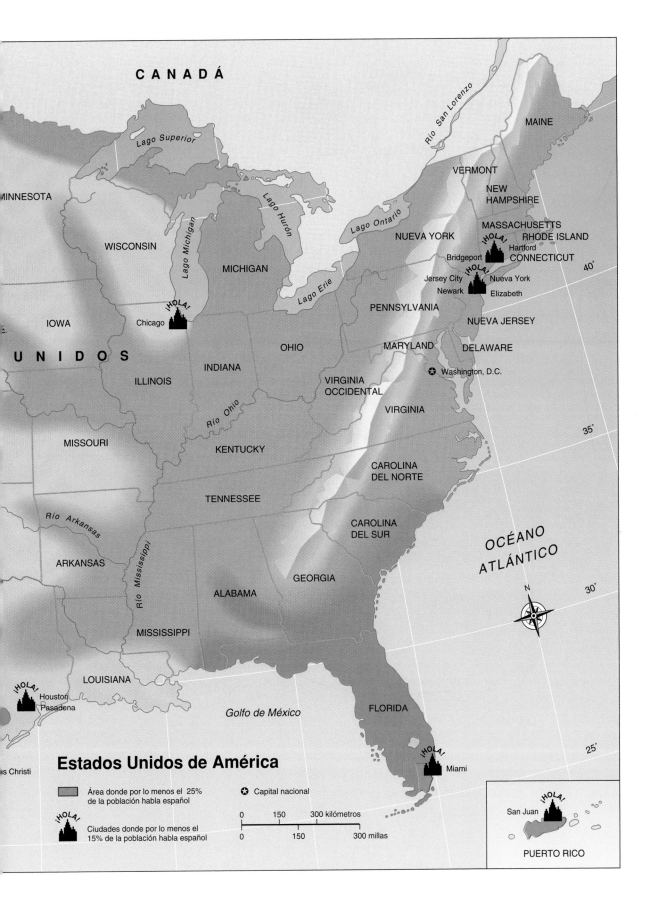

CANADÁ

Río San Lorenzo

MINNESOTA

Lago Superior

Lago Hurón

Lago Michigan

WISCONSIN

MICHIGAN

Lago Ontario

Lago Erie

MAINE

VERMONT

NEW HAMPSHIRE

MASSACHUSETTS

NUEVA YORK

RHODE ISLAND

¡HOLA!

Bridgeport

Hartford

CONNECTICUT

IOWA

¡HOLA!

Chicago

Jersey City

Newark

¡HOLA!

Nueva York

Elizabeth

UNIDOS

ILLINOIS

INDIANA

OHIO

PENNSYLVANIA

NUEVA JERSEY

MARYLAND

DELAWARE

Washington, D.C.

VIRGINIA OCCIDENTAL

VIRGINIA

Río Ohio

MISSOURI

KENTUCKY

CAROLINA DEL NORTE

35°

40°

Río Arkansas

TENNESSEE

CAROLINA DEL SUR

OCÉANO ATLÁNTICO

ARKANSAS

Río Mississippi

GEORGIA

ALABAMA

N

30°

MISSISSIPPI

LOUISIANA

¡HOLA!

Houston

Pasadena

Golfo de México

FLORIDA

¡HOLA!

Miami

25°

s Christi

Estados Unidos de América

Área donde por lo menos el 25% de la población habla español

✪ Capital nacional

¡HOLA!

Ciudades donde por lo menos el 15% de la población habla español

0   150   300 kilómetros

0   150   300 millas

¡HOLA!

San Juan

PUERTO RICO

OCÉANO
ÁRTICO

GROENLANDIA
(Dinamarca)

ALASKA
(EE.UU.)

CANADÁ

**AMÉRICA
DEL NORTE**

ESTADOS UNIDOS
DE AMÉRICA

OCÉANO
ATLÁNTICO

BAHAMAS

Trópico de C

MÉXICO

CUBA
JAMAICA
BELICE
HONDURAS
HAITÍ

REP. DOMINICANA
PUERTO RICO (EE.UU.)

HAWAI
(EE.UU.)

OCÉANO
PACÍFICO

GUATEMALA
EL SALVADOR

NICARAGUA

COSTA RICA
PANAMÁ

TRINIDAD Y TABAGO

VENEZUELA

GUYANA
SURINAM
GUAYANA FF
(Fr.)

Galápagos
(Ecuador)

COLOMBIA

ECUADOR

**AMÉRICA
DEL SUR**

NAURÚ

KIRIBATI

ISLAS
SALOMÓN

ISLAS TUVALU

VANUATU

NUEVA
CALEDONIA (Fr.)

ISLAS FIJI

PERÚ

BRASIL

BOLIVIA

PARAGUAY

CHILE

ARGENTINA

URUGUAY

NUEVA
ZELANDIA

Islas Malvinas
(R.U.)

ANTÁRTIDA

El Mundo

El español es la lengua oficial

¿Por qué estudiar español?

(Why study Spanish?)

- 300,000,000 people in the world speak Spanish.

- Spanish is spoken in Puerto Rico, Spain, and in the 18 countries of Latin America.

- You will learn a lot more about English as you learn Spanish.

- You will have career opportunities that you would not otherwise have.

◁ Gaudi's Cathedral in Barcelona

XXX

● You will enjoy traveling more when you can communicate in Spanish.

Peruvian Mask

● And you will expand your world as you meet people of a culture different from your own.

● In the United States, Spanish is the most commonly spoken language after English.

● You will make new friends and be able to speak to them in their language.

● As you read Spanish and talk with other people in Spanish, you will gain all kinds of information about subjects of great interest and importance.

XXXI

Consejos
Tips for Learning Spanish

- **Start by starting!** Don't wait until you think you have learned "enough" before you start communicating in Spanish. Start today!

- **Use what you already know.** Many Spanish words have their roots in words that you already know. You are going to see and hear some words that seem familiar. Take a guess at their meaning.

- **Listen.** You are going to hear a lot of Spanish spoken in your Spanish class. You may hear Spanish on your local radio station, on TV, or in the music that you play. Spanish may be spoken in your own neighborhood or city. Listen actively to Spanish whenever you have the chance.

- **Watch.** Look at the expressions, the gestures, and the movements of people who speak Spanish. Watch the way they say things. You will pick up many clues about what they are saying.

- **Relax.** You **are** going to learn Spanish. It will take time. As you are learning, don't worry. Make an effort, and you will make progress every day.

- **Take charge.** Be positive. Be assertive. Know that you can and will succeed. Ask questions when you don't understand what is said. Look up words that you don't know. Find Spanish magazines and newspapers to read. Look for a pen pal in a Spanish-speaking country. Look for opportunities. They are everywhere! The biggest factor that will contribute towards your success is, of course, you. Set goals. Take charge of your own learning!

- **Work with someone.** To communicate in Spanish, you need to talk with and listen to someone. *Juntos* has been designed to help you learn to speak and understand Spanish. You will have the chance to communicate with someone every day. Work with a friend, your teacher, an exchange student. And work together . . . *juntos!*

ENCUENTROS

Y ou are about to take off on a great adventure, an adventure that you will take with others, together . . . ¡Juntos!

This section of your book is called *Encuentros*, which means "meetings" or "get-togethers." Everything that you will learn in *Encuentros* is practical and useful. It contains the words and phrases that you will use throughout this school year and when you meet new friends who speak Spanish.

So get ready to meet the world . . . to say hello. Today is the day that you start communicating in Spanish. Start by starting. Use what you already know. Listen. Watch. Relax. Work with someone. Take charge! You will succeed!

EN EL AEROPUERTO

Objectives
- to show students how much Spanish they already know
- to explore similarities and differences between Spanish and English
- to introduce the use of context clues

Related Components

Activity Book p. 5	Audio Book Script: p. 6
	Audio tapes Listening 1A

GETTING STARTED

Before students open their books, ask what Spanish words they already know. Write these on the board.

Ask where and how they learned these words. Determine how many are words that we use in English, like *siesta* or *taco*.

Cognates

Ask how many words on the signs look like English words (*autobús, información, migración, oficina, servicios, taxi, teléfonos*). Develop cognate awareness by presenting them in the style of a television quiz game. Write the Spanish cognate on the board, erase the letters that do not match, and draw underlines to indicate the missing letters. If the English cognate has a different number of letters, add or subtract underlines.

```
t e l _ _ o n _ s
s e r v i c _ _ s
m i g r a _ i _ n
i n f o r m a _ _ _ n
```

Contexts

Now introduce the idea of context. Have students look at the page to see if they can figure out in what kind of place these signs are located. Have them look closely at the **migración** sign. What do the figures appear to be doing? (Clarify the meaning of **migración**, a word that is used instead of **inmigración** in some countries.)

EN EL AEROPUERTO
At the airport

¡Bienvenidos!
Welcome!

¡Hola! *Hi!*
- **¡Buenos días!** *Good morning!*
- **¡Buenas tardes!** *Good afternoon!*
- **¡Buenas noches!** *Good evening!* or *Good night!*
- **¡Adiós!** *Goodbye!*
- **¡Chau!** *Bye!*

$cambio$

información

el taxi

Taxi

migracion Immigration

2

TELÉFONO

Perdón, busco...
*Excuse me,
I am looking for . . .*

- el teléfono
- los servicios
- la salida
- el autobús

¡OJO!
Look at the airport signs on these pages. Do you see any punctuation marks that you wouldn't find on words in English? Anything else that's not familiar?

Servicios
Damas
Caballeros

SALIDA BUS
GRANADA-AEROPUERTO
LUNES No:131509
8'15 - 9'15 - 17'30 - 19'00
MARTES
8'15 - 9'15 - 17'30 - 19'00
MIERCOLES
8'15 - 9'15
JU
8'15 - 9'1
V
8'15 - 9'
S
8'15 - 9
D
17'30

autobús

En el aeropuerto.

Busca las palabras. *Look at the signs on these pages. Find the Spanish words for:*

- telephone
- restrooms
- information
- bus
- ladies
- gentlemen
- taxicab

3

Model the greetings aloud for students to listen to and repeat. Have partners exchange greetings.

Perdón, busco...

Model the three sentences (say them aloud in a normal speaking voice).
Ask what **el, los,** and **la** probably mean. Explain that Spanish—and many other languages—require more than one form of the word *the.* Return to the greetings in ¡Hola! Ask what is unusual about the first word in the greetings. (One time it ends in **-os,** the other times in **-as.**)
Explain that in Spanish, names of things are divided into two categories, called masculine and feminine. Emphasize that this does not necessarily reflect a "real" gender difference.

Accents and Other Marks

Ask about the ¡**Bienvenidos!** sign. What is the mark at the beginning of the word, and why do you think it is there?
Ask students to find letters on these pages that have marks over them, not just on the signs but also in the texts. A few:

autobús	días	información
perdón	teléfono	

Ask: What do we call that mark? Look at these letters. Are there any other letters you think might have accents sometimes? Why? (Because **e, i, o,** and **u** are vowels, it is likely that the letter **a** might also take an accent at times.)

How Accents Work

Model words that do not have accents, such as **taxi,** and **aeropuerto.** Which part of each word is stressed?
Model a few words that do have accents. Ask how these differ from the unaccented words. Which parts of these words are stressed? What rule can we make for words that have no written accents? (Emphasis normally falls on the syllable just before the last one.) Ask what accent marks are useful for. Why don't *all* words have accent marks? (An accent shows where to put the emphasis when a word does not follow the just-before-the-last-syllable rule.)

First have students examine one cartoon and try to figure out what is happening. Then model and act out the dialog.

Perdón

Have students pass around objects. At each exchange they should say *por favor, gracias,* and *de nada.* Offer new objects to different students to keep everyone busy.

Señor, Señora, Señorita

Before you finish with the first drawing, ask what the word **señora** probably means. Ask what other forms of address students know, eliciting **señor** and **señorita**. Explain that **señorito,** like master, is not commonly used any more. (Point out the difference between the accent mark and the *tilde,* the sign above the ñ in **señora** and other words.)

Perdón ¿dónde está el telefono?

Ask students where other students are. Tell them to answer by pointing and saying *Está aquí* or *Está allí.* Repeat with *Está a la izquierda/derecha.*

Está, están

Draw attention to the words' endings, and ask students to suggest why they are different.

¿Dónde están los servicios?

Have three volunteers move around the room, one alone, the others together. Ask others *¿Dónde está/están?* Students must point to the person or pair and make complete sentences using *está(n) aquí/allí a la derecha/izquierda.* As students catch on, add words they don't know to your questions, but continue to use *está/están.* (Examples: *¿Sabes dónde está el estudiante alto?,* or *¿Las dos personas, dónde están?*) This should help them concentrate on listening for key words.

¿DÓNDE ESTÁ...?
Where is . . . ?

Perdón *Excuse me*

- **Por favor.** *Please.*
- **Gracias.** *Thank you.*
- **De nada.** *You're welcome.*

Perdón, ¿dónde está el teléfono?
Excuse me, where is the phone?

- **Está aquí.** *It's over here.*
- **Está allí.** *It's over there.*
- **Está a la derecha.** *It's to the right.*
- **Está a la izquierda.** *It's to the left.*

¿Dónde están los servicios?
Where are the restrooms?

- **Aquí, a la izquierda.** ←
- **Allí, a la derecha.** →

4

1 ¿Dónde está?

Con tu compañero(a), mira los dibujos. *With your classmate, look at the pictures. Say what the people might be saying.*

2 Te toca a ti
It's your turn

En parejas, creen dos diálogos diferentes. *In pairs, create two different dialogs.*

A
greet ·······▶ B
greet back
A ◀······
ask
directions ·······▶ B
give directions
A ◀······
say
thank you ·······▶ B
say you're
welcome

PARA COMUNICARNOS MEJOR

☐ In Spanish, nouns are either masculine or feminine. This is called gender. The definite article **el** or **la** identifies the gender of the noun.

FEMININE	MASCULINE
la salida *the exit*	**el teléfono** *the telephone*
la señora *the woman*	**el señor** *the man*

☐ To form the plural of nouns ending in a vowel, add **-s.** When a noun ends in a consonant, add **-es.** Notice how the article changes.

las salidas *the exits*	**los teléfonos** *the telephones*
las señoras *the women*	**los señores** *the men*

5

Objective
• to use numbers and counting
• to correctly use Hispanic names
• to say what your name is

Related Components

Activity Book p. 6	Audio Book Script: p. 6
	Audio Tapes Listening: 1A

Señas de identidad
Have students read the **¿Sabes que...?** Have them find **Nombre** and **apellidos** on the passport, and figure out what these words probably mean. Point out that people use both last names for legal purposes, but many do not use two last names in everyday life.

Role Call
Have students make their own ID cards on index cards. Collect and shuffle. Read aloud the first address in Spanish. Have the person who has that address read the next address. Keep the cards for use in other activities.

Number Games
Know Your Number Have students count off in turn, *uno* through *diez,* and remember their numbers. Tell them to raise a hand whenever you call their number. Call out a series of numbers, including *cero.* Vary speed and accent.

Name That Number Have students close their eyes. Clap 0 to 10 times, and have the class or individuals say the number.

Not That Number! Write a number from 1 to 10 on the board or card, and have the class skip that number as they count aloud together.

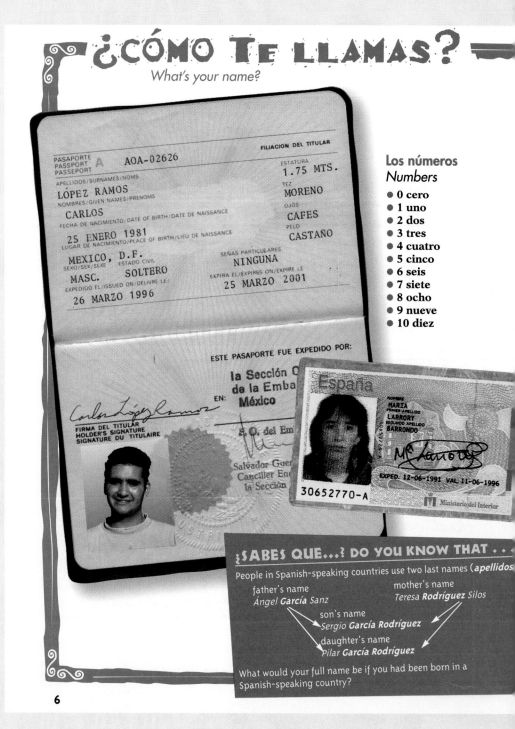

¿CÓMO TE LLAMAS?
What's your name?

Los números
Numbers

● 0 cero
● 1 uno
● 2 dos
● 3 tres
● 4 cuatro
● 5 cinco
● 6 seis
● 7 siete
● 8 ocho
● 9 nueve
● 10 diez

¡SABES QUE...? DO YOU KNOW THAT . . .

People in Spanish-speaking countries use two last names (*apellidos*

father's name
*Ángel **García** Sanz*

mother's name
*Teresa **Rodríguez** Silos*

son's name
*Sergio **García** Rodríguez*

daughter's name
*Pilar **García** Rodríguez*

What would your full name be if you had been born in a Spanish-speaking country?

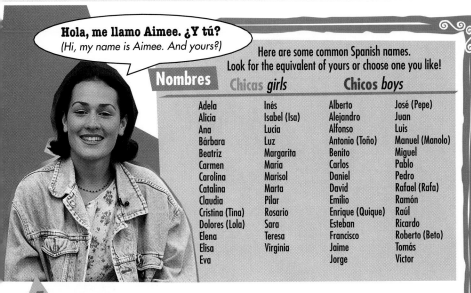

Hola, me llamo Aimee. ¿Y tú?
(Hi, my name is Aimee. And yours?)

Here are some common Spanish names.
Look for the equivalent of yours or choose one you like!

Nombres

Chicas *girls*		Chicos *boys*	
Adela	Inés	Alberto	José (Pepe)
Alicia	Isabel (Isa)	Alejandro	Juan
Ana	Lucía	Alfonso	Luis
Bárbara	Luz	Antonio (Toño)	Manuel (Manolo)
Beatriz	Margarita	Benito	Miguel
Carmen	María	Carlos	Pablo
Carolina	Marisol	Daniel	Pedro
Catalina	Marta	David	Rafael (Rafa)
Claudia	Pilar	Emilio	Ramón
Cristina (Tina)	Rosario	Enrique (Quique)	Raúl
Dolores (Lola)	Sara	Esteban	Ricardo
Elena	Teresa	Francisco	Roberto (Beto)
Elisa	Virginia	Jaime	Tomás
Eva		Jorge	Víctor

1 ¿Cómo te llamas?

Pregúntale a tu compañero(a). *Ask your classmate what his/her name is.*

— ¿Cómo te llamas?
— Me llamo Isabel. ¿Y tú?
— Me llamo Jorge.

2 ¿Cuál es tu dirección?
What's your address?

Habla con tu compañero(a).
Talk with your classmate about your name and address.

— ¿Cómo te llamas?
— Sergio García Rodríguez.
— ¿Cuál es tu dirección?
— Avenida Delicias, número tres-cuatro-ocho.
— ¿Qué ciudad?
— Madrid.

PARA COMUNICARNOS MEJOR

☐ To tell someone your name, say:
   Me llamo (Rosario).

☐ To ask another young person what his or her name is, say:
   ¿Cómo te llamas?

☐ To ask the same question of an adult, say:
   ¿Cómo se llama?

7

Nombres
Have students look at the list of names and find the names closest to their own. Assist those whose names are not on the list or whose names do not have Spanish equivalents (e.g., Tasha might become Tania and Jacqueline, Jacoba).

Chicos y chicas
Draw attention to the headings **Chicos** and **Chicas**. Have students listen with books closed as you say names aloud. Have the **chicos** hold up a hand when they think the name is masculine, the **chicas** when they think it is feminine. Say a few names that are not on the list but which are cognates or end in -a or -o (e.g., **Irene, Gabriela, Gerardo**). Ask for Hispanic names that are not on the list.

Compañeros
The Spanish instruction lines in activities 1 and 2 will be used often in this series. Model the sentences and have students repeat them.

ACTIVITIES

1. ¿Cómo te llamas ?
In this activity and the next, call attention to the question words. Have them use the answers to figure out what ¿**Cómo?** and ¿**Cuál?** mean.

2. ¿Cuál es tu dirección?
After modeling the exchange, have pairs perform it. Encourage them to invent new names, addresses, and cities each time they do it.

Mucho gusto

Have volunteers act out in English what two local teenagers would do and say when meeting for the first time. If the results are too informal, ask them to do it again as adults (or ambassadors) would. Model the exchange in the cartoon, and offer a few variations on it.

Me llamo

Tell students to choose a character to be, such as King Arthur or Mary Poppins, and choose one yourself. Introduce yourself to the first student in each row (imitate your character's voice, if possible), and have them continue the introductions down their rows. Those at the end of each row introduce themselves to each other.

¿Cómo estás? ¿Cómo está?

Have students read the *¿Sabes que...?* Explain that people in Spanish-speaking countries tend to be more formal. Have students pair up and flip a coin to determine whether they will be an adult (heads) or a child (tails). After acting out an introduction, they pair up with another person and repeat the process. Do several times.

Adiós

Have students mingle and say goodbye to each other. Tell them not to use the same phrases as the person to whom they are saying goodbye.

¿CÓMO ESTÁS?

How are you?

Mucho gusto *Nice to meet you*

- **Hola, ¿qué tal?** *Hi, what's up?*
- **Me llamo.** *My name is . . .*

¿Cómo estás (tú)?
¿Cómo está (usted)?

How are you?

- **Muy bien, gracias.** *Very well, thank you.*
- **Estoy bien, gracias.** *I'm fine, thanks.*
- **Mal.** *I am not doing well.*
- **Regular.** *So-so.*

Adiós *Goodbye*

- **Hasta luego.** *See you later.*
- **Hasta mañana.** *See you tomorrow.*

¡SABES QUE...?

In Spanish, there are two ways to address people: with *tú* or *usted. Tú* is used among most young people and among friends and is often called the "familiar" form. *¿Cómo estás tú? Usted* is often called the "polite" form. Use it with people older than you or people you don't know very well. *¿Cómo está usted?*

¿Cómo se llama...?

Con tu compañero(a), miren los dibujos. *With your classmate, look at the pictures. Ask questions about the people in them.*

— ¿Cómo se llama el chico?
— Se llama Toni.
— ¿Cómo se llama la chica?
— Se llama Ana.

 Hola, ¿cómo estás?

Con tu compañero(a), creen dos diálogos. *With your classmate, create two dialogs. Greet each other! Use your new Spanish names!*

— Hola, Daniel, ¿cómo estás?
— ¡Bien, gracias. ¿Y tú?
— Regular.

¡OJO!

To ask what the name of another person is, say:
¿Cómo se llama (el chico)?
To answer, say:
Se llama (Roberto).
To ask someone's name with the polite **usted** form, say:
¿Cómo se llama (usted)?

 Te toca a ti

En parejas, creen dos diálogos diferentes.
In pairs, create two different dialogs.

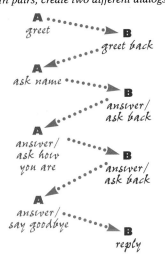

PARA COMUNICARNOS MEJOR

☐ *To tell how you are, say:*
Estoy bien. *I'm fine.*

☐ *To ask how a friend is, say:*
¿Cómo estás?

☐ *To ask the same question of an adult or someone you don't know well, say:*
¿Cómo está?

☐ *To ask how another person is, say:*
¿Cómo está Elena?
¿Cómo está Roberto?

1. ¿Cómo se llama?
Make sure students realize that **se** does not mean the same as **te**, and that the speakers in this dialog are referring to another person.
Expand by asking Student A the name of Student B, or show a photo of a famous person and ask who it is.

2. Hola, ¿cómo estás?
Possible variations for this dialog:
For **Hola** use **Buenos días**, etc.
For **Bien, gracias, ¿y tú?** use **mal.**

3. Te toca a tí
Possible Dialog
A: *Hola.*
B: *Buenos días*
A: *¿Cómo te llamas?*
B: *Me llamo Celestino, ¿y tú?*
A: *Me llamo Hipólita. ¿Qué tal?*
B: *Bien, gracias, ¿y tú?*
A: *Mal. Adiós.*
B: *Hasta luego.*
Have volunteers act out their dialogs for the class.

Objectives
• to say where you are from
• to say where something is
• to introduce yourself
• to say goodbye

Related Components

Activity Book	Audio Book
p. 7	Script: p. 6
	Audio Tapes
	Listening: 1A

Hola

Ask how many of the Spanish-speaking countries of Latin America students can name. Use a classroom map. Ask if anyone has ever been to any of them.

Soy de...

Model the statements of the people on this page. Point out that each one makes a statement that includes **Soy de...**, and ask what this probably means. Make sure they understand that **soy** combines *I* and *am,* and that the **yo** is not essential.

Thinking About Geography

On a classroom map, have a volunteer trace a general land route from the countries of Carmen to Jaime to Marta to Celia. Name each country the route crosses. Then point out Spain (Sergio) on a classroom map. Make sure everyone realizes that it is in Europe.

¿DE DÓNDE ERES?
Where are you from?

Hola, ¿qué tal? Me llamo Carmen. Soy de la Ciudad de México.

Hola, me llamo Jaime. Soy de San Salvador, la capital de El Salvador.

Hola, me llamo Marta. Soy de Bogotá, la capital de Colombia.

Hola, ¿qué tal? Me llamo Celia. Yo soy de Santiago de Chile.

¡Hola! Me llamo Sergio. Soy de Barcelona. Barcelona está en España.

10

¿De dónde eres?

Soy de España.

1 ¿De dónde es...?
Where is he/she from?

Con tu compañero(a), miren el mapa. *With your partner, look at the map. Talk about where the people are from.*

— *¿De dónde es Marta?*
— *Es de Colombia.*
— *¿De qué ciudad?*
— *De Bogotá.*

2 ¿Y tú? ¿De dónde eres?

Pregúntale a tu compañero(a) de dónde es. *Ask your classmate where he/she is from.*

— *¿De dónde eres?*
— *Soy de Nueva York.*

3 ¿Dónde está?

Con tu compañero(a), hablen sobre los lugares del dibujo. *With your classmate, talk about the places in the picture. Where are they? Ask about other places.*

— *¿Dónde está Santiago?*
— *Está en Chile.*
— *¿Dónde está San Antonio?*
— *Está en Texas, Estados Unidos.*

PARA COMUNICARNOS MEJOR

☐ *To ask where someone is from, use the appropriate form of the verb* **ser** *(to be) with* **de.**

¿Eres de Colombia? *Are you from Colombia?*

No, soy de Argentina. *No, I'm from Argentina.*

Mariana es de Colombia. *Mariana is from Colombia.*

☐ **Ser** *(to be) is the infinitve form of the verb. Note that in English, the infinitive has the word "to:" to sing, to read. In Spanish, a verb has a different form for each subject pronoun. Here are some of the forms of the verb* **ser:**

Subject pronoun	Form of ser	
yo	**soy**	*I am*
tú	**eres**	*you (familiar) are*
usted	**es**	*you (formal) are*
él, ella	**es**	*he, she is*

☐ *In Spanish, the subject pronouns are not always needed because the verb itself tells who the subject is:* **Yo soy Jaime** *has the same meaning as* **Soy Jaime.**

11

1. ¿De dónde es?
Expand this activity by adding people, cities, and countries on the board.

2. ¿Y tú? ¿De dónde eres?
Expand this activity by forming small groups and having students ask these questions in a circle. For example:
B: *¿De dónde eres?*
A: *Soy de California.*
B tells **C**
B: A *es de California.*
C: *¿Sí? ¿De dónde eres tú?*
B: *Soy de Montana.*
C tells **D**, and on and on, with everyone choosing a new place to be from each time they are asked. If groups become especially good at this, have them compete against the clock. See which team can complete ten questions in the shortest time with the fewest errors.

3. ¿Dónde está?
Expand this activity by having the person who answers give a wrong answer, and having the questioner (or a third person) correct it:
A: *¿Dónde está Santiago?*
B: *Está en México.*
A (or C): No, está en Chile.

Ser y estar

Few students will notice that both **ser** and **estar** both used on these pages, mean "to be." Because this duplication is confusing, it is better to begin by establishing some of the basic uses of both words. For example:
Teacher: *¿De dónde eres?*
Student A: *Soy de Miami.*
Ask a volunteer:
Teacher: *¿Dónde está Miami?*
Student B: *Miami está en Florida.*
Pronunciation and geography are not the point, so allow the use of English names. Use the correct pronunciation or word when questioning and confirming.

¿CUÁNTOS AÑOS TIENES?

Model the **¿Cuántos años tienes?** dialog at the top of the page. Model it again with a volunteer, and then have two volunteers do it. Then have all the students ask other students the same question.

Point out that when giving an age that ends with **uno**, the -**o** is dropped and the word becomes **un**.

Números del 11 al 99

Repeat the number games from page 6, using multiples of ten. Use a calendar to work with numbers beyond ten (and to introduce **años**).

Working with Ages

- Ask about the ages of the people in the photos on the student page.
- Name famous people and have students estimate their ages.
- Have small groups ask ages in turn in a circle. Each person has to answer with a slightly higher number than the previous person. Example:

A: *¿Cuántos años tienes?*
B: *Tengo treinta y un años.*
B: *¿Cuántos años tienes?*
C: *Tengo treinta y siete.*

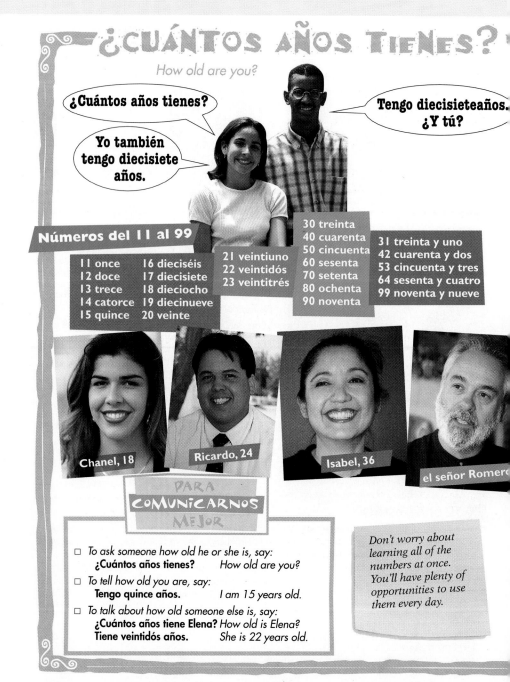

¿CUÁNTOS AÑOS TIENES?
How old are you?

¿Cuántos años tienes?

Tengo diecisieteaños. ¿Y tú?

Yo también tengo diecisiete años.

Números del 11 al 99

11 once	16 dieciséis
12 doce	17 diecisiete
13 trece	18 dieciocho
14 catorce	19 diecinueve
15 quince	20 veinte

21 veintiuno
22 veintidós
23 veintitrés

30 treinta
40 cuarenta
50 cincuenta
60 sesenta
70 setenta
80 ochenta
90 noventa

31 treinta y uno
42 cuarenta y dos
53 cincuenta y tres
64 sesenta y cuatro
99 noventa y nueve

Chanel, 18
Ricardo, 24
Isabel, 36
el señor Romero

PARA COMUNICARNOS MEJOR

☐ To ask someone how old he or she is, say:
   ¿Cuántos años tienes?   How old are you?

☐ To tell how old you are, say:
   Tengo quince años.   I am 15 years old.

☐ To talk about how old someone else is, say:
   ¿Cuántos años tiene Elena? How old is Elena?
   Tiene veintidós años.   She is 22 years old.

Don't worry about learning all of the numbers at once. You'll have plenty of opportunities to use them every day.

12

1 Lee los números

Read the following numbers aloud.

SEVILLA CICLOMOTOR
9309·2

GENERAL GZ
C. I. F. A-58146325
CAPSA - Barcelona
CAPSA - Barcelona
GENERAL GZO1
C. I. F. A-58146325
A 246160
Francisco-Barcelona

Floristería
JARDINES
DE
PONCE
Calle Mayor 321, Santurce
555-2595 • 555-2122 Fax 555-4406
555-2682

2 ¿Cuántos años tienes?

Ask three classmates how old they are.

3 Números

Con tu compañero(a), hablen de los números. *With your classmate, say (in Spanish!) what number you would associate with each of the following items. Can you think of any others?*

a bicycle (*dos*)	a week	your fingers
an octopus	a minute	a rectangle
February	the seasons	the months

4 Te toca a ti

Con tu compañero(a), creen dos diálogos diferentes.

A *say hi*
B *reply/ask how he or she is*
A *reply/ask back*
B *reply/ask where he/she is from*
A *answer/ask back*
B *answer*
A *ask age*
B *answer/ask back*
A *answer*

13

1. Lee los números
Expand this activity with sets of index cards numbered zero through nine. In pairs, one partner draws two cards from a pack and arranges them in any order. The other partner says that number aloud. Correct numbers are worth a point, errors cost a point.

2. ¿Cuántos años tienes?
To expand this activity, have one partner write down a number without the other person seeing, and give the other a ten-number range, saying, for example: **Es un número entre 33 y 42.** The other has three guesses. Roles change whenever someone guesses correctly.

3. Números
Expand this activity by asking students to come up with more words and phrases that suggest specific numbers, such as *tripod, octagon, United States, chessboard,* or *two football teams.*

4. Te toca a ti
This activity can include exchanges learned in earlier segments. You might suggest that students review pages 10–11 before continuing.
Possible Dialog
A: *Hola.*
B: *Buenos días. ¿Qué tal?*
A: *Bien, gracias, ¿y tú?*
B: *Mal. ¿De dónde eres?*
A: *Soy de Los Ángeles. ¿Y tú?*
B: *Soy de Omaha.*
A: *¿Cuántos años tienes?*
B: *Quince. ¿Y tú?*
A: *Dieciséis.*

¿QUIÉN ERES?

Objectives
- to say who you are
- to talk about your favorite things
- to say what you like to do

Related Components

Activity Book p. 8	Audio Book Script: p. 6
	Audio Tapes Listening: 1A

Explain that **¿Quién eres?** means "Who are you?" Ask if that means the same thing as asking **¿Cómo te llamas?** What kinds of things make up what a person *is*?

¿Quién es José?
Ask students to look at the information on José Martín Sanz and to figure out what this information means.

Color Games
Veo, veo One person picks an object and names its color. Another attempts to guess which object it is, pointing and using **aquí** or **allí**. Example:

A: *Veo, veo.*
B: *¿Qué ves?*
A: *El color rojo. ¿Dónde está?*
B: (points to a red book) *Allí.*

To expand, pick up the tempo. Those who take too long or make mistakes are out.

El color de... Form circles. Student A names an object in English and Student B names its color in Spanish. Example:

A: The sky.
B: *Azul.*
B: Chalk.
C: *Blanco.*

To expand, name objects with more colors (e.g., A zebra. *Blanco y negro*).

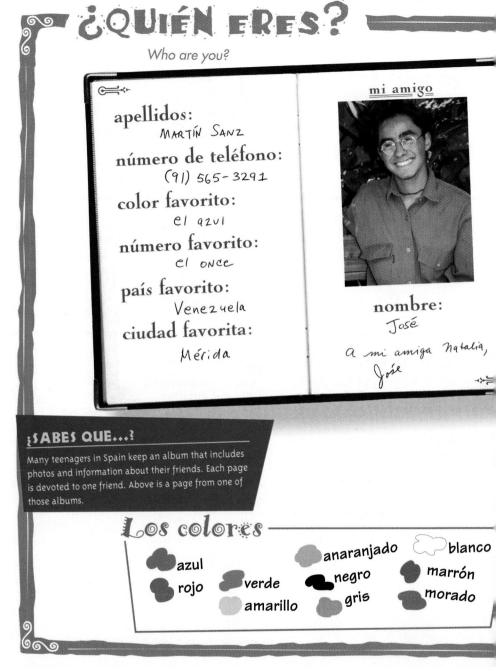

¿QUIÉN ERES?

Who are you?

apellidos:
MARTÍN SANZ

número de teléfono:
(91) 565-3291

color favorito:
el azul

número favorito:
el once

país favorito:
Venezuela

ciudad favorita:
Mérida

mi amigo

nombre:
José

a mi amiga Natalia,
José

¿SABES QUE...?

Many teenagers in Spain keep an album that includes photos and information about their friends. Each page is devoted to one friend. Above is a page from one of those albums.

Los colores

- azul
- rojo
- verde
- amarillo
- anaranjado
- negro
- gris
- blanco
- marrón
- morado

14

1 ¿Cuál es...?

Pregúntale a tu compañero(a). *Ask your classmate about the information in the diary.*

— ¿Cuál es su ciudad favorita?
— Mérida.

 2 ¿Y tu compañero(a)?

Pregúntale a tu compañero(a). *Ask your classmate at least six questions about himself/herself.*

— ¿Cuál es tu color favorito?
— El verde.

 3 ¿Quién es?

Find someone in your class who answers "yes" to the following statements.

- Mi color favorito es el verde. (*Daniel*)
- Mi número favorito es el trece.
- Mi ciudad favorita está en Europa.
- Mi país favorito es Estados Unidos.
- Mi nombre favorito tiene la letra "m".
- Mi número favorito es el 7.

 4 A escribir

Escribe seis oraciones. *Write six sentences about yourself. Include your name and some of your favorite things. Then trade this information with a classmate.*

Me llamo Isabel.
Mi color favorito es el morado.

PARA
COMUNICARNOS
MEJOR

☐ *In Spanish, you can use a possessive adjective (mi, tu, su) to tell what you have or own.*

¿Cuál es tu color favorito?
What is your favorite color?

Mi color favorito es el azul.
My favorite color is blue.

Su color favorito es el verde.
His/her/your favorite color is green.

 ¡OJO!

When talking about your favorite color or number use, the masculine article *el:*

Mi color favorito es el azul. (My favorite color is blue)

1. ¿Cúal es...?
Expand this activity by having each student pretend to be José and write simple sentences in the first person:
Me llamo José Martín Sanz.
Mi número de teléfono es....

2. ¿Y tu compañero(a)?
Expand this activity by having each person write a report about the other's answers. Example: *Su nombre es Amy Navratilova. Su color favorito es....*

3. ¿Quién es?
Expand this activity by having the class vote on favorite colors, numbers, and cities.

4. A escribir
Expand this activity by having partners select two famous people (one male, one female) and decide what those people's favorite colors, numbers, countries, and cities might be.

15

¿QUÉ TE GUSTA HACER?

¿Te gusta...?

Draw a happy face and a sad face on the board. Write **Sí, me gusta** and, **No, no me gusta** underneath. Ask individuals and/or the class about different subjects, eliciting a **me gusta** answer to each. Use Spanish when possible, English otherwise. Focus on establishing the response. Example: Pistachio ice cream: *¿Te gusta?*

Use **también** and **tampoco** to let them know how you feel about each item. After a while, shift the focus to other people, asking *¿A tí también/tampoco?*

¿Qué te gusta hacer el fin de semana?

Read aloud and act out a few vocabulary words or phrases. Ask volunteers to demonstrate the rest. Mime actions and have students identify them in Spanish.

Ask a few students *¿Te gusta leer?* and add check marks under one face or the other according to their answers. Have volunteers offer other likes and dislikes.

Thinking About Language

Ask students to identify as many cognates as they can in the small pictures. They should be able to come up with these:

americano	béisbol	bicicleta
cine	fútbol	gimnasio
montar	música	pizza
teléfono	televisión	voleibol

¿QUÉ TE GUSTA HACER?
What do you like to do?

¿Te gusta...? *Do you like . . .?*

- **Sí, me gusta mucho.**
  Yes, I like it very much.
- **No, no me gusta.**
  No, I don't like it.

¿Y a ti? *And you?*

- **A mí también.** *Me too.*
- **A mí tampoco.** *Me neither.*

¿Te gusta practicar deportes?

Sí, me gusta mucho.

¿Qué te gusta hacer el fin de semana?
What do you like to do on the weekend?

Me gusta...

 jugar al fútbol

 jugar al fútbol americano

 jugar al baloncesto

jugar al voleibol

 jugar al béisbol

No me gusta...

hablar por teléfono

 escuchar música

 mirar la televisión

 montar en bicicleta

leer

 ir al cine

dibujar

bailar

 jugar con videojuegos

 cocinar

 ir al gimnasio

comer pizza

You can choose your favorites from this menu of activities! Don't worry about learning every expression now. After all, your interests may change!

16

16

¿Te gusta...? *Do you like ...?*

Habla con tu compañero(a). *Talk with your classmates about what you like or dislike.*

— ¿Te gusta jugar al béisbol?
— Sí, me gusta mucho. ¿Y a ti?
— A mí también.

 ¿A quién le gusta...?
Who likes ...?

Find someone in your class who agrees with the statements below.

• **Me gusta escuchar música.**
• **No me gusta ir al cine.**
• **Me gusta cocinar.**
• **No me gusta jugar al béisbol.**
• **Me gusta dibujar.**
• **No me gusta comer pizza.**

 Encuesta *Survey*

Trabajen en grupos. *Work in groups. Vote on the most popular activity of your Spanish class. Then, inform your classmates.*

¡OJO!

The verbs that you use with *gustar* are all in the infinitive form. In Spanish, infinitives end in *-ar*, *-er*, and *-ir*. For example, *jugar* (to play) is an *-ar* verb, *comer* (to eat) is an *-er* verb, and *escribir* (to write) is an *-ir* verb.

 Te toca a ti

Con tu compañero(a), creen cuatro diálogos.

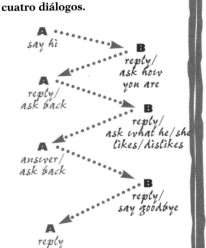

A — say hi
B — reply/ ask how you are
A — reply/ ask back
B — reply/ ask what he/she likes/dislikes
A — answer/ ask back
B — reply/ say goodbye
A — reply

PARA COMUNICARNOS MEJOR

Use the verb **gustar** *(to like) to talk about your likes and dislikes. Here are some of its forms:*

me gusta	*I like*
te gusta	*you like (familiar)*
le gusta	*you like (formal)*
le gusta	*he/she likes*

1. ¿Te gusta...?
Expand this activity by having students name three films or television shows they like a lot and three they don't like at all.

2. ¿A quién le gusta...?
Expand this activity by writing six verbs on index cards. Make a card for everyone in the class, but do not say exactly what the choices are. Students memorize their verb, then interview each other, as in the student text. Each person can ask three questions each time.
If the question is about the person's verb, he/she must answer *Sí, me gusta mucho.* If not, the person gives a negative answer. Do for several minutes. The person who finds the most me gusta answers wins.

3. Encuesta
Expand this activity by combining the reports from the groups and discussing the results.

4. Te toca a tí
Possible Dialog
A: *Hola.*
B: *Buenos días. ¿Qué tal?*
A: *Bien, gracias, ¿y tú?*
B: *Mal. ¿Te gusta leer?*
A: *No, no me gusta leer. ¿Y a ti?*
B: *Sí, me gusta leer. Adiós.*
A: *Hasta luego.*
Have volunteers act out their dialogs for the class.

17

Objectives
- to talk about friends and family
- to describe people and animals

Related Components

Activity Book p. 9	Audio Book Script: p. 7
	Audio Tapes Listening: 1A

Una Familia

Ask students to identify the illustration on this page. Have any of them ever made a family tree? Why is it called a "tree"?

¿Cúantos hermanos tienes?

Introduce ¿Cuántos? by displaying a few objects and doing simple math, saying and acting out each step. Example:
Un libro y un libro son dos libros.
Dos libros y un libro son....
¿Cuántos libros son?

Review the tree and the words for family members. Demonstrate how the tree works by talking about your own family or a fictitious one. Give the individuals names.

Ask the title question and a number of variations on it. Examples:
Tengo dos hermanos y tres hermanas.
¿Cuántos hermanos tengo?
¿Cuántos hermanos tiene tu hermana?

Have small groups poll themselves to determine how many brothers and sisters they have among them. Have each group report to the class. Add these on the board and talk about them. How many are brothers? How many are sisters?

You may also have to introduce **padrastro**, **madrastra**, and **medio hermano/a.** A list of words used for family members can be found in Chapter 3.
Ask *¿Cuántos años tienes?* and encourage students to understand the basis of that structure.

¿Tienes un gato?

Ask students to identify the animals in the list. Explain what a **mascota** is. Ask the title question and others. Be careful to avoid the more difficult plural *gustan.* Examples:
¿Te gusta el ratón?
¿Qué mascota es tu favorita?
Ask about pets that students have.

LA FAMILIA
The family

Una familia

la abuela   LOS ABUELOS   el abuelo

el padre (papá)   LOS PADRES   la madre (mamá)

la hermana   el hermano   la hermana
LOS HERMANOS

¿Cuántos hermanos tienes?
How many brothers and sisters do you have?
- **Tengo una hermana y un hermano.**
  I have a sister and a brother.
- **No tengo hermanos.**
  I don't have any brothers and sisters.

¿Tienes un gato?
Do you have a cat?
- **Sí, se llama Furia.**
- **No, pero tengo una tortuga.**
  No, but I have a turtle.

Las mascotas
pets

el gato

el pez

la tortuga

el pájaro

el ratón

el perro

PARA COMUNICARNOS MEJOR

You have used the verb **tener** to talk about age. **Tengo trece años.** (I am thirteen years old.) You can also use **tener** to talk about what you or other people have. Here are some of the forms of **tener.**

yo	tengo	I have
tú	tienes	you (familiar) have
usted	tiene	you (formal) have
él, ella	tiene	he/she has

18

Tu familia

En parejas, hablen sobre su familia.
With your classmate, talk about your family.

— ¿Cuántos hermanos tienes?
— Tengo una hermana.
— ¿Cómo se llama?
— Se llama Andrea.
— ¿Cuántos años tiene?
— Tiene once años.

Ésta es mi hermana...

Con tu compañero(a), creen dos diálogos. *With you classmate, create two dialogs. Take turns introducing different members of your family.*

— Ésta es mi hermana Pilar.
— Mucho gusto.

PARA COMUNICARNOS MEJOR

To introduce a boy or a man, say
Éste es... *(This is . . .)*

To introduce a girl or a woman, say
Ésta es... *(This is . . .)*

To introduce a friend, say **Éste(a) es mi amigo(a)...** *(This is my friend . . .)*

---

3 Ésta es mi familia

Habla de las fotos. *Bring a photograph of your family and friends and introduce them to the class.*

Ésta es mi mamá. Se llama Julia.
Éste es mi papá. Se llama Antonio.
Tengo tres hermanos.

PARA COMUNICARNOS MEJOR

The indefinite article **un** *or* **una** *identifies the gender of the noun.*

un chico	*a boy*
una chica	*a girl*

ACTIVITIES

1. Tu familia
Expand this activity by talking about pets, real and fictitious.

2. Ésta es mi hermana...
Provide several examples of introductions before groups begin. Expand this activity by having students introduce each other as famous people.

3. Ésta es mi familia
Expand this activity by forming circles of 6 to 10. Have students ask about others in the group and identify each as a family member. Example:
A points at anyone else, asks B:
A: ¿Quién es?
B: Es mi abuela.
Then B points at anyone else and asks C, the next person in the circle, about someone else.

Está, ésta
Resolve confusion over these forms by asking questions that will draw attention to the positions of the accents. Point out that all languages have words that look alike but have different meanings (e.g., *lead*, the metal, and *lead*, the action).

¿CÓMO ES?

Él es... Ella es...

Begin by describing yourself. Use words from all of the sections on this page, and don't be afraid to flatter yourself. Then follow up with either/or questions for students about someone else (e.g., *¿Es divertido o aburrido?*).

También es...

Launch this with a few comparisons (e.g., *Juan es alto. Guillermo también es alto.*) Use **tampoco** frequently.
Rate and compare inanimate objects, such as numbers. Is 33, for example, an interesting number? A fun one? Boring? This may lend itself to a class poll.

Tiene el pelo...

Introduce this by asking students to stand up as you call out combinations of color, length, and gender (e.g., *los chicos rubios que tienen pelo largo*).
Use this opportunity to introduce and practice *levántense*.

Busco a mi perro

Have students look at the lost dog ad and have a volunteer read it. Ask comprehension questions about the dog.
¿Cómo se llama el perro?
¿Cuántos años tiene?
¿Tiene el pelo corto or largo?
¿Cuál es el teléfono de Alberto?
¿Qué le gusta a Rufo?

¿CÓMO ES?
What is he/she like?

Él es... *He is . . .* **Ella es...** *She is . . .*

muy...		*very . . .*
simpático	simpática	*nice*
divertido	divertida	*fun*
aburrido	aburrida	*boring*
inteligente	inteligente	*intelligent*
interesante	interesante	*interesting*

¿Cómo es tu amigo?

Es muy guapo. Es bajo y tiene el pelo corto.

Busco a mi perro. Se llama Rufo. Tiene seis años. Tiene pelo corto. Le gusta mucho comer pizza. Es viejo, pero muy inteligente. Mi teléfono es 212-555-2892. (Me llamo Alberto.)

También es...

alto	alta	*tall*
bajo	baja	*short*
guapo	guapa	*handsome*
joven	joven	*young*
viejo	vieja	*old*
pelirrojo	pelirroja	*redhead*

Tiene el pelo...

negro   rubio

largo   castaño

corto

PARA COMUNICARNOS MEJOR

Adjectives have to agree with nouns in gender and number.

la chica (es) alta	las chicas (son) altas
el chico (es) alto	los chicos (son) altos

To form the plural of an adjective add **-s** *if it ends in a vowel and* **-es** *if it ends in a consonant.*

las chicas (son) simpáticas

las chicas (son) inteligentes

los chicos (son) simpáticos

los profesores (son) jóvenes

¿Cómo es tu familia?

Habla con tu compañero(a). *Talk about your friends and family.*

— ¿Cómo es tu amiga Lucía?
— Es baja y tiene el pelo negro. ¿Y tu amigo Teo? ¿Cómo es?
— También es bajo, pero tiene el pelo castaño.
— ¿Cómo son tus hermanos?
— Son muy simpáticos.

 ¿Cómo eres?

Habla con tu compañero(a). *Imagine you have arranged to meet someone, but you have never seen him or her before! You are on the phone. Describe yourself and ask all you need to know to recognize your telephone partner.*

— ¿Cómo eres?
— Soy alto y muy guapo. ¿Y tú?
— Soy rubia y baja.

 ¿Quién tiene...?

Find someone in your class whose answers "yes" the statements below.

- **Tengo tres hermanos.**
- **Tengo un perro viejo.**
- **No tengo un gato.**
- **Mi hermano(a) tiene el pelo rubio.**
- **Mis padres son altos.**
- **Mis abuelos son divertidos.**

Te toca a ti

Con tu compañero(a), creen cuatro diálogos diferentes.

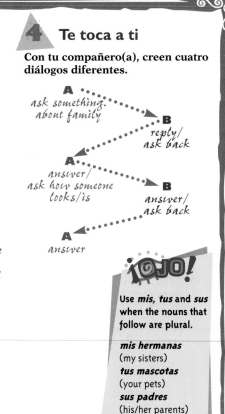

ask something about family → **B** reply/ask back

A answer/ask how someone looks/is → **B** answer/ask back

A answer

¡OJO!

Use *mis*, *tus* and *sus* when the nouns that follow are plural.

mis hermanas
(my sisters)
tus mascotas
(your pets)
sus padres
(his/her parents)

PARA COMUNICARNOS MEJOR

You have seen the singular forms of the verb **ser** *(to be). Here are the plural forms.*

Subject pronoun	Form of **ser**	
nosotros(as)	**somos**	we are
vosotros(as)	**sois**	you are
ustedes	**son**	you (plural) are
ellos/ellas	**son**	they are

1. ¿Cómo es tu familia?
Expand this activity by describing someone in the class and having them guess who it is.

2. ¿Cómo eres?
Distribute magazine photos of all kinds of people. Partners have to describe their photos without showing them. Exchange with others. Repeat several times.

3. ¿Quién tiene...?
Expand this activity by polling the class about which pets are boring, interesting, intelligent, etc.

4. Te toca a tí
Possible Dialog
A: *¿Cuántos hermanos tienes?*
B: *Tengo una hermana. ¿Y tú?*
A: *Tengo dos hermanos. ¿Cómo es tu hermana?*
B: *Es baja y aburrida. ¿Cómo son tus hermanos?*
A: *Son altos y aburridos.*
Expand by having volunteers act out their dialogs for the class.

Somos, sois, son
This is the first time students will see **sois**, commonly used in Spain but not in Latin America. Note that **sois** will appear in paradigms throughout this book, but it will not be actively presented.

Objectives

• to say what day it is
• to say when your birthday is
• to say what time it is

Related Components

Activity Book	Audio Book
p. 10	Script: p. 7
	Audio Tapes
	Listening: 1A

El calendario

Have students look at the Hispanic calendar in the book. Ask how this calendar is different from the ones they use. Display an American calendar, if necessary.
(In addition to the Spanish words, the week begins on Monday, not Sunday.)
Ask about the handwritten notes on the calendar. What do the entries for Beto and María probably mean? What does **cumpleaños** probably mean?

¿Qué mes?

Ask about the names of the months:
• which months are cognates?
  (All, although **Enero** may not appear to. It has the same root as *January,* but the Spanish word is based on the vulgate Latin **jenuarius,** and the **j** was lost.)
• Do any Spanish months have exactly the same spelling as English months?
  (no)
• Which spellings are the closest?
  (One letter differs in **abril,** and there is one extra letter in **mayo.**)
• What are the main differences in the Spanish and English spellings?
  (In January and February, **-ary** vs. **-ero;** in June and July, **-e** or **-y** vs. **-io;** in three of the last four months of the year, an additional **i** in Spanish, and in four of them, **-er** vs. **-re.**)

Los días de la semana

Review the days of the week. Point out that there are no cognates here because most English weekdays are translations from Latin to English (e.g., *Lunea dies* to *Moon day).*

¿QUÉ DÍA ES HOY?
What day is it today?

El calendario

septiembre

lunes	martes	miércoles	jueves	viernes	sábado	domingo
1 mi cumpleaños Natalia	2	3	4	5	6	7
8	9	10	11	12	13 María, 12 años	14
15	16	17 Beto, 22 años	18	19	20	21
22	23	24 el cumpleaños de Samuel	25	26	27 el cumpleaños de Isa	28
29	30					

¿Qué mes? What month?

- enero
- febrero
- marzo
- abril
- mayo
- junio
- julio
- agosto
- septiembre
- octubre
- noviembre
- diciembre

Many of the Spanish words for the months are very much like the English words. Words that are similar in two languages are called "cognates."

¿SABES QUE...?

In most Latin-American countries and in Spain, people write dates differently from the way they are written in the United States. The day comes first, followed by the month. The year is written last. This way, *11/3/98* would be the 11th of March.

In Spanish you do not capitalize the days of the week and the months.

22

22

1 ¿Qué día es hoy?

Pregúntale a tu compañero(a). *Ask your classmate what day it is today.*

— ¿Qué día es hoy?
— Hoy es jueves.

 2 ¿Cuándo es...?

Habla con tu compañero(a). *Talk about the calendar on page 22.*

— ¿Cuándo es el cumpleaños de Natalia?
— El dos de septiembre.
— Y el cumpleaños de María, ¿cuándo es?

 3 ¿Y tu cumpleaños?

Pregúntale a tu compañero(a). *Ask your classmate about his or her age and birthday.*

— ¿Cuántos años tienes?
— Tengo catorce años.
— ¿Cuándo es tu cumpleaños?
— Es el once de marzo.

 4 En tu calendario

Escribe tres fechas. *Write down three dates you always mark in your calendar or diary. Read them (in Spanish!) to your partner and explain (in Spanish or English) why you chose them.*

El 9 de julio es el cumpleaños de mi mamá.

To talk about days and dates, say:

¿Qué fecha es hoy?
What day is it today?

Hoy es viernes, doce de octubre.
Today is Friday, the 12th of October.

¿Cuándo es tu cumpleños?
When is your birthday?

Es el nueve de julio.
It's on the ninth of July.

Use *el* before the date when you're talking about an event.

Mi cumpleaños es el trece de abril.
(My birthday is on the 13th of April.)

¿SABES QUE...?

In several Spanish-speaking countries, the equivalent to April Fools' Day is December 28. It is called *El día de los Inocentes.* Tuesday the 13th (martes trece), not Friday, is considered an unlucky day.

23

---

1. ¿Qué día es hoy?
Expand this activity by having partners take turns picking a day on the calendar and asking what weekday it is. Example:
A: *¿Qué día es el seis de septiembre?*
B: *Es viernes.*

2. ¿Cuándo es...?
Mention that people in many Hispanic countries celebrate the day of the saint whose name they bear *(el día de tu santo)* instead of their birthdays.
Expand this activity by asking and answering questions about the saint's days of famous or imaginary people. (Allow any date—unless you have a calendar with saints' days on hand.) Example:
A: *¿Cuándo es el día del santo de Inés?*
B: *Es el once de septiembre.*

3. ¿Y tu cumpleaños?
Expand this activity by asking imaginative questions using vocabulary and structures from earlier pages in **Encuentros.**
Examples:
• *¿Cuál es tu día (mes) favorito?*
• *Qué día (mes) no te gusta?*

4. En tu calendario
Expand this activity by having ten groups make months for a Spanish calendar for the school year. Have them show national holidays, school events, holidays, and class birthdays. Display in classroom.

Dates for a Hispanic Calendar

21/9	*el día del estudiante, Argentina*
12/10	*día de la raza*
2/11	*día de los muertos*
20/11	*día de la revolución, México*
24/12	*nochebuena*
28/12	*día de los inocentes*
31/12	*año viejo*
6/1	*día de reyes*
14/2	*día de los enamorados*
*/3	*carnaval*
*/4	*semana santa*
*/4	*Feria de Abril, Sevilla, España*
5/5	*Cinco de Mayo, México*
24/6	*Intiraymi, Perú*

*Exact date varies from year to year.

La hora

Ask how many different basic expressions we use to tell the time in English.

Possible Answers:
It is [one] o'clock.
It is ten past/after [one o'clock].
It is one-ten.
It is [a] quarter past/after [one o'clock].
It is one-fifteen.
It is half-past [one o'clock].
It is one-thirty.
It is quarter to/of [two o'clock].
It is ten to/of [two o'clock].
It is one-fifty.
It is noon/midnight.

Ask how we know that something is going to happen at 9:00 at night, not 9:00 in the morning. (A.M. and P.M.)
Review the times in the illustration. Work on time expressions with a picture of a clock or a model that has movable hands.

Es la una, son las dos

Refer students to the drawing. Ask how the Spanish phrases for 1:00 and 1:20 differ from the other phrases. Does it make sense that **la una** is expressed with the singular verb **es** and **las dos** with the plural **son?**

Cuarto, media

Ask for ideas on why **cuarto** is masculine and **media** is feminine. (It is customary to speak of **un cuarto de hora** and **una media hora.**)

¿QUÉ HORA ES?
What time is it?

Son las once menos cuarto.
Son las dos menos veinte.
Es la una y veinte.
Son las ocho y diez.
¿Qué hora es?
Es la una.
Son las dos.
Son las once y media.
Son las once y cuarto.

Telling time in Spanish is different from telling time in English. Just don't be discouraged if learning to tell time in Spanish it takes a little time!

¿SABES QUE...?

In many Spanish-speaking countries digital clocks and schedules show the time in a different way.

In the U.S.		In most Spanish-speaking countries	
you read	you say	you read	you say
8:00 A.M.	It' eight A.M.	8:00	Son las ocho de la mañana.
2:00 P.M.	It's two P.M.	14:00	Son las dos de la tarde.
10:00 P.M.	It's ten P.M.	22:00	Son las diez de la noche.

24

Te gustaría ir al cine?

Sí, ¿a qué hora?

¿Te gustaría jugar al béisbol?
Would you like to play baseball?

Sí, ¡qué bueno! *Yes, great!*

Sí, ¿a qué hora?
Yes, what time?

No, tal vez otro día.
No, maybe some other day.

¡Que lástima! Tengo otro planes.
What a shame! I have other plans.

1 ¿Qué hora es?

Pregúntale a tu compañero(a).
Take turns asking what time it is.

5:30 p.m.   8:15 p.m.   1:00 p.m.

11:10 a.m.   6:45 a.m.   3:50 p.m.

2 ¿Te gustaría...?

Habla con tu compañero(a).
Invite your classmate to do something, and arrange the time. Create three short dialogs.

— ¿Te gustaría ir al cine?
— Sí, ¿a qué hora?
— A las ocho de la noche.
— ¡Qué bueno! Hasta luego.

PARA COMUNICARNOS MEJOR

1. To ask what time it is, say:
   ¿Qué hora es?
2. To tell the time, say: **Es la...** *(for one o'clock.)* **Son las...** *(for other hours):*
   Es la una. *It's one o'clock.*
   Son las siete. *It's seven o'clock.*
3. Use **y** for minutes past the hour:
   Son las nueve y diez. *It's ten minutes past nine.*
4. Use **menos** for minutes to the hour:
   Son las tres menos veinte. *It's twenty minutes to three.*
5. Use **media** for the half hour and **cuarto** for the quarter hour:
   Es la una y media. *It's one thirty.*
   Son las cinco menos cuarto. *It's a quarter to five.*
6. To ask at what time something happens, say:
   ¿A qué hora es (son)...?
7. To answer at what time something happens, say:
   A la una y cinco. *At five past one.*
   A las ocho y media. *At eight thirty.*

1. ¿Qué hora es?
Expand this activity by having students write numbers on index cards.
Set 1: the numbers 1 to 12 in random order
Set 2: the expressions and numbers
   y cuarto, y media, menos cuarto,
   5, 11, 18, 27, 35, 42, 45, 51, 59
Shuffle cards. Partners draw one card from each pile and state the time.

2. ¿Te gustaría...?
Expand this activity by having students ask what their partners are doing at different times on Saturday.

3. Te gustaría jugar al béisbol?
Have students vary this dialog according to their interest
Another Possible Dialog
A: *Hola*
B: *Buenos días.*
A: *¿Te gustaría jugar al fútbol?*
B: *Sí. ¿Qué día?*
A: *El viernes.*
B: *A qué hora?*
A: *A las cinco y cuarto.*
B: *Hasta luego.*
A: *Adiós.*
Have volunteers act out their dialogs for the class.

25

EN LA ESCUELA

Objectives
• to talk about the classes you take
• to talk about your schedule

Related Components

Activity Book p. 11	**Audio Book** Script: p. 7
	Audio Tapes Listening: 1A

Las materias
Ask about the student schedule to elicit days and times: *¿A qué hora es la clase de arte?*
Ask about students' own classes to elicit subject names: *¿Qué materias tienes martes a las once?*

¿Cuándo?
Use these terms as you continue to talk about this and other schedules.

Spelling Game
Creating and solving anagrams makes students more aware of spelling.
Have partners make a set of five-to-ten anagrams using words from any of the preceding pages of **Encuentros.** Have them print or type, so that you can photocopy selected words for the class to try to solve. Identify each set by a code name or number, and have the class vote on the best sets.

EN LA ESCUELA
At school

horas	lunes	martes	miércoles	jueves	viernes	sabado
9-10h	CIENCIAS	GEOGRAFÍA	LITERATURA	MATEMÁTICAS	LITERATURA	FÚTBOL
10-11h	MATEMÁTICAS	LITERATURA	MATEMÁTICAS	MATEMÁTICAS	INGLÉS	FÚTBOL
11-12:15h	GEOGRAFÍA	HISTORIA	INGLÉS	CIENCIAS	HISTORIA	
12:15-13:30h	HISTORIA	CIENCIAS	ESPAÑOL	HISTORIA	GEOGRAFÍA	
13:30-15h	EL ALMUERZO	EL ALMUERZO	EL ALMUERZO	EL ALMUERZO	EL ALMUERZO	
15-16:15h	LITERATURA	ARTE	EDUCACIÓN FÍSICA	ESPAÑOL	CIENCIAS	
16:15-17:30h	ESPAÑOL	ARTE	EDUCACIÓN FÍSICA	INGLÉS	ESPAÑOL	

Las materias *Subjects*

• **el arte** *art*
• **la geografía** *geography*
• **la historia** *history*
• **la educación física** *sports*
• **la literatura** *literature*
• **el español** *Spanish*
• **el inglés** *English*
• **las matemáticas** *mathematics*

¿Cuándo? *When?*

hoy *today*
mañana *tomorrow*
después *later*
esta semana *this week*

26

¡Qué materias tienes?

Pregúntale a tu compañero(a). *Ask your classmate what subjects he/she has.*

— ¿Qué materias tienes hoy?
— Tengo matemáticas, historia, geografía y ciencias.
— ¿Y qué materias tienes mañana?
— Tengo...

 Tu horario

Con tu compañero(a), hablen sobre el horario. *With your classmate, talk about the class schedule on page 26.*

— ¿Tienes clase de geografía?
— Sí, los lunes, los martes y los viernes.
— ¿A qué hora es la clase los lunes?
— A las nueve de la mañana.
— ¿Qué clase tienes después?
— Matemáticas.

 ¿Cómo es la clase?

Pregúntale a tu compañero(a). *Ask your classmate about his/her classes.*

— ¿Cómo es la clase de español?
— Es muy divertida.
— ¿Y la clase de matemáticas?
— Es un poco difícil.

 ¡Tu clase favorita?

Pregúntale a tu compañero(a). *Ask your classmate about his or her favorite class.*

— ¿Cuál es tu clase favorita?
— La clase de arte.
— ¿Por qué?
— Porque es divertida.

¿Cómo es...?
muy *very*
un poco *a bit*
fácil *easy*
divertido(a)
difícil *difficult*
aburrido(a)
interesante

 ¡OJO!

To say on Mondays, on Tuesdays, . . ., use *los lunes, los martes.* For Saturdays and Sundays, use *los sábados, los domingos.*

PARA COMUNICARNOS MEJOR

¿Por qué? *means "why."* **Porque** *means "because." What are the two differences between these words?*

1. ¿Qué materias tienes?
Encourage students to use expressions in the **¿Cuándo?** section.
Expand this activity by having partners make sentences about the student schedule and identifying which day it is.
Example:
A: *Son las doce y el estudiante tiene ciencias.*
B: *Es jueves.*

2. Tu horario
Expand this activity by asking such questions as: *¿Cuántas clases tienes los lunes?*

3. ¿Cómo es la clase?
Expand this activity by having students write up their own class schedules in Spanish, using the schedule on page 26 as a model. Have them describe each class with words like **fácil** and **divertida**.

4. ¿Tu clase favorita?
Expand this activity by polling the class to find out which classes students prefer and why.

En la clase

Have students describe what is going on. Make a few simple comments and questions about the picture and vocabulary. Examples:

¿Dónde está la pizarra? ¿Y aquí [in this classroom]?

¿Qué hay en el escritorio? ¿Y aquí?

Hay

Have students read the *Para comunicarnos mejor*. Make sure they realize that **hay** is a "catch-all" term that is used for both *there is* and *there are*.

Make statements/questions that use **hay** as both singular and plural. Examples:

¿Cuántas puertas hay en este salón de clases?

¿Cuántas ventanas hay?

¿Qué hay en mi escritorio? Libros, ¿no?

¿Cuántos libros hay? Uno.

Bien, yo tengo un libro y Juan tiene dos libros. ¿Cuántos libros hay?

¿QUÉ HAY EN LA CLASE?
What's in the classroom?

el cartel

la pizarra

el borrador

la tiza

la computadora

el lápiz

el escritorio

el cartel

el diccionario

el libro

la mesa

el cuaderno

la silla

el mapa

el bolígrafo

la mochila

la cinta

PARA COMUNICARNOS MEJOR

Use the word **hay** to talk about what is in the classroom.

En la clase hay una pizarra.
There is a chalkboard in the classroom.

Hay treinta estudiantes en la clase.
There are 30 students in the classroom.

28

¿Qué hay en la clase?

Habla con tu compañero(a). *Look around the classroom and talk about the things you see.*

muchos(as) *many*
pocos(as) *few*

— *¿Qué hay en la clase?*
— *Hay muchos escritorios y muchas sillas.*

 ¿Qué necesitas?

Pregúntale a tu compañero(a). *Take turns asking what items you need.*

— *¿Necesitas un diccionario?*
— *Sí, necesito uno.*
  (No, gracias, ya tengo uno.)

Use the verb **necesitar** *to talk about what you need. Here are some of its forms:*

yo	necesito	I need
tú	necesitas	you (familiar) need
usted	necesita	you (formal) need
él/ella	necesita	he/she needs

☐ *To ask if you need anything, use the expression* **¿Necesitas...?** *(Do you need . . .?)*

☐ *To answer the question, use one of the expressions:*
  • **No, ya tengo.** *(No, I already have it.)* or
  • **Sí, gracias.**

 ¿Qué es?

Describe something in the classroom. Your classmates have to guess what it is.

— *Es una cosa. Es grande,...*
— *¿De qué color es?*
— *Es verde. ¿Qué es?*
— *¡Es la pizarra!*

¿Cómo es?
grande *big*
pequeño(a) *small*
bonito(a) *pretty*
feo(a) *ugly*
nuevo(a) *new*
viejo(a) *old*

¿Qué es?
Es una cosa.
It's a thing.

¡OJO!
To ask what color something is, use the expression **¿De qué color es?** Remember that the gender of the adjective has to agree with the gender of the noun. **El libro es blanco. La tiza es blanca.**

1. ¿Qué hay en clase?
Expand this activity by having partners take turns holding one to three coins (or other small objects) in one hand and playing a guessing game. Example:
A: *¿Cuántas cosas [monedas] hay en mi mano?*
B: *Hay tres.*
A: *No, hay una.*

2. ¿Qué necesitas?
Expand this activity by having students ask questions about the number of things they need. For example:
A: *¿Cuántos lápices de colores necesitas?*
B: *Necesito tres lápices de colores: el rojo, el verde y el amarillo.*

3. ¿Qué es?
Expand this activity by having students rate the objects in the drawing as *¡Qué bueno!* or *¡Qué aburrido!*

29

¿CUÁNTO CUESTA?

Objectives
- to use numbers over 100
- to be able to buy things
- to say what you want

Related Components

Activity Book	Audio Book
p. 12	Script: p. 7
	Audio Tapes
	Listening: 1A

Cognados
Ask students to name any cognates they can find here. They should be able to find: **champú**, shampoo; **diccionario**, dictionary; **diente**, dental; **pasta**, paste; **refresco**, refreshment.

Números grandes
Besides focusing on prices, try dates and series of numbers. For example:
Dates: Ask: In what year did Columbus encounter the Americas? When did the United States declare its independence? When were you born?
Series: Have students supply numbers to complete a series. Examples:

111, 222, 333...	(444, 555...)
100, 200, 400...	(800, 1600...)
205, 210, 215...	(220, 225...)
123, 234, 345...	(456, 567...)
33, 66, 99...	(132, 165...)

Know Your Number: This game, used earlier to teach 1-10, can be adapted to higher numbers. Have students count off by hundreds *(cien, doscientos...)*. Call out numbers in each range *(ciento diez)* and have them raise a hand when they hear their own range. Again, vary speed and accent. It may help to assign ranges by row and have students close their eyes as you speak.

¿CUÁNTO CUESTA?
How much does it cost?

LAS CAMISETA[S]

$2.50 — LA PASTA DE DIENTES

$7.50

$26.30 — LA MOCHILA

$1.25

$6.25 — EL CHAMPÚ

$14.99 — EL DICCIONARIO

GRATIS — el refresco — EL REFRESCO

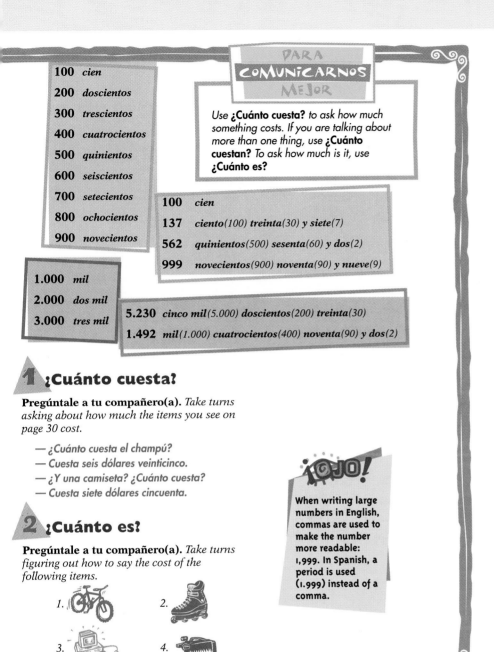

100	*cien*
200	*doscientos*
300	*trescientos*
400	*cuatrocientos*
500	*quinientos*
600	*seiscientos*
700	*setecientos*
800	*ochocientos*
900	*novecientos*

PARA COMUNICARNOS MEJOR

Use **¿Cuánto cuesta?** *to ask how much something costs. If you are talking about more than one thing, use* **¿Cuánto cuestan?** *To ask how much is it, use* **¿Cuánto es?**

100	*cien*
137	*ciento(100) treinta(30) y siete(7)*
562	*quinientos(500) sesenta(60) y dos(2)*
999	*novecientos(900) noventa(90) y nueve(9)*

1.000	*mil*
2.000	*dos mil*
3.000	*tres mil*

5.230	*cinco mil(5.000) doscientos(200) treinta(30)*
1.492	*mil(1.000) cuatrocientos(400) noventa(90) y dos(2)*

1 ¿Cuánto cuesta?

Pregúntale a tu compañero(a). *Take turns asking about how much the items you see on page 30 cost.*

— ¿Cuánto cuesta el champú?
— Cuesta seis dólares veinticinco.
— ¿Y una camiseta? ¿Cuánto cuesta?
— Cuesta siete dólares cincuenta.

2 ¿Cuánto es?

Pregúntale a tu compañero(a). *Take turns figuring out how to say the cost of the following items.*

1. 2. 3. 4.

¡OJO!
When writing large numbers in English, commas are used to make the number more readable: 1,999. In Spanish, a period is used (1.999) instead of a comma.

DE COMPRAS

Point out that *peseta* is the name of the unit of currency in Spain.

En la farmacia
Necesito...

Model the text and the variations. Talk about **necesitar,** and make sentences with **necesitas** and **necesita.** Point out that the full answer will be plural *(Son 159 pesetas)* because the verb refers to **pesetas** and not to **pasta.**

En la tienda
Quiero...
Model the text and the variations. Have students point to or show examples of these items. Make sentences with **quieres** and **quiere** as well.

En la cafetería
Por favor...
Model the text and the variations. Expand the activity by having students order more than one thing. Example:
Clerk: *¿Qué quiere Ud.?*
A: *Un batido y una pizza, por favor.*

DE COMPRAS
Going shopping

En la farmacia *At the drugstore*
Necesito... *I need . . .*
- champú
- pasta de dientes
- un cepillo de dientes
- un peine
- jabón

En la tienda *At the store*
Quiero... *I want . . .*
- una revista *a magazine*
- una tarjeta postal *a postcard*
- una camiseta *a T-shirt*
- un cartel *a poster*
- un bolígrafo *a pen*
- un diccionario español-inglés

En la cafetería *In the cafeteria*
Por favor,... *Please . . .*
- un batido de chocolate
  a chocolate milkshake
- un refresco *a softdrink*
- una limonada *a lemonade*
- una pizza
- una hamburguesa
- un sándwich

32

En la tienda

Con tu compañero(a), crea cuatro diálogos. *Take turns playing the roles of a clerk and the customer.*

— *Buenos días, quiero un bolígrafo, por favor. ¿Cuánto cuesta?*
— *Veinte pesetas.*
— *Gracias.*
— *De nada.*

 ## En la cafetería

Habla con tu compañero(a). *Imagine you are at a Spanish cafeteria. Take turns playing the roles of the clerk and the customer.*

— *Hola. Una limonada, por favor. ¿Cuánto cuesta?*
— *Diez pesos.*
— *Gracias.*
— *De nada.*

 ## En la farmacia

Con tu compañero(a), crea dos diálogos. *Take turns playing the roles of the clerk and the customer.*

— *Buenas tardes. Necesito champú, por favor. ¿Cuánto cuesta?*
— *Seis dólares veinticinco.*
— *Gracias.*
— *De nada.*

 ## Ahora tú

Trabajen en grupos pequeños. *With photos from magazines and brochures, create your own brochure. First, choose what kind of products you want to sell. Don't forget to include the prices!*

- *el dólar* **Estados Unidos**
- *la peseta* **España**
- *el peso* **México**

1. En la tienda
Expand this activity by having partners take turns as fortune-tellers. Instead of saying *Necesito champú*, partner A asks *¿Qué necesito?* and partner B predicts *Necesitas champú.*

2. En la cafetería
Expand this activity by having one play a clerk, the other a customer. The clerk makes suggestions, but the customer keeps turning them down. Example:
Clerk: *¿Le gusta un batido de chocolate?*
Client: *No, no me gustan los batidos.*

3. En la farmacia
Expand by having the customer ask for two to five of the same objects. Have the clerk answer by giving the total amount.

4. Ahora tú
Expand by having groups order from other groups' brochures.

Objectives

- to review useful words and phrases used in everyday situations
- to provide a single source for common vocabulary
- to learn phrases used in class

Related Components

Activity Book
p. 13-16

Palabras y Expresiones

Pages 34–36 of the student book summarize the most useful words and phrases introduced in the *Encuentros*. The list is organized by themes to make it easier to locate words. The same approach is used at the end of each chapter, in the *Vocabulario temático* section. Encourage students to use this section as necessary and review it frequently.

PARA TU REFERENCIA
(PALABRAS Y EXPRESIONES)

Greetings

- ¡Hola! *Hi!*
- Buenos días. *Good morning.*
- Buenas tardes. *Good afternoon.*
- Buenas noches. *Good evening/ Good night.*
- ¿Qué tal? *What's up?*
- ¿Cómo estás? *How are you? (familiar)*
- ¿Cómo está? *How are you? (formal)*
- Muy bien. *Very well.*
- Bien. *Fine.*
- Mal. *I'm not doing well.*

Meeting people

- Ésta/Éste es... *This is...*
- Mucho gusto. *Nice to meet you.*
- ¿Cómo te llamas? *What's your name?*
- Me llamo... *My name is...*
- ¿Cuál es tu apellido? *What's your last name?*
- ¿Cuál es tu dirección? *What's your address?*
- ¿Cuál es tu ... favorito(a)? *What's your favorite ...?*
- ¿Cuándo es tu cumpleaños? *When is your birthday?*
- ¿Cuántos años tienes? *How old are you?*
- Tengo ... años. *I'm ... years old.*
- ¿De dónde eres? *Where are you from?*
- Soy de... *I'm from...*
- ¿Y tú? *What about you?*

Polite expressions

- Perdón. *Excuse me.*
- Por favor. *Please.*
- Gracias. *Thank you.*
- De nada. *You're welcome.*

Likes and dislikes

- ¿Te gusta +infinitive? *Do you like to + infinitve?*
- Sí, me gusta mucho. *I like it very much.*
- No me gusta. *I don't like it.*
- ¿Qué te gusta hacer? *What do you like doing?*
- ¿Y a ti? *What about you?*
- A mí también. *Me too.*
- A mí tampoco. *Me neither.*

Favorite Activities

- bailar *to dance*
- cocinar *to cook*
- comer pizza *to eat pizza*
- dibujar *to draw*
- escuchar música *to listen to music*
- hablar por teléfono *to talk on the phone*
- ir al cine *to go to the movies*
- ir al gimnasio *to go to the gym*
- jugar al baloncesto *to play basketball*
- jugar al béisbol *to play baseball*
- jugar al fútbol *to play soccer*
- jugar al fútbol americano *to play football*
- jugar al voleibol *to play volleyball*
- leer *to read*
- mirar la televisión *to watch television*
- montar en bicicleta *to ride a bike*

Invitations

- ¿Te gustaría...? *Would you like to...?*
- Sí, ¡qué bueno! *Yes, great!*
- No, tal vez otro día. *No, maybe another day.*
- ¡Qué lástima! Tengo otros planes. *What a shame! I have other plans.*

34

Farewells

- Adiós. *Goodbye.*
- Chau. *Bye.*
- Hasta luego. *See you later.*
- Hasta mañana. *See you tomorrow.*

Expressions of time

- ¿Cuándo? *When?*
- después *later*
- hoy *today*
- mañana *tomorrow*
- esta semana *this week*

- ¿Qué hora es? *What time is it?*
- Son las.../Es la... *It is...*
- ... menos cuarto *quarter to...*
- ... y media *half past...*
- ... y cuarto *quarter past...*

- ¿A qué hora? *At what time?*
- A las... *At...*
- de la mañana *in the morning*
- de la tarde *in the afternoon*
- de la noche *in the evening*

Expressions of location

- ¿Dónde está? *Where is it?*
- ¿Dónde están? *Where are they?*
- A la derecha. *To the right.*
- A la izquierda. *To the left.*
- Está allí. *It's there.*
- Está aquí. *It's here.*

At the airport

- el autobús *bus*
- la salida *exit*
- los servicios *rest rooms*
- el taxi *taxicab*
- el teléfono *telephone*

Descriptions

- aburrido(a) *boring*
- alto(a) *tall*
- bajo(a) *short,*
- corto(a) *short*
- difícil *difficult*
- divertido(a) *funny, fun, amusing*
- fácil *easy*
- Fovorito(a) *favorite*
- grande *big, large*
- guapo(a) *good-looking*
- inteligente *inteligent*
- interesante *interesting*
- joven *young*
- largo(a) *long*
- nuevo(a) *new*
- pequeño(a) *small*
- viejo(a) *old*

Places

- la avenida *avenue*
- la cafetería *cafeteria*
- la calle *street*
- el cine *movie theater*
- la ciudad *city*
- la clase *classroom*
- la escuela *school*
- la farmacia *drugstore*
- el gimnasio *gym*
- el país *country*
- el restaurante *restaurant*
- la tienda *shop*

35

PARA TU REFERENCIA

You may also wish to focus on common classroom commands used in this book. Explain to students that these are commands directed at the whole class *(ustedes)*.

¿Qué dice la profesora/el profesor?
What does the teacher say?
Model and act out the following phrases. Provide the appopriate response to each command. Do not have students guess their English equivalents. Lead the class in TPR.

Abran el libro en la página…
Open your books to page…

¡Cierren los libros!
Close your books!

¡Digan/Escriban su nombre!
Say/Write your name!

¡Levanten la mano!
Raise your hand!

¡Saquen un lápiz!
Get a pencil!

¡Saquen un papel!
Get a piece of paper!

¡Señalen la puerta!
Point to the door!

¡Escuchen la cinta!
Listen to the tape!

¡Miren la pizarra!
Look at the chalkboard!

¡Pónganse de pie!
Get up!

¡Siéntense!
Sit down!

¡Hablen un poco más alto!
Speak a bit louder!

¡Vamos a hablar en español!
Let's speak in Spanish!

The following common phrases are useful responses and questions for students to have in class.

¿Qué dices tú?
Model the questions and phrases. Use these phrases where appropriate, such as answering questions in English from students by saying *no comprendo* or by asking other students *¿Qué dice Carlos?*

¿En qué página está?
On what page is it?

Más despacio, por favor.
Slower, please.

Tengo una pregunta.
I have a question.

No comprendo.
I don't understand.

¿Cómo?
Excuse me?/How?

¿Cómo se dice … en español?
How do you say … in Spanish?

No sé.
I don't know.

Perdón, ¿puede repetir la oración, por favor?
Excuse me, could you repeat the sentence, please?

¿Qué dice el profesor?
What is the teacher saying?

People

- la chica *girl*
- el chico *boy*
- el/la estudiante *student*
- el profesor *teacher*
- la profesora *teacher*

The family

- la familia *family*
- la abuela *grandmother*
- el abuelo *grandfather*
- los abuelos *grandparents*
- la hermana *sister*
- el hermano *brother*
- los hermanos *brothers and sisters*
- la madre *mother*
- el padre *father*
- los padres *parents*

Pets

- el gato *cat*
- el pájaro *bird*
- el perro *dog*
- el pez *fish*
- el ratón *mouse*
- la tortuga *turtle*

Foods and refreshments

- el batido de chocolate *chocolate milk-shake*
- la hamburguesa *hamburger*
- la limonada *lemonade*
- el refresco *soft drink*
- el sándwich *sandwich*

Going Shopping

- Necesito…. *I need. . .*
- Quiero… *I want. . .*
- la camiseta *T-shirt*
- el cepillo de dientes *toothbrush*
- el champú *shampoo*
- el jabón *soap*
- la pasta de dientes *toothpaste*
- el peine *comb*
- la revista *magazine*
- la tarjeta postal *postcard*

Classroom items

- el bolígrafo *pen*
- el borrador *eraser*
- el cartel *poster*
- la cinta *tape*
- la computadora *computer*
- el cuaderno *notebook*
- el diccionario *dictionary*
- el escritorio *desk*
- el lápiz *pencil*
- el libro *book*
- el mapa *map*
- la mochila *backpack*
- la pizzarra *chalkboard*
- la silla *chair*
- la tiza *chalk*

Question words

- ¿Cómo es? *What is it/he/she like?*
- ¿Cuál es…? *What is…?*
- ¿Cuándo? *When?*
- ¿Cuánto cuesta(n)? *How much is it?*
- ¿Cuántos(as)? *How many?*
- ¿Dónde? *Where?*
- ¿De qué color es? *What color is it?*
- ¿Por qué? *Why?*
- ¿Qué es? *What is it?*
- ¿Quién? *Who?*

Useful words

- pero *but*
- porque *because*
- también *also*
- y *and*
- o *or*

References

- *Colors page 14*
- *Days of the week page 22*
- *Months of the year page 22*
- *Numbers pages 6, 12, 31*

¿QUÉ DICEN LAS INSTRUCCIONES?

A
Adivina/Adivinen *Guess*
Anota/Anoten *Write down*
el anuncio *ad*

B
Busca/Busquen *Look for*

C
cada uno(a) *each one*
la carta *letter*
¿Cierto o falso? *True or false?*
Compara/Comparen *Compare*
Con tu compañero(a) *With your partner*
Corrige/Corrijan *Correct*
Crea/Creen *Create*

D
Decide/Decidan *Decide*
Describe/Describan *Describe*
Di/Digan *Say*
Diseña/Diseñen
el diálogo *dialog*
el dibujo *drawing*

E
En grupos *In groups*
la encuesta *survey*
la entrevista *interview*
Escoge/Escojan *Choose*
Escribe/Escriban *Write*

F
el folleto *brochure*

H
Habla/Hablen sobre/de *Talk about*
Haz/Hagan una lista *Make a list*
Haz/Hagan planes *Make plans*
Haz/Hagan preguntas *Ask questions*

I
Imagina/Imaginen *Imagine*
Informa/Informen a la clase *Inform the class*
Inventa/Inventen *Invent*

L
la lista *list*

M
Más popular *most popular.*
Menos popular *least popular.*
Mira/Miren *Look at.*

O
la oración *sentence*

P
el párrafo *paragraph*
Piensa/Piensen en *Think of*
Planea/Planeen *Plan*
Pon/Pongan *Put*
Pregúntale a tu compañero(a). *Ask your partner.*
Prepara/Preparen *Prepare*
Presenta/Presenten *Present*

Q
¿Qué ves en...? *What do you see in...?*

R
Representa/Representen *Act/Perform*
la respuesta *answer*
los resultados *results*

S
Según tu opinión *In your opinion*
el significado *meaning*

U
Usa/Usen *Use*

37

El abecedario español

Objective

• to practice listening to and writing letters of the Spanish alphabet

Related Components

Audio Book	Audio Tapes
Script: p. 8	Listening: 1B

To help students understand and use the Spanish alphabet, say aloud common words and phrases. As you say each word or phrase, have students spell it out loud, letter by letter. Some suggestions:

¡Hola!	*Está*
Bien	*Teléfono*
Mucho gusto	*Difícil*
Perdón	*Interesante*
Cuantos años	*Joven*
Bailan	*Calle*
Jugar	*Restaurante*
Mañana	*Perro*
Dónde	*Tarjeta*
Izquierda	*Porque*

Expand by having students work in pairs. One student reads common words or phrases from a list he or she has made. The other student spells aloud and/or writes the words correctly.

EL ABECEDARIO ESPAÑOL
(THE SPANISH ALPHABET)

• Since 1994, there have been 26 letters in the Spanish alphabet.
• The Spanish and English alphabets have 25 letters in common.
• The only letter of the English alphabet not included in the Spanish alphabet is "w." "W" appears only in foreign words.
• The Spanish alphabet has one letter that the English alphabet does not have: ñ.
• Before 1994, there were four more letters (for a total of 30) in the Spanish alphabet: "ch," "ll," "rr," and "w."

In dictionaries published before 1994, words that began with the letters "ch" and "ll" appeared in their own separate sections. Words beginning with "w" (foreign words) still do.

How to say the names of letters

The best way to learn the names of letters is to listen to your teacher, a friend who speaks Spanish, or your audio tape. But once you've done that, you can use this chart as a handy reminder of the approximate way to say the name of the letter.

Letter	Name	How to say the name of the letter	Letter	Name	How to say the name of the letter
a	"a"	like the "a" in "father"	n	"ene"	like "**en**-nay"
b*	"be"	like "bay"	ñ	"eñe"	like "**en**-yay"
c	"ce"	like "say"	o	"o"	like "oh"
(ch)*	"che"	like "chay" (rhymes with "day")	p	"pe"	like "pay"
d	"de"	like "day"	q	"cu"	like "coo"
e	"e"	the vowel sound in "day"	r	"ere"	like "**eh**-ray"
f	"efe"	sounds like "**ef**-fay"	(rr)*	"erre"	like "**ehr**-ray"
g	"ge"	like "hay"	s	"ese"	like "**es**-say"
h	"hache"	sounds like "**ah**-chay"	t	"te"	like "tay"
i	"i"	like the "ee" in "see"	u	"u"	like "oo" in "too"
j	"jota"	like "**hoe**-tah"	v	"ve"	like "bay"
k	"ka"	like "kah"	(w)*	"doble ve"	like "**doe**-blay-bay"
l	"ele"	like "**eh**-lay"	x	"equis"	like "**eh**-kees"
(ll)*	"elle"	like "y" in "yes"	y	"y griega"	like "yay"
m	"eme"	like "**em**-may"	z	"zeta"	like "**say**-tah"

Notes

* Technically, these are not separate letters of the alphabet. But they have names, and many Spanish speakers will refer to them as letters.

PRONUNCIACIÓN DE LAS LETRAS

The best way to learn how to pronounce Spanish words correctly is to listen to someone who speaks the language well. Your teacher will work with you on pronunciation throughout the year. However, here are some helpful pronunciation hints for your use when reading Spanish.

Pronouncing Spanish vowels

Spanish vowels are always—or nearly always—pronounced in the same way, regardless which syllable of the word is stressed. Use the alphabet chart on the left for pronunciation guidelines for the vowels. In English, vowels are typically pronounced with a following glide. That is not true in Spanish. Vowels in Spanish are short and pure.

The easiest consonants

Some Spanish consonants are pronounced approximately as they are in English: "b, c, d, f, k, l, m, n, p, q, s, t w, y."

Don't make a sound...

when you see the letter "h." In Spanish, the letter "h" is silent (except in the "ch" combination where it is pronounced as in English).

So you won't miss the sound of "h" . . .

the letter "j" in Spanish is pronounced approximately like the letter "h" in the English word "he."

Something familiar and not-so familiar . . .

In Spanish and in English, when "g" is followed by "a," "o," or "u," it has the same sound as in the English word "go." However, in Spanish when the letter "g" is followed by "e" or "i," it is pronounced like the letter "h" in the English word "he."

Nothing like it . . .

"ñ": English has no letter like it, but the sound is like the letters "n" and "y" in the English word "canyon."

"r" and "rr" are pronounced very differently from the English letter "r." Work with your teacher on these sounds.

Pronounce "ll" like the "l" "y" combination in "call you."

No guessing . . .

"x" can be pronounced in four different ways. Learn each word as you go.

You will never hear it . . .

The Spanish letter "v" is pronounced like the letter "b" in Spanish, never like the letter "v" in English. That sound doesn't exist in Spanish. The letter "z" in Spanish is pronounced like the letter "s" in the English word "sing." You'll never hear a sound like "zing."

Stress in the right place

In Spanish words, as in English, one syllable receives more stress than the others. The Spanish rules for stressing a syllable are easy:
- If a word has a written accent (´), stress the accented syllable ("rápido").
- If a word ends in a vowel ("rico"), an "n" ("comen"), or an "s" ("comes"), stress the next-to-the-last syllable.
- If a word has no written accent mark and ends in a consonant other than "n" or "s," stress the last syllable.

Pronunciación de las letras

For detailed background and instruction on correct pronunciation of Spanish vowels and consonants, consult the *Vocabulario temático* page at the end of each chapter of this book.

In this unit

We travel to Mexico, where a unique blend of indigenous and Spanish cultures captures the imagination of all who go there. Mexico's heart and capital, Mexico City, is the biggest city in the world, and a perfect place to explore the fast-paced ins and outs of Mexican urban life (Chapter 1). Our first meals lead to a survey of the city's amazing range of different foods and eating habits (Chapter 2). During a quick spin downtown, where Aztec temples and colonial churches face giant skyscrapers, we learn how to get around, where to go for what we want, and how to buy what we need. On the outskirts, we brush past archaeologists for a better look at the well-preserved ruins of Teotihuacán. Then we're off on a mouth-watering tour of markets, restaurants, and bustling *taquerías*.

Before leaving Mexico City, we'll visit Chapultepec Park—shown in the video for this unit and in the map in the *Adelante* section of the student book. Situated across the street from the Museum of Anthropology (which we visit in the video), the park is the largest open space in Mexico City and a favorite evening and weekend resort for *capitalinos* who crave the refreshment of grass and trees and lake breezes. Then, after waving goodbye to the *Ángel de la Independencia* high above the *Paseo de la Reforma*, we duck into a kitchen and try our hand at the unit project of making tacos.

VIDEO LINKS

Text	Video Segment
Unit Overview Unit Opener	**1. Introduction to Mexico** A whirlwind tour of Mexico City and its inhabitants
Chapter 1	**2. ¡Descubre la ciudad!** Mexico City old and new: getting around, where to go, what to do, how to buy, Teotihuacán grammar: verbs **ir** and **ir a** + infinitive; **-ar** verbs
Chapter 2	**3. ¿Qué vas a comer?** food and eating, dining out in Mexico City, Mexican menus, *taquerías* and restaurants grammar: **-er** and **-ir** verbs; **me/te/le gusta/gustan** + noun
Adelante	**4. Adelante**
Manos a la obra	Chapultepec Park **5. Manos a la obra** How to make tacos

Geography and Climate

Mexico has two mountain ranges, the Sierra Madre Oriental and the Sierra Madre Occidental, which run down from the US border and along the Gulf and Pacific coasts. Annual rainfall varies from 200 inches on parts of the Gulf coast to as little as 4 inches in the northern deserts. The central plateau, the historic heart of Mexico, has a pleasant climate year-round, with temperatures rarely rising above 80°F or falling below 50°F. Covering only 10% of the Mexican land mass, this temperate region contains half the population of almost 100 million.

History

The earliest known ancestors of today's indigenous Mexicans arrived on the subcontinent 20,000 years ago. By 6,000 B.C. squash and avocados were cultivated, and by 3,000 B.C. corn and beans were the backbone of the Mesoamerican diet. They still are.

Starting around 1,000 B.C., one great civilization follows another in Mexico. Ruins of cities built by Mayans, Toltecs, Zapotecs, and Olmecs bear eloquent testimony to their achievements, and when Cortés and his soldiers arrived in 1519 most population groups in Mexico were either tax-paying subjects of the Aztec emperor or in a chronic state of war with his armies. Playing one group against another with cunning, courage, treachery, and luck, Cortés overthrew the Aztec empire in 1521.

Mexico's independence from Spain came in 1821. Great instability followed. The US invaded in 1846 and took all Mexican territory north of the Rio Grande. In 1859 Benito Juárez, a poor Zapotec from the state of Oaxaca, was elected president. But foreign intervention, this time from France, kept him from consolidating his power until he defeated the French forces at Puebla in 1867.

In 1876 Porfirio Díaz established a dictatorship that lasted 35 years, creating both stability and enormous corruption. The *Porfiriato* was followed by a revolution that began in 1910 and took the lives of over one million Mexicans. Its reverberations are felt today.

Mexican Muralists

Perhaps the best record of the beliefs and passions that led to the Mexican Revolution, and then were transformed by it, are the murals created during the 1920s and '30s by Mexican artists José Clemente Orozco, Diego Rivera, and David Alfaro Siqueiros. Gigantic wall paintings such as *The Trench* (Orozco), *Zapata Leading the Agrarian Revolt* (Rivera), and *From Porfirio's Dictatorship to the Revolution* (Siqueiros) are attempts to communicate revolutionary ideals and history to a largely illiterate population. The murals influenced Pablo Picasso (when he painted *Guernica*), Jackson Pollock (who studied with Siqueiros in New York), and, much later, US inner-city graffiti muralists of the 1980s, as well as others.

Civilizaciones antiguas

HISTORY CONNECTION

Objective
- to explore early Mexican civilizations

Use
after Situaciones, pages 54–55

Materials
- 3" x 5" index cards
- 2 paper bags
- Transparency Unit 1, *Ruinas mayas en Palenque*
- overhead projector

Preparation
- Divide class into small groups and have each group research one of the ancient Mexican civilizations.
- Have groups fill out index cards, each with one fact they discover but without naming the culture. Example: They founded the city of Monte Albán. (Zapotecs)
- Show transparency and ask class what they've learned that might demonstrate that the ruin is Mayan and not Olmec, Toltec, Zapotec, or Aztec.

Activity
- Discuss the title of the activity with the class and invite group presentations of each civilization. Groups should emphasize the facts on their cards.
- Groups deposit their cards in a bag when they finish their presentations. After the presentations, each group picks a card and tries to identify the culture.
- If a group can't identify a culture, card is placed in bag for second game when first bag is empty.

FYI

Civilization	Major cultural center(s)
Olmec	La Venta
Toltec	Tula
Mayan	Palenque, Chichen Itzá
Zapotec	Monte Albán
Aztec	Templo Mayor

Cielito lindo

MUSIC CONNECTION

Objective
- to learn the words to a popular Mexican song

Use
any time during Unit 1

Materials
- TRB Activity Support Page 1, *Cielito lindo*

Activity
- Distribute song sheet and have students discuss the meaning of the lyrics. Which lyrics seem especially Mexican? Which lyrics remind them of popular US songs?

   Cielito lindo
   by Quirino Mendoza y Cortés

   Under my window each night
   rides a horseman
   who bravely serenades me,
   making me fall in love.
      (Refrain) Oh, oh, oh, oh, sing and don't cry,
               because singing makes hearts happy,
               little heavenly beauty.
   Oh, darling horseman, don't sing,
   I'm engaged to somebody else
   and his finding out that you want me
   could cost you your life.
      (Repeat refrain)
   Oh, horseman, before God,
   oh, leave me alone,
   and forget a love
   you'll never enjoy again.
      (Repeat refrain)
   A bird that leaves
   his first nest, his first nest,
   and comes back to find it taken,
   only gets what he deserves.

FYI
Quirino Mendoza y Cortés (1862-1957)—composer, musician, bandleader. He wrote *Cielito lindo* at the age of twenty. After years of teaching in rural Mexico, he joined Pancho Villa's revolutionary army in 1916.

En otras palabras— los aztecas

HISTORY CONNECTION

Objective
• to explore Náhuatl contributions to Spanish

Use
any time during Unit 1

Materials
• TRB Activity Support Page 2, *El imperio azteca en 1519* (map)
• Transparency Unit 1, *El imperio azteca en 1519*
• overhead projector
• posterboard or large pad
• thick marker

Activity
• Show the transparency and share the FYI below. Ask why the map is dated 1519.
• List Aztec and Spanish words on the posterboard and have students guess the English words that come from them. Why did these words travel from language to language?

Aztec (Náhuatl)	Spanish	English
aguacatl	aguacate	avocado
cacahuatl	cacao	cocoa
chillí	chile	chile
coyotl	coyote	coyote
ocelotl	ocelote	ocelot
tomatl	tomate	tomato
xocoatl	chocolate	chocolate

FYI
Originally from the north, the Aztecs spoke Náhuatl, a language closely related to those of the Pima, Shoshone, and Comanche tribes. When the Spaniards arrived in 1519, the Aztecs controlled an area from the Gulf of Mexico through the central mountains and southward to Guatemala. Their art, technology, and agriculture were very sophisticated. They used cocoa beans as money, and also cultivated pears, tomatoes, squash, tobacco, corn, beans, and peppers. Although enemies, Aztecs and Spaniards were influenced by each other This contact added new words to Spanish, and eventually to American English. Náhuatl dialects are spoken by one and a half million Mexicans today.

El bosque de Chapultepec

Objective
• to play a board game simulating a trip through Chapultepec Park

Use
during the Unit 1 *Adelante,* pages 78-87

Materials
• TRB Activity Support Page 3, *El bosque de Chapultepec* (map/board game)
• cardboard for game board (at least 18" x 18")
• drawings and magazine photos of woods
• crayons, magic markers, colored pencils

Preparation
• Read and discuss pages 78-82. Compare and contrast Chapultepec Park with a park you know.
• Discuss features of Chapultepec Park such as el castillo, el lago, el bosque, la feria y los juegos mecánicos, el monumento a los niños héroes, y el Papalote.

Activity
• Divide class into groups of four. Distribute activity sheet.
• Ask each group to devise a board game by copying the map and decorating it with pictures. Games can vary: one group might want to stop often; another group might want to get through the park quickly.
• Team members have specific roles. Possible roles include: designing game and game board, writing rules and testing them, presenting the finished game.
• Tell students they can write game rules in English, but the more Spanish they use in their game, the better.
• Challenge students to make games interesting with chance cards, animal sightings, sudden detours, etc.
• After all games have been presented, ask students which game they like best. Why?

Variations
• For *Situaciones,* pages 54-55, use Teotihuacán and its attractions for a board game.
• For *Para resolver,* pages 56-57, use Mexico City and its landmarks for a board game.

MÉXICO HOY

Communicative Objectives
• to introduce Mexico and its history
• to develop listening comprehension

Related Components

CD ROM	Video : Tape/Book
Unit 1	Unit 1: Seg. 1
Transparencies	
Unit 1	

Search to frame 1000807

GETTING STARTED

If any students have been to Mexico, ask them to describe the places they visited. If no one has been there, ask what they think they would find in Mexico. What would Mexico City be like? What would the weather be like? What kinds of food would people eat?

Using the Video
You may wish to show the first sequence of the Unit 1 video, a visual introduction to Mexico.

Using the Transparencies
To help orient students to Mexico, use the Locator Map Transparency. You may also want to review the other transparencies for Unit 1 at this time.

DISCUSS

Presenting Mexico
For more detailed information about Mexico, refer to pages 40A-40D.

Using the Text
English: Have students read the English introduction. Ask comprehension and critical-thinking questions. For example: How many people live in our city (state)? How much less (more) is that than Mexico City?
Spanish: Ask students to scan the text on the lefthand page for words they think they recognize. What do they think these chapters will probably be about?

UNIDAD 1

MEXICO HOY

En la unidad 1:

Capítulo 1	¡Descubre la ciudad!
Capítulo 2	¿Qué vas a comer?
Adelante	**Para leer:** Un paseo por Chapultepec
	Proyecto: Tortillas y tacos
	Otras fronteras: Ciencias, arte, historia y arqueología

40

Unit Components

Activity Book	Audio Book	CD ROM	Tutor Pages
p. 17-40	Script: p. 9-12;	Unit 1	p. 7-14
Assessment	17-20	**Conexiones**	**Video: Tape/Book**
Oral Proficiency:	Activities:	Chapters 1-2	Unit 1: Segments 1-5
p. 21-22	p. 13-16; 21-24	**Cuaderno**	
Listening Script:	**Audio Tapes**	p. 5-20	
p. 9-10	Chapter: 2A, 2B	**Magazine**	
Chapter Tests:	Adelante: 8A, 8B	Juntos en México	
p. 45-56	Assessment: 14A	**Transparencies**	
Portfolio: p. 33-34	Conexiones: 16A	Unit 1: Chapters 1-2	

You are about to enter Mexico City, a bustling capital with a population of over 23 million. As you walk through this modern city, you will see skyscrapers, parks, museums, fancy restaurants, fast food stands, and other symbols of a big city of today.

Mexico City is built on the ruins of Tenochtitlán, the ancient capital of the Aztec Empire, which flourished long before the voyages of Christopher Columbus. By the time the Spaniards arrived in 1519, the rich Aztec culture had been thriving for almost 3,000 years.

In this unit, you will stroll through Mexico City or visit Chapultepec Park and join Mexican teenagers for a fun day. You will go to a restaurant and learn how to order a delicious meal in Spanish. You'll even get to try your hands at making a taco! Finally, you'll return to Mexico's past and learn about the Aztec calendar—a great wonder of this ancient civilization. ¡Vamos!

"El Ángel", monumento a la Independencia, Ciudad de México.

41

Interdisciplinary Connections
To provide other perspectives, assign research projects like these:

Geography
How long is the border between Mexico and the United States? Which American states does it touch?

Math
If you took $100 to Mexico today, how many pesos would you get at the bank?

History
Who is the president of Mexico? How often are presidential elections held in Mexico?

Archaeology
What are some of the major archaeological sites in Mexico?

LOG BOOK
Have students write five things they'd like to learn about Mexico.

Para hispanohablantes

What cultures exist or once existed in the country your family came from? Share what you know about them with the class.

 CULTURE NOTE

The Aztecs called themselves the Mexicas (may-SHEE-kas), but the name we use for them refers to Aztlán, their original homeland. Aztlán was to the northwest of Mexico City.

▶▶▶ INTERNET LINK

For a broad collection of WWW links from the University of Guadalajara:
http://mexico.udg.mx:80/grafica.html

	Objetivos page 43	Conversemos pages 44-45	Realidades pages 46-47	Palabras en acción pages 48-49
Comunicación	• To talk about how to get around the city	Discuss different ways to get around the city		Activities 6, 8: Read cartoon, discuss how to go places in Mexico City; list how to go to places in your area
	• To talk about places to go and things to do	Discuss different places to go and things to do	Read text, answer questions, discuss places to go and things to do in Mexico City	Activities 3-5, 8: Read cartoon, discuss places to go in Mexico City, what to do, what to buy; make table of places in your area
	• To talk about giving simple directions	Answer questions about where places are and how to get to them		Activities 2, 6: Read cartoon, discuss where places are; discuss how to go to 3 places in Mexico City
Vocabulario temático	• To know the expressions for places in the city	Talk about different places in the city	Read text, answer questions, discuss places in Mexico City, make survey of class preferences	Activities 1-6: Read cartoon, make list of places; discuss where places are, where to go; what to do, what to buy; how to get there
	• To know the expressions for things to do	Talk about different things to do in the city	Read text, answer questions, discuss things to do in Mexico City	Activities 4, 5, 8: Read cartoon, discuss what to do; what to buy; make table of places and what to do there
	• To know the expressions for ways to get from place to place	Talk about how to get from one place to another		Activities 6, 8: Read cartoon, discuss and list how to go places
Estructura	• To talk about where you are going: the verb *ir + a* + name of place	Use *ir + a* + name of place to discuss where to go in the city	Read text, answer questions, discuss where to go in Mexico City	Activity 3: Read cartoon, discuss where to go
	• To talk about what you are going to do: the verb *ir + a* + an infinitive	Use *ir + a* + an infinitive to discuss what to do in the city	Read text, answer questions, discuss what to do in Mexico City	Activities 4, 8: Read cartoon, discuss what to do in Mexico City; make table
	• To talk about activities that you do: *-ar* verbs such as *comprar, pasear, visitar*	Use *-ar* verbs to talk about activities to do in the city		Activity 5: Read cartoon, discuss what to buy in Mexico City
Cultura	Aztec pyramids in Mexico City		Highlights of downtown Mexico City: Templo Mayor, Teatro Polifórum, discothéques, shopping	More places to go in Mexico City: Chapultepec Park, Teatro Nacional, Plaza Garibaldi
Integración		Places, likeable things to do, ways to travel	Describing places and things, likeable things to do	Places, ways to travel around the city, directions/locations

Para comunicarnos mejor (1) pages 50-51	Para comunicarnos mejor (2) pages 52-53	Situaciones pages 54-55	Para resolver pages 56-57	Notes
Activity 2: Discuss how friends and family go to places		Activities 1, 4: Read text, make plans to go to Teotihuacán; write sentences		
Activities 1-3: Discuss places to go and activities to do in Mexico City; discuss places in your area; make survey	Activities 1-3: Discuss activities to do downtown; discuss what to buy; make group list, ask other group questions	Activities 1-4: Read text, plan to go to Teotihua–cán; list places; discuss ones that will be visited; write sentences	Pasos 1-3: Read map, choose places to go; discuss where groups will go and what they will do; answer questions	
Activity 2: Discuss how friends and family get to places in your area		Activities 3, 4: Read text, discuss places that will be visited; write sentences		
Activities 1, 2: Discuss places in Mexico City; discuss places in your area	Activities 1, 2: Discuss things to do downtown; discuss where to buy things		Pasos 1-3: Read map, choose places to go in Mexico City; discuss where groups will go and what they will do; answer questions	
Activities 1, 3: Discuss things to do in Mexico City; make survey and report to class	Activities 1-3: Discuss things to do downtown, where to buy things; make group list, ask other group questions	Activities 1, 3, 4: Read text, make plans to go to Teotihuacán; discuss places that will be visited; write sentences	Pasos 2, 3: Read map, discuss where groups will go and what they will do; answer questions	
Activity 2: Discuss how familiar people get to places in your area		Activities 1, 4: Read text, plan to go to Teotihua-cán; write sentences		
Use all forms of *ir*. Activity 2: Discuss places to go in your city		Activities 1, 3, 4: Read text, make plans to go to Teotihuacán; discuss places; write sentences	Pasos 2, 3: Read map, discuss where groups will go and what they will do; answer questions	
Use all forms of *ir*. Activities 1, 3: Discuss things to do in Mexico City; make survey and report to class		Activities 1, 3, 4: Read text, make plans to go to Teotihuacán; discuss places that will be visited; write sentences	Pasos 2, 3: Read map, discuss where groups will go and what they will do; answer questions	
	Use all forms of *comprar*. Activities 1-3: Discuss things to do, where to buy things; make list, ask questions	Activities 3, 4: Read text, discuss places that will be visited in Mexico City; write sentences	Pasos 2, 3: Read map, discuss where groups will go and what they will do; answer questions	
		The mysterious history of Teotihuacán (Aztec for "home of the gods")	Using a map to find places in Mexico City	Entérate page 55 Teenagers in Mexico City: what they like to do, where they like to go
Activities that you do, time of day, days of week	Familiar people (family and friends), activities to do	Ways to travel, time of day, days of week, likeable things to do, places to go	Places in the city, locations	

El mapa de mi barrio

GEOGRAPHY CONNECTION

Objectives
- to draw and label a neighborhood map
- to discuss where places are, using the Chapter 1 *Vocabulario temático*

Use
after *Palabras en acción*, pages 48–49

Materials
- TRB Activity Support Page 4, *Papel cuadricu lado* (graph paper)

Preparation
- Set the scene by telling students that a Spanish-speaking friend is coming to visit. To help the visitor get around, they are going to draw and label a map of their neighborhood that includes the student's home, at least two means of transportation, and six places from the *Vocabulario temático* (shops, markets, etc.). You might want to draw a map of the school neighborhood on the chalkboard as a model.

Activity
- Have students use the completed maps to role-play in pairs, telling each other where places are. Host: *¿Dónde está el parque?* Friend: *El parque está cerca de la iglesia.* Host: *¿Dónde está la parada del autobús?* Friend: *Está a la derecha del museo.*
- Students then reverse roles and use the other map to ask more questions.
- Have the first pair work in front of the class. Help them along so the other students know how you expect each pair to play the game.
- Move around in the room during the activity to make sure students are on target.
- Have students take turns playing until time is up or until they have exhausted places to go, things to buy, etc.
- Display the labeled maps.

¿Adónde vas en la ciudad?

Objective
- to talk about going different places in a city, using Chapter 1 *Vocabulario temático*

Use
after *Palabras en acción*, pages 48-49

Materials
- TRB Activity Support Page 5, *Ruleta* (spinner)
- pencil, paperclip
- 3" x 5" index cards

Preparation
- Cut index cards in half. Write city places on them: *centro comercial, estadio, escuela, parada del autobús, estación del metro, librería, tienda de música, teatro, parque, museo, teatro.*

Activity
- Distribute spinner. Have students illustrate or label each section with a different means of transportation: *a pie, en autobús, en coche, en metro, en taxi, en bicicleta.*
- Have students practice using the spinner with a pencil for pivot and a paperclip for pointer.
- Students take turns picking a destination card, spinning to find out how they will get there, and creating a sentence with the information. For example, a student who picks *la librería* and spins *en coche* could say:—*Voy a la librería en coche.*

Variations
- Change the subject of the sentence to the third person. Example:—*Juan va al teatro en taxi.*

¿Qué hace la gente?

GAME

Objective
- to play a game about things we do, using **-ar** verbs

Use
after *Para comunicarnos mejor,* page 53

Materials
- TRB Activity Support Page 5, *Ruleta* (spinner)

Activity
- Distribute one spinner to each student and have students work in pairs.
- Display **-ar** verb and phrases on the board, and have students assign the verb or phrase to each section of one spinner. For example: *caminar, comprar, cantar, pasear, sacar fotos, visitar.*
- Assign personal pronouns to the other spinner. Display pronouns on the board: *yo, tú, él/ella, nosotros, Uds., ellos/ellas.*
- Each pair plays against another pair.
- Possible scenario: Student spins *visitar* on one spinner and *nosotros* on the other, and creates a sentence such as: *Nosotros visitamos el museo.*

Rules
- Pair gets 5 points for each correct sentence. Three points are subtracted for incorrect sentences.
- Sentences cannot be repeated.
- First pair to reach 25 points wins.

Variations
- Play game with other **-ar** verbs, such as *escuchar, necesitar, patinar, mirar, baitar.*
- Add when, where, or how often the activity takes place. E.g.: *Compro tarjetas en el mercado.*
- Play with **-er** or **-ir** verbs when you finish the *Para comunicarnos mejor* on pages 70–71 in Chapter 2.

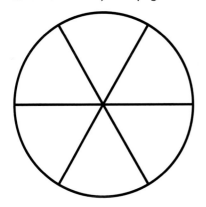

¿Qué vas a hacer mañana?

Objectives
- to plan daily activities, using **ir** and **ir a** + infinitive

Use
after *Para comunicarnos mejor,* page 51

Materials
- 3" x 5" index cards

Preparation
- Hand out index cards, one to each student, and have students draw an activity they plan to do the next day.
- Next to the drawing, have students write the time of day they plan to do the activity.

Activity
- Choose a volunteer to come forward and copy his/her activity and time from the card to the board, describing the plan while drawing the picture and writing the time. For example, the volunteer might draw someone getting into a bus, label the drawing 8 A.M., and say:— *A las ocho de la mañana, voy a la escuela.*
- When a volunteer finishes, students raise their hands to describe the plans in the third person, using the drawing and time as a guide. For example, after seeing antother drawing a student might say:—*A las dos de la tarde, Mariana va a sacar fotos.*
- Students who repeat the time and describe the drawing correctly, go next with a drawing and a time. If someone guesses incorrectly, another student tries to describe the activity.

Variation
- Students prepare activity cards with plural subjects and present their drawings to the class. For example:—*A las siete de la tarde, Carlos y yo vamos a un concierto.*

DESCUBRE LA CIUDAD

Introduce the chapter and its theme by asking a few questions about Mexico. You may wish to focus the discussion on the country's rich Pre-Columbian history and on the capital, Mexico City. Ask what activities people normally do in cities, and what students would expect to find in Mexico City.

Related Components

Audio Tapes	Conexiones
Conexiones: 16A, Ch. 1	Chapter 1
CD ROM	**Video: Tape/Book**
Chapter 1	Unit 1: Seg. 2

Search to frame 1012901

GETTING STARTED

Ask students if they can identify the buildings or the place in the photograph. Have any of them visited a place like this? Ask critical thinking questions. Suggestions: *¿Dónde está la Pirámide del Sol? Teotihuacán, ¿está cera o lejos de la Ciudad de México?*

Background

Places in Mexico City

La Alameda: A formal park in the center of the city. Nearby are the Palace of Fine Arts and a small museum that contains Diego Rivera's mural depicting the park.

La Basílica de Guadalipe: The site of an apparition of the Virgin Mary in 1531. There are two churches here: the original, badly damaged by earthquakes, and a new one.

La Ciudad Universitaria: The University of Mexico was founded in 1551, But its campus is very modern.

El Bosque de Chapultepec: The Central Park of Mexico City. It contains several museums and a large zoo.

El Paseo de la Reforma: The city's main street, running east-west.

Teotihuacán: The impressive ruins of an ancient city, about 50 kilometers north of Mexico City.

El Zócalo: The huge central square in front of the National Palace. The name means *pedestal,* apparently a reference to monuments that were planned for the square but never completed.

CAPÍTULO **1**

¡DESCUBRE LA CIUDAD!

La Pirámide del Sol en Teotihuacán, muy cerca de la Ciudad de México.

42

Chapter Components

Activity Book	Audio Book	CD ROM	Transparencies
p. 17-26	Script: p. 9-12	Chapter 1	Chapter 1
Assessment	Activities: p. 13-16	**Conexiones**	**Tutor Pages**
Oral Proficiency:	**Audio Tapes**	Chapter 1	p. 7-10
p. 21	Chapter: 2A	**Cuaderno**	**Video: Tape/Book**
Listening Script:	Assessment:	p. 5-12	Unit 1: Seg. 2
p. 9	14A, Ch.1	**Magazine**	
Chapter Test:	Conexiones:	Juntos en México	
p. 45-50	16A, Ch.1		

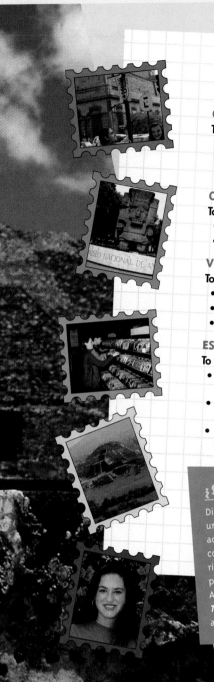

Objetivos

COMUNICACIÓN
To talk about:
- how to get around the city
- places to go and things to do
- giving simple directions

CULTURA
To learn about:
- places of interest in and around Mexico City
- what young Mexicans like to do

VOCABULARIO TEMÁTICO
To know the expressions for:
- places in the city
- things to do
- ways to get from place to place

ESTRUCTURA
To talk about:
- where you are going: the verb *ir* with *a* and the name of a place
- what you are going to do: the verb *ir* with *a* and the infinitive of another verb
- activities that you do: *-ar* verbs such as *comprar, pasear, visitar*

¿SABES QUE...?

Did you know that in Mexico you can find pyramids in the most unexpected places? If you visit the National University, you can admire the pyramid of Cuicuilco, excavated in 1922, after being covered with lava for thousands of years. If you take a subway ride to Pino Suárez Station, you will see the ruins of a round pyramid, discovered as the metro was being built. And the Aztec culture meets the twentieth century in the *Plaza de las Tres Culturas*, where the remains of an ancient pyramid face a seventeenth-century church and several modern buildings.

43

ACTIVITIES

Here are some additional activities that you may wish to use as you work through this chapter with your students.

Communication
Encourage after-class activities that may enhance student interest and proficiency. For example:
- speak to your students (or other teachers from the Spanish department) about how they were first introduced or became involved with the language

Culture
To encourage greater cultural understanding:
- show documentaries about Frida Khalo, Diego Rivera, and other artists
- create a learning center to explore the life and history of Mexico
- show the video that accompanies Unit 1 of this textbook

Vocabulary
To reinforce vocabulary, have students:
- make picture dictionaries

Structure
To reinforce the forms of **ir** plus **a** and verbs ending in **-ar**:
- make a grammar bulletin board and encourage students to write their observations about these verbs
- initiate oral pattern drills that incorporate all forms of the verb and new vocabulary

---

✓ CULTURE NOTE

Spanish grew out of a dialect of Latin spoken by the Roman soldiers who occupied the peninsula. That is why many Spanish words resemble those of other Romance (derived from Roman) languages, such as Italian and Portugese, as well as English words, many of which are loanwords from French and Latin.

Communicative Objectives
- to talk about places in the city
- to talk about things to do in the city
- to ask how to get somewhere

Related Components

Activity Book p. 17	Cuaderno p. 5
Audio Book Script: Seg. 1	Transparencies Ch. 1: Conversemos
Audio Tapes Chapter: 2A, Seg. 1	

GETTING STARTED

Ask students to imagine they are in Mexico City and are lost. What questions would they need to ask in order to find their way back to their hotel?

ACTIVITIES

These activities give students an opportunity to begin communicating with each other and with you, focusing on the theme and objectives of the chapter. The activities can be used as oral class activities, or, if you prefer, you can pair students to achieve more interaction. Additional activities integrate critical-thinking skills.

¿Qué te gusta hacer en la ciudad?
This is a class activity to review **me gusta** and **no me gusta** with known phrases. Have pairs ask each other what they like to do in the city.

¿Adónde vas?
Do a class activity to use transportation vocabulary. Say how to get to different places. Students use **generalmente** and forms of **ir** plus **a** to say how they usually get to the places on the chart.
Application: Answer with a negative.
¿Cómo vas a la escuela?
No voy en autobús, voy a pie.

CONVERSEMOS

¿ADÓNDE VAMOS?

Habla con tu compañero(a).

¿QUÉ TE GUSTA HACER EN LA CIUDAD?

Me gusta ir al cine.
No me gusta ir al gimnasio.

Me gusta...	No me gusta...
ir al cine	ir al gimnasio
bailar en la discoteca	ir a fiestas
ir al museo	comer en restaurantes

¿ADÓNDE VAS?
(Where are you going?)

Voy al centro. ¿Y tú?
(I'm going downtown. And you?)

al cine	a la escuela
al parque *(to the park)*	al centro *(downtown)*

¿Cómo vas al centro?
(How do you go downtown?)

Generalmente voy en coche.
(I usually go by car.)

- en metro
- en bicicleta
- a pie
- en camión*
- en coche
- en taxi

*Expresión de México. En otros países: **en autobús**.

—Voy en metro. ¿Y tú?
—Yo también.

44

MEETING INDIVIDUAL NEEDS

Including All Students

For Auditory Learners
Dictate the questions in these pages. Have pairs write them on cards, then record themselves as they ask each other.

For Visual Learners
Enlarge the symbols in *¿Adónde vas?* and *¿Qué vas a hacer?* Create sentences and have students find the symbols that go with them.

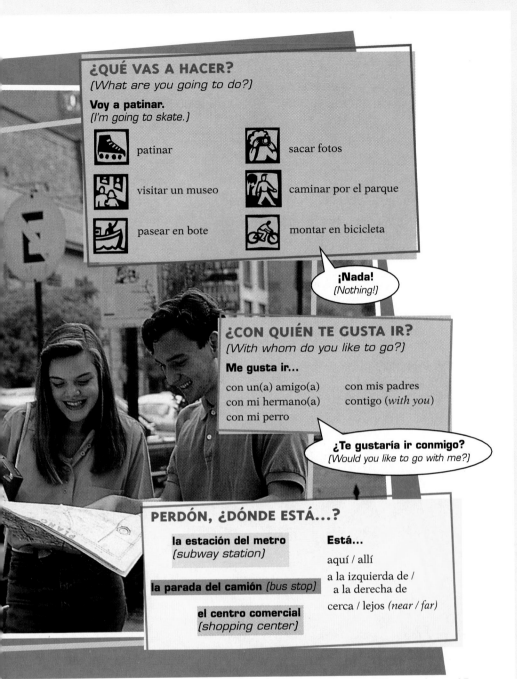

¿QUÉ VAS A HACER?
(What are you going to do?)

Voy a patinar.
(I'm going to skate.)

- patinar
- sacar fotos
- visitar un museo
- caminar por el parque
- pasear en bote
- montar en bicicleta

¡Nada!
(Nothing!)

¿CON QUIÉN TE GUSTA IR?
(With whom do you like to go?)

Me gusta ir...

con un(a) amigo(a)   con mis padres
con mi hermano(a)   contigo (*with you*)
con mi perro

¿Te gustaría ir conmigo?
(Would you like to go with me?)

PERDÓN, ¿DÓNDE ESTÁ...?

la estación del metro
(subway station)

la parada del camión *(bus stop)*

el centro comercial
(shopping center)

Está...

aquí / allí
a la izquierda de /
 a la derecha de
cerca / lejos *(near / far)*

¿Qué vas a hacer?
Class activity for students to use forms of **ir** plus **a** with infinitives to say what they are going to do.

¿Con quién te gusta ir?
Class activity for students to use **me gusta** to talk about with whom they like to do the above activity.

Perdón, ¿dónde está...?
Class activity for students to learn how to locate places in a city.
Challenge: Create a dialog in which one person is lost and finds a friend on the street. Use elements from these pages.

CHECK

- *¿Cómo vas a tu casa?*
- *¿Qué vas a hacer después de la escuela?*
- *Tu casa, ¿está lejos de aquí?*

LOG BOOK
Have students make a list of classroom objects that are **aquí/allí, a la derecha/izquierda,** and **cerca/lejos** based on where they are sitting.

Communicative Objectives

- to talk about places to go in Mexico City using forms of **ir a**
- to say what you would or would not like to do, using **me gustaría** and **no me gustaría**

Related Components

Activity Book p. 18	**Audio Tapes** Chapter Tape: 2A, Seg. 2
Audio Book Script: Seg. 2	**Cuaderno** p. 6

GETTING STARTED

Ask if anyone recognizes these places or can figure out what they are. Discuss the title and the words under it.

DISCUSS

Talk about the photographs and captions, and ask questions. Sample questions:

Mekano
Mira la palabra **discoteca.** *¿Qué es una discoteca?*
Dice que Mekano es una discoteca "¡padrísima!". ¿Padrísima es buena? ¿No es buena?

Plaza Garibaldi
Background Note:
Mariachis go to the Plaza Garibaldi to find work. Anyone who wants to hire a band can go there and select one.
Aquí está la Plaza Garibaldi.
La Plaza Garibaldi es un "lugar muy divertido".
¿Te gusta hacer cosas divertidas?
¿Conoces otro lugar divertido?
¿Qué hay en la Plaza Garibaldi?

Poliforum Theater
Background Note:
The theater contains an auditorium, art gallery, and handicraft museum. Its murals were designed by David Siqueiros, one of Mexico's best-known muralists.
¿Cómo se dice en inglés **concierto?**
¿y **moderno?**
¿Hay un teatro moderno aquí?
¿Qué lugares modernos hay en esta ciudad?

Templo Mayor
Background Note:
El Templo Mayor was the main religious pyramid in the Aztec city. Its foundations were recently discovered in the area next to the cathedral. Many of the recovered objects are on display near the site.
¿Como se dice en inglés **antiguo?**
Una persona, ¿es **antigua** *o* **vieja?**
¿Es moderno el Templo Mayor?

Open Air Market
Background Note:
Tianguis (street bazaars) and markets sell a variety of products. Here, price haggling is part of the experience. Arrive early for the best selection of goods.
Aquí hay un mercado.
¿Qué compran los chicos aquí?
¿Te gusta comprar libros?
¿Hay mercados aquí en [your city]?
Este lápiz cuesta 10 dólares. ¿Es barato?

REALIDADES
GUÍA DE MÉXICO

VISITA LA CIUDAD DE MÉXICO

ZONAS ARQUEOLÓGICAS. PARQUES Y PLAZAS. CINES Y DISCOTECAS... ¡Y MUCHO MÁS!

Los jóvenes en México van a bailar a Mekano. ¡Es una discoteca padrísima!

46

¿Vamos a caminar por la Plaza Garibaldi? Es un lugar muy divertido. Allí los mariachis tocan y cantan canciones típicas mexicanas. ▼

¿Te gustaría sacar fotos? El Templo Mayor está en el centro y es muy antiguo. ▼

◄ ¿Te gustaría escuchar música? Visita el Teatro Poliforum. Es un teatro muy moderno y los conciertos son muy buenos.

HABLA DE LA GUÍA

A. ¿Adónde van los jóvenes en la Ciudad de México?

Van a la discoteca.
Van...

B. ¿Qué es...?

divertido   barato
antiguo   moderno

C. ¿Adónde te gustaría ir? Pregúntale a tu compañero(a).

— ¿Adónde te gustaría ir?
— Me gustaría ir al teatro.
— ¿Qué vas a hacer allí?
— Voy a escuchar música.

▲ ¿Te gusta ir de compras? Muchos chicos compran discos compactos y artesanías en los "tianguis". ¡Allí todo es muy barato!

¿QUÉ OPINAS?

• ¿Qué tres lugares de la Ciudad de México te gustaría visitar? Pregúntales a otros estudiantes.
• Haz una tabla con los resultados. Usa el modelo.

Encuesta

lugar	yo	otros estudiantes
la Plaza Garibaldi	✓	
la discoteca Mekano		ℍℍℍ II
el Teatro Poliforum	✓	
el Templo Mayor		
los tianguis	✓	

Según tus compañeros, ¿cuál es el lugar más popular? ¿Y el menos popular?

¿SABES QUE...?

• The **Templo Mayor** was the central temple of the Aztec empire.

• **Plaza Garibaldi** is a city square famous for its restaurants, theaters, and especially for its mariachi bands.

• The outside of the **Teatro Poliforum** is decorated with a huge mural painted by more than thirty artists.

47

MEETING INDIVIDUAL NEEDS

Including All Students

For Auditory Learners
The class makes lists of vocabulary words related to each photo. Write each word as it is pronounced.

For Visual Learners
Draw simple pictures of the places in the poll. List activities for each place.

For Kinesthetic Learners
Charades: In teams, perform three vocabulary words that you would do or find at the places in the photos. Classmates guess the words.

ACTIVITIES

Habla de la guía

Individual and Pair Activities: Analysis and Evaluation
Answers: See model on student page.
A. Say where young people go in Mexico City.
B. Say which place fits each description.
Answers:
La Plaza Garibaldi es divertida.
El Templo Mayor es antiguo.
Todo es muy barato en los tianguis.
El Teatro Poliforum es moderno y tiene buenos conciertos.
C. Discuss the photos with a partner. Say which places you want to go to and what you will do there.
Extension: Create a dialog in which you and your partner talk about where you would like to go tomorrow.

¿Qué opinas?

Individual Activity: Taking a Survey
• Make a chart like the model and ask your classmates what three places they would like to visit in Mexico City.
• Put all the different answers in your chart.

Class Activity: Evaluation
What are the most and least popular places?
• Have a volunteer list the places on the board as other volunteers name them.
• Have another write the numbers for each place as representatives of the groups report on their polls.
• Add up the results.

CHECK

Indicate the photos and ask:
• *¿Adónde te gustaría ir?*
• *¿Cuál es tu actividad favorita?*
• *¿Qué vas a hacer el sábado?*

LOG BOOK
Have students list vocabulary they find especially difficult.

Para hispanohablantes

Compare these places to places you know in the country your family came from.

Communicative Objectives

To talk about:
- places in cities
- where places are in a city
- what you would like to do
- where you would like to go
- things to buy and where to buy them

Related Components

Activity Book p. 19-20	Transparencies Ch. 1: Palabras en acción
Cuaderno p. 7-8	

GETTING STARTED

Ask if anyone has ever given directions to a person who spoke very little English. How difficult was it? Why?

DISCUSS

Ask students to say where places are. Encourage them to use expressions like near, far, on your right, on your left, on the square... What would they have to say and understand in Spanish?

PALABRAS EN ACCIÓN

¿QUÉ HAY EN LA CIUDAD?

 1 ¿Qué hay en el dibujo?

Haz una lista de los lugares.

> el parque
> el museo
> la calle San Felipe...

2 ¿Dónde está?

Pregúntale a tu compañero(a) sobre cuatro lugares del dibujo. ¿Dónde están?

> —¿Dónde está el teatro?
> —Está en la calle San Felipe.

 3 ¿Adónde vamos?

Habla con tu compañero(a).

> —¿Adónde vamos?
> —Me gustaría ir a la tienda de música.

4 ¿Qué hacer?

Pregúntale a tu compañero(a).

> —¿Qué vas a hacer en el parque?
> —Voy a pasear en bote. ¿Te gustaría ir conmigo?
> —Sí, ¡padrísimo!

48

Para hispanohablantes

Some Spanish speakers in your class may use other expressions than the ones introduced in this chapter. Ask them to share with the class.

la tienda de artesanías
el quiosco
el periódico
el museo
el estadio
la iglesia
la biblioteca
la tienda de música
los discos compactos
la plaza
el camión

Me gusta sacar fotos.

¿Y tú?

Voy a patinar.

Me gustaría ir contigo.

---

5 ¿Qué compras?

Habla con tu compañero(a) sobre cuatro lugares del dibujo y di qué compras allí.

— ¿Qué compras en el quiosco?
— Compro tarjetas postales.

6 Miniteatro

Estás en la plaza. Habla con tu compañero(a).

— ¿Dónde está el museo?
— Aquí, a la izquierda.

7 Collage

Usa fotos de revistas para crear un collage de tu pueblo o ciudad. Escribe el nombre de cada lugar.

8 ¿Y tú?

Haz una lista de cinco lugares de tu pueblo o ciudad. Escribe cómo vas a cada lugar y qué vas a hacer allí.

Lugares	¿Cómo vas?	¿Qué vas a hacer?
el parque	a pie	patinar
el teatro	en metro	escuchar música

49

ACTIVITIES

1. Individual Activity

Make a list of things found in the city.
Extension: Write a list of your favorite places in your own town or city.

2. Pair Activity

Ask your partner where four places in the drawing are. Use locations from your list for *Activity 1*.
Analysis: Ask each other questions about places in your own town or city.

3. Pair Activity

Discuss with your partner to which places you would like to go.
Application: Say where you would not like to go.

4. Pair Activity

Ask your partner what he or she is going to do in different places. Then, your partner asks you whether you would like to go with him or her.

5. Pair Activity

Ask and answer questions about four places in the drawing. Say what you would buy there.
Analysis: Ask each other questions about places where you buy these things in your own town or city.

6. Pair Activity

You are at the *Plaza de la Independencia*. Ask your partner where other places are in the drawing.
Synthesis: Design a map to show where your school is located in relation to other places in the neighborhood, and explain to your partner where these places are.

Hands-On Activity

Homework for individuals or small groups: Use photos from magazines to create a collage of your town or city. Write captions.

Synthesizing Activity

Make a list of five places near your home, how to get to those places, and something that you are going to do in each.
For Kinesthetic Learners: Create and perform a skit in which you and a partner play a teenager trying to entertain a younger brother or sister. The older one asks such things as *¿Te gustaría ir al parque?* The younger one is difficult to please.

For students having difficulty talking about where they would like to go and what they would like to do or buy, you might consider:

• **The tutor page:** Pair the student with a native speaker or a more able student using the tutor page.
• **Actividades:** See page 42C: *¿Adónde vas en la ciudad?*

CHECK

• *¿Dónde está la librería?*
• *¿Qué vas a comprar allí?*
• *¿Adónde te gustaría ir mañana?*
• *¿Adónde vas a comprar el periódico?*

PORTFOLIO

Suggest that students draw a simple plan of a city or town they have visited and label objects and places.

Communicative Objectives
- to say that you are going somewhere, using **ir** plus **a** plus the name of a place
- to say what you are going to do, using **ir** plus **a** plus an infinitive
- to present the contraction **al**

Related Components

Activity Book p. 21-22	**Cuaderno** p. 9
Audio Book Script: Seg. 3 Activities: p. 13	**Tutor Page** p. 7
Audio Tapes Chapter: 2A, Seg. 3	

GETTING STARTED

Say "Tomorrow I am going to...," and ask for ways to complete the sentence. Point out that students are using the verb *to go* for many purposes: to talk about the future, to express destination, to indicate what they are going to do. Explain that **a** contracts with **el** to form **al.** Use examples such as:
*el parque. Voy **al** parque.*
*la plaza. Vamos **a** la plaza.*
*el teatro. Van **al** teatro.*

Language in Context
To demonstrate the use of **ir a**, say and then perform these and other sentences:
Mañana voy al museo.
Vamos a jugar al baloncesto.
Then have students perform a few sentences:
Ustedes van a escribir en la pizarra.
Tú vas a bailar y él va a jugar voleibol.
Nosotros vamos a pasear.

DISCUSS

Review vocabulary from *Encuentros* and introduce some of this chapter's new vocabulary with questions that incorporate **ir a.** For example:
¿Vas a jugar al béisbol hoy?
No, hoy vamos al teatro.
¿Y cuándo vas a estudiar?
Voy a estudiar mañana.

PARA COMUNICARNOS MEJOR
¿ADÓNDE VAS?

MUSEO NACIONAL DE ANTROPOLOGÍA
CIUDAD DE MÉXICO

PALACIO DE BELLAS ARTES
CIUDAD DE MÉXICO

To say that you are going somewhere, use a form of the verb *ir* (to go) with *a* and the name of the place.

Voy a la Ciudad de México.	I am going to Mexico City.

When *a* comes before *el*, the two words combine to form *al*.

Voy al Museo Nacional de Antropología.	I'm going to the National Museum of Anthropology.

To talk about what you are going to do, use a present-tense form of *ir* with *a* and an infinitive.

Voy a pasear por el parque.	I'm going for a walk in the park.
Vamos a visitar el Palacio de Bellas Artes.	We are going to visit the Palace of Fine Arts.

Here are the forms of the verb *ir* in the present tense.

¡OJO!

To ask where someone is going, use the question word **adónde**.

¿Adónde vas ahora?
(Where are you going now?)

ir (to go)			
yo	**voy**	nosotros(as)	**vamos**
tú	**vas**	vosotros(as)	**vais**
usted	**va**	ustedes	**van**
él/ella	**va**	ellos/ellas	**van**

Thinking About Language
Use this opportunity to remind students that nouns have genders in Spanish.

Reviewing Gender
1. Ask students if they remember the meaning of **el amigo** and **la amiga.**

2. Write **el teatro** and **la discoteca** on the board, and ask what they probably mean. Ask what makes one a *masculine* noun and the other a *feminine* noun. (In this case, the articles are determined by the endings of the words: **-o** and **-a.**)

3. Use other examples—like **el coche** and **la estación**—to establish that the gender of a noun cannot be taken literally.

1 En la Ciudad de México

¿Qué vas a hacer allí? ¿Cuándo? Pregúntale a tu compañero(a).

— ¿Qué vas a hacer ahora?
— Voy a caminar por la Plaza Garibaldi.
— ¿Y después?
— Voy a sacar fotos de la iglesia.

¿Qué vas a hacer?
visitar el Museo de Antropología
caminar por la Plaza Garibaldi
sacar fotos de la iglesia
bailar en la discoteca
comprar tarjetas postales

2 Lugares favoritos

¿Adónde van los fines de semana? ¿Cómo van? Pregúntale a tu compañero(a).

— ¿Adónde van tus amigos los fines de semana?
— Van al centro comercial.
— ¿Cómo van?
— Van en metro.

1. tus amigos(as)
2. tus hermanos(as)
3. tu compañero(a)
4. tus amigos(as) y tú
5. tus compañeros(as) de clase
6. ¿y tú?

3 Una encuesta

A. ¿Qué van a hacer el sábado? En grupo, hagan una encuesta. Usen el modelo.

	yo	Mariana	Juan	Ana
escuchar música		✓		
pasear por el parque	✓		✓	
bailar		✓		✓
ir de compras				
jugar al voleibol				
ir al teatro				

B. Informen a la clase.

Mariana va a escuchar música.
Juan y yo vamos a pasear por el parque.
Mariana y Ana van a bailar.

Museo
Restaurantes
Tiendas
Pirámides
Discotecas
Teatro

51

51

Communicative Objective
• to talk about things you do, using **-ar** verbs

Related Components

Activity Book p. 23-24	**Audio Tapes** Chapter: 2A, Seg. 4
Audio Book Script: Seg. 4 Activities: p. 14	**Cuaderno** p. 10
	Tutor Page p. 8

GETTING STARTED

Ask students what Spanish words they know that end in **-ar**. List these on the board as they say them.

Language in Context
Run through **comprar** with the class, pointing to yourself and others to illustrate **compro, compras,** etc. (This will also help kinesthetic learners.) Then use the paradigm to introduce the written forms of the present tense of **comprar**. Ask volunteers to apply the paradigm to the other **-ar** verbs.

DISCUSS

Review vocabulary from *Encuentros* and introduce some of this chapter's new vocabulary with questions that incorporate **-ar** verbs.

¿Qué compras en el cine?
¿Qué discos compactos escucha tu hermana?
¿Bailas con tu hermana?
¿Cuándo miran tus amigos la televisión?
Yo compro el periódico en el quiosco. ¿Y tú?
¿Compramos libros en una farmacia?
¿Qué cantan los mariachis?
Los fines de semana montamos en bicicleta.

PARA COMUNICARNOS MEJOR
¿QUÉ COMPRAS?

To talk about shopping and other activities, you can use many verbs that end in *-ar.*

Comprar (to buy), for example, is a verb that ends in *-ar.*

> *Compro muchos discos compactos.* I buy a lot of CDs.
> *Mis amigos compran revistas.* My friends buy magazines.

Here are the forms of the verb *comprar* in the present tense.

comprar (to buy)			
yo	compro	nosotros(as)	compramos
tú	compras	vosotros(as)	compráis
usted	compra	ustedes	compran
él/ella	compra	ellos/ellas	compran

Other *-ar* verbs that follow the same pattern are:

bailar *to dance*	**pasear** *to take a walk*
caminar *to walk*	**montar (en bicicleta)**
cantar *to sing*	*to ride (a bike)*
cocinar *to cook*	**patinar** *to skate*
escuchar *to listen*	**sacar (fotos)**
hablar *to speak*	*to take (pictures)*
mirar *to watch*	**visitar** *to visit*

Thinking About Language

Reviewing Gender
You may wish to offer these hints to your students:
Masculine nouns may end not just in **-o,** like **amigo** and **año** but also in:
-or, like **color** and **borrador**
-al, like **general, decimal, capital**
-ol, like **español, fútbol, béisbol**
-nte, like **restaurante** and **estudiante.**
Feminine nouns may end in **-a,** like **amiga** and **independencia,** but also in:
-ión, like **dirección** and **oración**
-dad, like **actividad** and **ciudad**
-cia, like **ambulancia** and **diferencia**

Point out that these are general rules and that there are exceptions. Not all words that end in **-o** are masculine—for example, **-o** words like **la soprano** and **la mano.** Nor are all words that end in **-a** feminine—for example, **-ista** words like **el artista** or **el dentista.**

1 En el centro

¿Qué haces en el centro? Pregúntale a tu compañero(a).

—¿Compras discos?
—Sí, compro discos de jazz.
(No, no compro discos. Compro libros.)

1. comprar discos
2. bailar en las discotecas
3. patinar
4. montar en bicicleta
5. escuchar música rock
6. sacar fotos
7. pasear por el parque
8. visitar museos

2 De compras

¿Qué compran? ¿Dónde?
Pregúntale a tu compañero(a).

—¿Qué compran tus padres
en el mercado?
—Compran artesanías.

1. tus padres
2. tus amigos(as) y tú
3. tu madre
4. tu padre
5. tus compañeros(as)
6. ¿y tú?

¿Dónde?
en el mercado
en el museo
en la librería
en la tienda de música
en el quiosco
en el cine

¿Qué?
artesanías
revistas
libros
discos compactos
tarjetas postales

3 En el parque

A. Generalmente ¿qué hacen en el parque?
En grupo, hagan una lista de actividades.

Actividades en el parque
pasear en bote
escuchar música
hablar con los amigos

B. ¿Qué hacen ustedes? Pregúntenle a
otro grupo.

—¿Qué hacen ustedes en
el parque?
—Montamos en
bicicleta y patinamos.
¿Y ustedes?
—Paseamos en bote.

Para hispanohablantes

Tell the class what you are going to do
this weekend. Try to use -ar verbs.

Students use **-ar** verbs to talk about things
they do and where to do them.

1. Pair Activity
Ask your partner what he or she does
downtown. Use the verbs in the list.
Answers:
1. See model on student page.
2. *bailas/bailo*
3. *patinas/patino*
4. *montas/monto*
5. *escuchas/escucho*
6. *sacas/saco*
7. *paseas/paseo*
8. *visitas/visito*

2. Pair Activity
Ask and answer questions about things
people buy and where they buy them. Use
the words in the lists to answer.
Answers:
1. See model on student page.
2. *compran/compramos*
3. *compra/compra*
4. *compra/compra*
5. *compran/compran*
6. *compras/compro*
Application: One partner makes incorrect
statements with **comprar.** The other partner corrects them.
*Compro discos compactos en el restaurante.
No, compras discos compactos en la tienda
de música.*

3. Group Activity
A. Make a list of things that you do in a
park.
B. Compare lists with another group.
For Kinesthetic Learners: In a group, create and act out four sentences with **-ar**
verbs showing two or more people doing
something. Example: *Ellos pasean en bote.*

For students having difficulty communicating what they do using **-ar** verbs, you
might consider:
•**The tutor page:** pair the student with a
 native speaker or a more able student
 using the tutor page.
•**Actividades:** See page 42D:
 ¿Qué hace la gente?

• ¿Qué música escuchas?
• ¿Quién compra libros de Stephen King?
• ¿Qué miras en la televisión?

LOG BOOK
Have students write all of the forms of
bailar and **hablar,** using the paradigm as a
model. They should divide each word into
stem and ending.

Objectives
Communicative: to talk about plans
Cultural: to learn about Teotihuacán

Related Components

Assessment Oral Proficiency: p. 21	**Conexiones:** 16A, Ch.1
Audio Book Script: Seg. 5 Activities: p. 15	**Conexiones** Chapter 1
	Magazine Juntos en México
Audio Tapes Chapter: 2A, Seg.5	**Tutor Page** p. 9

GETTING STARTED

Has any member of the class ever visited ruins of an ancient culture? If so, ask that person to talk about it. Ask what your town or city would be like if there were buildings from thousands of years ago next to recent buildings. Would people be more aware of that culture? Or would they be so used to seeing the ruins that they would pay no attention at all?

Students should now be able to use **ir a**, **–ar** verbs and all the chapter vocabulary correctly.

Read aloud the introduction, pausing to have students locate the *Calzada de los Muertos* and the *Pirámides del Sol y de la Luna* on the map. Refer to the map and photos as you ask questions with **ir a**. *¿Adónde vamos ahora? ¿Qué vamos a ver? ¿Y qué vamos a hacer?*

APPLY

1. Pair Activity
Talk about when and how you're going to Teotihuacán with your partner.
Answers: See model on student page.
Extension: Suggest ways of getting to Teotihuacán to a partner, who responds:
A. *¿Vamos a Teotihuacán en bicicleta?*
B. *No, vamos en coche.*

2. Pair Activity
Study the map and write a list of the places you can find in Teotihuacán.

SITUACIONES
UNA VISITA A TEOTIHUACÁN

PALACIO DE TEPANTITLA

PLANO GENERAL
ZONA ARQUEOLÓGICA DE TEOTIHUACÁN

PIRÁMIDE DE LA LUNA

PIRÁMIDE DEL SOL

PLAZA DE LA LUNA

PALACIO DE QUETZAL-PAPALOTL

RÍO SAN JUAN

CIUDADELA

CALZADA DE LOS MUERTOS

CONJUNTO PLAZA OESTE

CONJUNTO NORESTE DEL RÍO SAN JUAN

MUSEO

PARA TU REFERENCIA

la Calzada de los Muertos *Road of the Dead*
la Ciudadela *Citadel*
el conjunto *(building) complex*
la luna *moon*
el palacio *palace*
el sol *sun*
el templo *temple*
venden *sell*

HORAS DE VISITA: DE 8:00 a.m. A 5:00 p.m.
TRANSPORTE: CAMIONES Y TAXIS

Teotihuacán es una zona arqueológica muy antigua. Está cerca de la Ciudad de México. En Teotihuacán hay dos pirámides, la Pirámide del Sol y la Pirámide de la Luna. La calle principal se llama Calzada de los Muertos. En Teotihuacán también hay tiendas que venden artesanías, libros y tarjetas postales.

54

3. Pair Activity
Decide which places you will visit at the ruins.
Answers: See model on student page.
Application: Decide where you do not want to go.

4. Writing Activity
Use -ar verbs, ir a, and unit vocabulary to write your plans for visiting the ruins. Be sure to say with whom, where, when, and how you will go, and what you will buy.
Possible Answer:
Voy a visitar la Pirámide de la Luna el sábado. Voy a ir con mi hermano. Vamos a pie. Y vamos a comprar tarjetas postales.

For students having difficulty saying where something is and where they're going, you might consider:
•**The tutor page:** pair the student with a native speaker or a more able student using the tutor page.
•**Actividades:** See page 42C: *El mapa de mi barrio.*

1 Planes

Haz planes con tu amigo(a) para pasar un día en Teotihuacán. Decidan cuándo y cómo van a ir.

— ¿Te gustaría ir conmigo a Teotihuacán?
— Sí. ¿Cuándo vamos?
— El sábado por la mañana.
— ¿Cómo vamos a ir?
— En camión.

2 ¿Qué hay en Teotihuacán?

Miren el plano y hagan una lista de los lugares que hay en Teotihuacán.

3 ¿Adónde vamos?

Decidan adónde van a ir. Hablen de sus planes con sus compañeros.

— Vamos a visitar la Pirámide de la Luna.
— ¡Sí, padrísimo! ¿Y adónde vamos después?
— Me gustaría ir al museo y comprar tarjetas postales.

4 Tu excursión

Escribe cinco oraciones sobre tus planes. Usa las siguientes preguntas.

- ¿Con quién vas a ir?
- ¿Adónde?
- ¿Cuándo?
- ¿Cómo?
- ¿Qué vas a comprar?

TEOTIHUACÁN
CIUDAD DE MÉXICO

BOLETO DE ACCESO A MUSEOS Y ZONAS ARQUEOLÓGICAS

A

TEOTIHUACAN

INSTITUTO NACIONAL DE ANTROPOLOGÍA E HISTORIA

¿SABES QUE...?

Teotihuacán was one of the first urban centers built on the American continent. At its peak, about 500 A.D., it had between 125,000 and 200,000 residents. The city had been abandoned and was in ruins by the time the Aztecs found it. They named this site *Teotihuacán*, or "place of the gods."

55

CHECK

- ¿Dónde están las pirámides?
- ¿Qué van a hacer en Teotihuacán?
- ¿Qué cosas van a comprar en Teotihuacán?

PORTFOLIO

Have students make a map of a fictitious archaeological zone. Have them decide what streets, temples, and important buildings they will need to include, and where those places should be located.

Background

Teotihuacán (tay-oh-tee-wah-KAHN) is the name the Aztecs gave to a cultural, commercial, and religious center built by an earlier civilization of which little is known. At its peak, around 600 A.D., the city had a population of more than 150,000.

La Calzada de los Muertos The Aztecs called this the Street of the Dead because they assumed that the small buildings along the street were tombs. Archaeologists have determined, however, that they were small homes and temples.

La Pirámide del Sol The base of this structure is almost the same size as the Pyramid of Cheops in Egypt, but at 210 feet, it is only half as tall.

La Pirámide de la Luna The picture on the ticket shows the Pyramid of the Moon. This structure is smaller than the Pyramid of the Sun, but because it was built on higher ground, their tops are at the same level.

El Templo de Quetzalcóatl This smaller pyramid is named for the stone carvings on its side, which appear to be representations of the god. It is located in a large walled area known as the Citadel. The postcard shows one of the stone carvings. Quetzalcóatl, who is usually depicted as a plumed serpent, was probably the most important god of Central America. There are many versions of his myth.

Para hispanohablantes

Write a travel brochure for Teotihuacán. Read it to the class and answer their questions.

▶▶▶ **INTERNET LINK**

Usenet group: alt.archaeology

Objectives

Communicative: to make plans for a trip to Mexico City
Cultural: to learn about Mexico City

Related Components

Magazine	**Video: Tape/Book**
Juntos en México	Unit 1: Seg. 2
Transparencies	
Ch. 1: Para resolver	

Search to frame 1012901

GETTING STARTED

Ask students to rate their map skills. Have they served as a navigator for their parents on a car trip? Can they find their way around a city with a street map?

APPLY

Form groups. Explain that they are going to make plans for a weekend in Mexico City.

PASO 1: Lugares de la Ciudad de México
Use the map to pick five places to visit this weekend.
Extension: Make a list of all the museums you can find on the map.

PASO 2: ¿Adónde vamos?
Talk about where you want to go and when, where each place is, and what you'll do when you get there.
Answers: See model on student page.
Application: Make a sentence using **voy a** and another place from the map and say what you are going to do there.

PASO 3: ¿Y los otros grupos?
Compare plans with another group.
Answers: See model on student page.
Application: Pick a street and ask the other group where it is.

PASO 4: El centro de mi ciudad
Draw a map of the downtown area of your city or town. Include five places and say where each of them is.
Answers: See model on student page.
Extension: Use at least three forms of **ir** and **ir a** to say to what places in Latin America you would like to go.
Challenge: Play a simple map exercise by

selecting two landmarks and asking students to find them. In Spanish, ask them to name the streets they would take to go from one place to the other.

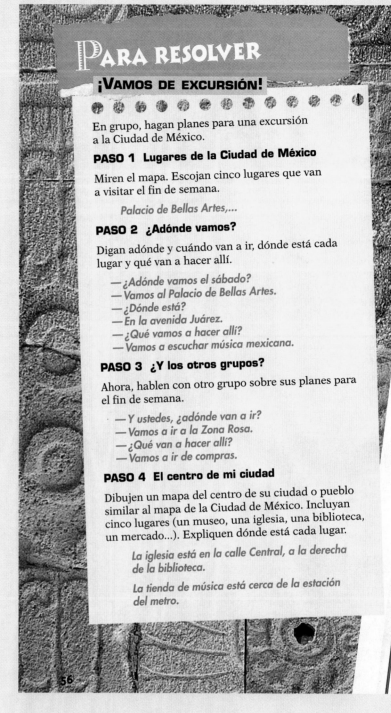

PARA RESOLVER
¡VAMOS DE EXCURSIÓN!

En grupo, hagan planes para una excursión a la Ciudad de México.

PASO 1 Lugares de la Ciudad de México

Miren el mapa. Escojan cinco lugares que van a visitar el fin de semana.

Palacio de Bellas Artes,...

PASO 2 ¿Adónde vamos?

Digan adónde y cuándo van a ir, dónde está cada lugar y qué van a hacer allí.

— ¿Adónde vamos el sábado?
— Vamos al Palacio de Bellas Artes.
— ¿Dónde está?
— En la avenida Juárez.
— ¿Qué vamos a hacer allí?
— Vamos a escuchar música mexicana.

PASO 3 ¿Y los otros grupos?

Ahora, hablen con otro grupo sobre sus planes para el fin de semana.

— Y ustedes, ¿adónde van a ir?
— Vamos a ir a la Zona Rosa.
— ¿Qué van a hacer allí?
— Vamos a ir de compras.

PASO 4 El centro de mi ciudad

Dibujen un mapa del centro de su ciudad o pueblo similar al mapa de la Ciudad de México. Incluyan cinco lugares (un museo, una iglesia, una biblioteca, un mercado...). Expliquen dónde está cada lugar.

La iglesia está en la calle Central, a la derecha de la biblioteca.

La tienda de música está cerca de la estación del metro.

56

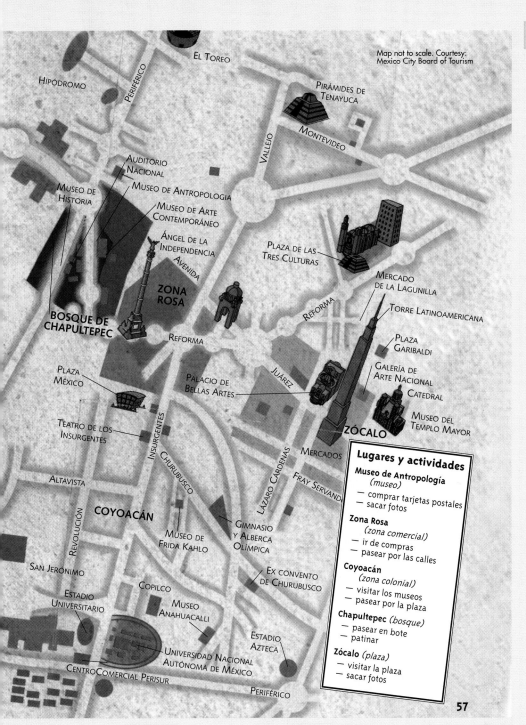

Map not to scale. Courtesy:
Mexico City Board of Tourism

EL TOREO

HIPÓDROMO

PERIFÉRICO

PIRÁMIDES DE
TENAYUCA

VALLEJO

MONTEVIDEO

AUDITORIO
NACIONAL

MUSEO DE ANTROPOLOGIA

MUSEO DE
HISTORIA

MUSEO DE ARTE
CONTEMPORÁNEO

ÁNGEL DE LA
INDEPENDENCIA

AVENIDA

PLAZA DE LAS
TRES CULTURAS

MERCADO
DE LA LAGUNILLA

ZONA
ROSA

REFORMA

TORRE LATINOAMERICANA

BOSQUE DE
CHAPULTEPEC

REFORMA

PLAZA
GARIBALDI

PLAZA
MÉXICO

PALACIO DE
BELLAS ARTES

JUAREZ

GALERÍA DE
ARTE NACIONAL

CATEDRAL

TEATRO DE LOS
INSURGENTES

INSURGENTES

CHURUBUSCO

MERCADOS

LÁZARO CÁRDENAS

FRAY SERVANDO

ZÓCALO

MUSEO DEL
TEMPLO MAYOR

ALTAVISTA

REVOLUCIÓN

COYOACÁN

MUSEO DE
FRIDA KAHLO

GIMNASIO
Y ALBERCA
OLÍMPICA

EX CONVENTO
DE CHURUBUSCO

SAN JERÓNIMO

COPILCO

ESTADIO
UNIVERSITARIO

MUSEO
ANAHUACALLI

ESTADIO
AZTECA

UNIVERSIDAD NACIONAL
AUTÓNOMA DE MÉXICO

CENTROCOMERCIAL PERISUR

PERIFÉRICO

Lugares y actividades

Museo de Antropología
(museo)
— comprar tarjetas postales
— sacar fotos

Zona Rosa
(zona comercial)
— ir de compras
— pasear por las calles

Coyoacán
(zona colonial)
— visitar los museos
— pasear por la plaza

Chapultepec (bosque)
— pasear en bote
— patinar

Zócalo (plaza)
— visitar la plaza
— sacar fotos

57

City Words

PLACES IN THE CITY
bakery *la panadería*
bank *el banco*
baseball field *el campo de béisbol*
courthouse *la corte*
hospital *el hospital*
hotel *el hotel*
post office *la oficina de correos*
shoe store *la zapatería*
shopping center *el centro comercial*
supermarket *el supermercado*

TRANSPORTATION
airplane *el avión*
highway *la autopista*
motorcycle *la motocicleta*
train *el tren*
ship *el barco*

ADJECTIVES
enormous *enorme*
expensive *caro*
fast *rápido*
inexpensive *barato*
luxurious *lujoso*
slow *lento*

MEETING INDIVIDUAL NEEDS

Including All Students

For Visual Learners
With the class, create a set of symbols for *sigue derecho, dobla a la derecha* and *dobla a la izquierda*. Write messages using the symbols to direct someone to a goal.

For Kinesthetic/Auditory Learners
Blindfold classmates from different teams and take turns reading the symbol messages. They should act according to what they hear.

Objectives

Communicative: to talk about favorite activities
Cultural: to learn about young people in Mexico City

Related Components

Audio Tapes	Conexiones
Conexiones: 16A, Ch1	Chapter 1

GETTING STARTED

Ask *¿Quiénes son las personas en las fotos?* Ask them to figure out what questions were asked in this *encuesta*. (*¿Cómo te llamas? ¿Cuántos años tienes? ¿Cuáles son tus actividades favoritas? ¿Qué actividad te gusta más?* or *¿Cuáles son tus lugares favoritos?* or *¿Qué lugares te gustan más?*)

DISCUSS

Using the Text

Ask questions about the three teenagers' preferences.
¿Qué le gusta hacer a cada chavo?
(Ir al cine.)
¿A quién le gusta ir de compras? (Luis)
¿Y a quién le gusta ir a conciertos? (Claudia)
¿A quién le gusta bailar? (Pablo)
Then ask about students' own preferences.

Cooperative Learning

Two students meet in the park and interview each other. Model a dialog with a volunteer. For example:
– *Buenos días. ¿Cómo te llamas?*
– *Buenos días. Me llamo Pablo Granados.*
– *¿Cuántos años tienes, Pablo?*
– *Tengo quince años.*
Synthesis: Invent other titles for this page. For example: *Tres chicos mexicanos.*

CHECK

LOG BOOK

Have students review the activities in the lesson and write the activities they are having difficulty with in their Log Books.

ENTÉRATE

CHAVOS° EN LA CIUDAD

ENCUESTA: ¿QUÉ HACEN LOS JÓVENES EN MÉXICO?

Éstas son las respuestas de tres chavos que viven en la Ciudad de México.

Nombre: Luis Daniel Mujica
Edad:° 16 años
Actividades favoritas: ir de compras, ir al cine y montar en bicicleta.
Lugares favoritos: el centro comercial La Torre y el Parque de Chapultepec.

Nombre: Claudia Rayón
Edad: 17 años
Actividades favoritas: ir al cine, ir a Coyoacán a escuchar música.
Lugares favoritos: el Palacio de Bellas Artes y el Centro Cultural Universitario, porque hay cine, salas de video y una cafetería fantástica.

Nombre: Pablo Granados
Edad: 15 años
Actividades favoritas: patinar, bailar, ir al cine y comer hamburguesas.
Lugares favoritos: las cafeterías Freeday y Hard Rock.

TE TOCA A TI

Escoge cinco actividades favoritas de los jóvenes de México.

¿Qué actividades te gustan? ¿Y a tus compañeros?

Haz una gráfica de barras.°

los chavos (Méx.) *teenagers*
la edad *age*
la gráfica de barras *bar graph*

58

Te toca a ti

Have the class choose five activities that the **chavos** enjoy doing. Conduct a poll to find out how popular these activities are in the class. Have five volunteers go to the front of the class and ask for a show of hands on each one's activity. (*¿A quién le gusta [patinar]?*) Have all students make a bar graph.

Para hispanohablantes

Interview another Spanish speaker in front of the class. Ask about favorite activities.

VOCABULARIO TEMÁTICO

Lugares de la ciudad
Places in the city
la biblioteca *library*
el centro *downtown*
el centro comercial
  shopping center
la discoteca *discotheque*
el estadio *stadium*
la estación del metro
  subway station
la iglesia *church*
el quiosco *newsstand*
la librería *bookstore*
el mercado *market*
el museo *museum*
la parada del camión *bus stop*
el parque *park*
la plaza *square*
el teatro *theater*
la tienda de artesanías
  craft shop
la tienda de música
  record store

¿Cómo vas?
How are you going?
a pie *on foot*
en camión *by bus*
en coche *by car*

en metro *by subway*
en taxi *by taxi*

¿Con quién vas?
With whom are you going?
con... *with. . .*
conmigo *with me*
contigo *with you*

¿Qué vas a hacer?
What are you going to do?
caminar *to walk*
cantar *to sing*
comprar *to buy*
ir a un concierto
  to go to a concert
ir de compras
  to go shopping
pasear en bote
  to take a boat ride
pasear (por) *to take a walk*
patinar *to skate*
sacar fotos *to take pictures*
visitar *to visit*

¿Qué vas a comprar?
What are you going to buy?
las artesanías *arts and crafts*

el disco compacto *compact disc*
el periódico *newspaper*

¿Cómo es?
antiguo(a) *ancient*
barato(a) *inexpensive*
moderno(a) *modern*

¿Dónde está?
cerca *near*
lejos *far*

Expresiones y palabras
¿Adónde te gustaría ir?
  Where would you like to go?
¿Con quién? *With whom?*
Me gustaría... *I would like . . .*
¿Adónde? *Where?*
generalmente *usually*
los jóvenes *young people*

Expresiones de México
¡Padrísimo! *Great!*
el camión *bus*
los chavos *teenagers*
el tianguis *outdoor market*

LA CONEXIÓN INGLÉS-ESPAÑOL

By now you have noticed that some Spanish words are very similar to some English words. Words in two languages that look alike and mean the same thing are called "cognates." One of the cognates you saw in this chapter was ***visitar***. Did you figure out what it meant when you saw it?

Look at the ***Vocabulario temático*** and make a list of other cognates you see. Look for cognates in phrases and in single words. Did you find cognates because of their spelling, their sound, or both?

La conexión inglés-español
Some cognates on this page are:
las fotos
el museo
el parque
el teatro

Some apparent cognates students may know or find on this page are:
(bookstore v. library)
(foot v. pie)
(car v. coach)

Objectives
• to review vocabulary
• to correctly pronunce words containing the letter **d**

Related Components

Activity Book	Audio Tapes
Chapter Review: p. 25-26	Chapter: 2A, Seg. 6 Assessment: 14A, Ch. 1
Assessment Listening Script: p. 9 Chapter Test: p. 45-50	**Cuaderno** p. 11-12
Audio Book Script: Seg. 6 Activities p. 16	**Tutor Page** p. 10

Pronunciation: "d"
• Use this page to review the pronunciation of the letter "d." Remind students that the Spanish "d" is pronounced like the English "d" in "day" when it appears at the beginning of a sentence or after a pause or after the letters "l" or "n."

"d" after "l" or "n"
tienda, grande, Maldonado, el disco

"d" as first word of a sentence
Daniel tiene 17 años.

"d" after a pause
Los últimos tres días de la semana son viernes sábado, y...domingo.
• In all other positions in a word or sentence, the letter "d" is pronounced like the "th" of the English word "then."

"d" in other positions
mercado, parada, moderno, estadio, periódico, verdad, sed
• In the sentence *¿Adónde te gustaría ir?* the first "d" is pronounced like the "th" in "then," whereas the second "d" is pronounced like the "d" in "day."

LOG BOOK
Have students write down any words they had difficulty pronouncing. Also have them write down their favorite tongue twisters.

	Objetivos page 61	Conversemos pages 62-63	Realidades pages 64-65	Palabras en acción pages 66-67
Comunicación	• To talk about foods you like or dislike	Discuss foods that are liked and disliked	Read text, answer questions, discuss foods liked or disliked	Activities 1-8: Read menu, list foods; describe foods; discuss foods; discuss drinks and desserts; list foods eaten; write dialog; make and label collage; make list
	• To talk about favorite restaurants		Read text, list foods from different restaurants	
	• To talk about ordering something to eat	Practice different things to say when ordering something to eat	Read text, list foods from different restaurants	Activity 6: Write dialog for waiter and restaurant customer
Vocabulario temático	• To know the expressions for food and drinks	Practice the names of different foods and drinks	Read text, answer questions, discuss foods liked or disliked	Activities 1-8: Read menu, list foods; describe foods; discuss foods; discuss drinks and desserts; list foods eaten; write dialog; make and label collage; make list
	• To know the expressions for places where you can eat	List the names of different places to eat	Read text, list foods from different restaurants	
	• To know the expressions for table settings	Learn the names of the items in a table setting		
Estructura	• To talk about foods you like: the verb *gustar* + noun	Use the verb *gustar* + noun to discuss foods that are liked	Read text, answer questions, discuss foods liked or disliked	Activity 1: Read menu, list foods liked
	• To talk about meals: the verbs *comer* and *compartir*	Use the verbs *comer* and *compartir* to talk about meals	Read text, answer questions, discuss meals liked or disliked	Activity 5: List foods for each meal
Cultura	*Taquerías*		The Mexican word for tomato	The new peso
Integración		Places in a city or town, things that are liked, describing things	Enjoyable things to do, describing things	Describing things, naming favorite things, time of day, greetings

Para comunicarnos mejor (1) pages 68-69	Para comunicarnos mejor (2) pages 70-71	Situaciones pages 72-73	Para resolver pages 74-75	Notes
Activities 1-3: Talk about foods and drinks liked or disliked; make a survey and report to class	Activities 1-3: Have partners discuss what they eat and drink in restaurants; list what they eat for meals, and ask others what they eat; discuss cafeteria eating habits	Activities 1, 2, 4: Read text, make plans to go to a restaurant; make ads for favorite restaurants; make plans for a class meal	Pasos 1-6: Read menu, choose different menus; prepare group menu; invent surprise dish; discuss ingredients; compare menus; vote for favorite surprise dish	
		Activity 2: Make ads for favorite restaurants		
Activities 1, 3: Talk about foods and drinks liked or disliked; make survey and report to class	Activities 1, 3: Have partners discuss what they eat and drink in restaurants; list what they eat for meals, ask others what they eat; discuss cafeteria eating habits	Activities 1, 2, 4: Read text, make plans to go to a restaurant; make ads for favorite restaurants; make plans for a class meal	Pasos 1-6: Read menu, choose different menus; prepare group menu; invent surprise dish; discuss ingredients; compare menus; vote for favorite surprise dish	
	Activities 1, 2: Have partners discuss what they eat and drink in restaurants; discuss cafeteria eating habits	Activities 1, 2: Read text, make plans to go to a restaurant; make ads for favorite restaurants		
Activities 1-3: Talk about foods and drinks liked or disliked; make a survey and report to class		Activity 1: Read text, make plans to go to a restaurant		
	Use all forms of *comer* and *compartir*. Activities 1-3: Have partners discuss what they eat and drink in restaurants; list what is eaten at home, ask others what they eat; discuss cafeteria eating habits	Activities 1, 3, 4: Read text, make plans to go to a restaurant; discuss different meal times in U.S. and Mexico; make plans for a class meal	Pasos 1, 3: Read menu, choose different menus for other weekdays; prepare group menu and draw it; invent surprise dish and name it	
		Eating in the afternoon: *la comida, la merienda, la cena*	Sidewalk fruit drinks: *jugos, aguas frescas, licuados*	Entérate page 76 Basic Mexican cuisine/The early history of chocolate
Saying what is liked, costs of items, describing things	Describing recurring activities	Where to go, what to do, activities and things enjoyed, time of day, costs	Costs, describing things	

Tengo

GAME

Objective

• to play a bingo game, using Chapter 2 *Vocabulary*

Use

after *Palabras en acción,* pages 66–67

Materials

• TRB Activity Support Page 6, (grid)
• TRB Activity Support Page 7, *Yo tengo* (food pictures)
• glue sticks

Activity

• Distribute *Tengo* grids and food pictures.
• Have students cut out pictures, run glue stick over blank grids, and paste down pictures in any order they like.
• Say a word from the *Vocabulario temático* and use it in a sentence. Repeat word and sentence.
• Students mark an X through each word called.
• The winner is the first student with 5 X's in a straight line—horizontal, vertical, or diagonal.

Variations

• Play with 16 boxes (4 x 4) instead of 25.
• Have students write vocabulary words in the blank grid boxes; you call out English definitions of words, and students draw X's through the words defined.
• Play with any vocabulary you want to review.
• Play until the border is filled.
• Play until all 25 (or all 16) boxes are filled.

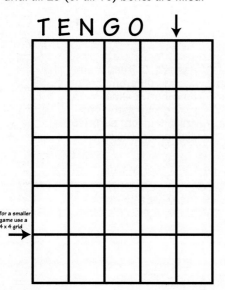

T E N G O ↓

for a smaller game use a 4 x 4 grid →

Comidas y colores

GAME

Objective

• to play a game about food and colors, using Chapter 2 *Vocabulario temático*

Use

after *Palabras en acción,* pages 66–67

Materials

• 2 English-Spanish dictionaries

Activity

• Appoint a scorekeeper.
• Divide students into teams A and B and have them work at opposite ends of the classroom. Each team selects a recorder and a spokesperson.
• Call out two colors, e.g., *rojo y verde.*
• Each recorder writes down all the red and green foods his/her team thinks of: *manzana, chile rojo, chile verde, lechuga, verduras, tomate,* etc.
• After 5 minutes, spokespersons come to the front and show their lists to the scorekeeper. The spokesperson for the team with the longest list reads first.
• Both teams get credit for all correct items, but the second spokesperson only reads items that weren't named by the first spokesperson.
• The team with the most items wins.

Variations

• Assign each team a color. The team makes a poster of foods that color and labels them.
• Select a color and have students either write down or say aloud objects of that color in the classroom.

Como, tomo, comparto

GAME

Objective
• to play a game, using -er and -ir verbs and Chapter 2 Vocabulary

Use
after *Palabras en acción,* pages 66–67

Materials
• TRB Activity Support Page 7, *Yo tengo* (food pictures)
• 3" x 5" index cards

Preparation
• Use pictures to make sets of 4 food and beverage flash cards, duplicating one item in each set. For example: *naranja, manzana, leche, leche.*

Activity
• Divide class into teams of 4.
• Have a team come to the front and give each member one card from their set. Then have them make sentences, using the verb *comer* or *tomar* for a unique food or beverage and the verb *compartir* for the duplicated food or beverage.
• After looking at the team cards, Maria might begin: *Yo como una naranja. Carlos toma un vaso de leche. Gloria y Ana comparten una manzana.* Then Gloria would say: *Ana y yo compartimos una manzana. María come una naranja. Carlos toma un vaso de leche, etc.*
• Students score 1 point for each correct sentence, or a maximum of 3 points per turn.
• After each team has played once, tally points and announce *El equipo ganador.*

Me gusta mucho

GAME

Objective
• to play a game about favorite foods and beverages, using the verb *gustar*

Use
after *Para comunicarnos mejor,* pages 68–69

Activity
• Have students select a favorite food or beverage.
• One after another, students name their favorite food or drink as well as the favorites of the students before them. For example, Ana might say:—*A mí me gustan las hamburgesas.* Enrique could follow up: *A Ana le gustan las hamburgesas y a mí me gusta el pollo.*
• The correct form of *gustar* must accompany each food, but foods and beverages may be repeated. The student who puts together the longest string of foods and beverages is the winner.

Variations
• List foods in alphabetical order, with each student selecting a food that begins with a subsequent letter of the alphabet. Student A:—*Me gusta el arroz.* Student B:—*Me gusta el arroz y me gusta la carne.* Student C:—*Me gusta el arroz, me gusta la carne y me gustan los plátanos,* etc.
• Play game with names of things to buy, places to go, places in the city, activities you can do, sports, etc.

¿QUÉ VAS A COMER?

Introduce the chapter and its theme by asking students if they have ever eaten Mexican food. You may wish to have them make lists of Mexican foods and their ingredients and to add foods as they study this chapter. You may also wish to read them the descriptions of Mexican foods in the list that follows.

Related Components

Audio Tapes	Conexiones
Conexiones: 16A, Ch. 2	Chapter 2
	Video: Tape/Book
CD ROM	Unit 1: Seg. 3
Chapter 2	

Search to frame 1061913

GETTING STARTED

Ask students if they can identify any of the foods in the photograph. Ask critical thinking questions. For example: *¿De donde son típicos el mole y las enchiladas?*

Background

Mexican Meals

Desayuno
This early meal is the lightest of the day. It may consist simply of bread and coffee or include heavier foods like these:
atole drink of finely ground corn, often sweetened with chocolate or fruit
frijoles pinto beans that have been boiled, mashed, and fried
huevos mexicanos scrambled eggs with tomatoes, onions, and chilis
huevos rancheros fried eggs served on tortillas and covered with salsa picante

Comida/Cena
In most places, *la comida,* the principal meal, is eaten between 1:00 and 3:00 P.M. In urban Mexico, the evening meal, *la cena,* may be the largest. Some specialties:
chiles rellenos chilis stuffed with cheese or other food, dipped in egg whites, and fried
pollo en mole chicken covered with a thick sauce made of chili, cinnamon, squash seeds, and chocolate
tamal (tamales) corn dough stuffed with meat, beans, and chili, wrapped in corn husks and steamed

CAPÍTULO 2

¿QUÉ VAS A COMER?

60

Almuerzo
Un almuerzo is similar to *una comida,* but lighter. Some typical foods:
enchilada any combination of beans, beef, cheese, chicken, or seafood seasoned with salsa or chili, wrapped in a tor-tilla, baked, and covered with cream, cheese, or salsa
quesadilla flour tortilla topped or filled with cheese and other ingredients
taco soft or crisp corn tortilla wrapped around the same fillings as an enchilada

Chapter Components

Activity Book p. 27-36	Audio Book Script: p. 17-20 Activities: p. 21-24	16A, Ch. 2	Magazine Juntos en Mexico
Assessment Oral Proficiency: p. 22 Listening Script: p. 10 Chapter Test: p. 51-56	**Audio Tapes** Listening: 2B Assessment: 14A, Ch. 2 Conexiones:	**CD ROM** Chapter 2 **Conexiones** Chapter 2 **Cuaderno** p. 13-20	**Transparencies** Chapter 2 **Tutor Pages** p. 11-14 **Video: Tape/Book** Unit 1: Seg. 2

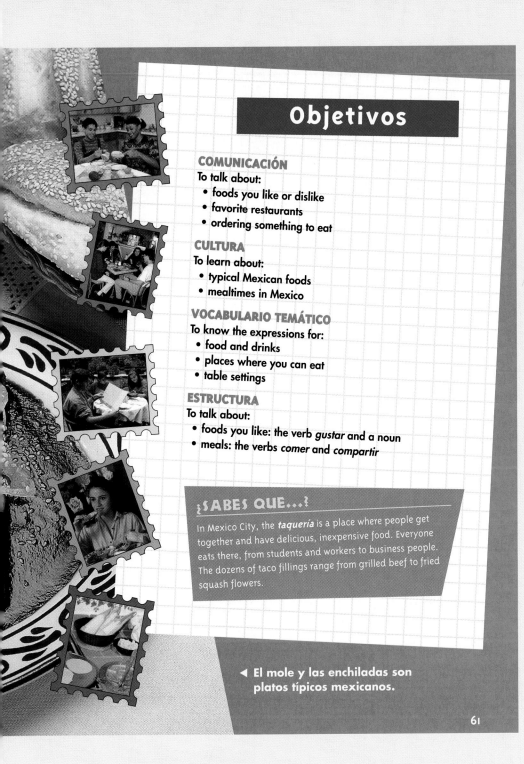

Objetivos

COMUNICACIÓN
To talk about:
- foods you like or dislike
- favorite restaurants
- ordering something to eat

CULTURA
To learn about:
- typical Mexican foods
- mealtimes in Mexico

VOCABULARIO TEMÁTICO
To know the expressions for:
- food and drinks
- places where you can eat
- table settings

ESTRUCTURA
To talk about:
- foods you like: the verb *gustar* and a noun
- meals: the verbs *comer* and *compartir*

¿SABES QUE...?
In Mexico City, the **taquería** is a place where people get together and have delicious, inexpensive food. Everyone eats there, from students and workers to business people. The dozens of taco fillings range from grilled beef to fried squash flowers.

◄ **El mole y las enchiladas son platos típicos mexicanos.**

61

Communicative Objectives

To talk about:
- types of food
- what foods you like or don't like
- what you eat and drink

Related Components

Activity Book	**Cuaderno**
p. 27	p. 13
Audio Book	**Transparencies**
Script: Seg. 1	Ch. 2: Conversemos
Audio Tapes	
Listening: 2B, Seg. 1	

GETTING STARTED

Ask students to identify the objects and activities on the page using just the pictures.

You may wish to talk about the times of the day at which people usually eat. See the **Background** information on page 60.

ACTIVITIES

These activities give students an opportunity to begin communicating with each other and with you, focusing on the theme and objectives of the chapter. The activities can be used as oral class activities, or, if you prefer, you can pair students to achieve more interaction. Additional activities integrate critical-thinking skills.

¿Dónde vas a comer hoy?
Class activity to review **ir a** with known words and cognates. Pairs of students ask each other where they are going to eat. Encourage the use of alternative answers, such as the name of a local restaurant.

En el desayuno, ¿qué comes?
¿Qué tomas?
Class activity to introduce breakfast foods and drinks, and **comes/como** and **tomas/tomo.** Model the exercise by asking the questions and giving the response in the title. Then ask students the questions, and have them answer using words from the list of breakfast foods and drinks.

¿Y en el almuerzo? ¿Y en la cena?
¿Qué te gusta?
Class activity to introduce some lunch and dinner vocabulary. You may want to ask the title questions separately and have students list foods they eat at home and in school.

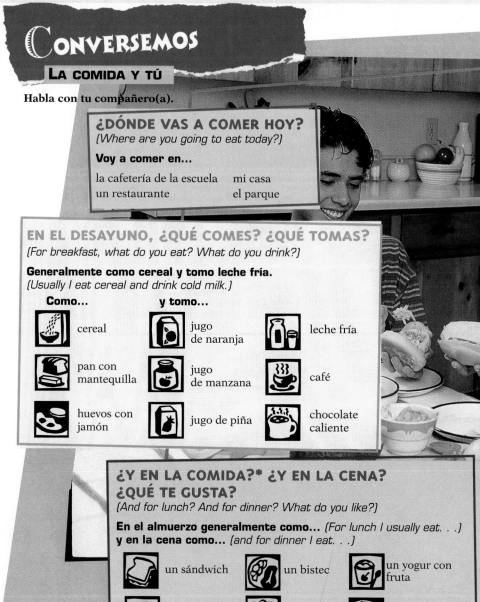

CONVERSEMOS

LA COMIDA Y TÚ

Habla con tu compañero(a).

¿DÓNDE VAS A COMER HOY?
(Where are you going to eat today?)

Voy a comer en...

la cafetería de la escuela   mi casa
un restaurante   el parque

EN EL DESAYUNO, ¿QUÉ COMES? ¿QUÉ TOMAS?
(For breakfast, what do you eat? What do you drink?)

Generalmente como cereal y tomo leche fría.
(Usually I eat cereal and drink cold milk.)

Como...

cereal

pan con mantequilla

huevos con jamón

y tomo...

jugo de naranja

jugo de manzana

jugo de piña

leche fría

café

chocolate caliente

¿Y EN LA COMIDA?* ¿Y EN LA CENA?
¿QUÉ TE GUSTA?
(And for lunch? And for dinner? What do you like?)

En el almuerzo generalmente como... *(For lunch I usually eat. . .)*
y en la cena como... *(and for dinner I eat. . .)*

un sándwich

una ensalada

un bistec

una pizza

un yogur con fruta

arroz con pollo

*Expresión de México. En otros países: **el almuerzo.**

62

Analysis: Pair Activity. Partners take turns naming a food and saying at what meal they would eat or drink it.
A: *Huevos con jamón.*
B: *Generalmente, como huevos con jamón en el desayuno.*

MEETING INDIVIDUAL NEEDS

Reaching All Students

For Auditory Learners
Pronounce the vocabulary words and have students locate them on these pages.

For Visual Learners
Have pairs create a table setting using real objects. One student names objects, the other indicates which object it is.

For Kinesthetic Learners
Small groups pantomime situations in a restaurant. Other members of the class speak for the characters.

¿QUÉ COMIDAS TE GUSTAN?
(What foods do you like?)

Me gusta el pescado. **Me gustan las verduras.**

el queso

el pescado

la sopa

las hamburguesas

las papas fritas

las verduras*

Las hamburguesas son deliciosas, ¿verdad?
(Hamburgers are delicious, aren't they?)

*Expresión de México. En otros países: **los vegetales, las legumbres.**

EN EL RESTAURANTE, ¿QUÉ DICES?
(At the restaurant, what do you say?)

¿Qué vas a pedir? *(What are you going to order?)*

¿Quieres compartir un postre? *(Do you want to share a dessert?)*

¿Tienes mucha hambre / sed? *(Are you very hungry / thirsty?)*

¿Algo más? *(Something else?)*

¿Cómo es la comida? *(What's the food like?)*

fresca *(fresh)*   picante *(spicy)*   horrible *(awful)*
rica *(tasty)*   dulce *(sweet)*   deliciosa *(delicious)*

No, gracias. No quiero nada.
(No, thanks. I don't want anything.)

un vaso

una taza

Mesero, una servilleta, por favor.
(Waiter, may I have a napkin, please?)

una servilleta

una cuchara

un tenedor

un plato

un cuchillo

63

¿Qué comidas te gustan?
Class activity to introduce food vocabulary and distinguish between **gusta** and **gustan**.

En el restaurante, ¿qué dices?
Class activity to introduce expressions used in restaurants and at mealtimes, as well as table-setting vocabulary.
Extension: Incorporate these expressions with other vocabulary on this page.
Example: *Me gusta el pollo. Yo quiero un sandwich de pollo y un té frio.*
Analysis: List foods and have students say what utensils they will need to eat them.

CHECK

- *¿Qué vas a comer para la cena?*
- *¿Qué necesitas cuando comes pescado?*
- *¿Cómo es la comida en la escuela?*

LOG BOOK
For one day, have students list the foods they eat, the utensils they use, and the comments they have about the food.

Communicative Objective
• to talk about the markets, restaurants, and foods of Mexico

Related Components

Activity Book	Audio Tapes
p. 28	Listening Tape: 2B, Seg. 2
Audio Book	**Cuaderno**
Script: Seg. 2	p. 14

GETTING STARTED

Ask what these photographs show. Are students familiar with any of these foods and places? What can people find at each of these places? How are these places different from each other? How do they compare to the places where students usually eat?

DISCUSS

Talk about the photographs and captions, and ask questions. Sample questions:

Introduction
Yo tengo mucha hambre.
¿Y Uds.? ¿Tienen hambre?
¿Vamos a comer?

Fruit & Vegetable Market
¿Qué hay aquí? Yo veo unas frutas.
¿Qué frutas? Naranjas, plátanos...
A mí me gustan las naranjas.
¿Te gustan las frutas?
¿Qué fruta te gusta más?

Fast-Food Restaurant
¿Qué quiere decir rápida?
¿Comen Uds. comida rápida?
¿Cuáles son las comidas rápidas?

Taquería
¿Dónde compran Uds. pizza?
En una pizzería, ¿no?
¿Y qué compran en una taquería?
Pues, tacos, claro.

Outdoor Restaurant
Miren, ellos van a comer al restaurante.
¿Qué te gustaría comer aquí?

REALIDADES

LA COMIDA EN MÉXICO

¡VAMOS A COMER EN MÉXICO!

TAQUERÍAS, RESTAURANTES, CAFETERÍAS DE COMIDA RÁPIDA, MERCADOS DE FRUTAS Y VERDURAS. ¡Y MUCHO MÁS!

► En esta cafetería venden comida rápida. ¿Te gustan las hamburguesas? ¿y las papas fritas? ¡Aquí son deliciosas!

◄ ¿Te gusta la comida picante? En las taquerías los mexicanos compran tacos, enchiladas y tortillas. ¡La comida es padrísima! Y no es cara. ¡Buen provecho!

En México hay muchos restaurantes al aire libre. Hay restaurantes italianos, chinos y vegetarianos. ¿Qué te gustaría comer? ¿Pescado, bistec o pollo? ▼

▲ En este mercado hay frutas y verduras frescas. ¿Te gustan los tomates? ¡Qué ricos!

64

MEETING INDIVIDUAL NEEDS

Reaching All Students

For Auditory Learners
In a small group, take turns asking simple food questions. For example: *Tacos, tacos, ¿a quién le gustan los tacos?*

For Visual Learners
Bring in foods mentioned in the text and use them as "flashcards."

For Kinesthetic Learners
Volunteers act out where they are (e.g., **en la taquería**). Others guess where they are and what foods they are probably eating.

 **INTERNET LINK**

La Comida Mexicana:
http://www.udg.mx:80/Cocina/menu.html

HABLA DE LA REVISTA

A. Di qué te gustaría comer en cada lugar.

En la taquería: tacos...

En la cafetería:
En el restaurante al aire libre:
En el restaurante de comida rápida:

B. Busca una comida para cada descripción.

Los tacos son picantes.

picantes frescas deliciosas ricos padrísima

C. Habla con tu compañero(a) de las comidas de las fotos.

— ¿Qué te gustaría comer?
— Me gustaría comer enchiladas.

— A mí me gustan mucho los tacos. ¿Y a ti?
— A mí también. ¡Son deliciosos! ¿Verdad?

¿QUÉ OPINAS?

• Mira la lista. ¿Qué comidas te gustan?
• ¿Y a tu compañero(a)?
• ¿Qué comidas favoritas tienen en común?
• Haz un diagrama. Usa el modelo.

COMIDAS FAVORITAS EN COMÚN

tú   tu compañero(a)

tacos   pollo   pizza

Comidas	
tacos	piña
guacamole	pizza
hamburguesas	huevos
pescado	bistec
pollo	papas fritas
ensaladas	naranjas
jamón	¿otras comidas?

65

ACTIVITIES

Habla de la guía

Individual and Pair Activity:
A. Say what you would like to eat in each place.
B. Say which foods are spicy, fresh, delicious, good, and great.
Answers: See model on student page.
C. With a partner, talk about the foods in the photos that you would like to eat.

¿Qué opinas?

Pair Activity: Making a Venn Diagram
• Look at the list and decide which foods you would like to eat.
• Find out which foods your partner likes.
• Which foods do you both like?
• Make a Venn diagram to compare foods that both of you like and foods that only one of you likes.
Evaluation: Class Activity. Use the information from the completed diagrams to rank the most popular foods.

CHECK

Point to the photos and ask:
• ¿Qué frutas te gustan?
• ¿Dónde compramos tacos?
• ¿Qué comida te gusta más?

LOG BOOK

Have students list vocabulary they find especially difficult.

Para hispanohablantes

Write a paragraph describing your favorite kind of fast food. Read aloud what you have written to the class.

Communicative Objectives

To talk about:
• foods and how they taste
• foods you like and don't like
• being hungry and thirsty

Related Components

Activity Book p. 29-30 Cuaderno p. 15-16	Transparencies Ch. 2: Palabras en acción Tutor Page p. 11

GETTING STARTED

Ask students to look at the menu and identify the words they know or are able to recognize. (More than 20 are simple cognates.)

DISCUSS

Run through the menu with the class, asking in English for the next word that anyone recognizes. If you wish, switch to Spanish after a few words.

A few words deserve special attention:
jamón: ask what it sounds like
carne: elicit *carnivorous*
arroz: ask what it sounds like
pastel: elicit *pastry*

Discuss the similarities of the cognates and ask personal-experience questions about the Mexican food names.

PALABRAS EN ACCIÓN
EL MENÚ DEL DÍA

 1 ¿Qué te gusta?

Haz una lista.

Me gusta: *la sopa de pollo*
Me gustan: *los tacos*

 2 ¿Cómo es?

Describe las comidas del menú.

frío(a)	caliente	dulce	picante
helado	café		

 3 ¿Tienes hambre?

Habla con tu compañero(a) sobre el menú.

— *Tienes hambre, ¿verdad?*
— *Sí, quiero un sándwich de queso. ¿Y tú?*
— *Yo quiero una ensalada.*

 4 Bebidas y postres

Habla con tu compañero(a).

— *¿Tienes sed?*
— *Sí, quiero un refresco.*
— *Y de postre, ¿qué vas a comer?*
— *Quiero un pastel de chocolate.*

66

Para hispanohablantes

Some Spanish speakers in your class may use other expressions than those introduced in this chapter. Have them share with the class. A few variations:

el aguacate: la palta
el atún: la tuna
el bistec: la carne de res, el biftec
¡Buen provecho!: ¡Qué le aproveche!
el helado: el mantecado
el jugo: el zumo
las papas: las patatas
el pastel: el bizcocho, la torta
la piña: el ananás
el plátano: el guineo, la banana
la sopa de verduras: la sopa de vegetales

For students that need additional help, you might consider:
• **The tutor page:** Pair the student with a native speaker or with a more able student using the tutor page.
• **Actividades:** see page 60C: *Comidas y colores*

SÁNDWICHES
NS15⁰⁰ de atún
NS12⁰⁰ de queso
NS10⁰⁰ hamburguesas
NS5⁰⁰ papas fritas

FRUTAS
NS3⁰⁰ piña y naranjas
NS5⁰⁰ melón
NS5⁰⁰ manzanas
NS3⁰⁰ plátanos

POSTRES
NS8⁵⁰ flan
NS9⁵⁰ helado de chocolate / helado de vainilla
NS10⁵⁰ pastel de chocolate
NS6⁵⁰ yogur

BEBIDAS
NS3⁵⁰ agua mineral
NS4⁵⁰ café o té
NS6⁵⁰ refrescos y batidos

---

5. ¿Qué comes? ¿Qué tomas?

Completa la tabla.

	Como...	y tomo...	hora
desayuno	*2 huevos,...*	*chocolate*	a las *7:00*
comida (almuerzo)	___	___	___
cena	___	___	___

6. En un restaurante

Escribe un diálogo entre un(a) mesero(a) y un(a) cliente(a).

Mesero(a): *Buenos días, ¿qué va a pedir?*
Cliente(a): *Quiero un sándwich de atún.*
Mesero(a): *¿Y para tomar?*
Cliente(a): *Un vaso de leche.*
Mesero(a): *¿Algo más?*
Cliente(a): *No, gracias.*

7. Collage

Usa fotos o dibujos para crear un collage de tus comidas y bebidas favoritas. Escribe el nombre de cada comida o bebida.

8. ¿Y tú?

Haz una lista de las comidas que te gustan.

¡SABES QUE...?

The **peso** is the basis of the Mexican currency. In 1993, the new **peso** (abbreviated as N$) was introduced. Its value is 1000 times greater than the old **peso**.

67

ACTIVITIES

1. Individual Activity
Look at the menu and list the foods that you like.
Evaluation: Rate the foods on a scale of 1-3 (1 being foods you like). Compare your list with another student.

2. Individual Activity
Write foods from the menu under the word that best describes them.
Extension: Choose other adjectives (e.g. colors) to describe the foods on the list.

3. Pair Activity
Speak with your partner about the menu.
For Auditory Learners: Pair activity. Say five food words while your partner writes them down. Switch roles and correct each other's work.

4. Pair Activity
Speak with your partner about the drinks and desserts on the menu.
Application: Write a sentence about three of your favorite desserts and drinks from this menu.

5. Individual Activity
Make a chart that shows what you eat and drink at each meal and when you eat.
For Auditory Learners: Ask the student next to you *¿Qué comes para el desayuno/almuerzo/cena?* He or she answers, then asks the next student. Repeat the process with the question *¿Qué tomas para ...?*

6. Individual Activity
Write a dialog between a waiter and a customer.
Synthesis: Share dialogs. Form groups and use the best ideas for a new script.

7. Hands-On Activity
Use photos and drawings of your favorite foods to create a collage. Label each food with its name.

8. Writing Activity
List the foods you like.

CHECK

- *¿Qué te gusta comer de postre?*
- *Describe la comida en el menú de la escuela.*
- *¿Qué te gusta tomar cuando tienes sed?*

PORTFOLIO
Create a bilingual menu for a Mexican restaurant. Use this menu as a model.

Communicative Objective
- to use **gustar** to talk about things you or other people like or dislike

Related Components

Activity Book p. 31-32	**Audio Tapes** Listening: 2B, Seg. 3
Audio Book Script: Seg. 3 Activities: p. 21	**Cuaderno** p. 17
	Tutor Page p. 12

GETTING STARTED

Ask students to name one restaurant they like and one they don't like, using **me gusta** and **no me gusta**. Decide which restaurants the class likes best and which they like least.

Language In Context

Vocabulary Note: Ask students to think of English words that might be related to **gustar.** Try to elicit *gusto* and *disgust.* Ask them to use those English words in sentences. Ask if the words seem positive or negative. Explain that *gusto* and *disgust* (like **gustar**) come from a Latin word *(gustare)* that means "taste." Ask for other **dis-** words that mean the opposite of something (e.g., *disagree, disadvantage*).

Grammar Note: Remind students that **gustar** is unusual. Most verbs refer to a person who perfoms an action—for example, *yo como tacos.* **Gustar,** however, refers to the object that receives the action (in this case, the taco): *me gusta comer tacos.* In English, this would be: *It pleases me to eat tacos.*

DISCUSS

Review vocabulary from previous chapters and introduce some of this chapter's new food vocabulary with questions and statements that use forms of **gustar.**
Por la mañana me gusta el café.
En la caferería de la escuela me gustan las ensaladas.
Y me gustan mucho las hamburguesas.
Pero no me gusta el pollo.
Y a ti, ¿te gusta el pollo?
No, no me gusta el pollo.
A mis hermanos tampoco les gusta el pollo.

PARA COMUNICARNOS MEJOR
¿QUÉ TE GUSTA?

To talk about things you like or dislike, use the verb *gustar* and a noun.

☐ To say that you or another person likes or dislikes one thing, use ***gusta*** followed by a singular noun.

Me gusta el pollo.	I like chicken.
No me gusta el bistec.	I don't like steak.

¿RECUERDAS?

To say that you like to do something, use ***me gusta*** and the infinitive of another verb.

Me gusta compartir la pizza.

☐ To say that you or another person likes or dislikes more than one thing, use ***gustan*** followed by a plural noun.

Me gustan las hamburguesas.	I like hamburgers.
No me gustan los postres.	I don't like desserts.

☐ ***Le gusta/le gustan*** can mean *you* (formal) *like, he likes,* and *she likes.*

Le gustan las verduras.	You like vegetables.
Le gusta la sopa.	He likes soup.
Le gusta el jugo de naranja.	She likes orange juice.

☐ Use ***a mí, a ti, a usted, a él, a ella***, or ***a*** and a name for emphasis or clarity.

A mí me gusta el flan.	I like flan.
A ti te gusta el helado.	You like ice-cream.
A Eva le gusta el té frío.	Eva likes iced tea.

¡OJO!

If you ask "who likes. . . ?" remember to begin the question with **a.**

¿A quién le gustan las ensaladas?

For students needing help using **gustar,** you might consider:
- **The tutor page:** Pair the student with a native speaker or a more able student using the tutor page.
- **Actividades:** see page 60D: *Me gusta mucho*

1 Taquería del Sol

La Taquería del Sol tiene un menú del día.
¿Qué ensalada te gusta? ¿qué taco? ¿qué
sándwich? ¿qué jugo? ¿qué postre?
Pregúntale a tu compañero(a).

— ¿Qué ensalada te gusta?
— Me gusta la ensalada de tomate.

2 En un restaurante mexicano

¿Qué comidas te gustan? Pregúntale a tu
compañero(a).

— ¿Te gustan los tacos?
— Sí, son muy ricos. Me gustan mucho.
  (No, no me gustan.)

1. los tacos
2. el arroz con pollo
3. el guacamole
4. los frijoles
5. las enchiladas
6. el flan

3 El menú de la escuela

A. En grupo, preparen una tabla con las comidas y bebidas que hay
en la cafetería de la escuela. Anoten qué le gusta a cada uno.

	a mí	a María	a Andrés	a Eva
pescado	no	sí	sí	no
pizza				
pollo				
papas fritas		sí	sí	

B. Informen a la clase.

A mí no me gusta el pescado y a Eva tampoco.
A María le gustan las papas fritas y a Andrés también.

TAQUERÍA
DEL SOL
MENÚ DEL DÍA
ensalada: de tomate o
           de lechuga
taco: de pollo, de carne
      o de verduras
sándwich: de jamón o
          de queso
jugo: de manzana o
      de naranja
postre: helado o flan
N$10.⁰⁰

69

Students use **gustar** to talk about food.

1. Pair Activity
Ask each other which of the options on the
Taquería del Sol menu you like.
Answers: See model on student page.
Extension: Do the activity in the plural:
A: *¿Qué ensaladas te gustan?*
B: *Me gustan las ensaladas de tomate y de
lechuga.*

2. Pair Activity
Ask each other whether or not you like
each of these dishes.
Possible Answers:
1. See model on student page.
2. ¿Te gusta el arroz con pollo?
   No, no me gusta.
3. ¿Te gusta el guacamole?
   ¡No, qué horrible! No, no me gusta.
4. ¿Te gustan los frijoles?
   ¡No, qué horribles! No, no me gustan.
5. ¿Te gustan las enchiladas?
   Sí, me gustan las enchiladas.
6. ¿Te gusta el flan?
   ¡Ay, qué rico! ¡Me gusta muchísimo!
Extension: Form groups of three. Have the
groups follow the model below, changing
roles from time to time.
A: (to B) *¿Te gusta el flan?*
B: (Nods "yes" or "no")
A: (to C) *A mi amigo no le gusta el flan.*

3. Group Activity
A. Use the model to make a chart of the
foods and drinks in your school cafeteria.
Write down what members of the group
say they like or dislike.
B. Report the results to the class in complete sentences.
Answers: See model on student page.
Synthesis: Imagine that you are in charge
of the menu for your school cafeteria. What
changes would you make? Design a menu
in Spanish that includes the prices.

¿Qué comidas les gustan a tu compañero(a)?
¿Qué libro no te gusta?
¿Qué bebida te gusta mucho?

Write about your favorite foods and
what it is that you like about them.

Communicative Objective
• to talk about eating, sharing, and other everyday activities using **-er** and **-ir** verbs.

Related Components

Activity Book p. 33-34	**Audio Tapes** Chapter: 2B, Seg. 4
Audio Book Script: Seg.4 Activities: p. 22	**Cuaderno** p. 18
	Tutor Page

GETTING STARTED

Ask students to name **-er** and **-ir** verbs they know. Write these on the board. (comer, escribir, ir, leer, salir, ser, tener.)

Language In Context
Point to the fruits and talk about eating. For example:
¿Qué te gusta comer?
¿Comes manzanas?
Yo también como manzanas.
José, ¿comes manzanas?

Grammar Note: Read aloud the text and examples. Explain that Spanish verbs end in **-ar, -er,** or **-ir.** Use the paradigms to review **-er** and **-ir** endings.

DISCUSS

Review vocabulary from *Encuentros* and Chapter 1 and introduce some of this chapter's new food vocabulary with questions that incorporate *comer* and *compartir.* For example:
¿Con quién compartes las papas fritas?
¿Qué comes?
¿Compartimos una piña?
Los mexicanos comen muchas tortillas. ¿Y tú?
Comparto el sandwich con mi hermano.
¿Vas a comer pescado o carne esta noche?
Cuando voy al parque, como un helado de chocolate. Y tú, ¿qué tipo de helado comes?

PARA COMUNICARNOS MEJOR
¿QUÉ COMES?

To talk about everyday activities, you will use many verbs that end in -er and -ir.

Comer *(to eat)*, for example, is a verb that ends in **-er.**

— *Por la mañana como fruta.* In the morning, I eat fruit.
¿Y ustedes? And you?
— *Comemos cereal con leche.* We eat cereal with milk.

Compartir *(to share)* is a verb that ends in **-ir.**

Siempre comparto el postre. I always share dessert.

Look at the forms of the verbs ***comer*** and ***compartir*** in the present tense. Note that the endings are the same, except in the ***nosotros(as)*** and ***vosotros(as)*** forms.

	comer (to eat)	compartir (to share)
yo	com**o**	compart**o**
tú	com**es**	compart**es**
usted	com**e**	compart**e**
él/ella	com**e**	compart**e**
nosotros(as)	com**emos**	compart**imos**
vosotros(as)	com**éis**	compart**ís**
ustedes	com**en**	compart**en**
ellos/ellas	com**en**	compart**en**

Some other **-er** and **-ir** verbs that you have already seen are ***leer*** *(to read)* and ***escribir*** *(to write).*

70

For students needing help using **-er** and **-ir** verbs, you might consider:
• **The tutor page:** Pair the student with a native speaker or a more able student using the tutor page.
• **Actividades:** see page 60D: *Como, bebo, comparto.*

1 Los restaurantes del centro

¿Qué comes en los restaurantes? ¿Qué tomas?
Pregúntale a tu compañero(a).

— ¿Qué comes en un restaurante italiano?
— Como pizza.
— ¿Y qué tomas?
— Tomo agua mineral.

en un restaurante vegetariano
en un restaurante italiano
en un restaurante mexicano
en un restaurante de comida rápida
en una taquería

2 Desayuno, almuerzo y cena

A. ¿Qué comen en cada comida? Con tu compañero(a),
preparen una lista.

desayuno: *cereal con leche...*
almuerzo (comida): *un sándwich de...*
cena: *pollo con papas fritas...*

B. Ahora, pregúntenles a otros compañeros(as).

— ¿Qué comen ustedes para el desayuno?
— Comemos huevos con jamón. ¿Y ustedes?
— Nosotros comemos cereal con leche.

3 En la cafetería de la escuela

Pregúntale a tu compañero(a).

— Generalmente, ¿qué comes en la cafetería de
la escuela?
— Como un sándwich.

1. ¿Qué comes?
2. ¿Qué tomas?
3. ¿Comes pan con la comida?
4. Generalmente, ¿qué comes de postre?
5. Generalmente, ¿compartes la comida? ¿Con quién?
6. ¿Te gusta comer en la cafetería de la escuela?

ACTIVITIES

Students use forms of **comer.**

1. Pair Activity
Ask each other what you eat and drink at
each restaurant on the list.
Answers: See model on student page.
Application: Each player makes a sentence
with: *Yo como...* After all have taken a turn,
players repeat what everyone eats.

2. Pair Activity
A. List the foods that both of you eat at
breakfast, lunch, and dinner.
Answers: See model on student page.
B. Compare your list with other students.
Be sure to use plural forms of **comer.**
Answers: See model on student page.
For Auditory Learners: Several players take
turns speaking simple sentences. Each sub-
stitutes a new noun. Example:
Player A. *Como una naranja.*
Player B. *Como un tomate.*
When players can't think of any new
nouns, start again with a new sentence.

3. Pair Activity
Ask and answer the questions in the list.
Possible answers:
1. See model on student page.
2. *Tomo un batido de chocolate.*
3. *Sí, como pan con la comida.*
4. *Como flan.*
5. *No, no comparto la comida.*
6. *Sí, me gusta mucho comer en la cafetería
de la escuela.*
Application: Make up sentences about a
person and a place, using **compartir.**
Example: *En el parque, los chavos comparten
la bicicleta con sus hermanos.*

CHECK

Ask students to name:
• *tres cosas que comes todos los días*
• *tres cosas que no compartes con tus amigos*
• *tres comidas que te gusta comer y que no
quieres compartir*

LOG BOOK
Have students write down the endings of
comer and **compartir** and write a brief
sentence about the differences.

Para hispanohablantes

Act out a scene in which you and your
friends order and share different dishes at
a restaurant.

Communicative Objective
• to talk about what and where you are going to eat

Related Components

Assessment Oral Proficiency: p. 22	**Conexiones** Chapter 2
Audio Book Script: Seg. 5 Activities: p. 23	**Magazine** Juntos en Mexico
Audio Tapes Listening: 2B, Seg.5 Conexiones: 16A, Ch. 2	**Tutor Page** p. 14

GETTING STARTED

Read aloud the title of this page. Have students look at the ads and figure out what foods are served in each restaurant. Follow up with such questions as:

¿Qué es comida internacional? Los tacos, ¿son comida internacional?

¿Hay hamburguesas en Puros Tacos?

¿En qué país están los tres restaurantes?

APPLY

1. Pair Activity
Pick a restaurant and make plans to go there with a friend.
Answers: See model on student page.
Extension: Write or say when you are going to go to each of these restaurants.
Example: *Voy a Los Guajolotes mañana.*

2. Individual Activity
Design a restaurant ad in Spanish for your favorite restaurant. Give the foods, prices, hours, address, and telephone number.
Answers: See models on student page.
Analysis: Exchange advertisements with other students, and ask questions about their restaurants.

3. Pair Activity
Compare the times of meals in Mexico with those where you live.
Answers: See model on student page.

4. Pair activity
Plan a meal for the class. Decide on a soup, main course, dessert, and beverage. Determine what you need to buy for the meal, what you need to set the table, and who will act as the waiter.
Possible Answer: *Vamos a comer sopa de verduras, bistec con papas, y flan. Vamos a*

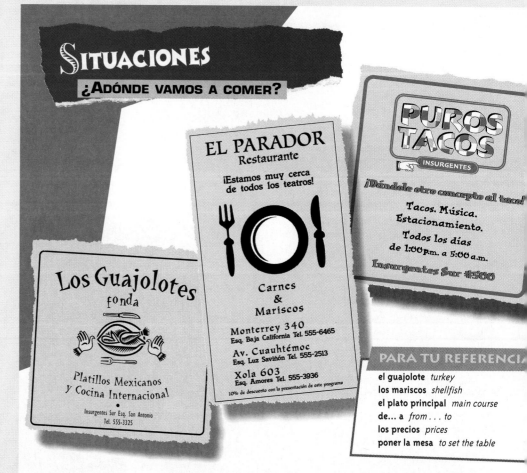

SITUACIONES
¿ADÓNDE VAMOS A COMER?

EL PARADOR
Restaurante

¡Estamos muy cerca de todos los teatros!

Carnes & Mariscos

Monterrey 340
Esq. Baja California Tel. 555-6465

Av. Cuauhtémoc
Esq. Luz Saviñón Tel. 555-2513

Xola 603
Esq. Amores Tel. 555-3936

10% de descuento con la presentación de este programa

PUROS TACOS
INSURGENTES

¡Dándole otro concepto al taco!

Tacos. Música.
Estacionamiento.
Todos los días
de 1:00 p.m. a 5:00 a.m.

Insurgentes Sur #500

Los Guajolotes
fonda

Platillos Mexicanos y Cocina Internacional

Insurgentes Sur Esq. San Antonio
Tel. 555-3325

PARA TU REFERENCIA

el guajolote *turkey*
los mariscos *shellfish*
el plato principal *main course*
de... a *from . . . to*
los precios *prices*
poner la mesa *to set the table*

 1 Decisiones

Mira los anuncios y haz planes para ir a comer con un(a) amigo(a).

— ¿Adónde vamos? ¿A Puros Tacos?
— Sí, ¡padrísimo! Me gustan mucho los tacos.
  (No, no me gustan mucho los tacos. ¡Vamos a El Parador!)

 2 Haz un anuncio

Haz un anuncio de tu restaurante favorito con las comidas, los precios, el horario, la dirección y el teléfono.

72

tomar café y agua mineral. Necesitamos carne, verduras, agua mineral, platos cuchillos, cucharas y tenedores. Yo voy a ser el mesero.
Application: Say what you are going to eat at home this evening. Example: *Hoy voy a comer carne y ensalada.*

For students needing help, you might consider:
• **The tutor page:** Pair the student with a native speaker or a more able student using the tutor page.
• **Actividades:** see page 60C: *Tengo*

 **INTERNET LINK**

Especialidades de México:
http://mexico.udg.mx:80/Cocina/Tipico.html

3 La hora de las comidas

Con tu compañero(a), comparen la hora de las comidas en México y en Estados Unidos.

— ¿A qué hora es la comida (el almuerzo) en México?
— En México la comida es de 1:00 a 3:00 de la tarde.
— ¿Y en Estados Unidos?

 4 Una comida en la clase

Hagan planes para una comida en la clase. Decidan:

• Qué van a comer (incluyan sopa, plato principal y postre)
• Qué van a tomar
• Quién va a ser el/la mesero(a)
• Qué necesitan para poner la mesa
• Qué necesitan para la comida

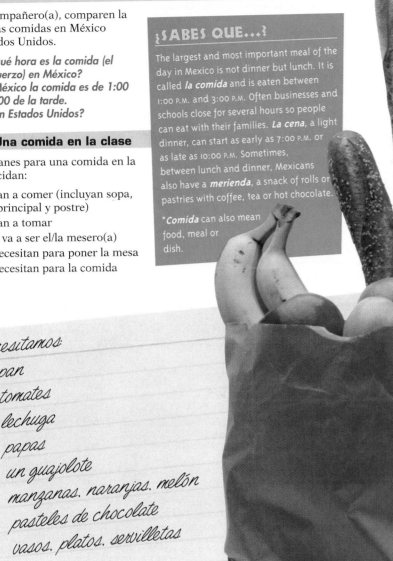

¿SABES QUE...?

The largest and most important meal of the day in Mexico is not dinner but lunch. It is called *la comida* and is eaten between 1:00 P.M. and 3:00 P.M. Often businesses and schools close for several hours so people can eat with their families. *La cena*, a light dinner, can start as early as 7:00 P.M. or as late as 10:00 P.M. Sometimes, between lunch and dinner, Mexicans also have a *merienda*, a snack of rolls or pastries with coffee, tea or hot chocolate.

*Comida can also mean food, meal or dish.

Necesitamos:

pan
tomates
lechuga
papas
un guajolote
manzanas, naranjas, melón
pasteles de chocolate
vasos, platos, servilletas

73

Para hispanohablantes

Write a newspaper review of the food at a Mexican restaurant.

CHECK

• ¿A qué restaurante te gusta ir?
• ¿Qué comidas te gustan más?
• ¿A qué hora te gusta comer?

Thinking About Language

You can use this opportunity to discuss with your students that Spanish is not spoken similarly throughout the world, nor even in Mexico alone.

What Is a Spanish Accent?

1. Ask students to identify accents they have heard on television or in real life. Ask why everyone in the US does not speak the same way. What things might have led to all these different accents?
(A few reasons: different colonies were started by English speakers with a variety of regional or class accents; others were established by people who spoke other languages—e.g., Dutch influenced the Brooklyn accent.)

2. Ask:
• Do you think the Spanish of Spain is likely to be different from Mexican Spanish, the way British English differs from American English?
• Do you think there is as much or more variety in Spanish as there is in English?
• What do you think might cause that?
(Some reasons why there is much variety in Spanish: the dates the Spanish arrived in an area; how hard and long they tried to colonize an area; Native American languages and languages spoken in nearby colonies; the languages of the next waves of settlers.)

LOG BOOK

Have students write down important things they had with this lesson.

Communicative Objectives
• to plan a menu
• to talk about kinds of food

Related Components

Video: Tape/Book
Unit 1: Seg. 3

Search to frame 1061913

GETTING STARTED

Talk about your school's cafeteria. Do students feel that the foods are varied enough? Do they make special menus to celebrate holidays or community events? What kinds of foods do they serve then?

APPLY

Form groups. Explain that each group will plan one week's menu for the school cafeteria.

PASO 1: El menú de la semana
Choose one of these menu topics for each day.
Extension: Describe your menu idea.
Example: *El menú para vegetarianos va a tener muchas verduras.*

PASO 2: El menú del día
Prepare your menu for one day (soups, daily special, sandwiches, and desserts), give the prices in dollars. Make a drawing of the menu.
Answers: See sample menu on student page.

PASO 3: El plato sorpresa
Create a surprise dish and give it an unusual name.
Answers: See model on student page.
Extension: Exchange names with other groups and figure out what's in each dish.

PASO 4: Ingredientes
Name the ingredients and prices of the dishes you chose.
Application: Exchange menus and order food from another group. One student from each group acts as another's waiter.

PASO 5: Encuesta
Compare menus and decide which is the overall favorite, the least expensive, most expensive, tastiest, and spiciest and which is the overall favorite surprise dish.

74

PARA RESOLVER
EL MENÚ DE LA CAFETERÍA

Con tu clase, planeen el menú de la cafetería de la escuela para toda la semana.

PASO 1 El menú de la semana
En grupos, escojan un menú para cada día de la semana.

• *Menú vegetariano: lunes*
• *Menú para atletas:*
• *Menú de comidas rápidas:*
• *Menú mexicano:*
• *Menú italiano:*

PASO 2 El menú del día
Preparen el menú del día: sopas, plato del día, postres, bebidas, precios en dólares... Hagan un dibujo del menú.

PASO 3 El plato sorpresa
En grupos, inventen un plato sorpresa para el menú. ¿Cómo se llama?

Pan, aguacate, lechuga y tomate verde.
Se llama sándwich "verde, verde, verde".

PASO 4 Los ingredientes
¿Qué hay en el menú y cuánto cuesta? Digan cuáles son los ingredientes de cada plato.

Ensalada "¡Viva México!"
(Aguacate, tomate y frijoles)
Cuesta $2.50

PASO 5 Encuesta
Con la clase, comparen todos los menús. ¿Cuál es el menú favorito de la clase? ¿Cuál es el más barato? ¿Cuál es el más caro? ¿Cuál es el más rico? ¿Cuál es el más picante? ¿Cuál es el plato sorpresa favorito de la clase?

74

¿SABES QUE...?

In Mexico, *jugos*, or fruit juices, are usually freshly squeezed by street vendors. You can also get an *agua fresca*, which is a fruit juice mixed with water and sugar. For an extra burst of energy, try a *licuado*, a fruit milk shake which is sometimes mixed with an egg.

MEETING INDIVIDUAL NEEDS

Reaching All Students

For Auditory Learners
Name two foods and have others guess to which meal you are referring.

For Kinesthetic Learners
Suggest different foods with shapes of clay, and use the shapes to present a menu to the class.

MENÚ VEGETARIANO

Lunes

SOPAS

sopa de verduras $1.20
sopa de tomate $1.00

PLATOS DEL DÍA

pasta $3.00
arroz con frijoles $2.00
ensalada "¡Viva México!" $2.50
(aguacate, tomate y frijoles)

PLATO SORPRESA

sándwich "verde, verde, verde" $2.50
(pan, aguacate, lechuga y tomate verde)

POSTRES

flan de mango $1.20
ensalada de frutas $1.25

BEBIDAS

jugo de piña $1.00
refrescos $1.00
chocolate caliente $1.00

75

PORTFOLIO

Have students write a menu for a restaurant they would like to own.

More Food Words
appetizer *el aperitivo*
entree *el plato fuerte*

bake *cocer*
boil *hervir*
fry *freír*
marinate *marinar*
roast *asar*
stew *guisar*

rare *poco asado, casi crudo*
medium *medio asado, bien cocido*
well-done *bien asado, bien cocido*

 **CULTURE NOTE**

Bocadillo, a word used in Spain for small sandwich; has been replaced by **sandwich** in many places. Where both words exist, **bocadillos** may be made of a roll-like bread and **sandwiches** of sliced white bread.

Para hispanohablantes

Ask about and write down a family recipe and, if possible, a story about someone who cooked or ate it.

Objectives
Communicative: to learn about typical Mexican foods
Cultural: to talk about important ingredients in Mexican cooking

Related Components

Audio Tapes	Magazine
Conexiones: 16A, Ch. 2	Juntos en Mexico
Conexiones Chapter 2	

GETTING STARTED

Ask students to talk about these three foods. Have they tried all three? Which do they like best? Why?

DISCUSS

Using the Text
Ask comprehension and critical-thinking questions after each paragraph. Examples:

Introduction
¿Es importante el color en la comida?
¿Te gustaría comer una comida con muchos colores?

El maíz
(For information about *tamales* and *atole*, see page 73.)
Los mexicanos usan el maíz en muchas comidas. ¿Con qué comes tú el maíz? ¿De qué se hace una tortilla?

El chocolate en las comidas
Los mexicanos usan chocolate en salsas para el pollo y la carne. ¿Y tú? ¿Qué salsa te gusta más?

Chilemanía
Comer un chile muy picante, ¿es bueno o es malo?
¿Con qué te gusta comer los chiles?
¿Con qué comidas usan los mexicanos los chiles? (Don't forget chocolate.)

CHECK

Use **Te toca a ti** to check comprehension.

Te toca a ti
Answers:
1. *Falsa. Los mexicanos preparan mole con chocolate y chiles.*

ENTÉRATE
LA COMIDA MEXICANA

La comida mexicana es color, sabor° y tradición. El maíz,° el chocolate y los chiles° son ingredientes típicos° de la comida mexicana.

CHILEMANÍA

¿Son todos los chiles rojos y picantes? No. Hay chiles amarillos, verdes y de otros colores. También hay chiles menos picantes. Los chiles son muy populares en México. Los mexicanos usan chile con pan, salsas, pastas, frutas y también con las papas fritas. ¡Es una chilemanía!

EL MAÍZ

El maíz se usa° para hacer sopas, comidas, postres como el tamal dulce° y bebidas como el atole.° Pero lo más° importante es la tortilla, que es como el pan en otras culturas.

EL CHOCOLATE EN LAS COMIDAS

¿Chocolate con carne? ¿Chocolate con chiles? En México preparan muchas comidas con *mole poblano*, una salsa° con chocolate, chiles y muchos ingredientes más.

¿SABES QUE...?

Chocolate is made from cocoa beans. The cocoa tree was cultivated by the Aztecs. They believed cocoa to be a source of strength and wisdom. Today, **chocolate** is a basic ingredient in Mexican cooking, not only for desserts, but also for main dishes and drinks.

el atole *sweet drink made of milk and cornstarch*
los chiles *chili peppers*
lo más *the most*
el maíz *corn (maize)*
el sabor *flavor*
la salsa *sauce*

TE TOCA A TI

Di qué oraciones son ciertas y cuáles son falsas. Corrige las oraciones falsas.

1. Los mexicanos preparan *mole* con maíz.
2. Todos los chiles son rojos y picantes.
3. El maíz se usa para hacer tortillas.
4. El *mole poblano* es una salsa con chocolate.

se usa *is used*
el tamal dulce *sweet maize dough wrapped up in maize or banana leaves*
típicos *typical*

76

---

2. *Falsa. Hay chiles de muchos colores y no todos son picantes.*
3. *Cierta.*
4. *Cierta.*

LOG BOOK
Have students write the names of all the foods they can remember from the chapter.

 CULTURE NOTE

Chocolate, corn, and chilis are not just typical of Mexican cuisine, they are native to Mexico. All three were unknown in Europe until the Aztecs introduced the Spaniards to their bitter *tchocolatl*, spicy *chillis*, and corn. (*Maíz* is a Taíno word, *corn* an English one.)

VOCABULARIO TEMÁTICO

Lugares para comer
Places to eat

el restaurante al aire libre
outdoor restaurant

el restaurante de comida rápida
fast food restaurant

la taquería taco shop

En el desayuno
For breakfast

el cereal cereal
los huevos eggs
la mantequilla butter
el pan bread

**En el almuerzo
y en la cena**
For lunch and for dinner

el aguacate avocado
el arroz rice
el atún tuna
el bistec steak
la carne meat
la ensalada salad
los frijoles beans
el jamón ham
la lechuga lettuce
las papas potatoes
las papas fritas French fries
la pasta pasta
el pescado fish
el pollo chicken
el queso cheese
la sopa soup
el tomate tomato
las verduras vegetables

Las frutas *Fruits*
la manzana apple
el melón melon
la naranja orange
la piña pineapple
el plátano banana

Las bebidas *Drinks*
el agua mineral mineral water
el batido shake
el café coffee
el chocolate (caliente)
(hot) chocolate
el jugo juice
la leche milk
el té tea

Los postres *Desserts*
el flan flan
el helado de vainilla
vanilla ice-cream
el pastel cake
el yogur yogurt

En el restaurante
el cliente/la clienta customer
la comida food, meal, dish
la cuchara spoon
el cuchillo knife
el menú menu
el mesero/la mesera
waiter/waitress
el plato del día daily special
el plato plate
la servilleta napkin
la taza cup
el tenedor fork
el vaso glass

¿Cómo es?
caro(a) expensive
delicioso(a) delicious
dulce sweet
fresco(a) fresh
horrible awful
picante spicy
rico(a) tasty

Expresiones y palabras
¿Algo más? Something else?
¡Buen provecho!
Enjoy your meal!
No quiero nada.
I don't want anything.
¿Qué vas a pedir?
What are you going to order?
¿Tienes hambre/sed?
Are you hungry/thirsty?
Tengo mucha hambre/sed.
I'm very hungry/thirsty.
caliente hot
compartir to share
frío(a) cold, iced
o or
¿verdad? Isn't it?, aren't they?,
right?
tomar to drink

**Platos típicos
mexicanos**
la enchilada enchilada
el guacamole guacamole
el mole mole
el taco taco
la tortilla tortilla

Expresión de México
la comida lunch

LA CONEXIÓN INGLÉS-ESPAÑOL

It was easy to recognize the word ***delicioso*** because it looks like *delicious*. Other cognates may not be as obvious. Look at these words in the ***Vocabulario temático***: ***ensalada***, ***jamón***, ***bistec***, ***plato***. How can their connection to English help you understand what they mean?

77

La conexión inglés-español
Not all Spanish cognates which end in -**oso/a** have English cognates which end in -**ous** (e.g., *talentoso/talented* or *musculoso/muscular*).
However if a word ends in -**oso** or -**osa**, cover the ending to see if it looks like an English word. If it does, the most likely English ending is -**ous**.

VOCABULARIO TEMÁTICO

Objectives
• to review vocabulary
• to correctly pronounce words containing the letter "c" in Spanish

Related Components

Activity Book	Audio Book
Chapter Review: p. 35-36	Script: Seg. 6 Activities p. 24
Assessment	**Audio Tapes**
Listening Script: p. 10	Listening: 2B, Seg. 6
Chapter Test: p. 51-56	Assessment: 14A, Ch. 2
	Cuaderno p. 19-20

Pronunciation: "c"
• The letter "c" is pronounced like the English "c" in the word "cat" (but without the accompanying aspiration) at the end of a word or when it is followed by an "r," "l," "a," "o," or "u."

"ca" - carne, aguacate, café
"co" - comida, compartir,
"cu" - cuchara, cuchillo,
"cl" - cliente
"cr" - creer

final consonant in a syllable or word: *bistec*
The first "c" in the word *acción*.

• The letter "c" is pronounced like the English "s" in "say" before an "i" or "e."
before "e" - *cereal , dulce*
before "i" - *delicioso*

• Before the letter "h," the "c" and "h" are pronounced together like the "ch" in the English word "church." Before 1994 "ch" was regarded as a separate letter of the alphabet and had its own section in the dictionary.

chocolate, leche, cuchara, cuchillo

Language Note
In Spain, the "c" before an "e" or "i" is pronounced like the "th" in the English word "thick."

▶▶▶INTERNET LINK

Chile Pepper Magazine:
http://www.hot.presence.com:80/g/p/H3/ chilepepper/
All about chocolate: http://www.qrc.com/~sholubek/choco/faq.htm

ADELANTE

Objectives

Pre-Reading Strategy: to elicit meaning from photographs and captions

Cultural: to introduce students to Mexico City's Chapultepec Park

Related Components

CD ROM Unit 1: Adelante	**Video:** **Tape/Book** Unit 1: Seg. 4
Magazine Juntos en méxico	

Search to frame 1110707

GETTING STARTED

Ask some questions about public parks. Why were they invented? Are they worth-while? What should they be used for?

Using the Video

Show Segment 4 of the Unit 1 video, the introduction to Chapultepec.

Antes de leer

Read aloud the paragraphs. Ask compre-hension questions. Examples:
¿Chapultepec es grande o pequeño?
(670 hectares is about 2.6 square miles)
¿Hay museos en Chapultepec?
¿Qué más hay?

Information for Travelers

The park is located at the western end of the Paseo de la Reforma, not far from the Zona Rosa. The Metro stop Chapultepec is near the main entrance. The park is free and open every day.

ADELANTE

ANTES DE LEER

Es domingo, ¿adónde vamos? ¡Al Bosque° de Chapultepec! Está en el centro de la Ciudad de México. Son 670 (seiscientas setenta) hectáreas de parque. Hay teatros, museos, lagos,° un zoológico, un parque de diversiones° ¡y un castillo!°

Mira las páginas 78–81. Di qué actividades te gustaría hacer en el Bosque de Chapultepec.

◄ La famosa estatua° de Tláloc, dios de la lluvia,° está a la entrada° del **Museo Nacional de Antropología, en el Bosque de Chapultepec.**

el bosque *woods*	la entrada *entrance*
el castillo *castle*	la estatua *statue*
el dios de la lluvia *god of rain*	los lagos *lakes*
	el parque de diversiones *amusement park*

Adelante Components

Activity Book p. 37-40	**Audio Tapes** Adelante: 8A, 8B	**Magazine** Juntos en México	**Video: Tape/Book** Unit 1: Seg. 4-5
Assessment Portfolio: p. 33-34	**CD ROM** Unit 1: Adelante	**Transparencies** Unit 1: Adelante	

◄ En náhuatl, la lengua° de los aztecas, chapultepec quiere decir "monte de los chapulines".

◄ Muchos chicos y chicas van a patinar al Bosque de Chapultepec.

◄ En el parque, los cacahuates° con chile, con sal° o con azúcar,° son muy populares.

el azúcar *sugar*
los cacahuates *peanuts*
la lengua *language*

el monte de los chapulines
   grasshopper hill
la sal *salt*

Using the Photos

Tláloc

Tláloc was the god of rain. (His name means "He Who Makes Things Sprout.") This 167-ton, 25-foot-tall statue was discovered near Teotihuacán. Although we call the statue by an Aztec name, it was probably created by an earlier civilization.

History Link: Why do you think the god of rain was important to the Aztecs?

Grasshopper

The Aztecs lived on Chapultepec Hill in the fourteenth century, before building their city on the lake. Emperor Maximilian lived on Chapultepec Hill, as did several Mexican presidents. (The presidents now live in a different part of the park.)

Language Link: The Aztec language was classical Nahuatl. Modern dialects of this language are still spoken by a million people in central and western Mexico.

Peanuts

The peanut is native to tropical areas of the Americas. Today it is grown mostly for its edible oil. The word **cacahuate** comes from Nahuatl and originally meant "cocoa from the earth."
¿Te gusta comer cacahuates?
¿Prefieres los cacahuates con azúcar o con sal?

►►►INTERNET LINK

Links to the Aztecs: http://kira.pomona.claremont.edu/mesoamerica.html

Objectives

Reading Strategy: to identify the main idea and details

Cultural: to observe Chapultepec Park's contributions to recreation, ecology, and the preservation of Mexican history

Related Components

Activity Book p. 37	Audio Tapes Adelante: 8A

GETTING STARTED

Ask if any students have been to a park like Chapultepec. If so, ask them to describe the attractions and activities in the park. Ask students what kinds of theme parks they want to explore.

Background

About Chapultepec Park

Chapultepec is one of the most diverse public parks in the world and the official home of the President of Mexico.
The park was created in several stages. The oldest section, and the one closest to the center of the city, is the Bosque de Chapultepec. It contains most of the major attractions, including the castle, museums of art and anthropology, several theaters, two lakes, a botanical garden, a zoo, and Los Pinos, the "Mexican White House. "The newer sections are called Chapultepec Nuevo (which has three science museums) and Chapultepec section 3 (an amusement park).

Thinking About Language

Ask: What English words do the words **montaña rusa** resemble? Try to elicit *mountain* and *Russia*.
Ask students to suggest reasons why a roller coaster would be called a "Russian Mountain. "(The name refers to a twisting ice-toboggan slide first built in Russia.)
Ask students to suggest where our word *roller coaster* might have come from. (Early roller coasters did not have wheels, but coasted over rollers.)

Comidas

¿Te gustaría comer en un restaurante de Chapultepec?
¿Qué te gusta más, los tacos o las enchiladas?
¿Comes frutas con chile en tu ciudad?

UN PASEO POR
CHAPULTEPEC

Chapultepec Mágico

Es el nombre del parque de diversiones de Chapultepec. La montaña rusa° es una de las diversiones favoritas.

◄ La montaña rusa de este parque tiene forma de serpiente.°

▼ En el parque venden° deliciosas frutas con chile.

Comidas

Chapultepec es un lugar ideal para hacer picnics. Aquí venden comida mexicana deliciosa: tacos, enchiladas y frutas con chile. También venden refrescos, jugos y helados.

Las calles

Como° no hay coches en las calles del parque, patinar es muy divertido.

El Castillo

El Castillo está en la cima° del Monte de Chapultepec. Este edificio° histórico es hoy el Museo Nacional de Historia.

Teatros

En el Auditorio Nacional, la Casa del Lago y el Teatro del Bosque hay conciertos y obras de teatro.°

como *since*
el edificio *building*
en la cima *on the top*
la montaña rusa *roller coaster*
las obras de teatro *theater plays*
la serpiente *snake*
venden *they sell*

80

El Castillo

¿Qué es el Castillo de Chapultepec?
¿Dónde está?

History Link: Chapultepec Castle was built in 1787. In 1841 it was made into a military academy, and later it became the residence of Maximillian of Hapsburg, whom the French installed as emperor while trying to take over Mexico in the 1860s. Until 1944, the castle was the residence of the President of Mexico.

Muchos jóvenes visitan el zoológico de Chapultepec.▼

El parque zoológico

En el zoológico ¡hay más de° 2.500 (dos mil quinientos) animales! Es un centro de protección de animales, como el lobo° mexicano, el panda gigante, el orangután, el gorila, el jaguar, el puma y el águila.°

Papalote:° Museo del Niño

En el Papalote hay exposiciones de ciencia y tecnología. En Chapultepec también hay museos de arte y un museo de antropología.

el águila *eagle*
el lobo *wolf*
más de *more than*
el niño *child*
el papalote *kite*

▲ **En el zoológico de Chapultepec hay jaguares mexicanos.**

◄ **En el Papalote: Museo del Niño, hay muchas exposiciones interesantes.**

These activities can be done as classwork or as homework.

Objectives

Organizing Skills: writing lists; using lists to organize information
Communication Skills: writing sentences; designing logos

Related Components

Activity Book	Assessment
p. 38	Portfolio: p. 33-34

ACTIVITIES

1. Tu cartel de Chapultepec
Group Activity Make a poster of Chapultepec Park with drawings of places there. Include:
- the name of each place
- what you can do at each place

2. Categorías
Group Activity Divide the places in Chapultepec Park into four categories—recreation, art, history, and science.
Possible Answers:
Recreation: *el parque zoológico, el lago, Chapultepec Mágico, el Auditorio Nacional*
Art: *el Museo Nacional de Antropología*
History: *el Castillo de Chapultepec, el Museo Nacional de Antropología*
Science: *El Papalote, el Museo Nacional de Antropología, el parque zoológico*

3. ¡Diseña tu logo!
Individual Activity Choose three places in Chapultepec Park and design a logo for each place.

4. Compruébalo
Individual Activity Choose the correct ending for each sentence.
1. c   **2.** b   **3.** a   **4.** e   **5.** d

❶ Tu cartel de Chapultepec
Mira el mapa de Chapultepec. En grupo, van a hacer un cartel del Bosque. Usen dibujos para ilustrar su cartel. Incluyan:
- el nombre de cada lugar
- actividades para hacer

❷ Categorías
Ahora, pongan los lugares de Chapultepec en cuatro categorías:

Diversión	montaña rusa
Arte	
Historia	
Ciencias	

❸ ¡Diseña tu logo!
Ahora, escoge tres lugares de Chapultepec y diseña un logo para cada uno.

❹ Compruébalo
Haz oraciones con elementos de las dos columnas.

En el zoológico hay más de 2.500 animales.

En...
1. el zoológico
2. el Papalote
3. la cima del monte
4. el Auditorio Nacional
5. el parque de diversiones

hay...
a. un castillo
b. exposiciones de ciencia y tecnología
c. más de 2.500 animales
d. una montaña rusa
e. conciertos

82

1. EN LA CIUDAD DE MÉXICO

Tu horario

Escribe qué lugares te gustaría visitar en la Ciudad de México. Haz un horario para un fin de semana. Por ejemplo:

	sábado	domingo
por la mañana	9:00–11:00 visitar el Museo de Antropología	
por la tarde	2:00 comer	
por la noche		

¿Adónde vas a ir? ¿Cuándo? ¿Qué vas a hacer allí?

Escribe las respuestas. Por ejemplo:

El sábado por la mañana voy a ir al Museo de Antropología. Voy a sacar fotos.

2. ¿QUÉ HAY EN EL BOSQUE DE CHAPULTEPEC?

A. Escribe las respuestas a estas preguntas.

- ¿Dónde está el Bosque de Chapultepec?
- ¿Qué lugares te gustaría visitar allí?
- ¿Qué cosas te gustaría hacer allí?
- ¿Qué animales hay en el zoológico?
- ¿Qué comidas mexicanas te gustaría comprar allí?

B. Ahora diseña el parque que te gustaría tener en tu pueblo o ciudad. Incluye lugares, actividades ¡y tus logos!

3. UN COLLAGE

Haz un collage sobre la Ciudad de México. Incluye:

- lugares interesantes para visitar
- actividades que te gustaría hacer
- comidas mexicanas
- animales de México

83

TALLER DE ESCRITORES

Objectives
Organizing Skills: making a schedule
Writing Skills: answering questions

Related Components

Activity Book p. 39	Assessment Portfolio: p. 33-34

ACTIVITIES

1. En la Ciudad de México
Individual Activities You can extend these activities by having students ask questions about one another's work.

Tu horario
Students will list places they would like to visit in Mexico City and make a weekend schedule.
Answers: See model on student page.

¿Adónde vas a ir? ¿Cuándo? ¿Qué vas a hacer allí?
Students will answer these questions.
Answers: See model on student page.

2. ¿Qué hay en el Bosque de Chapultepec?
Individual Activities You can extend these activities by having students compare their diaries and drawings.
A. Students will write responses to the bulleted questions in their diaries.
Possible Answers:
- *Está en la Ciudad de México.*
- *Me gustaría visitar El Papalote y el castillo.*
- *Me gustaría pasear en bote.*
- *En el zoológico hay pandas y gorilas.*
- *Me gustaría comprar tacos y jugos.*

B. Students will make a drawing of a park they would like to have where they live. They should include places of interest, activities, and their own logos.

3. Un collage
Group Activity Students will make a collage for Mexico City, including:
- interesting places to visit
- activities they would like to do
- Mexican foods
- Mexican animals

Objectives
Communicative: to listen to and understand directions
Cultural: to learn about Mexican foods
TPR: to have students make their own tacos

Related Components

Assessment	Transparencies
Portfolio: p. 33-34	Unit 1: Project
CD Rom	**Video:**
Unit 1: Manos a la obra	Tape/Book
	Unit 1: Seg. 5

Search to frame 1142327

Materials
- 1 lb. ground beef
- 1 onion
- 2 tbsp. oil
- 12 corn tortillas
- 1/2 lb. cheese
- 1/2 cup sour cream
- 1 head lettuce
- 2 tomatoes

(To taste)
- Cilantro
- Parsley
- Chili powder salt, and pepper

GETTING STARTED

In this exercise, encourage students to use their eyes more than their ears. Tell them to concentrate on the action and listen only for clues, not for each separate word. If possible, show the taco-making segment of the Unit 1 video.
How many students have tried tacos? Do they like them? Point out that tacos are becoming very popular in the United States. Why is this so? Are our tastes changing? If so, why?

DISCUSS

Read the introduction aloud. Ask comprehension questions. Examples:
¿De qué habla el libro, de la comida o de los lugares de la ciudad?
¿De qué comida habla, de la carne o del maíz?
¿De dónde es el maíz?
¿Dónde comen tortillas de maíz?
¿Qué ingredientes tienen los tacos?
¿Te gustaría comer tacos con mucho chile?
¿Qué vas a cocinar primero, la carne o la salsa?

84

MANOS A LA OBRA

¡Tortillas y tacos!
¡Mmmm... deliciosos!

La tortilla es la comida fundamental de México y toda América Central. Se hace° con maíz.° Los tacos son tortillas con carne o pollo, verduras, queso y chile.
El maíz

- es una planta originaria de México.
- su nombre azteca es "toconayo".

TE TOCA A TI

Invita a tus amigos a comer tacos. Son deliciosos y fáciles de hacer.

84

el aceite *oil*	la cucharada	el maíz *corn*
la cebolla *onion*	*(measure) tablespoon*	el perejil *parsley*
la crema (Méx.)	la libra *pound*	la pimienta *pepper*
sour cream		se hace *it is made*

✔ CULTURE NOTE

People began cultivating maize, or corn, around 5,000 years ago. Cornmeal was prepared by soaking it in limewater, then grinding it into flour with an oblong stone held in both hands.
The word **maíz** comes from a Taíno word. It is believed that Columbus first encountered corn in Cuba or Puerto Rico.

1 **Para preparar la salsa:** poner°
los tomates, la cebolla, el
cilantro, el perejil, chile, sal y
pimienta en la licuadora° por
unos minutos.

2 **Para preparar la carne:** freír°
la carne en aceite con sal y
pimienta. Después, mezclar°
un poco de salsa con la carne.

3 **Para hacer los tacos:** poner
una cucharada de carne en cada
tortilla.

4 **Para decorar los tacos:**
poner la crema primero,
después la salsa, la lechuga
y el queso.

freír *to fry*   mezclar *to mix*
la licuadora *blender*   poner *to put*

85

Using the directions in the book, lead students through the creation of a taco.
1. Make a taco as you give the instructions. If you do not have real materials, use clay, colored paper, or other substitutes.
2. After you have done this several times, invite volunteers to do it as you read aloud.
3. Do this as TPR with the whole class.

CHECK

To check the understanding of students, have them act out each step of taco-making as you read it aloud, but give the instructions for steps in a different order.

LOG BOOK
Have students write down the ingredients and preparation steps.

Para hispanohablantes

Describe how you would make a super-taco with all your favorite ingredients.

Thinking About Language
Read aloud Step 1 of the recipe and ask if anyone knows what the word **salsa** means. Here it is "sauce, "but many people think of it as a spicy condiment. (Some may also know salsa as a dance style popularized by musicians from the Caribbean.) Ask what makes the salsa in the recipe spicy (and why the dance might have been named for the sauce).

▶▶▶INTERNET LINK

The burrito isn't a taco, but it has its own web site: http://www.infobahn. com:80/pages/rito.html

Objectives

Communicative: to expand reading comprehension

Cultural: to relate the study of Spanish to other disciplines

Related Components

Activity Book p. 40	**Audio Tapes** Adelante: 8B
Assessment Portfolio: p. 33-34	**Video:** Tape/Book Unit 1: Seg. 4

Search to frame 1110707

Monarca, mariposa maravillosa

About the Monarch Butterfly
The winter nesting grounds of the monarch were discovered in the state of Michoacán a few years ago. The location was kept secret for fear that tourism would lead to the site's destruction.
Monarchs migrate north each spring, laying eggs along the way. The parents die, and the new generation finds its way to Mexico in the fall. No one knows how.

Possible Answers:
- *Las monarcas emigran a México.*
- *Emigran de Canadá y los Estados Unidos*
- *Son de color negro, anaranjado y blanco*

Other Questions:
¿Qué tipo de animal es la monarca?
¿Por qué es especial este animal?

Math Link: *¿Cuántas millas son 5.000 kilómetros? (1 km = 5/8 mi; 5,000 km = ±3125 miles)*

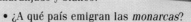

▶▶▶ INTERNET LINKS

Monarch Migration
http://www.ties.k12.mn.us:80/~jnorth/
migrations/students/monarch.html
Mexican Art
http://unicornio.cencar.udg.mx:80/
cultfolk/pinturas/pintores.html
The Aztec Calendar
http://napa.diva.nl/~voorburg/aztec.html
Mexican Flag and related topics
http://www.udg.mx:80/cultfolk/bandera/
bandera.html

CIENCIAS

MONARCA, MARIPOSA° MARAVILLOSA

Todos los años, millones de mariposas *monarcas* emigran° desde Canadá y Estados Unidos hasta° México (más de 5.000 kilómetros). Las *monarcas* son de color negro, anaranjado y blanco.

- ¿A qué país emigran las *monarcas*?
- ¿De dónde emigran?
- ¿De qué color son?

ARTE

TIENDA DE LEGUMBRES°

Este cuadro° se llama *Tienda de legumbres.* Es de la artista mexicana Elena Climent (1955). Los cuadros de Climent representan situaciones de la vida diaria° de los mexicanos. Hoy día, Elena vive y trabaja° en la ciudad de Nueva York.

- ¿Por qué el cuadro se llama Tienda de legumbres?
- ¿Qué frutas y verduras hay en este cuadro?
- ¿Qué colores hay en el cuadro?
- ¿De dónde es Elena Climent? ¿Dónde vive?

el cuadro *painting*
emigran *migrate*
hasta *up to*
las legumbres *vegetables*
la mariposa *butterfly*
trabaja *works*
la vida diaria *daily life*

86

Tienda de legumbres

About the Artist
Elena Climent depicts subjects such as contrasts (and conflicts) between plastic items of modern Mexican life and traditional ones of her country's past.
Some of the items in the painting: **dulces** (candies) and **juguetes** (toys).

Possible Answers:
- *Se llama* Tienda de Legumbres *porque es de una tienda de legumbres.*
- *Hay plátanos, manzanas, naranjas, una piña, aguacates y tomates.*
- See photo on student page.
- *Elena Climent es de México y vive en Nueva York.*

Art Link: Ask students if they have reproductions of favorite paintings. What are the paintings? Why did they choose them?

ARQUEOLOGÍA

EL CALENDARIO AZTECA

Los aztecas eran° grandes astrónomos. El calendario azteca está en el Museo de Antropología de la Ciudad de México. Allí están representados el sol y todos los planetas, los años, los meses y los días.

- ¿Quiénes eran grandes astrónomos?
- ¿Dónde está el calendario azteca?
- ¿Qué cosas están representadas en el calendario azteca?

HISTORIA

EL ÁGUILA Y LA SERPIENTE

La bandera° de México es verde, blanca y roja. En el centro hay un águila, un cacto y una serpiente. Según la tradición, los aztecas fundaron° Tenochtitlán (hoy Ciudad de México) donde encontraron° un águila en un cacto devorando° una serpiente. El águila simboliza prosperidad.

- ¿De qué color es la bandera de México?
- ¿Qué animales hay en la bandera?
- ¿Qué simboliza el águila?

la bandera *flag*	eran *were*
devorando *devouring*	fundaron *founded*
encontraron *(they) found*	

87

- *Los aztecas eran grandes astrónomos.*
- *El calendario azteca está en el Museo de Antropología de la Ciudad de México.*
- *En el calendario azteca están representados el sol, los planetas, los años, los meses y los días.*

History Link: Why was the study of astronomy important to ancient peoples? (A few ideas: early peoples had to be able to predict seasonal changes for farming; early religions were often attempts to explain seasonal changes and other celestial events.)

Historia: El águila y la serpiente

About the Symbol
Near the end of the 1300s, the Aztecs searched for a place where a prophecy predicted they would see an eagle on a cactus eating a snake. That place was an island in Lake Texcoco.
The image of the eagle, cactus, and snake became the official symbol of the country of Mexico in 1821, the year in which it won independence from Spain.

Possible Answers:
- *La bandera de México es verde, blanca y roja.*
- *Hay un águila y una serpiente.*
- *El águila simboliza prosperidad.*

Other Questions:
¿De qué colores es la bandera de los Estados Unidos?
¿Te gustaría vivir en un lugar con serpientes?
¿Qué animal es un símbolo de los Estados Unidos?

El calendario azteca

About the Calendar
The Sun Stone is not really a calendar, even though it has signs representing each of the 20 days of the Aztec month. (A year was 18 months plus 5 supplementary days.) In fact, it represents the predicted death of the fifth—and last—sun. The face of the sun god Tonatiuh is at the center of the stone.
The Sun Stone was carved from volcanic rock in the late 1400s. Spanish priests had it buried shortly after the conquest, but it was recovered in 1790.
Answers:

UNIDAD 2 TEXAS: CONSERVANDO LA HERENCIA HISPANA

 In this unit

We visit Texas to explore an important part of our country's long Spanish heritage. We start by going to a series of family parties and celebrations (Chapter 3), and then we take a tour of Hispanic homes, Spanish missions, and Mexican-American neighborhoods (Chapter 4). We drop into a birthday party after school, and we dance at a *quinceañera*. We plan parties of our own—and keep our eyes peeled for skeletons on the Day of the Dead! And we design a dream home after exploring Hispanic neighborhoods in old San Antonio, in border-town El Paso, and in modern mile-high Dallas.

Getting into Hispanic life in Texas involves listening and dancing to many different kinds of good music, and we explore recent Tex-Mex music in the *Adelante* section of the student book. In the unit video, we listen not to one but to *two* mariachi bands—an amateur school group during practice and the supersonically professional Campanas de América. Finally, we complete the unit project of making party *piñatas*.

VIDEO LINKS

Text	Video Segment
Unit Overview Unit Opener	**1. Introduction to Texas**
	flag, location, size, history of Hispanic people north of the Río Grande
Chapter 3	**2. Celebraciones**
	birthday party, *quinceañera*, ranch barbecue
	grammar: adjective/noun agreement; verbs **ser, hacer, conocer,** and **conocer a**
Chapter 4	**3. ¿Dónde vives?**
	private homes, Spanish missions, El Paso's Chihuahuita, Dallas by air and San Antonio by water
	grammar: the verb **estar** + location expressions; possessive adjectives
Adelante	**4. Adelante**
	an after-school mariachi band and the professional Campanas de América
Manos a la obra	**5. Manos a la obra**
	How to make a *piñata*

Geography and Climate

Covering 267,338 square miles, Texas is the second largest state in the US, and larger than Spain or any other European country outside Russia. The state's size makes it a land of vivid geographical contrasts: in east Texas you find rolling hills, thick pine forests, and a Gulf coast littoral thick with plant life; in west Texas you're surrounded by huge areas of flat, dry prairieland stitched by gullies, arroyos, and mountain ranges. Overall, summers are long and winters short, but January temperatures in the Rio Grande Valley can reach the high 90s (F) while blizzards block highways in the northern Panhandle.

History

Native American hunters built camps in western Texas at least 37,000 years ago; later, tribes were able to establish permanent farming villages in the more fertile east. The first Spaniards arrived in 1528, but the land was too hard to work to encourage settlement by anyone except army and church. Texas was still part of Mexico when Mexico became an independent country in 1821.

Fifteen years later, led by Stephen Austin and Sam Houston, Anglo-American and Mexican Texans issued a declaration of independence, seceding from Mexico and creating the free and independent Republic of Texas. In February 1836 a Mexican army under General Santa Anna besieged Texas troops in San Antonio's Alamo mission, and on April 21, at San Jacinto, Sam Houston's troops defeated the Mexican army and captured Santa Anna.

Ten years later, Texas gave up its independence to become the 28th state. After the Civil War, farming and cattle ranching dominated the state's economy until the first oil well blew in at Spindletop in 1901 and the Texas petroleum industry was born.

Hispanic Texas Today

Up to 25% of Texas's 11 million residents are of Mexican-American descent, and the state's long Hispanic history is especially evident all along the Rio Grande. You see it in the public and private architecture, in the names of streets and parks, in the names of Tex-Mex dishes and in newspapers and magazines. You hear it in the nonstop Spanish spoken on the streets of Corpus Christi, Brownsville, Laredo, San Antonio, and El Paso, and in accordion-powered *conjunto* music and strings-and-brass mariachi music, both of them popular not only in Texas but also in northern Mexico, New Mexico, Arizona, southern California, New York City, and anywhere else there's a sizeable Mexican-American, or Chicano, population.

Exploradores españoles

HISTORY CONNECTION

Objective
- to play a game about Spanish explorers of the United States and Mexico

Use
any time during Unit 2

Materials
- TRB Activity Support Pages 8A-8B, *Exploradores españoles* (fact sheets)
- TRB Activity Support Page 9, *Exploradores españoles*
- 8 1/2" x 11" rectangles of cardboard
- TRB Activity Support Page 5, *Ruleta* (spinner)
- different-colored push pins

Preparation
- Divide class into groups of 6 and give each group an activity sheet on a different explorer.
- Have groups assign a positive (+) or negative (–) value to each statement about the explorer's life. They mark their sheet and discuss their reasons.
- Make copies of all marked sheets for each group.
- Groups make game boards by placing cardboard under map. They number spinner sections 1-6.

Activity
- Review the route of each explorer.
- Each group chooses a reader; each of the other group members selects an explorer and a push pin. They decide which explorer goes first.
- The reader reads the statements about the different explorers in group order: the 1s first, then the 2s, etc.
- Explorer players go forward if a statement is positive, backward if a statement is negative. For example, a positive value (+) has been assigned to statement 7 about Ponce de León. If a Ponce de León player spins 4, he/she advances 4 spaces. If the statement had been assigned a negative value (-), the player would have gone back 4 spaces.
- The first student to complete a route wins.

FYI
Other important Spanish explorers include Francisco Pizarro (1475-1541), Vasco Núñez de Balboa (1475-1519), Juan Rodríguez Cabrillo (1500-1543), and Juan de Oñate (1550-1625).

¿Qué hay en un nombre?

GEOGRAPHY CONNECTION

Objective
- to recognize the Spanish names of places in Texas and geographical features

Use
any time during Unit 2

Materials
- reference books (atlas, encyclopedia, book of road maps, etc.)
- paper plates,cups, plastic flatware, a tabelcloth

Activity
- Have students look up maps of Texas and search for places and geographical features with Spanish names: towns, cities, rivers, lakes, mountains, etc.
- Give students 5 minutes to compile a list of Spanish names.
- One at a time, have each student read his/her list, omitting places or geographical features already mentioned. Write names on the board and discuss their meanings.

Variations
- Have students consult maps of other states with Spanish heritages (California, Colorado, New Mexico, Arizona, Nevada, Florida) and create simple pictograms of places with Spanish names. For example: Mesa Verde can be a green table, Los Angeles can be a choir of angels, and Boca Raton can be a mouse with an arrow pointing to its mouth.
- Discuss and display the pictograms.

FYI
In the United States over 2,000 towns, cities, rivers, mountains, and states have Spanish names. Some better-known ones: Amarillo, Colorado, Sierra Nevada, Las Vegas, Las Cruces, Rio Grande, San Antonio, San Francisco, Sangre de Cristo, Santa Fe, Montana. Smaller cities with Spanish names include Agua Caliente AZ, Alma NY, Bonita KA, Buena Vista Il, Los Alamos NM, Perdido AL, and Punta Gorda FL.

Sopaipillas

HANDS ON: COOKING

Objective
- to make and eat a batch of *sopaipillas* (Tex-Mex fried bread puffs)

Use
any time during Unit 2

Ingredients
- 4 cups flour
- 1 1/4 tsp. salt
- 3 tsp. baking powder
- 3 tbs. sugar
- 2 tbs. shortening
- 1 1/4 cups milk
- vegetable oil

Supplies
- flour sifter or strainer
- bowl
- towel
- rolling pin
- pastry board
- electric frying pan
- paper towels

Preparation
- Sift flour, measure, and sift again, adding salt, baking powder, and sugar.
- Cut in shortening and add milk to make a dough that's soft but firm enough to roll.
- Cover dough and let stand for one hour. (Mix dough before class so that it's ready to roll out and fry.)
- Roll dough 1/4" thick on lightly floured board and cut in diamond-shaped pieces.
- Heat 1" of oil and add a few pieces of dough at a time, turning them once they puff to brown on both sides.
- Drain on paper toweling.
- Dribble honey on them or powder with sugar. Makes 4 dozen.

FYI
The Mexican presence in the southwestern United States has led to the cuisine we call Tex-Mex. It's Mexican cooking with a Texan twist. Here are some other popular Tex-Mex foods: burritos (flour tortillas filled with meat, chicken, beans, or cheese), chiles rellenos (peppers stuffed with cheese or meat), fajitas (strips of chicken or steak, marinated in lime juice and grilled over a fire), guacamole (avocado dip), nachos (crisp tortilla chips covered with refried beans or cheese with salsa), salsa (a sauce of chopped tomato, onion, chile, and cilantro).

Fiesta fabulosa

SOCIAL STUDIES CONNECTION

Objective
- to research and prepare a holiday party with Tex-Mex dishes, decorations, and music

Use
any time during Unit 2

Materials
- construction paper, markers or colored pencils
- paper plates; cup; plastic flatware, a table cloth

Activity
- Have students research Mexican holidays and choose one to celebrate: *el Día de la Raza* (Oct. 12), *el Día de los Muertos* (Nov. 1–2), *el Día de la Independencia* (Sept. 16), or any other holiday that's suitable.
- Discuss the holiday's significance.
- Decide whom to invite to the *fiesta*—other classes, parents, etc.
- Prepare invitations.
- Make decorations appropriate to the holiday. These might include banners, masks, and costumes.
- Prepare food if you like. It can be simple: salsa, tortilla chips, and cola. Or go all out and prepare *sopaipillas,* using the recipe on this page, and some of the dishes in Chapter 2 of *Juntos.*
- If you can, bring in tapes or CDs of Tex-Mex music.
- *¡Que disfruten mucho!*

Variations
- Have each student prepare a Hispanic dish.
- Turn their recipes into a bilingual cookbook that includes drawings and photographs of the dishes.
- Have students prepare skits for a *Teatro Tex-Mex*, present the skits to the class, and vote on a favorite.
- Use the party as a fund-raiser for a class trip: sell food, drinks, copies of the cookbook, etc.

TEXAS

Objectives

- to introduce the Hispanic heritage of the state of Texas
- to develop listening comprehension

Related Components

CD ROM	Video: Tape/Book
Unit 2	Unit 2: Seg. 1
Transparencies	
Unit 2	

Search to frame 1172226

GETTING STARTED

Create a list of things students know about Texas, such as food, music, cities, and history. What are their impressions of Texas? Do they know where their ideas about Texas came from?

Using the Video

Show Segment 1 of the Unit 2 video, an introduction to **Texas**.

Using the Transparencies

To help orient students to Texas, use the Locator Map Transparency. You may also want to review the other transparencies for Unit 2 at this time.

DISCUSS

Presenting Texas

For more information about Texas, refer to pages 88A–88D.

Using the Text

English: After students have read the introduction, ask comprehension and critical-thinking questions. Examples:
When was "a hundred years before the Pilgrims landed"? (1520)
What other parts of the US are strongly influenced by other cultures? (A few: Minnesota, Scandinavian; New England, English; Southern Florida, Cuban.)
Spanish: Ask what the Unit's subtitle means. If no one can figure it out, elicit the English cognate of **conservando**. Read the chapter descriptions aloud and ask questions such as:
Where do you think the word **Hispana** comes from? (from the Latin name for Spain, *Hispania*.)

UNIDAD 2

TEXAS

CONSERVANDO LA HERENCIA HISPANA

En la unidad 2:

Capítulo 3	Celebraciones
Capítulo 4	¿Dónde vives?
Adelante	**Para leer:** Ritmos de Texas

Proyecto: ¡A romper la piñata!

Otras fronteras: Prensa, geografía, idioma y arte

88

Unit Components

Activity Book	Audio Book	Conexiones: 16B	Transparencies
p. 41-64	Script: p. 25-28; 33-36	**CD ROM**	Unit 2: Chapters 3-4
Assessment	Activities: p. 29-32; 37-40	Unit 2	**Tutor Pages**
Oral Proficiency: p. 23-24		**Conexiones**	p. 15-22
Listening Script: p. 11-12	**Audio Tapes**	Chapters 3-4	**Video: Tape/Book**
Chapter Tests: p. 57-68	Listening: 3A, 3B	**Cuaderno**	Unit 2: Segments 1-5
Portfolio: p. 35-36	Adelante: 9A, 9B	p. 21-36	
	Assessment: 14A, 14B	**Magazine**	
		Juntos en Texas	

The state of Texas, known as the Lone Star State, is so big that it has two time zones! Texas lies north of Mexico, separated from it by the Rio Grande.

Texas has a rich Hispanic heritage. Spanish explorers first came to the region nearly a hundred years before the Pilgrims landed in New England. Spain occupied the area until the early 1800's when Mexican-born Spanish settlers revolted and gained independence. Around that time, Anglo settlers began arriving and soon outnumbered the Hispanic population. In 1845, Texas became the 28th state of the United States.

Today, many Texans speak Spanish as well as English. Many Texan street names, buildings, and arts reveal a strong Hispanic influence. In this unit you will take part in the celebrations of Mexican-Americans whose families have lived in Texas for many generations. You will also enjoy fiestas and mariachi music, tour the city of San Antonio, make plans for a weekend in El Paso, and learn how to make a *piñata*.

Parque Nacional Big Ben, Texas

89

ACTIVITIES

Interdisciplinary Connections

To provide other perspectives, assign brief research projects like these:

History
Who were the first Europeans to reach Texas? What were they searching for?

Weather
What is the weather like in Texas?

Geography
How long would it take you to get to Texas by car? How long would it take to cross Texas by car, from east to west?

Economics
Guess what the three most important industries in Texas are. Then look up the information and compare your answers. (The top three have traditionally been manufacturing, tourism, and oil—in that order. Natural gas, minerals, and livestock were the next three.)

 CULTURE NOTE

The word *Texas* is derived from *taysha,* a Native American (Caddoan) word for "friend" or "ally".

 **INTERNET LINK**

State of Texas Homepage: http://www. texas.gov:80/TEXAS_homepage.html

CAPÍTULO 3: PLAN

	Objetivos page 91	Conversemos pages 92-93	Realidades pages 94-95	Palabras en acción pages 96-97
Comunicación	• To talk about how you plan to celebrate an event	Discuss how to plan a birthday celebration	Read text, answer questions, plan party and present plan	Activity 4: Read cartoon, compare a familiar birthday celebration with celebration in cartoon
	• To talk about whom you are going to invite	Discuss whom to invite to a birthday celebration	Read text, answer questions, decide whom to invite to party, present list	Activities 2, 5: Read cartoon, describe guests; make party invitations
	• To talk about what you are going to do	Discuss what to do at parties	Read text, answer questions, decide what to do at a party and present info to class	Activity 3: Read cartoon, discuss enjoyable things to do at parties
	• To talk about what you need to buy or make	Discuss what is needed to make or buy for parties	Read text, answer questions, decide what to make or buy for party, present info to class	Activity 1: Read cartoon, make list of party items, describe them
Vocabulario temático	• To know the expressions for parties and celebrations	Talk about different parties and celebrations	Read text, answer questions, discuss different parties and celebrations	
	• To know the expressions for party activities	Talk about different party activities	Read text, answer questions, decide which activities to do at a party and present list	Activity 3: Read cartoon, discuss characters and enjoyable things to do at parties
	• To know the expressions for things to buy or make for a party	Talk about different things to make or buy for a party	Read text, decide what to make or buy for party, present info to class	Activity 1: Read cartoon, make list of party items and describe them
	• To know the expressions for describing people and things	Describe the people to invite to a party		Activities 1, 2, 8: Read cartoon, make list of party items and describe them; describe guests; write and present dialog
Estructura	• To talk about events, people, places, and things: adjectives	Use adjectives to describe people to invite to a party		Activities 1, 2, 8: Read cartoon, list and describe party items; describe guests; write and present dialog
	• To talk about what you do or make: the verb *hacer*	Use *hacer* to discuss what to do for a birthday, what to make for a party	Read text, answer questions, discuss what others do at parties, what to do at parties	Activity 3: Read cartoon, discuss characters and enjoyable things to do at parties
	• To talk about people you know: the verb *conocer*			Activity 6: Present people to each other
Cultura	The extended family in Hispanic cultures		*La quinceañera:* a party to celebrate a young woman's fifteenth birthday	
Integración		Enjoyable activities, familiar people, activities to do, describing things	Dates, time, activities to do, making plans, types of food, familiar people	Dates, time, days of the week, describing things, making plans, enjoyable things to do, locations, age

CELEBRACIONES

Para comunicarnos mejor (1) pages 98-99	Para comunicarnos mejor (2) pages 100-101	Situaciones pages 102-103	Para resolver pages 104-105	Notes
		Activities 3, 4, 5: Interview friends, report to class; create ad; respond to invitation	Paso 1: Choose event to celebrate and decide when and where to have class party	
			Paso 2: Decide whom to invite to class party and why	
	Activities 1A, 1B: Discuss party and make table; report to class	Activities 4, 5: Create ad; respond to party invitation		
Activity 1: Discuss what to take to a party		Activity 4: Create ad	Pasos 3-5: Make invitation and menu for class party; list items needed	
		Activities 2-5: Describe photos; interview friends, report to class; create ad; respond to invitation		
		Activities 1, 3, 4: Describe photos; interview friends, report to class; create ad		
Activity 1: Discuss what to take to a party	Activities 1A, 1B: Discuss party and make table; report to class	Activities 1, 4: Describe people in photos; create ad	Pasos 3-5: Make invitation and menu for class party; list items needed	
Activities 2A, 2B, 3: partners Draw and describe partners; each other; describe class; identify family mem-	bers, others		Activity 1: Describe people in photos	Paso 2: Decide whom to invite to class party and why
Activities 2A, 2B, 3: Describe drawings of partners; describe class; identify family, others	Activity 3B: Use *ser* + adjectives in a group discussion of famous people	Activities 1, 3: Describe photos; interview friends about party and report to class		
	Activities 2A, 2B, 3B: Make list of what people do; discuss what they do; talk about famous people	Activities 1, 3, 4: Describe photos; interview friends and report to class; create ad		
	Activities 2A, 2B, 3A, 3B: Make list of what friends and family do; discuss what they do; talk about famous people	Activities 1, 3, 4: Describe photos; interview friends and report to class; create ad		
				Entérate page 106 The Day of the Dead
Describing things and people, what will be done	Describing familiar people, telling how well activities can be done, activities that are done	Describing familiar people, describing things, telling favorite activities	Activities that are going to be done, dates, time, food and beverages, necessities	

☐ ¿El mundo es redondo, no?   ☐ ¿Quien es?

GAME

Objective
• to play a matching game using sentences that demonstrate noun/adjective agreement

Use
after *Para comunicarnos mejor,* page 98

Materials
• 3" x 5" index cards in two colors

Activity
• Have each student write a singular or plural noun on a card of one color—blue, for example. (To play two rounds, they'll need two blue cards, etc.)
• On each of the other-colored cards, write an adjective from the *Vocabulario temático* you've had so far. Though listed in masculine singular form, adjectives should agree with their nouns.
• Collect all noun cards, shuffle, and redistribute.
• Place the adjective cards face down on your desk.
• Player 1 picks an adjective card and tries to make a sentence with the noun already dealt. For example, player 1 has the noun *hermana,* picks the adjective *simpático,* and makes this sentence: *Mi hermana es simpática.*
• Each player plays until he/she uses all 10 adjectives or can't make up a sentence. The game continues until everyone has had a turn.
• The player who makes up the most sentences wins.

GAME

Objective
• to describe a famous person, using the verb *ser* with adjectives

Use
after *Para comunicarnos mejor,* page 98

Preparation
• Students write several sentences about a famous Hispanic person without naming that person. At least three of the sentences should use the verb *ser* and an adjective.

Activity
• Have a volunteer, student A answer questions from student B about the person he/she had described.
• If student B doesn't identify the famous person after five questions, another student, C, tries to guess the identity of student A's famous person.
• Here is a sample scenerio.
Student B: *¿Es hombre o mujer?*
Student A: *Es mujer.*
Student B: *¿Tiene el pelo negro?*
Student A: *Sí.*
Student B: *¿Es vieja o joven?*
Student A: *Es joven.*
Student B: *¿De dónde es?*
Student A: *Es cubana.* Student B: *¿Es Celia Cruz?* Student A: *No, Celia Cruz no es joven.* Another student, C, asks questions. Student C: *¿Canta en Miami Sound Machine?* Student A: *Sí.* Student C: *¿Es Gloris Estefán?* Student A: *¡Sí!*

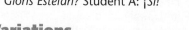

Variations
• Have students describe a teacher at school, or a favorite doll, stuffed animal, or toy they remember.
• If students describe a favorite object, have them bring it to class to see if their classmates think the description is accurate.

¿A quién conoces?

GAME

Objective
- to play a sentence-making game, using the verb *conocer* + *a* and Chapter 3 *Vocabulario temático*

Use
after *Para comunicarnos mejor,* page 100

Materials
- TRB Activity Support Page 5, *Ruleta* (spinner)
- 3" x 5" index cards, cut in half

Activity
- Distribute spinner and have students write pronouns in the six sections: *yo, tú, él/ella, nosotros/as, Uds., ellos/ellas.* Show them how to make a pointer.
- Give students one card each and have them write a noun or noun phrase referring to a person or persons. For example: *mi tía, los doctores, mi abuelo, las amigas de Clara, el presidente de los Estados Unidos.*
- Collect cards and divide class into two teams.
- Team A player selects a card, then spins for a subject. For example, the player draws *mi tía* and spins a *yo.* The sentence could be:—*Yo conozco a mi tía muy bien.*
- A player from team B takes a turn.
- Play continues until all cards have been used.
- Tally points and announce the winning team.

Rules
- Each correct sentence is worth 5 points.
- Sentences cannot be repeated.
- If a student is stumped, his/her team loses its turn.

Variations
- Have the players on each team make a sentence negative for extra points
- After Unit 3, Chapter 5, make cards with beach activities and water sports. Have students create sentences with these cards and the verb *saber.*

¿Qué haces?

GAME

Objective
- to play a question-and-answer game, using the verb *hacer* and Chapter 3 *Vocabulario temático*

Use
after *Para comunicarnos mejor,* page 100

Activity
- This game can be played by individuals or teams, with or without a dictionary.
- Give students 3 minutes to answer the question *¿Qué haces?* by listing things they make or do. For example: *Hago un sándwich. Hago un cartel. Hago una piñata. Hago un menú para mi compleaños..*
- Have each student read an item from the list without repeating any sentences read before.
- Play until there are no new sentences to read.

Variations
- Have students make answers more specific by defining the activity and the occasion. For example: *¿Qué haces para tu fiesta de cumpleaños?—Hago la lista de invitados.*

CELEBRACIONES

Ask students how their families celebrate family days like Thanksgiving, birthdays, or weddings.

Related Components

Audio Tapes Conexiones: 16B, Ch. 3	**Conexiones** Chapter 3
CD ROM Chapter 3	**Video: Tape/Book** Unit 2: Seg. 2

Search to frame 1181201

GETTING STARTED

Ask students if they have visited a place like that shown in the photograph. Ask critical thinking questions, such as:
¿Qué hay en el paseo del Río en San Antonio?

Background

People of Spanish-speaking background in Texas often celebrate holidays in different ways from those of non-Hispanic communities.

Hispanic Holidays

Personal Holidays

El día del santo Instead of birthdays, many people celebrate the day of a saint with their same name. This is the result of an earlier tradition of naming children for the saint on whose day they were born.

Civic Holidays

Las fiestas patronales Some cities honor a patron saint with festivities. San Antonio, Texas, enthusiastically celebrates its patron and namesake for ten days in April.
El día de independencia Most countries have them, and so does Texas (March 2, when it broke with Mexico and became a territory).
El día de la raza (October 12) The United States calls this Columbus Day, but Latin American countries celebrate *la raza,* the indigenous population.

Religious Holidays

El día de los reyes (January 6th) This celebrates the day *los reyes magos* reached Bethlehem. It is the day children receive their Christmas gifts.
Carnaval This colorful secular celebration, with music, costumes, and dancing, comes just before Lent, a period of fasting and penitence.

CAPÍTULO **3**

CELEBRACIONES

90

Semana Santa In parts of the Hispanic world, Easter lasts an entire week. It is often celebrated by carrying holy images from the churches in solemn parades.

Las Navidades Christmas lasts from early December through *reyes.* On the 24th, *Nochebuena,* families may perform traditional acts, such as placing a figure of baby Jesus in the *nacimiento* (nativity scene).

Chapter Components

Activity Book p. 41-50	**Audio Book** Script: p. 25-28 Activities: p. 29-32	**CD ROM** Chapter 3	**Transparencies** Chapter 3
Assessment Oral Proficiency: p. 23 Listening Script: p. 11 Chapter Test: p. 57-62	**Audio Tapes** Listening: 3A Assessment: 14A, Ch. 3 Conexiones: 16B, Ch. 3	**Conexiones** Chapter 3 **Cuaderno** p. 21-28 **Magazine** Juntos en Texas	**Tutor Pages** p. 15-18 **Video: Tape/Book** Unit 2: Seg. 3

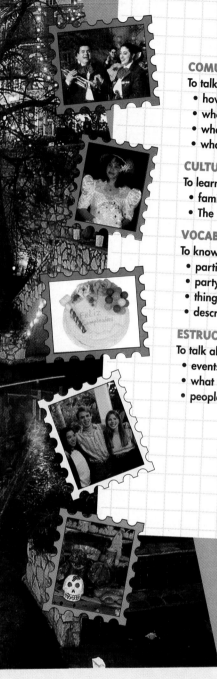

Objetivos

COMUNICACIÓN

To talk about:

- how you plan to celebrate an event
- whom you are going to invite
- what you are going to do
- what you need to buy or make

CULTURA

To learn about:

- family celebrations in Texas
- The Day of the Dead celebration

VOCABULARIO TEMÁTICO

To know the expressions for:

- parties and celebrations
- party activities
- things to buy or make for a party
- describing people and things

ESTRUCTURA

To talk about:

- events, people, places and things: adjectives
- what you do or make: the verb *hacer*
- people you know: the verb *conocer*

¿SABES QUE...?

In the Spanish-speaking world, *la familia* refers to the extended family. This can include uncles, aunts, first, second and even third cousins, nieces, nephews, grandparents, and anyone related to them. Children's godfathers and godmothers are also included.

◄ **Paseo del Río en San Antonio, Texas.**

91

Here are some editorial activities that you may wish to use as you work through the chapter with your students.

Communication

Encourage after-class activities that may enhance student interest and proficiency. Some ideas:

- encourage students to find a native speaker in their class or neighborhood with whom they can practice
- ask native speakers to make simple audio tapes that describe members of their family; have others listen to them

Culture

The long historic relationship between Texas and Mexico has influenced the culture on both sides of the border. To encourage greater understanding:

- show the video that accompanies Unit 2 of this textbook
- have the *Fiesta fabulosa* described on page 88D

▶▶▶INTERNET LINK

A Usenet group about food history: rec.food.historic

Communicative Objectives
- to talk about celebrations and guests
- to accept or turn down an invitation

Related Components

Activity Book p. 41	Cuaderno p. 21
Audio Book Script: Seg. 1	Transparencies Ch. 3: Conversemos
Audio Tapes Listening: 3A, Seg. 1	

GETTING STARTED

Ask students to name as many kinds of celebrations as they can.

DISCUSS

These activities give students an opportunity to begin communicating with each other and with you, focusing on the theme and objectives of the chapter. The activities can be used as oral class activities, or, if you prefer, you can pair students to achieve more interaction. Additional activities integrate critical-thinking skills.

¿Qué te gusta hacer en una fiesta?
Class activity to review **me gusta** and **no me gusta.**

¿Qué vas a hacer para tu cumpleaños?
Class activity to introduce vocabulary and review **ir a.** Ask the title question and have students use these and other answers. For example: *Voy a comer en mi restaurante favorito.*

¿A quién vas a invitar?
Class activity to introduce vocabulary for relatives and adjectives.

CONVERSEMOS
LAS CELEBRACIONES Y TÚ

Habla con tu compañero(a).

¿QUÉ TE GUSTA HACER EN UNA FIESTA?

Me gusta...	No me gusta...
bailar	escuchar música
cantar	hablar con mis amigos
comer	sacar fotos

¿QUÉ VAS A HACER PARA TU CUMPLEAÑOS?

Voy a...

- hacer una fiesta
- hacer un picnic
- hacer una barbacoa
- jugar con videojuegos
- comer en un restaurante
- tocar la guitarra

Nada especial.
[Nothing special.]

92

✓ CULTURE NOTE

Literally, a *compadre* or *comadre* is a close friend or relative who acts as a godparent (*padrino/madrina*), but in some places it means much more. *El compadrazgo* is the friendship and trust that makes people consider someone part of the family even though that person is not a relative.

MEETING INDIVIDUAL NEEDS

Reaching All Students

For Visual Learners
Draw pictures of preparations for a party and the party itself. Put them in a logical order and say what each activity is.

For Auditory Learners
Record conversations using the questions in *¿Vienes a mi fiesta de cumpleaños?*

For Kinesthetic Learners
Have students describe members of their family and act out each description.

¿A QUIÉN VAS A INVITAR?

**Voy a invitar a mi amigo Juan.
Juan es muy divertido.**

INVITADOS *(Guests)*

mi amigo / mi amiga *(my friend)*

mi novio / mi novia
(my boyfriend / my girlfriend)

mi primo / mi prima
(my cousin)

mi tío / mi tía
(my uncle / my aunt)

mis parientes
(my relatives)

mi vecino / mi vecina
(my neighbor)

mi padrino / mi madrina
(my godfather / my godmother)

¿Cómo es?

simpático(a)
divertido(a)
genial *(cool)*
inteligente
interesante
popular

¿QUÉ HACES PARA TU FIESTA?

Hago la lista de invitados.

Hago una piñata.
Hago un menú.
Invito a mis amigos.
Compro la comida.
Preparo la comida.

Escribo las invitaciones.
Decoro la casa.
Selecciono los discos
   compactos.

¿VIENES A MI FIESTA DE CUMPLEAÑOS? ¿A MI SANTO?

¿Qué contestas?

¿Cuándo es? *(When is it?)*

¿Una fiesta? ¡Qué bien!
(A party? Great!)

¡Claro que sí! *(Of course!)*

Sí, ¿a qué hora?
(Yes, at what time is it?)

Lo siento, no puedo.
(Sorry, I can't.)

93

¿Qué haces para tu fiesta?
Class activity to introduce the first-person form of **hacer** and words for throwing a party.
For Kinesthetic Learners: Name the activities in any order and have class members act out each one.

¿Vienes a mi fiesta de cumpleaños? ¿A mi santo?
Class activity to introduce accepting, declining, and asking questions about an invitation.
Synthesis: Create a party invitation, with date, time, activities, and theme.

Communicative Objective
• to talk about family celebrations

Related Components

Activity Book p. 42	**Audio Tapes** Listening Tape: 3A, Seg. 2
Audio Book Script: Seg. 2	**Cuaderno** p. 22

GETTING STARTED

Ask what types of celebrations are shown on this page and whether anyone has had a similar event to celebrate recently. Ask what *noticias* probably means in the title **Noticias de San Antonio**.

DISCUSS

Read aloud the captions and ask questions about each photo, using gestures to clarify new words.

Wedding
¿Quiénes celebran su boda? Lucía Lara y Juan Pastor, ¿verdad?
¿En qué día celebran su boda?
¿Qué hay después de la ceremonia?
¿Donde es la fiesta?

✓ CULTURE NOTE

Missions were the first form of Spanish settlement in the Southwest. Both fortress and church, missions were used to colonize new areas and to spread the Catholic faith. San Antonio de Valero, better known as El Alamo, is one of five missions that still exist in the San Antonio area.

Wedding Anniversary
¿Qué celebran Roberto y Sara Gallardo, su cumpleaños, su boda?
Celebran su aniversario número cincuenta, ¿verdad?
¿Cómo se dice en inglés aniversario?

"Sweet Fifteen"
¿Cuántos años va a tener Aracelia? ¿Cómo va a celebrar su cumpleaños?
¿Qué música es la de su fiesta? ¿Qué van a hacer los invitados en esa fiesta?

ℝEALIDADES

DIARIO AHORA, Viernes 18 de Julio

NOTICIAS DE SAN ANTONIO *Celebraciones*

Esta semana en San Antonio muchas familias celebran ocasiones muy especiales. ¡Felicidades!

Quinceañera

Aracelia, hija de Patricio y Josefa Lugo, va a celebrar sus quince años el domingo 20 de julio a las 6:00 p.m., en el restaurante Casa Río. Hay una gran fiesta con la famosa banda de música tejana La Diferenzia.

Boda

Lucía Lara y Juan Pastor celebran su boda en la iglesia de San Antonio, el sábado 19 de julio a las 8:00 p.m. Después de la ceremonia hay una fiesta con música y una cena en casa de la familia Lara.

Día del santo

Santiago Pereda celebra el día de su santo el viernes 25 de julio. Hay una comida en honor de Santiago en casa de sus padrinos a las 2:00 de la tarde.

Graduación

Ana Luisa Martínez celebra su graduación del Memorial High School el día 21 de julio. Después de la graduación hay una barbacoa para la familia y los amigos en el parque Fiesta Texas a las 4:00 p.m.

Cincuentaōs

Roberto y Sara Gallardo celebran su aniversario de bodas el 25 de julio en el salón de fiestas La Rotonda. Van a celebrar la ocasión con una comida deliciosa para la familia y los amigos.

✓ CULTURE NOTE

The *Quinceañeras* seem to have begun in Latin America (it is unknown in Spain). *Quinces* are often more elaborate and expensive than Aracelia's (although the band at her party, La Diferenzia, has a national reputation). Among Cuban-Americans, for example, professionally choreographed musical productions (starring the birthday girl) are popular.

Graduation
¿Cómo va a celebrar su graduación Ana Luisa?
Aquí dice "barbacoa", ¿es una celebración?
¿Para quién es la barbacoa?

Saint's Day
¿Qué va a celebrar Santiago?
¿Qué va a hacer y dónde?

▶▶▶ INTERNET LINK

A bilingual newspaper in San Antonio:
http://www.hispanic.com:80/LaPrensa/headlines.html

HABLA DEL PERIÓDICO

A. ¿Qué ocasiones especiales celebran las personas de las fotos?

Roberto y Sara Gallardo celebran su aniversario de bodas.

B. Con tu compañero(a), hablen de las fiestas.
¿Quién va a celebrar qué? ¿Cuándo? ¿Dónde?

— *Lucía Lara y Juan Pastor van a celebrar
   su boda.*
— *¿Cuándo?*
— *El sábado 19 de julio.*
— *¿A qué hora?*
— *A las ocho.*
— *¿Dónde?*
— *En la iglesia de San Antonio.*

PLANEA UNA FIESTA

A. Usa el modelo para planear tu fiesta ideal.
¿Qué necesitas para tu fiesta? ¿A quién vas a invitar?
¿Dónde vas a celebrar la fiesta? ¿Qué te gustaría hacer?

Invitados
mi prima Ana

Fiesta
mi cumpleaños

Día y hora
6 de octubre a las 7:00 p.m.

Comida
tacos

Actividades
escuchar música

Lugar
mi casa

B. Presenta la información a la clase.

ACTIVITIES

Habla del periódico

Pair Activity:
Comprehension and Evaluation
A. Discuss what special occasions these people are celebrating.
Answers: See model on student page.
B. Talk about these celebrations. Say who is celebrating what, when and where they will do it, and what they are going to do.
Answers: See model on student page.

Planea una fiesta

Individual Activity: Planning
A. Make a copy of the graphic organizer, and complete each of the categories. (Some require more than one entry.)
Possible Answers:
Actividades: bailar, cantar, hablar, tocar la guitarra; Comida: jugos, refrescos, pollo; Lugar: un restaurante.
B. Present your party plan to the class.
Extension: Conduct a poll. Ask which types of parties class members like to attend, what foods and activities they prefer, and what day and time they like best.

CHECK

- *¿Qué fiesta te gustaría celebrar?*
- *¿Qué fiestas le gusta celebrar a tu familia?*
- *¿Cómo vas a celebrar tu cumpleaños?*

LOG BOOK
Have students list vocabulary they find especially difficult.

MEETING INDIVIDUAL NEEDS

Reaching All Students

For Auditory Learners
Say who is in each photo and what each person is celebrating. For example:
Es una foto de Aracelia. Va a celebrar sus quince años.

For Visual Learners
Make a bulletin-board display about family celebrations.

For Kinesthetic Learners
Form groups and act out different types of celebrations. Have other groups guess what kind of party it is.

Para hispanohablantes

Do you know about any other celebrations that are not included in the photos? Tell the class about them.

Communicative Objectives

To talk about:
- party activities
- what people look like
- who people are and how to introduce them

Related Components

Activity Book p. 43-44	Transparencies Ch. 3: Palabras en acción
Cuaderno p. 23-24	Tutor Page p. 15

GETTING STARTED

Ask students which of the activities in the drawing they saw in photos earlier in the unit. Which ones are new?

DISCUSS

Comment on the people in the picture and what they look like. For example:
Aquí está Mariana en su fiesta de cumpleaños.
También está la familia de Mariana: esta chica que tiene pelo largo es la hermana de Mariana.

Para hispanohablantes

Some Spanish speakers in your class may use other vocabulary than that introduced in this chapter. Ask them to share with the class. A few variations:

los abuelos: los tatas
la boda: el matrimonio
el globo: la bomba, la vejiga
el novio: el enamorado
el pelo: el cabello
el/la rubio/a: el/la güero/a, el/la catire/a

PALABRAS EN ACCIÓN
¡FELIZ CUMPLEAÑOS!

1 ¿Qué ves en el dibujo?

¿Qué cosas hay en la fiesta? ¿Cómo son? Haz una lista.

Cosas	¿Cómo son?
globos	amarillos y azules
una piñata	bonita

2 ¿Cómo son los invitados?

Pregúntale a tu compañero(a) sobre el dibujo. Describe a cinco invitados.

— ¿Cómo es la prima de Mariana?
— Es baja y muy simpática.
— ¿Cómo es Isabel?
— Es joven y...

96

3 Actividades en la fiesta

¿Qué hace cada invitado? ¿Qué te gusta hacer a ti en una fiesta? Habla con tu compañero(a).

— ¿Qué hace el primo de Mariana?
— Baila.
— Y a ti, ¿te gusta bailar en las fiestas?
— Sí, me gusta mucho.

4 Cumpleaños

Compara tu cumpleaños con el cumpleaños de Mariana. Contesta las preguntas.

- **Mariana hace una fiesta, ¿y tú?**
- **Ella invita a su familia, ¿y tú?**
- **Ella tiene una piñata, ¿y tú?**

For students having difficulty talking about party activities or who people are and what they look like, you might consider:
- **The tutor page:** Pair the student with a native speaker or a more able student using the tutor page.

Quiero romper
la piñata.

Eva, ¿vienes a mi
casa mañana?
Voy a hacer una
barbacoa.

Lo siento,
Pedro,
no puedo.

la piñata

los globos

Tía Ester, ¿conoces a
mi novia Isabel?

¡No, Susana, son
para Mariana!

No.
Mucho gusto.

el hermano
de Mariana

Quiero abrir
los regalos.

Encantada.

las velas

los regalos

la abuela
de Mariana

1. Individual Activity
Make a list of things you see at the party, and describe them.
For Visual Learners: Make your own picture dictionary of the list.

2. Pair Activity
Describe five people in the drawing.
For Auditory Learners: Take turns describing other students and guessing who they are.

3. Pair Activity
Talk about what the guests are doing and which of those activities you enjoy.
For Kinesthetic Learners: Perform each activity as you mention it.

4. Pair Activity
Compare Mariana's birthday party with one of yours.
Application: Take turns naming things people do at parties that you like or don't like. Use **me gusta** and **no me gusta**.

5. Pair Activity
Decide what kind of party to have, and invite your partner.
For Kinesthetic Learners: Describe a party with words or gestures, and have your partner guess the kind of party.

6. Group Activity
Introduce someone to your partner.
Extension: Introduce a character from a TV program.

7. Hands-On Activity
Make a collage of a party or celebration. Write three sentences to describe it.
Extension: Make a page of pictures of a family and write captions that describe the relationships between the people.

8. Pair Activity
Write a dialog about a favorite relative. Present it to the class.
Extension: Write a dialog in which you invite your partner to a party. Describe who is going to be there.

 Invitaciones

Imagina que vas a hacer una fiesta. Invita a tu compañero(a).

— ¿Vienes a mi fiesta de graduación?
— ¡Claro que sí! ¿Cuándo es?
— Es el sábado.
— ¿Dónde?
— En mi casa.

 Presentaciones

Presenta una persona a tu compañero(a).

Ana: Pedro, ¿conoces a mi amigo David?
Pedro: No. Encantado.
David: Mucho gusto.

 Collage

Con fotos o dibujos, haz un collage de una fiesta o celebración. Escribe tres oraciones para describir la fiesta.

 Tú eres el autor

Escribe un diálogo sobre tu pariente favorito. Presenta el diálogo a la clase.

— ¿Quién es tu pariente favorito?
— Es mi padrino.
— ¿Cuántos años tiene?
— Tiene...
— ¿Cómo es?
— Es...

97

CHECK

Indicate the drawing and ask students:
• ¿Qué celebra Mariana?
• ¿Qué hacen en la fiesta de Mariana?
• Describe la familia de Mariana.

LOG BOOK
Have students write a list of whom they would invite to a party. Then write a word next to each which describes her/him.

Communicative Objective

• to describe events, people, places, or things, using *ser* and an adjective

Related Components

Activity Book p. 45-46	Audio Tapes Listening: 3A, Seg. 3
Audio Book Script: Seg. 3 Activities: p. 29	Cuaderno p. 25
	Tutor Page p. 16

GETTING STARTED

Tell the class that you are going to describe someone they know from the movies. Choose an actress, but do not use the pronouns *she* or *her*. Do use *beautiful* and other adjectives that are traditionally applied to women. Once the class has figured it out, ask how they knew that you were speaking of a woman. Explain that something similar happens in Spanish.

Language in Context

Point out the list of adjectives on this page. Then select one to describe yourself (e.g., **soy alta**). Ask individual students to do the same. Continue until the **soy** pattern is firmly established.

Ask questions and make comments in Spanish about people, places, events, and things, using forms of **ser**. *Sí/no* questions are probably best. For example:

¿Eres rubio? ¿Eres pelirrojo?
¿Cómo es Texas, grande o pequeño?
¿Cómo va a ser la fiesta?

Note: the *Thinking About Language* at the beginning of Chapter 4 will deal with the difference between *¿Cómo es?* and *¿Cómo está?* You may wish to refer to it at this time.

DISCUSS

Review vocabulary from previous chapters and introduce some of this chapter's new vocabulary with questions that incorporate forms of **ser**.

¿Cómo eres?
¿Quién es pelirroja?
¿Quién es aburrido?
¿Son ustedes grandes o pequeños?
¿Cómo es la escuela?
¿Son divertidas las fiestas?

PARA COMUNICARNOS MEJOR

¿CÓMO ES LA FIESTA?

To describe events, people, places, or things, use adjective.

Adjectives must have the same gender and number as the nouns they describe.

La fiesta es divertida.	The party is fun.
El pastel es delicioso.	The cake is delicious.
Los invitados son simpáticos.	The guests are friendly.

To form the plural of an adjective that ends in *-o*, *-a*, or *-e*, just add *-s* to the singular form.

	masculine	feminine
singular	Juan es alto. Él es inteligente.	María es alta. Ella es inteligente.
plural	Los chicos son altos. Ellos son inteligentes.	Las chicas son altas. Ellas son inteligentes.

Most adjectives that end in a consonant refer to both male and female nouns. To form their plural, add *-es*.

Carlos es genial.	*María es genial.*
Ellos son geniales.	*Ellas son geniales.*

Here are some adjectives you know.

alto(a)	**grande**	**azul**
bajo(a)	**caliente**	**especial**
divertido(a)	**dulce**	**genial**
guapo(a)	**inteligente**	**joven**
simpático(a)	**interesante**	**popular**

¿RECUERDAS?

Adjectives that end in *-o* describe masculine nouns. Adjectives that end in *-a*, describe feminine nouns. Adjectives that end in *-e* describe both feminine and masculine nouns.

98

Thinking About Language

You can use this opportunity to discuss barbecues in Texan celebrations, and the origin of the word *barbecue*.

Food Words

1. Ask a volunteer to describe a barbecue. (Broiling or roasting meat over an open fire, usually outdoors)

2. Ask for reasons why barbecues are so popular in Texas. (Possible reason: cattle-raising is a major business there.)

3. Explain that *barbecue* comes from the Spanish **barbacoa**, which was not originally a Spanish word. Ask students where the word might have come from. (It is a Native American word. The Taínos of Puerto Rico used it to refer to the frame on which they grilled meat.)

4. Meat had been grilled in Europe for thousands of years. Why did the Spaniards adopt the Taíno word? (Possibly because it was done outdoors or because it was associated with feasts.)

For students having difficulty describing someone or something using **ser** and an adjective, or with noun and adjective agreement, you might consider:

• **The tutor page:** Pair the student with a native speaker or a more able student using the tutor page.

1 De fiesta

¿Qué vas a llevar a la fiesta?

Voy a llevar globos rojos.

rojo	grande
frío	pequeño
delicioso	azul
caliente	popular

1. 2. 3.
4. 5. 6.

2 Descripciones

A. Haz un dibujo de un(a) compañero(a) y describe cómo es.
Pregúntale a otro(a) compañero(a) quién es.

B. Describe tu clase. Usa los adjetivos apropiados.

Somos inteligentes y divertidos.

3 ¿En quién piensas?

Mira la lista de adjetivos y piensa en
personas famosas o miembros de tu familia.

Mis primos son geniales.

¿Quién es...?
genial   joven
interesante   guapo(a)
simpático(a)   popular

99

• **Actividades:** see page 90C:
¿El mundo es redondo, no? and *Fiestas de los famosos*

• **Actividades:** see page 90C:

✓ CULTURE NOTE

The polite form of address, *Usted*,
evolved in the 1600s as a contraction of
vuestra merced (your Grace or your
Worship). The longer form had earlier
replaced the use of *vos* (from *vosotros*) as
the polite singular form.

ACTIVITIES

Students use forms of **ser** to describe
events, people, places or things.

1. Individual Activity
Say what you will bring to the party.
Possible answers:
1. See model on student page.
2. *Voy a llevar (unas) galletas delisiosas.*
3. *Voy a llevar (unas) velas.*
4. *Voy a llevar (unos) discos compactos.*
5. *Voy a llevar (unos) sandwiches calientes.*
6. *Voy a llevar un pastel delicioso.*
Possible Answer for 8:
Voy a llevar un frisbi.
Application: Name three places where you
would like to have a fiesta, and describe
them.

2. Class and Pair Activities
A: Draw a picture of a classmate and write
a description. Then ask another classmate
who it is. When you describe people or
things, make sure the adjectives you use
have the same gender and number as the
nouns.
Possible Adjectives: *alto/a, bajo/a,
inteligente, guapo/a, genial*
B: Describe the class.
Answers: See model on student page.
Analysis: In groups of five or six, compare
your drawings and describe students with
similar traits.

3. Individual Activity
Use the list of adjectives to describe famous
people or family members.
Answers: See model on student page.
Application: Write three sentences about
people whom the adjectives in the list do
not describe. Example:
Sean Connery no es joven.

CHECK

• *¿Cómo son ustedes?*
• *¿Cómo es el salón de clases?*
• *¿Cómo eres, rubio o pelirrojo?*
• *¿Cómo soy yo, alto o bajo?*
• *¿Cómo somos los profesores?*

LOG BOOK
Have students make up a rule that will help
them remember when to use the different
forms of the verb **ser**.

Communicative Objectives
• to say what you make or do using **hacer**
• to say whether you know or are familiar with someone using **conocer**

Related Components

Activity Book p. 47-48	**Audio Tapes** Listening: 3A, Seg. 4
Audio Book Script: Seg.4 Activities: p. 30	**Cuaderno** p. 25
	Tutor Page p. 17

GETTING STARTED

Remind students of the expression *hacer una fiesta*. How would they say this in English? Then ask the same question about *hago una piñata*. Why do they say *have* in one case and *make* in the other?

Language in Context

Hacer
Explore the two senses of **hacer** by asking: Do you *do* your homework or *make* your homework?
Ask for the Spanish phrases for "to do homework" and "to make the bed." Make sure they realize that **hacer la tarea** and **hacer la cama** are parallel constructions, and that in English we say *to do* in one case and *to make* in the other.
Examples of the *do* sense of **hacer**:
¿Que haces con tus amigos? ¿Vas al cine? ¿Qué más hacen Uds.?
Examples of the *make* sense of **hacer**:
¿Vamos a hacer una fiesta?
Bien, yo hago las decoraciones.

Conocer
Explain that **conocer** (plus **a**) is used to talk about knowing a person, never about knowing a fact. Ask what Spanish word is used to talk about knowing facts. (It is **sabre**).

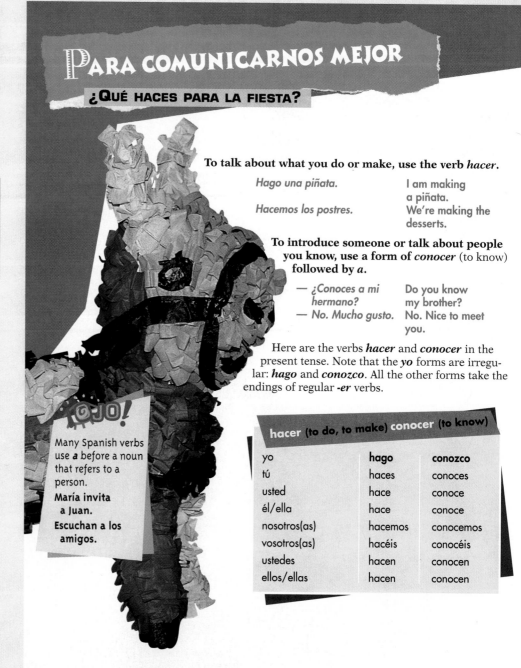

PARA COMUNICARNOS MEJOR

¿QUÉ HACES PARA LA FIESTA?

To talk about what you do or make, use the verb *hacer*.

Hago una piñata.	I am making a piñata.
Hacemos los postres.	We're making the desserts.

To introduce someone or talk about people you know, use a form of *conocer* (to know) followed by *a*.

— *¿Conoces a mi hermano?*	Do you know my brother?
— *No. Mucho gusto.*	No. Nice to meet you.

Here are the verbs **hacer** and **conocer** in the present tense. Note that the **yo** forms are irregular: **hago** and **conozco**. All the other forms take the endings of regular **-er** verbs.

¡OJO!
Many Spanish verbs use **a** before a noun that refers to a person.
María invita a Juan.
Escuchan a los amigos.

hacer (to do, to make)		conocer (to know)
yo	**hago**	**conozco**
tú	haces	conoces
usted	hace	conoce
él/ella	hace	conoce
nosotros(as)	hacemos	conocemos
vosotros(as)	hacéis	conocéis
ustedes	hacen	conocen
ellos/ellas	hacen	conocen

100

DISCUSS

Review vocabulary from previous chapters and introduce some of this chapter's new vocabulary with questions that use **conocer** and **hacer**.
¿Conoces a Eduardo? ¿Qué hace Eduardo? Sí. Estudia.
¿Y tú qué haces? ¿También estudias?
¿Conoces a Emilio Estevez? ¿Qué hace Emilio Estevez? Sí. És actor de cine.
Y Emilio, ¿te él conoce a ti? ¿No?
¿Quieres hacer una fiesta mexicana?
Para hacer la fiesta, hay que hacer tacos.

1 La fiesta de la escuela

A. ¿Qué hace cada estudiante para la fiesta de la escuela? En grupo, hagan una tabla.

— *Irene, ¿qué haces para la fiesta?*
— *Hago las ensaladas.*

B. Informa a la clase.

Irene hace las ensaladas.
Javier y yo hacemos los carteles.

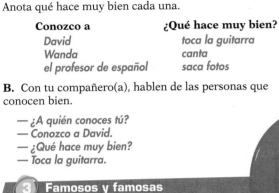

	yo	Irene	Javier	Bill
las ensaladas		✓		
los carteles	✓		✓	
el menú			✓	✓
los postres				
las hamburguesas				
la piñata				

2 ¿A quién conoces?

A. Haz una lista de tres personas que conoces de la escuela. Anota qué hace muy bien cada una.

Conozco a	**¿Qué hace muy bien?**
David	toca la guitarra
Wanda	canta
el profesor de español	saca fotos

B. Con tu compañero(a), hablen de las personas que conocen bien.

— *¿A quién conoces tú?*
— *Conozco a David.*
— *¿Qué hace muy bien?*
— *Toca la guitarra.*

3 Famosos y famosas

A. Con tu compañero(a), consulten una revista de cine o de televisión. Hagan una lista de las personas famosas que conocen.

Conocemos a: los Barrio Boyzz, Gloria Estefan,...

B. Con otro grupo, hablen de las personas de la lista. Digan qué hacen y cómo son.

— *¿A quién conocen?*
— *Conocemos a los Barrio Boyzz.*
— *¿Qué hacen?*
— *Cantan muy bien.*

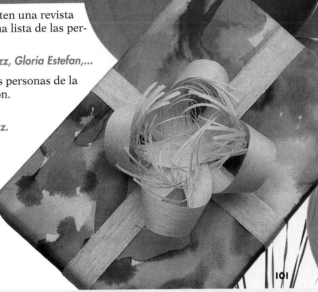

For students having difficulty using **hacer** or **conocer**, you might consider:
• **The tutor page:** Pair the student with a native speaker or a more able student using the tutor page.
• **Actividades:** see page 90D:
   ¿A quién conoces? and *¿Qué haces?*

ACTIVITIES

Students use **conocer** and **hacer** to say who they know and what they do.

1. Group Activity
A. Decide what each of you will make or do for a school party. Make a chart.
B. Share your plans with the class.
Answers: See models on student page.
Extension: Think of four more things you might need for the party, and decide which class members should do them.

2. Individual and Pair Activities
A. Make a list of three people in your school and what each does well.
B. With your partner, talk about people you each know.
Answers: See models on student page.
Application: Write a dialog in which two people meet and discover that they have mutual friends.

3. Pair and Group Activities
A. Look at an entertainment magazine and make a list of famous people you know of.
B. With other pairs, describe the people on your list and what they do.
Answers: See models on student page.

CHECK

• ¿Qué haces en una fiesta?
• ¿Quién hace unas decoraciones bonitas?
• ¿Cuándo vamos a hacer tacos?
• ¿Conoces al actor Jimmy Smits?
• ¿Conocen ustedes a mi prima?
• ¿Conozco a tus padres?
• ¿Quién conoce a mi hermana?

LOG BOOK
Have students write down sentences using each form of **hacer** and **conocer** that does not follow the general rules for **-er** verbs.

Para hispanohablantes

Have a Spanish-speaking student tell the class about a person he or she admires.

SITUACIONES

Communicative Objective
• to talk about parties and celebrations

Related Components

Assessment Oral Proficiency: p. 23	**Conexiones** Chapter 3
Audio Book Script: Seg. 5 Activities: p. 31	**Magazine** Juntos en Texas **Tutor Page** p. 18
Audio Tapes Listening: 3A, Seg.5 Conexiones: 16B, Ch. 3	

GETTING STARTED

At this point, students should be able to correctly use adjectives and the verbs **hacer** and **conocer**.
Ask students how they celebrate their birthdays. Are their celebrations the same as those in the photos? What birthday customs do they follow?

APPLY

1. Individual or Pair Activity
Write a description of each photo.
Possible Descriptions:
Los chicos y las chicas son jóvenes y guapos. Cinco chicos y chicas son rubios. Los chicos son altos. Hay chicas altas. Hay otras chicas bajas. Ellos rompen la piñata. La chica del cumpleaños abre los regalos. Los chicos y las chicas comparten la comida.
Synthesis: With a partner, design and write an invitation for the party in the photos.

2. Individual Activity
Make a photo album of some of your parties, using the list for suggestions. Describe three photos from one of your parties.
Possible answers:
Es mi fiesta de cumpleaños. Mis amigos rompen la piñata.
Tomamos refrescos. Y comemos pastel.
Aquí mis amigos y yo bailamos.
Analysis: Exchange descriptions with someone and decide which photos that person described.

SITUACIONES
FOTOS Y RECUERDOS

1 Fotos y fiestas
¿Quiénes son las personas de las fotos? ¿Cómo son? ¿Qué hacen?

2 Tu álbum de fotos
Haz tu álbum. Describe tres fotos de una fiesta de la lista.

• una fiesta de cumpleaños o del santo
• fiesta de Fin de Año.
• un picnic de graduación
• un aniversario de bodas
• una fiesta de Navidad

PARA TU REFERENCIA

el Fin de Año *New Year's Eve*
la Navidad *Christmas*
querido(a) *dear*
los recuerdos *memories*
los servicios *services*

102

3. Group Activity
Ask two classmates to describe their favorite kinds of celebrations and what they do. Let them share that with the class.
Answers: See model on student page.
For Kinesthetic Learners: Act out activities at a specific type of family celebration. Have the class guess what celebration it is.

4. Hands-On Activity
Make a poster for a business that organizes all kinds of parties. Label the parties and describe the photos. For ideas, see the *Vocabulario temático* and *Realidades* pages.
Synthesis: With a small group, create a television ad for a party-planning service. Perform your commercial in class.

Answer a friend's invitation to a New Year's Eve party. Say why you cannot attend and what your plans are.

Answers: See model on student page.

For Visual Learners: Make a party invitation. Substitute photos or drawings for as many of the words as you can. Trade invitations with a partner and read them aloud to each other.

For students having difficulty talking about parties or celebrations, you might consider:

•**The tutor page:** Pair the student with a native speaker or a more able student using the tutor page.

CHECK

- *¿Cuál es tu celebración favorita?*
- *¿Qué haces en una fiesta?*
- *¿Cómo celebras el Año Nuevo?*

LOG BOOK

Have students write the forms of **hacer** and **conocer** that they have found difficult.

---

3 Entrevista

Habla con dos amigos. Pregúntales cuál es su fiesta favorita. ¿Qué hacen? Informa a la clase.

El día de Fin de Año es muy especial para mis amigos. Por la mañana hacen un picnic en el parque. Por la noche celebran con la familia y después van a bailar a su discoteca favorita.

4 Cartel

Eres una persona que organiza diferentes tipos de fiestas (de cumpleaños, de graduación, de Fin de Año...). Haz un cartel con fotos o dibujos. Incluye tipos de fiestas y servicios.

¿Quieres celebrar una fiesta?

Somos especialistas en: escribir las invitaciones, decorar la casa, seleccionar la música, preparar la comida, sacar las fotos y también ¡compramos los regalos!

Organizamos

fiestas de bodas,

aniversarios, graduaciones

y otras ocasiones especiales

5 Una invitación

Contesta la invitación de un amigo a una fiesta de Fin de Año.

Querido Jimmy:

Gracias por tu invitación. Me gustaría mucho celebrar el Fin de Año con tu familia, pero no puedo. Mis padres y yo vamos a San Antonio a visitar a mis abuelos.

Tu amiga,
Margarita

103

Communicative Objectives
• to talk about planning a party
• to describe the guests
• to write party invitations

Related Components

Transparencies	Video: Tape/Book
Ch. 3: Para resolver	Unit 2: Seg. 2

Search to frame 1181201

GETTING STARTED

Ask students what they think the *¡Fiesta!* card is. Ask if they can figure out what is on the computer screen. (It is the model for *PASO 5.*)

APPLY

Form small groups. Each group will plan a class party.

PASO 1: ¿Qué van a celebrar?
Decide what, where, and when you will celebrate.
Answers: See model on student page.
Extension: Write five activities for the party. Exchange with others and agree on the five best.

PASO 2: Los invitados
Decide whom you are going to invite to the party and say why.
Answers: See model on student page.
Application: Pick five famous people you will not invite to the party, and say why:
No invitamos a Mel Gibson y Sandra Bullock porque no hablan español.

PASO 3: Una invitación
Make an invitation. Follow the model.
Analysis: Exchange invitations with another group and ask each other questions about the party.

PASO 4: El menú
Plan a menu.
Possible answers:
Comida: *sandwiches (de atún, de queso), pollo con arroz, hamburguesas*
Bebidas: *batidos, agua mineral, café*
Postres: *flan, pastel de chocolate, piña*

PARA RESOLVER
PLANES PARA UNA FIESTA

En grupo, hagan planes para una fiesta de la clase.

PASO 1 ¿Qué van a celebrar?
Decidan qué van a celebrar, cuándo y dónde.

• El fin de los exámenes
• Una fiesta sorpresa
• La victoria de un equipo

> *Vamos a celebrar la victoria del equipo de fútbol. La fiesta es el domingo en el gimnasio.*

PASO 2 Los invitados
Decidan a quién van a invitar a la fiesta y por qué.

> *Vamos a invitar a personas simpáticas y divertidas.*

> *Vamos a invitar a Roberto porque baila muy bien.*

PASO 3 Una invitación
Hagan una invitación para la fiesta. Usen el modelo.

PASO 4 El menú
Hagan un menú para la fiesta.

> **MENÚ**
> **Comidas:** *tacos, enchiladas,...*
> **Bebidas:** *refrescos, jugos,...*
> **Postres:** *helados, frutas,...*

PASO 5 Los planes finales
Hagan una lista de las cosas que necesitan y decidan quién va a comprar cada cosa.

PASO 5: Los planes finales
Make a list of the things you need and who will bring them.
Answers: See model on student page.
Extension: Describe the party you have planned. For example:
La fiesta de mi grupo es divertida porque hay salsa y merengue.

Group Project:
Learn the words to *Cumpleaños feliz.*
> *Cumpleaños feliz,*
> *te deseamos a ti,*
> *que los cumplas,*
> *que los cumplas,*
> *que los cumplas feliz.*

PLANES FINALES

DECORACIONES
Globos
Flores

MÚSICA
Discos compactos
Cintas
Videos

COMIDAS Y BEBIDAS
Refrescos
Tacos
Enchiladas

QUIÉN
NANCY

PARA TU REFERENCIA

las cintas *tapes*
las decoraciones *decorations*
el equipo *team*
el fin *end*
la sorpresa *surprise*
la victoria *victory*

105

PORTFOLIO

Have students make invitations to a party that will celebrate their favorite color. Clothing, food, and entertainment should all have to do with that color.

Family Words
Here are additional words that students may be interested in knowing:

adopted children *hijos adoptivos*
first cousin *primo hermano/a*
second cousin *primo segundo*
distant cousin *primo lejano*
grandson/daughter *nieto/a*
great-grandfather/mother *bisabuelo/a*
great-grandson/daughter *bisnieto/a*
great-uncle/aunt *tío/a abuelo/a*
great-great-grandchild *tataranieto/a*
great-great-grandparent *tatarabuelo/a*
half-brothers/sisters *medios-hermanos/as*
nephew/niece *sobrino/a*
stepbrother/sister *hermanastro/a*
stepfather *padrastro*
stepmother *madrastra*
stepson/daughter *hijastro/a*
in-laws *familia política*
daughter-in-law *nuera*
son-in-law *yerno*
father/mother-in-law *suegro/a*
brother/sister-in-law *cuñado/a*
brother/sister-in-law's spouse *concuñado/a*
godfather/godmother *padrino/madrina*

Para hispanohablantes

Describe to the class a party that you would like to have. Try to use the words **ser, conocer,** and **hacer.**

▶▶▶ INTERNET LINK

There are many geneaology sites on the Internet. Some of your students may be interested in this Usenet group:
soc.genealogy.hispanic

Related Components

Audio Tapes	Magazine
Conexiones: 16B, Ch. 3	Juntos en Texas
Conexiones Chapter 3	

GETTING STARTED

Ask what Halloween is and where it came from. Are students aware that in many countries Halloween is part of a religious celebration on which people remember the dead?

Background Note

Customs, beliefs and calendar dates of holidays around Halloween time differ somewhat from country to country. The celebration was brought to Latin America from Spain. In Mexico, Catholic customs blended with Aztec traditions to create a three-day holiday.

Celebrations last from All Saints Eve (Halloween) through November 2nd, the Day of the Dead. On the afternoon of the 2nd, families clean and decorate relatives' graves. As evening falls, they light candles and think about the dead.

Like Halloween, which mixes Catholic customs with Celtic practices brought to the U.S. by Irish immigrants, the Day of the Dead is made more appealing to children through toys and candles that make death seem less frightening.

DISCUSS

Using the Text

Read aloud each paragraph, then ask comprehension, critical-thinking, and culture-awareness questions such as:

El Día de los Muertos
¿Quién celebra el Día de los Muertos?

La foto
¿Qué forma tienen los dulces, los panes, y las galletas?
Has anyone ever eaten a Halloween candy shaped like a skull or a bone?

La celebración en Texas
¿Qué ponen las familias en los altares?

ENTÉRATE

EL DÍA DE LOS MUERTOS°

...e los Muertos es el 2 de noviembre. Es una celebración popular muy importante ... mexicanos y los mexicano-americanos. En este día las familias honran° a los ...dición muy antigua.

LA CELEBRACIÓN EN TEXAS

Las ... ...rios° y hacen altares° con ... ...arientes muertos. Los altares tienen flores, tarjetas postales, velas, ..., especialmente la comida favorita del muerto. A veces hay fotos de ...

En este día hacen muchas cosas en forma de esqueletos:° galletas, panes, dulces...° ¡y juguetes° también!

TE TOCA A TI

Completa las oraciones según el artículo.

1. El Día de los Muertos es el...
2. Las familias visitan...
3. Los altares tienen...
4. Hay galletas, panes, dulces y juguetes en forma de...

los altares *altars*	honran *they honor*
los cementerios *cemeteries*	los juguetes *toys*
los dulces *candies*	los muertos *the dead*
los esqueletos *skeletons*	

106

CHECK

Te toca a ti
Answers:
1. *dos de noviembre.*
2. *los cementerios.*
3. *flores, tarjetas postales, velas, frutas, pan y muchas otras comidas.*
4. *esqueletos.*

LOG BOOK

Have students list the Day of the Dead customs they find most appealing.

Para hispanohablantes

Tell the class how your family celebrates the Day of the Dead. Do you follow the customs of the place your family came from, or do you celebrate Halloween? Do you combine the two sets of customs?

▶▶▶ INTERNET LINK

About the Day of the Dead in Mexico:
http://mexico.udg.mx:80/Tradiciones/Muertos/muertos.html

Vocabulario Temático

Fiestas y celebraciones
Parties and celebrations

el aniversario anniversary
la boda wedding
el día del santo saint's day
la graduación graduation
la quinceañera sweet fifteen

¿Qué vas a hacer para tu fiesta?
What are you going to do for your party?

decorar la casa to decorate the house
escribir las invitaciones to write the invitations
hacer la lista de invitados to make out the guest list
invitar a los amigos to invite friends
jugar con videojuegos play videogames
seleccionar los discos compactos to choose the CDs
tocar la guitarra to play the guitar

¿Qué vas a comprar para la fiesta?
What are you going to buy for the party?

las flores flowers
las galletas cookies
los globos balloons
las velas candles

Los invitados
Guests

el hijo/la hija son/daughter
la madrina godmother
el novio/la novia boyfriend/girlfriend
el pariente/la parienta relative
el padrino godfather
el primo/la prima cousin
el tío/la tía uncle/aunt
el vecino/la vecina neighbor

Actividades en la fiesta
Party activities

abrir los regalos to open the presents
hacer una barbacoa to have a barbecue
hacer un picnic to have a picnic
romper la piñata to break the piñata

¿Cómo es?

especial special
famoso(a) famous
genial cool
popular popular

Expresiones y palabras

¡Claro que sí! Of course!
¿Conoces a...? Do you know...?
Encantado(a) Delighted
¡Felicidades! Congratulations!
¡Feliz cumpleaños! Happy birthday!
hacer una fiesta to have (give) a party
Lo siento, no puedo. Sorry, I can't.
Nada especial. Nothing special.
¡Qué bien! Great!
¿Vienes...? Are you coming...?
celebrar to celebrate
conocer to know
hacer to do, to make
la ocasión occasion

LA CONEXIÓN INGLÉS-ESPAÑOL

Spanish words ending in *-ción*, like *invitación*, usually have English cognates. To make the plural form of these words, drop the accent on the *o* and add *-es*: for example, *invitación* becomes *invitaciones*. It's also helpful to know that these words are always feminine.

Look at the list for other such words. What are their cognates in English?

107

La conexión inglés-español

Ask for English words ending in **-tion** that have cognates ending in **-ción** (e.g., *nation* and *education*.)
Write **colección** and **dirección** on the board, and ask how they differ from **invitación** and **graduación**. Make sure students understand that, as a rule, Spanish cognates that end in **-cción** change to **-ction** in English.
Possible Rule: Some Spanish words that end in **-ción** have English cognates that end in **-tion**.

VOCABULARIO TEMÁTICO

Objectives
- to review vocabulary correctly pronounce words containing the letter "r" and the double "rr"
- to review vocabulary

Related Components

Activity Book	Audio Book
Chapter Review: p. 49-50	Script: Seg. 6 Activities p. 32
Assessment	**Audio Tapes**
Listening Script: p. 11	Listening: 3A, Seg. 6 Assessment: 14A, Ch. 3
Chapter Test: p. 57-62	**Cuaderno** p. 27-28

Pronunciation: "r" and "rr"

Words containing the letter "r" and the double "rr" are best learned by imitating your teacher.

- The letter "r" is produced with a single tap of the underside of the tongue against the gum ridge above the upper teeth (i.e. the alveolar ridge), except when the letter "r" occurs at the beginning or end of a word.
flores, madrina, primo, claro

- "rr" is produced by making multiple taps (i.e. a trill) in the same area of the mouth.
carro, perro, arre

- The "r" at the beginning and end of a word closely resembles the pronunciation of the "rr."
romper, rápido, hacer, popular

Have the student imitate the sound of a car when starting (rrum, rrrum) and use this sound when pronouncing words like *carro*.

The distinction between the two sounds "r" and "rr" within a word is very important as *"carro"* means "car," whereas *"caro"* means expensive. Similarly *"pero"* means "but" whereas *"perro"* means dog.

Language Note

In some countries (like Puerto Rico), the "rr" is pronounced like the English "h" in "hill."

107

	Objetivos page 109	Conversemos pages 110-111	Realidades pages 112-113	Palabras en acción pages 114-115
Comunicación	• To talk about where you live	Have students discuss where they live		Activity 8: Read cartoon, write sentences about bedrooms
	• To talk about where things are in your house and neighborhood	Discuss where things are in the neighborhood		Activity 8: Read cartoon, write sentences about bedrooms
Vocabulario temático	• To know the expressions for types of homes	Talk about different types of homes		Activity 7: Make, label, and present collage of different types of homes
	• To know the expressions for places in your neighborhood	Talk about different places in the neighborhood		
	• To know the expressions for rooms and furniture in a house			Activities 1-5: Read cartoon, make list; discuss inside and outside, location of an object, rooms and their locations
	• To know the expressions for locations	Talk about different places in the neighborhood	Read map and text, answer questions, decide which statements are true and which are false	Activities 2, 3, 5, 6, 8: Read cartoon, discuss inside and outside, location of an object, rooms and their locations, where pets are; write sentences
Estructura	• To talk about where things are: the verb *estar* and expressions to show location	Use *estar* + location expressions to talk about where homes are	Read map and text, answer questions, talk about buildings	Activities 3, 5, 6: Read cartoon, discuss location of an object; describe where each room is; describe where pets are
	• To talk about things that people own, relationships among people: possessive adjectives	Use possessive adjectives to talk about homes and neighborhoods		
Cultura	The Spanish-Mexican heritages of different Texan cities		*Paseo del Río:* walking along the San Antonio River	
Integración		Asking and telling where things are, where to go, what to do, places in a neighborhood	Locations, what people would like to do, directions	Locations, expressing ownership

Para comunicarnos mejor (1) pages 116-117	Para comunicarnos mejor (2) pages 118-119	Situaciones pages 120-121	Para resolver pages 122-123	Notes
	Activities 1, 3: Discuss homes; fill out survey; have students discuss choices with each other	**Activity 2: Have students tell visiting friends where rooms and furniture in their homes are**	**Pasos 2-4: With group, discuss ideal home, draw floor plan, and present to class**	
Activity 2: Discuss locations of buildings near school	**Activity 1: Discuss homes**	**Activity 2: Have students tell visiting friends where rooms and furniture in their homes are**	**Pasos 2-4: With group, discuss ideal home, draw floor plan, and present to class**	
	Activity 2: Talk about members of a family and where they live		**Paso 2: With group, discuss where ideal home would be**	
Activity 2: Discuss locations of buildings near school	**Activity 3: Fill out survey for neighborhood party, have students discuss choices with each other**		**Pasos 2, 4: With group, discuss where ideal home would be; present ideal home to class**	
Activity 3: Describe locations of furniture in ad	**Activity 1: Discuss homes**	**Activity 2: Have students tell visiting friends where rooms and furniture in their homes are**	**Pasos 3, 4: Decide what ideal home would be like and draw floor plan; present ideal home to class**	
Activities 1-3: Read map and describe where a person is; discuss locations of buildings near school; describe locations of furniture in ad	**Activity 2: Talk about members of a family and where they live**	**Activity 2: Have students tell visiting friends where rooms and furniture in their homes are**	**Pasos 1-4: Discuss floor plan in book; discuss ideal home and draw floor plan; present ideal home to class**	
Activities 1-3: Read map and describe where a person is; discuss locations of furniture in ad		**Activity 2: Have students tell visiting friends where rooms and furniture in their homes are**	**Pasos 1-4: Discuss floor plan in book; discuss ideal home and draw floor plan; present ideal home to class**	
	Activities 1, 2, 3B: Discuss homes; talk about members of a family and where they live; discuss survey choices	**Activity 2: Have students tell visiting friends where rooms and furniture in their homes are**	**Pasos 3, 4: Decide what ideal home would be like and draw floor plan; present ideal home to class**	
		El Paso and El Camino Real		**Entérate page 124 San Antonio's mission trail**
Locations, places in a neighborhood	**People that you know, describing things, expressing ownership or relationships**	**Days, dates, time, numbers, addresses, periods of the day**	**Locations, numbers, describing things, expressing ownership**	

¡Qué familia!

SOCIAL STUDIES CONNECTION

Objective
- to invent imaginary families, using Chapter 4 *Vocabulario temático*

Use
after *Palabras en acción,* pages 114–115

Materials
- newspapers or magazines
- scissors
- glue sticks
- posterboard or cardboard

Activity
- Divide class into 3 groups. Each group is an extended family.
- Groups decide which of them play the different family members, deciding on personality, age, and other characteristics.
- Students look through magazines for photos like their chosen characters and glue them to posterboard or cardboard.
- Students present their characters to the class, describing them physically and talking about their personalities. One student might say:—*Soy Sandra María Fernandez Colón. Tengo 15 años. Estoy en el grado diez en la escuela superior Martín Lutero King. Soy pequeña y tengo el pelo largo. Me gusta ir con mis amigos a bailar a la discoteca. Me gustaría ser profesora,* etc.
- One student in each group introduces the family members.—*Aquí les presento la familia Sanchez Colón: el abuelo Ernesto Sanchez Gil, la abuela María Elena Silva de Sanchez, el padre Raúl Sanchez Silva,* etc.
- After the characters have been presented, they ask the class questions about themselves. For example: *Soy uno de los hijos, ¿cómo me llamo?,* etc.
- Use these family members again in *¿Dónde está mi familia?* and *Mi telenovela,* page 108D.

¿Cómo es la casa?

SOCIAL STUDIES CONNECTION

Objective
- to design and present homes for the characters from *¡Qué familia!,* using the verb *estar* + location expressions

Use
after *Para comunicarnos mejor,* page 116

Materials
- interior design/home fashion magazines
- craft paper (1 yard per group)
- glue sticks

Activity
- Have each member of the families from *¡Qué familia!* select a room from a magazine and present it to the class, describing colors and using location expressions to tell where the furniture is.
- Make sure each family has the basic components of a home: kitchen, bedroom, living room, etc.
- Have students arrange the rooms by floor and glue the rooms to craft paper.
- Each family presents its home to the class, describing rooms and other features as if they were selling the home to prospective buyers.
- Display the homes, and save them for *¿Dónde está mi familia?* and *Mi telenovela* on page 108D.

Variations
- On graph paper, have students draw and label floor plans of their dream home—*Mi casa ideal.* Ask them to talk about how these homes are similar to and different from their real homes.
- Have them write a short description of their dream home.—*Mi casa es un apartamento. Vivo en el segundo piso. Mi casa tiene dos dormitorios, una cocina, un baño, una sala y un comedor,* etc.
- Pair students and have them use their floor plans to discuss their dream homes' similarities and differences.
- Have students describe their bedroom or any other favorite room or place in their dream home.

¿Dónde está mi familia?

Objective
- to discuss where family members are, using possessive adjectives and the verb *estar*

Use
after *Para comunicarnos mejor,* page 118

Materials
- the families created for *¡Qué familia!* (page 108C)
- the floor plans created for *¿Cómo es la casa?* (page 108C)

Activity
- Have students take turns placing their characters randomly in the house created for *¿Cómo es la casa?*
- A member of the family playing stands near the house and tells where he/she is and where the rest of the family members are. For example, the student who role-plays Sandra María Fernández Colón might say:—*Estoy en mi dormitorio. Mi hermana está en su dormitorio. Mi madre está en la cocina. Mi padre está en el patio. Mis abuelos están en la sala,* etc. Then she asks classmates:—*¿Dónde está mi padre?* The first volunteer might answer:—*Tu padre está en el patio.* (If a student answers incorrectly, another classmate tries.)
- When all the family members have been located in their home, the next family goes to the front and places their family members in the rooms of their home.
- Play until all the families have been situated in their homes.

Mi telenovela

ART/WRITING CONNECTION

Objectives
- to write an episode of a *telenovela,* or TV soap opera, using the verb *estar* + location expressions and Chapter 4 *Vocabulario temático*

Use
after completing the 3 previous activities

Materials
- the families created for *¡Qué familia!*
- the floor plans created for *¿Cómo es la casa?*
- TRB Activity Support Page 10, *Storyboard*

Activity
- Have students display their floor plans and reintroduce their characters to the rest of the class. Tell them they are going to create a *telenovela* about their character and any other characters they choose—including members of other families. The story can be set in one house, two houses, or all three houses.
- Distribute storyboard. Have students draw the story on the storyboard and write captions and talk balloons. If they would rather not draw, they can write different scenes into the storyboard panels.
- Dramas should be exciting, funny, imaginative. Captions and dialog should refer to rooms and furniture, using the verb *estar* + location expressions.
- Videotape the *telenovelas,* if possible, and present the best tapes to other Spanish classes.

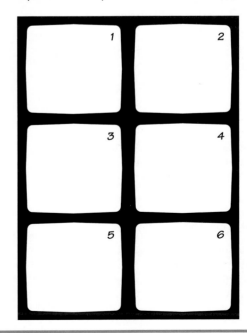

¿DÓNDE VIVES?

Introduce the chapter and its theme by asking students to describe their homes and neighborhoods.

Related Components

Audio Tapes	Conexiones
Conexiones: 16B, Ch. 4	Chapter 4
	Video: Tape/Book
CD ROM	Unit 2: Seg. 3
Chapter 4	

Search to frame 1212900

GETTING STARTED

Ask students to look at the photograph and to identify what is there according to the caption. Ask critical-thinking questions, such as: *Según tu opinión, ¿por qué muchos civdades en Texas tienen nombres españoles?*

Thinking About Language

You can use this opportunity to discuss with your students the importance of the Spanish language.

Who Speaks Spanish?

How important is Spanish? Have a contest. Invite students to estimate:

1. How many people in the world speak Spanish as their first language?
(There are around 330,000,000 first-language speakers.)

2. How many people in the United States speak Spanish as their first language?
(22,400,000 in the U.S. according to 1990 census)

3. How many people in Africa speak Spanish as their first language?
(100,000 Spanish-speakers live in Africa; it is the official language of Equatorial Guinea, a former Spanish colony.)

4. What country has the largest number of Spanish speakers?
(Mexico, with 85,000,000 people)

5. How many people speak Spanish as a second language?
(Around 50,000,000 people speak it as a second language.)

Where Do They Speak It?

Spanish is spoken as a first language by a majority or a fairly large minority in many countries.

CAPÍTULO 4

¿DÓNDE VIVES?

108

Andorra	Argentina	El Salvador	Equatorial Guinea
Australia	Belize	France	Guatemala
Bolivia	Colombia	Honduras	Mexico
Chilie	Cuba	Morocco	Nicaragua
Costa Rica	Dominican Republic	Ecuador	Panama

Chapter Components

Activity Book	Audio Book	CD ROM	Transparencies
p. 51-60	Script: p. 33-36	Chapter 4	Chapter 4
Assessment	Activities: p. 37-40	**Conexiones**	**Tutor Pages**
Oral Proficiency:	**Audio Tapes**	Chapter 4	p. 19-22
p. 24	Chapter: 3B	**Cuaderno**	**Video: Tape/Book**
Listening Script: p. 12	Assessment:	p. 29-36	Unit 2: Seg. 2
Chapter Test:	14B, Ch. 4	**Magazine**	
p. 63-68	Conexiones:	Juntos en Texas	
	16B, Ch. 4		

Objetivos

COMUNICACIÓN

To talk about:
- where you live
- where things are in your house and neighborhood

CULTURA

To learn about:
- places of interest in San Antonio
- typical weekend activities in El Paso
- the history of missions in Texas

VOCABULARIO TEMÁTICO

To know the expressions for:
- types of homes
- places in your neighborhood
- rooms and furniture in a house
- locations

ESTRUCTURA

To talk about:
- where things are: the verb *estar* and expressions to show location
- things that people own, relationships among people: possessive adjectives

¿SABES QUE...?

The cities of San Antonio and El Paso were founded by Spanish explorers in the 1700s. Other Texas cities such as Austin, Dallas, and Houston were established by Anglo-American settlers in the 1800s. Whether their founders were of Spanish or Anglo-American origins, the life and culture of all these cities have been profoundly influenced by Latin American communities. Throughout Texas, Mexican and other Latin American influences are everywhere. The decorative ironwork on doors, covered porches, patios, tile roofs, and outdoor murals all owe their distinctive look to Texas' Spanish heritage.

◀ **Una calle de San Antonio, Texas.**

109

▣ ACTIVITIES

Here are some additional activities that you may wish to use as you work through this chapter with your students.

Communication

Encourage after-class activities that may enhance student interest and proficiency. Some ideas:
- have students browse through such magazines as *Buenhogar* looking for house and furniture vocabulary
- ask a Spanish speaker to give a house or apartment tour

Culture

To encourage greater understanding of the strong Hispanic heritage in Texas:
- suggest that students explore the city of San Antonio by using the Internet Link on this page
- show the video that accompanies Unit 2 of this textbook

Vocabulary

To reinforce vocabulary, have students:
- use magazine photos or drawings to create their own picture dictionaries
- invite Spanish speakers to talk about the houses they grew up in

Peru
Spain
Venezuela
Paraguay

Philippines
Uruguay
USA

▶▶▶ INTERNET LINK

An excellent set of San Antonio links:
http://www.electrotex.com:80/span/sp.sa.html

Communicative Objectives

• to discuss places where people live
• to describe a location
• to talk about where you have to go

Related Components

Activity Book p. 51	**Cuaderno** p. 29
Audio Book Script: Seg. 1	**Transparencies** Ch. 4: Conversemos
Audio Tapes Listening: 3B, Seg. 1	

☐ GETTING STARTED

Ask students to identify the objects and phrases on the pages using just the pictures.

☐ DISCUSS

These activities give students an opportunity to begin communicating with each other and with you, focusing on the theme and objectives of the chapter. The activities can be used as oral class activities or, if you prefer, you can pair students to achieve more interaction. Additional activities integrate critical-thinking skills.

¿Dónde vives?

This is a class activity on how to give an address. Ask students where they live.

¿Vives en un apartamento?

Class activity to introduce vocabulary for places where people live. Ask a few students the question in the title. Extend with questions that use the four locations in the list and words from earlier chapters. For example:
¿Donde está tu casa, en el centro?
¿Está lejos de la escuela?

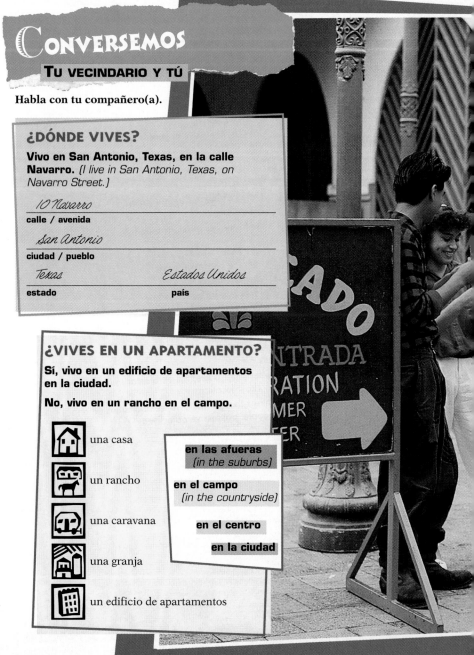

CONVERSEMOS

TU VECINDARIO Y TÚ

Habla con tu compañero(a).

¿DÓNDE VIVES?

Vivo en San Antonio, Texas, en la calle Navarro. *(I live in San Antonio, Texas, on Navarro Street.)*

10 Navarro
calle / avenida

San Antonio
ciudad / pueblo

Texas   _Estados Unidos_
estado   país

¿VIVES EN UN APARTAMENTO?

Sí, vivo en un edificio de apartamentos en la ciudad.

No, vivo en un rancho en el campo.

- una casa
- un rancho
- una caravana
- una granja
- un edificio de apartamentos

en las afueras
(in the suburbs)

en el campo
(in the countryside)

en el centro

en la ciudad

110

Location Words

Draw a class plan on the board and use it from the students' viewpoint (Ana is on the left, Pepe is on the right). Label the front of the room so you can use *delante/detrás*.

Possible questions:
¿Quién está detrás de María José?
¿Quién está lejos de Pepe?
¿Quiénes están cerca de Pepe?
¿Pedro está a la izquierda de... ¿quién?

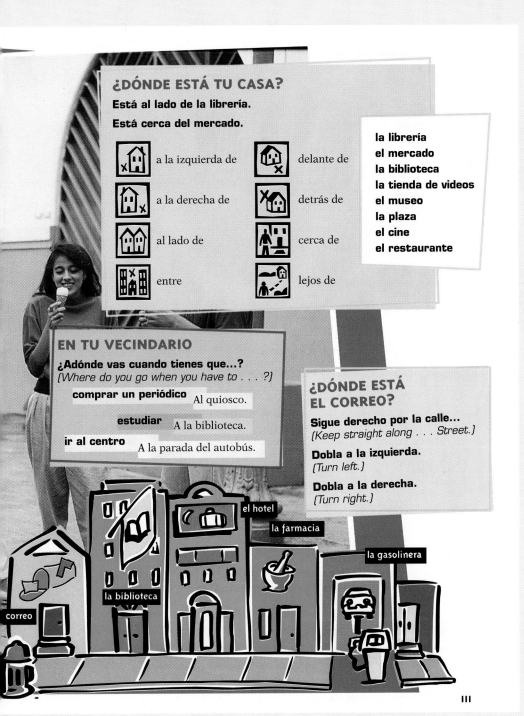

¿DÓNDE ESTÁ TU CASA?

Está al lado de la librería.

Está cerca del mercado.

	a la izquierda de		delante de
	a la derecha de		detrás de
	al lado de		cerca de
	entre		lejos de

la librería
el mercado
la biblioteca
la tienda de videos
el museo
la plaza
el cine
el restaurante

EN TU VECINDARIO

¿Adónde vas cuando tienes que...?
(Where do you go when you have to . . . ?)

comprar un periódico
Al quiosco.

estudiar
A la biblioteca.

ir al centro
A la parada del autobús.

¿DÓNDE ESTÁ EL CORREO?

Sigue derecho por la calle...
(Keep straight along . . . Street.)

Dobla a la izquierda.
(Turn left.)

Dobla a la derecha.
(Turn right.)

el hotel
la farmacia
la gasolinera
la biblioteca
correo

III

¿Dónde está tu casa?
Class activity to introduce location expressions. Have students use location expressions to form answers to the sample questions.
For Visual Learners: One partner thinks of a classroom object and gives clues to the other using only location expressions.

En tu vecindario
Class activity to introduce **tener que**. Ask these and similar questions, then present other examples of **tener que**, such as: *Tengo que comer* or *Tienes que estudiar*.
Analysis: Have pairs write five questions and answers using **tener que**. After they ask and answer their own questions, have them exchange questions with other pairs.

¿Dónde está el correo?
Class activity to practice giving directions.

CHECK

- ¿Dónde vive tu mejor amigo?
- ¿Qué está al lado de tu escritorio?
- ¿Adónde tienes que ir el sábado?

LOG BOOK
Have students write sentences about where they sit in class using location expressions.

Objectives
Communicative: to discuss locations and give directions using a map
Cultural: to become familiar with the city of San Antonio

Related Components

Activity Book p. 52	**Audio Tapes** Listening Tape: 3B, Seg. 2
Audio Book Script: Seg. 2	**Cuaderno** p. 30

GETTING STARTED

Ask if any of the locations numbered on the map have familiar names. Does the center of San Antonio resemble the town you live in? How is it different?

DISCUSS

Talk about the map and the captions, and ask questions. Sample questions:

El centro de San Antonio
Aquí está el centro de San Antonio.
¿Qué hay en el centro?
¿Tiene muchos o pocos lugares históricos?
¿Hay lugares históricos en nuestro pueblo?

La plaza del Mercado
¿Qué hace la gente en la plaza del Mercado?
¿Qué más hay aquí?

El Paseo del Río
¿Dónde está el Paseo del Río?
¿Qué tiene?
¿Qué es un taxi acuático?

Centro de Información para visitantes
¿Dónde está el Centro de Información?
¿Quién usa el Centro de Información?

La Plaza de El Álamo
¿Qué hay en la Plaza de El Álamo?
¿Qué lugar en la Plaza es famoso en la historia de Texas?

El Hemisfair Arena
¿Es el centro de convenciones un edificio antiguo?

La Torre de las Américas
¿Cuántos pisos tiene la Torre de las Américas?
¿Cómo es la vista desde aquí?

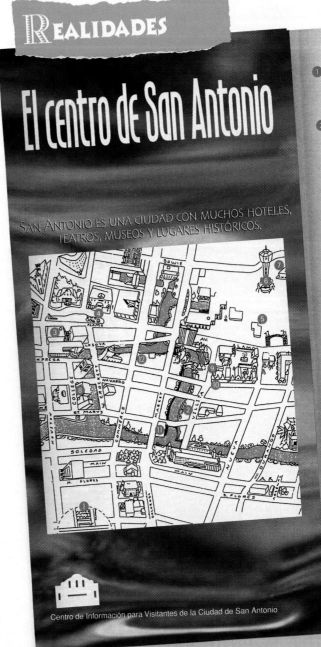

REALIDADES

El centro de San Antonio

SAN ANTONIO ES UNA CIUDAD CON MUCHOS HOTELES, TEATROS, MUSEOS Y LUGARES HISTÓRICOS.

① LA PLAZA DEL MERCADO
Esta plaza es un lugar importante para celebraciones. Hay tiendas de artesanías y restaurantes típicos.

② EL PASEO DEL RÍO
Este lugar popular está en el centro de la ciudad. Hay muchas tiendas y cafés al aire libre. ¿Te gustaría pasear por el río en un taxi acuático? ¡Es muy divertido!

③ EL CENTRO DE INFORMACIÓN PARA VISITANTES
El Centro de Información de San Antonio está en el 317 de la Plaza de El Álamo. Horario: de 8:30 a.m. a 5:00 p.m. todos los días. Tel. (512) 555-9145.

④ LA PLAZA DE EL ÁLAMO
En esta plaza están el centro comercial Rivercenter y El Álamo. El Álamo es el lugar más famoso de la historia de Texas.

⑤ EL HEMISFAIR PLAZA
El Hemisfair Plaza es un centro de convenciones.

⑥ LA TORRE DE LAS AMÉRICAS
La famosa Torre de las Américas tiene 75 pisos. Desde aquí hay una vista panorámica de San Antonio. ¡Es sensacional!

OTROS LUGARES...

⑦ EL INSTITUTO DE CULTURAS TEJANAS

⑧ EL HOTEL LA MANSIÓN DEL RÍO

⑨ EL TEATRO RÍO ARNESON

⑩ EL AUDITORIO DE CONVENCIONES VILLITA

⑪ LA BIBLIOTECA CENTRAL

⑫ EL RESTAURANTE CASA RÍO

Centro de Información para Visitantes de la Ciudad de San Antonio

112

MEETING INDIVIDUAL NEEDS

Reaching All Students

For Auditory Learners
Take turns asking questions about places. For example: *¿Dónde hay taxis acuáticos?*

For Visual Learners
Make flashcards with pictures of places on one side and the names on the other. Quiz each other in small groups or pairs.

For Kinesthetic Learners
Volunteers act out simple statements by class members. Example: *Melisa está al lado de Gerardo y a la derecha de Nati.*

A. Di qué lugar te gustaría visitar. ¿Por qué?

Me gustaría visitar la Plaza de El Álamo porque es un lugar histórico.

B. Estás en el Centro de Información para Visitantes. ¿Cómo vas a cada lugar? Da direcciones.

Para ir al restaurante Casa Río, sigue derecho por la avenida Álamo y después dobla a la derecha en la calle Commerce.

¿Al hotel La Mansión del Río?

¿A la Biblioteca Central?

¿A la Torre de las Américas y al Hemisfair Plaza?

¿Al Teatro Río Arneson?

C. Paseas en taxi acuático por el río San Antonio. Di qué edificios hay.

A la izquierda está la Biblioteca Central.
A la derecha está el Auditorio de Convenciones Villita.

¿CIERTO O FALSO?

Di qué oraciones son ciertas y cuáles son falsas. Corrige las oraciones falsas.

1. El Instituto de Culturas Tejanas está al lado de la Torre de las Américas.
2. El Auditorio de Convenciones Villita está detrás del Teatro Río Arneson.
3. El Hemisfair Plaza está a la izquierda del Instituto de Culturas Tejanas.
4. El Centro de Información está lejos de la Plaza de El Álamo.
5. La Plaza del Mercado está cerca del Hemisfair Plaza.

¿SABES QUE...?

The **Paseo del Río** is a place where you can take a walking tour along the bank of the San Antonio River. As you stroll along, you will see markers and monuments of the city's rich history as well as its modern, bustling business district. For a change of pace, you can enjoy the scenery by boat!

porque están muy lejos del Centro de Información. Dobla a la derecha por la Avenida de el Alamo, dobla a la izquierda en la calle Market hasta la calle Bowie. Allí, dobla a la derecha.

Para ir al teatro Río Arneson, doble a la derecha por la avenida de El Álamo, dobla a la derecha en la calle Market y después dobla a la izquierda en la calle N. Presa. El teatro está al lado del río. Allí está también el Auditorio de Convenciones Villita.

C. You are taking the river tour. Describe the buildings you see along the way.
Answers: See models on student page.
Analysis: Give each other directions from one point on the map try to follow them.

¿Cierto o falso?

Individual Activity: Using a Map
Use the map to decide if the sentences are true or false. Correct false statements.
1. *Cierto.*
2. *Cierto.*
3. *Cierto.*
4. *Falso. El Centro de Información está cerca de la Plaza de El Álamo.*
5. *Falso. La Plaza del Mercado está lejos del Hemisfair Plaza.*
Challenge: Write false statements and exchange them with others. Correct one another's sentences.

CHECK

Point to the map and ask students:
• *¿Qué lugar en San Antonio te gustaría visitar?*
• *¿Qué lugares están al lado del río?*
• *¿Qué está cerca de la Torre de las Américas?*

PORTFOLIO
Have students draw simple pictures or create collages that illustrate location expressions.

113

ACTIVITIES

Habla del mapa de San Antonio

Pair Activity: Conversing
A. Say what place on the map you would like to visit and why.
B. You are at the Information Center (3). Take turns asking and giving directions to the places on the list.

Possible Answers:
See model on student page.
Para ir al hotel La Mansión del Río, dobla a la derecha por la avenida de El Álamo, dobla a la derecha en la calle Crockett y dobla a la derecha en la calle Navarro. El hotel está al lado de la calle College.
La Biblioteca Central está lejos del Centro de Información para ir a pie. En coche o en taxi, dobla a la derecha por la avenida de El Álamo. Después dobla a la drecha en la calle Market hasta la calle St. Mary's. La Biblioteca está al lado del río.
Para ir al Hemisfair Arena, a la Torre de las Américas, al Instituto de Culturas Tejanas y al parque Hemisfair tienes que ir en taxi

Para hispanohablantes

Hide an object in the classroom while one non-Spanish speaking student is outside. Spanish speakers take turns giving directions.

Communicative Objectives

To talk about:
- the rooms of a house
- the furniture and objects in the house
- houses, using location expressions

Related Components

Activity Book	Transparencies
p. 53-54	Ch. 4: Palabras en acción
Cuaderno	
p. 31-32	**Tutor Page**
	p. 19

GETTING STARTED

Give the class a tour of the house in the picture. Pronounce the name of each room as you refer to it, and comment briefly on each place. Move your body and use gestures to indicate where you are in the house.

DISCUSS

Comment on the rooms and objects in the picture, using location expressions. For example:

En esta casa hay cocina, baño, sala, comedor y dormitorio.

Abajo, en la cocina está la estufa.

Para hispanohablantes

Some may use expressions other than the ones introduced in this chapter. Ask them to share those with the class. A few variations:

las afueras los suburbios
el apartamento el departamento
el cuarto de baño el excusado, el water
la cómoda el gavetero, la coqueta
el dormitorio la alcoba, la recámara, el cuarto, la habitación
la finca la estancia, la granja
el garage la cochera
la gasolinera la bomba de gasolina
el refrigerador la nevera
el ropero el armario
la sala la sala de estar, el living
el sofá el diván

① ¿Qué cuartos hay?

Haz una lista de los cuartos que hay en la casa.

> *la sala,...*

② Dentro y fuera de la casa

¿Qué hay fuera de la casa? ¿Y qué hay dentro? Habla con tu compañero(a).

> — *¿Qué hay fuera de la casa?*
> — *Hay un árbol,...*
> — *¿Y dentro?*
> — *Hay...*

③ ¿Qué es?

Escoge una cosa del dibujo. Di dónde está. Tu compañero(a) va a adivinar qué es.

> — *Está en la cocina. ¿Qué es?*
> — *Es el refrigerador.*

④ ¿Cómo es?

Habla con tu compañero(a) sobre los cuartos del dibujo.

> — *¿Cómo es el comedor?*
> — *Es pequeño.*
> — *¿Qué hay en el comedor?*
> — *Hay una mesa.*

114

For students having difficulty communicating about houses and families in them you might consider:
- **The tutor page:** pair the student with a native speaker or a more able student using the tutor page
- **Actividades:** see page 108C: *¡Qué familia!*

EL CUARTO DE BAÑO   **EL DORMITORIO**

el espejo

el inodoro

la cómoda

la bañera

¿Dónde está el teléfono?

Está en la sala, encima de la mesa.

los muebles

la cama

el escritorio

la radio

ARRIBA

ABAJO

la pared

LA COCINA

el fregadero

la estufa

la lámpara

el refrigerador

el lavaplatos

Está arriba, debajo de la cama.

el sillón

EL COMEDOR

la silla

la mesa

EL JARDÍN

Rufo

EL SÓTANO

---

5 **¿Dónde está...?**

Describe dónde está cada cuarto. Habla con tu compañero(a).

— ¿Dónde está el cuarto de baño?
— Está arriba, al lado del dormitorio.
— ¿Dónde está la cocina?
— Está...

6 **¿Dónde están las mascotas?**

Busca las mascotas en el dibujo y di dónde están.

El perro está fuera de la casa.

7 **Collage**

Haz un collage de diferentes tipos de casas. Identifica cada uno. Presenta el collage a la clase.

8 **Mi dormitorio**

¿Qué tienes en tu dormitorio? Escribe cinco oraciones.

Tengo una cama y una cómoda.
Tengo un escritorio delante de la ventana.
Tengo...

115

ACTIVITIES

1. Individual or Pair Activity
Make a list of the rooms in this house.
Analysis: When one partner names a piece of furniture, the other names the room where it is found.

2. Pair Activity
Use **dentro** and **fuera** to ask about objects inside or outside the house.
For Kinesthetic Learners: In pairs, take turns putting objects next to each other. Partners have to make a simple sentence describing the relationships. For example: *El lápiz está a la derecha del libro.*

3. Pair Activity
Pick an object in the drawing, say where it is, and have your partner identify it.
Analysis: Repeat the activity using objects in the classroom or school.

4. Pair Activity
Talk about one of the rooms in the house.
Application: Talk about a room in your house.

5. Pair Activity
Discuss where each room is located.
Application: Ask where rooms are in your partner's house.

6. Pair Activity
Tell your partner where the pets are in or outside the house.

7. Hands-On Activity
Make a collage of pictures of different kinds of houses. Identify each type. Present your collage to the class.
For Auditory Learners: Write the names of friends on stickers and tell others where to put them on the collage.

8. Writing Activity
Write five sentences describing what you have in your room.
Synthesis: Make up a skit in which you talk to one of your parents about what furniture you want in your room.

CHECK

- ¿Qué cuartos tiene esta casa?
- ¿Qué hay dentro de la sala de esta casa?
- ¿Dónde están la radio y el televisor?

PORTFOLIO
Draw a floor plan of your home. Instead of drawing the furniture, write the name of each piece where it belongs.

Communicative Objective
• to use **estar** to say where someone or something is

Related Components

Activity Book p. 55-56	Audio Tapes Listening: 3B, Seg. 3
Audio Book Script: Seg. 3 Activities: p. 37	Cuaderno p. 33
	Tutor Page p. 20

GETTING STARTED

As students enter the class, greet each one by asking *¿Cómo estás?* and *¿Y dónde estás?* Elicit such responses as: *Estoy bien* or *Estoy en la clase.*

Language in Context
Read aloud the questions and answers about the church. Run through the **estar** paradigm, and write examples. Remind students that **ser** and **estar** both mean "to be." Explain that **estar** is used to talk about location and also to describe characteristics of something or someone that are not lasting. **Ser**, on the other hand, is used to describe more permanent characteristics—and time. To illustrate this, ask students to help explain the distinction between *¿Cómo estás?* (How are you?) and *¿Cómo eres?* (What are you like?)

DISCUSS

One way to introduce **estar** and location is to bring a toy animal to class. Give it a name, put it in different places, and ask simple location questions that review previous vocabulary and introduce some of this chapter's vocabulary.
¿Dónde está Pepe? ¿Está cerca de la puerta? ¿Y ahora? ¿Está encima del escritorio o al lado del escritorio?
¿Dónde estoy, delante de Pepe o detrás de Pepe? ¿Y ahora?
¿Quiénes están a la derecha de Pepe? ¿y a la izquierda?
¿Quiénes están entre Pepe y Juan?
¿Y ahora, Pepe está arriba o abajo del escritorio?
¿Dónde estoy, a la derecha o a la izquierda de Pepe?

PARA COMUNICARNOS MEJOR
¿DÓNDE ESTÁ?

¡OJO!

The word *de* followed by *el* becomes *del*.

La farmacia está detrás del correo.

To say where something or someone is, use the verb *estar*.

— ¿Dónde está la iglesia? — Está cerca del Centro de Convenciones.	Where is the church? It is near the Convention Center.
— Y tú, ¿dónde estás? — Estoy en el Café Rex, al lado de la biblioteca.	And where are you? I am at the Café Rex, next to the library.

Here is the verb *estar* in the present tense. Note that the *yo* form is irregular: *estoy*. All the other forms have an accent except the *nosotros(as)* form.

estar (to be)

yo	**estoy**	nosotros(as)	estamos
tú	estás	vosotros(as)	estáis
usted	está	ustedes	están
él/ella	está	ellos/ellas	están

Here are some expressions you can use with *estar* to show location:

abajo *downstairs*	**dentro de** *inside*
arriba *upstairs*	**detrás de** *behind*
a la izquierda de *to the left of*	**en** *in, on, at*
a la derecha de *to the right of*	**encima de** *on top of*
al lado de *next to*	**entre** *between*
cerca de *near*	**fuera de** *outside*
debajo de *under*	**lejos de** *far from*
delante de *in front of*	

116

For students having difficulty using **estar,** you might consider:
• **The tutor page:** Pair the student with a native speaker or more able student using the tutor page
• **Actividades:** see page 108C: *¿Cómo es la casa?*

1 En un teléfono público

Mira el mapa. Escoge un teléfono y explícale a tu compañero(a) dónde estás.

Hola, María. Estoy en la calle Salinas, entre una librería y un cine.

2 El vecindario de la escuela

¿Dónde está...? Pregúntale a tu compañero(a).

— ¿Dónde está el correo?
— Está al lado de la biblioteca.

1. el correo
2. la tienda de videos
3. la farmacia
4. la iglesia
5. el teléfono público
6. el cine

3 Muebles Confortables

Mira el anuncio. ¿Dónde están las cosas?

El sillón está entre el escritorio y la lámpara.

1. el sillón
2. la lámpara
3. la computadora
4. los libros
5. los estantes
6. el sofá

Muebles Confortables

Avenida Alameda n°510, El Paso, Teléfono 555-7700

117

ACTIVITIES

Students use **estar** to say where something or someone is located.

1. Pair Activity
Choose one of the telephones on the map and describe where you are.
Possible Answers:
Estoy en la calle Salinas cerca de la calle Santa Rosa y al lado de un cine.
Estoy en la calle Salinas entre las calles San Jóse y Santa Rosa.
Estoy en la calle Santa Rosa cerca del correo.
Synthesis: Describe the location of an imaginary telephone booth in or near the school for others to guess.

2. Pair Activity
Ask and answer questions about where each place is in your neighborhood.
Answers: See model on student page.

3. Individual or Pair Activity
Give the location of items in the advertisement. Various answers are possible for some items.
Possible Answers:
1. See model on student page.
2. *La lámpara está al lado del sillón.*
3. *La computadora está encima del escritorio.*
4. *Los libros están en los estantes.*
5. *Los estantes están a la derecha del sofá.*
6. *El sofá está entre el escritorio y los estantes.*
Application: Use **estar** and location expressions to tell volunteers where to find an object.

CHECK

- *¿Dónde está la cocina en tu casa?*
- *¿Dónde estoy ahora?*
- *¿Dónde están tus libros?*
- *¿Qué está encima de mi escritorio?*
- *¿Quiénes de nosotros estamos cerca de la puerta?*

LOG BOOK
Have students write sentences that describe some of the differences between the ways that **estar** and **ser** are used.

Communicative Objectives

Use possessive adjectives to:
• say what people own
• talk about relationships

Related Components

Activity Book p. 57-58	**Audio Tapes** Listening: 3B, Seg. 4
Audio Book Script: Seg.4 Activities: p. 38	**Cuaderno** p. 34
	Tutor Page p. 21

 GETTING STARTED

Indicate the drawing and ask whose room it probably is. Ask how teenagers' rooms are different from the rooms of their parents or younger siblings.

Language in Context

Use students' books and other objects to review **mi** and **tu**. Begin mixing in **su**, **sus**, and **nuestro**. For example:
¿Es mi libro? No. ¿Es tu libro? No.
Es el libro de él. Es su libro.
Review the possessive adjectives in the paradigms. Remind students to use singular adjectives with singular nouns, and plural adjectives with plural nouns.
Point out that **nuestro** also has masculine and feminine forms that correspond to the noun that follows.

 **DISCUSS**

Review vocabulary from previous chapters and introduce some of this chapter's vocabulary with questions and statements that use possessive adjectives.
¿Dónde está la casa de tu familia?
Mi familia y yo vivimos en un apartamento.
Conocemos bien nuestros vecinos.
¿Conocen Uds. a sus vecinos?
Nuestros vecinos tienen un perro grande.
¿Tienen perros tus vecinos?
¿Y tu familia, tiene un perro?
¿Cómo se llama su perro?
Me gustaría tener tres perros, pero nuestro apartamento es pequeño.

PARA COMUNICARNOS MEJOR

¿QUÉ TIENEN EN SU DORMITORIO?

To talk about things that people own and relationships among people, use possessive adjectives.

Mi hermana y yo tenemos dos camas, un escritorio y muchos libros.	My sister and I have two beds, a desk, and many books.
Nuestro dormitorio es grande.	Our bedroom is big.

☐ Remember to use ***mi***, ***tu***, and ***su*** when the noun that follows is singular, and ***mis***, ***tus***, and ***sus*** when the noun that follows is plural.

		singular		plural
my	mi		mis	
your	tu	} casa/cuarto	tus	} casas/cuartos
your, his, her	su		sus	

☐ ***Su(s)*** can also mean *their*.

Mis primos viven en El Paso. Su casa es grande y muy bonita.	My cousins live in El Paso. Their house is big and very pretty.

☐ ***Nuestro***, ***nuestra*** and ***nuestros***, ***nuestras*** (*our*) have the same gender and number as the noun that follows them.

	singular	plural
masculine	nuestro vecino	nuestros vecinos
feminine	nuestra bicicleta	nuestras bicicletas

118

For students having difficulty using possessive adjectives, you might consider:
• **The tutor page:** Pair the student with a native speaker or more able student using the tutor page
• **Actividades:** see page 108D: *¿Dónde está mi familia?*

1 Mi casa

¿Cómo es tu casa? Pregúntale a tu compañero(a).

— ¿Cómo es tu dormitorio?
— Mi dormitorio es pequeño. Tiene una cama y un escritorio.

1. dormitorio
2. cocina
3. cuarto de baño
4. sala
5. comedor
6. sótano

¿Cómo es...?
pequeño(a)
grande
moderno(a)
feo
bonito
viejo(a)

2 Su familia

Habla de la familia de personas que conoces.

Mi amiga vive en Amarillo. Su hermano vive en las afueras de El Paso.

1. mi amiga
2. mi primo y mi prima
3. mis vecinos
4. mi amigo
5. mis tíos

sus parientes
hermano   tíos
madrina   abuelos
primos   hermanas
hijo(a)

¿Dónde viven?
en las afueras de...
en el campo
en la ciudad
en una granja
en un apartamento
en una caravana

3 El festival del vecindario

A. Con tu compañero(a), contesten la siguiente encuesta sobre sus preferencias para un festival del vecindario.

Festival del vecindario Encuesta

Preferencias

lugar favorito para el festival	la plaza
música favorita	el rock
comida favorita	
postres favoritos	
actividades favoritas	
bebidas favoritas	

B. Hablen con otros estudiantes de sus preferencias para el festival.

— ¿Cuál es su lugar favorito?
— Nuestro lugar favorito es la plaza.
— ¿Cuál es su música favorita?
— Nuestra música favorita es el rock.

119

ACTIVITIES

Students **use** possessive adjectives to talk about things people own or relationships among people.

1. Pair Activity
Ask each other about these places in your homes.
Possible Answers:
1. See model on student page.
2. *Mi cocina es pequeña. Tiene una estufa blanca.*
3. *Mi cuarto de baño es azul. Tiene dos espejos.*
4. *Mi sala es bonita. Tiene una silla verde muy grande.*
5. *Mi comedor es amarillo. Tiene una mesa grande.*
6. *Mi sótano es feo. Tiene nuestras bicicletas.*

2. Pair Activity
Talk about the families of people you know. Use the lists for vocabulary.
Possible Answers:
1. See model on student page.
2. *Mi primo y mi prima viven en el campo. Sus abuelos viven en el centro.*
3. *Mis vecinos viven en un apartamento. Su hijo vive en una caravana.*
4. *Mi amigo vive en un apartamento. Su madrina vive en una casa.*
5. *Mis tíos viven en una granja. Sus primos viven en una garanja.*

3. Pair Activity
A. Students complete a survey on their preferences for a block or neighborhood party.
B. Discuss your answers with other pairs of students.
Answers: See models on student page. Suggest that students use the topics listed on the chart.

CHECK

• *¿Cuáles son tus lugares favoritos?*
• *¿Cuáles son los lugares favoritos de tu familia?*
• *¿Voy a cenar en mi casa o en su casa?*
• *¿De quién son estos libros?*
• *¿Cuáles son sus comidas favoritas?*

LOG BOOKS
Use possessive adjectives to write about your best friends and your favorite activities to do together.

Communicative Objective
• to talk about what you have to do, using **tener que**
• to talk about where things are

Related Components

Assessment Oral Proficiency: p. 24	16B, Ch. 4 **Conexiones** Chapter 4
Audio Book Script: Seg. 5 Activities: p. 39	**Magazine** Juntos en Texas
Audio Tapes Listening: 3B, Seg.5 Conexiones:	**Tutor Page** p. 22

GETTING STARTED

At this point, students should be able to use **estar**, **tener que**, possessive adjectives, and all of the chapter vocabulary correctly. Ask students if they recognize the phrase in this section's title. If not, can they figure out what it means? Ask for sayings about homes or houses in English. (A few: My home is your home; there's no place like home; home is where the heart is.) Have volunteers read aloud the letters on the student page. Ask comprehension questions.

APPLY

1. Individual Activity
Make a list of things you have to do before a friend comes to visit.
Possible Answers:
cocinar, hacer una piñata, decorar la casa, invitar a los amigos
Analysis: Decide which of the things on the list you like or dislike doing, and replace **tener que** with **me gusta/no me gusta**.

2. Individual or Pair Activity
Tell your friend in which room he or she will be sleeping, and how to get there. Explain where other rooms are.
Note: Students should use their own homes for this exercise, or you may wish to draw a floor plan on the board to help them.
For Kinesthetic Learners: Pick an object in the classroom and direct someone to it using **estar** and location expressions.

3. Individual or Pair Activity
Look at the ads in the El Paso newspaper and plan your weekend.

SITUACIONES
MI CASA ES TU CASA

Querida Ana:
Este fin de semana voy a ir a El Paso y me gustaría mucho conocer tu vecindario. Saludos.
Sara

Querida Sara:
¡Qué bien que vienes a El Paso! Tienes que venir a nuestra casa. Este fin de semana hay muchas cosas para hacer en nuestra ciudad. Hay un mercado al aire libre, conciertos, fiestas y mucho más. ¡Hasta pronto!
Ana

PARA TU REFERENCIA

alemanes
German

antes de
before

la feria del libro
book fair

gratis
free

el patinaje
rollerblading

todas las edades
all ages

 Antes de la visita

Haz una lista de las cosas que tienes que hacer antes de la visita de un amigo(a).

Tengo que comprar refrescos, tengo que...

2 Bienvenido(a) a mi casa

Explícale a tu amigo(a) dónde está su dormitorio y otras partes de la casa.

Tu dormitorio está arriba, a la derecha. Yo comparto el dormitorio de la izquierda con mi hermano. El cuarto de baño está al lado de nuestro dormitorio. ¿Quieres usar el teléfono? Está en...

120

Possible Answers:
Sábado por la mañana: patinar en el parque.
Sábado por la tarde: comer en La Cascada.
Sábado por la noche: ir al cine.
Challenge: Review your plans. Write sentences about what you must do in order to do each activity. Use **tener que**.

For students having difficulty talking about what they have to do or where things are, you might consider:
• **The tutor page:** Pair the student with a native speaker or more able student using the tutor page
• **Actividades:** see page 108D: *Mi telenovela*

- ¿Qué tienes que hacer hoy?
- ¿Dónde está mi libro de español?
- ¿Tienes que ir a la escuela los sábados?

LOG BOOK

Write about everything you will do on Saturday.

Background

El Paso is located about as far west as one can go and still be in Texas, near the point where the Rio Grande stops being the border and wanders off into New Mexico. Although its population is only about half a million, El Paso is one of the larger Texas cities.

The first recorded mention of the mountain pass at El Paso is from 1581, when a Spanish expedition passed through to explore the north. It was not given a name, however, until seventeen years later. The first Spanish mission in the region, Nuestra Señora de Guadalupe, was built on the southern side of the river in 1659, in what is now called Ciudad Juárez. It was not until 1691 that a mission was built on the northern side.

Para hispanohablantes

Assist other students with their Log Book activities.

 3 ¿Qué hacemos en El Paso?

Miren los anuncios del periódico de El Paso. Decidan el plan para el fin de semana.

	sábado	domingo
por la mañana	patinar en...	
por la tarde	jugar al béisbol	
por la noche		

33

RESTAURANTES EN EL PASO

$ no muy caro; $$ muy caro

Americanos $
Café Río, 101 S. El Paso
La Cascada, 1600 Airway Blvd. $$

Mexicanos $$
El Rancho Escondido, 14549 Montana
Taco Salsa, 3535 N. Mesa $

Alemanes $
Schnitzel Factory, 1550 Hawkins Blvd.
Günther's Edelweiss, 11055 Gateway West $$

JUAN GABRIEL presenta su nuevo disco *Gracias por esperar* este sábado a las 8:00 p.m.

CINES EN EL PASO
Cine Galaxy: *La familia Pérez,*
4:30, 6:30, 8:30 y 10:30

Cine Embassy: *Batman Forever,*
3:45, 5:30, 7:30 y 10:00

Este fin de semana
feria del libro
en tu biblioteca local,
de 10:00 a.m. a 4:00 p.m.

sábado

10:00 a.m. Patinaje con música en el parque.

12:30 a.m. Clases de fotografía gratis para jóvenes de 12 a 18 años. Centro de cultura La Familia.

6:00 p.m. Teatro en el parque.

7:00 p.m. Fiesta en la discoteca Sol.

domingo

11:00 a.m. a 6:00 p.m. Mercado en la calle Río Grande.

1:30 p.m. a 6:00 p.m. Exposición de arte "Jóvenes Hispanos" en el Museo de Arte de El Paso (tel. 555-4040).

4:00 p.m. Béisbol para todos con la Comunidad de El Paso.

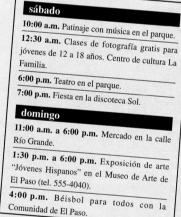

¿SABES QUE...?

El Paso (originally called **El Paso del Norte**) is a city in west Texas, close to the Rio Grande and the border with Mexico. Four hundred years ago, Spanish conquistadors built the last section of **El Camino Real**, or the Royal Road, through this site. **El Camino Real** connected Mexico City with Santa Fe, and it was the longest road in North America when it was built. **El Paso** is still strongly tied to Mexico. A large portion of the city's population is Hispanic, and many of its important events are sponsored by local Hispanic organizations.

121

✔ CULTURE NOTE

Juan Gabriel is a talented musician with a following in both Mexico and the US. The singer/composer's music ranges from soft rock to *norteñas* to commercial ballads.

 ▶▶▶ INTERNET LINK

Background on El Paso: http://cs.utep.edu:80/elpaso/ephistory.html

121

Communicative Objectives

to talk about:
- rooms in a house
- household objects
- where things are

Related Components

Transparencies	Video: Tape/Book
Ch. 4: Para resolver	Unit 2: Seg. 2

Search to frame 1212900

GETTING STARTED

Ask what they think the title means. Tell students what your favorite room of your home is and why you like it. Then ask what room(s) they like best and why.

APPLY

PASO 1: Describan el plano
In groups, use the floor plan to answer these questions:
- How many rooms are there? What are they?
- What furniture is in each room? Make a list. Where is each piece of furniture?

Possible Answers:
- *Hay ocho cuartos. Hay cuatro cuartos abajo y cuatro cuartos arriba. Abajo están el comedor, la cocina, una sala y un cuarto de baño. Arriba están dos dormitorios, otra sala y otro baño.*
- See floor plan.

Locations:
Some Possible Answers:
El comedor: *Las sillas están cerca de la mesa.*
La sala: *Las sillas es tán al lado del sofá.*
El dormitorio 1: *Las mesas de noche están al lado de la cama.*

PASO 2: ¿Dónde está su casa ideal?
Say where your ideal house would be.
- Would it be in the country, city, or suburbs?
- What would you like to have in your neighborhood? (Parks, libraries, movie theaters, pizzerias, etc.)

Possible Answers:
- *Mi casa ideal está en el campo.*
- *En el vecindario hay un parque y una taquería.*

Analysis: Ask a partner other questions about the floor plan, such as:

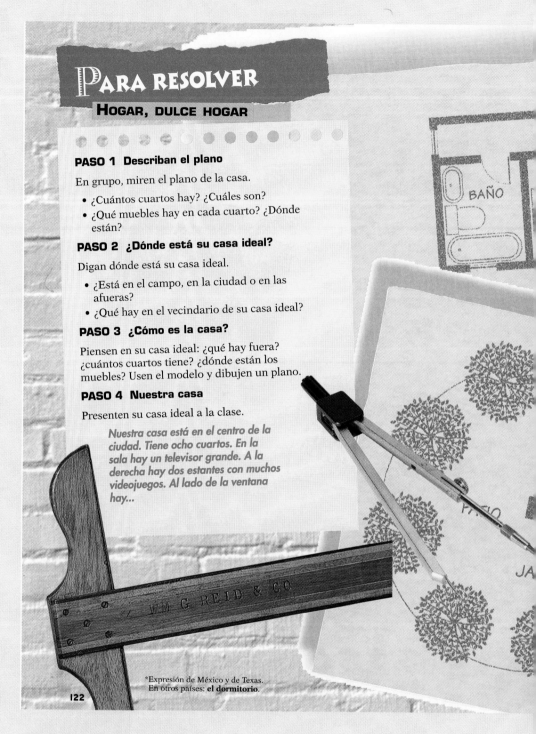

PARA RESOLVER

HOGAR, DULCE HOGAR

PASO 1 Describan el plano

En grupo, miren el plano de la casa.

- ¿Cuántos cuartos hay? ¿Cuáles son?
- ¿Qué muebles hay en cada cuarto? ¿Dónde están?

PASO 2 ¿Dónde está su casa ideal?

Digan dónde está su casa ideal.

- ¿Está en el campo, en la ciudad o en las afueras?
- ¿Qué hay en el vecindario de su casa ideal?

PASO 3 ¿Cómo es la casa?

Piensen en su casa ideal: ¿qué hay fuera? ¿cuántos cuartos tiene? ¿dónde están los muebles? Usen el modelo y dibujen un plano.

PASO 4 Nuestra casa

Presenten su casa ideal a la clase.

Nuestra casa está en el centro de la ciudad. Tiene ocho cuartos. En la sala hay un televisor grande. A la derecha hay dos estantes con muchos videojuegos. Al lado de la ventana hay...

BAÑO

*Expresión de México y de Texas. En otros países: **el dormitorio**.*

122

¿Cuántas ventanas hay en la sala?

PASO 3: ¿Cómo es la casa?
Imagine your ideal house. Decide what is outside, how many rooms it will have, and where the furniture will go. Draw a floor plan.
For Kinesthetic Learners: Give a guided tour of your ideal home.

PASO 4: Nuestra casa
Describe your ideal house to the class.
Answers: See model on student page.
For Auditory Learners: Read aloud the sample description. Have your partner transcribe it. Check your partner's text and correct mistakes.

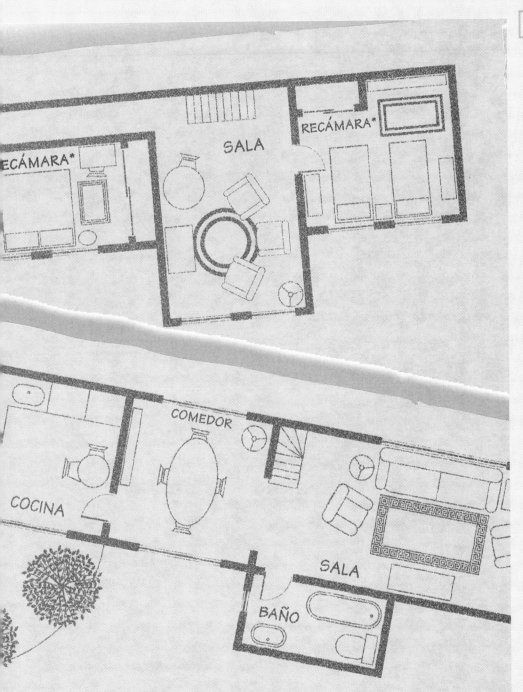

SALA

RECÁMARA*

ECÁMARA*

COMEDOR

COCINA

SALA

BAÑO

LOG BOOK
Use location expressions to describe where a room in your home is.

House Vocabulary
attic *el ático*
banister *el pasamano*
brick *el ladrillo*
ceiling *el techo*
cement *el cemento*
chimney *la chimenea*
curtains *las cortinas*
door *la puerta*
doorknob *el tirador, el pomo*
first floor *la planta baja*
floor *el piso, la planta*
keyhole *el ojo de la cerradura*
lock *la cerradura*
maildrop *el buzón*
plaster *el yeso*
roof *el techo, la cubierta*
sash *el marco*
second floor *el primer piso*
shutter *la contraventana*
stairs *las escaleras*
stucco *el estuco*
terrace *la terraza*
window *la ventana*
windowpane *el cristal*
wood *la madera*

Para hispanohablantes

In a group, plan and draw a two or three-family home.

ENTÉRATE

Objective
Cultural: to learn about San Antonio's missions and the Spanish influence on the city.

Related Components

Audio Tapes	Magazine
Conexiones: 16B, Ch. 4	Juntos en Texas
Conexiones Chapter 4	

GETTING STARTED

Ask which states have names that come from Spanish. List the states on the board as they are named and discuss why they have Spanish names.

California: the name of an island in the Spanish romance *Las Serges de Esplandian,* which was written in 1510
Colorado: "red," first applied to the muddy Colorado River
Florida: Ponce de Leon arrived on *Pascua Florida,* Easter Sunday, 1513
Montana: "mountainous"
Nevada: "snowy," for its mountains (Sierra Nevada)
Note: Texas, Arizona, and (New) Mexico come from Native American names.

DISCUSS

Using the Text
Read aloud the introduction to "El Camino de las Misiones.". Ask both comprehension and critical-thinking questions.
Suggestions:
¿Dónde es evidente la herencia hispana?
¿Cuántas misiones hay en San Antonio?
¿Dónde están situadas las misiones?
¿Cuál es la misión más importante?
¿Cuántos años tiene el acueducto?
¿Es grande la ciudad de San Antonio?

CHECK

Te toca a ti

Answers:
1. *la presencia española en San Antonio.*
2. *su religión, su cultura y nuevos métodos de agricultura a los habitantes de la zona.*
3. *a lo largo del río.*
4. *"El Álamo".*
5. *lleva agua a las granjas locales.*

ENTÉRATE

EL CAMINO DE LAS MISIONES°

La herencia hispana es muy importante en Texas. Es evidente en los nombres de sus ciudades, calles y pueblos, y también en los nombres de sus habitantes. Las misiones son un ejemplo de la presencia española en San Antonio. Las misiones eran° comunidades° fundadas° en el siglo° XVIII. Allí los misioneros° españoles enseñaban° religión, cultura y métodos de agricultura a los habitantes de la zona. En San Antonio hay cinco misiones españolas. Están situadas a lo largo° del río.

La misión más importante es la misión de San Antonio Valero, que hoy se llama El Álamo. Está en el centro de la ciudad y es un museo histórico.

En la misión de San Francisco de la Espada hay un acueducto de 200 años que todavía lleva° agua a las granjas locales.

a lo largo de *along*
el camino de las misiones *mission trail*
las comunidades *communities*
enseñaban *taught*
eran *(they) were*
fundadas *founded*
los misioneros *missionaries*
el siglo *century*
todavía lleva *still carries*

124

¿SABES QUE...?

The five Spanish missions in San Antonio are San Antonio Valero, Concepción, San Juan Capistrano, San Francisco de la Espada y San José. These communities were the foundation of the city in the 18th century. Today, San Antonio has become one of the ten largest cities in the United States.

TE TOCA A TI

Completa las oraciones.
1. Las misiones son un ejemplo de...
2. Los misioneros españoles enseñaban...
3. Las cinco misiones de San Antonio están situadas...
4. La misión más importante se llama...
5. El acueducto de San Francisco de la Espada todavía...

PORTFOLIO
Research what life was like in an early Spanish mission in the southwestern United States. Write a brief report.

Para hispanohablantes
Make a list of names of streets and other places in your town or state that have Spanish names. Find out why those places were given those names, and report to the class.

 CULTURE NOTE

The five missions form the 850-acre San Antonio Missions National Historic Park, which was established in 1978.

▶▶▶ INTERNET LINK
The San Antonio Missions Home Page: http://www.nps.gov/parklists/index/saan.html

VOCABULARIO TEMÁTICO

¿Dónde vives?
Where do you live?

las afueras *suburbs*
el campo *countryside*
la caravana *trailer*
el edificio de apartamentos
  apartment building
la granja *farm*
el pueblo *town*
el rancho *ranch*

¿Qué hay en tu vecindario?
What's in your neighborhood?

el correo *post office*
la gasolinera *gas station*
el hotel *hotel*

Fuera de la casa
Outside the house

el árbol *tree*
el garaje *garage*
el jardín *garden*

Dentro de la casa
Inside the house

la cocina *kitchen*
el comedor *dining room*
el cuarto *room*
el cuarto de baño *bathroom*
el dormitorio *bedroom*
los muebles *furniture*
la pared *wall*

la puerta *door*
la sala *living room*
el sótano *basement*
la ventana *window*

En la cocina
In the kitchen

la estufa *stove*
el fregadero *sink*
el lavaplatos *dishwasher*
el refrigerador *refrigerator*

En la sala
In the living room

la alfombra *rug*
la lámpara *lamp*
la mesa *table*
la radio *radio*
el sillón *armchair*
el sofá *sofa*
el televisor *television set*

En el dormitorio
In the bedroom

la cama *bed*
la cómoda *chest of drawers*
el espejo *mirror*
los estantes *shelves*
la mesa de noche *night table*
el ropero *closet*

En el cuarto de baño
In the bathroom

la bañera *bathtub*
el inodoro *toilet*

¿Dónde está?
Where is it?

al lado de *next to*
a la derecha de *to the right of*
a la izquierda de *to the left of*
abajo *downstairs*
arriba *upstairs*
cerca de *near*
debajo de *under the*
delante de *in front of*
dentro de *inside of*
detrás de *behind*
en *in/on/at*
encima de *on top of*
entre *between*
fuera de *outside of*
lejos de *far from*

Expresiones y palabras

Dobla a la derecha. *Turn right.*
Dobla a la izquierda. *Turn left.*
Sigue derecho por la calle...
  Keep straight along . . . Street
Tengo que/tienes que...
  I have to/you have to . . .
del *of the*
nuestro(a), nuestros(as) *our*
su(s) *your/their*

Expresiones de Tejas

la recámara *bedroom*
tejano(a) *Texan*

LA CONEXIÓN INGLÉS-ESPAÑOL

The Spanish word **granja** is a cognate of the English *grange*, an old word for *farm*. Notice that the *j* in the Spanish corresponds to the *g* in the English.

Look at the **Vocabulario temático**. What other pairs of cognates show this same *j-g* pattern? How could the pattern help you figure out the meaning of certain Spanish words?

Objectives
- to review vocabulary
- to correctly pronounce words containing the letter "g"

Related Components

Activity Book	Audio Tapes
Chapter Review: p. 59-60	Listening: 3B, Seg. 6
Assessment	Assessment: 14B, Ch. 4
Listening Script: p. 12	**Cuaderno**
Chapter Test: p. 63-68	p. 35-36
Audio Book	
Script: Seg. 6	
Activities p. 40	

Pronunciation: "g"

- Before an "i" or "e," the "g" is pronounced somewhat like the "h" in the English word "hill." The difference between the two sounds is that the Spanish "h" is typically pronounced with greater friction. This Spanish sound can be approximated by narrowing the distance between the back of the tongue and the roof of the mouth while pronouncing the English "h" sound.

agencia, agente, álgebra, gitano, agitación

- The letter "g" is pronounced like the "g" in the English word "go" when:• it precedes an "l" or "r" *globo, granja*

- comes at the beginning of a sentence or after a pause and is followed by an "a," "o," or "u."
Gomez es un apellido común.
Los mejores alumnos son Machado, Gomez, y Tapias.

- it is preceded by an "n" and followed by "a," "o," or "u."
tengo, vengo, Durango, angustia

- In all other situations before "a," "o," or "u," the hard "g" is pronounced midway between an English "h" and "g." To produce this sound, position your mouth as if to say "g" (as in "go"), but allow the air to escape slowly as in the pronunciation of an English "h:"
la gasolinera, fregadero, amigos, te gustaría, hago

LOG BOOK
Have students write their own tongue twisters.

ADELANTE

Objectives

Pre-Reading Strategy: to elicit information from photographs
Cultural: to learn about the Mexican-American music of Texas
Interdisciplinary: to learn about different musical styles

Related Components

CD ROM Unit 2: Adelante	**Video:** Tape/Book Unit 2: Seg. 4
Magazine Juntos en Texas	

GETTING STARTED

Ask if anyone listens to Tex-Mex or Tejano music. If so, ask that person to describe it. If possible, play a Tex-Mex or Tejano tape and ask students what kinds of music they think influenced these musicians.
For influences and recordings, see *About the Music,* and *Music & Musicians* below.

Using the Video

Show Segment 4 of the Unit 2 video, the introduction to Tex-Mex music.

Antes de leer

After students look at the photos on these pages, read aloud the questions. Make sure they understand what they are to do. Discuss each of the answers. See page 129 for more on instruments.

About the Music

Tex-Mex music—often called *conjunto*—has strong roots in Mexico's lively *norteño* and sentimental *ranchera* music. One of the major influences is the polka, brought to Texas by German immigrants. That tradition contributed both the accordion and the danceable "oompah" backbeat.
Other popular forms that *conjunto* music encompasses include the syncopated *cumbia,* originally from Colombia, and the slow *corrido* ballad.
Tejano is also a form of *conjunto,* with a younger and more urban sound. In this branch, the synthesizer has replaced the accordion, and rock is a primary influence.

ANTES DE LEER

Texas es un centro musical muy importante. Todos los años en San Antonio hay un festival de conjuntos° tejanos, un festival de mariachis y el famoso *Texas Music Awards.*

Mira las fotos de las páginas 126-129. Contesta:

* ¿Conoces la música tejana?
* ¿Conoces a los cantantes?°
* ¿Conoces los instrumentos que tocan?

los cantantes *singers*
los conjuntos *bands*

126

Adelante Components

Activity Book p. 61-64	**Audio Tapes** Adelante: 9A, 9B	**Magazine** Juntos en Texas	**Video: Tape/Book** Unit 2: Seg. 4-5
Assessment Portfolio: p. 35-36	**CD ROM** Unit 2: Adelante	**Transparencies** Unit 2: Adelante	

◄ Campanas de América son los reyes° de la música mariachi en San Antonio. ¡Son padrísimos! Tocan música mexicana tradicional y moderna.

◄ Flaco Jiménez es un acordeonista y cantante tejano de fama internacional. Él recibió° dos premios Grammy.

◄ La guitarra es uno de los instrumentos típicos de la música mariachi.

los reyes *kings*
recibió *received*

127

Campanas de América

This traditional mariachi band has also recorded Tex-Mex music.
Geography Link: Why does the mariachi group call itself **Campanas de America?** (Because the name "América" refers to all countries in the western hemisphere.) Have students use a dictionary to find the terms for people from the United States (**estadounidense**), Canada (**canadiense**) and the United States or Canada (**norteamericano/a**).

Flaco Jiménez

Flaco (Leonardo) Jiménez, born in San Antonio in 1939, is a musician and song-writer who showed the world that the accordion can be an exciting instrument. His father, Santiago Jiménez, Sr., helped shape the sound of conjunto. Flaco has worked with Willie Nelson, Bob Dylan, Carlos Santana, and others.

Music & Musicians

Some other Tex-Mex musicians:
The Texas Tornados is a group of veteran rockers that includes accordionist Flaco Jiménez and singer Freddy Fender. Their album, *Texas Tornados* (Warner), is available in English and Spanish.
Los Lobos is a California group, but they also play norteño and conjunto music, which they blend with a rock sound. Paul Simon included them on his album *Graceland.* They hit the big time in 1988, performing for the Ritchie Valens bio-film *La Bamba.*
Mazz, from Brownsville, is one of the best Tejano rock-conjunto bands. They record on the EMI Latin label.
Selena was headed for national success when she was murdered in 1995. Her last record, *Dreaming of You* (EMI Latin), hit number one on the national pop charts.
La Diferenzia was named "Best New Artist" at the Texas Music Awards of 1995. They record with Arista.
Elida Reyna sings border music in both tra-ditional and modern styles. Her album *Atrévete* gives a pop touch to Tex-Mex.

■ DISCUSS

Using the Photos

Texas Music Awards

These awards are given annually in San Antonio. About 25 groups perform, and the concert has been shown on television. The date varies.
¿Te gustaría ir a los Texas Music Awards?
¿A quién te gustaría oír cantar en los Texas Music Awards?

Tell the class what you know about conjunto or other Hispanic music.

The Tejano Music Web Page: http://ra.oc.com:2157/tejano/tejano.html

Objectives

Cultural: to learn about Mexican-American music and musicians
Reading Strategy: to identify a main idea

Related Components

Activity Book p. 61	Audio Tapes Adelante: 9A

⬛ GETTING STARTED

Ask students to look at the photos and say which instruments seem to be the most popular.

Background

Mariachis

The mariachi style developed from the traditional music of the state of Jalisco in western Mexico. Today mariachi bands play polkas, cumbias, and all the other popular music forms. A band will usually know more than a thousand songs.

The first mariachi bands were all string instruments: harp, violin, guitar, and guitarrón. Trumpets came later; the harp has now disappeared.

The word *mariachi* is believed to date from the French occupation of Mexico in the 1860s. At that time it was a tradition to hire a group to play local music at weddings, and the name may come from the French word *mariage.* Or it may refer to the fact that the same groups played at celebrations in honor of the Virgin Mary.

⬛ DISCUSS

Suggestions for discussion:

Ritmos de Texas

¿Cuál es el corazón de la cultura mexico-americana?
¿Qué ritmos son populares en Texas?
¿Saben Uds. cómo es la música mariachi?
¿Que música es parte de tu herencia cultural?
¿Cómo se llama?

Los instrumentos

¿Qué instrumentos son tradicionales de México?
¿Creen que los grupos musicales necesitan batería?
¿Te gusta la música del sintetizador?

Ritmos° de Texas

La música es el corazón° de la cultura mexico-americana. Los ritmos más populares de Texas son la música tex-mex y la mariachi. "La música es nuestra herencia cultural",° dicen los tejanos. "Cantamos en inglés y en español porque somos mexico-americanos".

La música tex-mex
¡Jazz, blues, country, rock, salsa y ritmos mexicanos! La música tex-mex tiene muchos ritmos.

◄ **El guitarrón es una guitarra grande de sonido grave.° Tiene seis cuerdas.°**

▲ **El grupo Mariachi Internacional es uno de los favoritos en Texas. Su música conserva la tradición musical mexicana.**

Los instrumentos
La guitarra, el acordeón y el bajo sexto son instrumentos tradicionales de México. Otros, como los sintetizadores y la batería,° vienen de° la música country y rock.

la batería *drums*
el corazón *heart*
las cuerdas *strings*

la herencia cultural *cultural heritage*
los ritmos *rhythms*
el sonido grave *low pitch*
vienen de *come from*

128

Tex-mex en la radio

En Texas hay estaciones de radio que ponen° música tex-mex todo el día. Las canciones° de Gary Hobbs, Elsa García y Selena triunfan° en todo el país. Por primera vez° en 1995, dos canciones tex-mex fueron° las más populares de los Estados Unidos.

Una ceremonia importante

La ceremonia de los *Texas Music Awards* (TMA) es más grande que° la ceremonia de los Grammy, los *MTV Music Awards* y los *American Music Awards*. A la ceremonia de los *TMA* van más de 15.000 espectadores.

Otro instrumento de la música popular mexicana es el acordeón. ▶

¿Mariachis en la escuela?

¡Sí! En muchas escuelas de Texas los chicos aprenden° a tocar música mariachi. Las clases son en inglés y en español. Los chicos escogen su instrumento favorito y aprenden a tocar en grupo. Los profesores son mariachis de grupos famosos, como los Campanitas de Oro.

En un grupo de música mariachi siempre hay un violín.
▼

◀
Una clase de músician música mariachi en una escuela de Texas.

La vihuela es una guitarra pequeña de sonido agudo.° Tiene cinco cuerdas.
▼

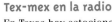

aprenden *learn*
las canciones *songs*
fueron *were*
más grande que *bigger than*

ponen *play*
por primera vez *for the first time*
el sonido agudo *high pitch*
triunfan *succeed*

129

Tex-mex en la radio

¿Qué música tocan algunas estaciones de radio en Texas?
¿Conoces la música de Selena?
¿Qué pasó por primera vez en 1995?
(Dos canciones de Selena, No me quieras más *y* Fotos y recuerdos, *fueron las más populares de los Estados Unidos.)*

Una ceremonia importante

¿Los Texas Music Awards *es una ceremonia grande o pequeña?*
¿Van muchos o pocos espectadores a los Awards? *¿Cuántos?*

¿Mariachis en la escuela?

¿Qué hacen los jóvenes en las clases de música mariachi?
¿Quiénes son sus profesores?
¿Qué es Campanitas de Oro?

Music Link: Ask students to identify the instruments in English. What do they think each sounds like? Do any students play one of these instruments? What kind of music does he or she play?

Note: A vihuela is an older form of the guitar, with a higher pitch; a **guitarrón** is a large or bass guitar; a **bajo sexto** is a 12-string bass guitar.

CHECK

- *¿De dónde es la tradición musical de los mariachis?*
- *¿Dónde hay mucha música tex-mex en la radio?*
- *¿Es grande la vihuela?*
- *¿Qué instrumentos usan los mariachis?*

LOG BOOK

Have students make a list, in Spanish, of things they learned about Tex-Mex music and instruments.

Para hispanohablantes

Listen to a few Tex-Mex songs and write Spanish and English lyrics for one. If the song does not already have lyrics, make them up.

▶▶▶ INTERNET LINK

Mariachis on the Web: http://mexico. udg.mx:80/Udg/Extuniv/mariachi

These activities can be done as classwork or as homework.

Objectives
Organizing Skills: classifying vocabulary
Communication Skills: writing lists

Related Components

Activity Book p. 62	Assessment Portfolio: p. 35-36

ACTIVITIES

1. ¡Escuchen bien!
Individual Activity Listen to a Tejano song in Spanish. Write down:
• what instruments are played
• whether the song is traditional or modern
• whether or not it is a love song

2. Tu música favorita
Individual Activity Write six sentences about your favorite music. Tell the class:
• what kind of music it is
• what instruments the musicians play
• the names of the group(s)

3. ¡Cuántos instrumentos!
Individual Activity Classify the instruments mentioned on pages 126-129. Write their names in Spanish, and include the proper article for each one.
Answers:
de viento: *el acordeón, la trompeta*
de cuerda: *el bajo sexto, la guitarra, el guitarrón, la vihuela, el violín*
de percusión: *la batería*
otros: *el sintetizador,*

4. ¿Cierto o falso?
Individual Activity Say whether each statement is true or false. Correct the false statements.
Possible Answers:
1. *Falso. La música tex-mex es muy popular.*
2. *Cierto.*
3. *Falso. La ceremonia de los* Texas Music Awards *es más grande que la ceremonia de los Grammy.*
4. *Cierto.*

130

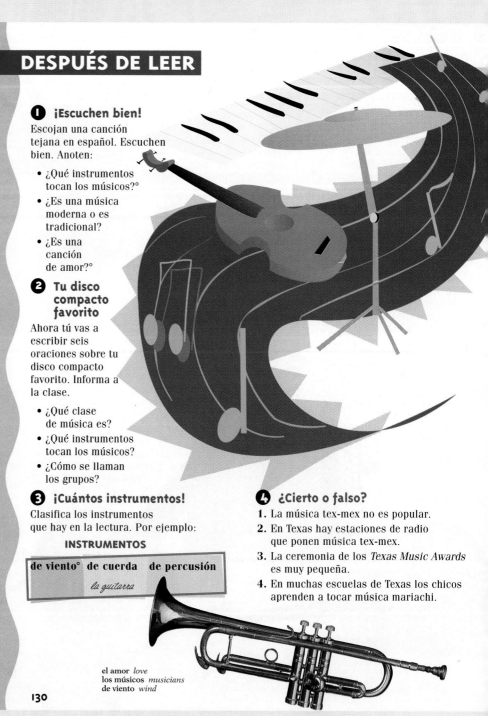

DESPUÉS DE LEER

❶ ¡Escuchen bien!
Escojan una canción tejana en español. Escuchen bien. Anoten:
• ¿Qué instrumentos tocan los músicos?°
• ¿Es una música moderna o es tradicional?
• ¿Es una canción de amor?°

❷ Tu disco compacto favorito
Ahora tú vas a escribir seis oraciones sobre tu disco compacto favorito. Informa a la clase.
• ¿Qué clase de música es?
• ¿Qué instrumentos tocan los músicos?
• ¿Cómo se llaman los grupos?

❸ ¡Cuántos instrumentos!
Clasifica los instrumentos que hay en la lectura. Por ejemplo:

INSTRUMENTOS

de viento°	de cuerda	de percusión
	la guitarra	

❹ ¿Cierto o falso?
1. La música tex-mex no es popular.
2. En Texas hay estaciones de radio que ponen música tex-mex.
3. La ceremonia de los *Texas Music Awards* es muy pequeña.
4. En muchas escuelas de Texas los chicos aprenden a tocar música mariachi.

el amor *love*
los músicos *musicians*
de viento *wind*

130

TALLER DE ESCRITORES

1. DISEÑA LA TAPA° DE UN DISCO COMPACTO

Tus amigos y tú tienen un grupo musical y van a grabar° un disco compacto. En grupo, escriban:

- el título° del disco compacto
- el nombre del grupo y el tipo de música
- los nombres de los músicos y los cantantes

Y ahora... ¡a diseñar la tapa!

2. NOTICIAS SOCIALES

Con tu compañero(a), escribe una noticia social para un cumpleaños, una quinceañera, una graduación o una boda. La noticia es para un periódico. Usa una foto. Escribe:

- la celebración
- el nombre de la(s) persona(s)
- la fecha y el lugar

3. MÚSICA TEJANA

Escribe un párrafo sobre la música tejana que conoces. Incluye:

- nombres de grupos o cantantes
- las canciones que cantan
- los instrumentos que tocan

Presenta tu informe a la clase

4. UNA CARTA

Escribe a un(a) amigo(a). Describe tu vecindario y tu casa.

_____ de _____ de _____

Querido(a) _____:

Yo vivo en _____. Es un vecindario muy _____ en las afueras de la ciudad. Tiene muchas tiendas, _____ y _____. Mi casa está en la calle _____, número _____. Yo vivo allí con mis padres y _____. Mi cuarto es _____. Tiene una cama, _____ y _____. Y tú, ¿cuándo vienes a mi casa? Contesta pronto. Tu amigo(a),

_____

(tu nombre)

grabar *to record*
la tapa *cover*
el título *title*

131

TALLER DE ESCRITORES

Objectives
- to practice writing
- to use vocabulary from this unit

Related Components

Activity Book p. 63	Assessment Portfolio: p. 35-36

ACTIVITIES

1. Diseña la tapa de un disco compacto
Group Activity Students will create the cover of a CD by their own musical group. It should include:
- the title
- their group's name and musical style
- the instrumentalists and singers

Note: Suggest that they create titles by putting together words from both of this Unit's *Vocabularios temáticos.* Examples:
La abuela baila tex-mex
¿Dónde están los mariachis?
Arriba y abajo

2. Noticias sociales
Pair Activity Students will write a newspaper announcement of a birthday, **quinceañera**, graduation, or wedding. They should use a photo and include:
- what the celebration is
- who is celebrating the event
- the date and place

3. Música tejana
Individual Activity Students will write a paragraph about Tejano music they are familiar with and report to the class. They should include:
- the names of groups or singers
- the songs they sing
- the instruments they play

Edit: Have pairs exchange, review, and edit each other's reports. Have them work together to prepare final drafts.

Present: Students read their final drafts to the class.

4. Una carta
Individual Activity Students will write a letter to a friend, describing their neighborhood and house.

Objectives
Communicative: to listen to and understand directions
Cultural: to replicate a Mexican tradition
TPR: to make a piñata

Related Components

Assessment	Transparencies
Portfolio: p. 35-36	Unit 2: Project
CD Rom	**Video:**
Unit 2: Manos a la obra	Tape/Book
	Unit 2: Seg. 5

Search to frame 1301311

Materials
- paste, a mixture of flour and water
- a balloon
- scissors
- strips of newspaper
- paints and brushes
- crepe paper

GETTING STARTED

Encourage students to use their eyes more than their ears. Rather than try to understand every word, they should focus on actions and listen only for clues.
Introduce this exercise with a brief TPR session in which you cut up a piece of paper and glue the pieces together. If possible, show the piñata-making segment of the Unit 2 video.

DISCUSS

Read aloud each paragraph, then ask a few comprehension and critical-thinking questions, such as:

Introduction
¿Qué es el arte popular? ¿Es el arte que hace un artista famoso o es arte que hace una persona que no es famosa?
¿Las tradiciones son cosas que hacemos muchas o pocas veces?
Todas las familias tienen tradiciones, ¿no?¿Qué tradiciones hay en tu familia?

Dulces y sorpresas
¿Qué hay dentro de una piñata?
¿Qué formas tienen muchas piñatas?
¿Qué personaje popular te gustaría para una piñata?

Las celebraciones
¿En qué celebraciones hay piñatas en México?
¿Te gustaría romper una piñata para otra celebración? ¿Qué celebración?
Las piñatas son muy populares en México. ¿En qué otros lugares son populares?

¡A ROMPER LA PIÑATA!°

Hacer piñatas es una artesanía popular de México. En Texas y otros estados del suroeste, las familias de origen mexicano mantienen esta tradición.

DULCES Y SORPRESAS
Las piñatas están decoradas con papel de muchos colores. Dentro de la piñata hay dulces, frutas y otras sorpresas. Las piñatas tienen forma de° animales, frutas o personajes° populares.

LAS CELEBRACIONES
En México y en Texas, siempre° hay piñatas en cumpleaños, en primeras comuniones,° en aniversarios y en otras celebraciones. Hoy en día,° las piñatas son también populares en otras partes de Estados Unidos y en muchos países latinoamericanos.

TE TOCA A TI

Haz una piñata. Decide cómo va a ser y de qué color. ¡Usa tu imaginación!

¡A romper la piñata! *Let's break the piñata!*
la forma de *the shape of*
hoy en día *nowadays*

los personajes *characters*
las primeras comuniones *first communions*
siempre *always*

132

MATERIALES

engrudo (una mezcla° de harina y agua)
un globo
tijeras°
tiras° de papel de periódico
pinturas° y pinceles°
papel crepé

tijeras

un globo

pinturas y pinceles

1 Infla° el globo.

2 Pon° las tiras de papel de periódico en el engrudo un momento.

3 Pega° el papel al globo. Deja secar° el papel. Repite este paso 3 ó 4 veces.

4 Usa el papel crepé, las pinturas, los pinceles y tu imaginación para hacer tu piñata.

5 Corta° un círculo.° Rellena° la piñata. Pega el círculo en su lugar.

6 Cuelga° la piñata... ¡y a romperla!

el círculo *circle*   infla *inflate*   pon *place*
corta *cut*   la mezcla *mixture*   rellena *fill*
cuelga *hang*   pega *glue*   las tiras *strips*
deja secar *leave to dry*

133

HANDS-ON

Using the directions in the book, lead students through the creation of a piñata.
1. Make a piñata as you read aloud the instructions.
2. After you have done this several times, invite volunteers to do it as you read the directions aloud .
3. Do this as TPR with the whole class.

Te toca a ti
Assign as homework. Make sure students understand that they will design their piñatas according to the particular celebration of their choice.

CHECK

Ask students to perform these actions as you say them:
• *Pega una tira de papel a otro papel.*
• *Corta un círculo de papel.*
• *Pon las tijeras en tu escritorio.*

LOG BOOK
Have students look at the captions and write down all of the commands.

✓ CULTURE NOTE

Before the piñata became a party pot, it was a clay pot that hung in the kitchen. (Party piñatas used to be made of clay.) The name may come from the fact that those hanging pots looked like pinecones, or *piñas* (*pigné* in Italian). Remind students that *piña* also means pineapple (Chapter 2). Does a pineapple resemble a piñata?

Para hispanohablantes

Describe to the class how you would make a piñata out of some other material, and say what you would put inside it.

Objectives
- to expand reading comprehension
- to relate the study of Spanish to other disciplines

Related Components

Activity Book p. 64	Audio Tapes Adelante: 9B
Assessment Portfolio: p. 35-36	Video: Tape/Book Unit 2: Seg. 4

Search to frame 1270820

Informar en español

About Spanish Papers in Texas
Although Hispanics account for about one-quarter of the population of Texas, most of the state's Spanish-language papers are small. About half are located in Dallas, Houston, Fort Worth, and San Antonio. The first newspaper published in Texas was in Spanish, *La Gaceta de Texas,* in Nacogdoches, launched in May 1813.

Activity
Read aloud the paragraph. Ask comprehension questions such as:
¿Cuántos periódicos hispanos tiene Dallas?
¿Cuál es el periódico semanal más antiguo de Texas?

INTERNET LINKS

La Jornada of Mexico City http://www. infosel.com. mx/pub/reformae.html
The Texas Rivers Project http://chico. rice.edu/armadillo/Ftbend/rivers.html
The Spanish Language http://csgwww. uwaterloo.ca:80/~dmg/espanol/ gramatica.html
Luis Jiménez http://press-gopher. uchicago.edu:70/CGI/cgi-bin/hfs.cgi/21/ new_mexico/93073295.ctl

---

 PRENSA

INFORMAR EN ESPAÑOL

En el estado de Texas hay muchas publicaciones en español. Dallas publica° ocho periódicos hispanos. Estos periódicos tienen información internacional, nacional y local. *El Sol de Texas* es la publicación semanal más antigua° del estado.

- ¿Lees el periódico?
- ¿Hay periódicos en español en tu ciudad?

 GEOGRAFÍA

RÍO GRANDE O RÍO BRAVO

El Río Grande es uno de los ríos más largos° de América del Norte. Forma la frontera entre Estados Unidos y México. Pasa° por Colorado, Nuevo México y Texas. En México se llama Río Bravo *("fierce river").* Este río es importante porque provee de° agua a los dos países.

- ¿Por qué estados pasa el Río Grande?
- ¿Cómo se llama este río en México?
- ¿Por qué es importante el Río Grande?

más antigua *oldest*
más largos *longest*
pasa *(it) passes*
provee de *it supplies*
publica *publishes*

Río Grande o Río Bravo

About the River
In 1582, a Spanish explorer named this river the *Río del Norte;* later it was named the *Rio Grande.* Mexicans now call it the *Rio Bravo (del Norte.)*
So much of the water is used for agriculture that much of the river seems neither *grande* nor *bravo.* In places like the canyons of Big Bend National Park, however, it can be spectacular.

Activity
Read aloud the selection. Ask the bulleted questions and critical-thinking questions, such as: Why do there have to be treaties about water usage? (The river also belongs to Mexico.)
Answers:
- *El Río Grande pasa por Colorado, Nuevo México y Texas.*
- *En México el río se llama Río Bravo.*
- *Es importante porque provee de agua a Estados Unidos y México.*

VAQUEROS° TEJANOS

Muchos palabras que asociamos con la vida° de los vaqueros tejanos vienen del español: corral , rodeo, rancho, cañon y muchas más.

- ¿Conoces otras palabras de inglés que vienen de otro idioma? ¿Cuáles?

ARTE

ESCULTURA° DE COLORES

Luis Jiménez es un artista de origen mexicano de El Paso, Texas. Jiménez hace esculturas grandes de colores vivos.° Sus esculturas representan° la vida en la frontera y las experiencias de los inmigrantes. Sus obras° están en plazas, parques y museos de todo el país. La escultura de la foto se llama *Sodbuster* y está en Santa Fe.

- ¿Quién es Luis Jiménez?
- ¿Hay esculturas en tu vecindario? ¿Dónde están?

los colores vivos *bright colors*	las obras *works*
la escultura *sculpture*	representan *represent*
la vida *life*	los vaqueros *cowboys*

135

Activity
Ask students if they recognize these Spanish words that are (or were) used in the American West:

el arroyo arroyo (stream)
el calabozo calaboose (jail; Spanish means dungeon)
el cañón canyon
el juzgado hoosegow (jail, orig. court)
la reata lariat (from *reatar,* to tie again)
loco loco (crazy)
la mesa mesa (flat-topped hill, Spanish means table)
el estampido stampede (Spanish means explosion)
vamos vamoose (let's get out of here)
Discuss the kinds of words that were adopted in the old West, and why they were. (A few ideas: landscape features such as mesas and canyons were named by Spanish explorers; Mexican **vaqueros** were the original cowboys.)

Escultura de colores

About Luis Jiménez
Born in El Paso in 1940, Jiménez received his earliest training from his father, a maker of neon signs. In college, he first studied architecture, then art.
Jiménez has created public sculptures for Houston, Wichita, and other cities. He works with bronze and other traditional materials as well as industrial materials like fiberglass.
Possible Answers:
- *Luis Jiménez es un artista mexicano de Texas.*
- Answers will vary.

Other Questions
What animals are in the sculpture? (oxen)
What is a sodbuster? (Sod is the surface layer of dirt and roots that Great Plains farmers must break through—bust—in order to plant.)

Vaqueros tejanos

About Cowboy Words
Many "cowboy" words were originally Spanish. **Vaquero** itself turned into *buckaroo*—a word now heard only in movies but once synonymous with "cowboy."
Possible Answers:
- Some of the food vocabulary is of Native American origin. A few words: avocado, barbeque, chocolate, guacamole, tomato
- Answers will vary.

3 PUERTO RICO
ISLA DEL ENCANTO

In this unit

We visit the beautiful island of Puerto Rico. And it's hard to imagine a better spot to explore water and beach activities (Chapter 5) and weather (Chapter 6). Puerto Rico's 300 miles of beaches offer great swimming, fishing, snorkeling, diving, parasailing, windsurfing—plus some of the world's best waves for surfing. ¡Qué chévere! Except for snow, the weather in Puerto Rico offers nearly every kind of condition you can think of, from seemingly endless sunny days to drenching rains and even hurricanes.

Before leaving Puerto Rico, we'll make two stops that are highlighted in both the lively video for this unit and the *Adelante* section of the student book. The first stop is El Yunque, Puerto Rico's beautiful tropical rain forest. There we see how a special combination of sunlight and intensive rainfall contributes to the formation of an environmental resource that is also an ideal location for hiking and observing nature firsthand. After completing the unit project of making kites (*chiringas*), we leave Puerto Rico as we found it—on the hills above El Morro, a magnificent 16th-century fortress. Here breezes are always blowing and the daytime sun nearly always shines brightly.

VIDEO LINKS

Text	Video Segment
Unit Overview Unit Opener	**1. Introduction to Puerto Rico** El Morro, Old San Juan, El Yunque, the beaches and people
Chapter 5	**2. Arena, sol y mar** beach sports, international surfing and sailing competition
Chapter 6	**3. ¿Cómo te afecta el tiempo?** weather words, hurricanes, which clothes to wear, rainy day activities, weather forecast grammar: the verb **saber** + infinitive; negative words
Adelante	**4. Adelante** El Yunque rain forest, Moses the manatee grammar : the verb **querer** + infinitive; **querer** + noun
Manos a la obra	**5. Manos a la obra** How to make a kite

Geography and Climate

Volcanic in origin, the island of Puerto Rico is 100 miles long and 30 miles wide. There is a narrow band of flat land along the shores, then coastal plain and, lengthwise across the island, two ranges of mountains. Prevailing winds from the south cool as they cross these mountains, producing daily rain showers over most of the central region. The temperature in Puerto Rico hardly ever falls below 70 °F or rises above 95 °F.

History

Puerto Rico was first settled by people from Central and South America over 6,000 years ago. The Taínos created the first important civilization on the island about 1000 A.D.

The Taíno population may have been as high as 100,000 when Columbus landed on the island in 1493, during his second voyage to the New World. San Juan was settled in 1521 by Juan Ponce de León, who later explored Florida. Most of the Taínos soon died from overwork or disease, and slaves were brought from Africa to replace natives as laborers.

Spanish dominance in Puerto Rico did not end until the Spanish-American War of 1898, when the island became a US protectorate. In 1917 Congress voted to give US citizenship to Puerto Ricans, and in 1947 passed a law allowing islanders to elect their governors.

Political Status

Although Puerto Ricans elect their governor, they cannot vote in mainland elections and have no elected representatives in the US Senate or House of Representatives. Puerto Ricans do not pay US federal taxes, but are eligible for service in the US armed forces. Plebiscites are held periodically on the island to determine whether to continue the commonwealth status, seek independence, or become a state. All these positions have strong support.

Island Music

Made famous by musicians such as Tito Rodriguez and Ray Barretto, *salsa* is only one of many combinations of Taíno, African, and Spanish music that have made Puerto Rico a capital of 20th-century pop music and dancing. Other well-known names include bandleader Tito Puente and singer José Feliciano. Nor is pop music the only kind of music that thrives here. Classical music received a great boost when Catalan cellist Pablo Casals moved to the island in 1956–the same year that another exile from Spain, poet Juan Ramón Jiménez, learned at his home in San Juan that he had won the Nobel Prize for literature.

El escudo de Puerto Rico

HISTORY CONNECTION

Objectives
- to explore the historical significance of the shield of Puerto Rico
- to create a personal shield

Use
any time during Unit 3

Materials
- Transparency Unit 3, *El escudo de Puerto Rico*
- overhead projector
- TRB Activity Support Page 11, *Mi escudo* (blank shield)

Activity
- Share the FYI information below, then show transparency and discuss symbols on shield.
- Hand out copies of the activity and have students design shields for themselves, using personal symbols and, if they like, Spanish words.
- Have students describe their shields to classmates—in Spanish, if possible.
- Display *escudos* in classroom.

FYI
The marriage in 1469 of Isabella, queen of Castile, and Ferdinand, king of Aragon, united two large kingdoms into what is still modern Spain. The Catholic king and queen went on to expand their domain further by annexing huge amounts of land in the Americas. Their emissary, Christopher Columbus, landed on the island of Borinquen (so called by the Taínos, its indigenous inhabitants) on November 19, 1493, during his second voyage to the New World. Columbus renamed the island San Juan Bautista (St. John the Baptist) in honor of the Catholic saint and Ferdinand and Isabella's son John. San Juan Bautista is still Puerto Rico's patron saint, and San Juan the name of its capital and largest city.

Instrumentos borinqueños

MUSIC CONNECTION

Objective
- to identify Puerto Rican musical instruments by sight and to explore their origins

Use
any time during Unit 3

Materials
- TRB Activity Support Page 12, *Instrumentos borinqueños*
- Puerto Rican musical instruments

Activity
- Hand out activity support page and share the FYI below. Have students discuss what kind of sound they think each instrument would make.
- Have students try to play any available Puerto Rican instruments.

los claves (los palillos)

el cuatro

el bongó

el pandero

FYI
Six of the instruments pictured were brought to Puerto Rico from other cultures. The *cuatro,* named for its 4 strings, is adapted from the Spanish guitar, as is the small high-pitched *tiple.* The *tambor,* originally made from a tree trunk, the *bongó,* the *pandero,* and the *claves* came from Africa. The *güiro,* a hollow gourd with grooves rasped into its side and played with a steel comb, is of indigenous Taíno origin. So are the *maracas.*

Tostones islennos

HANDS ON: COOKING

Objective
- to cook and eat *tostones* (fried green plantains) with *mojito* (garlic sauce)—one of Puerto Rico's favorite dishes

Use
any time during Unit 3

Supplies
- paper towels
- electric frying pan
- drinking glass
- serving dish
- garlic press

Ingredients
Tostones
- 6 green plantains
- water
- salt
- oil

Mojito
- 8 large cloves of garlic
- 1/2 cup olive oil
- chopped cilantro or parsley

Preparation
Tostones
- Peel plantains, cut into 1" slices, and soak in salted water for 15 minutes. Drain and dry on paper towels.
- Heat enough oil in frying pan to cover slices. Fry for 2 minutes on each side.
- Drain on paper towels, flatten each slice with the base of a glass, and fry again until browned.
- Drain on serving dish with paper towels.
- Salt to taste and cover while cooking *mojito*.

Mojito
- Peel garlic cloves and mash in garlic press.
- Heat oil, add mashed garlic, and sauté until golden brown.
- After adding chopped cilantro or parsley, pour hot mixture lightly over *tostones*. ¡Buen provecho!

La bandera de Puerto Rico

HISTORY CONNECTION

Objective
- to explore the Puerto Rican flag and anthem
- to review the names for colors

Use
any time during Unit 3

Materials
- TRB Activity Support Page 13, *La bandera de Puerto Rico*
- crayons or markers

Activity
- Distribute activity support page and share FYI below.
- Give directions for coloring the flag.
  —*Colorea la bandera según las instrucciones:*
  Deja la estrella en blanco.
  Colorea el triángulo de color azul.
  Colorea la franja de arriba de color rojo.
  Colorea la franja del centro de rojo.
  Colorea la franja de abajo también de rojo.
  Deja las franjas 2 y 4 en blanco.
- Have students read the island's official anthem, *La borinqueña,* and discuss its vocabulary and meaning. Ask students why they think people respond so strongly to their homeland's flag and anthem.

FYI
The Puerto Rican flag was designed during the 1890s, before the Spanish-American War, by Puerto Rican nationalists living in New York City and planning a future with fellow exiles from Cuba. The two groups decided to use the same design, and the Cuban flag is identical to the Puerto Rican flag except that the triangle is red and the stripes are blue. The colors for both flags were inspired by the flag colors of the exiles' temporary home. The early history of the US had been an inspiration to revolutionary movements for a century by the early 1890s. As for the official Puerto Rican anthem, *La borinqueña*, its name derives from the Taíno word for the island: *Borikén* or *Borinquen*. In *La borinqueña,* Puerto Rico is the daughter of sun and sea, just as the sons and daughters of this Caribbean island call themselves *borinqueños, borinqueñas* or *boricuas* in honor of their land.

PUERTO RICO

Communicative Objectives
- to introduce Puerto Rico
- to establish the location of Puerto Rico
- to develop listening comprehension

Related Components

CD Rom Unit 3	**Video: Tape/Book** Unit 3: Seg. 1
Transparencies Unit 3:	

Search to frame 1322427

▢ GETTING STARTED

Ask if anyone has ever been to Puerto Rico. If so, ask about it. If no one has, ask students what they'd expect to see while vacationing on a tropical island. What would the weather be like? What kind of clothing would they wear? What would they expect to do there?

Using the Video

Show Segment 1 of the Puerto Rico video, an introduction to the country.

Using the Transparencies

To help orient students to Puerto Rico, use the Locator Map Transparency. You may also want to review the other transparencies for Unit 3 at this time.

▢ DISCUSS

Presenting Puerto Rico

For more information about Puerto Rico, refer to pages 136A–136D.

Using the Text

English: After students have read the introduction, ask comprehension and critical-thinking questions. For example: What are four things you can find or do in Puerto Rico?
Do you think many tourists visit Puerto Rico? Why?
Spanish: Ask students what they think the subtitle, *isla del encanto,* means. Encourage them to play with the letters to find English cognates.

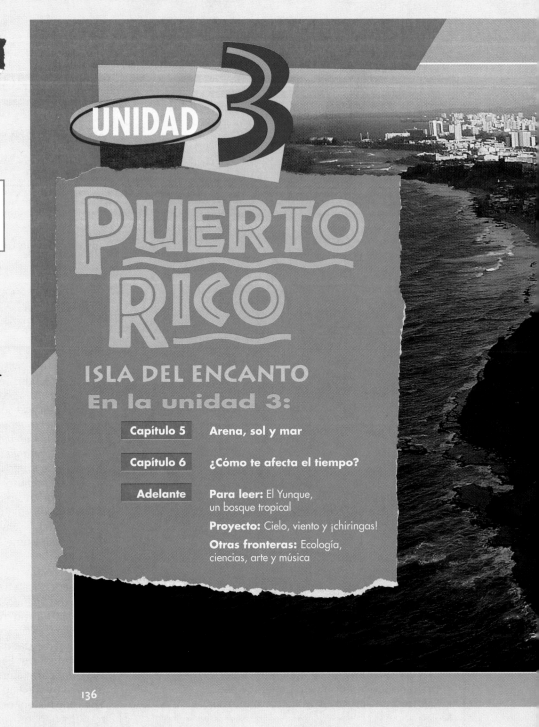

UNIDAD **3**

PUERTO RICO

ISLA DEL ENCANTO
En la unidad 3:

Capítulo 5	Arena, sol y mar
Capítulo 6	¿Cómo te afecta el tiempo?
Adelante	**Para leer:** El Yunque, un bosque tropical
	Proyecto: Cielo, viento y ¡chiringas!
	Otras fronteras: Ecología, ciencias, arte y música

136

Unit Components

Activity Book p. 65-88	Audio Book Script: p. 41-44; 49-52	CD ROM Unit 3	Transparencies Unit 3: Chapter 5-6
Assessment Oral Proficiency: p. 25-26	Activities: p. 45-48; 53-56	**Conexiones** Chapter 5-6	**Tutor Pages** p. 23-30
Listening Script: p. 13-14	**Audio Tapes** Listening: 4A, 4B	**Cuaderno** p. 37-52	**Video: Tape/Book** Unit 3: Segments 1-5
Chapter Tests: p. 69-80	Adelante: 10A, 10B Assessment: 14B	**Magazine** Juntos en Puerto Rico	
Portofolio: p. 37-38	Conexiones: 17A		

If you like water sports, you will like Puerto Rico. It has 300 miles of shoreline and just about every water sport from scuba diving to parasailing. And you can enjoy these sports almost every day of the year because Puerto Rico has a tropical climate.

In Puerto Rico you can find colonial-style towns, modern cities, and a tropical rain forest. And there is El Morro, a sixteenth-century fortress that guards San Juan harbor.

The original inhabitants of Puerto Rico were the Tainos, who came to the Caribbean from South America. In 1508 Puerto Rico was colonized by Spain. Today, Puerto Rico is a commonwealth of the United States.

This unit will be your guide to Puerto Rico. You will visit the beaches, explore the rainforest, and get plenty of sun. See you at the beach! Terrific! ¡Qué chévere!

El castillo de El Morro en San Juan, Puerto Rico.

137

 ## ACTIVITIES

INTERDISCIPLINARY CONNECTIONS

To provide other perspectives, assign brief research projects like these:

Archaeology
What have archaeologists discovered about the original inhabitants of the island?

Weather
Find out the average temperature in Puerto Rico. How many days each year is the temperature as high—or higher—in your town? (Sources vary; average is ±78°.)

Economics
How much would it cost to fly from here to Puerto Rico? Find the lowest price.

History
In what year did Spain lose Puerto Rico to the United States? Who was our President then? How many presidents have we had since then? (Counting McKinley, Clinton would be the 18th).

Geography
What U.S. state is the closest to the size of Puerto Rico? (Connecticut).

Math
If you phoned San Juan at noon our time, what time would it be there? (The same as Eastern Standard Time—except during daylight savings, when it's one hour later).

✓ CULTURE NOTE

When Columbus reached the island of Borinquen, he renamed it San Juan Bautista. When Ponce de León established a colony at the place we call San Juan, he named it Puerto Rico.

 **▶▶▶ INTERNET LINK**

General Introduction to Puerto Rico:
http://www.lib.ox.ac.uk/internet/news/faq/archive/puerto-rico-faq.html

	Objetivos page 139	Conversemos pages 140-141	Realidades pages 142-143	Palabras en acción pages 144-145
Comunicación	• To talk about sports and activities you want to do	Discuss water sports and how to do them	Read text, answer questions, discuss water sports	Activities 4, 8: Read cartoon, discuss activities; write dialog
	• To talk about sports and activities you know how to do	Talk about sports and activities you want to do	Read text, answer questions, discuss water sports, survey class preferences	Activities 2, 5, 6, 8: Read cartoon, discuss activities; act out a water sport; write dialog
	• To talk about the beach and water sports	Brainstorm list of things needed at the beach	Read text, answer questions, discuss water sports, survey class preferences	Activities 1, 3, 7: Make list; talk about things needed at beach; make collage
Vocabulario temático	• To know the expressions for beach activities	Talk about beach activities		Activities 1-2, 5,7-8: Read cartoon, make lists; discuss beach activities; talk about sports; make collage; write dialog
	• To know the expressions for water sports	Talk about water sports	Read text, discuss water sports, survey class preferences	Activities 1, 4, 7: Read cartoon, make lists; talk about sports; ask about water sports; make collage
	• To know the expressions for sports equipment	Talk about sports equipment		Activities 1, 5, 8: Read cartoon, make lists; talk about sports; act out water sports; make collage; write dialog
	• To know the expressions for things to take to the beach	Talk about things to take to the beach		Activities 1, 3, 6-8: Read cartoon, make lists; talk about things needed at beach; act out water sports; make collage; write dialog
Estructura	• To talk about what you know how to do: the verb *saber* + infinitive	Use *sé* to discuss sports and activities you know how to do	Read text, answer question about water sports	Activity 4: Read cartoon, discuss activities
	• To talk about what you want to do: the verb *querer* + infinitive	Use *querer* + infinitive to talk about sports you'd like to learn	Read text, answer questions, discuss water sports	Activities 5, 6, 8: Read cartoon, talk about sports; act out water sports you want to learn; write dialog
Cultura	• Special political status of Puerto Rico as part of US		La Parguera phosphorescent bay	
Integración		What you like to do, items to take with you	Describing activities, what you would like to do	What you are going to do, items that you have or don't have

Para comunicarnos mejor (1) pages 146-147	Para comunicarnos mejor (2) pages 148-149	Situaciones pages 150-151	Para resolver pages 152-153	Notes
Activities 1-3: Talk about water sports; make list; survey skills		Activities 1B, 5.1: Read text, make list of sports and activities to do; write in diary		
	Activities 1, 3: Talk about activities to do; make table, interview classmates	Activities 1A, 1B, 3, 5.3: Read text, answer questions; make list; make weekend beach plans; write in diary	Pasos 1-5: Read map, discuss where to go and what to do; make a list; analyze list; present and compare results	
	Activity 2: Discuss things to take to beach, and make group list	Activity 1C: Read text, identify water sports and beach activities by equipment	Paso 2: Make a list of clothes, sports equipment, and other things to take to beach	
	Activity 1: Talk about activities to do	Activities 1, 3: Read text, answer questions, make lists; identify beach activities; make plans	Pasos 1-5: Read map, discuss where to go what to do; analyze list; present results	
Activity 1: Talk about water sports you know how to do	Activity 1: Talk about activities to do	Activities 1, 3: Read text, answer questions; make lists; identify water sports; make plans	Pasos 1-5: Read map, discuss where to go, what to do; analyze list; present results	
	Activity 2: Discuss things to take to beach, and make group list	Activities 1C, 5.2: Read text, identify beach activities, water sports; write in diary	Pasos 1-5: Read map, discuss where to go, what to do; analyze list; present results	
	Activity 2: Discuss things to take to beach, and make group list	Activities 1C, 5.2: Read text, identify beach activities, water sports; write in diary	Pasos 1, -5: Read map, discuss where to go, what to do; analyze list; present results	
Use all forms of saber. Activities 1-3: Talk about water sports you/partner know how to do; make list; survey skills		Activities 1B, 5.1: Read text, write list of activities you know how to do; write in diary		
	Use all forms of querer. Activities 1-3: Talk about activities to do; make list; make table, interview classmates	Activities 1A, 1B, 2, 3, 5.3: Read text, answer questions about sports; make list; talk about where to go; make weekend beach plans; write in diary	Pasos 1-5: Read map, discuss where to go and what to do; make list; analyze list; present and compare results	
		Special resort beaches called *balnearios*		Entérate page 154 Puerto Rican baseball stars/The Caribbean League and mainland players
Activities to do, reactions, telling how well something is done	People you know, activities to do, days of week, time of day	Locations, activities to do, days of week, time of day	Items you need for a trip, what to do, numbers, cost	Describing people and activities, direction words, numbers, dates

Mi postal puertorriqueña

WRITING CONNECTION

Objective
• to make a postcard using information about Puerto Rico, Chapter 5 *Vocabulario temático,* and the verbs **saber** and **querer** + infinitive

Use
after *Para comunicarnos mejor,* page 147

Materials
• postcard-sized posterboard
• crayons, colored pencils, markers
• magazine pictures of Puerto Rico
• clothesline and clothespins

Preparation
• Share cultural, geographical, and historical information about Puerto Rico.
• Discuss places in Puerto Rico and reasons to go.

Activity
• Have students make a postcard from Puerto Rico by illustrating one side of the posterboard with a drawing or magazine photo.
• On the other side, students write a note to a friend or family member. It should include location, date, salutation, the weather, what they are doing and with whom, their date of return, a closing, etc. For example:

San Juan, Puerto Rico
25 de noviembre

Hola, Linda:

Estoy en el Castillo de El Morro. Juan y Eric están aquí también. Son las dos de la tarde y hace mucho sol. Voy a la playa todos los días. Llevo el protector solar y los lentes de sol. Sé hacer un poco de surf, pero no sé bucear. Quiero practicar tabla y vela. ¡Me gusta San Juan tanto como Brooklyn!

Hasta pronto, tu amiga,
Suzanne

• Have students read their cards aloud and pin them on the clothesline.

FYI
Here are some other words that may be useful: *querido(a), un beso, un abrazo fuerte, chau, besos y abrazos, hasta la vista.*

Y los ganadores son...

HANDS ON: COLLAGE

Objective
• to discuss swimsuits, using Chapter 5 *Vocabulario temático*

Use
after *Palabras en acción,* page 143

Materials
• pictures of swimsuits from newspapers and magazines
• posterboard

Activity
• Have each student describe a swimsuit picture, first in writing and then to the class.—*Es un traje de baño rojo de señora. Tiene grandes flores amarillas y naranjas. Cuesta 48 dólares.*
• Make a swimsuit poster by taping swimsuits and descriptions to posterboard.
• Give poster a title: *Los ganadores del año.*
• Take a vote and give awards for *lo más bonito, lo más feo, lo más grande, lo más gracioso, lo más diferente,* etc.

Variations
• While teacher describes a swimsuit from the posterboard, students either draw and color it or guess which one it is and point it out.

FYI
In different countries, different words may be used to name the same beachwear.

bañador	
traje de baño	1-piece swimsuit
malla enteriza	
bikini	bikini
short	trunks
traje de dos piezas	
bañador de dos piezas	2-piece swimsuit
malla de dos piezas	

Busca pares

GAME

Objective
• to play a memory game, using words from Chapter 5 *Vocabulario temático*

Use
after *Palabras en acción,* pages 144–145

Materials
• 15 sealed envelopes, cut in half and numbered 1–30
• glue stick
• foam-core board
• 30 3" x 5" index cards

Preparation
• Glue numbered envelope halves to foam-core board.
• Using an index card for each word, make sets of matched pairs: Spanish word on one card, English translation on another; or, drawing or magazine picture on one card and Spanish word on second card.

Activity
• Pass cards around for students to look at. Then shuffle and randomly place one in each pocket.
• Player 1 asks for two numbers:—*Quiero el número 1 y el número 16.*
• If the two cards match, student uses the Spanish word in a sentence, keeps the cards, and chooses two more numbers.
• No match? Next person gets a turn.
• The player who makes the most matches wins.

Variations
• Save the game board to review other words: beach items, beach activities, water sports, etc.

¿Qué sabes hacer?

GAME

Objectives
• to talk about what we know how to do, using the irregular verb **saber** + infinitive
• to talk about what we want to do, using the irregular verb **querer** + infinitive

Use
after *Para comunicarnos mejor,* page 147

Materials
• masking tape

Activity
• Students bring in magazine pictures of an activity they know how to do (and name in Spanish) and one they want to do. For example: *nadar, jugar béisbol, tocar la guitarra, bucear,* etc.
• Divide the chalkboard into two sections, labeled *saber hacer* and *querer saber.*
• John, volunteer 1, comes to the board and tapes his pictures under the appropriate headings.
• Olga, volunteer 2, tries to identify the pictures.—*John sabe jugar béisbol y quiere hacer surf.* If she guesses incorrectly volunteer 3, Sally, tries to identify the pictures.
• After everyone's pictures are on the chalkboard, students tally the activities and then each presents one conclusion orally. For example, John might say:—*Seis personas saben jugar béisbol.* Olga:—*Tres personas quieren hacer tabla y vela.* Sally:—*Diez personas saben nadar,* etc.

Variations
• Have students make a chart or a graph, using their tallies and the pictures on the chalkboard.

ARENA, SOL Y MAR

Introduce the chapter and its theme by asking students to draw a few conclusions about Puerto Rico. Elicit the fact that it is an island, that it has a warm climate all year round, and that people—tourists as well as Puerto Ricans—practice and enjoy ocean-based water sports.

Related Components

Workbook	Video Tape/Book
Chapter 5	Unit 3: Seg. 2
Conexiones	
Chapter 5	

Search to frame 1322427

GETTING STARTED

Ask students if they recogonize or have done the activity shown in the photographer (surfing). Possible critical thinking question: Ests joven hace surf. ¿Qué opinas, es fácil o difícil hacer surf?

Thinking About Language

You can use this opportunity to discuss with your students how and why languages borrow words from other languages.

Loanwords

1. Do you think the word **surf** is an original Spanish word? Why not?
(Introduce the term *loanword*.)

2. Why do you suppose Spanish speakers use the English word *surf* instead of the Spanish word **oleaje?**
(The sport was probably well-established before it reached Spanish-speaking countries.)

3. What other water sports can you name?
(Several sports will be mentioned in this chapter, among them sailing, jet skiing, parasailing, waterskiing, skindiving, surfing, and windsurfing.
Only the most recent, **jet ski** and **parasailing**, are English loanwords—and **Jet Ski** is a trademark. **Esquí** is from Norwegian and **buceo** from a Portuguese word for an underwater snail.)

4. Why do languages sometimes use loanwords instead of creating new words? Why don't they always use loanwords?
(Encourage interpretations and discussion.)

CAPÍTULO 5

ARENA, SOL Y MAR

Hacer surf es muy popular en Puerto Rico.

138

Chapter Components

Activity Book p. 65-74	Audio Book Script: p. 41-44 Activities: p. 45-48	CD ROM Chapter 5	Transparencies Chapter 5
Assessment Oral Proficiency: p. 25 Listening Script: p. 13 Chapter Test: p. 69-74	**Audio Tapes** Listening: 4A Assessment: 14B, Ch. 5 Conexiones: 17A, Ch. 5	**Conexiones** Chapter 5 **Cuaderno** p. 37-44 **Magazine** Juntos en Puerto Rico	**Tutor Pages** p. 23-26 **Video: Tape/Book** Unit 3: Seg. 2

Objetivos

COMUNICACIÓN
To talk about:
- sports and activities you want to do
- sports and activities you know how to do
- the beach and water sports

CULTURA
To learn about:
- leisure activities of Puerto Rican teenagers
- baseball in Puerto Rico
- key locations in Puerto Rico using a map

VOCABULARIO TEMÁTICO
To know the expressions for:
- beach activities
- water sports
- sports equipment
- things to take to the beach

ESTRUCTURA
To talk about:
- what you know how to do: the verb *saber* with the infinitive of another verb
- what you want to do: the verb *querer* with the infinitive of another verb

¿SABES QUE...?

Puerto Rico is part of the U.S., but not a state in the traditional sense. It is called an *Estado Libre Asociado*, or "Free Associated State." Puerto Ricans are American citizens. They elect a governor and a legislature as in any other state, but they do not elect national representatives or senators. Instead, Puerto Ricans choose a Residential Commissioner who speaks for them, but who may not vote in the U.S. Congress.

ACTIVITIES

Here are some additional activities that you may wish to use as you work through the chapter with your students.

Communication
Encourage after–class activities that may enhance student interest and proficiency. Some ideas:
- suggest that they watch a soccer match on Spanish-language television
- ask Spanish speakers to make simple audio tapes that describe what it would be like to do one of the sports in this chapter; have others listen to them

Culture
The written word can only hint at what life is like in other lands. To encourage greater understanding:
- take a trip to a restaurant that serves Spanish Caribbean food
- lend students tapes of *salsa*, *plena*, and other Puerto Rican dance music
- show the video that accompanies this textbook

Vocabulary
To reinforce vocabulary, have students:
- use magazine photos or drawings to create their own picture dictionaries

Structure
To reinforce the forms of **saber** and **querer**:
- make a grammar bulletin board and encourage students to write their observations about these verbs

INTERNET LINK

My Puerto Rican Homepage:
http://gwis2.circ.gwu.edu/~jacobino/
puerto-rico.html

CONVERSEMOS

Communicative Objectives
- to talk about sports and beach activities
- to respond with typical expressions

Related Components

Activity Book p. 65	**Cuaderno** p. 37
Audio Book Script: Seg. 1	**Transparencies** Ch. 5: Conversemos
Audio Tapes Chapter: 4A, Seg. 1	

GETTING STARTED

Ask students to identify the objects and activities pictured here. A few, like the ones in *¿Adónde vas a nadar?* may be difficult. In that particular case, you might suggest that they first look for the word **nadar** in the second activity.

ACTIVITIES

These activities give students an opportunity to begin communicating with each other and with you, focusing on the theme and objectives of the chapter. The activities can be used as oral class activities, or, if you prefer, you can pair students to achieve more interaction. Additional activities integrate critical-thinking skills.

¿Qué actividades te gusta hacer?
Class activity to review **me gusta** and **te gusta** with known verbs. Ask the question in the title and other questions, such as *¿A quién le gusta jugar fútbol?* Also ask questions that will allow the student to express a preference. For example: *¿Te gusta jugar baloncesto? Prefiero leer.*

¿Qué deportes acuáticos sabes hacer?
Class activity to introduce **sé, no sé, quiero aprender a**, and sports vocabulary. Demonstrate the use of the three terms. Ask the question in the title.

Homework: Make three sentences for each item. For example: *Sé bucear. No sé bucear. Quiero aprender a remar.*

¿Adónde vas a nadar?
Class activity to introduce use of **ir a** and new vocabulary.

Application: Ask students to identify the water sports they can do in each place. *¿Qué deporte haces en una piscina?*

CONVERSEMOS
LA PLAYA Y TÚ

Habla con tu compañero(a).

¿QUÉ TE GUSTA HACER?

Me gusta...	No me gusta...
jugar al béisbol	patinar
jugar al fútbol	leer
ir al gimnasio	comer

Prefiero bailar.
(I prefer to dance.)

¿QUÉ DEPORTES ACUÁTICOS SABES HACER?

Sé...	No sé...	Quiero aprender a...

Sé nadar. Quiero aprender a bucear.
(I know how to swim. I want to learn how to dive.)

bucear — navegar
nadar — hacer tabla a vela
remar — hacer jet ski

¿ADÓNDE VAS A NADAR?

Voy...

al mar — al lago
a la piscina — al río

140

MEETING INDIVIDUAL NEEDS

Reaching All Students

For Visual Learners
Use photographs to present the vocabulary in *¿Adónde vas a nadar?*

For Auditory Learners
Have one partner read vocabulary aloud while the other acts out each word.

For Kinesthetic Learners
Tell them to use exaggerated body language when using the expressions in *¡Vamos a la playa!* Ask other questions. For example: *¿Quieres más tarea?*

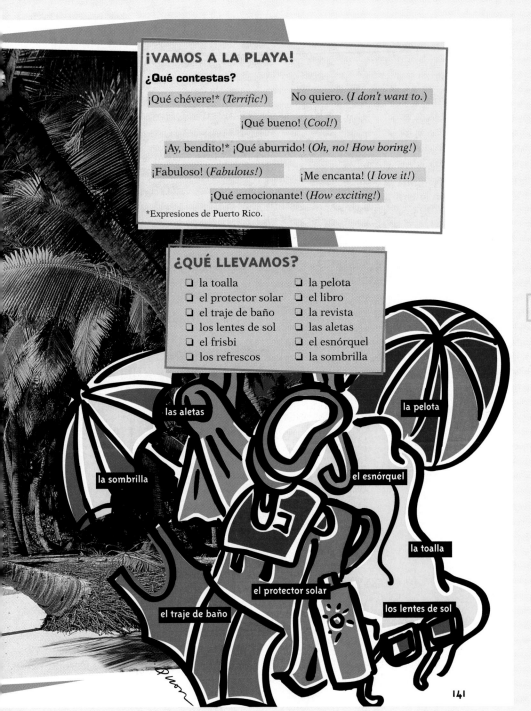

¡VAMOS A LA PLAYA!

¿Qué contestas?

¡Qué chévere!* (*Terrific!*)   No quiero. (*I don't want to.*)

¡Qué bueno! (*Cool!*)

¡Ay, bendito!* ¡Qué aburrido! (*Oh, no! How boring!*)

¡Fabuloso! (*Fabulous!*)   ¡Me encanta! (*I love it!*)

¡Qué emocionante! (*How exciting!*)

*Expresiones de Puerto Rico.

¿QUÉ LLEVAMOS?

- ❏ la toalla
- ❏ el protector solar
- ❏ el traje de baño
- ❏ los lentes de sol
- ❏ el frisbi
- ❏ los refrescos
- ❏ la pelota
- ❏ el libro
- ❏ la revista
- ❏ las aletas
- ❏ el esnórquel
- ❏ la sombrilla

las aletas

la pelota

la sombrilla

el esnórquel

la toalla

el protector solar

el traje de baño

los lentes de sol

141

¡Vamos a la playa!
Class activity to learn popular expressions. Model the phrases. Then say *¡Vamos a la playa!* and select a student to respond. That person then repeats the pattern with another person, and so on.
Analysis: Name sports and other activities and have volunteers use the phrases to express how they feel about that activity.

¿Qué llevamos?
Class activity to introduce new vocabulary by using the illustrations on this page. Ask the question in the title. Also take this opportunity to review words by asking such questions as:
¿Qué comida vas a llevar?
¿Y qué libro?

CHECK

- *¿Sabes bucear?*
- *¿Dónde haces surf, en el mar o en la piscina?*
- *¿Vamos a la piscina?*

LOG BOOK
Have students choose one expression from *¡Vamos a la playa!* and write activities they associate with it.

REALIDADES

Communicative Objectives
- to talk about watersports
- to talk about Puerto Rico

Related Components

Activity Book	Audio Tapes
p. 66	Chapter Tape:
Audio Book	4A, Seg. 2
Script: Seg. 2	**Cuaderno**
	p. 38

GETTING STARTED

Ask what these activities are and if anyone has ever done any of them. If so, have that person tell the class about it. If not, talk about them yourself. (See *Descriptions of Water Sports,* page 151.) Use gestures and body language to act out or clarify.

DISCUSS

Talk about the photographs and captions, and ask questions. Suggestions:

Introduction
Tell students that each photo was taken in a different part of Puerto Rico. Ask them to look at the captions and find the names of these places. (Humacao, Rincón, Isla Verde, Fajardo, Vieques).

Sailboat
Aquí hay una foto de unos veleros.
Este es un velero con dos velas.
Vela, velero; los veleros tienen velas.
Hay una regata de veleros.
¿Qué es una regata?

Surfer
¿Saben Uds. hacer surf?
Dice aquí que es "un poco peligroso" hacer surf. ¿Es cierto?
¿En qué lugares de Estados Unidos hacen surf? (California, Florida, Hawaii, etc.).

Windsurfers
Estas personas hacen tabla a vela.
Dicen que "es un deporte emocionante".
¿Qué quiere decir la palabra emoción*?*

Skindivers
¿Quiénes aprenden a bucear?
¿En qué lugar de Puerto Rico están?

Waterskiing
Esta mujer no hace surf, ¿verdad?
¿Qué hace?
¿Quién sabe hacer esquí acuático?

Playa y Mar

REALIDADES

DEPORTES ACUÁTICOS EN

PUERTO RICO

Isla tropical. Playas de arena blanca. Temperatura ideal. ¡Y gran hospitalidad!

La regata de veleros en Humacao es emocionante.

Hacer surf es un poco peligroso. Pero este chico no tiene miedo. En Rincón hay olas perfectas.

¿Sabes hacer tabla a vela? Muchas personas van a hacer tabla a vela a Isla Verde. Es un deporte muy chévere.

Fajardo es un lugar ideal para hacer esquí acuático. Es un deporte muy fácil y divertido.

¿Quieres bucear? Chicos y chicas aprenden a bucear en Vieques. El mar es azul y transparente.

142

▶▶▶ INTERNET LINK

For images of Puerto Rico, including a regatta in San Juan Harbor:
http://www.astro.lsa.umich.edu/users/salgado/HTML/images_pr.html

HABLA DE LA REVISTA

A. Di qué saben hacer las personas de las fotos.

Saben navegar.

B. Según tu opinión, ¿qué deporte acuático es fácil?

¿Y divertido?   ¿Y chévere?

¿Y emocionante?   ¿Y peligroso?

C. Habla con tu compañero(a) sobre los deportes acuáticos.

— ¿Sabes bucear?

— Sí, sé bucear.
  (No, no sé, pero me gustaría aprender.)

— ¿Quieres navegar o hacer tabla a vela?

— Quiero navegar.

¿QUÉ OPINAS?

• ¿Qué tres deportes acuáticos te gustaría hacer?

• Pregúntales a otros estudiantes: ¿Cuál es tu deporte acuático favorito?

Haz una tabla con los resultados. Usa el modelo.

ENCUESTA

Deporte	yo	otros estudiantes
nadar		
hacer tabla a vela	✓	III
bucear		
hacer surf		
navegar	✓	
hacer jet ski	✓	
hacer esquí acuático		

Según la encuesta, ¿cuál es el deporte más popular? ¿Y el menos popular?

¿SABES QUE...?

For only a few dollars, you can go for an evening boat ride in **La Parguera**, the most famous of Puerto Rico's several phosphorescent bays. The light comes from billions of aquatic microorganisms that give off a green glow when the waters are disturbed.

143

Communicative Objectives

To talk about:
• beach activities you like to do
• things you need to take to the beach
• things you know how to do
• sports you want to play

Related Components

Activity Book p. 67-68	Transparencies Ch. 5:
Cuaderno p. 39-40	Palabras en acción
	Tutor Page p. 23

GETTING STARTED

Ask students which of the activities in the drawing they saw in photos earlier in the unit. Which ones are new?

DISCUSS

Comment on what the people in the drawing are wearing or doing. For example, contrast two characters:
El hombre tiene lentes de bucear, pero la mujer tiene lentes de sol.

Para hispanohablantes

Some Spanish speakers in your class may use other expressions than the ones introduced in this chapter. Ask them to share with the class. A few variations:
el bote: el barco, la lancha, la nave
hacer surf: practicar tabla hawaiana
hacer tabla a vela: hacer surf a vela
los lentes: las gafas, los anteojos
los lentes de bucear: la máscara
el/la salvavidas: el/la guarda playas
la sombrilla: el parasol, el quitasol
la tabla: el acuaplano, la tabla hawaiana
el traje de baño: el bañador
el velero: el bote a vela, el barco de vela

PALABRAS EN ACCIÓN
EN LA PLAYA

1 ¿Qué ves en el dibujo?

Haz cuatro listas. Compara tus listas con las listas de tus compañeros(as).

¿Qué ves? los remos,...
¿Qué hacen? navegar,...
¿Qué llevan? la toalla,...
¿Qué alquilan? las aletas,...

2 Actividades en la playa

¿Qué te gusta hacer en la playa? Habla con tu compañero(a) de cuatro actividades.

— ¿Qué te gusta hacer en la playa?
— Me gusta jugar al frisbi. ¿Y a ti?
— A mí me gusta hacer esquí acuático.

3 ¿Qué necesitas?

Habla con tu compañero(a) de cuatro cosas que necesitan en la playa.

— ¿Necesitas el protector solar?
— Claro que sí. Hoy quiero tomar el sol.

4 ¿Qué sabes hacer?

Habla de cuatro actividades.

— ¿Sabes bucear?
— Sí, bastante bien. ¿Y tú?
— Más o menos. ¿Sabes navegar?
— No, pero sé hacer surf.

144

For students having difficulty talking about the beach and beach activities you might consider:
• **The tutor page:** Pair the student with a native speaker or a more able student using the tutor page.
• **Actividades:** see page 138D: *Y los ganadores son...*

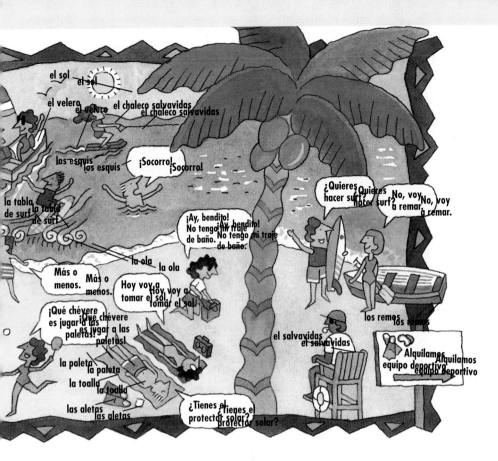

el sol
el velero
el chaleco salvavidas
los esquis
¡Socorro!
la tabla de surf
¿Quieres hacer surf?
No, voy a remar.
¡Ay, bendito! No tengo mi traje de baño.
Más o menos.
la ola
Hoy voy a tomar el sol.
¡Qué chévere es jugar a las paletas!
la paleta
la toalla
las aletas
¿Tienes el protector solar?
los remos
el salvavidas
Alquilamos equipo deportivo

---

5 ¿A qué quieren jugar?

Escoge cuatro deportes para jugar con tus compañeros(as).

— *María, ¿quieres jugar al voleibol?*
— *Sí, ¡qué chévere! ¡Me encanta jugar al voleibol! ¿Y tú, Luis?*
— *No, ¡qué aburrido! Prefiero jugar a las paletas.*

6 Charada

Representa frente a la clase el deporte acuático que quieres hacer.

7 Collage

Usa fotos de revistas para hacer un collage de la playa. Describe el collage a la clase.

8 Tú eres el autor

Con tu compañero(a), escriban un diálogo sobre las actividades en la playa. Presenten el diálogo a la clase.

— *¿Te gusta hacer tabla a vela?*
— *A mí me encanta. ¿Y a ti?*
— *Yo quiero aprender. ¿Es peligroso?*
— *No, es emocionante.*

145

Communicative Objective
• to say what you know how to do, using **saber** and the infinitive of another verb

Related Components

Activity Book p. 69-70	**Audio Tapes** Listening: 4A, Seg. 3
Audio Book Script: Seg. 3 Activities: p. 45	**Cuaderno** p. 39
	Tutor Page p. 24

 GETTING STARTED

Ask students to name a few action verbs. Write them on the board. (See lists below.)

Language in Context

Read aloud what the girl in the photo is asking. Ask the class what she might say about herself, eliciting the word **sé**.
For example:
Yo sé hacer surf, pero no muy bien.
Point out that **sé** and **sabes** are related, even though they don't look very similar. Ask what other words are part of the **saber** "family." Use the paradigm to review the forms of **saber**.

 DISCUSS

Review action verbs from previous chapters and introduce some of this chapter's new verbs with questions that incorporate **saber** plus an infinitive.
For example:
¿Saben jugar al béisbol?
María, ¿sabes tocar piano?
¿Quiénes saben bailar salsa?
¿Sabemos todos hacer pizza?
¿Saben Uds. que yo sé cantar rap?
¿Qué deporte sabes jugar?
¿Sabes cómo se llama este libro?
¿Quién sabe bucear?

PARA COMUNICARNOS MEJOR
¿QUÉ SABES HACER?

¿Sabes hacer surf? ¡Es emocionante!

¡OJO!

Saber is not used to mean "to know a person or a place." **Conocer** is used for that purpose.

To say that you know how to do something, use a form of the verb *saber* (*to know how*) and the infinitive of another verb.

Sé hacer surf.	I know how to surf.
¿Saben nadar?	Do you know how to swim?

All forms of the verb ***saber*** are like the forms of regular *-er* verbs, with one exception: *yo sé*.

saber (to know how)

yo	**sé**	nosotros(as)	sabemos
tú	sabes	vosotros(as)	sabéis
usted	sabe	ustedes	saben
él/ella	sabe	ellos/ellas	saben

For students having difficulty using **saber** plus an infinitive to say what they know how to do, you might consider:
• **The tutor page:** Pair the student with a native speaker or a more able student using the tutor page.

1 Deportes acuáticos

¿Qué deportes acuáticos sabes hacer? Pregúntale a tu compañero(a).

— ¿Sabes bucear?
— Sí, sé bucear bastante bien. ¡Es divertido!
  (No, no sé bucear. No me gusta.)

1. bucear
2. navegar
3. hacer surf
4. hacer esquí acuático
5. remar
6. nadar

> *Expresiones útiles*
> muy bien
> más o menos
> bastante bien
> bien
> ¡Es divertido!
> ¡Es emocionante!
> ¡Es peligroso!
> ¡Me encanta!
> ¡No me gusta!

2 Para tu diario

Prepara una lista de ocho cosas que sabes hacer.

> Sé montar en bicicleta.
> Sé bailar salsa.

3 La fiesta del Club de Español

A. El Club de Español va a hacer una fiesta y necesita voluntarios(as). En grupo, preparen una tabla con los nombres de los compañeros(as) y las actividades que saben hacer.

¿Quién sabe...?	yo	Pedro	Juana
hacer pasteles		✓	
tocar la guitarra	✓		✓
sacar fotos	✓		

GRAN FIESTA DEL CLUB DE ESPAÑOL

SÁBADO, 25 DE FEBRERO A LAS 5:30

NECESITAMOS VOLUNTARIOS(AS) PARA:

- Hacer arroz con pollo, pasteles y galletas
- Preparar jugos y refrescos
- Tocar la guitarra
- Sacar fotos
- Decorar el gimnasio
- Escribir las invitaciones

B. Informen a la clase.

- Pedro sabe hacer pasteles.
- Juana y yo sabemos tocar la guitarra.
- Yo sé sacar fotos.

147

ACTIVITIES

Students use **saber** plus an infinitive to say that they know how to do something.

1. Pair Activity
Use **saber** to talk about water sports you know how to do, and use expressions that tell how well you can do them and how much you enjoy them.
Possible Answers:
1. See model on student page.
2. No, no sé navegar. No me gusta.
3. No, no sé hacer surf. ¡Es peligroso!
4. Sí, sé hacer esquí acuático. ¡Es chévere!
5. Si, sé remar muy bien. No es aburrido.
6. Sé nadar bastante bien. ¡Me encanta!
Application: In pairs, make lists of things you both know how to do well and things that neither of you knows how to do well. Write sentences about these.

2. Individual Activity
Make a list of eight things you know how to do.
Possible Answers:
Sé cocinar. Sé cantar. Sé tocar la guitarra. Sé escribir cartas. Sé hacer pizza.
Analysis: You need someone to help with a party. What questions would you ask a friend who offers to help?

3. Group Activity
A. Use the model to prepare a chart of things to be done for the **fiesta**. Discuss which of you can do these things, list their names, and make a checkmark.
(Other tasks: *hacer arroz con pollo, hacer galletas, preparar jugos y refrescos, decorar el gimnasio, escribir las invitaciones.*)
B. Tell the class who will do what.
Answers: See model on student page.

CHECK

- ¿Qué deporte sabes hacer?
- ¿Qué sabemos hacer bien?
- ¿Qué saben bailar tus amigos?
- ¿Saben Uds. si yo sé cantar?
- ¿Quién sabe nadar?

LOG BOOK
Write how the conjugation of **saber** does not follow the general rules you learned for **-er** verbs.

Para hispanohablantes

Interview your classmates to find out what activities they know how to do.

Communicative Objective
• to say what you want to do by using **querer** and the infinitive of another verb

Related Components

Activity Book p. 71-72	**Cuaderno** p. 40
Audio Book Script: Seg.4 Activities: p. 46	**Tutor Page** p. 25
Audio Tapes Listening: 4A, Seg. 4	

GETTING STARTED

Ask what students think the ads on these pages offer.

Language in Context
Ask questions and make comments about the advertisements. Use forms of **querer** with infinitives when possible. For example:
¿Quieres llevar una bicicleta a la playa?
¿No? ¿Y un kayak?

Point out that a person normally uses **querer** and the infinitive of another verb to say that he or she wants to do something. Ask how we say the same thing in English. Ask what other words are part of the **querer** "family."

Have students write sentences using forms of **querer** with infinitives.

DISCUSS

Review action verbs from previous chapters and introduce some of this chapter's new verbs with questions that incorporate **querer** plus an infinitive.
¿Quieren llevar comida a la playa?
¿Quién quiere nadar con las aletas?
¿Quieres jugar al béisbol esta tarde?
¿Qué película quieren ver?
¿Quién quiere ir de compras esta tarde?
¿Qué instrumento quieres tocar?
¿Quieres cocinar tacos y enchiladas?
¿Queremos comer ahora?

PARA COMUNICARNOS MEJOR

¿QUÉ QUIERES HACER?

LA BICI FANTÁSTICA
•Alquiler •Venta •Reparación
•Bicicletas de todas las marcas
•Los mejores precios del mercado
Teléfono: 555-4987
San Juan de Puerto Rico

DEPORTES
LA OLA
Venta de kayaks y accesorios
Alquiler por hora, por día y por semana
Clases de remo
Abierto de lunes a domingo de 7:00 a.m. a 9:00 p.m.
555-6735
Balneario de Luquillo
Luquillo, Puerto Rico

LA CASA DEL BUCEO
VENTA, REPARACIÓN, ALQUILER DE EQUIPO DE BUCEO
LA ESCUELA DE BUCEO MÁS GRANDE DE PUERTO RICO
TELÉFONO:
555-5442
Avenida Jesús T. Piñero 293
Río Piedras, P. R. 00926

To talk about what you want to do, use a form of the verb *querer* (*to want*) **and the infinitive of another verb.**

—Quiero ir a la playa.	I want to go to the beach.
—¿Quieren alquilar un bote a motor?	Do you want to rent a motor boat?
—No, queremos alquilar un kayak.	No, we want to rent a kayak.
—Y tú, ¿qué quieres hacer?	And you, what do you want to do?
—Quiero jugar al voleibol.	I want to play volleyball.

Here are the forms of the verb *querer* in the present tense. Note that the stem *(quer-)* changes from *e* to *ie* in all forms except *nosotros(as)* and *vosotros(as)*.

querer (ie) (to want)

yo	quiero	nosotros(as)	queremos
tú	quieres	vosotros(as)	queréis
usted	quiere	ustedes	quieren
él/ella	quiere	ellos/ellas	quieren

148

For students having difficulty using **saber** or **querer** plus an infinitive to say what they know how to do, you might consider:
• **The tutor page:** Pair the student with a native speaker or a more able student using the tutor page.
• **Actividades:** see page 138C: *Mi postal puertorriqueña* and *Quiero hacer más*

 **En la playa**

¿Qué quieren hacer? Pregúntale a tu compañero(a).

—*¿Qué quieren hacer tus amigos?*
—*Quieren hacer surf.*

1. tus amigos   3. tus amigos y tú   5. tu hermano

2. tu amiga   4. los jóvenes 6. ¿y tú?

2 Tus compañeros y tú van a la playa

A. ¿Qué quieres llevar? Pregúntales a seis compañeros(as).

—*Mariana, ¿qué quieres llevar a la playa?*
—*Quiero llevar el frisbi y las paletas.*
—*Y tú, Roberto, ¿qué quieres llevar?*
—*Quiero llevar la red.*

B. Hagan una lista de las cosas que quieren llevar.

Queremos llevar el frisbi,...

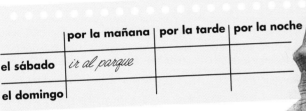

¿Qué llevamos?
las paletas
la red
los lentes de sol
el frisbi
la pelota
la guitarra
el protector solar
la sombrilla

3 Actividades para el fin de semana

A. ¿Qué quieres hacer el fin de semana?

	por la mañana	por la tarde	por la noche
el sábado	*ir al parque*		
el domingo			

B. ¿Qué quieren hacer? Pregúntales a tus compañeros(as).

—*Quiero ir a la playa el sábado por la mañana. ¿Quieren ir conmigo?*
—*Sí, quiero ir, pero por la tarde.*
—*No, yo quiero ir al parque.*

149

149

Communicative Objectives
• to talk and write about sports activities and equipment
• to invite a friend to go somewhere
• to respond to invitations

Related Components

Assessment: Oral Proficiency: p. 25	**Conexiones** Chapter 5
Audio Book Script: Seg. 5 Activities: p. 47	**Magazine** Juntos en Puerto Rico
Audio Tapes Listening: 4A, Seg.5 Conexiones: 17A, Ch.1	**Tutor Page** p. 26

GETTING STARTED

At this point, students should be able to use **saber** and **querer** and all of the chapter vocabulary correctly.
Review vocabulary and grammar with the realia and such questions as:
¿Qué deportes saben hacer?
¿Qué deportes quieren jugar?

APPLY

1. Individual or Class Activities
A. Answer questions about the Club.
Answers:
El club está en Humacao, Puerto Rico.
El club tiene ocho canchas.
(Possible answer) *Quiero aprender natación, buceo, tabla a vela y navegación.*
B. List activities you know how to do and activities you want to learn to do.
Possible Answers:
Quiero aprender a navegar.
Sé hacer esquí acuático.
Challenge: Make a sentence for each of the icons. Use a different form of **saber** each time. Example: *Mi hermano no sabe jugar a las paletas.*
C. Decide which sport goes with each word, then write a sentence saying that you need this object to play that sport.
Answers:
Necesito una pelota para jugar al tenis.
Necesito remos para remar.
Necesito lentes de bucear para bucear.

Club deportivo Borinquen
Humacao, Puerto Rico

Con dos piscinas, ocho canchas de tenis y una marina que acomoda toda clase de botes, el club deportivo Borinquen ofrece una gran variedad de clases: natación, buceo, tabla a vela y navegación. También alquila equipo deportivo.

1 Actividades en el club deportivo

A. Lee el anuncio del club deportivo Borinquen y contesta las preguntas.

> *¿Dónde está el club?*
> *¿Cuántas canchas tiene?*
> *¿Qué deportes quieres aprender en el club?*

B. Mira los dibujos del anuncio y haz una lista de las actividades que sabes hacer y otra lista de las actividades que quieres aprender.

> *Sé jugar al tenis.*   *Quiero aprender a bucear.*

C. ¿Qué equipo necesitas? Di para qué deporte o deportes necesitas estas cosas.

> *Necesito aletas para bucear.*

una pelota	un velero
remos	esquís
lentes de bucear	una tabla
una red	un paracaídas
un traje de baño	

PARA TU REFERENCIA

acomoda
holds
la cancha
court
la natación
swimming
la navegación
sailing
ofrece
offers
toda clase de
all kinds of

150

Necesito una red para jugar al voleibol.
Necesito un velero para la navegación.
Necesito esquís para hacer esquí acuático.
Necesito una tabla para hacer surf.
Necesito un paracaídas para hacer parasailin

2. Pair Activity
Ask where your partner wants to go Saturday. Say what the two of you will do.
Answers: See model on student page.

3. Pair Activity
Make plans to go to the beach this weekend.
• Ask if your partner wants to go to the beach.
• Discuss two or three activities you'll do there.
• Decide what day and time you'll go.
Sample Dialog:
—*¿Quieres ir a la playa el domingo por la mañana?*
—*Sí. ¿Qué vamos a hacer?*
—*Yo quiero tomar el sol y nadar.*
—*Y yo quiero hacer surf. Vamos.*

2 ¿Adónde quieres ir?

Pregúntale a tu compañero(a) adónde quiere ir el sábado.
Di qué van a hacer.

—¿Adónde quieres ir el sábado?
—Al lago.
—Chévere, me encanta nadar.

¿Adónde?
al lago
al río
a la piscina
a la playa

 3 Un fin de semana en la playa

Haz planes con tu compañero(a) para ir a la playa este
fin de semana.

• Pregúntale a tu compañero(a) si quiere ir a la playa este
  fin de semana.
• Hablen de dos o tres actividades que quieren hacer allí.
• Decidan el día y la hora.

 4 Entrevista

Entrevista a un(a) compañero(a) que practica deportes. Pregúntale
dónde y cuándo practica el deporte. Informa a la clase.

*A María Hernández le gusta jugar al voleibol. Sabe jugar
muy bien. Practica en el parque por la mañana.*

 5 Tu diario: mi deporte favorito

En tu diario, contesta las siguientes preguntas:

1. ¿Cuál es tu deporte favorito? ¿Cuándo practicas? ¿Dónde?
   ¿Con quién?
2. ¿Qué necesitas para practicar tu deporte favorito?
3. ¿Qué deporte quieres aprender? ¿Por qué?

 **¿SABES QUE...?**

Swimming and surfing are favorite
after-school activities in Puerto Rico. By
law, all of Puerto Rico's beaches are
public. Special resort beaches, called
balnearios, have facilities such as
dressing rooms and picnic grounds. If
you don't bring your own equipment,
rentals are available in many of these
balnearios.

151

---

4. Pair Activity
Interview an athlete about his or her
sport. Then write answers in Spanish.
Share your answers with the class.
Answers: See model on student page.
Synthesis: Write a fictional interview with
your favorite sports figure.

5. Homework or Classwork
1. Write about your favorite sport, when
and where you play it, and with whom.
2. What do you need in order to play
your sport?
3. What sport would you like to learn?
Why?

CHECK

¿Qué deporte sabes hacer bien?
¿Qué necesitas para jugar tenis?
¿Quieres ir a la playa este fin de semana?

LOG BOOK
Have students use their Log Books to write
down the paradigms of any verbs they
have difficulty using.

Background

Descriptions of Water Sports

Jet Skiing: A jet ski is a 6-foot-long boat-
frame with an engine. It is ridden like a
motorcycle (there are sit-down and stand-
up versions) and can reach speeds up to 60
mph. Invented in the late 1960s.

Parasailing *(hacer parasailing)*: Sailers are
towed by a motorboat and lifted by a parafoil, a flexible cloth kite that resembles a
sport parachute. The parafoil was invented
in 1963.

Sailing *(navegar)*: Most recreational or racing vessels are sloops (one mast, two sails).
They range from 10 to 70 feet in length.

Skindiving *(bucear)*: Shallow-water diving
is done with a mask and snorkel (a short
tube). Deeper dives require air tanks and a
facemask. Jacques Cousteau invented
scuba gear.

Surfing *(hacer surf)*: Surfers ride along or
just under a breaking wave. Boards range
from 4 to 12 feet, and larger ones have a
stabilizing fin. Surfing was invented in
Hawaii more than 500 years ago.

Waterskiing *(hacer esquí acuático)*: Skiers
are towed behind a motorboat. In competition, they slalom around buoys and
jump ramps. Invented on the French
Riviera, 1920s.

Windsurfing *(hacer tabla a vela)*: A sailboard is a surfboard with sail, footstraps,
and small keel. Record speed is just over 45
knots (about 52 mph). Developed in
California in the 1960s.

For students having difficulty talking
about beach activities, using **saber** and
querer, you might consider:
• **The tutor page:** Pair the student with a
  native speaker or a more able student
  using the tutor page.
• **Actividades:** see page 138D:
  Busca pares

Communicative Objectives
• to discuss taking a trip
• to use a map to decide where to go
• to talk about how much money you need

Related Components

Transparencies	Video: Tape/Book
Ch. 5: Para resolver	Unit 3: Seg. 2

Search to frame 1340917

GETTING STARTED

Ask students if they have ever planned a trip. What were some of the problems they faced? How did they solve them?

APPLY

Form small groups. Have each of the groups select a city that is *not* marked with a sports symbol. They will use these cities as bases for these activities.

PASO 1: ¿Adónde quieren ir?
Decide what activities all of you want to do on a weekend trip, and choose a place on the map where you can do all of those things.
Answers: See model on student page.
Application: Name a place you don't want to go to and say why.

PASO 2: ¿Qué quieren llevar?
List the clothes, equipment and other things you are going to take on the trip.
Possible Answers:
Ropa: un traje de baño, una camiseta
Accesorios: la toalla, los lentes de sol
Equipo deportivo: la pelota, las paletas
Analysis: Player one says several words that have a common link. Player two says one word that links them. Examples: *mar, piscina, lago, río (nadar)*
arena, agua, sol (playa)

PASO 3: ¿Cuánto dinero necesitan?
Use the advertisements to find the best prices for equipment and classes. Write how much money you'll need.
Answers: See model on student page.
Application: You have a budget of $100. Write down what equipment you will rent and what classes you will take.

PASO 4: ¿Cuáles son los resultados?
Report the results to the class.

PASO 5: Comparen los resultados
Compare your findings.
• Which were the three most popular places? Why?
• Which group wanted to bring the most clothing? The most equipment?
• Which group needed the most money? Which needed the least?

PARA RESOLVER
PLANES PARA UNA EXCURSIÓN

PASO 1 ¿Adónde quieren ir?

En grupo, escojan un lugar del mapa adonde quieren ir el fin de semana. Digan por qué quieren ir allí.

• *Queremos ir a Fajardo el sábado.*
• *Luis y Roberto quieren nadar.*
• *Beatriz quiere aprender a hacer esquí acuático.*
• *Yo quiero tomar el sol.*

PASO 2 ¿Qué quieren llevar?

Ahora, hagan una lista de la ropa, equipo deportivo y otras cosas que van a llevar.

PASO 3 ¿Cuánto dinero necesitan?

Miren la lista de precios para decidir qué van a alquilar y cuánto dinero van a necesitar. Anoten las respuestas.

> *Queremos bucear con esnórquel tres horas el sábado y dos el domingo. Vamos a alquilar aletas, esnórquel y lentes de bucear. Necesitamos $75 por persona.*

PASO 4 ¿Cuáles son los resultados?

Presenten los resultados de su grupo a la clase.

PASO 5 Comparen los resultados.

• ¿Cuáles son los tres lugares más populares? ¿Por qué?
• ¿Qué grupo quiere llevar más ropa o más cosas?
• ¿Qué grupo necesita más dinero? ¿Y menos dinero?

PARA TU REFERENCIA

el alquiler *rental*
la aventura *adventure*
el buceo *diving*
el dinero *money*
los precios *prices*
la ropa *clothing*
el tanque *oxygen tank*

152

PUERTO RICO

OCÉAN

PUNTA BORINQUEN
Isabella
Camuy
Quebradillas
Río Guajataca
Aguadilla
GUAJATACA
PUNTA HIGÜERO
Moca
Aguada
San Sebastián
CUEVAS DE CAMU
• **Rincón**
Río Añasco
Añasco
Las Marías
Mayagüez
Maricao
AÑASCO
• Hormigueros
MARICAO
Río Guanajibo
Cabo Rojo
San Germán
PORTA COELI
• Lajas
Saban
VALLE LAJAS
BOQUERÓN
La Parguera
DE

BAHÍA FOSFORESCENTE

PRINT FILM
Multi-Purpose
CANON LENS

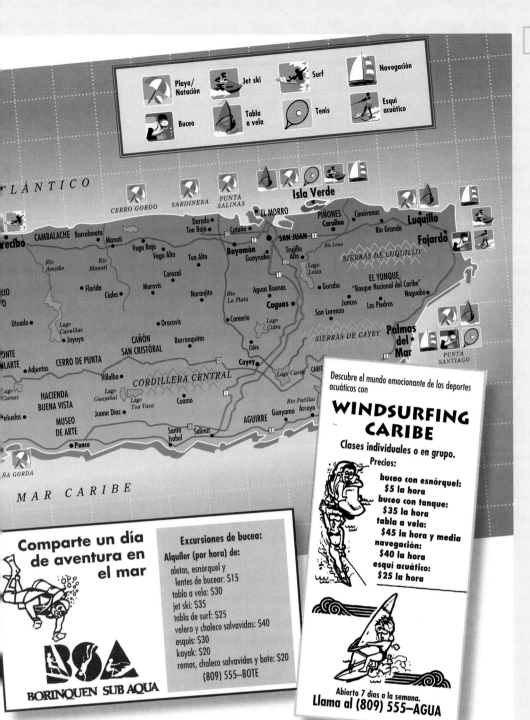

PORTFOLIO

Have students present the information they obtained from *Paso 5* in the form of a pie chart or a bar or line graph.

Water Sports Words

PARASAILING
chute *el paracaídas*
harness *el arnés*

SAILING
boom *la botavara*
keel *la orza*
mast *el mástil*
rudder *el timón*
sloop *la balandra*
wheel *la rueda*

SKINDIVING
air hose *el tubo respirador*
air tank *el tanque de oxígeno*
depth gauge *la sonda marina*
valve *la válvula*
wetsuit *el traje isotérmico*

SURFING/WINDSURFING
fin (skeg) *la aleta*
footstraps *las correas*
surfer *el/la surfista*
tube *el tubazo*

WATERSKIING
slalom *slalom*
towline *la cuerda de arrastre*

Para hispanohablantes

Using the realia as a model, write an advertisement for a hotel in Guánica.

▶▶▶ INTERNET LINK

There are hundreds of water sports pages on the World Wide Web. These two have links to many others:
windsurfing
http://www.dsg.cs.tcd.ie:80/dsg_people/afcondon/windsurf/windsurf_home.html
skindiving
http://www.3routes.com:80/SCUBA/home.html
A few of the sports Usenet groups:
rec.windsurfing
rec.sport.waterski
rec.sport.swimming

Objectives
- **Communicative:** to talk about baseball
- **Cultural:** to learn about Puerto Rico's baseball stars

Related Components

Audio Tapes	Magazine
Conexiones: 17A, Ch. 5	Juntos en Puerto Rico
Conexiones Chapter 5	

GETTING STARTED

Ask if anyone knows more about these players. Do they know the names of any other Hispanic players in the United States?

DISCUSS

Using Context Clues
Use this exercise to practice learning from context clues. Ask, for example, what **promedio de bateo** probably means. At least a few students should be able to work it out by looking at the numbers. **Jonrones**, on the other hand, can be understood if one tries to say it aloud.

Thinking About Language
Use the cards to ask such questions as what article should go with **equipo** or what the infinitive form of **lanza** is.

Critical Thinking
Have students create questions that compare and contrast the cards. For example:
¿Quién tiene más carreras impulsadas?
¿Quién tiene más años, González o Baerga?

Cooperative Learning
Research and vote on an all-star Hispanic team, then create a set of cards. Students may wish to include these cards in their portfolios.

Para hispanohablantes

Narrate an imaginary baseball game for the class as if you were a sportscaster.

ENTÉRATE
DEPORTISTAS BORICUAS°

ESTRELLAS° DEL BÉISBOL

El béisbol es uno de los deportes más populares de Puerto Rico. Jóvenes y adultos practican béisbol en la calle, en parques y estadios. Muchos puertorriqueños° juegan° en la Liga Caribeña° y en las Ligas Mayores.

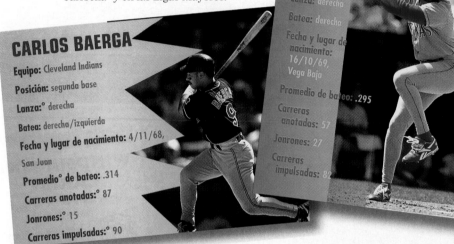

CARLOS BAERGA

Equipo: Cleveland Indians

Posición: segunda base

Lanza:° derecha

Batea: derecha/izquierda

Fecha y lugar de nacimiento: 4/11/68, San Juan

Promedio° de bateo: .314

Carreras anotadas:° 87

Jonrones:° 15

Carreras impulsadas:° 90

JUAN GONZÁLEZ

Equipo: Texas Rangers

Posición: jardinero

Lanza: derecha

Batea: derecha

Fecha y lugar de nacimiento: 16/10/69, Vega Baja

Promedio de bateo: .295

Carreras anotadas: 57

Jonrones: 27

Carreras impulsadas: 32

TE TOCA A TI

¿Cierto o falso?

1. Juan González es jardinero de los Cleveland Indians.
2. El béisbol no es popular en Puerto Rico.
3. El cumpleaños de Juan González es en octubre.
4. Carlos Baerga es de San Juan.
5. Juan González y Carlos Baerga tienen 19 jonrones.

¿SABES QUE...?

The Caribbean League's season stretches from October to March. Many professional ball players from the United States join the Caribbean professional players during that time.

boricuas *from Puerto Rico*
las carreras anotadas *runs scored*
las carreras impulsadas *runs batted in*
las estrellas *stars*
el jardinero *outfielder*
los jonrones *home runs*
juegan *play*
lanza *throws*
la Liga Caribeña *Caribbean League*
el promedio *average*
los puertorriqueños *Puerto Ricans*

154

CHECK

¿Cierto o falso?
Answers:
1. *Falso. Juan González es jardinero de los Texas Rangers.*
2. *Falso. El béisbol es muy popular en Puerto Rico.*
3. *Cierto.*
4. *Cierto.*
5. *Falso. Carlos Baerga tiene 15 jonrones y Juan González tiene 27.*

PORTFOLIO
Have students create Spanish baseball cards of themselves.

Additional Baseball Words
pitcher *lanzador*
catcher *receptor*
first base *primera base*
second base *segunda base*
shortstop *jardinero corto*
third base *tercera base*
outfielder *jardinero (izquierdo, central y derecho)*
single *sencillo*
double *doble*
triple *triple*
strikeout *ponche*
inning *entrada*

VOCABULARIO TEMÁTICO

En la playa
At the beach

la arena *sand*
el bote a motor *motorboat*
la ola *wave*
el/la salvavidas *lifeguard*
el sol *sun*
el velero *sail boat*

Actividades en la playa
Activities at the beach

jugar al frisbi *to play frisbee*
jugar a las paletas
to play paddle ball
jugar con la arena
to play in the sand
tomar el sol *to sunbathe*

Los deportes acuáticos
Water sports

bucear *to dive*
hacer esquí acuático
to water-ski
hacer jet ski *to jet ski*
hacer parasailing *to parasail*
hacer surf *to surf*
hacer tabla a vela *to windsurf*
nadar *to swim*
navegar *to sail*
remar *to row*

El equipo deportivo
Sports equipment

las aletas *flippers*
el chaleco salvavidas *life jacket*
el esnórquel *snorkel*
los esquís *skis*
el frisbi *frisbee*
los lentes de bucear
diving mask
la paleta *paddle*
el paracaídas *parachute*
la pelota *ball*
la red *net*
los remos *oars*
la tabla a vela *sailboard*
la tabla de surf *surfboard*

Cosas para la playa
Things for the beach

los lentes de sol *sunglasses*
el protector solar *sunscreen*
la sombrilla *beach umbrella*
la toalla *towel*
el traje de baño *bathing suit*

Lugares para ir a nadar
Places to go swimming

el lago *lake*
el mar *sea*
la piscina *swimming pool*
el río *river*

Expresiones y palabras

bastante bien *quite well*
Es peligroso. *It's dangerous.*
¡Fabuloso! *Fabulous!*
más o menos *just so so*
¡Me encanta! *I love it!*
¡Qué emocionante!
How exciting!
¡Socorro! *Help!*
alquilar *to rent*
aprender a *to learn to*
llevar *to carry*
prefiero... *I prefer*
querer *to want*
saber *to know how*

Expresiones de Puerto Rico

¡Ay, bendito! *Oh, no!*
¡Qué chévere! *Terrific!*

LA CONEXIÓN INGLÉS-ESPAÑOL

Many words that begin with *s-* in English begin with **es-** in Spanish. For example, you know that the Spanish words **especial** and **estación** mean *special* and *station* in English. What words in the *Vocabulario temático* of this chapter begin with **es-**? Did you know their meaning when you first saw them?

155

Objectives
• to review vocabulary
• to correctly pronounce words containg the lettewrs "v" and "b"

Related Components

Activity Book	Audio Book
Chapter Review: p. 73-74	Script: Seg. 6 Activities p. 48
Assessment	**Audio Tapes**
Listening Script: p. 13 Chapter Test: p. 69-74	Listening: 4A, Seg. 6 Assessment: 17A, Ch. 5
	Cuaderno p. 43-44

Pronunciation: "b" and "y"

• Remind students that at the beginning of a sentence, after a pause, or after an "m" or "n", both letters are pronounced like the "b" in the English word "boy."
• at the begining of a sentence.
Bolivia es un país.
Venezuela es un país.
b) after "m" or "n"
ambos, combinación, convite, convidar
• At all other times, the Spanish "b" and "v" are pronounced halfway between an English "b" and "v." This sound is best approximated by trying to say an English "v" with both lips rather than with the upper teeth and lower lip.
Quiero bucear
Estoy bastante bien.
Fabuloso!
saber, el frisbi, el bote a motor

LOG BOOK
Have students copy their three favorite tongue-twisters.

La conexión inglés-español

Ask what other words begin with this sound. When a student suggests one that begins with an **s** rather than an **es** (e.g., **salvavidas**), ask what is different about it. (**S** plus a consonant never appears at the beginning of a Spanish word.)
Possible Rule: If a word begins with an **es** and a consonant, cover the **e** to see if it reminds you of an English word.
This rule does not apply just to cognates but to all Spanish words. Ask for other examples.

	Objetivos page 157	Conversemos pages 158–159	Realidades pages 160–161	Palabras en acción pages 162–163
Comunicación	• To talk about the weather and the seasons	Discuss the local weather and favorite seasons	Read text, discuss weather forecast, talk about where to go, make weather chart, discuss where to go and what to do	Activities 1, 5-7: Read cartoon, make table; talk about weather; act out a season scene; make collage
	• To talk about what to do and what to wear	Discuss what to do and wear in different kinds of weather	Read text and weather chart, discuss where to go and what to do	Activities 2, 3: Read cartoon, talk about what people do, what people wear
Vocabulario temático	• To know the expressions for weather and seasons	Brainstorm different seasons and weather expressions	Read text, discuss weather in Puerto Rico	Activity 8: Read cartoon, write letter about seasons and weather locally
	• To know the expressions for the cardinal points		Read text, discuss weather forecast, make weather chart, talk about where to go and what to do	Activities 1-5: Read cartoon, make table; discuss characters; talk about what they are wearing; discuss where to go; create dialogs
	• To know the expressions for clothing	Talk about choosing what to wear according to the weather forecast		Activity 2: Read cartoon, talk about what characters are wearing
	• To know the expressions for pastimes	Discuss different pastimes suited for different kinds of weather	Read text, discuss weather forecast, talk about sports and activities	Activity 3: Read cartoon, talk about what people do
Estructura	• To talk about what you and other people like to do: the verb *gustar* and an infinitive	Use the verb *gustar* and an infinitive to talk about different kinds of weather	Read text, discuss weather forecast, talk about activities	Activity 4: Read cartoon, discuss where to go
	• To talk about games or sports you play: the verb *jugar*			Activity 3: Read cartoon, describe what people do
	• To talk about giving advice: informal commands, the verb *tener* with *que* and an infinitive	Use the verb *tener* with *que* and an infinitive to give advice about what to do in different kinds of weather		Activity 5: Read cartoon, give advice about what to do in different places
Cultura	Puerto Rico's two seasons: dry and rainy		The Fahrenheit scale in Puerto Rico	
Integración		Favorite activities, what is going to happen	Days of week, times of day, numbers, what is going to happen, activities to learn	Making plans, places to go

¿CÓMO TE AFECTA EL TIEMPO?

Para comunicarnos mejor (1) pages 164–165	Para comunicarnos mejor (2) pages 166–167	Situaciones pages 168–169	Para resolver pages 170–171	Notes
Activities 1, 2: Discuss what people like to do during different seasons; make list of seasonal weekend activities	Activities 1-3: Discuss weather forecast, give advice; discuss what to do and what not to do during bad weather	Activities 1-4: Make storm lists; discuss newspaper weather report; write and present weather forecast; write weather conversations	Pasos 2, 4: Make table of weather conditions during a single season; make poster	
Activities 1, 2: Discuss what people like to do in different seasons; make list of seasonal weekend activities	Activities 1-3: Discuss weather forecast, give advice; discuss what to do and what not to do during bad weather	Activities 1, 3, 4: Make storm lists; write and present weather forecast; write weather conversations	Pasos 1, 3, 4: Talk about seasonal activities; make list of seasonal clothing	
Activities 1, 2: Discuss what people like to do in different seasons; make list of seasonal weekend activities	Activity 3: Discuss what not to do during bad weather	Activity 3: Write and present weather forecast	Pasos 1, 2, 4: Talk about seasonal activities; make table of weather conditions; make poster	
		Activities 2,4: Discuss newspaper weather report; write weather conversations	Pasos 1, 4: Talk about seasonal activities; make poster	
	Activity 2: Discuss clothing to wear in bad weather	Activity 4: Write weather conversations	Pasos 3, 4: Make list of seasonal clothing; make poster	
Activity 2: Make list of seasonal weekend activities	Activity 3: Discuss what not to do during bad weather	Activities 3, 4: Write and present weather forecast; write weather conversations	Pasos 1, 4: Talk about seasonal activities; make poster	
Activities 1, 2: Discuss what people like to do in different seasons; make list of seasonal weekend activities			Pasos 1, 4: Talk about seasonal activities; make poster	
Activity 3: Talk about games or sports; make table	Activity 3: Discuss what not to do during bad weather	Activity 4: Write weather conversations	Pasos 1, 4: Talk about seasonal activities; make poster	
	Activity 1-3: Discuss weather forecast, give advice; discuss what to do and what not to do during bad weather	Activities 1, 3, 4: Make storm lists; write and present weather forecast; write weather conversations		
		The Spanish version of "Let a smile be your umbrella"	About Fahrenheit scale	Entérate page 172 Interview with a Puerto Rican TV weather reporter/The Caribbean wind god *Juracán*
Family and friends, favorite activities	Possessions, days of week, places to go, friends, what is going to happen	Items in the house, things to buy, greetings and good-byes	Numbers, how things are named, locations, transportation	Favorite activities, destinations, describing things to do, times of day

Nos gusta todo

GAME

Objective

- to play a game about favorite things, using *gustar* + infinitive and Chapter 6 *Vocabulario temático*

Use

after *Para comunicarnos mejor*, page 164

Materials

- 19 3" x 5" index cards (4 one color, 6 another color, 9 a third color)
- marker
- 3 small paper bags, numbered 1, 2, and 3

Preparation

- Prepare three different-colored groups of index cards: group 1 for the four seasons (*primavera, verano, otoño,* and *invierno*), group 2 for six plural subjects (*mi amigo y yo, mis amigos, mi familia y yo, mi perro y yo, mis abuelos, mis abuelos y mis padres*), and group 3 for nine words and phrases about the weather (*buen tiempo, mal tiempo, calor, fresco, viento, nublado, soleado, llueve, nieva*).

Activity

- Slip each group of cards into its bag and place bags on a table. Select a scorekeeper and form two teams.
- A pair from each team comes to the front and chooses one card from each bag.
- Each pair adds information to the words selected in order to make a sentence in two minutes or less. For example, pair 1 from team A selects *invierno, mis amigos y yo,* and *mal tiempo*. They make the following sentence:—*En el invierno, cuando hace mal tiempo, a mis amigos y a mí nos gusta jugar al ajedrez en casa.* Then pair 1 from team B goes. Teams return cards to bags after each sentence and play until each card has been used at least once.
- The same word can be used more than once, but not the same sentence.
- The team that makes the most sentences wins.

Variations

- Paste weather pictures to cards instead of using the weather phrases.

¡A Puerto Rico!

GAME

Objective

- to play a game about what to do on a Puerto Rican vacation, using informal commands and the verb *tener que* + infinitive

Use

after *Para comunicarnos mejor*, page 166

Preparation

- Brainstorm regular verbs studied so far and list them on chalkboard: *bucear, comer, compartir, comprar, escuchar, jugar, llevar, nadar, navegar, pasear, patinar, remar, sacar fotos, tomar, tomar el sol, visitar.*

Activity

- Set the scene by telling students that a friend or relative is getting ready for a vacation in Puerto Rico. This person wants to know what to pack, where to go, and what to do.
- Have students work in groups of five. First they decide whom they are advising, then they spend five minutes jotting down advice. For example:
  No debes tomar el sol sin un gorro.
  Escribe en tu diario todos los días.
  Come platos puertorriqueños.
  Tienes que comprar un regalo para tus abuelos.
  Usa protector solar en la playa.
  Debes visitar al Viejo San Juan.
  Escribe muchos postales.
  Saca muchas fotos en El Yunque, etc.
- Groups present their advice, alternating turns until a group runs out of fresh advice.
- Groups play until only one remains—the winner of the game.

¿En casa o al aire libre?

GAME

Objective
• to play a game about indoor and outdoor activities, using irregular verbs *jugar* and *hacer* and Chapter 6 *Vocabulario temático*

Use
after *Para comunicarnos mejor,* page 166

Activity
• Divide class in half by rows— team A for indoor activities and team B for outdoor activities. Appoint someone to keep track of how many activities each side names.
• Give teams five minutes to write down activities.
• Start the game by saying *jugar.* Someone from team A might begin:—*Juego al ajedrez en casa cuando hace frío.* Team B:—*Juego al tenis en el parque cuando hace buen tiempo.* Team A:—*Juego con mi hermano José en casa cuando hace mucho frío.* Team B:—*Esquío en las montañas cuando hace buen tiempo.* Team A:—*Juego con videojuegos en la casa de un amigo cuando hace mal tiempo,* etc.
• Play continues in this way until one team is unable to go on. The other team then finishes listing its activities.
• Start round 2 with the verb *hacer.* The winners of round 1, e.g., team B, might begin:—*Hago surf todos los días cuando hace buen tiempo.* Team A:— *Hago sopa para tomar en la cena cuando hace frío.* Students play as they did with *jugar.*
• The team that names the most activities wins. Activities that can be done indoors and out may be used more than once if qualified properly. For example, team B could say:—*Juego al baloncesto en el parque cuando hace buen tiempo.* And team A could say:—*Juego baloncesto en el gimnasio de la escuela cuando hace mal tiempo.*

¡Qué calor! ¡Qué frío!

GAME

Objective
• to play a weather game, using informal commands and exclamations from the Chapter 6 *Vocabulario temático*

Use
after *Para comunicarnos mejor,* page 166

Activity
• Stand in front and exclaim:—*¡Qué calor!* Ask students to think of commands that, if obeyed, might cool you off. Encourage the class to be as creative and as funny as possible.
• Give students five minutes to write down as many of these commands as they can think of. For example, player 1 might say:—*Toma hielo con té.* Player 2:—*Nada al*  *polo norte para tomar un refresco frío.* Player 3:—*Compra el polo norte y vive allí.*
• Continue in this manner until players have no more suggestions to offer, then change the exclamation to *¡Qué frío!* and repeat the activity.
• Play until all exclamations listed in the Chapter 6 *Vocabulario temático* have been used.

Variations
• Play the game with *Voy a* or *Tengo que* + infinitive instead of *informal* commands.

¿CÓMO TE AFECTA EL TIEMPO?

Introduce the chapter and its theme by having students compare Puerto Rico to any cold place they know of. Ask in what ways weather affects people (clothing, outdoor sports, food, housing, ecology, moods). Elicit the idea that talking about the weather is a universal concern.

Related Components

Audio Tapes	Conexiones
Conexiones: 17A, Ch. 6	Chapter 6
	Video: Tape/Book
CD ROM	Unit 3: Seg. 3
Chapter 6	

Search to frame 1381418

GETTING STARTED

Direct students' attention to the photograph. Suggestions for questions:
¿Te gusta la lluvia?
¿Qué ves en la foto?

Thinking About Language

You can use this opportunity to introduce and discuss informal commands in Spanish.

Tú Commands

Students may be unnecessarily confused by the similarity of the command form and the third-person singular of the present tense. One way to avoid confusion is to begin by reviewing English commands. For example, write:

You listen.   You, listen.

Model both of the sentences. Ask: How do we know that one spoken sentence is a statement and the other is a command? What about the written sentences? How do you know?
Next, write the Spanish equivalents under the English ones and say them aloud.

Tú escuchas.   Tú, escucha.

Ask: How are these sentences different? Do not draw attention to the similarities between **escucha** and the third-person singular. Instead, emphasize the fact that the difference between the command and the statement is clearer in Spanish than it is in English.

156

Now point out that there is a simpler way to write or speak commands in both languages.

¡Escucha!   Listen!

Finish up by having volunteers make short statements and commands with these **-ar** verbs: **andar, bailar, cantar, estudiar.**

Chapter Components

Activity Book p. 75-84	Script: p. 49-52 Activities: p. 53-56	Chapter 6 **Conexiones** Chapter 6	Tutor Pages p. 27-30
Assessment Oral Proficiency: p. 26 Listening Script: p. 14 Chapter Test: p. 75-80	**Audio Tapes** Listening: 4B Assessment: 14B, Ch. 6 Conexiones: 17A, Ch. 6	**Cuaderno** p. 45-52 **Magazine** Juntos en Puerto Rico	**Video: Tape/Book** Unit 3: Seg. 2
Audio Book	**CD ROM**	**Transparencies** Chapter 6	

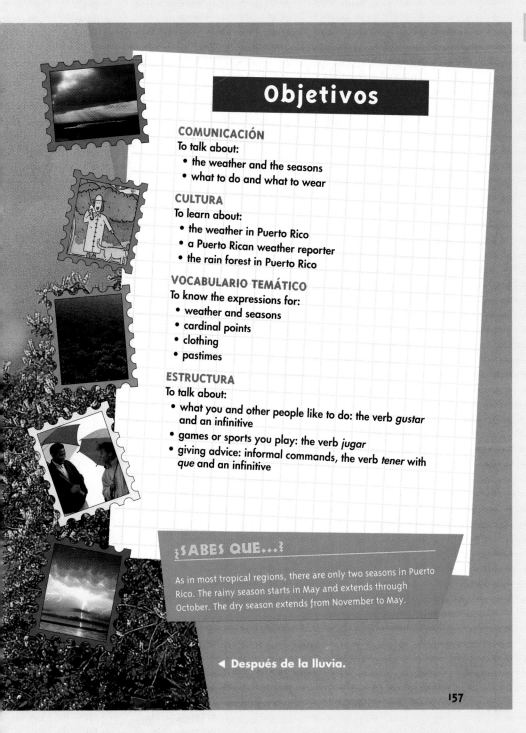

Objetivos

COMUNICACIÓN
To talk about:
* the weather and the seasons
* what to do and what to wear

CULTURA
To learn about:
* the weather in Puerto Rico
* a Puerto Rican weather reporter
* the rain forest in Puerto Rico

VOCABULARIO TEMÁTICO
To know the expressions for:
* weather and seasons
* cardinal points
* clothing
* pastimes

ESTRUCTURA
To talk about:
* what you and other people like to do: the verb *gustar* and an infinitive
* games or sports you play: the verb *jugar*
* giving advice: informal commands, the verb *tener* with *que* and an infinitive

¿SABES QUE...?

As in most tropical regions, there are only two seasons in Puerto Rico. The rainy season starts in May and extends through October. The dry season extends from November to May.

◀ **Después de la lluvia.**

157

■ ACTIVITIES

Here are some additional activities that you may wish to use as you work through this chapter with your students.

Communication
Encourage after-class activities that may enhance student interest and proficiency. Some ideas:
* have students listen to a weather forecast on Spanish television
* bring a Spanish newspaper to class and post the weather report map

Culture
The written word can only hint at what life is like in other lands. To encourage greater understanding:
* listen to cassettes of Puerto Rican *salsa*, *plena*, or *merengue* music
* show the video that accompanies Unit 3 of this textbook

Vocabulary
To reinforce vocabulary, have students:
* use photos to make clothing flashcards
* use Log Books to keep track of difficult vocabulary

Structure
To reinforce **tú** commands:
* make talk balloons with commands and paste them on photos of people talking

▶▶▶ INTERNET LINK
Forecasts in Spanish for Puerto Rico:
gopher to geograf1.sbs.ohio-state.edu

Communicative Objectives
• to talk about the weather
• to talk about clothing and weather

Related Components

Activity Book p. 75	**Cuaderno** p. 45
Audio Book Script: Seg. 1	**Transparencies** Ch. 6: Conversemos
Audio Tapes Listening: 4B, Seg. 1	

GETTING STARTED

Name the seasons and ask for a show of hands to indicate which students like each season best. Ask volunteers to say why they prefer that season.

ACTIVITIES

These activities give students an opportunity to begin communicating with each other and with you, focusing on the theme and objectives of the chapter. The activities can be used as oral class activities, or, if you prefer, you can pair students to achieve more interaction. Additional activities integrate critical-thinking skills.

¿Qué estación del año te gusta más?
Class activity to review **a mí me gusta** and **a mí no me gusta**, and introduce the seasons. This time, ask students to rank the seasons in writing:
   A mí me gusta más [la primavera]
   A mí me gusta...

Donde tú vives, ¿qué tiempo hace en cada estación?
Class activity to introduce weather vocabulary and time expressions. Go through the seasons asking *¿Qué tiempo hace en [la primavera]?* Point out that weather verbs are always singular.
Analysis: Have partners ask each other about weather conditions in other parts of the United States.

MEETING INDIVIDUAL NEEDS

Reaching All Students

For Visual Learners
In groups, write and illustrate a tourist brochure for an imaginary place known for having a warm or cold climate.

For Kinesthetic Learners
In groups of four, think of movements or mime activities that suggest each of the seasons and types of weather. Perform these for the class.

For Auditory Learners
Make up a simple song that mentions the seasons and their weather.

¿QUÉ LES GUSTA HACER CUANDO HACE BUEN TIEMPO? ¿Y CUANDO HACE MAL TIEMPO?

Cuando llueve, nos gusta jugar al ajedrez.
(When it rains, we like to play chess.)

 volar chiringas*

 jugar con la nieve

 jugar al ajedrez

 patinar sobre hielo

 jugar al béisbol

 esquiar

 nadar

 mirar la televisión

* Expresión de Puerto Rico. En otros países: **papalotes**.

PRESTA ATENCIÓN AL PRONÓSTICO DEL TIEMPO. ¿QUÉ ACONSEJAS? *(What do you advise?)*

Hace fresco. Lleva el suéter. *(It's cool. Wear/Take your sweater.)*

Está nublado.

Hace sol.

Hace fresco. *(It's cool.)*

Va a llover. *(It's going to rain.)*

Viene una tormenta. *(A storm is coming.)*

Va a nevar. *(It's going to snow.)*

Llueve a cántaros. *(It's raining cats and dogs.)*

Viene un huracán. *(A hurricane is coming.)*

 el impermeable

 las botas

 los lentes de sol

 el gorro

 el suéter

 los guantes

 el abrigo

 el paraguas

No debes salir sin el gorro.
(You shouldn't go out without your hat.)

Quédate en casa.
(Stay home.)

Ten cuidado.
(Be careful.)

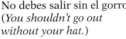

159

¿Qué les gusta hacer cuando hace buen tiempo? ¿Y cuando hace mal tiempo?
Class activity to talk about what students like to do in good and bad weather. Have them answer the title questions using the example and words from the list or any others they know.
Possible Answers:
Cuando hace viento, me gusta volar chiringas.
Cuando hace buen tiempo, me gusta jugar al béisbol.
Cuando hace calor, me gusta nadar.
Cuando nieva, me gusta esquiar.

Presta atención al pronóstico del tiempo. ¿Qué aconsejas?
Class activity to introduce **tú** commands with weather and clothing vocabulary. After modeling the activity, have pairs take turns advising each other on how to prepare for the weather.
Possible Answers:
Está nublado. Lleva el abrigo.
Hace sol. Lleva los lentes de sol.
Va a nevar. Quédate en casa.
Viene un huracán. Ten cuidado.
Viene una tormenta. No debes salir sin el impermeable y las botas.

CHECK

- ¿Qué tiempo hace en el verano?
- ¿Qué haces cuando llueve mucho?
- ¿Qué ropa llevo cuando hace frío?

LOG BOOK
Have students list activities and phrases they associate with their favorite season and their least-favorite season.

Communicative Objective
• to talk about the weather

Related Components

Activity Book p. 76	**Audio Tapes** Listening Tape: 4B, Seg. 2
Audio Book Script: Seg. 2	**Cuaderno** p. 46

GETTING STARTED

Draw a few of the easier weather symbols on the board and ask students what they think the symbols mean.

DISCUSS

Talk about the weather map page. Suggestions:

El tiempo
¿Qué quiere decir la palabra tiempo*?*
¿Qué ves en el dibujo?
¿De qué país es este mapa?

Pronóstico: San Juan, Norte y Este
¿Cómo se dice en inglés pronóstico*?*
¿Dónde está San Juan? ¿En el sur?

Ponce y Sur
¿Y qué ciudad está en el sur?
¿Qué es Ponce?
¿Cuándo va a hacer sol en el sur?
¿Hace calor o hace frío en esta ciudad?

Mayagüez, Oeste
¿Dónde está Mayagüez?
¿Qué tiempo va a hacer en Mayagüez por la mañana? ¿Y por la tarde?

El mar
¿Qué son olas? Dibuja olas en la pizarra.
¿Las olas van a ser grandes o pequeñas?

Leyenda
Examine the legend with students, asking them to describe in English the type of weather each symbol represents.

✓ CULTURE NOTE

Two Puerto Rican cities have nicknames that reflect their location: Ponce, *la perla del sur,* and Mayagüez, *la estrella del oeste.*

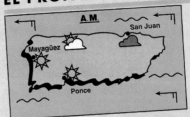
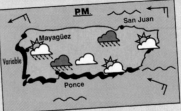

REALIDADES

El tiempo en Puerto Rico

EL TIEMPO

EL PRONÓSTICO PARA MAÑANA

A.M.
San Juan
Mayagüez
Ponce

P.M.
San Juan
Mayagüez
Variable
Ponce

Leyenda
Mar de 2/4 pies
Mar de 3/6 pies
Mar de 5/9 pies
Mar de 9 pies
VIENTO: intensidad y dirección
*1 barra = 10 mph
**1/2 barra = 5 mph

Sol   Poco nublado   Nublado   Lluvias   Nubes

Norte
Oeste   Este
Sur

EL MAR: Olas de 2 a 4 pies; vientos del este

San Juan, Norte y Este: Por la mañana, va a estar nublado y fresco. Por la tarde, va a estar nublado con mucho viento. Hay probabilidades de tormenta. Por la noche, va a llover. Temperatura máxima: 76 °F; mínima: 73 °F.

Ponce, Sur: Por la mañana, va a hacer sol y mucho calor. Por la tarde y por la noche, va a llover. Temperatura máxima: 93 °F; mínima: 82 °F.

Mayagüez, Oeste: Por la mañana, va a hacer sol. Por la tarde y por la noche, va a estar nublado, con probabilidades de lluvia. Temperatura máxima: 92 °F; mínima: 80 ° F.

160

▶▶▶ INTERNET LINK
Today's weather all around the world:
Usenet: clari.apbl.weather

HABLA DEL TIEMPO EN PUERTO RICO

A. Con tu compañero(a), hablen del pronóstico.

— *¿Qué tiempo va a hacer en Mayagüez por la mañana?*
— *Va a hacer sol.*
— *¿Qué tiempo va a hacer en San Juan por la noche?*
— *Va a llover.*

B. Estás en Puerto Rico. Di adónde quieres o no quieres ir y por qué.

Quiero ir a Ponce.
No quiero ir a San Juan porque hay probabilidades de tormenta.

LA TABLA DEL TIEMPO

A. Haz una tabla del tiempo en Puerto Rico.

	Mañana	Tarde	Noche	Temperatura Mínima/Máxima
Mayagüez	sol			80 °F / 92 °F
Ponce				
San Juan				

B. Ahora, pregúntale a tu compañero(a) qué actividades le gustaría hacer según el tiempo. Usen la información de la tabla.

— *¿Qué te gustaría hacer en Mayagüez por la mañana?*
— *Me gustaría nadar y hacer tabla a vela.*

¿SABES QUE...?

In Puerto Rico, as in the rest of the United States, the Fahrenheit scale is used to determine the temperature. Most Spanish-speaking countries use the Celsius scale. Freezing is 32° on the Fahrenheit scale and 0° on the Celsius. Here are the formulas for conversion.
Celsius to Fahrenheit: $F = 9/5 \times C + 32$
Fahrenheit to Celsius: $C = (F - 32) \times 5/9$

161

ACTIVITIES

Habla del tiempo en Puerto Rico

Pair Activity: Conversing
A. Talk about the weather in Puerto Rico.
B. Discuss where you would like to go or not go in Puerto Rico and why.
Answers: See models on student page.

La tabla del tiempo

Pair Activity: Classifying
A. Make a weather chart for Puerto Rico based on the report.
B. Using the weather information in the chart, ask and answer questions about activities you would like to do in different places in Puerto Rico.
Answers: See chart and model on student page.
Application: Say what you can or cannot do if there is bad weather where you live.

CHECK

Indicate the weather page and ask:
• *¿Qué ciudad en Puerto Rico tiene buen tiempo? ¿Por qué?*
• *¿Dónde va a llover?*
• *¿Cuál va a ser la temperatura más alta? ¿y la más baja?*

LOG BOOK
Have students list vocabulary they find especially difficult.

MEETING INDIVIDUAL NEEDS

Reaching All Students

For Auditory Learners
Listen to weather forecasts on a Spanish television channel or radio station.

For Visual Learners
In a group, make weather symbols, place them on a map, and describe the weather in those places.

For Kinesthetic Learners
In a group, create a weather forecast for a "reporter" to present while the others act out the symbols.

Para hispanohablantes

Present the daily weather report to the class in the style of Spanish-speaking TV forecasters.

Communicative Objectives

To talk about:
- weather in different places and seasons
- weather and the clothes people wear
- weather and the activities people do

Related Components

Activity Book	Transparencies
p. 77-78	Ch. 6: Palabras en
Cuaderno	acción
p. 47-48	**Tutor Page**
	p. 27

GETTING STARTED

Ask students to describe today's weather in Spanish. How did the weather affect what they wore to school?

DISCUSS

Contrast what the people in the drawing are wearing or doing. Use gestures to indicate objects, actions, or attitudes to the weather. For example:
Miren el perro. ¿Por qué lleva un gorro? Sí, porque llueve.

PALABRAS EN ACCIÓN

¿QUÉ TIEMPO HACE?

Aquí llueve a cántaros.

el impermeable

las botas

Seattle

San Francisco

Phoenix

Hace mucho sol.

la mujer

el hombre

el gorro

los guantes

el niño

ESTADOS UNIDOS

Montana

patinar
sobre hielo

esquiar

Denver

Ten cuidado.
Usa el protector solar.

Aquí nieva. David juega con la nieve.

el abrigo

el suéter   la nieve

Minneapolis

Miami

¡Qué tormenta!

Nueva York

¡Hace mucho calor!
¡Cien grados!

---

1 ¿Qué tiempo hace en...?

Completa la tabla.

Lugares	Tiempo
Nueva York	*hay tormenta*

2 ¿Qué hacen?

Habla con tu compañero(a) de cuatro personas del dibujo.

— ¿Qué hace el hombre de Guayama?
— Juega al ajedrez.
— ¿Y el niño de Minneapolis?
— Juega con la nieve.

3 ¿Qué ropa llevan?

Mira las personas del dibujo. ¿Qué ropa llevan? Habla con tu compañero(a).

— ¿Qué ropa lleva la mujer de Seattle?
— Lleva...

4 ¿Adónde les gustaría ir?

En grupos, decidan qué lugares del dibujo les gustaría visitar. Hablen con otro grupo.

— ¿Qué lugar les gustaría visitar?
— Nos gustaría visitar Mayagüez.
— ¿Qué tiempo hace allí?
— Hace buen tiempo. Hace sol y mucho calor.

162

Challenge:
Students make flashcards with Spanish weather words (categories: weather conditions, months, and seasons) on one side and a photo on the other. Use for association games of varying degrees of difficulty. Examples:
julio = Verano, hace mucho sol.
primavera = En la primavera llueve mucho.

For students having difficulty communicating about the weather you might consider:
- **The tutor page:** Pair the student with a native speaker or a more able student using the tutor page.

Hace buen tiempo. Ana nada en el mar.

la niña

la lluvia

el norte

San Juan

PUERTO RICO

Palmas del Mar

el oeste ⟵◇⟶ el este

Mayagüez

Ponce   Guayama

el sur

¡Hay un huracán!

Quiero volar la chiringa, pero no hace viento.

Aquí está nublado.

la chiringa

el ajedrez

5 ¿Qué me aconsejas?

Haz cuatro diálogos sobre el tiempo.

— *Voy a Denver. ¿Qué tiempo hace allí?*
— *Nieva mucho. Lleva botas.*

6 Charada

Usa una expresión para describir qué tiempo hace. La clase tiene que adivinar qué estación es.

— *¡Hace mucho frío!*
— *Es invierno.*

7 Collage

Haz un collage de tu estación favorita. Usa fotos o dibujos de revistas y periódicos. Incluye tres errores. La clase tiene que adivinar cuáles son.

8 Tú eres el autor

Un(a) amigo(a) va a ir a vivir a tu pueblo o ciudad. En una carta, dile qué tiempo hace en cada estación y qué ropa tiene que llevar.

Querido(a)...

En invierno aquí siempre hace mal tiempo. Llueve a cántaros y tienes que llevar impermeable y botas.

163

1. Individual Activity
Make a chart of the places in the drawing and the weather in each location.

2. Pair Activity
Talk about what four people in the drawing are doing.
For Kinesthetic Learners: Speak and perform the activities the people in the drawing are doing.

3. Pair Activity
Talk about the clothes each person in the drawing is wearing.
For Visual Learners: Make clothing flash cards with drawings or photos.

4. Group Activity
Decide which places in the drawing you would like to visit, and talk about the weather in each place. Discuss your choices with another group.
Application: Talk about places in the drawing you don't want to visit and why:
No queremos visitar Phoenix en el verano porque hace mucho calor.

5. Individual Activity
Write four dialogs about the weather.
Application: Give weather advice. Use *tener que* in each piece of advice.

6. Roleplay Activity
In groups, act out short weather scenes. Have the class guess which season it is.
Analysis: Ask students to name one month of the year that is associated with each of the weather scenes.

7. Hands-On Activity
Make a collage of your favorite season. Include three errors for the class to find.
Analysis: Compare your collages with others who chose the same season.

8. Synthesizing Activity
A friend is moving to your town. Write a letter saying what the weather is like in each season and what clothes to bring.
For Auditory Learners: One person reads his or her letter while another writes it down. When both have written, check and correct each other's work.

CHECK

Point to the drawing and ask:
• *¿Qué tiempo hace en Seattle?*
• *¿Qué llevas cuando hace mucho calor?*
• *¿Qué hacen tus amigos cuando llueve?*

LOG BOOK
Have students write down any vocabulary they have difficulty remembering.

Communicative Objectives
- to talk about things you like to do, using **nos gusta** and **les gusta**
- to talk about playing, using **jugar**

Related Components

Activity Book p. 79-80	**Audio Tapes** Listening: 4B, Seg. 3
Audio Book Script: Seg. 3 Activities: p. 53	**Cuaderno** p. 49
	Tutor Page p. 28

GETTING STARTED

Ask for the names of sports and games that are played only in certain seasons. Why are they only played at certain times? What games are played all year?

Language in Context

Nos/les gusta
Review **me/te/le gusta** and the phrase "[something] is pleasing to me/you/ or him/her."
Clarify **les gusta/n** and **nos gusta/n** by talking about three classroom groups. Define by clothing color, for example:
A Uds. les gusta el rojo y a ellos les gusta el azul. A nosotros nos gustan el blanco y el amarillo.
Emphasize the need to use **a** before a person's name or a pronoun.

Jugar
Point out that pronunciation does not follow rules written in books. It is what people feel comfortable with. For that reason a strong sound like **juegan** will displace a softer one like *jugan*.

Language Note
In some countries, people drop the **a** and use a noun immediately after **jugar**.

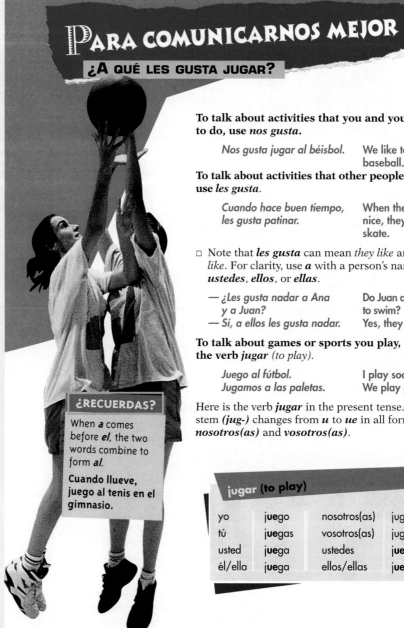

To talk about activities that you and your friends like to do, use *nos gusta*.

Nos gusta jugar al béisbol.	We like to play baseball.

To talk about activities that other people like to do, use *les gusta*.

Cuando hace buen tiempo, les gusta patinar.	When the weather is nice, they like to skate.

☐ Note that ***les gusta*** can mean *they like* and *you* (plural) *like*. For clarity, use ***a*** with a person's name or with ***ustedes***, ***ellos***, or ***ellas***.

— *¿Les gusta nadar a Ana y a Juan?*	Do Juan and Ana like to swim?
— *Sí, a ellos les gusta nadar.*	Yes, they like to swim.

To talk about games or sports you play, use a form of the verb *jugar* (to play).

Juego al fútbol.	I play soccer.
Jugamos a las paletas.	We play paddleball.

Here is the verb ***jugar*** in the present tense. Note that the stem *(jug-)* changes from *u* to *ue* in all forms except ***nosotros(as)*** and ***vosotros(as)***.

¿RECUERDAS?

When **a** comes before **el**, the two words combine to form **al**.

Cuando llueve, juego al tenis en el gimnasio.

jugar (to play)			
yo	ju**e**go	nosotros(as)	jugamos
tú	ju**e**gas	vosotros(as)	jugáis
usted	ju**e**ga	ustedes	ju**e**gan
él/ella	ju**e**ga	ellos/ellas	ju**e**gan

DISCUSS

Review vocabulary from previous chapters and introduce some of this chapter's new vocabulary with questions that incorporate **jugar** and **nos/les gusta**.
¿Quiénes juegan al fútbol americano?
¿A Uds. les gusta jugar al ajedrez?
Yo juego al frisbi todos los sábados.
¿Quién juega con videojuegos?
Rosa y Tina juegan al baloncesto.
¿Jugamos al baloncesto con ellas?
¿A quiénes no les gustan los videojuegos?

1 Las estaciones

¿Qué les gusta hacer a ustedes en las diferentes estaciones?
Pregúntale a tu compañero(a).

— ¿Qué les gusta hacer a ustedes en el otoño?
— Nos gusta volar chiringas.

¿Cuándo?
En el otoño
En el invierno
En el verano
En la primavera

1.   3.   5.

2.   4.   6.

2 Actividades de fin de semana

A. ¿Qué les gusta hacer los fines de semana a las personas que conoces? Haz una tabla.

B. Habla con tu compañero(a).

— ¿Qué les gusta hacer a tus padres los fines de semana?
— En el verano les gusta ir a la playa y en el invierno les gusta esquiar.

ACTIVIDADES DE FIN DE SEMANA

Personas	En el verano	En el invierno
a mis padres	ir a la playa	esquiar
a mi amiga		
a mis primos		
a mis vecinos		
a mi abuelo		

3 Juegos y deportes

A. ¿A qué juegan? ¿Cuándo juegan? En grupo, hagan una tabla.

juego o deporte	todos los días	los fines de semana	a veces
ajedrez	Yolanda Lisa	yo	

B. Hablen con sus compañeros(as) de sus respuestas.

— ¿Quién juega al ajedrez?
— Yolanda, Lisa y yo jugamos al ajedrez.
— ¿Cuándo?
— Yolanda y Lisa juegan todos los días. Yo juego los fines de semana.

165

For students having difficulty using **gustar** to talk about what they like to do, you might consider:
- **The tutor page:** Pair the student with a native speaker or a more able student using the tutor page.
- **Actividades:** see page 156C: *Nos gusto todo*

Students **use nos/les gusta to say what they and others like to do.**

1. Pair Activity
Ask what your partner and his or her friends like to do during each season. Use the picture clues to tell which season it is.
Possible Answers:
1. See model on student page.
2. ...el invierno? ...jugar en la nieve.
3. ...el invierno? ...patinar sobre hielo.
4. ...el otoño? ...jugar al ajedrez.
5. ...la primavera? ...bucear.
6. ...el verano? ...nadar.
Analysis: With a partner, make lists of Spanish words that go with each season.

2. Individual and Pair Activities
A. Make a list of things that people you know like to do on weekends.
Possible Answers:
escuchar música
ir al cine
ir al centro
ir a un concierto
hablar por teléfono
jugar al béisbol
B. Talk about your list with a partner.
Answers: See model on student page.

3. Group Activity
A. Using the model as an example, make a chart of the sports you like to play and how often you like to play them.
B. Discuss your answers with your partners.
Answers: See models on student page.
Evaluation: Have volunteers present each group's results to the class. Rank the sports on the board according to how often they're played and discuss.

CHECK

- ¿Les gusta la lluvia?
- ¿Nos gustan la nieve y el hielo?
- ¿Juegas al baloncesto?
- ¿Va a llover, jugamos al béisbol?
- Yo juego al tenis con Gabriela Sabatini todos los días. ¿Sabes quién gana?

LOG BOOK
Ask students to write a sentence describing the use of the verb **jugar**.

Para hispanohablantes

Ask another Spanish speaker what he or she likes to do on the weekends and why. Write down the entire answer.

Communicative Objectives
- to tell a friend to do something, using **tú** commands
- to talk about what people have to do, using **tener que**
- to talk about what people should do or not do, using **deber** and an infinitive

Related Components

Activity Book p. 81-82	**Cuaderno** p. 50
Audio Book Script: Seg.4 Activities: p. 54	**Tutor Page** p. 29
Audio Tapes Listening: 4B, Seg. 4	

GETTING STARTED

Write this lesson's verbs: **comprar, llevar, jugar, leer, compartir,** and **escribir.** Use them for TPR. For example:
Lleva tu libro. Escribe en tu cuaderno.
Write the command forms next to the verbs as the class performs each action.

Language in Context

Tú Commands
Write simple commands using **comprar, leer,** and **escribir** so students can see command forms in context. Ask what rule appears to apply to -ar verbs. Repeat for -er verbs and -ir verbs. Have volunteers produce the command forms of **compartir, llevar,** and **jugar,** using the three sentences as models.
Have others produce forms for **bailar, cantar, aprender, comer,** and **abrir.** Warn students that the **tú** commands of some of the more basic verbs do *not* follow these rules. (For example, they just learned **ten cuidado.**)

Tener que and Deber
Ask for different ways to say that you feel it is necessary/important to read (I must read, I have to read, I ought to read, I should read, etc.).
Compare *I should read* and **debo leer,** emphasizing the absence of the *to* in the English construction. Compare *I have to read* and **tengo que leer,** emphasizing the additional **que.**

PARA COMUNICARNOS MEJOR
¡LLEVA EL PARAGUAS!

To tell a friend to do something, use the informal (*tú*) command.

¡Lleva el paraguas!	Take the umbrella!
¡Lee el pronóstico del tiempo!	Read the weather forecast!

Note that the ***tú*** command forms are the same as the present tense forms used for ***usted, él,*** or ***ella.***

informal commands			
-ar verbs: **-a** ending		**-er/-ir** verbs: **-e** ending	
comprar	compr**a**	leer	lee
llevar	llev**a**	compartir	comparte
jugar	jueg**a**	escribir	escribe

☐ To tell a friend to do something, you can also use a form of ***tener*** followed by ***que*** and an infinitive.

Hace frío. Tienes que llevar el abrigo.	It's cold. You have to wear your coat.

☐ To tell a friend not to do something, you can use ***no debes*** and the infinitive of another verb.

No debes salir sin las botas cuando llueve.	You should not go out without your boots when it rains.

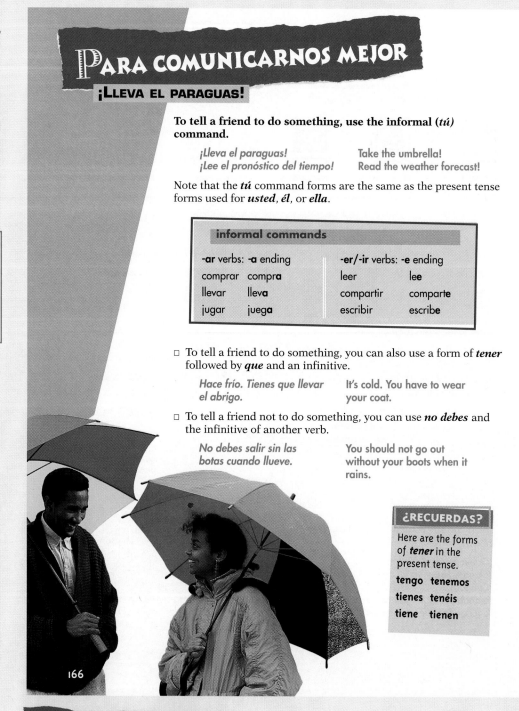

¿RECUERDAS?

Here are the forms of *tener* in the present tense.

tengo	tenemos
tienes	tenéis
tiene	tienen

DISCUSS

Review vocabulary from previous chapters and introduce some of this chapter's new vocabulary with questions that incorporate **tener que** and **deber.**
Mañana va a llover mucho. ¿Debo llevar un paraguas?
¿Debo comprar lentes de sol mañana?
En una tormenta de nieve, ¿vuelo chiringas o miro la televisión?
Si voy al parque, ¿juego con la nieve o patino?
Hace frío. Tengo que comprar un abrigo.

1 El pronóstico de la semana

Mira el pronóstico del tiempo. Luego, contesta la pregunta de tu compañero(a) y escoge un consejo según el tiempo.

— ¿Qué tiempo va a hacer el jueves?
— El jueves va a llover. Lleva el paraguas.

El pronóstico
de la semana

lunes   martes   miércoles   jueves   viernes

2 ¿Qué tiene que hacer?

Dile a tu compañero(a) qué tiene que hacer según el tiempo.

Va a nevar. Tienes que usar botas.

1. un niño
2. la profesora
3. los estudiantes
4. nosotros(as)
5. los vecinos
6. ¿y tú?

Consejos
llevar el paraguas
usar el protector solar
nadar en la piscina
patinar en el lago
aprender a navegar
usar botas
llevar un impermeable
tener cuidado

3 Cuando hace mal tiempo

Dile a tu compañero qué no debe hacer cuando hace mal tiempo.

— *Este fin de semana va a hacer mal tiempo. No debes ir a la playa.*

1. hacer mal tiempo
2. hacer mucho calor
3. hacer mucho frío
4. hacer mucho sol
5. llover a cántaros
6. nevar

No debes...
ir a la playa
abrir las ventanas
jugar en el parque
tomar el sol
salir sin el abrigo
hacer una barbacoa

167

ACTIVITIES

Students **use deber and tener que to talk about the weather.**

1. Pair Activity
Use the weather forecast to ask and answer questions and to give advice.
Possible Answers:
El lunes va a hacer sol. Usa el protector solar.
El martes viene una tormenta. Lleva el impermeable.
El miércoles viene un huracán. Quédate en casa.
El jueves ...(see model on student page).

El viernes va a hacer sol. Aprende a navegar.
Application: Substitute **deber** for the commands in your answers. Example: *Debes nadar en la piscina.*

2. Pair Activity
Ask and answer questions about what each of these people should do in each type of weather.
Possible Answers:
1. See model on student page.
2. *Viene una tormenta. ¿Qué tiene que hacer la profesora? Tiene que prestar atención al pronóstico.*
3. *Va a hacer mucho frío. ¿Qué tienen que hacer los estudiantes? Tienen que patinar en el lago.*
4. *Viene un huracán. ¿Qué tenemos que hacer? Tenemos que tener cuidado.*
5. *Va a llover a cántaros. ¿Qué tienen que hacer los vecinos? Tienen que llevar los impermeables.*
6. *Va a hacer viento. ¿Qué tengo que hacer? Tienes que aprender a navegar.*

3. Pair Activity
Tell your partner what he or she should not do when the weather is bad.
Possible Answers:
1. See model on student page
2. *...No debes tomar el sol.*
3. *...No debes salir sin el abrigo.*
4. *...No debes jugar en el parque.*
5. *...No debes abrir las ventanas.*
6. *...No debes hacer una barbacoa.*

CHECK

- ¿Qué le dices a un amigo cuando...
  ...va a llover?
  ...hace mucho sol?
  ...va a salir?
- ¿Qué debo hacer si...?
  ...tengo hambre?
  ...tengo frío?
  ...estoy aburrido?

For students having difficulty using informal commands, **deber**, and **tener que**, you might consider:
- **The tutor page:** Pair the student with a native speaker or a more able student using the tutor page.
- **Actividades:** see page 156C: *¡A Puerto Rico!*

Para hispanohablantes

Listen to another native speaker of Spanish. How often does that person use commands? Write a few examples of those commands.

167

Communicative Objectives
• to give advice
• to talk about the weather

Related Components

Assessment Oral Proficiency: p. 26	**Conexiones** Chapter 6
Audio Book Script: Seg. 5 Activities: p. 55	**Magazine** Juntos en Puerto Rico
Audio Tapes Listening: 4B, Seg.5 Conexiones: 17A, Ch.6	**Tutor Page** p. 30

GETTING STARTED

At this point, students should be able to use **tú** commands, **tener que, deber, gustar, jugar,** and **all of the chapter vocabulary** correctly. Ask if anyone has been in a hurricane or tropical storm. What was it like? (You may wish to refer to the weather information on page 169.)

APPLY

1. Group Activity
Based on the article, make a list of three things to do and three things not to do before and during a storm.
Possible Answers:
Tienes que comprar comida. No debes estar cerca de un árbol.
Tenemos que escuchar el pronóstico del tiempo. No debemos abrir las ventanas.
For Auditory Learners: Create and record weather forecasts, and exchange with other groups. Listen to their tapes and write down as much as you can.

2. Pair Activity
Use today's weather report to answer the following questions about the weather in the United States and your area.
Possible Answers:
La temperatura de hoy es 52°F.
La temperatura máxima es 58°F. La temperatura mínima es 47°F.
En el norte del país, nieva....
Hace más frío en Colorado.
Hace más calor en Arizona.
Llueve más en Florida y Georgia.
Nieva en Montana y Minnesota.

SITUACIONES
A MAL TIEMPO, BUENA CARA

23A

VIENE GRAN TORMENTA TROPICAL
Vientos de 60 millas por hora

• Lluvias intensas
• Posibles emergencias de agua y electricidad
• Peligro de inundación

Antes de la tormenta aconsejamos:
• conservar agua y electricidad
• escuchar el pronóstico del tiempo
• comprar comida en lata
• comprar velas y pilas

Durante la tormenta no deben:
• usar el televisor, el refrigerador, el teléfono y otros aparatos eléctricos
• salir cuando hace mucho viento
• abrir las ventanas
• estar cerca de un árbol

168

3. Individual Activity
Use your answers to Activity 2 to create a forecast for tomorrow's weather. Present your forecast to the class.
Answers: See model on student page.
For Kinesthetic Learners: Act out various pieces of advice for different weather situations.

4. Individual Activity
Write what you think these characters are saying to each other about the weather.
Possible Dialog:
A: *¡Llueve!*
B: *Debemos llevar un paraguas.*

A: *¡Qué día más bonito!*
B: *Hace sol. Voy a hacer surf.*

A: *¿Tienes frío?*
B: *Sí, ¡Tengo mucho frío!*
Challenge: What if one of the characters in one of these cartoons came from some other planet? What would this visitor say to the other person? Write a new dialog.

Viene una tormenta tropical

Miren el artículo sobre la tormenta tropical. En grupo, hagan una lista de tres cosas que tienen que hacer y tres cosas que no deben hacer cuando viene una tormenta.

Tenemos que conservar agua. No debemos salir cuando hace mucho viento.

 ¿Qué tiempo hace aquí?

Con tu compañero(a), contesten las siguientes preguntas sobre el tiempo donde ustedes viven y en otras partes del país. Busquen la información en el periódico.

- ¿Cuál es la temperatura de hoy?
- ¿Cuál es la temperatura máxima? ¿y la mínima?
- ¿Qué tiempo hace en el norte del país? ¿y en el sur? ¿y en el este? ¿y en el oeste?
- ¿En qué estado hace más frío?
- ¿En qué estado hace más calor?
- ¿En qué estados llueve más?
- ¿En qué estados nieva?

 Tu pronóstico

Usa las respuestas de la actividad 2 para escribir el pronóstico del tiempo. Luego presenta el pronóstico a la clase.

> **Saluda:** *Buenas tardes/noches.*
> **Di tu nombre:** *Soy...*
> **Anuncia:** *Aquí está el pronóstico del tiempo para hoy...*
> **Aconseja:** *Lleva... No debes...*
> **Saluda:** *Muchas gracias. Hasta mañana.*

 Vamos a hablar del tiempo

Con tu compañero(a), escriban dos diálogos sobre el tiempo. Presenten los diálogos a la clase.

¿SABES QUE...?

In Spanish, the expression *A mal tiempo, buena cara* is very popular. It means that even in dark moments you should be optimistic. It is similar to the English expression "Let a smile be your umbrella on a rainy day."

PARA TU REFERENCIA

conservar *to conserve*
durante *during*
la electricidad *electricity*
gran *great*
en lata *canned*
la inundación *flood*
no deben *you (plural) should not*
saluda *greet*

169

- *¿Qué tiempo hace hoy?*
- *¿Dónde va a hacer buen tiempo en Puerto Rico?*
- *¿Qué debo hacer cuando llueve?*

LOG BOOK

Have students write a description of the weather for each day of an entire week.

Background

Hurricane (*huracán*): A violent tropical storm created by a low-pressure area. Its winds move in a circular pattern at more than 73 miles an hour. It is often accompanied by heavy rainfall.

Lightning (*rayos*): A flash of light caused by the discharge of atmospheric electricity between one cloud and another or between one cloud and the Earth.

Thunder (*truenos*): The sound caused by the sudden heating and expansion of air by the electrical discharge (lightning).

Rainbow (*arco iris*): An arc of color formed by the refraction, reflection, and dispersion of the sun's rays in water droplets, for example in mist or falling rain.

Tornado (*tornado*): A funnel-shaped column of high-speed whirling winds.

Geography Note

The weather in Puerto Rico is not always perfect. Hurricane season lasts from June to November. Serious storms hit the island about once every ten years.

Para hispanohablantes

Make a short comic strip for the class. Use weather vocabulary and expressions from this chapter.

For students having difficulty talking about the weather or giving informal commands, you might consider:

- **The tutor page:** pair the student with a native speaker or a more able student using the tutor page.
- **Actividades:** see page 156D: *¿En casa o al aire libre?* and *¡Qué calor! ¡Qué frío!*

 **INTERNET LINK**

Hurricanes, general: http://thunder.met.fsu.edu:80/explores/tropical.html
Up-to-date information on hurricanes: http://www.sims.net/links/hurricane.html

Communicative Objectives

- to discuss weather, climate, and appropriate clothing for a city or state
- to talk about information that should go in a poster about a place in your state

Related Components

Transparencies	Video: Tape/Book
Ch. 6: Para resolver	Unit 3: Seg. 3

Search to frame 1381418

 GETTING STARTED

Have volunteers read aloud the El Yunque poster. Then ask comprehension and experience questions. For example:
¿Qué necesitas llevar a El Yunque?
¿Les gusta hacer un picnic? ¿Dónde?

APPLY

Form groups, and prepare to have each group create a poster similar to the El Yunque poster. It should promote a place in your city or state and be aimed at students in other countries.
Try to ensure that a range of seasons and weather conditions is represented. Groups can divide up the roles (researcher, artist, etc.).

PASO 1: ¿Qué lugar es?
Select a place and write about it. Include:
- the name
- what there is to see
- where it is
- seasonal activities
- nearby places of interest
- how to get there
- other information

PASO 2: ¿Cómo es el tiempo?
Choose a season. What is the weather like then? What is the temperature? Find out and write down the answers.
Application: Name your favorite season and explain why you like it. For example:
Me gusta más el otoño porque los árboles tienen muchos colores.

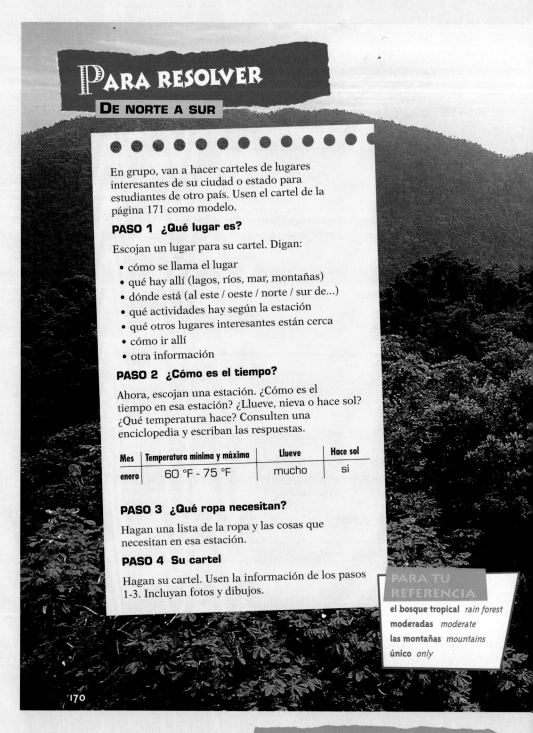

PARA RESOLVER

DE NORTE A SUR

En grupo, van a hacer carteles de lugares interesantes de su ciudad o estado para estudiantes de otro país. Usen el cartel de la página 171 como modelo.

PASO 1 ¿Qué lugar es?

Escojan un lugar para su cartel. Digan:

- cómo se llama el lugar
- qué hay allí (lagos, ríos, mar, montañas)
- dónde está (al este / oeste / norte / sur de...)
- qué actividades hay según la estación
- qué otros lugares interesantes están cerca
- cómo ir allí
- otra información

PASO 2 ¿Cómo es el tiempo?

Ahora, escojan una estación. ¿Cómo es el tiempo en esa estación? ¿Llueve, nieva o hace sol? ¿Qué temperatura hace? Consulten una enciclopedia y escriban las respuestas.

Mes	Temperatura mínima y máxima	Llueve	Hace sol
enero	60 °F - 75 °F	mucho	sí

PASO 3 ¿Qué ropa necesitan?

Hagan una lista de la ropa y las cosas que necesitan en esa estación.

PASO 4 Su cartel

Hagan su cartel. Usen la información de los pasos 1-3. Incluyan fotos y dibujos.

PARA TU REFERENCIA

el bosque tropical *rain forest*
moderadas *moderate*
las montañas *mountains*
único *only*

170

PASO 3: ¿Qué ropa necesitan?
Make a list of the clothes and other things visitors should bring for that season.
Analysis: List the clothing and equipment visitors would need for a trip in one of the other seasons.

PASO 4: Su cartel
Use the information you have gathered to create a poster. Include photos and drawings.
Challenge: Look at the *Vocabulario temático* of other chapters for words and expressions to use in the poster.

MEETING INDIVIDUAL NEEDS

Reaching All Students

For Auditory Learners
Take turns saying words associated with a season or weather condition and naming the season or weather.

For Visual Learners
Think of ways in which *hace sol* and *hace frío* could be used in Puerto Rico. Illustrate and write a caption for each idea.

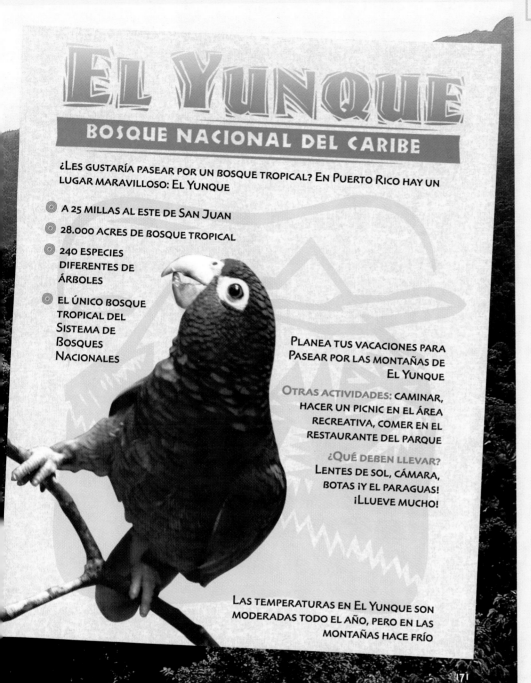

El Yunque

BOSQUE NACIONAL DEL CARIBE

¿LES GUSTARÍA PASEAR POR UN BOSQUE TROPICAL? EN PUERTO RICO HAY UN LUGAR MARAVILLOSO: EL YUNQUE

- A 25 MILLAS AL ESTE DE SAN JUAN
- 28.000 ACRES DE BOSQUE TROPICAL
- 240 ESPECIES DIFERENTES DE ÁRBOLES
- EL ÚNICO BOSQUE TROPICAL DEL SISTEMA DE BOSQUES NACIONALES

PLANEA TUS VACACIONES PARA PASEAR POR LAS MONTAÑAS DE EL YUNQUE

OTRAS ACTIVIDADES: CAMINAR, HACER UN PICNIC EN EL ÁREA RECREATIVA, COMER EN EL RESTAURANTE DEL PARQUE

¿QUÉ DEBEN LLEVAR? LENTES DE SOL, CÁMARA, BOTAS ¡Y EL PARAGUAS! ¡LLUEVE MUCHO!

LAS TEMPERATURAS EN EL YUNQUE SON MODERADAS TODO EL AÑO, PERO EN LAS MONTAÑAS HACE FRÍO

171

CHECK

PORTFOLIO
If students wish, they may add copies or photos of their poster to their portfolios.

Weather Words

CONDITIONS
clear *despejado*
cloudy *nublado, cubierto*
drizzle *la llovizna*
dew *el rocío*
fog *la niebla*
partly cloudy *muy nuboso*
rainy *lluvioso*
squall *el chubasco*
sunny *soleado*
windy *ventoso*

CLOUDS
altocumulus *altocúmulo*
cirrocumulus *cirrocúmulo*
cirrostratus *cirrostrato*
cirrus *cirro*
cumulonimbus *cumulonimbo*
cumulus congestus *cúmulo congestus*
stratocumulus *estratocúmulo*
stratus *estrato*
thunderhead *la nube de tormenta*

EQUIPMENT
barometer *el barómetro*
solar panel *el panel solar*
thermometer *el termómetro*
weathervane *la veleta*

PREDICTIONS
barometric pressure *la presión barométrica*
dew point *el punto de rocío*
front, cold/warm *el frente frío/cálido*
front, stationary *el frente estacionario*
hail *el granizo*
humidity *la humedad*
isobars *isobaras*
precipitation *precipitación*
pressure, low/high *bajas/altas presiones*
weather map *el mapa meteorológico*

Para hispanohablantes

Ask a family member about the weather where he or she grew up. Write a short description of it.

Objectives
Communicative: to learn weather and journalism vocabulary
Cultural: to learn about a Puerto Rican TV personality

Related Components

Audio Tapes	Conexiones
Conexiones: 17A, Ch. 6	Chapter 6
	Magazine
	Juntos en Puerto Rico

GETTING STARTED

Ask whether some television weather forecasters seem more reliable or better-informed than others. Do students think that forecasters are trained meteorologists or simply TV personalities?

DISCUSS

Using the Text

Perform the interview. Take the role of Susan, and have volunteers ask you the questions.
Ask comprehension questions about the text. Suggestions:
¿Qué hace Susan en la televisión?
¿Por qué va Susan a otros países?

Using Context Clues

Ask questions that require critical thinking:
¿Qué es Teleonce? ¿Por qué tiene ese nombre? (It combines *Tele[visión]* and [Channel] 11.)
¿Cuántas horas creen Uds. que trabaja Susan en un día? (If we assume that she works from 2:30 to the end of the 10:00 news, with a half-hour to eat, 8 hours.)

Cooperative Learning

In groups, choose a weather word such as *huracán*, find out its characteristics, and prepare a weather forecast for Puerto Rico. Include suggestions for what to do during the event. Present your report to the class.

Para hispanohablantes

Do a "TV-style" weather forecast for the class. Use visual aids to demonstrate.

ENTÉRATE
EL PRONÓSTICO PARA HOY...

¡EL TIEMPO NOS UNE A TODOS!°

Susan Soltero presenta el pronóstico del tiempo en Teleonce, un canal de televisión° de Puerto Rico. En esta entrevista, Susan habla de su trabajo.°

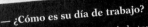

— ¿Cómo es su día de trabajo?

— Voy al canal a las 2:30 de la tarde. Leo los mapas y escribo el pronóstico. Presento el tiempo a las 6:00 de la tarde y a las 10:00 de la noche.

— ¿Le gusta su trabajo?

— ¡Me encanta! Porque el tiempo nos une a todos. Los pronósticos son muy importantes.

— ¿Qué tiene que estudiar una persona para trabajar° en televisión?

— Tiene que estudiar periodismo° y aprender un idioma.°

— ¿Cuál fue° su pronóstico más emocionante?

— El huracán Hugo, con vientos a más de 72 millas por hora° y lluvias torrenciales.°

TE TOCA A TI

1. Susan Soltero trabaja...
2. A ella le gusta...
3. Su pronóstico más emocionante fue...
4. Para trabajar en la televisión, una persona...

aprender un idioma *to learn a language*
el canal de televisión *tv station*
fue *it was*
las lluvias torrenciales *torrential rain*
millas por hora *miles per hour*
el periodismo *journalism*
el tiempo nos une a todos *the weather brings us together*
el trabajar *to work*
el trabajo *job/work*

CHECK

Te toca a ti
Answers:
1. *...para Teleonce, un canal de televisión de Puerto Rico.*
2. *...su trabajo.*
3. *...el huracán Hugo.*
4. *...tiene que estudiar periodismo y aprender un idioma.*

Language Note

What is the difference between a hurricane and a typhoon? Mainly linguistic—they are the same kind of tropical storm, but each is native to a different part of the world. The storms that originate in the Atlantic or the eastern Pacific are named for the Taíno god of the wind. Those of the South Pacific take their name from the Chinese phrase *tai fung*, which means "great wind."

LOG BOOK

Have students list all words from the **Entérate** that are cognates.

VOCABULARIO TEMÁTICO

El tiempo
The weather

está nublado *it's cloudy*
hace buen tiempo
  the weather is nice
hace calor *it's hot*
hace fresco *it's cool*
hace frío *it's cold*
hace mal tiempo
  the weather is bad
hace sol *it's sunny*
hace viento *it's windy*
llueve *it rains/it's raining*
nieva *it snows/it's snowing*

Las estaciones del año
The seasons of the year

la primavera *spring*
el verano *summer*
el otoño *fall*
el invierno *winter*

La ropa
Clothing

el abrigo *coat*
las botas *boots*
el gorro *cap*
los guantes *gloves*
el impermeable *raincoat*
el suéter *sweater*

Consejos para el tiempo
Weather advice

Lleva el paraguas.
  Take an umbrella.

No debes salir sin...
  *You shouldn't go out
  without . . .*
**Presta atención al pronóstico
  del tiempo.** *Pay attention to
  the weather forecast.*
Quédate en casa.
  Stay at home.
Ten cuidado. *Be careful.*

Actividades para cada estación
Activities for each season

esquiar *to ski*
jugar al ajedrez *to play chess*
jugar con la nieve
  to play in the snow
patinar sobre hielo
  to ice-skate

¿Cuándo?
When?

a veces *sometimes*
nunca *never*
siempre *always*
todos los días *every day*

El pronóstico del tiempo
The weather forecast

el este *east*
el grado *degree*
la lluvia *rain*
la nieve *snow*
el norte *north*

el oeste *west*
el sur *south*
**la temperatura
  mínima/máxima**
  low/high temperature
va a llover/nevar
  it is going to rain/snow
**viene una tormenta/un
  huracán** *a storm/a hurricane
  is coming*

Expresiones y palabras

¿Cómo te afecta? *How does it
  affect you?*
Llueve a cántaros.
  It's raining cats and dogs.
les gusta(n) *they like*
nos gusta(n) *we like*
¿Qué aconsejas?
  What do you advise?
¡Qué tormenta!
  What a storm!
el hombre *man*
llevar *to wear; to take*
la mujer *woman*
el niño/la niña *boy/girl*
usar *to use*

Expresiones de Puerto Rico

volar chiringas *to fly kites*

LA CONEXIÓN INGLÉS-ESPAÑOL

Some Spanish words, like **suéter**, look or sound a lot like their English cognates. Other connections are harder to spot. For example, **fresco** is related to the English word *fresh*.

Look at the **Vocabulario temático** for other words that sound similar to English words.

173

VOCABULARIO TEMÁTICO

Objectives
• to review vocabulary
• to correctly pronounce words containing the letters "s", "x", "z"

Related Components

Activity Book	Audio Book
Chapter Review: p. 83-84	Script: Seg. 6 Activities p. 56
Assessment Listening Script: p. 14 Chapter Test: p. 75-80	**Audio Tapes** Listening: 4B, Seg. 6 Assessment: 14B, Ch. 6
	Cuaderno p. 51-52

Pronunciation: "s," "x," "z"

In most of the Spanish-speaking world, the letters "s" and "z" are pronounced like the "s" in the English word "send."
ajedrez, haz, empezar, guantes, sol, fresco, suéter

Language Note

In Spain, the letter "z" (like the letter "c" before "e" or "i") is pronounced like the "th" in the English word "think."

Unlike most Spanish letters, the letter "x" is pronounced in a variety of unpredictable ways:
"h" as in "he"—*México, Ximena*
"sh" as in "she"—*Uxmal*
"ks" as in "books"—*máximo, examen, excursión, experimento, exilio*
"s" as in "sit"—*Xochimilco.*

The pronunciation of the "x," therefore, should be learned for each word in which it appears.

LOG BOOK

Have the class make up tongue twisters. Then have students write down their three favorite ones.

La conexión inglés-español

Some words related to **fresco:** *freshman, fresh, fresco, freshet,* which are related to a German word for "bold" or "impudent."
Some words related to **calor:** *calorie, caloric, caldarium, caldera, calm, caldron,* and *calefaction,* which are related to a Latin word for "heat."
Some words related to **sol:** *solar, solarium, solstice,* and *parasol,* which are related to an Indo-European word for "sun."

173

ADELANTE

Objectives

Pre-Reading Strategy: to elicit meaning from photographs and captions
Cultural: to learn about the El Yunque Rain Forest
Interdiciplinary: to teach students about Puerto Rico's environment and indigenous species

Related Components

CD ROM	Video:
Unit 3: Adelante	Tape/Book
Magazine	Unit 3: Seg. 4
Juntos en Puerto Rico	

Search to frame 1433811

GETTING STARTED

Ask students about the animals and plants pictured here. What are they? Where do the animals live? What are they like?

Using the Video

Show Segment 4 of the Puerto Rico video, the introduction to El Yunque.

Antes de leer

Read aloud the first paragraph and ask a few comprehension questions. Examples:
¿Dónde está El Yunque?
¿Qué hay en El Yunque?
Read aloud the second paragraph. Have students look at the photos on these pages and the next two pages.
Read the choices aloud and ask about each in turn. For example:
¿Hay serpientes y otros reptiles?

About the Park

When Columbus reached Puerto Rico in 1493, its mountains were covered with rain forests. Spain made the Luquillo mountains a protected area in 1876, but fewer than 20 square miles of rain forest remain on the island.
The Caribbean National Forest—which includes El Yunque—is the only tropical rain forest that is part of the National Forest System of the United States.

ADELANTE

ANTES DE LEER

El Yunque es un bosque tropical cerca de San Juan, Puerto Rico. Tiene más de° 28.000 acres y una gran variedad de flora y fauna.
Mira las páginas 174-177. Según las fotos y los títulos,° ¿cuál es el tema principal de este artículo?

    a. serpientes y otros reptiles
    b. un bosque tropical
    c. cómo sacar fotos en un bosque

El múcaro de Puerto Rico° vive en El Yunque. ▶

más de *more than*
el múcaro *Puerto Rican owl*
los títulos *titles*

174

Adelante Components

Activity Book	Audio Tapes	Magazine	Video: Tape/Book
p. 85-88	Adelante: 10A, 10B	Juntos en	Unit 3: Seg. 4-5
Assessment	**CD ROM**	Puerto Rico	
Portfolio: p. 37-38	Unit 3: Adelante	**Transparencies**	
		Unit 3: Adelante	

◀ La cotorra° puertorriqueña es un ave° en peligro de extinción.°

◀ En El Yunque hay flores° exóticas, como las orquídeas.

◀ El coquí es una rana° muy pequeña.

el ave *bird*
la cotorra *parrot*
en peligro de extinción *in danger of extinction*
las flores *flowers*
la rana *frog*

175

Using the Photos

Puerto Rican Owl

The **múcaro,** or Puerto Rican owl, is a small, nocturnal bird that feeds mainly on insects.

Culture Link: In Puerto Rican popular culture, birds of prey such as the owl are believed to be bad omens. Can you think of any similar beliefs in your culture? Why do such beliefs exist?

Puerto Rican Parrot

These parrots, native only to Puerto Rico, grow to be about 12 inches long. Once abundant, there are now only about fifty living in the wild, all in or near El Yunque.

Environmental Link: The Puerto Rican parrot was hunted for food and because it ate crops. Can you suggest other reasons why birds become extinct?

Orchids

Not all orchids have showy flowers. The most conspicuous orchids in El Yunque are epiphytes, or air plants, which grow on trees but take water and nutrients directly from the damp air and the debris that falls on their petals.

Agriculture Link: Would you eat an orchid? (You may have. Vanilla flavoring comes from the orchid called *vanilla*.) What flowers do you eat? (The most common: artichokes, broccoli, and cauliflower. The spices clove and saffron are made from flowers. Some people eat parts of roses, marigolds, dandelions, and squash flowers.)

The Coquí

The **coquí,** named for the sound it makes, is a tree frog found only on this island. It has become a symbol of Puerto Rico.

Culture Link: What other animals are symbols of countries, cities, or particular groups? Why do people adopt certain animals as symbols?

 **INTERNET LINK**

The Caribbean National Forest page:
http://www.gorp.com:80/gorp/resource/US_National_Forest/pr_carib.html

Objectives

Cultural: to learn about the El Yunque Rain Forest
Reading Strategy: to elicit meaning from context

Related Components

Activity Book p. 85	Audio Tapes Adelante: 10A

GETTING STARTED

Ask if anyone has been to a tropical rain forest. If so, ask what it was like. If not, have students describe these photos. Elicit such details as the prevalence of green and the thickness of the vegetation.

Background

What makes a forest a rain forest? Lots of rain. The annual rainfall in El Yunque is over 200 inches per year—about ten to twenty times as much as most parts of the continental United States get.

Not all rain forests are tropical. There is another North American rain forest in Washington and Oregon, where moist Pacific winds cool as they cross the Cascade mountain range.

Types El Yunque has four types of rain forest, each at a different altitude and each with different plants, weather, and animals. At the top of the mountain there is an almost constant cloud cover. Here the temperature is the coolest and the vegetation the smallest.

Importance Rain forests help regulate the world's climate and produce oxygen, and are home to about half the world's plant and animal species. Some rain forest plants have led scientists to cures for diseases. Others are a potential source of food.

Threats The two greatest threats to rain forests are agriculture and urbanization. Incursions are difficult to stop, for they provide homes and income for the poor.

DEL MUNDO HISPANO

El Yunque

El Yunque es un parque nacional muy especial. Tiene muchos tipos de animales y plantas. Los árboles de El Yunque son muy altos. Muchos miden° más de 100 pies.

Caminar por El Yunque es una aventura.° Es como un laberinto° con árboles, ríos y senderos.° ¡Y llueve más de cuatro veces° al día!

▼ Estas orquídeas son típicas de El Yunque.

▲ En El Yunque hay helechos° gigantes.

Flores tropicales

En El Yunque hay flores tropicales de todos los colores. Existen más de 20 tipos de orquídeas.

Animales únicos

El Yunque tiene animales únicos en el mundo. La boa puertorriqueña es muy larga. Mide hasta° 7 pies. La cotorra puertorriqueña es un ave típica de El Yunque.

La boa puertorriqueña está en peligro de extinción. ▶

la aventura *adventure*	más de cuatro veces
hasta *up to*	*more than four times*
los helechos *ferns*	mide(n)... pies *measure(s)...feet*
el laberinto *maze*	los senderos *paths*

176

DISCUSS

Suggestions for discussion:

El Yunque

¿Por qué es especial El Yunque?
Cuánto miden muchos de los árboles?
¿Qué es un laberinto? ¿Quién puede dibujar un laberinto en la pizarra?
¿Y cómo es "un laberinto con árboles, ríos y senderos"?

Math Link: *¿Y cuántas veces llueve en el mes de septiembre? (más de 120 veces)*

Flores tropicals

¿Cuántos tipos de orquídeas hay en el parque de El Yunque?
Miren la foto de las orquídeas de El Yunque. ¿Qué colores ven?
¿Son como éstas todas las orquídeas? ¿Creen que sí? ¿Creen que no?

Animales únicos

¿Qué animal ven Uds. en esta página? ¿Es grande una boa puertorriqueña? ¿Quién tiene un animal en casa? ¿Cómo es?, ¿grande,? ¿pequeño?, ¿peligroso?

▼ **La cascada La Mina es un lugar muy popular de El Yunque.**

En El Yunque también hay millones de ranas que cantan ¡coquí! ¡coquí! Estas ranas son muy pequeñas: ¡miden menos de una pulgada!°

Lugares para visitar

En El Yunque hay maravillosas cascadas° y también un pico° muy alto. Se llama El Toro y tiene 3.523 pies.

Consejos para los visitantes°

- Consulta un mapa de El Yunque.
- Camina siempre con un(a) guía.°
- No cortes° flores ni plantas.
- No molestes° a los animales.

Y recuerda que llueve todos los días.

Así que... ¡lleva el paraguas!

LOS ANIMALES DE EL YUNQUE

NOMBRE	ESTADO	ABUNDANCIA
Mangosta *Sm. Indian mongoose*	I	C
Culebra corredora *Ground snake*	N	R
Salamanquita *Dwarf gecko*	N	C
Lagartijo jardinero *Upland grass lizard*	N	C
Sapo común *Giant toad*	I	R
Múcaro *Puerto Rican owl*	N	C
Cotorra puertorriqueña *Puerto Rican parrot*	N	R
Sapito de labio blanco *White-lipped toad*	N	C
Rata parda *Norway rat*	I	C
Murciélago frutero *Fruit bat*	N	C

Fuente: Bosque Nacional del Caribe

CLAVE / *KEY*

ESTADO	ABUNDANCIA
N-nativo	C-común
I-introducido	R-raro

las cascadas *falls*
el/la guía *guide*
menos de una pulgada
  less than an inch
no cortes *don't cut*
no molestes *don't disturb*
pico *(mountain) peak*
los visitantes *visitors*

177

Lugares para visitar

¿Cuántos pies tiene El Toro? (3.523)
Miren el número. ¿Hay algo diferente?
Sí, tiene un punto y no una coma.

Weather Link: Why do clouds exist at the top of the mountain? (They result from the cooling of warm, water-filled winds as they move over the mountain.)

Consejos para los visitantes

Discuss the advice.
Punto número uno: Consulta un mapa de El Yunque. (Anoten: un mapa, no una.)
¿Por qué tenemos que consultar un mapa?
Porque El Yunque es como un laberinto, ¿verdad? .

Los animales de El Yunque

Discuss the list.
¿Qué hay en la primera columna? Los nombres de los animales de El Yunque.
En el bosque de El Yunque, ¿Sólo viven estos animales, o hay muchos más animales? No, hay muchos más animales.
La segunda columna se llama estado.
¿Qué quiere decir estado?
Miren la clave. Hay dos letras: una es N *y una es* I.
¿Qué quiere decir la letra N? *¿Y la letra* I?
¿Qué es un animal nativo?

CHECK

- *¿Qué es El Yunque?*
- *¿Qué hay en El Yunque?*
- *¿Qué consejos hay en el libro?*

LOG BOOK

Have students write three or four sentences describing El Yunque.

 **INTERNET LINK**

Scientific research is being done in the Luquillo Experimental Forest.
http://geochange.er.usgs.gov/pub/info/html/wrd/larsen.html

These activities can be done as classwork or as homework.

Objectives

Organizing Skills: making graphs; making a graphic organizer
Communication Skills: writing sentences

Related Components

Activity Book p. 86	Assessment Portfolio: p. 37–38

ACTIVITIES

1. Cuatro preguntas

Group Activity Write four questions and take turns asking and answering another group's questions. Write down their answers to your questions.
Groups win one point per correct answer. If a group cannot answer, it loses its turn.
Possible Questions:
¿Dónde vive el múcaro?
¿Dónde está El Yunque?
¿Qué es un coquí?
¿Hay muchos coquíes en Puerto Rico?

2. Gráficas del tiempo

Individual Activity Convert the table to two bar graphs.

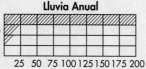

Lluvia Anual

El Yunque
Ciudad de México
Santiago de Chile
Mi pueblo o ciudad

25 50 75 100 125 150 175 200

Temperatura promedio en julio

El Yunque
Ciudad de México
Santiago de Chile
Mi pueblo o ciudad

30° 40° 50° 60° 70° 80° 90° 100°

3. ¡Clasifica los animales!

Individual Activity Classify the animals mentioned in the Adelante.

Reptiles	Mamíferos
la boa	*la mangosta*
la culebra	*el murciélago*
el largartijo	*la rata*
la salamanquita	

Anfibios	Aves
el coquí	*la cotorra*
el sapito	*el múcaro*
el sapo	

---

❶ Cuatro preguntas

En grupo, escriban cuatro preguntas sobre El Yunque. Hagan las preguntas a otro grupo. Anoten las respuestas.
Reglas del juego:°

- Los grupos ganan un punto° por cada respuesta correcta.
- Si un grupo no sabe la respuesta, pierde el turno.°

	lluvia (pulgadas/año)	temperatura promedio° en julio (Fahrenheit)
El Yunque	200	88°
Ciudad de México	23	64°
Santiago de Chile	14	48°
Mi pueblo o ciudad	¿?	¿?

❷ Gráficas del tiempo

Ya sabes que en El Yunque llueve mucho. Usa la información de la tabla de arriba para hacer dos gráficas de barras,° una para la lluvia y otra para la temperatura.

Lluvia anual

El Yunque
Ciudad de México
Santiago de Chile
Mi pueblo o ciudad

pulgadas 0 25 50 75 100 125 150 175 200

❸ ¡Clasifica los animales!

Mira los animales de El Yunque. Clasifica cada animal. Puedes consultar una enciclopedia.

Reptiles *la boa*
Mamíferos°
Anfibios°
Animales de El Yunque
Aves

❹ Compruébalo

Busca la descripción correcta.

1. La cotorra puertorriqueña...
2. El Toro...
3. La boa puertorriqueña...
4. Muchos árboles de El Yunque...
5. Las orquídeas...
6. El coquí...

a. miden más de 100 pies.
b. es un ave en peligro de extinción.
c. son flores exóticas.
d. es una rana muy pequeña.
e. mide hasta siete pies.
f. es un pico muy alto de El Yunque.

los anfibios *amphibians*
ganan un punto *win a point*
las gráficas de barras *bar graphs*
los mamíferos *mammals*

pierde el turno *loses a turn*
el promedio *average*
las reglas del juego *rules of the game*

---

4. Compruébalo

Individual Activity Choose the correct ending for each sentence.
1. b **2.** f **3.** e **4.** a **5.** c **6.** d

TALLER DE ESCRITORES

1. UN CARTEL

Con tu compañero(a), diseñen un cartel turístico sobre El Yunque.
Incluyan:

- una descripción del bosque
- una lista de los animales
- fotos y dibujos de revistas
- qué llevar
- consejos para los visitantes

2. INTERCAMBIO° ELECTRÓNICO

En grupo, preparen preguntas para una clase en Puerto Rico.
El tema: actividades favoritas. Por ejemplo:

> ¿Cuáles son las actividades favoritas de la clase?
>
> ¿Qué les gusta hacer en...?
>
> ¿Cuándo van a... ?
>
> ¿Qué les gusta hacer cuando llueve o...?

Usen el correo electrónico° para mandar° sus preguntas.

3. AMIGOS POR CORRESPONDENCIA

En una carta, invita a tu amigo(a) a visitar un lugar interesante de tu
ciudad o estado. Incluye: una descripción del lugar, dónde está, qué
hay, qué temperatura hace, qué ropa va a necesitar y qué actividades
van a hacer. Por ejemplo:

Miami, 10 de noviembre de 1996

Querida Luisa:

*¡Qué chévere, vas a visitar mi país! Aquí hay un lugar
fantástico que se llama Los Everglades. Es un parque
nacional.*

*Aquí en diciembre no hace calor. Vas a necesitar un suéter
y un abrigo. También vamos a ir al cine y a patinar. Miami
es muy divertido.*

Tu amigo,

Sam

el correo electrónico *E-mail*   mandar *to send*
el intercambio *exchange*

179

TALLER DE ESCRITORES

Objectives
- to practice writing
- to use vocabulary from this unit

Related Components

Activity Book p. 87	Assessment Portfolio: p. 37-38

ACTIVITIES

1. Un cartel
Pair Activity Students will design a simple tourist poster advertising El Yunque. They should include:
- a description of the forest
- a list of animals
- photos and drawings
- what to bring
- advice for visitors

2. Intercambio electrónico
Group Activity Groups will write questions about favorite activities for a Puerto Rican class to answer. For Example: What are the favorite activities of the class? What do you like to do in …? When do you go to …? What do you like to do when its raining? Ask each group to read aloud its two or three best questions. Write some of these on the board, and have the class correct them if necessary. Encourage discussion of the questions.
Have the class pick the three best questions and write answers for them.

3. Amigos por correspondencia
Individual and Pair Activity Individuals will write letters inviting someone to visit a place in their city or state. They should include: a description of the place, its location, what is there, the temperature, what clothes are needed, and what activities are available.
Edit: Pairs exchange letters and review and edit each other's work. They should circle words they think are misspelled, and make notes about other possible errors. Have them work together to check the spelling and grammar, and to prepare final drafts.
Present: Students read their final drafts aloud to another person.

PORTFOLIO
Encourage students to select one of these assignments to add to their portfolios.

Objectives
Communicative: to listen to and understand directions
Cultural: to learn about a popular pastime
TPR: to have students make their own kites

Related Components

Assessment	Transparencies
Portfolio: p. 37-38	Unit 3: Project
CD Rom	**Video:**
Unit 3: Manos a la obra	Tape/Book
	Unit 3: Seg. 5

Search to frame 1481224

Materials
- 2 fine sticks of balsa wood
- Paper of different colors
- Paints
- Markers
- String
- Glue
- Scissors

GETTING STARTED

In this exercise, students should use their eyes more than their ears. Rather than try to understand every word, they should concentrate on the images and listen only for clues.

Before students open their books, try a brief TPR session showing how to tie a shoe. This will introduce and practice several key words used in the kite video. If possible, show the kite-making segment of the Unit 3 video.

DISCUSS

Read the first two paragraphs aloud and ask comprehension, experience, and analysis questions. For example:
¿Qué es una chiringa, un pájaro?
¿Cómo se llama una chiringa en México?
Read aloud each segment of the *Historia y usos* section. Use the information underneath the boxes to expand on the material.

Math Link: The world record for kite height is 31,955 feet (over five miles). It was set in Germany in 1919.

CIELO,° VIENTO Y ¡CHIRINGAS!

Volar chiringas es una actividad que comparten niños, adolescentes y adultos del mundo hispano.

Chiringa es una palabra puertorriqueña. En España las chiringas se llaman *cometas*, en México *papalotes*, en Venezuela *papagayos*, en Argentina *barriletes*, en Nicaragua *lechuzas* y en Chile *volantines*.

HISTORIA Y USOS

Las chiringas tienen más de 3.000 años y vienen de China. Con las chiringas es posible hacer muchas cosas.

- Los científicos° usan chiringas para estudiar la electricidad en el cielo y para otros experimentos. ¡Muchas chiringas ascienden hasta 2 millas!°

- Con una chiringa también es posible hacer deportes. El paracaídas es un tipo de chiringa.

- En Guatemala hacen chiringas para las ceremonias religiosas.

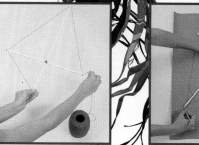

1 Cruza° las dos cañas y átalas° con el cordel. Ata las 4 puntas° con el cordel para formar la estructura.

2 Pon° la estructura sobre el papel. Marca las puntas y corta° el papel un poco más grande que la estructura.

3 Dobla° los bordes del papel para darle° forma. Usa el pegamento para pegar los bordes a la estructura.

180

ascienden hasta 2 millas *they go as high as 2 miles*	el cielo *sky*	cruza *cross*	pon *place*
átalas *tie them*	los científicos *scientists*	darle *to give (it)*	las puntas *ends*
	corta *cut*	dobla *fold*	

Science
Strong, lightweight materials like Mylar (a type of polyester which is thin, strong, and flexible) enable kites to fly higher and to carry instruments. The electrical experiment mentioned in the text took place in the Galápagos Islands, off the coast of Ecuador. One reason for going there was the reduced risk of collisions with commercial airplanes.

Sport
Thrill-seekers have hitched their wagons, skateboards, skis, and other vehicles to high-tech kites. The parafoil (parasail) is a soft, air-filled kite.

Ceremony
In Santiago Sacatepéquez, in Guatemala, people fly large circular kites above the cemetery to celebrate el día de los muertos (the Day of the Dead).

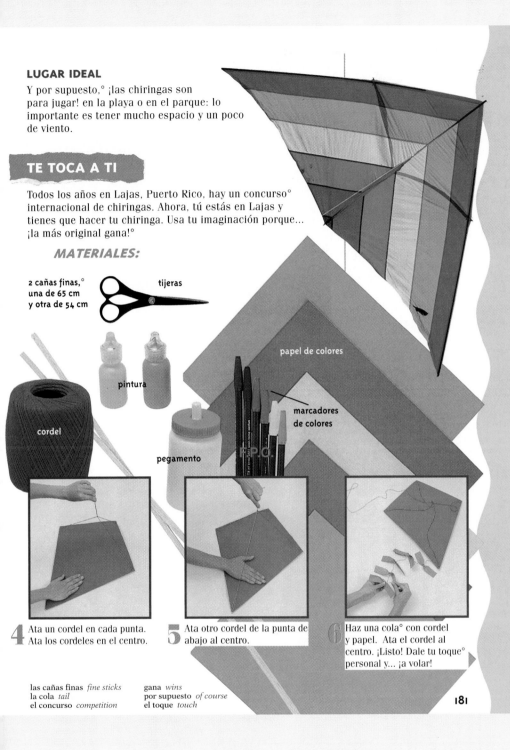

LUGAR IDEAL

Y por supuesto,° ¡las chiringas son para jugar! en la playa o en el parque: lo importante es tener mucho espacio y un poco de viento.

TE TOCA A TI

Todos los años en Lajas, Puerto Rico, hay un concurso° internacional de chiringas. Ahora, tú estás en Lajas y tienes que hacer tu chiringa. Usa tu imaginación porque… ¡la más original gana!°

MATERIALES:

2 cañas finas,° una de 65 cm y otra de 54 cm

tijeras

pintura

cordel

papel de colores

marcadores de colores

pegamento

4 Ata un cordel en cada punta. Ata los cordeles en el centro.

5 Ata otro cordel de la punta de abajo al centro.

6 Haz una cola° con cordel y papel. Ata el cordel al centro. ¡Listo! Dale tu toque° personal y… ¡a volar!

las cañas finas *fine sticks*
la cola *tail*
el concurso *competition*

gana *wins*
por supuesto *of course*
el toque *touch*

181

Para hispanohablantes

Describe the kite-making process in your own words while working with the materials. Do not look at the photos.

Chiringa is derived from an all-purpose word meaning "little thing."
A **cometa** is a "comet." (*Kome* is a Greek word that means "hair," a reference to a comet's tail.) **Papalote**, an Aztec word, means "butterfly." A **papagayo** is a parrot and a **lechuza** is an owl. A **barrilete** is a type of barrel-shaped kite. **Volantín**, related to **volar**, originally meant "acrobat."
Ask if anyone can guess where the English word *kite* came from.
(Like the words **lechuza** and **papagayo**, it is the name of a bird, in this case one of the hawk family.)
Ask students why there are so many names for one object.
(Possibly because these countries were relatively isolated during colonial times. In a few cases it is because indigenous names were adopted—or adapted.)
Ask Spanish speakers if they know other names for kites.

HANDS-ON

Using the directions in the book, lead students through the creation of a kite.
1. Act out the process as you read aloud the instructions. If you do not have kite-making materials, use something similar.
2. After you have done this several times, invite volunteers to do it as you read.
3. Do this as TPR with the whole class.

Te toca a ti

Ask students to make "tourism kites" with texts and images that advertise a beach or other place in Puerto Rico. To encourage creativity, ask what place the butterfly kite might be used to advertise. Display the kites. This activity can be assigned as homework.

CHECK

Ask students to perform these actions as you describe them:
• *Ata un cordel en cada punto.*
• *Coloca la estructura sobre el papel.*
• *Haz una cola.*

PORTFOLIO

Have students draw a picture of a kite and label each part (paper, cord, sticks, and so on).

▶▶▶ INTERNET LINK

For links to world of kite-making and flying: http://www.kfs.org/kites

Objectives

• to expand reading comprehension
• to relate the study of Spanish to other disciplines

Related Components

Activity Book p. 88	Audio Tapes Adelante: 10B
Assessment Portfolio: p. 37-38	Video:Tape/Book Unit 3: Seg. 4

Search to frame 1433811

Manatíes en peligro

About Manatees

The manatee (man-uh-TEE), or sea cow, is a mammal that grows to be about 14 feet long and 1500 pounds. Moisés (of the video) is a West Indian manatee (**manatí antillano**), a type found from the southeastern United States to northeastern South America.

Activity

Show the segment about Moisés. Ask comprehension questions:
¿Qué tipo de animal es Moisés?
Have a volunteer read the text. Ask more comprehension questions. Example:
¿Qué tipo de animal es el manatí?
Ask analysis questions. For example:
¿Qué quiere decir la palabra marino?
(Que es del mar).
¿Por qué le llaman el manatí antillano?
(Porque es de Las Antillas).
Possible Answers:
Some endangered species: bald eagle, grizzly bear, alligator, gorilla, giant panda.
Some groups: American Society for the Prevention of Cruelty to Animals, World Society for the Protection of Animals.

▶▶▶INTERNET LINKS

Manatees http://www.satelnet.org/manatee/html
The Arecibo Radiotelescope http://www.naic.edu/general/aovef.html
Caribbean Music Usenet: rec.music.afro-latin
Puerto Rican Artists http://www.upr.clu.edu:80/cuarto/ mundo.html

182

ECOLOGÍA

MANATÍES EN PELIGRO

El manatí antillano° es un mamífero acuático que vive en las costas de Puerto Rico. Es de color gris o marrón y come plantas acuáticas. Hoy día, hay sólo 78 manatíes en Puerto Rico. Muchos han muerto° en redes de pescadores° o en accidentes con botes a motor.

• ¿Qué otros animales en peligro de extinción conoces?
• ¿Conoces grupos que trabajan para la protección de animales en peligro de extinción? ¿Cómo se llaman?

ARTE

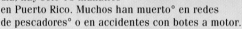

PINTEMOS° CON PALABRAS

Este cuadro,° *Paisaje doble,*° del artista puertorriqueño Rafael Ferrer (1933) representa un paisaje de Puerto Rico. ¿Puedes describir este cuadro?

• ¿Dónde está la mujer?
• ¿Qué hace?
• ¿Qué tiempo hace?
• ¿Qué colores hay en el cuadro?
• ¿Por qué se llama *Paisaje doble*?

182

antillano *Antillean*	el paisaje doble
el cuadro *painting*	*double landscape*
han muerto *have died*	los pescadores *fishermen*
	pintemos *let's paint*

Pintemos con palabras

About the Artist

Rafael Ferrer was born in Santurce. He was educated in the United States and lives in Philadelphia and Puerto Rico. His style is intentionally primitive, featuring bright colors and strong contrasts. Puerto Rican landscapes and themes are not his only subject matter.

Activity

Have volunteers read and answer bulleted questions.
Possible Answers:
• *La mujer está en la playa.*
• *La mujer pinta.*
• *Hace muy buen tiempo.*
• *Azul, verde, etc.*
• *Hay dos paisajes: el paisaje que mira la mujer y el paisaje que pinta la mujer.*

¡BIP! * ¡BIP! * ¡BIP!

MENSAJES°
DE LAS GALAXIAS

En Arecibo, Puerto Rico, está el radiotelescopio más grande del mundo.° Este instrumento da° información sobre estrellas,° planetas, otras galaxias y tormentas.

- ¿Qué planetario conoces en Estados Unidos? ¿Dónde está?
- ¿Te gustaría mandar un mensaje a otros planetas?
- Usa tres adjetivos para describir nuestro planeta.

MÚSICA

LA BOMBA AFRICANA

La bomba es un baile de origen africano que bailan en la costa de Puerto Rico. Los hombres y las mujeres bailan en grupo o separados al ritmo° de los tambores.° El nombre *bomba* viene del instrumento musical *bombo,* un tipo de tambor.

- ¿Qué es la bomba?
- ¿Qué es un bombo?

al ritmo *to the rhythm*	más grande del mundo *biggest in the world*
las estrellas *stars*	los mensajes *messages*
da *gives*	los tambores *drums*

183

Mensajes de las galaxias

About Radiotelescopes

Radiotelescopes gather radio waves in much the same way optical telescopes gather light. (Light and radio waves are both electromagnetic, but the latter are longer.) They can detect radio activity up to fifteen billion light years away—much farther than optical telescopes. The Arecibo telescope is 1,000 feet in diameter, the world's largest single-dish radio telescope. The reflected waves focus on the triangular object suspended above the bowl.

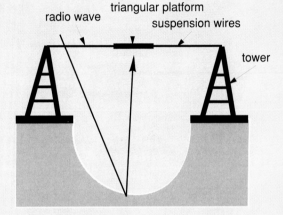

radio wave — triangular platform — suspension wires — tower

La bomba africana

About the bomba

La bomba originated with the Ashanti people of the west coast of Africa, some of whom were brought to Puerto Rico as slaves in the 15th to 17th centuries. Today, the words to the songs are in Spanish and the musicians also use *maracas,* which were invented by the Arawak Indians of Puerto Rico, but the other instruments, rhythms, and intonations are clearly African in origin.

In this unit

We visit Spain, a country as strikingly beautiful as the language that grew up there. After a quick introduction to Spain's main regions, we spend a day at a Spanish high school (Chapter 7) and get ready to go out for a night of dancing (Chapter 8). The school in Seville is a perfect place to discuss one of Federico García Lorca's ravishing poems about Andalusia, and it's fascinating to watch Spanish students struggle with English just like we struggle with Spanish. And as long as we're dancing in Seville, what better dance could we try than the flamenco?

Before leaving Andalusia we stop off in Granada, an enchanting town featured in both the unit video and the *Adelante* section of the student book. The first place we go is the Alhambra, a marvelously ornate fortified palace that is one of the world's finest specimens of Arabic architecture. Afterward we visit a nearby flower garden and tea house, and sit down to a fine local meal, both Spanish and Arabic, of fried vegetables and couscous. That leaves just enough time to tackle the unit project of making a tile (*azulejo*) with the guidance of one of Andalusia's world-renowned tilemakers. *¡Muchas gracias, señor!*

VIDEO LINKS

Text	Video Segment
Unit Overview Unit Opener	**1. Introduction to Spain** A glance at Spain's main regions and Spanish scenery
Chapter 7	**2. La vida estudiantil** Going to high school in Seville: discussing a poem by García Lorca, studying English as a foreign language grammar: preterite of -**ar**, -**er**, and -**ir** verbs; preterite of irregular verb **hacer**
Chapter 8	**3. Preparándose para salir** Getting ready to go out for the evening, choosing something to do, dancing the flamenco at a *discoteca* grammar: verbs **poder** and **salir**; reflexive verbs
Adelante	**4. Adelante** The Alhambra and other places to go and things to do in Granada
Manos a la obra	**5. Manos a la obra** How to paint a tile the Andalusian way

Geography and Climate

Separated from France and the rest of Europe by the Pyrenees Mountains, Spain takes up 85% of the Iberian peninsula and is almost as large as California and Georgia combined. The main geographic feature of Spain's 194,884 square miles (504,750 square kilometers) is the Meseta, a broad central plateau bordered by mountains on all sides. Summers are hot there, winters long and sometimes severe. The northern Pyrenees region receives much more rain than the Meseta, while the climate along the southern and eastern coasts is warm and moist. Southern Spain is hot and dry, and regions such as Murcia and Almeria are virtual deserts.

History and Government

The original inhabitants of Spain called themselves Iberians. Beginning around the 3rd century B.C. Spain was colonized by many foreign peoples, including Carthaginians, Romans, Visigoths, and Moors. After 711 A.D. Moors from Arabia and North Africa dominated Spain for 700 years. By the tenth century Moorish Spain was the richest and most civilized country in Europe. Gradually the Moors were driven out of Spain by Catholic monarchs who, beginning in 1469, united the many kingdoms within Spain into a single nation. Spain grew even wealthier and more powerful by colonizing vast amounts of land in North and South America. The country's fortunes declined during the wars and rebellions for independence of the 18th and 19th centuries. In 1936, a civil war erupted between fascists and republicans. The war lasted three years and ended with a fascist victory. Six hundred thousand Spaniards were killed, and General Franco became dictator. In 1978, three years after Franco's death, the country reverted to monarchy and adopted a parliamentary constitution. Since the 1980s many regions of Spain have had strong local governments. However, there is still pressure from Catalonian and Basque nationalists for increased self-government in their regions.

Spain's 20th-Century Voice

Born in Granada, Federico García Lorca (1898–1936) found his deepest inspiration in the craft and passion of his native region's folk songs and legends, which he brought up to date and then projected into the future like sunlight flashing from a thrown dagger. All of Andalusia haunts García Lorca even when he writes about New York in the '20s (*Poeta en Nueva York*) or the death of a bullfighter in Madrid ("Llanto por Ignacio Sánchez Mejias"). His magnificent body of poetry extends from *Romancero gitano* to *Diván del Tamarít* and includes plays such as *Bodas de sangre.* With him, you ride dusty roads by moonlight, you endure family tragedies, you smell bittersweet lemon flowers at dawn, you watch gypsies dancing by campfires, you hear the cool fall of water in fountained courtyards, and you wrap homesickness around your shoulders like a black winter cape.

Dentro de la Alhambra

HISTORY CONNECTION

Objective
• to explore the Arabic influence on Spanish architecture

Use
after beginning Unit 4

Materials
• Transparency Unit 4, *Dentro de la Alhambra*
• TRB Activity Support Page 14, *Dentro de la Alhambra* (fact sheet)

Preparation
• Project the transparency without identifying the Alhambra's location or architectural style.

Activity
• Share the FYI below. On the map, show students how the Arabs came to Spain from North Africa and locate cities in Andalusia with noteworthy Arabic architecture: Seville, Cordoba, Malaga, and Granada.
• Have students discuss how Arabic desert architecture was readily adaptable to the climate of Andalusia: In summer, thick white-washed walls keep out heat, shaded porches provide relief from the sun, tiled floors and walls keep interiors cool; in winter, upper-floor windows let in sunlight, carpets and braziers are portable sources of warmth, etc.
• Distribute activity support page and have students fill in the names of the architectural elements. (*Answer key;* left lines 1(*4*), 2(*2*), 3(*9*), 4(*7*); right lines 1(*1*), 2(*3*), 3(*10*), 4(*5*).

FYI
An army of Arabs and Berbers from North Africa landed on the Iberian peninsula in 711 A.D. The Muslim invaders eventually controlled the entire Spanish peninsula except for the northern regions of Galicia and Asturias. Arabs were a force in Spain until 1492, when Ferdinand and Isabella's troops took the Alhambra in the Battle of Granada and the last Arab ruler was banished.

Jugamos alquerque

GAME

Objectives
• to play a game brought to Spain by the Arabs
• to explore Spanish words of Arabic origin

Use
after beginning Unit 4

Materials
• TR, Activity Support Page 15, *Alquerque* (game board)

Preparation
• Have students discuss the Spanish words derived from Arabic that are listed on the activity support page. Point out that many words beginning with *al-* come from Arabic. (In Arabic, *al-* means *the.*)

Activity
• Distribute the activity support page for use as a game board. For game pieces, students can use coins or cut out the markers from the top of the sheet.
• Have them place game pieces as shown on inset. Players alternate moves; pieces can move in any direction.
• First player moves one piece to center point.
• Players can move a piece to an empty intersection or jump and capture an opponent's piece if there's an empty intersection directly behind the piece.
• Before jumping a piece, a player must call out a Spanish-Arabic word from the activity sheet.
• Players who capture all an opponent's pieces win.

FYI
From 711 A.D. until Columbus's first voyage, Spain experienced a remarkable flowering of the arts under Islamic rulers. Arab traders and settlers brought musical instruments, games, clothing, foods, and poetry. Over 4,000 Spanish words are derived from Arabic. *Alquerque,* a game that originated in ancient Egypt, appears to be an early form of checkers. The word *alquerque* means *the snap* or *the crack*—the sound of wooden game pieces striking a wooden board. Brought to *Al-Andalus* in the tenth century, *alquerque* is still played in some parts of Spain and in Central America.

MUSIC CONNECTION

Objective
• to explore a musical instrument that is uniquely identified with Spain

Use
after beginning Unit 4

Materials
• TR, Activity Support Page 16, *La guitarra*

Activity
• Share the FYI information below.
• Distribute activity support page and talk about the drawing. Ask students to discuss the differences between a classical acoustic guitar and other stringed instruments, such as the violin, the banjo, and the electric guitar.

Variations
• Ask students if any of them play the guitar or know someone who does. Arrange a classroom recital followed by questions and answers.
• Have students bring in tapes or CDs of guitarists.

FYI
The guitar is a plucked string instrument that probably originated early in the sixteenth century. It developed from an Arabic instrument, the *oud,* that came to Spain after the Moorish invasion of 711. By the end of the 19th century, the shape and size of the modern classical guitar had been fixed, and the guitar's six strings were tuned E, A, D, G, B, and E, still the standard tuning. Always a popular instrument among Hispanics—crucial, for instance, to Andalusia's flamenco and Argentina's tango—the guitar was an exotic novelty in non-Hispanic pop music until the advent of rock and roll in the 1950s. The classical repertory includes guitar transcriptions of Bach and Mozart by virtuosos Andrés Segovia and Julian Bream, and extended original pieces by composers Manuel de Falla, Heitor Villa-Lobos, and Pierre Boulez.

ART CONNECTION

Objective
• to make a different kind of portrait, after exploring the work of a well-known Spanish artist

Use
after beginning Unit 4

Materials
• Transparency Unit 4, *Busto de Sylvette*
• overhead projector
• paper, pencils, pens, markers

Preparation
• Show students the transparency and discuss it, sharing facts from the FYI below plus any other information you have about Picasso and cubism.

Activity
• Have students pair up and draw cubist portraits of their partners. Then have them exchange portraits.
• Each student describes his/her partner's drawing to the class. For example:—*Estos son mis ojos. Mi pelo está aquí,* etc. Partners confirm or modify the descriptions.
• Make sure students understand that the subjects of the best portraits may not be immediately recognizable.

FYI
In realistic art, when we see both eyes face on, we see only the edges of the ears, and if the head is turned even slightly one ear disappears completely. But in cubist art we can see everything on one plane and in any order, shape, and size the artist chooses. A mouth may open above a nose, ears may look like mailboxes, and eyelashes may be longer than ponytails. Late in the 19th century, a group of revolutionary French artists cleared the way for cubism by using simple geometric shapes in their paintings. Inspired by these works and by the abstract features of African masks, Barcelona-born Pablo Picasso (1881-1973) spun cubes, spheres, and pyramids all the way around and finished the first cubist painting in Paris in 1907. Picasso made cubist sculpture over the years, too, and New York's *Bust of Sylvette* (1968) was fabricated from a drawing with his approval.

ESPAÑA

Communicative Objectives
- to introduce Spain and its history
- to discuss how students spend their time in and out of the classroom

Related Components

CD ROM	Video
Unit 4	Unit 4: Seg. 1
Transparency	
Unit 4	

Search to frame 1000813

GETTING STARTED

Before they have a chance to read this page, ask students for words that they associate with Spain. In addition to bull-fights and flamenco, try to elicit colors, adjectives, and other less obvious words.

Using the Video

You may wish to show Segment 1 of the Unit 4 video, an introduction to Spain.

Using the Transparencies

To help orient students to Spain, use the Locator Map Transparency. You may also want to review the other transparencies for Unit 4 at this time.

DISCUSS

Presenting Spain

For more information about Spain, refer to pages 184A-184D.

Using the Text

English: After students have read the introduction, ask comprehension and critical-thinking questions. For example: Has anyone ever seen flamenco dancing? Have you ever heard of Maimonides, Magellan, or Picasso? What do you think Spanish high school students think about their own history and culture?

UNIDAD 4

ESPAÑA

DÍA A DÍA
En la unidad 4:

Capítulo 7	La vida estudiantil
Capítulo 8	Preparándose para salir
Adelante	**Para leer:** Maravillas de Andalucía

Proyecto: Azulejos españoles

Otras fronteras: Ecología, tecnología, juegos y literatura

184

Unit Components

Activity Book p. 89-108	Audio Book Script: p. 57-60; 65-68	CD ROM Unit 4 Conexiones Chapters 7-8	Transparencies Unit 4: Chapters 7-8
Assessment Oral Proficiency: p. 27-28 Listening Script: p. 15-16 Chapter Tests: p. 81-92 Portfolio: p. 39-40	Activities: p. 61-64; 69-72 **Audio Tapes** Chapter: 5A, 5B Adelante: 11A, 11B Assessment: 15A Conexiones: 17B	**Cuaderno** p. 53-68 **Magazine** Juntos en España	**Tutor Pages** p. 31-38 **Video: Tape/Book** Unit 4: Segments 1-5

Plaza de España, en Sevilla.

In Spain you will find a rich combination of ancient traditions, and today's modern trends. Spain echoes with the beat of traditional flamenco music and pulses with rock and disco rhythms of teen culture. In the cities, you can see buildings that are hundreds—even thousands—of years old as well as modern skyscrapers. Spain is marked by history, but it's also racing into the twenty-first century.

Students in Spain have an adventurous past to learn about. For centuries, Spain has given the world artists, authors, builders, doctors, and explorers. Their names are known around the world: Maimonides, Goya, Picasso, and so many more.

But Spanish students don't just learn about yesterday. They're also part of what's happening today. And, like you, they're acquiring skills they'll use in the world of tomorrow.

In this unit, you will meet the teenagers of Seville. You will see what their average day is like, and you will discover how schools in Spain compare and contrast with schools in the United States.

At the end of the school day, you will go out and have some fun with the teenagers of Seville. You may even learn to dance the flamenco. ¡Olé!

185

INTERDISCIPLINARY CONNECTIONS

To provide other perspectives, assign research projects like these:

Geography

- How many countries have common borders with Spain? (France, Andorra, Portugal, Morocco—with the Spanish colonies, Ceuta and Melilla—and Great Britain's colony, Gibraltar.)
- Use a globe or atlas to find out what U.S. cities are on the same latitude as these Spanish cities: San Sebastián, Madrid, Seville. (a few on the east coast: Portland, ME; New York, NY; Richmond, VA)

Arts

Don Quixote, Carmen, and Don Juan are three of the most famous characters in literature. What works did they appear in and who created them? (*Don Quixote,* novel by Miguel de Cervantes, 1605; *Carmen,* novel by Frenchman Prosper Mérimée, 1846, later an opera by Georges Bizet, 1875, which takes place in Seville; Don Juan, appeared in *El burlador de Sevilla,* by Tirso de Molina, and has been used by other authors.)

 CULTURE NOTE

The Iberian Peninsula takes its name from the Ebro River, which the Greeks called the Iberus. The name España comes from the Latin *Hispania,* which originally comes from a Semitic word meaning "remote".

▶▶▶ **INTERNET LINK**

For many of the best WWW links:
http://www.yahoo.com/text/Regional/Countries/Spain/

	Objetivos page 187	Conversemos pages 188-189	Realidades pages 190-191	Palabras en acción pages 192-193
Comunicación	• To talk about school subjects and schedules	Have students talk about subjects they are taking this year and their schedule	Read text, answer questions, talk about subjects and activities, discuss this year's subjects, make survey, report to class	Activities 1-3, 5, 8: Read cartoon, make list; discuss classrooms; talk about characters; discuss homework; write schedule
	• To talk about activities in school		Read text, answer questions, students discuss what they did in school last year	
	• To talk about making excuses	Talk about reasons for not doing homework		Activity 4: Give reasons for not doing homework
Vocabulario temático	• To know the expressions for school subjects	Have students talk about subjects they are taking this year	Read text, answer questions, talk about subjects and activities, discuss this year's subjects, make survey, report to class	Activities 3, 5, 8: Read cartoon, talk about characters; discuss homework; write schedule
	• To know the expressions for places in school		Read text, answer questions, talk about school last week; partners discuss what they did last year	Activities 1, 2, 7: Read cartoon, make list; discuss classrooms; make map
	• To know the expressions for school equipment	Have students talk about what they did in school yesterday	Read text, answer questions, talk about school last week; partners discuss what they did last year	Activities 1, 2, 5-7: Read cartoon, make list; discuss classrooms and homework; make map
	• To know the expressions for excuses	Talk about excuses for not doing homework		Activity 4: Give excuses for not doing homework
Estructura	• To talk about what you did: preterite of -ar verbs including spelling-changing verbs such as *sacar, jugar,* and *empezar*	Use the preterite of -ar verbs to talk about school yesterday	Read text, answer questions, talk about school last week; partners discuss what they did last year	Activities 3, 4: Read cartoon, talk about characters; give reasons for not doing homework
	• To talk about other activities you did: preterite of -er and -ir verbs and preterite of verb *hacer*	Talk about school yesterday and reasons or excuses for not doing homework	Read text, answer questions, talk about school last week; partners discuss what they did last year	Activities 3, 4: Read cartoon, talk about characters; give reasons for not doing homework
Cultura	The Spanish school day		The Spanish home room: *el salón de clase*	
Integración		Times of day, days of week, numbers, describing events, school courses, school supplies	Describing activities, days of week, school courses, reactions	Classroom items, reactions, school supplies, school courses

 # LA VIDA ESTUDIANTIL

Para comunicarnos mejor (1) pages 194-195	Para comunicarnos mejor (2) pages 196-197	Situaciones pages 198-199	Para resolver pages 200-201	Notes
Activities 1-3: Talk about school equipment; have partners discuss what they did yesterday; make class list	Activity 1: Discuss homework, make table	Activities 3, 4: Read text, answer questions, write letter about club activities; interview a senior, report to class	Pasos 1, 3-4: Look at poster, make list; design collage	
Activity 3: Make class list of last year's subjects and grades		Activity 5: Read text, answer questions, write ad	Pasos 1-4: Look at poster, make list; choose event, make table; design collage	
	Activity 2B: Give reasons for not doing homework			
Activities 1-3: Talk about school equipment; have partners discuss what they did yesterday; make class list	Activity 1: Discuss homework, make table	Activities 3, 4: Read text, answer questions, write letter about club activities; interview a senior, report to class	Pasos 1-4: Look at poster, make list; choose event, make table; design collage	
Activity 1: Talk about school equipment		Activity 2: Read text, have partners discuss sports they played last week	Pasos 1, 3, 4: Look at poster, make list; design collage	
Activity 1: Talk about school equipment	Activities 1, 3: Discuss homework, make table; make group table, report to class	Activity 4: Read text, answer questions, interview a senior, report to class	Pasos 1, 3, 4: Look at poster, make list; design collage	
	Activity 2B: Give excuses for not doing homework			
Use all present and preterite forms of *estudiar.* Activities 1-3: Talk about school equipment; discuss yesterday; make class list		Activities 1-5: Read text, answer questions, talk about school clubs; discuss sports; write letter about club activities, interview a senior, report to class; write ad	Pasos 2-4: Look at poster, choose an event, make table; design collage	
Activity 2: Have partners discuss what they did yesterday	Use all preterite forms of *hacer, aprender,* and *escribir.* Activities 1-3: Discuss homework, make graph; give reasons for not doing homework; make group table, report to class	Activities 1, 3-5: Read text, answer questions, talk about school clubs; write letter about club activities; interview a senior, report to class; write ad	Pasos 3, 4: Look at poster, design and present collage	
				Entérate page 202 The Spanish school system (ages 6-18)
Things to do, school supplies, reactions, school courses, things to buy	School courses, friends, favorite activties	Favorite activities, sports activities, numbers, items to take along	Dates, sports and other activities, celebrations	Numbers, things that need to be done

☐ ¡Vale!

GAME

Objective
• to play a game using exclamatory expressions from Chapters 1–7 of *Juntos I*

Use
after *Palabras en acción,* pages 192–193

Materials
• copies of *Juntos I*
• 3" x 5" index cards
• paper bag

Activity
• Divide class into seven groups. Assign each group one of the chapters in *Juntos* studied so far.
• Groups refer to the *Vocabulario temático* for their chapter and write each exclamatory expression on a separate index card.
• Put all cards in the bag and mix.
• Choose a scorekeeper to keep track of points.
• A player from group 1 picks a card from the bag and reads it aloud. For example:—*¡Qué suerte!* Player then creates a sentence that would elicit the exclamation—*¡Yo saqué una buena nota! ¡Qué suerte!* If the group 1 player can't think of a sentence, the card is given to group 2. Otherwise, a player from group 2 selects a new card.
• Players return cards to the bag after use.
• When everyone has had a turn, points are tallied and the winning team announced.

Variations
• Display and discuss additional exclamations for students to use, such as *¡No me digas! ¡Qué desgracia! ¡Así es! ¡Así se dice! ¡Así se hace! ¡Tremendo! ¡Fantástico! ¡Increíble!*

☐ Ayer hice mucho

GAME

Objective
• to play a game about school, using preterite verbs

Use
after *Para comunicarnos mejor,* page 194

Preparation
• Students form teams by rows and select a scorekeeper.
• Write these questions on the board: *¿Quiénes? ¿Qué cosa(s)? ¿A qué hora? ¿Dónde? ¿Por qué?*

Activity
• Ask students:—*¿Qué hiciste ayer en la escuela?*
• Give students 3 minutes to write down all the school activities they can think of.
• When time is up, call teams in row order: A1, B1, C1, etc. Each player turns an activity into a complete sentence and shares it with the class A1:—*Estudié tres lecciones de matemáticas para mi examen.* B1:—*Comí en la cafetería con mis amigos,* and so on.
• When all school activities have been used, change the question to:—*¿Qué hiciste ayer después de la escuela?*
• Tally points and announce the winning team. Teams receive 1 point per basic sentence, e.g.,—*Comí en la cafetería.* No points are given for repeated sentences. Teams receive 1 extra point per sentence for each answer to a question from the board. For example: *Mis amigos y yo comimos en la cafetería a la una de la tarde* receives 3 points because it answers *¿Quiénes?* and *¿A qué hora?* Or: *Mis amigos y yo comimos burritos y refrescos en la cafetería a la una* gets 4 points because it answers *¿Qué cosa(s)?* as well.

¿Qué notas sacaste?

SOCIAL STUDIES CONNECTION

Objective
- to talk about school subjects and grades, using preterite verbs

Use
after *Para comunicarnos mejor,* page 194

Materials
- posterboard or manila paper

Activity
- Pair students and have them design a report card for a fictitious school they attended in Spain last year. Have them include the school's name and location, as well as spaces for subjects, grades, days absent or late, teachers' comments, etc.
- Partners interview each other to find out what subjects they took last year, and enter the subjects on the report cards. They use the preterite when asking and answering questions. For example:—*¿Qué materias estudiaste en el año pasado?—Estudié historia, arte, álgebra, informática y literatura española.—¿Cuál te gustó más?*
- Read the FYI below and have partners give each other grades and write comments on the grades, using the numbers or letters of the Spanish scale.
- Students exchange report cards and change partners. New partners ask each other: *¿Qué nota sacaste en* (subject)*?,* again using the preterite.
- Display the finished report cards. Use them again later for skits about school and grades.

Variations
- Have students play the roles of teacher and student. Students can challenge unsatisfactory grades and comments.—*Sra. Gómez, ¿por qué saqué una nota baja en geometría? Hice la tarea todos los días,* etc. Teachers can explain the grades and comments.—*Sí, pero usted sacó una nota muy mala en el examen.*
- Have students role-play parents' reactions to the report cards.

FYI
In Spain tests are marked on a scale of 1-10. Letter grades are as follows: S (*Sobresaliente, 9–10*), N (*Notable, 8–9*), B (*Bien 7–8*), SF (*Suficiente, 5–7*), IN (*Insuficiente, 4–5*), or MD (*Muy deficiente, 0–3*).

Cuéntame un cuento

WRITING CONNECTION

Objective
- to create and tell a story, using the preterite of verbs ending in -**ar**, -**er**, and -**ir**

Use
after *Para comunicarnos mejor,* page 196

Materials
- note pads

Activity
- Divide class into four groups and give each a note pad.
- Have each group pick a leader and a topic and decide on a story line. Display a list of possible topics: *¿Qué pasó el año pasado en...? Un cuento divertido?* etc.
- Students pass the pad, each writing the next sentence of the story. Sentences refer to actions that took place in the past. Begin with *Había una vez . . .*
- When the story is finished, the group revises it, gives it a title, and writes three questions based on it.
- Group members take turns reading the story aloud and asking the questions.
- After the readings, have students illustrate the stories and staple them together. If they have access to a computer, they can input their anthology and print out copies for everyone.

Variations
- Cut up a copy of each group's story into sentences; distribute them to the rest of the class. Have students reorder the sentences or use the verbs again to create a new story.
- Have students select ten verbs from previous chapters and use them to write another story.
- Have students illustrate each other's stories and retell them from the pictures.

LA VIDA ESTUDIANTIL

Introduce the chapter and its theme by asking students what they would do if school did not exist. Would they work? What jobs are they qualified for? At what age would they have begun working?

Related Components

Audio Tapes	Conexiones
Conexiones: 17B, Ch. 7	Chapter 7
CD ROM	**Video: Tape/Book**
Chapter 7	Unit 4: Seg. 2

Search to frame 1000813

GETTING STARTED

Ask students to look carefully at the photograph of high school students in Seville. Suggestions for critical thinking questions:
¿ De qué hablan estos estudiantes?
¿ De los libros del instituto?

Thinking About Language

You can use this opportunity to discuss verb tenses with your students.

Past, Present, and Future

Some students are not aware that they use tenses in English. As the preterite is introduced in this chapter, this would be a good time to draw attention to tenses.

1. Make three columns on the board, and fill in the center one:

YESTERDAY	TODAY	TOMORROW
	I cook.	

2. Ask: Suppose I expect to cook tomorrow. What would I say? Write "I am going to cook" on the board.
Now ask for the Spanish equivalents and write them in the appropriate columns.

YESTERDAY	TODAY	TOMORROW
	I cook.	I am going to cook.
	Yo cocino.	Yo voy a cocinar.

3. Ask: How would I tell you in English about cooking yesterday? How is "I cooked" different from "I cook"? Add both to the list:

YESTERDAY	TODAY	TOMORROW
I cooked.	I cook.	I am going to cook.
Yo cociné.	Yo cocino.	Yo voy a cocinar.

Explain that differences in time are called tenses, and that these are the preterite, the present, and the future. Ask volunteers to suggest the first-person preterite forms of a

few regular **-ar** verbs, such as **bailar**, **escuchar**, and **nadar.**Point out that these are regular **-ar** verbs, and that the **-er** and **-ir** verbs will follow different rules, as they do in the present tense.

Chapter Components

Activity Book p. 89-98	Audio Book Script: p. 57-60 Activities: p. 61-64	CD ROM Chapter 7	Transparencies Chapter 7
Assessment Oral Proficiency: p. 27 Listening Script: p. 15 Chapter Test: p. 81-86	**Audio Tapes** Listening: 5A Assessment: 15A, Ch. 7 Conexiones: 17B, Ch. 7	**Conexiones** Chapter 7 **Cuaderno** p. 53-60 **Magazine** Juntos en España	**Tutor Pages** p. 31-34 **Video: Tape/Book** Unit 4: Seg. 3

CAPÍTULO 7

LA VIDA ESTUDIANTIL

186

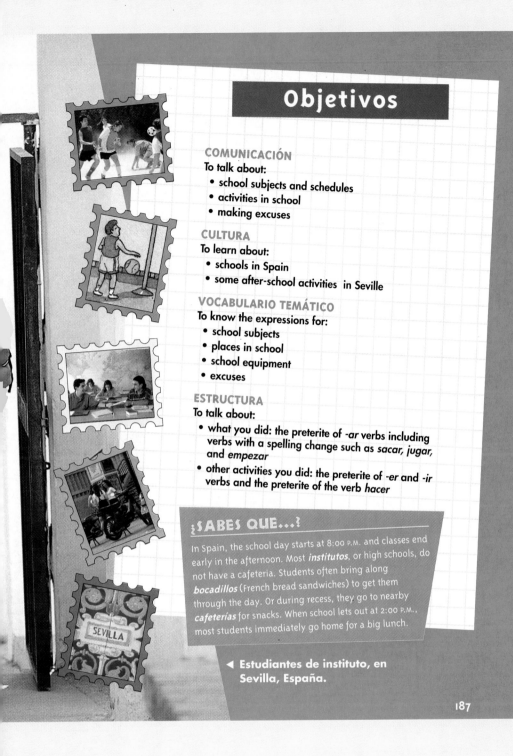

Objetivos

COMUNICACIÓN
To talk about:
- school subjects and schedules
- activities in school
- making excuses

CULTURA
To learn about:
- schools in Spain
- some after-school activities in Seville

VOCABULARIO TEMÁTICO
To know the expressions for:
- school subjects
- places in school
- school equipment
- excuses

ESTRUCTURA
To talk about:
- what you did: the preterite of *-ar* verbs including verbs with a spelling change such as *sacar, jugar,* and *empezar*
- other activities you did: the preterite of *-er* and *-ir* verbs and the preterite of the verb *hacer*

¿SABES QUE...?

In Spain, the school day starts at 8:00 P.M. and classes end early in the afternoon. Most *institutos,* or high schools, do not have a cafeteria. Students often bring along *bocadillos* (French bread sandwiches) to get them through the day. Or during recess, they go to nearby *cafeterías* for snacks. When school lets out at 2:00 P.M., most students immediately go home for a big lunch.

◄ **Estudiantes de instituto, en Sevilla, España.**

187

ACTIVITIES

Here are some additional activities that you may wish to use as you work through this chapter with your students.

Communication
Encourage after-class activities that may enhance student interest and proficiency. Some ideas:
- use the Internet to learn about issues of interest in different countries
- visit a local travel agency or consulate to get information on Spain

Culture
The written word can only hint at what life is like in other lands. To encourage greater understanding:
- listen to music from Andalusia or attend a flamenco performance
- show the video that accompanies Unit 4 of this textbook

Vocabulary
To reinforce vocabulary, have students:
- invent class schedules for famous people
- role-play classroom situations

Structure
To reinforce preterite forms of **-ar, -er,** and **-ir** verbs:
- make a display that shows the conjugation of regular verb forms
- try oral-pattern drills that use all forms of **-ar, -er,** and **-ir** verbs

▶▶▶ INTERNET LINK

UNO: Andalucía Datos Básicos:
http://www.cica.es/0iae199?/0esp/datos 199?.html [replace ? with current year]

Communicative Objectives
- to talk about your classes
- to talk about what you did in school
- to talk about exams and homework

Related Components

Activity Book p. 89	Cuaderno p. 53
Audio Book Script: Seg. 1	Transparencies Ch. 7: Conversemos
Audio Tapes Listening: 5A, Seg. 1	

GETTING STARTED

Ask students to imagine they are in Spain on a study program. It is the first day of school. How would they find out what classes they are expected to take?

ACTIVITIES

These activities give students an opportunity to begin communicating with each other and with you, focusing on the theme and objectives of the chapter. The activities can be used as oral class activities, or, if you prefer, you can pair students to achieve more interaction. Additional activities integrate critical-thinking skills.

¿Qué materias tienes este año?
Class activity to introduce school subjects. Ask several students the question, and then have pairs ask each other. You might also want to have them list the classes they are taking this year.

¿Qué tarea hiciste ayer?
Class activity to introduce preterite forms of some -ar, -er, and -ir verbs. After modeling the sentences and vocabulary, ask students to create sentences. Expand by encouraging them to make sentences with multiple verbs and other numbers (*Escribí tres poemas y leí dos revistas*).

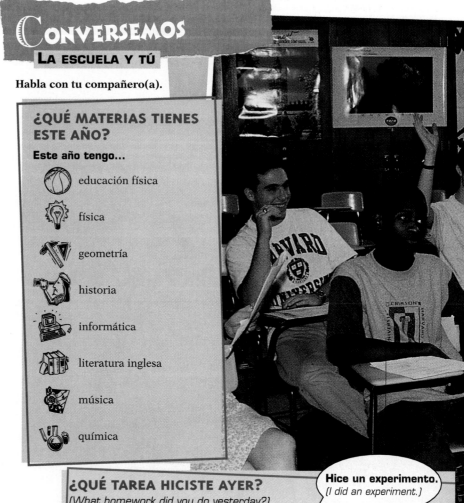

CONVERSEMOS
LA ESCUELA Y TÚ

Habla con tu compañero(a).

¿QUÉ MATERIAS TIENES ESTE AÑO?

Este año tengo...
- educación física
- física
- geometría
- historia
- informática
- literatura inglesa
- música
- química

¿QUÉ TAREA HICISTE AYER?
(What homework did you do yesterday?)

Hice un experimento. *(I did an experiment.)*

Escribí un informe. *(I wrote a paper.)*
- ❑ una composición
- ❑ un poema

Leí un cuento. *(I read a short story.)*
- ❑ una novela
- ❑ una revista
- ❑ un periódico en español

Estudié los apuntes de historia. *(I studied the history notes.)*
- ❑ las fórmulas de química
- ❑ el vocabulario de español / de francés
- ❑ un capítulo del libro de literatura

188

¿Cómo es tu horario?
Class activity to practice names of subjects and review days of the week. Ask students to use the table to answer your questions. Later, ask them to answer questions about their own schedules. Also: have students write sentences about all the classes they take on one day of the week. Example: *Los miércoles tengo biología a las 10:30.*

MEETING INDIVIDUAL NEEDS

Reaching All Students

For Auditory Learners
What would characters on a show like *Beverly Hills 90210* say about school if they spoke Spanish? Act out your dialogs.

For Visual Learners
Create drawings to represent each class. Shuffle these and match them up with other cards with class names on them.

¿CÓMO ES TU HORARIO?

Tengo álgebra todos los días. *(I have algebra every day.)*

Tengo alemán los lunes, miércoles y jueves.
(I have German on Mondays, Wednesdays, and Thursdays.)

Hora	lunes	martes	miércoles	jueves	viernes
8:10	álgebra	álgebra	álgebra	álgebra	álgebra
9:10	alemán	biología	alemán	alemán	historia

¿CUÁNDO FUE TU ÚLTIMO EXAMEN DE ESPAÑOL?

Fue ayer. *(It was yesterday.)*
❑ la semana pasada *(last week)*
❑ el lunes pasado *(last Monday)*
❑ el mes pasado *(last month)*

¿Cómo fue?

¡Fue horrible! Saqué una mala nota.
(It was horrible! I got a bad grade.)

¡Fue fatal!
(It was awful!)

¡Fue fácil! Saqué una buena nota.
(It was easy! I got a good grade.)

¡Qué mala suerte!
(What bad luck!)

¡Qué rollo!*
(What a bore!)

¡Qué suerte!
(What good luck!)

* Expresión de España.

¿HICISTE LA TAREA?

Claro que sí.
Todavía no. *(Not yet.)*

¿Por qué?

Porque tuve que estudiar para un examen.
(Because I had to study for a test.)

Porque no comprendí las preguntas.
(Because I didn't understand the questions.)

Porque anoche estuve enfermo(a).
(Because I was sick last night.)

Porque dejé los libros en el armario.
(Because I left my books in the locker.)

189

Class activity to introduce **fue** in conjunction with *cómo* and *cuándo* with several time expressions, and to introduce exclamations. Expand with words from earlier chapters, like **cumpleaños**.
Note: Fue is taught as an expression used to describe something that happened. The complete preterite of **ser** will not be introduced in this level.

¿Hiciste la tarea?

Class activity to introduce preterite forms, including **estuve, tuve,** and **hiciste**. After modeling the sentences, have pairs do teacher-student exchanges. Expand by varying these sentences (*¿Por qué no estudiaste para el exámen?*) and creating others.

CHECK

- ¿Qué materias tienes mañana?
- ¿Cómo es tu horario el lunes por la tarde?
- ¿Escribiste una composición la semana pasada? ¿El mes pasado? ¿Para qué materia?
- ¿Cómo fue tu último examen de historia?

LOG BOOK

Have students write their daily schedule.

Communicative Objectives

To talk about:
- past events
- school subjects and activities
- emotions or opinions

Related Components

Activity Book p. 90	**Audio Tapes** Listening Tape: 5A, Seg. 2
Audio Book Script: Seg. 2	**Cuaderno** p. 54

 GETTING STARTED

Ask what the most important thing that happened in school last year was. What words or phrases would someone need to know to describe that event in Spanish?

 DISCUSS

Talk about the photographs and captions, and ask questions. Suggestions:

El primer día de clase
¿Adónde fue Grace? ¿Cómo llegó?
¿Crees que es genial andar en moto?
Yo creo que es fatal. ¿No?

La excursión a la Alhambra
¿Qué es la Alhambra? ¿Dónde está?
¿Cómo fue la excursión a la Alhambra?
¿Te gustaría ir a la Alhambra?

Un momento emocionante
¿Jugar al fútbol es emocionante?
Y ganar, ¿es emocionante?
Y tú, ¿jugaste al fútbol el año pasado?
¿Por qué dicen: "¡Qué suerte!"? ¿Es porque su equipo es malo?

En la clase de informática
¿Quiénes pasaron mucho tiempo en la case de informática?
¿Qué materia es?

MI ÁLBUM DE LA ESCUELA

El día que empezaron las clases, Grace llegó a la escuela en su moto nueva. ¡Qué genial!

Toda la clase hizo una excursión a la Alhambra de Granada. Fue maravillosa.

INFORMÁTICA

¡Un momento emocionante! En diciembre, nuestro equipo jugó un partido de fútbol y ganó tres a dos. ¡Qué suerte!

En febrero, Pedro y Reyes pasaron muchas horas en la clase de informática. ¡Qué rollo!

Clase de inglés: Marta y Curro leyeron un cuento de Mark Twain. ¡Qué divertido!

En la Feria de abril, María Luisa y Rosa bailaron sevillanas hasta la una de la mañana. ¡Qué divertido!

190

En la clase de inglés
¿Qué hicieron Marta y Curro?
¿Cómo fue?
¿Qué es lo contrario de divertido?
¿Todos los cuentos son divertidos?
¿Qué cuento no es divertido?

 CULTURE NOTE

The April Fair is a week-long celebration that comes shortly after Easter. Sevillanos hold parties in large tents called **casetas**, wear traditional costumes, ride horses through the fairgrounds, dance, and generally take life easy.

En la Feria de Abril
¿Qué hacen estas chicas?
¿Dónde bailaron sevillanas?
¿Cómo fue?

 CULTURE NOTE

La Alhambra is an Arab fortress-palace built on a hilltop in Granada during the 13th and 14th centuries. (For more information, see the Unit 4 *Adelante*.)

HABLA DE LAS FOTOS DEL ÁLBUM

A. Con tu compañero(a), hablen de las cosas que hicieron los estudiantes. Usen expresiones de la lista.

— Grace llegó a la escuela en su moto nueva.
— ¡Qué genial!

B. ¿Qué actividades hiciste tú la semana pasada? ¿Cuáles no hiciste?

Leí un poema. No jugué al fútbol.

Leí...   Jugué...
Llegué...   Bailé...
Hice...   Empecé...
Escribí...   Estudié...

¡Qué aburrido!
¡Qué divertido!
¡Qué genial!
¡Qué interesante!
¡Qué maravilloso!
¡Qué rollo!
¡Qué suerte!

C. Con tu compañero(a), habla de las cosas que hicieron el año pasado.

— ¿Qué estudiaste el año pasado?
— Estudié matemáticas, historia y biología.
— ¿Qué otras cosas interesantes hiciste?
— Hice experimentos en el laboratorio. También leí una novela muy emocionante.

¿QUÉ OPINAS?

¿Cuántos estudiantes hicieron estas cosas la semana pasada? Haz una encuesta.

ENCUESTA

Actividad	Número de estudiantes
hicieron una excursión	III
bailaron en una fiesta	III
jugaron un partido de fútbol	IIII
llegaron a la escuela en moto	II
leyeron un cuento	
hicieron un experimento	

¡SABES QUE...?

In most Spanish schools, the students stay in the same classroom for much of the school day. They go to other rooms only for their music, gym or science classes. The room in which they take most of their subjects is called **la clase** or *el salón de clase*. The people who move from classroom to classroom are the teachers!

191

ACTIVITIES

Habla de las fotos del álbum

Pair Activities: Conversing
A. Use the list of expressions to talk about what the students in the photos did.
Possible Answers:
Marta y Curro leyeron un cuento. ¡Qué emocionante!
El equipo de fútbol ganó tres a dos. ¡Qué maravilloso!
Pedro y Reyes pasaron muchas horas en la clase de informática. ¡Qué aburrido!
María Luisa y Rosa bailaron sevillanas. ¡Qué genial!
La clase hizo una excursión a la Alhambra. ¡Qué interesante!
B. Which activities in the photos did you do or not do last week?
Possible Answers:
Leí un cuento. No jugué al fútbol.
Llegué a la escuela en moto. No escribí un poema.
Hice una excursión muy interesante. No bailé hasta la una de la mañana.
Jugué al fútbol. No ganamos tres a dos.
Bailé sevillanas. No leí un poema.
Empecé un cuento. No hice una excursión.
C. Talk about things you did last year.
Answers: See model on student page.

¿Qué opinas?

Group Activity: Taking a Poll
How many of you did any of the activities in the chart last week? Form groups, make charts, and fill them in. Discuss your findings with other groups, and then create a class chart.
Analysis: Compare the class chart with the example. Discuss the differences.

CHECK

- ¿Qué estudiaste el año pasado?
- ¿Cuál materia fue fatal?
- ¿Cuál fue muy interesante?
- ¿Qué actividades hiciste ayer?

LOG BOOK
Have students write a paragraph about photographs they would like to take.

Para hispanohablantes

Think of other expressions that describe how you feel about school subjects. Make a list. Next to each expression, write in Spanish what it means.

PALABRAS EN ACCIÓN

Communicative Objectives

To talk about:
- the names of classrooms
- things found in classrooms
- what you did in school yesterday
- why you did not do something

Related Components

Activity Book p. 91-92	Transparencies Ch. 7: Palabras en acción
Cuaderno p. 55-56	Tutor Page p. 31

GETTING STARTED

Invite students to compare the school in the picture with their own. Does your school have all of these classrooms? What others does it have?

DISCUSS

Ask what the characters in the picture are saying, and model the dialogs. Have students act out the dialogs.

PALABRAS EN ACCIÓN

AYER EN LA ESCUELA

Tarea para mañana:
Hacer los problemas 1 a 10
de la página 120.
$a + b + y =$

¡Vale!

¿Quieres mis apuntes, Lola?

la pizarra

la carpeta

el lápiz

EL SALÓN DE CLASE

los apuntes

la calculadora

la canasta

la pelota

EL LABORATORIO

la fórmula química
~ H_2O ~

El cuerpo humano

el microscopio

los tubos de ensayo

¿Hiciste la tarea, Eva?

¡Claro que sí!

la red

EL PATIO

1 ¿Qué ves en el dibujo?

Escoge tres lugares de la escuela. Haz una lista de las cosas que ves allí. Compara tu lista con la lista de tu compañero(a).

Lugar	Cosas
laboratorio	*tubos de ensayo,* *microscopios,...*
salón de clase	*pizarra,...*

2 Actividades en la escuela

¿Qué hiciste en la escuela? Habla con tu compañero(a) de las cosas que hicieron en los diferentes salones de clase.

— ¿Qué hiciste en el salón de actos?
— Canté en el coro.

3 ¿Qué hicieron?

Según los diálogos del dibujo, ¿qué hicieron ayer los estudiantes? Pregúntale a tu compañero(a).

— ¿Qué hizo Eva?
— Hizo la tarea.

4 Excusas

¿Por qué no hiciste la tarea? Da tres excusas.

— ¿Por qué no hiciste la tarea?
— Porque dejé los libros en el armario.

192

For students having difficulty saying what they did or did not do in school, or using exclamatory expressions, you might consider:

- **The tutor page:** Pair the student with a native speaker or a more able student using the tutor page.
- **Actividades:** see page 186C: *¡Vale!*

192

1. Pair Activity

Choose three places in the drawing. Make a list of things found in those places. Compare lists.

Analysis: One partner names a classroom, and another names an object found there.

2. Pair Activity

Talk about what each one of you did in each classroom.

Extension: Partners take turns naming things that are done in a particular class. The other says whether it is true or false.

3. Pair Activity

Ask and answer questions about what each of these students studied yesterday.

Application: Change the dialogs to be the opposite. Example: *Saqué una mala nota.* becomes *Saqué una buena nota.*

4. Individual Activity

Why didn't you do your homework? Give three excuses.

5. Pair Activity

Talk to your partner about yesterday's homework.

Extension: Talk about last year's classes, and what the homework was like.

6. Roleplay Activity

In pairs, act out school activities. The class guesses what you are doing and where.

For Visual Learners: Draw pictures or symbols for each subject, classroom, or object. Use as flashcards.

7. Hands-On Activity

Make a floor plan of your school for a new student. Write the names of the rooms and what things are found in each.

8. Synthesizing Activity

Write your class schedule from yesterday. Say what you did.

Analysis: Compare it with a partner.

CHECK

- *¿Qué salones de clase hay en la escuela?*
- *¿Qué hay en el salón de español?*
- *¿Qué hiciste en la escuela ayer?*

LOG BOOK

Have students write down any vocabulary they have difficulty remembering.

---

5 ¿Cuál fue la tarea?

Habla con tu compañero(a) sobre las tareas de ayer.

— *¿Cuál fue la tarea de español?*
— *Leer dos páginas del libro y aprender el verbo "hacer".*
— *¡Qué rollo!*

6 Charada

Con tu compañero(a), representa una actividad en la escuela. La clase va a decir qué actividad es.

7 Un plano de tu escuela

Haz un plano de tu escuela para un(a) estudiante nuevo(a). Escribe el nombre de cada lugar y anota qué cosas hay allí.

8 Tú eres el autor

¿Cómo fue tu horario ayer? ¿Qué hiciste?

Materia	¿Qué hiciste?
Física	Estudié para un examen.
Informática	Tomé apuntes en la biblioteca.
Matemáticas	Hice cinco problemas.

193

PARA COMUNICARNOS MEJOR

Communicative Objective
• to say what you did in the past, using the preterite tense of **-ar** verbs

Related Components

Activity Book p. 93-94	**Audio Tapes** Listening: 5A, Seg. 3
Audio Book Script: Seg. 3 Activities: p. 61	**Cuaderno** p. 57
	Tutor Page p. 32

GETTING STARTED

Ask for words and phrases that tell us that something happened in the past, such as *yesterday, before,* or *an hour ago.*

Language in Context

Ask questions and make comments in Spanish using the preterite of **estudiar** and familiar vocabulary. For example:
Ayer estudié esta lección.
Y tú, ¿estudiaste esta lección ayer?
¿Estudiaron Uds.?
Si no estudiaste el español, ¿qué estudiaste?
Have students compare the present and the preterite forms of **estudiar**. What generalizations can they make about the preterite of verbs that end in -ar?
When discussing **-car, -gar,** and **-zar** verbs, you may wish to remind students of the pronunciation taught in Chapters 2 and 6. Point out that in some cases letters change in order to keep the original sound.

DISCUSS

Review vocabulary from previous chapters and introduce some of this chapter's new vocabulary with questions that incorporate the preterite of **-ar** verbs. For example:
¿Estudiaste ayer?
¿Sabes que hablé con tu padre ayer?
¿Llegaste tarde a la clase esta mañana?
¿Sacaste buenas notas en inglés?
¿Qué hiciste anoche, estudiaste o bailaste?
¿Tomaron jugo de naranja en la mañana?

PARA COMUNICARNOS MEJOR
¿QUÉ ESTUDIASTE AYER?

To talk about past events, use the preterite tense.

Estudié español.	I studied Spanish.
Nosotros compramos un diccionario	We bought a dictionary.

Compare the present and preterite forms of the **-ar** verb **comprar** as they appear in the chart below.

comprar (to buy)

	Present	Preterite
yo	compr**o**	compr**é**
tú	compr**as**	compr**aste**
usted	compr**a**	compr**ó**
él/ella	compr**a**	compr**ó**
nosotros(as)	compr**amos**	compr**amos**
vosotros(as)	compr**áis**	compr**asteis**
ustedes	compr**an**	compr**aron**
ellos/ellas	compr**an**	compr**aron**

Note that the **nosotros(as)** form is the same in both tenses.

Verbs ending in **-car, -gar,** and **-zar** have a spelling change in the **yo** form in the preterite.

sacar *to get*	—>	(yo) sa**qué**
jugar *to play*	—>	(yo) ju**gué**
empezar *to start*	—>	(yo) empe**cé**

194

For students having difficulty using the preterite to talk about school subjects and grades, you might consider:
• **The tutor page:** Pair the student with a native speaker or a more able student using the tutor page.
• **Actividades:** see page 186D: *¿Qué notas sacaste?*

1 ¿Qué compraron?

Con tu compañero(a), hablen sobre las cosas que compraron estas personas para la escuela.

Mi amigo compró una computadora.

1. mi amigo

4. la profesora de música

2. yo

5. nosotros(as)

3. mis compañeros

6. tú

2 En la escuela

Con tu compañero(a), hablen de las cosas que pasaron ayer en la escuela. Usen expresiones de la lista.

— *Estudié geometría toda la tarde.*
— *¡Qué rollo!*

1. estudiar geometría toda la tarde
2. llegar tarde a la escuela
3. dejar la tarea en el armario
4. pasar tres horas en el laboratorio
5. jugar un partido de baloncesto
6. sacar una buena nota en química

¡Qué bueno!
¡Qué rollo!
¡Qué aburrido!
¡Qué suerte!
¡Qué lástima!
¡Qué mala suerte!

3 Nuestras notas

A. En grupo, hagan una lista de las materias de este año. Anoten en qué materias sacó buenas notas cada uno.

Materias	yo	Juan	Margarita	Luisa
álgebra	✓	✓		
español		✓		✓

B. Informen a la clase.

Juan y yo sacamos buenas notas en álgebra.

195

Para hispanohablantes

Observe the class quietly for about five minutes. Write a paragraph about things that individuals did during that time, and read it to the class.

Students use the preterite of **-ar** verbs to talk about the past.

1. Pair Activity
Talk to your partner about the things these people bought for school.
Answers:
1. See model on student page.
2. *Yo compré un cuaderno.*
3. *Mis compañeros compraron unas carpetas.*
4. *La profesora de música compró un piano.*
5. *Nosotras compramos un microscopio.*
6. *Tú compraste una calculadora.*
Application: Say when each bought these things. For example: *Mi amigo compró la computadora ayer por la tarde.*

2. Pair Activity
What did you do in school yesterday? Answer the questions. Use exclamations from the list to comment on them.
Possible Answers:
1. See model on student page.
2. *Llegué tarde a la escuela. ¡Qué lástima!*
3. *Dejé la tarea en el armario. ¡Qué mala suerte!*
4. *Pasé tres horas en el laboratorio. ¡Qué aburrido!*
5. *Jugué un partido de baloncesto. ¡Qué bueno!*
6. *Saqué una buena nota en química. ¡Qué suerte!*
Application: Say what you did not do.

3. Group Activity
A. Make a chart like this one of subjects that you are studying this year. Check off those in which you received a good grade.
B. Share the results with the class.
Analysis: Examine and comment on the results. Are there some classes in which many students do well? Are there any in which many students do poorly?

CHECK

- ¿Cuándo estudiaste tus apuntes?
- ¿Qué compró tu familia en la tienda?
- ¿De qué materia hablamos ayer?
- ¿Quién trabajó esta semana?¿Cuándo?
- ¿Quién no habló español hoy?

LOG BOOK
Have students compare the past and present forms of **-ar** verbs, and write down their observations.

Communicative Objectives
- to use the preterite of **-er** and **-ir** verbs
- to talk about things you did in the past, using the verb **hacer**

Related Components

Activity Book p. 95-96	Audio Tapes Listening: 5A, Seg. 4
Audio Book Script: Seg.4 Activities: p. 62	Cuaderno p. 58
	Tutor Page p. 33

GETTING STARTED

Ask students what did they did yesterday. Write some of the English verbs whose past tense ends in **-ed** and some that have irregular changes, such as *did* or *bought*. Ask students to comment on the formation of the past tense in English.

Language in Context

Review the preterite of **-ar** verbs. Then have students look at and compare the paradigms of **-er** and **-ir** verbs.
Use **hacer** and time expressions to elicit things the students did in the past. For example:
¿Qué hiciste ayer en la clase de español?
¿Y en la clase de álgebra?
¿Hicieron ustedes la tarea anoche?
Daniel, ¿a qué hora hiciste la tarea?
¿Quién hizo la tarea de inglés?

DISCUSS

Review vocabulary from previous chapters and introduce some of this chapter's new vocabulary with questions that use the preterite. For example:
¿Qué hizo ella anoche?
Ella hizo el informe.
Ellos no hicieron la tarea.
¿Hiciste arroz para la cena de ayer?
¿Cuándo leíste este artículo?
¿Qué aprendimos ayer?
¿Aprendiste esta lección?
¿Qué escribieron Uds. en la clase de química?
Escribí las fórmulas en el cuaderno.

PARA COMUNICARNOS MEJOR

¿QUÉ HICISTE AYER EN LA ESCUELA?

To talk about past events, you will also need to know the preterite of -er and -ir verbs.

Aprendí un poema.	I learned a poem.
Escribí un informe.	I wrote a report.

Here are the forms of the **-er** verb *aprender* and the **-ir** verb *escribir* in the preterite. Note that they have the same endings.

¡OJO!

Note that *leer* has a spelling change in some forms of the preterite.

leí	leímos
leíste	leísteis
leyó	leyeron

aprender (to learn) escribir (to write)

	aprender	escribir
yo	aprendí	escribí
tú	aprendiste	escribiste
usted	aprendió	escribió
él/ella	aprendió	escribió
nosotros(as)	aprendimos	escribimos
vosotros(as)	aprendisteis	escribisteis
ustedes	aprendieron	escribieron
ellos/ellas	aprendieron	escribieron

The verb **hacer** *(to do, to make)* is irregular in the preterite.

hacer (to do)

yo	hice	nosotros(as)	hicimos
tú	hiciste	vosotros(as)	hicisteis
usted	hizo	ustedes	hicieron
él/ella	hizo	ellos/ellas	hicieron

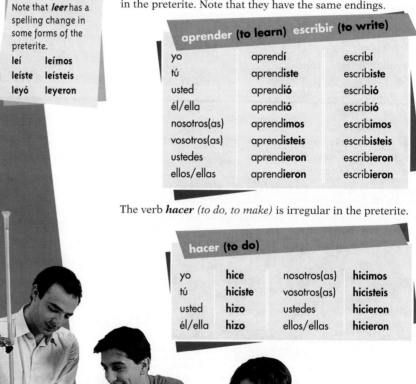

For students having difficulty using the preterite to talk about what they did in school, you might consider:
- **The tutor page:** Pair the student with a native speaker or a more able student using the tutor page.
- **Actividades:** see page 186C: *Ayer hice mucho*

1 La tarea

A. ¿Qué tarea hiciste anoche? Haz una gráfica como el modelo.

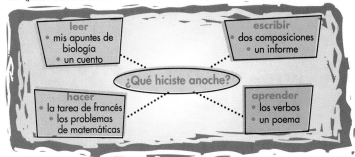

leer
- mis apuntes de biología
- un cuento

escribir
- dos composiciones
- un informe

¿Qué hiciste anoche?

hacer
- la tarea de francés
- los problemas de matemáticas

aprender
- los verbos
- un poema

B. Usa la gráfica para hablar con tu compañero(a) sobre la tarea.

— ¿Qué leíste anoche?
— Leí mis apuntes de biología. ¿Y tú?

2 Un día de clase

A. Hoy es un mal día para la clase. ¿Qué pasó? Haz oraciones negativas.

Mi compañero(a) no hizo la tarea.

1. mi compañero(a)		comprender los problemas
2. yo		escribir el informe
3. nosotros(as)	**no**	hacer la tarea
4. muchos estudiantes		aprender las fórmulas
5. mis compañeros(as)		leer el capítulo de historia
6. tú		ganar el partido de baloncesto

3 En mi tiempo libre

A. En grupo, hagan una tabla de sus actividades favoritas. Escriban quiénes y cuándo hicieron esas actividades.

actividades	quién	cuándo
escribir cartas	María, Jorge	ayer
leer revistas	yo	anoche
comer en un restaurante		

B. Presenten los resultados a la clase.

María y Jorge escribieron cartas ayer.

Para hispanohablantes

Write about one funny, interesting, or exciting thing that you did recently. Use as many details as possible.

SITUACIONES

Communicative Objectives
- to talk about school activities
- to talk about the past

Related Components

Assessment Oral Proficiency: p. 27	**Conexiones** Chapter 7
Audio Book Script: Seg. 5 Activities: p. 63	**Magazine** Juntos en Espana
Audio Tapes Listening: 5A, Seg. 5 Conexiones: 17B, Ch. 7	**Tutor Page** p. 34

GETTING STARTED

Students should now be able to use the preterite of simple -ar, -er, and -ir verbs, and all of the chapter vocabulary correctly. Ask students what school clubs they take part in and what they do there.

APPLY

1. Individual or Class Activity
Read the announcements in the school's newsletter and answer the questions.
Possible Answers:
- *Hay cuatro clubes en el Instituto.*
- *Leyeron una novela de Rosa Chacel.*
- *Invitaron al Club de Ecología.*
- *Hicieron una excursión al Coto de Doñana.*
- *El equipo de baloncesto ganó todos los partidos.*

2. Pair Activity
Talk about sports you played last week. Say:
- with whom you played
- where you played
- which teams played
- which team won and when

Possible Answers:
- *Jugué al fútbol con mis amigos.*
- *Jugamos en el parque.*
- *Jugaron el equipo rojo y el equipo azul.*
- *El equipo azul jugó el viernes pasado.*

Application: Talk to your partner about the sports you played last year.

3. Individual or Pair Activity
Write to a friend about what you did in a school club last week.
Answers: See model on student page.
Analysis: Exchange letters with your partner and edit each other's work.

4. Individual Activity
Interview another student about what he or she did in school last year. Ask:
- in what courses he or she got good or bad grades
- what sports he or she played and how many games the team won
- what clubs he or she belonged to and what he or she did there
Share what you found out with the class.
Answers: See model on student page.

For students having difficulty grasping the preterite, you might consider:
- **The tutor page:** Pair the student with a native speaker or a more able student using the tutor page.
- **Actividades:** see page 186D: *Cuéntame un cuento*

SITUACIONES

LA REVISTA ESCOLAR

ACTIVIDADES DEL INSTITUTO VELÁZQUEZ

CLUB DE LECTORES
Si te gusta leer, el Club de Lectores es para ti. El mes pasado leímos una novela muy interesante de la escritora española Rosa Chacel.

CLUB DE ECOLOGÍA
¿Te gustan los animales y las plantas? ¿Te interesan los problemas del medio ambiente? En el Club de Ecología hicimos una excursión al Coto de Doñana para estudiar los animales y las plantas de la región.

CLUB DEPORTIVO
¿Te gustan los deportes? En el Club Deportivo practicamos baloncesto, fútbol, atletismo y voleibol. El mes pasado, el equipo de baloncesto del Instituto ganó todos los partidos.

CLUB DE FOTOGRAFÍA
¿Quieres sacar buenas fotos? Los miembros del Club de Fotografía sacaron fotos muy interesantes de pájaros y árboles del Coto de Doñana. Invitaron al Club de Ecología a su exposición.

PARA TU REFERENCIA
el atletismo *track and field*
el/la escritor(a) *writer*
la exposición *exhibition*
¿Te interesan...? *Are you interested in . . .?*
los lectores *readers*
el medio ambiente *environment*
los miembros *members*

1 **Actividades en la escuela**

Lee la revista escolar y contesta las preguntas.
- ¿Cuántos clubes hay en el Instituto Velázquez?
- ¿Qué leyeron el mes pasado los miembros del Club de Lectores?
- ¿A quién invitaron los miembros del Club de Fotografía?
- ¿Qué hicieron el mes pasado los miembros del Club de Ecología?
- ¿Quién ganó los partidos?

Un evento deportivo

Habla con tu compañero(a) sobre los deportes que practicaron la semana pasada. Digan:

- con quién practicaron el/los deporte(s)
- dónde practicaron el/los deporte(s)
- qué equipos jugaron
- qué equipo ganó

 Amigos por correspondencia

Escríbele a un(a) amigo(a) sobre tus actividades de la semana pasada en un club.

> *Querido Esteban:*
>
> *Estoy muy bien. El viernes pasado empecé las clases de fotografía. Saqué unas fotos muy bonitas de mi perro. Llevé mis fotos al Club de Fotografía para una exposición en junio. Hasta pronto. Tu amiga,*
>
> *Clara*

 Una entrevista

Entrevista a un(a) estudiante. Pregúntale:

- en qué materias sacó buenas/malas notas el año pasado
- qué deportes practicó y cuántos partidos ganó su equipo
- en qué club(es) participó y qué hizo allí

Informa a la clase.

> *Eduardo Serna sacó buenas notas en español. Jugó al béisbol y ganó todos los partidos. En el Club de Lectores leyó Los cuentos de la Alhambra de Washington Irving.*

 Un club divertido

Tu club necesita más miembros. Escribe cuatro oraciones para un anuncio en el periódico escolar sobre las actividades que hicieron en el club el año pasado.

> - *Sacamos fotos de la ciudad.*
> - *Hicimos una excursión al Parque Nacional.*
> - *Escribimos un informe sobre los animales de la región.*
> - *Leímos dos libros sobre el medio ambiente.*

Communicative Objectives
- to talk about memorable events of the school year
- to present a collage to the class

Related Components

Transparencies	Video: Tape/Book
Ch. 7: Para resolver	Unit 4: Seg. 2

Search to frame 1021014

GETTING STARTED

Ask students to name some of the highlights of this school year. Winning a football game? A dance?

APPLY

PASO 1: Un año especial
Discuss the important school events of this year. List suggestions on the board.
Answers: See model on student page.
Analysis: Create a timeline of the events on the list. Write one sentence for each event. Use the preterite tense. Example:
Ganamos el partido de fútbol en septiembre.

PASO 2: Momentos para recordar
Form groups for the last three activities. Choose several outstanding moments from the list. Use the table on this page as a model and fill in the information.

PASO 3: ¡A trabajar!
Design a collage with photos or drawings of each event. Write:
- sentences about the photos
- the date of the events
- the title of the collage
- the names of your group's members

PASO 4: Nuestro año escolar
Present your group's collage to the class, and talk about the events of the year.
Analysis: Compare and contrast collages. Find three similarities and three differences between your collage and those of other groups.

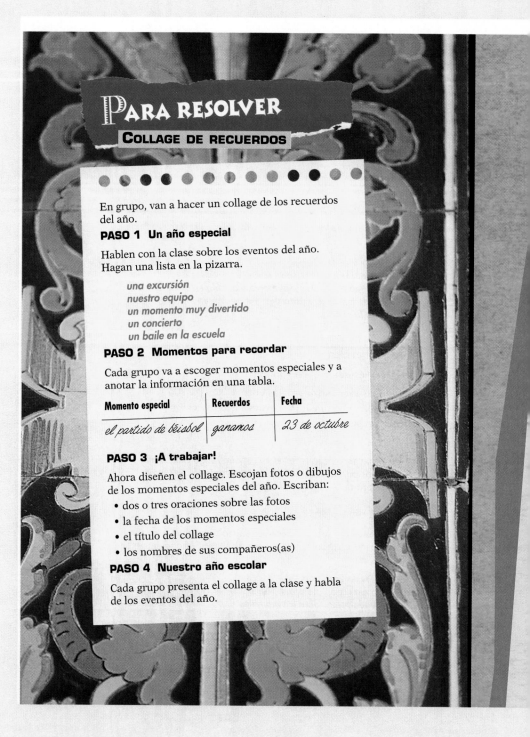

PARA RESOLVER
COLLAGE DE RECUERDOS

En grupo, van a hacer un collage de los recuerdos del año.

PASO 1 Un año especial

Hablen con la clase sobre los eventos del año. Hagan una lista en la pizarra.

una excursión
nuestro equipo
un momento muy divertido
un concierto
un baile en la escuela

PASO 2 Momentos para recordar

Cada grupo va a escoger momentos especiales y a anotar la información en una tabla.

Momento especial	Recuerdos	Fecha
el partido de béisbol	ganamos	23 de octubre

PASO 3 ¡A trabajar!

Ahora diseñen el collage. Escojan fotos o dibujos de los momentos especiales del año. Escriban:
- dos o tres oraciones sobre las fotos
- la fecha de los momentos especiales
- el título del collage
- los nombres de sus compañeros(as)

PASO 4 Nuestro año escolar

Cada grupo presenta el collage a la clase y habla de los eventos del año.

200

Recuerdos del año

7 de septiembre

La primera foto que sacó Elena para el Club de Fotografía.

15 de mayo

SEVILLA

Miguel Ángel, el día de su cumpleaños. Invitó a toda la clase a un picnic en el parque. ¡Fue genial!

25 de abril

Curro, Lola, Ana María y Grace pasaron un día en el Parque de María Luisa. ¡Qué divertido!

LOG BOOK

Think of other special moments you had with your family, friends, or pets. Make a table like the one in *Paso 2*.

School Words

Subjects

calculus *el cálculo*
dance *el baile, la danza*
ethics *la ética, la moral*
fine arts *las bellas artes*
health education *la clase de salud*
history *la historia*
home economics *la economía doméstica*
humanities *las humanidades*
industrial arts *las artes industriales*
physical education *la educación física*
physics *la física*
social studies *los estudios sociales*
theater *el teatro*
trigonometry *la trigonometría*

People, Places, and Activies

academic advisor *el/la orientador/a académico/a*
break *el recreo, el receso*
janitor *el conserje*
lunch break *la hora del almuerzo*
lunchroom *la cafetería*
school band *la banda escolar*
school team *el equipo de la escuela*
science fair *la feria científica*
suspension *la suspensión*
uniform *el uniforme*
yard *el patio*

Objectives

Communicative: to learn more school vocabulary
Cultural: to talk about education in Spain

Related Components

Audio Tapes	Conexiones
Conexiones: 17B, Ch. 7	Chapter 7
	Magazine
	Juntos en España

GETTING STARTED

Ask students if they think everyone should study exactly the same subjects. How much variety should be allowed? Why?

DISCUSS

Using the Text

After each paragraph, ask comprehension and critical-thinking questions, such as:
¿Hasta que edad tienen que ir a la escuela los jóvenes de España?
¿Qué tienen que estudiar?
¿Qué escogen si quieren seguir con sus estudios?
¿Qué aprenden en la Formación Profesional, por ejemplo?
¿Qué estudian cuando quieren ir a la universidad?

Cooperative Learning

In Spanish, make a graphic organizer of your school system to show what courses students follow and why.

CHECK

Te toca a ti
Answers:

1. ...*hasta los 16 años.*
2. ...*aprenden un oficio.*
3. ...*escogen el Bachillerato.*
4. ...*artes, ciencias de la naturaleza, salud, de humanidades, de ciencias sociales, y tecnología.*
5. ...*la carrera que piensan estudiar.*

ENTÉRATE

¿QUÉ ESTUDIAN LOS JÓVENES DE ESPAÑA?

En España es obligatorio° ir a la escuela hasta los 16 años. Después de los estudios primarios y secundarios, los estudiantes que quieren seguir,° escogen el Bachillerato o la Formación Profesional.

En la Formación Profesional los estudiantes aprenden un oficio° (mecánico(a),° electricista,° etc.). En el Bachillerato, se preparan° para ir a la universidad. Hay seis tipos de Bachillerato. Los estudiantes tienen que escoger uno, según° la carrera° que piensan estudiar.

EDUCACIÓN PRIMARIA
6 años (de los 6 a los 12)

EDUCACIÓN SECUNDARIA
4 años (de los 12 a los 16)

FORMACIÓN PROFESIONAL
2 años (de los 16 a los 18)

BACHILLERATO
2 años (de los 16 a los 18)
- en artes
- en ciencias de la naturaleza
- en salud°
- en humanidades
- en ciencias sociales
- en tecnología

TE TOCA A TI

Completa las oraciones.

1. En España, es obligatorio ir a la escuela...
2. En la Formación Profesional los estudiantes...
3. Para ir a la universidad los jóvenes...
4. Hay Bachilleratos en...
5. Los estudiantes tienen que escoger un tipo de Bachillerato, según...

la carrera *major, career*	se preparan *they get ready*
el/la electricista *electrician*	la salud *health*
el/la mecánico(a) *mechanic*	seguir *to continue*
obligatorio *mandatory*	según *depending on*
el oficio *trade*	

PORTFOLIO

Make an identification card in Spanish. Include your name, address, year of graduation, name of your school, an ID number, and other relevant information.

Para hispanohablantes

If you have studied in a different school system, or know someone who went to school in another country, tell the class how that school was different from yours.

 INTERNET LINK

Information about Spain's educational system: http://www.civeng.carelton.ca/SiSpain/educatio/enlargem.html

VOCABULARIO TEMÁTICO

En la escuela
At school

el armario *locker*
el fichero *card catalogue*
la fuente *water fountain*
el laboratorio *laboratory*
la oficina del director
principal's office
el pasillo *hallway*
el patio *courtyard*
el salón de actos *auditorium*
el salón de clase *classroom*

En el salón de clase
In the classroom

los apuntes *notes*
la calculadora *calculator*
la carpeta *folder/binder*

En el laboratorio
In the lab

el microscopio *microscope*
la planta *plant*
los tubos de ensayo *test tubes*

Las materias
Subjects

el alemán *German*
el álgebra *algebra*
la biología *biology*
la física *physics*
el francés *French*
la geometría *geometry*
la informática *computer science*

la literatura inglesa
English literature
la química *chemistry*

¿Qué hiciste en la escuela?
What did you do in school?

la composición *composition*
el examen (los exámenes)
exam(s)
el experimento *experiment*
la fórmula *formula*
el informe *report*
el problema *problem*
la tarea *homework*
el vocabulario *vocabulary*
la excursión *excursion, outing*
cantar en el coro
to sing in the choir
estudiar *to study*
ganar el partido
to win the game
sacar una buena/mala nota
to get a good/bad grade

¿Qué leíste?
What did you read?

el capítulo *chapter*
el cuento *short story*
la novela *novel*
la página *page*
el poema *poem*

¿Cuándo?

anoche *last night*

ayer *yesterday*
el lunes pasado *last Monday*
el mes pasado *last month*
la semana pasada *last week*

Excusas
Excuses

Estuve enfermo(a). *I was sick.*
Tuve que... *I had to . . .*

Expresiones y palabras

¿Cómo fue...? *How was . . . ?*
¿Cuándo fue...?
When was . . . ?
¡Fue fatal! *It was awful!*
¡Fue horrible! *It was horrible!*
¡Qué mala suerte!
What bad luck!
¡Qué suerte! *What good luck!*
Todavía no. *Not yet.*
la canasta
basket (as in basketball)
comprender *to understand*
dejar *to leave behind, to forget*
empezar *to begin*
el equipo *team*
llegar *to arrive*
la moto *motorcycle*
pasar *to spend time/to happen*
último *last*

Expresiones de España

¡Qué genial! *How cool!*
¡Qué rollo! *What a bore!*
¡Vale! *Sure!*

LA CONEXIÓN INGLÉS-ESPAÑOL

Many words that end in *-em* in English end in **-ema** in Spanish. For example, the word *poem* in English is **poema** in Spanish. Note that most Spanish words ending in **-ema** are masculine.

Look at the *Vocabulario temático*. Can you find another word like **poema**?

VOCABULARIO TEMÁTICO

Objectives
• to review vocabulary
• to correctly pronounce words containing the "n," "m," and "ñ"

Related Components

Activity Book	Audio Book
Chapter Review: p. 97-98	Script: Seg. 6 Activities p. 64
Assessment Listening Script: p. 15 Chapter Test: p. 81-86	**Audio Tapes** Listening: 5A, Seg. 6 Assessment: 15A, Ch. 7
	Cuaderno p. 59-60

Pronunciation

• The Spanish letters "n" and "m" should present no problem to English speakers since they are pronounced in more or less the same manner in Spanish. Though the consonant following a nasal sound affects the pronunciation of the nasal sound somewhat, this phenomenon also occurs in English and thus does not require special attention here.

armario, moto, comprender, notas, novela, genial

• It should be noted, however, that the letter "n" is pronounced like the "ng" in the English word "finger ":
• before a hard 'c': *blanco*
• before a hard "g": *mango*
• when the "n" is the last letter in the word: *salón, examen*
• The "ñ" is always pronounced like the "ny" in the English word "canyon." *año, otoño, baño, cañón, España*

PORTFOLIO
Have students make a **sopa de letras** with words that have the letters **n** or **ñ**.

La conexión inglés-español

Answer: *el problema*
Note: Many masculine nouns with **-ema** or **-ama** endings were originally Greek. Many are also cognates. Examples: *diagrama, dilema, esquema, panorama, programa, telegrama*

	Objetivos page 205	Conversemos pages 206-207	Realidades pages 208-209	Palabras en acción pages 210-211
Comunicación	• To talk about making plans to go out	Have students discuss whom they go out with, making plans, and getting ready to go out	Read text, answer questions, talk about going out; call friend to make plans; leave phone message for friend	Activities 1, 2, 5: Read cartoon, discuss getting ready to go out; give partner advice
	• To talk about what to wear	Have students discuss what they are going to wear when they go out	Read text, answer questions, call friend to make plans to go out, and talk about what to wear	Activities 1-4, 7: Read cartoon, discuss getting ready to go out; discuss clothing; make collage
	• To talk about leaving and receiving phone messages	Discuss leaving/receiving messages on answering machine	Read text, answer questions, leave phone message for friend	Activities 6, 8: Read cartoon, act out phone conversation; create message for answering machine
Vocabulario temático	• To know the expressions for getting dressed and other daily routines	Have students talk about how they get ready to go out and what they wear	Read text, answer questions, call friend to make plans and talk about what to wear	Activities 1-4, 7: Read cartoon, discuss getting ready to go out; describe clothing; discuss clothing; make collage
	• To know the expressions for calling on the telephone	Practice talking on phone, leaving/receiving messages on answering machine	Read text, answer questions, call where you're going for information	Activities 6, 8: Read cartoon, act out phone conversation; create message for answering machine
Estructura	• To talk about what you can or can't do: the verb *poder* and the infinitive of another verb	Use *poder* + the infinitive to make plans to go out; practice talking on phone, leaving/receiving messages on answering machine	Read text, answer questions, talk about going out; call friend, make plans; leave phone message; interview partner	Activity 6: Read cartoon, act out phone conversation
	• To talk about going out: the verb *salir*	Use *salir* to talk about plans to go out; practice talking on phone, leaving/receiving messages on answering machine	Read text, answer questions, talk about going out; call friend to make plans; leave phone message for friend	Activities 1, 2, 6: Read cartoon, discuss getting ready to go out; act out phone conversation
	• To talk about daily routines: reflexive verbs and pronouns	Use reflexive verbs and pronouns to talk about getting ready to go out	Read text, answer questions, call friend to make plans, and talk about what to wear	Activities 1, 2, 4, 5, 7: Read cartoon, discuss getting ready to go out; discuss clothing; give advice; make collage
Cultura	Teenage social life in Spain			
Integración		Familiar people, daily activities, numbers, what to do, greetings, polite terms	Dates, days of week, time of day, numbers, where to go, what to do, places to go	Locations, greetings, polite terms, places to go, daily activities

PREPARÁNDOSE PARA SALIR

Para comunicarnos mejor (1) pages 212-213	Para comunicarnos mejor (2) pages 214-215	Situaciones pages 216-217	Para resolver pages 218-219	Notes
Activity 2: Have partners interview each other, make table	**Activities 1-3: Discuss what people do before going out; practice talking on phone; discuss daily routines**	**Activities 2, 4: Read ad, create dialog; call gym, practice talking on phone**	**Pasos 1-4: Read travel ad, make plans; create dialog for customer and travel agent; discuss clothing; make map**	
	Activity 2: Practice talking on phone	**Activity 4: Read ad, call gym, practice talking on phone**	**Pasos 2, 3: Read travel ad, create dialog for customer and travel agent; discuss clothing**	
Activity 2: Have partners interview each other; make table	**Activities 1-3: Discuss what people do before going out; practice talking on phone; discuss daily routines**	**Activities 1, 3, 4: Read ad, answer questions; discuss activities; call gym, practice talking on phone**	**Pasos 2, 3: Read travel ad, create dialog for customer and travel agent; discuss clothing**	
	Activity 2: Practice talking on phone	**Activity 4: Read ad, call gym, practice talking on phone**	**Paso 2: Read travel ad, create dialog for customer and travel agent**	
Use all forms of *poder.* Activities 1, 3: Discuss not being able to go out tonight; talk about ways to solve problems		**Activities 2, 5: Read ad, create dialog; give advice to people with different interests**	**Paso 1: Read travel ad, make plans for trip**	
Use all forms of *salir.* Activities 1, 2: Discuss not being able to go out tonight; interview partners, make table	**Activities 1, 2: Discuss what people do before going out; practice talking on phone**	**Activity 2: Read ad, create dialog**	**Pasos 2, 4: Read travel ad, create dialog for customer and travel agent; make and present map**	
	Use *ponerse.* Activities 1-3: Discuss what to do before going out; practice talking on phone; discuss daily routines	**Activities 2, 4: Read ad, create dialog; call gym, practice talking on phone**	**Paso 3: Read travel ad, discuss clothing**	
		***Sevillanas:* Andalusian folk dances**		**Entérate page 220 Motorbikes in Spain**
Daily activities, familiar people, times of day, places to go	**Numbers, times, daily activities, descriptive words, saying what to do**	**Activities, numbers, time of day, subjects, saying what to do, descriptions**	**Activities people like to do and are going to do, places to go, time of day**	

¿Puedes o no puedes?

Objective
- to talk about things we can do, using the irregular verb *poder*

Use
after *Para comunicarnos mejor,* page 212

Activity
- Each student lists five activities he/she can do well.
- During the sharing of lists, students listen carefully to find someone who can do something they would like to be able to do.
- When all lists have been shared with the class, students pair off with students whom they can show how to do something, and from whom they can learn how to do something. For example:—*Yo no puedo hacer el experimento de química. Ana sí puede hacer el experimento. Ana me puede ayudar en la case de química.*

Variations
- Have one student list activities on the board while classmates make their presentations. Afterward, students can discuss similarities and differences. For example:—*Paul y Steven pueden escribir un poema muy bien, y Tom y Carol pueden escribir un cuento.*
- Have students take notes during the activity and write up their conclusions.

Puedo No puedo

Salgo mucho

Objective
- to talk about going out, using the irregular verb *salir*

Use
after *Para comunicarnos mejor,* page 212

Activity
- Select a class recorder.
- Have students brainstorm places to go and things to do. The recorder writes places and activities on the board. For example: *Salgo con los amigos todos los sábados. Salgo con mi novia al cine. Salimos antes de la cena. Salgo a comer pizza con los amigos.*
- Each student votes for a favorite place to go. The recorder records each vote, adds them up, and announces the class's five favorite places to go.
- Now invite students to discuss what they wear when they go to their favorite places. For example:—*Cuando salgo con mis amigas, me pongo una falda, una blusa y mis negros zapatos,* etc.

Variations
- Write student names on cards. Put one name on some cards, several names on others. Each student chooses a card and makes the person(s) named the subject of a sentence with the verb *salir.*
- Change the focus of the activity by using *salir de*—to physically leave a place. Brainstorm new lists.

¿Cuándo te lavas el pelo?

MATH CONNECTION

Objective
- to talk about daily activities, using reflexive verbs

Use
after *Para comunicarnos mejor,* page 214

Preparation
- Question students about their daily habits. Have them write down answers to questions such as: *¿Cuándo te bañas? ¿Cuándo te cepillas los dientes?* On the board, write the reflexive verbs you use *(bañarse, cepillarse)* as well as other reflexive verbs that you could have used, e.g., *despertarse, vestirse, mirarse en el espejo, acostarse.*

Activity
- Select a class recorder.
- Have the other students form groups of five. Each group selects a secretary/spokesperson and chooses a playing order for the other four members.
- Group members ask each other the same questions the teacher asked, and answer with their previously written answers. The secretary/spokesperson tracks the responses and reports them to the class. For example:—*En nuestro grupo, dos personas se cepillan los dientes al despertarse. Otra se cepilla los dientes después del desayuno y la cena. Una se cepilla después del desayuno.*
- The class recorder tallies the reports on the board.
- The class discusses the findings. For example:—*En nuestra clase, 20 estudiantes se cepillan los dientes al despertarse y 3 después del desayuno y la cena. Cinco personas se cepillan solamente después del desayuno.*

Variations
- Have students display the information in a graph or chart which they can label and present.
- When you finish Chapter 8, go back to the Chapter 7 activity *Hice mucho ayer* (186C). Students can review reflexive verbs by answering a new question: *¿Qué haces/hiciste antes de ir a la escuela?*

Nuevo y fabuloso

MEDIA CONNECTION

Objective
- to create original TV commercials, using reflexive verbs and Chapter 8 *Vocabulario temático*

Use
after *Para comunicarnos mejor,* page 214

Materials
- Newspaper or magazine pictures of people getting ready to go out—brushing teeth, combing hair, putting on shoes, etc.
- TRB Activity Support Page 10, *Storyboard*

Activity
- Have students form teams of five to make a television commercial.
- Place all the pictures on a table and have each team select a picture that can be used to promote a specific product.
- Team members choose roles: scriptwriter, director, actor, actress, etc.
- Teams invent a name for their product, write a short commercial (5–8 sentences) with reflexive verbs, sketch a sequence of visuals on the storyboard, and present their commerical to the class. For example, team A selects toothpaste—*Cuando me ducho pienso en Jabónflor. Siempre me baño con Jabónflor. También me lavo el pelo con Jabónflor.*
- After the commercials have been presented, ask students which products they would buy, which they wouldn't buy, and why. Possible answers:—*Voy a comprar Jabónflor porque quiero usar un nuevo jabón; no voy a comprarlo porque no quiero ir al supermercado hoy,* etc.
- Have students vote for the commercial they think is most effective.

Variations
- Use props and make videotapes of the commercials.
- Have each team make a print version of their commercial by pasting the picture to posterboard and writing a narrative advertisement based on the storyboard and the script underneath.

PREPARÁNDOSE PARA SALIR

Introduce the chapter and its theme by asking what American teenagers typically do after school or on weekends. Do students know if (or think that) these activities are the same as those of teenagers in other countries? What do they think Spanish teenagers do?

Ask students how long it takes them to get ready to go out. What do they have to do? How does where they are going affect how long they take to get ready?

Related Components

Audio Tapes	Conexiones
Conexiones: 17B, Ch. 8	Chapter 8
CD ROM	**Video: Tape/Book**
Chapter 8	Unit 4: Seg. 3

Search to frame 1065901

 GETTING STARTED

Have students look at the photograph. Ask them what about this discotheque is the same or different from American discotheques they have visited. Ask critical thinking questions: *¿Te gustaría ir a esta discoteca de Sevilla? ¿Por qué?*

Thinking About Language

You can use this opportunity to introduce the use of reflexive verbs and pronouns in Spanish to indicate actions we do to ourselves.

Reflexive Verbs and Pronouns
1. You can introduce reflexive verbs by saying and acting out a few sentences:
Yo me lavo las manos.
Yo me cepillo los dientes.
Ask **sí/no** questions with the same verbs:
¿Tú te lavas las manos?
¿Ustedes se cepillan los dientes?
Follow up with this comparison:
Yo miro la televisión.
Yo "me" miro en el espejo.
Ask if anyone noticed anything unusual about your sentences.

2. Explain that if you use a "self" word or phrase, such as *wash yourself* or *look at myself,* it must be accompanied by a pronoun—**me, te, se, nos,** or **os.** These pronouns serve a function that is similar to the "self" words.

CAPÍTULO **8**

PREPARÁNDOSE PARA SALIR

3. Ask students to mention other "self" words (*himself, herself, itself, ourselves, yourselves, themselves*). Ask them to make up an English sentence for each of these words. Explain that these "self" pronouns are called reflexive pronouns—they *reflect* the action back upon the person who performs the action.

Chapter Components

Activity Book	Audio Book	CD ROM	Transparencies
p. 99-108	Script: p. 65-68	Chapter 8	Chapter 8
Assessment	Activities: p. 69-72	**Conexiones**	**Tutor Pages**
Oral Proficiency:	**Audio Tapes**	Chapter 8	p. 35-38
p. 28	Listening: 5B	**Cuaderno**	**Video: Tape/Book**
Listening Script: p. 16	Assessment: 15A,	p. 61-68	Unit 4: Seg. 2
Chapter Test:	Ch. 8	**Magazine**	
p. 87-92	Conexiones: 17B,	Juntos en España	
	Ch.8		

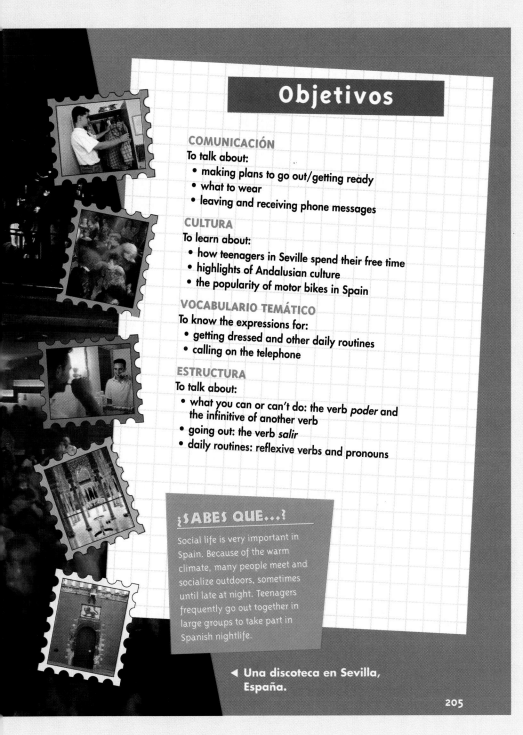

Objetivos

COMUNICACIÓN
To talk about:
- making plans to go out/getting ready
- what to wear
- leaving and receiving phone messages

CULTURA
To learn about:
- how teenagers in Seville spend their free time
- highlights of Andalusian culture
- the popularity of motor bikes in Spain

VOCABULARIO TEMÁTICO
To know the expressions for:
- getting dressed and other daily routines
- calling on the telephone

ESTRUCTURA
To talk about:
- what you can or can't do: the verb *poder* and the infinitive of another verb
- going out: the verb *salir*
- daily routines: reflexive verbs and pronouns

¿SABES QUE...?
Social life is very important in Spain. Because of the warm climate, many people meet and socialize outdoors, sometimes until late at night. Teenagers frequently go out together in large groups to take part in Spanish nightlife.

◀ **Una discoteca en Sevilla, España.**

205

CONVERSEMOS

Communicative Objectives
- to invite a friend to go out
- to say how you get ready to go out
- to say what you wear
- to answer a phone and leave messages

Related Components

Activity Book p. 99	**Cuaderno** p. 61
Audio Book Script: Seg. 1	**Transparencies** Ch.8: Conversemos
Audio Tapes Listening: 5B, Seg. 1	

GETTING STARTED

Ask students to identify the activities and objects. Model the Spanish phrase for each of the activities.

ACTIVITIES

These activities give students an opportunity to begin communicating with each other and with you, focusing on the theme and objectives of the chapter. The activities can be used as oral class activities, or, if you prefer, you can pair students to achieve more interaction. Additional activities integrate critical-thinking skills.

Generalmente, ¿con quién sales?
Class activity to introduce **salir**. Students use **salgo** to say with whom they go out. Encourage the use of alternative answers. Vary this with questions and statements that use days of the week and other vocabulary. Try not to use forms other than **salgo** and **sales**. Examples:
¿Sales los miércoles? ¿Con quién sales?
Yo salgo los sábados por la noche. Y tú, ¿con quién sales? Salgo con mi esposo.

¿Qué haces antes de salir?
Class activity to introduce reflexive pronouns and the vocabulary of personal grooming. Model the sentences while acting out the actions. Ask students to name actions in Spanish while you or volunteers perform them. Vary this by doing three activities in the wrong order (e.g., dry hair, shower, wash hair) and having students correct you.

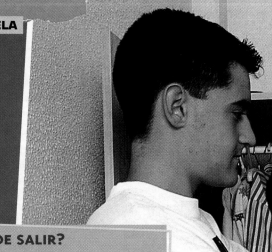

CONVERSEMOS
DESPUÉS DE LA ESCUELA

Habla con tu compañero(a).

GENERALMENTE, ¿CON QUIÉN SALES?

Salgo con mis amigos.
[I go out with my friends.]

- ❏ mis amigos
- ❏ mi familia
- ❏ mi hermano(a)
- ❏ solo(a) *(alone)*

¿QUÉ HACES ANTES DE SALIR?

Me baño, me peino y me pongo la ropa.
[I take a bath, comb my hair, and I get dressed.]

 me cepillo los dientes   me seco el pelo

 me ducho   me peino

 me lavo el pelo   me pongo la ropa

> **¿En cuánto tiempo te duchas?**
> *[How long does it take you to shower?]*

HOLA... ¿QUIERES SALIR?

¡Vale*! ¿Dónde nos encontramos?
(OK! Where shall we meet?)

Sí, estoy listo(a).
(Yes, I am ready.)

¡Claro que quiero salir!
¿Adónde vamos?
*(Of course I want to go out!
Where shall we go?)*

* *Expresión típica de España*

No puedo. Tal vez otro día.
(I can't. Perhaps another day.)

No, no tengo ganas.
(No, I don't feel like it.)

No, todavía no estoy listo(a).
(No, I am not ready yet.)

No puedo. Tengo que trabajar.
(I can't. I have to work.)

206

Hola...¿quieres salir?
Class activity to teach students how to accept or decline an invitation to go out. Work with the class to create a skit in which two people talk on the phone about what to do on Saturday night.

POR TELÉFONO

¿Qué dices?

Hola, ¿puedo hablar con...?
(Hello, may I speak with . . . ?)

Dile/Dígale que me llame,
por favor.
(Tell him/her to call me, please.)

¿Qué contesta la otra persona?

No está. ¿Quiere(s) dejar un mensaje?
*(He/She is not in. Would you like
to leave a message?)*

Sí, un momento, por favor.
(Yes, one moment, please.)

No está, pero va a volver pronto.
*(He/She is not in but will be back
soon.)*

EL CONTESTADOR AUTOMÁTICO

¿Qué escuchas?

"En este momento no puedo contestar el teléfono.
Por favor, deja un mensaje después de la señal".
*("I can't answer the phone right now. Please leave a
message after the beep.")*

¿Qué dices?

Oye, no te olvides del concierto. ¿Qué vas a ponerte?
Llámame. ¡Hasta luego!
*(Listen, don't forget the concert. What are you going to
wear? Call me. Bye!)*

¿QUÉ VAS A PONERTE?

Voy a ponerme vaqueros y una camisa.
[I'm going to wear jeans and a shirt.]

la camisa   la chaqueta   el suéter   la falda

los vaqueros   los tenis   los zapatos   el chaleco

207

CULTURE NOTE

The word **tío** comes from the word **tipo**,
"type," and is a slang term for "guy." It is
used by close friends. Do not call someone **tío** or **tía** if you do not know the
person well.

Por teléfono
Class activity to teach how to give and get
information on the telephone. Ask how this
activity is different from the previous one.
(This is not the person you are trying to
reach; it is someone else.) Model the
exchanges with a volunteer. Have pairs try
exchanges.

El contestador automático

¿Qué escuchas?
Class activity to create a message for a tele-
phone-answering machine. Ask what the
title probably means. If students have trouble with **contestador**, write it on the board
and cover the **-dor**. You may have to ask
for the meaning of **computadora** or
refrigerador.
Model these sentences. Have pairs create a
few brief messages of both types. Invite
them to perform these for the class.

¿Qué dices?
Class activity for leaving messages on
answering machines. Model the message
on the student page. Have volunteers create messages. Expand this activity by making the messages specific (e.g., *Hola, soy
Arnold Schwarzenegger. No estoy en casa,
pero... voy a volver pronto.)*

¿Qué vas a ponerte?
Class activity to introduce **ponerse** and
other new vocabulary.
Ask volunteers to read aloud the names of
the clothing and to point to classmates
who are wearing them. Ask variations on
the question in the title, such as:
El sábado por la noche, ¿qué vas a ponerte?

CHECK

* *¿Qué vas a ponerte mañana?*
* *¿Con quién sales este sábado?*
* *¿Qué dejas en un contestador automático?*

LOG BOOK
Have students write down all of the expressions that use reflexive pronouns.

Communicative Objective
• to talk about places to go

Related Components

Activity Book p. 100	**Audio Tapes** Listening Tape: 5B, Seg. 2
Audio Book Script: Seg. 2	**Cuaderno** p. 62

GETTING STARTED

Ask what activities your students think most American teenagers do on weekends. Do students recognize the activities in these pages? Are these the same kinds of things they like to do on weekends?

DISCUSS

Talk about the entertainment listings and ask questions. Suggestions:

Arte
Aquí dice "arte". ¿Qué es "arte" en inglés?
¿Dónde hay una exposición de arte?
¿Cuánto cuesta la entrada?
¿Qué palabra en inglés es como "entrada"?

Baile
¿Qué actividad hay en la academia?
¿A qué hora es?
¿A qué número de teléfono puedes llamar para más información?

Cine
¿Qué película hay en el cine?
¿A qué hora?

Conciertos
¿Cómo se llama la banda?
¿Qué música van a tocar en el concierto?
¿Dónde va a ser el concierto?

Deportes
¿A qué van a jugar en el estadio?
¿Cómo se llaman los equipos?
¿Es barato ir al partido?

Discotecas
¿Cómo se llama la discoteca?
¿A qué hora puedes ir a la discoteca?

Teatro
¿Cómo se llama esta obra de teatro?
¿Sabes lo qué hace una violetera?

REALIDADES
GUÍA DE ESPECTÁCULOS

LA SEMANA EN Sevilla

CINE
Flamenco de Carlos Saura. En la sala Rialto, de martes a viernes a las 16:00, 18:15, 20:30 y 22:45 hrs. Entrada: 400 pesetas.

ARTE
Exposición de Arte de Sevilla en el Museo de Bellas Artes. De martes a domingo, de 9:00 a 18:00 hrs. Entrada: 150 pesetas.

CONCIERTOS
Famosa banda de rock La Lola, en la plaza de San Francisco. Viernes y sábado a las 21:00 hrs. Entrada: 600 pesetas.

BAILE
Baile de sevillanas en la Academia Manolo Marín. De lunes a jueves, de 18:00 a 20:00 hrs. Para más información, llamar al 437–25–12.

DEPORTES
Partido de fútbol entre el Betis y el Sevilla en el estadio Benito Villamarín. El sábado a las 14:00 hrs. Entrada: 2.500 pesetas.

208

✓ CULTURE NOTE

The **Sevillanas** is a folkloric dance for pairs. Four pieces of music have the same theme and different steps.
Carlos Saura, one of Spain's best-known writer-directors, has been making movies since the end of the 1950s.
La violetera is a Spanish musical about a cabaret singer. *Violeteras* sold violets.

▶▶▶INTERNET LINK
Turista virtual de Sevilla http://www.cica.es/~masa/0tvs/0esp/tvs.htm

HABLA DE LA GUÍA

A. Con tu compañero(a), hagan planes para ir a uno de los espectáculos de la guía.

> — *¿A qué hora es La Violetera?*
> — *A las ocho de la noche.*
> — *¿Cuánto cuesta la entrada?*
> — *Dos mil pesetas.*
> — *Vale. ¡Vamos!*

B. Llama a un(a) amigo(a) por teléfono para hacer planes.

> — *¡Hola, Irene! ¿Puedes salir este sábado?*
> — *Sí, ¿adónde quieres ir?*
> — *Al museo.*
> — *¿Dónde nos encontramos?*
> — *En la cafetería.*
> — *¿Qué vas a ponerte?*
> — *Los vaqueros negros y la blusa blanca.*

C. Quieres ir al teatro con tu compañero(a). Deja un mensaje en el contestador automático.

> *"Hola Juan. ¿Puedes salir conmigo esta tarde? Me gustaría ir al teatro. Va a llover. No te olvides del paraguas. ¡Hasta luego!"*

¿QUÉ OPINAS?

¿Qué puedes hacer en tu pueblo o ciudad? ¿Cuándo? ¿A qué hora? ¿Qué actividades no puedes hacer? ¿Por qué? Pregúntale a tu compañero(a).

Haz una tabla con los resultados. Usa el modelo.

		Actividades	Día	Hora	¿Por qué no puedes?
Yo	puedo	ir a la discoteca	el viernes	a las 21:00 hrs.	
	no puedo	ir al teatro	—		es muy caro
Luisa	puede	ir al cine	el sábado	a las 18:00 hrs.	
	no puede	ir a la playa	—		está muy lejos

Los números del 1.000 al 10.000

1.000 mil	2.000 dos mil
1.100 mil cien	3.000 tres mil
1.500 mil quinientos(as)	10.000 diez mil

209

Habla de la guía

Pair Activities: Interpreting
Look at the announcements.
A. Make plans to attend an event listed in the magazine.
Answers: See model on student page.
B. Call a friend to make plans to attend an event.
Answers: See model on student page.
C. You want to go to the theater. Make up a message to leave on a friend's answering machine, asking if he or she is free and wants to go.
Answers: See model on student page.
Math Link
You and a friend each have 4,500 pesetas to spend in Sevilla this weekend. How many things can you do together?

¿Qué opinas?

Individual and Pair Activities: Evaluation
1. Which of the activities on the other page can you do where you live? On what days can you do them? At what time? Are there any activities that you cannot do? Which ones? Why can't you do them?
2. Ask your partner the same questions.
3. Use the answers to make a chart like the model.
Analysis: Compare your chart with those of other pairs.

CHECK

Point to the Sevilla events page and ask:
• *¿Te gusta más el cine o el teatro?*
• *¿A qué lugar te gustaría ir en Sevilla?*
• *¿Es posible ir a la discoteca el lunes?*
• *¿Cuánto cuesta la entrada en ese lugar?*

LOG BOOK
Have students list vocabulary they find especially difficult.

MEETING INDIVIDUAL NEEDS

Reaching All Students

For Auditory Learners
Students create and respond to recorded phone messages inviting them to go out.

For Visual Learners
Write a note (with a map) reminding a friend when and where you will be going.

For Kinesthetic Learners
Volunteers act out activities from the list. Others guess what they are doing and where they are.

Para hispanohablantes

Make a newspaper page like this one. List things that people can do for fun in your town this week.

Communicative Objectives
- to talk about clothing
- to talk about getting ready to go out
- to answer the phone
- to leave messages

Related Components

Activity Book p. 101-102	Transparencies Ch. 8: Palabras en acción
Cuaderno p. 63-64	Tutor Page p. 35

GETTING STARTED

Ask what this sequence of drawings seems to represent. Is this typical of the way many teenagers get ready to go out on a Saturday night?

DISCUSS

Suggest a few ways to group the people in the drawings (e.g., boys and girls, those talking on the phone and those talking directly to each other). Ask students to suggest other groupings (e.g., those who talk a lot, those who are getting ready and those who are ready, those who know what they are going to do and those who don't).

Para hispanohablantes

Some Spanish speakers in your class may use other expressions than the ones introduced in this chapter. Ask them to share with the class. A few variations:

está ocupado: está comunicando
la entrada: el billete, el boleto
un momento: un ratito
el peine: la peinilla
prepararse: alistarse
el contestador automático: la máquina contestadora
los tenis: las zapatillas
tener una cita con: encontrarse con, tener un compromiso con
el vestido: el traje

PALABRAS EN ACCIÓN
ANTES DE SALIR

¡Hola, Sofía! ¿Puedes salir esta noche?

Frente a la Giralda, a las 8:30.

¿Federico? ¡Vale! ¿Dónde nos encontramos?

¡Hola! ¿Puedo hablar con Cristina, por favor?

Ahora no. Tiene que secarse el pelo. Llama más tarde.

Muy bien. ¡Hasta luego!

FEDERICO LLAMA A SOFÍA POR TELÉFONO

Cristina se seca el pelo.

Pablo se ducha.

María se peina.

Andrés se cepilla los dientes.

1 ¿Qué hacen las chicas?

Mira las escenas del dibujo. Haz una lista de las cosas que hacen las chicas.

Sofía habla con Federico por teléfono.
Cristina se seca el pelo.

2 ¿Y qué hacen los chicos?

Mira las escenas del dibujo. ¿Qué hacen los chicos antes de salir? Habla con tus compañeros(as).

— ¿Qué hace Pablo antes de salir?
— Se ducha.

3 ¿Qué llevan?

Mira las escenas del dibujo. Habla con tu compañero(a) sobre la ropa que lleva cada uno.

— ¿Qué lleva Ramón?
— Lleva vaqueros, tenis y un chaleco negro.

4 ¿Qué te pones para ir a...?

Habla con tu compañero(a) sobre la ropa que te pones cuando vas a una fiesta, a un baile, a un concierto y a la escuela.

— ¿Qué te pones para ir a una fiesta?
— Generalmente me pongo una blusa y una falda corta. ¿Y tú?
— Me pongo vaqueros y un chaleco.

210

For students having difficulty talking about what they do before going out and what they wear to go out, or communicating on the phone, you might consider:
- **The tutor page:** Pair the student with a native speaker or a more able student, using the tutor page.

¿Qué me pongo, el vestido rojo o la falda negra con la blusa blanca?

el abrigo

el vestido   la blusa

la falda

los zapatos   las botas

LUISA ESCOGE LA ROPA

¿Vas a ponerte el chaleco negro?

¡Claro que sí! Está de moda.

la camisa

la chaqueta

el chaleco

los pantalones

los vaqueros

los tenis

RAMÓN SE PONE LA ROPA

el dinero

las llaves

Ana, no te olvides el dinero y las llaves.

No te olvides de llamar.

ANA SE PREPARA PARA SALIR

211

5 Antes de salir

¿Qué consejos le das a tu amigo(a) antes de salir?

> No te olvides del dinero.
> No te olvides...

6 Por teléfono

Llamas por teléfono a un amigo(a) para salir y contesta otra persona. Con tu compañero(a), haz un diálogo.

> — Hola. ¿Puedo hablar con Eva?
> — No está, pero va a volver pronto. ¿Quieres dejar un mensaje?
> — Dile que me llame, por favor.

7 Collage

Diseña la página de anuncios de una revista de modas. Usa dibujos y fotos de revistas. Escribe los anuncios y luego describe la ropa a la clase.

> *Esta primavera los chicos se ponen camisas negras con tenis blancos. Las chicas se ponen vestidos largos con botas.*

8 Tú eres el/la autor(a)

Prepara un mensaje para un contestador automático.

> *Hola. En este momento no puedo contestar el teléfono. Voy a volver pronto. Por favor, deja un mensaje después de la señal.*

ACTIVITIES

1. Individual Activity
Look at the cartoon and make a list of the things the girls are doing.
Extension: Make a list of all the places in the cartoon.

2. Individual and Group Activity
Talk with your classmates about what the boys are doing before going out.

3. Pair Activity
Talk about what each character in the last scene of the cartoon is wearing.
For Auditory and Kinesthetic Learners: First, one volunteer acts out getting ready to go to a party while another describes the actions in Spanish. Later, the actor performs what the speaker describes.

4. Pair Activity
Talk about the clothes you wear to go to a party, a dance, a concert, and school.
For Auditory Learners: One describes what someone in class is wearing, and the other guesses who that person is.

5. Pair Activity
Give your partner advice about what to do before going out.
Analysis: Make a list of things to do before going to a party.

6. Roleplay Activity
Create a skit in which you telephone one person but have to leave a message with another person who answers the phone.
Extension: Write "While you were out" notes for all the messages read in class and answer them.

7. Hands-On Activity
Homework for individuals or small groups. Use photos or drawings to design a page of ads for a fashion magazine. Write text for the ads and describe the clothes to the class.
For Auditory Learners: Create a radio announcement for your fashions.

8. Individual Activity
Make up a message for your own answering machine.
Application: Exchange messages. Write a response to your partner's message.

CHECK

- *¿Qué te pones para salir?*
- *¿Qué haces antes de salir?*
- *¿Qué mensaje tienes en tu contestador automático?*

PORTFOLIO

Class project. Make a comic book or a **fotonovela** about two brothers or sisters getting ready to go out. (**Fotonovelas** tell soap-opera-like stories with photos of the characters and printed talk balloons.)

Communicative Objectives
• to say what you can or cannot do, using **poder**
• to talk about going out, using **salir**

Related Components

Activity Book p. 103-104	**Audio Tapes** Listening: 5B, Seg. 3
Audio Book Script: Seg. 3 Activities: p. 69	**Cuaderno** p. 65
	Tutor Page p. 36

GETTING STARTED

Introduce these pages with a telephone monologue that uses **salir** and **poder** in different ways. For example:
Oye, Donna, ¿quieres salir conmigo esta noche? ¿No puedes? ¿Cuándo puedes salir? ¿El sábado?

Language in Context

Poder: Remind students that when **saber** is used with an infinitive, it means that you *know how* to do something. Explain that **poder** is used with an infinitive to say that you *can* do something.

Salir: Explain that **salir** means "to go out" in the sense of "to leave a place." Ask for examples in English (e.g., to go out the door). Make sure they do not confuse it with *"to leave something"* (e.g., a message). Point out that while **salir** can be used to talk about going out in general, *to go out with* or *to date* is **salir con.**

DISCUSS

Review vocabulary and introduce some of this chapter's vocabulary with questions that incorporate **poder** and **salir:**
¿Salen Uds. esta noche?
¿Puedo salir con Uds.?
¿Pueden salir de casa por la noche?
¿Cúando sales de la casa para la escuela?
Mi marido y yo salimos muy pronto.
Salgo de la escuela a las cuatro de la tarde. Y Uds.? ¿A qué hora salen?

To say what someone can or cannot do, use a form of the verb *poder* followed by the infinitive of another verb.

No, esta noche no puedo salir.   No, tonight I can't go out.

Here are the forms of the verb *poder* in the present tense. Note that the stem *(pod-)* changes from *o* to *ue* in all forms except *nosotros(as)* and *vosotros(as)*.

poder (ue) (to be able to)

yo	puedo	nosotros(as)	podemos
tú	puedes	vosotros(as)	podéis
usted	puede	ustedes	pueden
él/ella	puede	ellos/ellas	pueden

□ Other verbs with the same stem change as *poder* are *costar* (to cost) and *volver* (to come back).

To say that someone is going out, use the verb *salir*.

Los sábados salgo con mis amigos.   On Saturdays I go out with my friends.

Here is the verb *salir* in the present tense. Note that the *yo* form is irregular: *salgo*.

salir (to go out)

yo	**salgo**	nosotros(as)	salimos
tú	sales	vosotros(as)	salís
usted	sale	ustedes	salen
él/ella	sale	ellos/ellas	salen

212

For students having difficulty using **poder** and **salir** to talk about what they can do or about going out, you might consider:
• **The tutor page:** Pair the student with a native speaker or a more able student, using the tutor page.
• **Actividades:** see page 204C: *¿Puedes o no puedes?* and *Salgo mucho*

1 ¿Salen esta noche?

Pregúntale a tu compañero(a).

— ¿Salen tus amigos esta noche?
— No, no pueden. Tienen que estudiar.

1. tus amigos
2. tu prima
3. tu hermana y tú
4. tu amigo
5. tus padres
6. ¿y tú?

Tener que...
estudiar
escribir un informe
trabajar
hacer la tarea
cocinar
escribir cartas

2 ¿Salen mucho?

A. Pregúntale a cinco compañeros qué días salen, a qué hora salen y adónde van generalmente. Anota las respuestas en una tabla.

¿Quién?	¿Qué días sale?	¿A qué hora?	¿Adónde?
Marta	miércoles y sábados	por la noche	al cine
José	domingos	por la tarde	a la discoteca

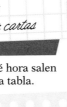

B. Presenta los resultados a la clase.

Marta sale los miércoles y los sábados por la noche. Va al cine.
José sale los domingos por la tarde. Va a la discoteca.

3 Problemas de cada día

¿Qué puedo hacer? Pregúntale a tu compañero(a).

— *Quiero aprender más español. ¿Qué puedo hacer?*
— *Puedes mirar la televisión en español.*

1. Quiero aprender más español.
2. Quiero sacar buenas notas.
3. Quiero jugar bien al tenis.
4. No quiero llegar tarde a la escuela.
5. Quiero hablar con mi prima.
6. Quiero invitar a un compañero a una fiesta.

¿Qué puedes hacer?
mirar la televisión en español
llamar por teléfono
escribir una invitación
practicar más
estudiar más
ir en autobús

213

---

3. ¿Salen tu hermana y tú esta noche? No, no podemos. Tenemos que hacer la tarea.
4. ¿Sale tu amigo esta noche? No, no puede. Tiene que escribir cartas.
5. ¿Salen tus padres esta noche? No, no pueden. Tienen que decorar la sala.
6. ¿Sales tú esta noche? No, no puedo. Tengo que cocinar.
Challenge: Write a skit in which one person keeps asking another to go out and the other makes unusual excuses.

2. Individual Activity
A. Ask five classmates on what days they go out, at what time, and where they usually go. Make a chart like this one.
B. Present your results to the class.
Answers: See models on student page.

3. Pair Activity
These people have problems. Ask a partner what each of them can do.
Possible Answers:
1. See model on student page.
2. ...¿Qué puedo hacer? Puedes estudiar más.
3. ...¿Qué puedo hacer? Puedes practicar más.
4. ...¿Qué puedo hacer? Puede ir en autobús.
5. ...¿Qué puedo hacer? Puedes llamar por teléfono.
6. ...¿Qué puedo hacer? Puedes escribir una invitación.

CHECK

- ¿Sales este fin de semana?
- ¿Por qué no podemos hacer una fiesta?
- ¿A qué hora sales de la escuela?
- ¿Pueden salir con sus amigos los lunes por la noche?
- ¿Con quién sale tu hermano?

LOG BOOK
Have students write sentences using the forms of **poder** and **salir** that do not follow the general rules for -**er** and -**ir** verbs.

ACTIVITIES

Students use **salir** and **poder** to talk about going out and what they can or cannot do.

1. Pair Activity
Take turns asking each other if these people are going out tonight and saying why they cannot go. Use **poder** and then explain what they have to do.
Possible Answers:
1. See model on student page.
2. ¿Sale tu prima esta noche? No, no puede. Tiene que escribir un informe.

Para hispanohablantes

Tell the class about a time you wanted to go out with friends, but could not because you had to do other things.

213

Communicative Objective
• to talk about daily routines, using reflexive verbs

Related Components

Activity Book p. 105-106	**Audio Tapes** Listening: 5B, Seg. 4
Audio Book Script: Seg.4 Activities: p. 70	**Cuaderno** p. 66
	Tutor Page p. 37

GETTING STARTED

Ask students to think of English verbs that are usually followed by the word *myself*, such as *hurt myself*. They should be able to make a long list. (Some ideas: helped myself, kicked myself, forgot myself, got myself into trouble.)

Language in Context

You may wish to introduce reflexive verbs with the suggestions in the *Thinking About Language* on the opening page of this chapter (p. 204).
Tell students that certain Spanish verbs that are used with the pronouns **me, te, se, nos,** and **os** are known as reflexive verbs. One group of these describes washing, grooming, and dressing. Students may find it easier to think of these as meaning to wash oneself, to comb one's hair, and so on.

DISCUSS

Review vocabulary from previous chapters and introduce some of this chapter's new vocabulary with questions that incorporate reflexive verbs.
Buenos días, Bill. ¿Qué te pones hoy?
Mira, Bill se pone una camiseta negra.
¿Me pongo la falda azul o la falda roja?
¿Con qué te cepillas los dientes, Margarita?
¿Con chocolate?
¿Se ponen pantalones negros los mariachis?
Los chicos van al gimnasio. ¿Qué hacen después? Se duchan. ¿No te gusta el agua fría? No te laves el pelo.

PARA COMUNICARNOS MEJOR
¿CÓMO TE PREPARAS PARA SALIR?

To talk about daily routines, use reflexive verbs.

Reflexive verbs are used with the pronouns *me, te, se, nos,* and *os.* Reflexive pronouns usually come before the verb and correspond to the subjects: *(yo) me, (tú) te, (usted/él/ella) se,* and so on.

Me cepillo los dientes y me peino.	I brush my teeth and comb my hair.
Me pongo una falda y una blusa.	I put on a skirt and a blouse.

☐ Reflexive pronouns may also be attached to an infinitive.

— *Teresa, ¿qué vas a ponerte hoy?*	Teresa, what are you going to wear today?
— *Voy a ponerme el vestido azul.*	I am going to wear my blue dress.

Here are the forms of the verb *ponerse* in the present tense. Note that the *yo* form is irregular: *pongo.*

ponerse (to put on, to wear)

yo	**me** pongo	nosotros(as)	**nos** ponemos
tú	**te** pones	vosotros(as)	**os** ponéis
usted	**se** pone	ustedes	**se** ponen
él/ella	**se** pone	ellos/ellas	**se** ponen

Here are other reflexive verbs.

bañarse *to take a bath*	**peinarse** *to comb one's hair*
cepillarse *to brush (one's hair/teeth)*	**ponerse** *to put on, to wear*
ducharse *to take a shower*	**prepararse** *to get ready*
lavarse *to wash (one's hair/hands)*	**secarse** *to dry off*

214

For students having difficulty using reflexive verbs, you might consider:
• The tutor page: Pair the student with a native speaker or a more able student, using the tutor page.
• Actividades: see page 204D: *¿Cuándo te lavas el pelo?*

1 Antes de salir de casa

¿Qué hacen? Pregúntale a tu compañero(a).

— ¿Qué hacen los chicos antes de salir de casa?
— Los chicos se peinan.

1. los chicos

4. tu amiga y tú

2. la chica

5. el chico

3. los niños

6. ¿y tú?

2 ¿Estás listo(a)?

Tu amigo(a) te llama por teléfono antes de salir.
Crea un diálogo con tu compañero(a).

— Patricia, ¿estás lista?
— No, todavía no. Tengo que lavarme el pelo.
— ¿Qué vas a ponerte hoy?
— Voy a ponerme la camisa azul.

Voy a ponerme...
las botas
la camisa azul
los zapatos rojos
los vaqueros
la blusa verde
el chaleco negro

3 ¿En cuánto tiempo...?

A. En grupo, hablen de cuánto tiempo necesita cada uno para hacer cada cosa.

¿En cuánto tiempo...?	Romina	Félix	yo
te duchas/te bañas	10 minutos	15 minutos	25 minutos
te pones la ropa			
te cepillas los dientes			
te preparas para salir			

B. Informen a la clase.

— ¿En cuánto tiempo se duchan?
— Romina se ducha en diez minutos. Félix se ducha en quince minutos. Yo me ducho en veinticinco minutos.

215

ACTIVITIES

Students use reflexive pronouns and verbs to talk about preparing to go out.

1. Pair Activity
Ask each other what the people in the pictures are doing.
Possible Answers:
1. See model on student page.
2. ¿Qué hace la chica antes de salir de casa? La chica se cepilla el pelo.
3. ¿Qué hacen los niño antes de salir de casa? Los niños se cepillan los dientes.
4. ¿Qué hacen tu amiga y tú antes de salir de casa? Mi amiga y yo nos secamos el pelo.
5. ¿Qué hace el chico antes de salir de casa? El chico se baña.
6. ¿Qué haces tú antes de salir de casa? Yo me pongo la ropa.

2. Pair Activity
A friend calls you before going out. Make up a conversation with your partner about what you are going to wear and where you are going to meet.
Answers: See model on student page.
Extension: Pick a color and look for five classmates who are wearing a piece of clothing that color. Write a sentence about the person and the clothing.

3. Group Activity
A. Talk with group members about how much time each of these activities takes. Make a chart like this one that shows how long each activity takes each person.
B. Compare results with another group.
Answers: See model on student page.
Evaluation: Class activity. Compare the results of all the groups.

CHECK

- ¿A qué hora nos encontramos?
- ¿Te cepillas los dientes cada día?
- ¿Saben con quién me encuentro hoy?
- ¿Qué te pones primero, la camisa o los pantalones?

LOG BOOK
Have students write down all the forms of any relexive verbs they have trouble with.

MEETING INDIVIDUAL NEEDS

Reaching All Students

For Visual Learners
Have students make three sets of flashcards: one with personal pronouns, another with reflexive pronouns, and a third with simple drawings of figures performing reflexive actions.
Student A selects any picture and any pronoun, and places them on the table in any order. Student B must select the other pronoun and correctly complete the sentence. Experiment with variations.

Para hispanohablantes

Make up a short story about a student who does not want to get up and get ready for school on Monday morning.

Objectives

Communicative: to talk about extracurricular activities

Cultural: to explore typical after-school activities of students in Sevilla

Related Components

Assessment Oral Proficiency: p. 28	**Conexiones** Chapter 8
Audio Book Script: Seg. 5 Activities: p. 71	**Magazine** Juntos en España
	Tutor Page p. 38
Audio Tapes Listening: 5B, Seg. 5 Conexiones: 17B, Ch. 8	

GETTING STARTED

Students should now be able to use **poder, salir**, reflexive verbs and pronouns, and all of the chapter vocabulary correctly.
Have volunteers read aloud the ads in the *Periódico Estudiantil.* After each, ask simple comprehension questions. For example: *¿Qué bailes de salón puedes aprender?*

APPLY

1. Pair Activity
Create a dialog in which one person asks if another wants to go out this afternoon. The other person responds that it is not possible because of an after-school class.
Answers: See model on student page.
Synthesis: Write an advertisement for a class that you could teach. Say when and where the class is, how much it costs to go, and give a phone number to contact.

2. Pair Activity
Discuss the activities in the ads.
Answers: See model on student page.
Evaluation: List after-school activities in a column and rate each activity.

3. Pair Activity
You're going to an after-school class with your partner. Call and ask if he or she is ready.
Answers: See model on student page.

SITUACIONES

¡ACTIVIDADES PARA TODOS!

PERIÓDICO ESTUDIANTIL número 2   febrero

 Piano/Guitarra Academia de música Triana. Clases privadas. Todos los niveles. ☎ 443-85-75

 Bailes de salón Clases de tango, salsa, fox-trot y cha-cha-chá. Todos los niveles. Sra. Tosca. ☎ 490-10-98

ACADEMIA MANOLO MARÍN

Aprende flamenco con Manolo Marín. Todos los niveles. También hay clases de danza clásica española y sevillanas

437-25-12

 Gimnasio Hércules. Clases de gimnasia, karate, judo, yoga, natación y tenis. Si tomas clases dos veces por semana puedes usar la piscina y las máquinas de ejercicios. ☎ 444-22-11 Abierto todos los días de 7:00 a 21:00 horas.

 Informática Lotus, WordPerfect. Horario flexible. Llama a Daniel al ☎ 456-22-90.

 Idiomas Francés/inglés. Profesores nativos. Cursos intensivos. Clases privadas y en grupos. ☎ 443-42-22

 Pintura/Dibujo/Cerámica En la Academia de Bellas Artes. Clases de lunes a viernes a las 18:00 y 20:00 horas. Llama al ☎ 425-11-12.

 Tutora ¿Sacaste malas notas? ¿Necesitas ayuda en matemáticas o química? Llama a María del Pilar. ☎ 435-28-29

¿SABES QUE...?

Sevillanas are a folkloric dance from the region of Andalusia. *Sevillanas* are very popular throughout Spain.

216

For students having difficulty talking about after-school activities, you might consider:

• **The tutor page:** Pair the student with a native speaker or a more able student, using the tutor page.
• **Actividades:** see page 204D: *Nuevo y fabuloso*

¿Puedes salir?

Tu compañero(a) te pregunta si puedes salir esta tarde. Tú no puedes porque tomas una clase extraescolar. Crea un diálogo.

— ¿Puedes salir esta tarde?
— Lo siento, pero no puedo. Los lunes, miércoles y viernes voy al gimnasio. Tomo clases de karate. Tal vez otro día.

 ¿Qué quieres aprender?

Habla con tu compañero(a) sobre las actividades de los anuncios.

— ¿Tú sabes bailar el tango?
— No, pero me gustaría aprender.

 ¿Estás listo(a)?

Vas a salir con tu compañero(a). Llama por teléfono y pregúntale si está listo(a).

— ¿Estás lista?
— Todavía no. Tengo que ducharme.
— ¿Qué vas a ponerte?
— Una camisa, unos pantalones y los tenis.

 ¿Qué aconsejas?

¿Qué aconsejas...?

> Puedes ir al Gimnasio Hércules y tomar clases de karate.

• a un(a) amigo(a) que quiere ser deportista
• a un chico que quiere aprender francés
• a una chica que quiere aprender a usar la computadora
• a un estudiante que sacó malas notas en química
• a un amigo que baila muy mal

PARA TU REFERENCIA

la ayuda *help*
los bailes de salón *ballroom dancing*
las clases privadas *tutoring*
las máquinas de ejercicios *exercise machines*
mismo(a) *same*
los niveles *levels*
la pintura *painting*

217

4. Individual Activity
Give advice to these people, all of whom have different interests.
Questions and Possible Answers:
• a friend who likes sports
  (See model on student page.)
• a boy who wants to learn French
  Puedes llamar al 443-42-22. Hay profesores nativos y cursos intensivos.
• a girl who wants to learn how to use a computer
  Puedes llamar a Daniel en el 456-22-90. Él da clases de informática.
• a student who got bad grades in chemistry
  Puedes llamar a María del Pilar. Es tutora de química.
• a friend who dances badly
  Puedes aprender a bailar con la señora Tosca. Su número es el 490-10-98.
Challenge: Write new advice for these people without using any form of **poder**.

 CHECK

• ¿Cuándo sales de la escuela?
• ¿Dónde nos encontramos esta tarde?
• ¿Te gustaría estudiar francés después de la escuela?

LOG BOOK
Have students write down any vocabulary they are having difficulty with.

Para hispanohablantes

Write an ad for a private school or gym that teaches a sport, skill, or activity.

Communicative Objectives
• to talk about places in Andalucía
• to plan where to go and what to wear

Related Components

Transparencies	Video: Tape/Book
Ch. 8: Para resolver	Unit 4: Seg. 3

Search to frame 1065901

GETTING STARTED

Have students locate each destination on a map.

APPLY

In these activities, students work in pairs, in groups, and individually to make plans for visiting places in Andalusia.

PASO 1: ¿Adónde podemos ir?
Your group is going to spend three days in Andalusia. Read the ads and talk about the trips. Decide:
• where you want to go
• what you want to do there
Answers: See model on student page.

PASO 2: Clientes y agentes
With a partner, create a dialog between a travel agent and a client. Include:
• what day(s) you want to go
• how many people are going
• what you can do there
• when the trip begins and ends
Possible Dialog:
T: *¿Cuándo quiere Ud. salir de Sevilla?*
C: *Quiero salir el sábado.*
T: *¿Cuántas personas van?*
C: *Vamos cinco.*
T: *Vale.*
C: *¿Qué podemos hacer en Córdoba?*
T: *Uds. pueden visitar la Mezquita, el Alcázar y el barrio judío, que tiene una sinagoga muy antigua. Después pueden comprar artesanías en el mercado de cerámica.*
C: *¿Cuándo sale la excursión?*
T: *Sale a las seis de la mañana y vuelve a las nueve y media de la noche.*
C: *Gracias.*

PARA RESOLVER
ANDALUCÍA, ¡QUÉ MARAVILLA!

Tú y tus compañeros(as) van a estar tres días en Andalucía. Planeen qué lugares van a visitar.

PASO 1 ¿Adónde podemos ir?

En grupo, lean todos los anuncios. Hablen de las diferentes excursiones. Decidan:

• adónde quieren ir
• qué pueden hacer allí

— *A mí me gustaría ir a Granada porque allí podemos ver...*
— *Yo prefiero ir a Sierra Nevada porque...*

PASO 2 Clientes y agentes

Con un(a) compañero(a), hagan un diálogo entre un(a) cliente(a) y un(a) agente de viajes. Incluyan:

• qué día quieren ir
• cuántas personas van a ir
• qué pueden hacer allí
• a qué hora sale la excursión y a qué hora vuelve

PASO 3 ¿Qué vas a ponerte?

Hagan una lista de la ropa que va a ponerse cada uno para la excursión.

Voy a ponerme vaqueros...

PASO 4 Vamos a ir a...

Presenten sus planes a la clase.

El viernes vamos a ir a Córdoba para visitar la mezquita y la sinagoga. Salimos por la mañana a las seis y volvemos a las...

El Alcázar: palacio árabe, en Sevilla

Bosque de columnas de la Mezquita de Córdoba.

PARA TU REFERENCIA

el agente de viajes *travel agent*
gitano *gypsy*
las obras de arte *works of art*
judío *Jewish*
la mezquita *mosque*
la sinagoga *synagogue*

218

PASO 3: ¿Qué vas a ponerte?
Make a list of the things you are going to wear on your trip.
Answers: See model on student page.
Application: Use the form **voy a.** with reflexive verbs to talk about other things you will do to get ready for your trip. For example:
Voy a ducharme por la mañana.

PASO 4: Vamos a ir a...
Present your plans to the class.
Answers: See model on student page.
Extension: Class Activity. Students make statements about your travel plans that are **cierto** or **falso**. Give the correct information if it is **falso**.

ANDALUCÍA AYER Y HOY

Todas las excursiones salen de SEVILLA

El Patio de los Leones, en la Alhambra.

Los caballos andaluces son famosos en todo el mundo.

Granada y la Alhambra

Vamos a visitar el maravilloso palacio de la Alhambra. Por la noche, flamenco en el barrio gitano del Sacromonte. Salimos a las 5:00. Volvemos al día siguiente a las 11:00 de la mañana.
10.000 ptas. Con desayuno, almuerzo y cena.

Sierra Nevada

Dos días de sol, nieve y paisajes espectaculares. Excelente para esquiar. Salimos el sábado a las 6:00. Volvemos el domingo a las 23:00 horas.
20.000 ptas. Con desayuno, almuerzo y cena.

Sevilla: historia y cultura

La Catedral, la Giralda, el Alcázar, la tumba de Cristóbal Colón, obras de arte donde pueden admirar la historia y la cultura de Andalucía. Salimos a las 8:00. Volvemos a las 18:00 horas.
2.000 ptas. Con almuerzo.

Córdoba

Vamos a visitar la Mezquita, el Alcázar y el barrio judío, que tiene una sinagoga muy antigua. Después, vamos a visitar un mercado de cerámica donde pueden comprar artesanías. Salimos a las 6:00. Volvemos a las 21:30 horas.
5.000 ptas. Con desayuno, almuerzo y cena.

Para más información, llamar al 555-30-00

Sierra Nevada está a pocos minutos de Granada.

219

PORTFOLIO

Add the description of the trip you planned to your portfolio.

Background

Places in *Andalucía*

Several of these cities will also be dealt with in this unit's *Adelante*.

Granada was once a major Arab city. The **Alhambra,** a hilltop stronghold built between 1238 and 1358, was once the palace of Moorish kings. The **Sacromonte,** or Holy Mountain, is a primarily Gypsy neighborhood on a hillside across from the Alhambra. It is known for its caves, which were once used as homes but are now mainly bars and flamenco clubs.

The **Sierra Nevada** range lies southeast of Granada. Spain's third-highest peak is here, and there is skiing in the winter.

Sevilla was once a busy seaport-gateway to the Americas. It is still the country's fourth-largest city and is the capital of *Andalucía*. Its huge Gothic **catedral,** one of the largest in the world, incorporates a Moorish minaret, the **Giralda,** as its belltower. During the Moorish period, **Córdoba** was the largest city in Europe. Its **Mezquita** is a former mosque with a Christian church inside. The **Alcázar** is a fortified palace.

Thinking About Language

Several thousand Spanish words are loanwords from Arabic. Those that begin with **al-,** such as **Alhambra** and **Alcázar,** are usually of Arabic origin.

Para hispanohablantes

Pick one of these Spanish cities and write a paragraph about spending a day there. Do not say what city it is. Read your paragraph to the class and have them guess the city.

Objectives
Communicative: to talk about how to go places
Cultural: to learn about how Spanish students go places

Related Components

Audio Tapes	Conexiones
Conexiones: 17B, Ch. 8	Chapter 8
	Magazine
	Juntos en España

GETTING STARTED

Ask students how they get to school. Do any of them ride a moped or scooter? Why are mopeds more popular in some areas than others?

DISCUSS

Using the Text

After reading aloud each paragraph, ask some comprehension and critical-thinking questions. Suggestions:
¿Por qué no va en autobús Concha Gorospe?
¿Qué quiere decir "Y nunca llego tarde"?
¿Los exámenes para una licencia de manejar una moto son fáciles o difíciles?

Thinking About Language

Ask why **moto**, which ends with an **-o**, is feminine. If no one figures out that it is an abbreviation of **motocicleta**, ask what it means in English. To reinforce the point, ask if **foto** is used with **el** or **la**—and why. (Both motorscooters and motorcycles are called **motos** in Spain, but there are not many of the latter.)

CHECK

Te toca a ti
Answers:
1. *moda.*
2. *tener 4 años.*
3. *ir a la escuela, para salir por la noche, para ir de excursión. en fin, para todo.*
4. *más o menos 2.000 dólares.*

ENTÉRATE

LA MOTO ESTÁ DE MODA

Muchos piensan que una moto es la solución para el tráfico del futuro. En España es el vehículo de moda. Hay miles de motos en todas las ciudades.

"Nunca tomo el autobús", dice Carmen Gorospe, una chica de San Sebastián. "Con mi moto voy por toda la ciudad en pocos minutos. Y nunca llego tarde. Las motos son divertidas, fáciles de manejar° y puedes aparcar° en cualquier lugar".°

En España, los jóvenes usan las motos cada vez más°. Usan motos para ir a la escuela, para salir de noche, para ir de excursión, en fin, para todo. Los exámenes para tener una licencia de manejar son muy fáciles. ¡Y sólo° tienes que tener 14 años!

Claro, tener una moto es un lujo°. Una buena moto española o italiana cuesta más o menos 2.000 dólares. Y la gasolina, el aceite° y las reparaciones°, 50 dólares por mes. No todos los jóvenes tienen moto, pero a todos les gustaría tener una.

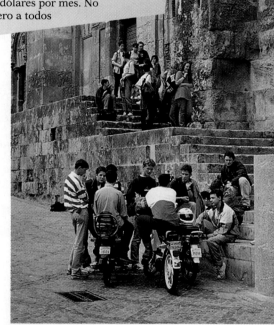

TE TOCA A TI

Completa las oraciones.

1. En España, la moto es el vehículo de...
2. Para manejar una moto en España, tienes que...
3. Los jóvenes usan las motos para...
4. Tener una moto cuesta...

el aceite *(motor) oil*
aparcar *to park*
cada vez más *more and more*
el lujo *luxury*
en cualquier lugar *anywhere*
manejar *to drive*
las reparaciones *repairs*
sólo *only*

220

✔ CULTURE NOTE

Spanish teenagers have to be eighteen before they can get a driver's license. Teens who can afford a **moto** prefer one to a bicycle, particularly in larger cities, like Sevilla, or places with steep hills, like San Sebastián. By and large, bicycles are considered to be for racing.

PORTFOLIO

Have students find at least four new cognates in the text and write a sentence with each, making the sentences work together as a paragraph, if they can. (New cognates include: **aparcar, gasolina, licencia, solución, tráfico, vehículo.**)

VOCABULARIO TEMÁTICO

¿Qué vas a ponerte?
What are you going to wear?

la blusa *blouse*
la camisa *shirt*
el chaleco *vest*
la chaqueta *jacket*
la falda *skirt*
los pantalones *pants*
los tenis *sneakers*
los vaqueros *jeans*
el vestido *dress*
los zapatos *shoes*

Antes de salir
Before going out

bañarse *to take a bath*
cepillarse (los dientes)
to brush (one's teeth)
ducharse *to take a shower*
lavarse (el pelo)
to wash (one's hair)
peinarse *to comb one's hair*
ponerse *to put on, to wear*
prepararse *to get ready*
secarse *to dry oneself*

**Los números
del 1.000 al 10.000**
mil *1,000*

mil cien *1,100*
mil quinientos(as) *1,500*
dos mil *2,000*
diez mil *10,000*

Por teléfono
On the phone

Deja un mensaje después
de la señal. *Leave
a message after the beep.*
Dile/Dígale que me llame, por
favor.
Tell him/her to call me, please.
Llama más tarde. *Call later.*
Llámame. *Call me.*
No está. *He/She is not in.*
¿Puedo hablar con...?
May I speak with . . .?
¿Quiere(s) dejar un mensaje?
*Would you like to leave a
message?*
Un momento, por favor.
One moment, please.
Va a volver pronto.
He/She will come back soon.

Expresiones y palabras
antes de *before*
¿Dónde nos encontramos?
Where shall we meet?

¿En cuánto tiempo...? *How long
does it take . . . ?*
en este momento *right now*
estar de moda *to be in fashion*
estar listo(a) *to be ready*
No te olvides... *Don't forget . . .*
No tengo ganas.
I don't feel like it.
Oye,... *Listen, . . .*
Tal vez otro día.
Perhaps another day.
el baile *dance*
el contestador automático
answering machine
contestar el teléfono
to answer the phone
costar *to cost*
el dinero *money*
encontrarse *to meet*
la entrada *admission ticket*
la exposición de arte *art exhibit*
llamar por teléfono
to call (on the telephone)
las llaves *keys*
poder *to be able*
salir *to go out*
solo(a) *alone*
trabajar *to work*
volver *to come back*

LA CONEXIÓN INGLÉS-ESPAÑOL

You have just learned the verb *ponerse, to put on* or *to wear*. Like
many other Spanish verbs, *ponerse* ends in *-se,* meaning *self.* The
verbs describe actions that a person does for himself or herself.

Look at the *Vocabulario temático.* What other verbs end in *-se?* Do
you think these verbs follow the same pattern?

221

Objectives
• to review vocabulary
• to correctly pronounce words containing "h," the silent "u," and "j"

Related Components

Activity Book	Audio Tapes
Chapter Review: p. 107-108	Listening: 5B, Seg. 6 Assessment: 15A, Ch. 8
Assessment Listening Script: p. 16 Chapter Test: p. 87-92	**Cuaderno** p. 67-68
Audio Book Script: Seg. 6 Activities p. 72	

Pronunciation: "h," the silent "u,"and "j"

There are two silent letters in Spanish:

• the "h," which is never pronounced:
(except after the letter "c")
haz, hacer, hacha, haga;

• the "u" in "gue," "gui," "que," and "qui":
*tianguis, guiso, sigue, pague,
aquí, quien, que, querido*

The silent "u" gives a hard pronunciation to the preceding "g," which would have to be pronounced as the "h" in "hill" if it occured directly before an "e" or "i".

• If the "u" sound is desired when it comes after a "g" and before an "e" or an "i," a dieresis (umlaut) must be placed over it:
vergüenza

• The letter "j" in Spanish is pronounced like the "h" in the English word "hill" but with greater friction.

LOG BOOK
Have students write pronunciation rules for **h, u** and **j** in their own words.

La conexión inglés-español

Other verbs in the list that involve action on oneself include *bañarse, ducharse, peinarse, secarse.* Reflective verbs can also have a second object besides the "self"— such as *dientes* or *cepillarse los dientes* and *pelo* in *lavarse el pelo.*

221

ADELANTE

Objectives

Pre-Reading Strategy: to elicit meaning from photographs and captions

Interdisciplinary: to learn about the region of Spain called Andalusia

Related Components

CD ROM	**Video:**
Unit 4: Adelante	**Tape/Book**
Magazine	Unit 4: Seg. 4
Juntos en España	

Search to frame 1113806

GETTING STARTED

Ask volunteers to read aloud the *Antes de leer* introduction. Ask: How long did the Arabs stay in Spain? How long has it been since 1492?

Using the Video

Show Segment 4 of the Unit 4 video, the introduction to Andalusia.

Antes de leer

Have students identify the themes on these pages (Arab influences on Spanish architecture, music, and dance).
Ask comprehension questions. Examples:
¿Qué puedes ver en el sur de España?
¿Cómo se llama el sur de España hoy día?
¿Qué crearon los árabes en Andalucía?

About Andalusia

The region of **Andalusia** is the largest (about one-fifth of the country) and most populous of Spain. Because the Sahara is so close, **Andalusia** has a subtropical climate. The Arab invasion of 711 was part of a holy war of conversion that had begun after the prophet Muhammad revealed the teachings of Islam a century earlier. Arab armies reached the south of France before being turned back in 732.
The Arabic name **al-Andalus** probably means "country of Vandals," a reference to the Germanic people who settled in southern Spain in the fifth century. *Moor* comes from the Roman name for the people of northeastern Africa, *maurus.*

ANTES DE LEER

Si visitas el sur de España vas a ver la influencia islámica° por todas partes.° Los árabes llegaron a la península Ibérica° en el año 711 y vivieron allí hasta el año 1492. A la región del sur la llamaron Al-Andalus. Por eso, hoy día el sur de España se llama Andalucía.

El tema principal de este artículo es la influencia árabe en Andalucía. Mira las fotos de las páginas 222–225. Haz una lista de cuatro aspectos de la influencia árabe que, en tu opinión, vas a encontrar en este artículo.

islámica *Islamic*   por todas partes *everywhere*
la península Ibérica *Iberian Peninsula*

222

Adelante Components

Activity Book	**Audio Tapes**	**Magazine**	**Video: Tape/Book**
p. 109-112	Adelante: 11A, 11B	Juntos en España	Unit 3: Seg. 4-5
Assessment	**CD ROM**	**Transparencies**	
Portfolio: p. 39-40	Unit 4: Adelante	Unit 4: Adelante	

◄ Los árabes crearon sistemas de irrigación para toda Andalucía. La Alhambra de Granada y sus jardines tienen el mismo° sistema de irrigación desde el año 1238. ¡Y todavía funciona!°

◄ Los azulejos° de los edificios de Andalucía tienen diseños geométricos.

◄ La música de Andalucía se llama flamenco. El flamenco combina elementos de la música árabe, gitana° y judía.°

los azulejos *tiles*
gitana *Gypsy*
el mismo *the same*

judía *Jewish*
¡Y todavía funciona! *And it still works!*

223

Using the Photos

La Alhambra
Begun in 1238, the Alhambra was intended to be both a palace and a fortress. Its name, **Al Qal'a al Hambra,** means "red fort." It is located on the top of a hill in the center of Granada.

Literature Link: Washington Irving lived in the Alhambra for a few months in the 1820s. He worked on two books there, *The Conquest of Granada* (published in 1829) and *The Alhambra* (1832). The latter is a collection of stories about the Arab period. Why do you think an American would write about life in Spain a thousand years earlier?

Azulejos
The Spanish word for ceramic tiles comes from **al zulaich,** an Arabic word that means "little stone." That word originally referred to mosaics. The tiles we now call *azulejos* were first made in the fourteenth century, shortly before the building of the Alhambra. They soon replaced mosaics as the decoration of choice.

Architecture Link: Most modern buildings have some form of ceramics. Where and how do they use them? What are the advantages of using tiles?

Flamenco
Flamenco is a form of music, song, and dance developed by gypsies about the end of the 1700s. It was influenced by a diverse mix of cultures, drawing from such sources as Greek psalms, Persian melodies, Jewish laments, Castilian romances, and Gregorian chants.

Arts Link: Where do the dances that you know come from? What influenced them?

▶▶▶ INTERNET LINK

Informacion turistica sobre Andalucía:
http://www.cica.es/Infor_gral.html
On Flamenco: http://www.teleport.com/
~jdimick/fg/flamarts.html

223

Objectives
Cultural: to learn about the Islamic influence in Andalusia
Reading Strategy: to identify the main idea and details
Content: to acquire new information through Spanish

Related Components

Activity Book p. 109	Audio Tapes Adelante: 11A

GETTING STARTED

Ask students to list ways in which one culture can affect another. Review the list after reading these pages.

Background

Culture Religious fervor gave way after the initial conquest of Spain by the Arabs, and a more secular state gradually emerged. In the mid-800s there was a growth of interest in philosophy and the sciences—notably botany, medicine, and astronomy—as well as in music, poetry, and architecture. In the 900s, sometimes called the "Dark Ages" in the rest of Europe, the Arab city of Cordoba was one of the world's great centers of culture.

The Jews of al-Andalus Although they had been persecuted by the Christians, the Jews were given important positions in the Arab government and were hired as scholar-teachers. So many eastern Jews immigrated to al-Andalus during this time that Cordoba became one of the great centers of Hebrew learning. One of the most important Jewish figures was the physician/philosopher Maimonides (1135–1204).

DISCUSS

Suggestions for discussion:

Maravillas de Andalucía

¿Dónde puedes ver la influencia islámica en Andalucía?
Los musulmanes vivieron en Andalucía.
¿Quiénes vivieron allí también?
¿Qué influencia tuvieron?

DEL MUNDO HISPANO

Maravillas°
DE ANDALUCÍA

Durante más de 700 años (711–1492) vivieron en Al-Andalus judíos, cristianos y musulmanes.° Fue una época de esplendor cultural.

La influencia de árabes y judíos fue muy importante en las ciencias, la literatura y la filosofía. Podemos ver la influencia islámica en la artesanía, la comida, la danza y, especialmente, en la arquitectura, la música y el idioma de España.

La arquitectura

En ciudades como Granada, Córdoba y Sevilla hay edificios que son únicos en el mundo:

La Alhambra

La Alhambra está en una colina° en el centro de Granada. Tiene una fortaleza° y varios palacios con patios, fuentes y jardines maravillosos.

La Alhambra fue el centro del gobierno y la residencia del rey° de Granada.

La Giralda

La Giralda era la torre° de una mezquita.°

Hoy día, la Giralda, es parte de la Catedral de Sevilla.

La Mezquita de Córdoba

La Mezquita de Córdoba se construyó° a lo largo de° 200 años. Fue la primera mezquita de Europa. En esa época Córdoba era uno de los grandes centros culturales del continente europeo.

a lo largo de *along*	los musulmanes *Moslems*
la colina *hill*	el rey *king*
la fortaleza *fortress*	se construyó *was built*
las maravillas *wonders*	la torre *tower*
la mezquita *mosque*	

224

La arquitectura

¿Quiénes tuvieron más influencia en la arquitectura?
¿En qué ciudades hay edificios únicos en el mundo?

La Alhambra

¿En que ciudad está la Alhambra?
¿Dónde?
¿Qué creen que es una colina?
¿Qué hay en la Alhambra?

La Giralda

La Giralda was once the tower of Sevilla's great mosque. The name is owed to a statue at the top that functions as a weathervane (**el giraldillo**, "something that turns").
¿Qué es la Giralda hoy?

La Mezquita de Córdoba

This ancient structure is a labyrinth of 850 double-arched red-and-white columns.
¿En cuántos años se construyo la mezquita?

La Mezquita de Córdoba se empezó en el año 786 y se terminó° 200 años más tarde.

La artesanía

La decoración de la Giralda, la Mezquita de Córdoba y la Alhambra es un extraordinario trabajo de artesanía. Los diseños geométricos y la caligrafía árabe están en todos sus techos° y paredes.

El laúd es un instrumento de cuerdas que viene del *al-'oud* árabe.

La música

¿Sabes de dónde viene la guitarra? La guitarra y el laúd° vienen de un instrumento árabe de cuerdas que se llama *al-'oud*. Hoy día, la guitarra es el instrumento principal del flamenco.

El patio andaluz. Muchas casas de Andalucía tienen un patio con azulejos en las paredes.

El idioma

El árabe tuvo una gran influencia° en los idiomas del sur de Europa. El español tiene más de 4.000 palabras que vienen del árabe.

PALABRAS QUE VIENEN DEL ÁRABE	
alfombra	azul
álgebra	cero
algodón	jazmín
arroz	naranja

el laúd *lute*
se terminó *was finished*
los techos *ceilings*

tuvo una gran influencia
had a great influence

225

La música

¿Cómo se dice laúd en inglés? (lute)
¿Qué tipo de instrumento es la guitarra?
¿Para qué música es muy importante la guitarra hoy día?
¿Y para qué otra música? (country and western, rock, classical, etc.)

El idioma

¿Cuántas palabras en español vienen del árabe?
¿En qué idiomas influyó el árabe especialmente?
(Spanish, Portuguese, Italian, and French)

Language Link: Which of these words of Arabic origin have reached English? Think of likely ones and look them up in a dictionary. (*Algebra, azure, cotton, orange,* and *zero* come from Arabic.)

CHECK

• ¿Qué maravillas hay en Andalucía?
• ¿En qué vemos la influencia árabe?
• ¿Qué lugar de Andalucía te gustaría visitar?

PORTFOLIO

Have students draw one of the *Maravillas de Andalucía* and write a few sentences describing it.

Para hispanohablantes

If buildings on these pages were in the town where you live, would you think of them as **maravillas?** Write what you would say about these places or things.

▶▶▶INTERNET LINKS

Photos of the Alhambra http://rubens. anu.edu.au/slides.xmosaic/bycountry/ Part18.html
Córdoba http://www.uco.es:80/cordoba/ estable/arcos.html

These activities can be done as classwork or as homework.

Objectives
Organizing Skills: using graphs and categorizing terminology
Communication Skills: creating dialogs, writing sentences

Related Components

Activity Book p. 110	Assessment Portfolio: p. 39-40

ACTIVITIES

1. La influencia árabe
Pair Activity Use a graphic organizer to organize the information on the preceding pages about the Islamic influence in Andalusia. Follow the model.
Possible Answers:

Arquitectura	**Palabras**
La Alhambra	*Andalicía*
La Giralda	*laúd*
La Mezquita	*alfombra*
patio	*álgebra*
Música/Danza	*algodón*
flamenco	*arroz*
laúd	*azul*
Artesanía	*cero*
azulejos	*naranja*
caligrafía	*tarea*

Talk with a partner about which of the four influences you think is the most interesting. Explain why.

2. Los datos
Individual Activity Answer the questions.
1. *El nombre de la región que ocuparon los árabes es Andalucía.*
2. *Los musulmanes vivieron en Andalucía durante más de 700 años.*
3. *Los árabes llamaron a la región del sur de España Al-Andalus.*
4. *Hoy día la Giralda es parte de la Catedral de Sevilla.*
5. *La Alhambra fue el centro del gobierno y la residencia del rey de Granada.*

DESPUÉS DE LEER

❶ La influencia árabe
Usa una gráfica para organizar la información sobre la influencia árabe en Andalucía. Sigue el modelo.

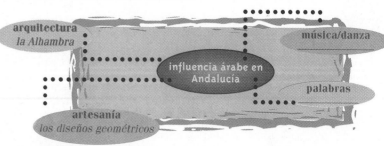

En tu opinión, ¿qué es interesante de la influencia árabe? ¿Por qué? Habla con tu compañero(a).

❷ Los datos
Contesta las preguntas.
1. ¿Cuál es el nombre de la región del sur de España?
2. ¿Quiénes vivieron en Andalucía durante más de 700 años?
3. ¿Cómo llamaron los árabes a la región del sur de España?
4. ¿Qué es hoy día la Giralda?
5. ¿Qué era la Alhambra?

❸ Decorar con palabras

La Alhambra y muchos otros edificios de Andalucía están decorados con caligrafía árabe.

Escribe una palabra o una oración corta en español. Diseña las letras de esa oración o palabra. ¡Usa colores y tu imaginación!

226

3. Decorar con palabras
Individual Activity Write a Spanish word or short sentence, and then design it, using calligraphy, colors, and your imagination. A few words and phrases from this unit that may lend themselves to this activity:
Deja un mensaje después de la señal, España, flamenco, fórmula, geometría, Granada, informática, jardín, literatura española, no tengo ganas

TALLER DE ESCRITORES

1. UNA CIUDAD DE ANDALUCÍA

Escoge una ciudad de Andalucía. Busca información en la biblioteca. Haz un folleto con fotos y dibujos. Incluye:

- dónde está
- datos históricos importantes
- lugares interesantes para visitar
- cosas para hacer allí

2. ¿QUÉ ESTÁ DE MODA ENTRE LOS JÓVENES?

Un(a) estudiante de otro país va a vivir en tu ciudad durante un mes. Escríbele una carta. Incluye información sobre:

- qué puede hacer después de la escuela y durante el fin de semana: actividades favoritas de los jóvenes
- dónde se encuentran los jóvenes: los lugares de moda
- qué se ponen: la ropa de moda
- cómo es tu escuela: las materias y los profesores más populares
- qué excursiones puede hacer desde tu ciudad: los lugares de interés
- qué tipo de ropa necesita para las excursiones

3. ¡HOLA! ¿QUIÉN HABLA?

Mira los dibujos. Describe las escenas y escribe los diálogos. Usa la lista de verbos.

peinarse	cepillarse	encontrarse
llamar	lavarse	secarse

227

Objectives
- to practice writing
- to use vocabulary from this unit

Related Components

Activity Book p. 111	Assessment Portfolio: p. 39-40

ACTIVITIES

1. Una ciudad de Andalucía
Individual Activity Students will look for information about a city in Andalusia and make a brochure with illustrations. They should include:
- where it is
- historical facts
- places of interest
- what they would like to do there

2. ¿Qué está de moda entre los jóvenes?
Individual or Pair Activity Students will write a letter to a foreign student who is coming to live in their city for a month. They should include information about:
- favorite after-school and weekend activities
- popular places to meet
- the latest clothing styles
- the best subjects and teachers at school
- places of interest for excursions
- types of clothing and other things one should bring on trips

3. ¡Hola! ¿Quién habla?
Individual and Pair Activity Students will describe each scene in one or two sentences, then write dialogs for each picture, using the list of verbs.
Edit: Pairs exchange texts and edit each other's work. They should make notes about possible errors, then work together to prepare final drafts.
Present: Students act out their dialogs for the class.

PORTFOLIO
Encourage students to select one of these assignments to add to their portfolios.

227

MANOS A LA OBRA

Objectives

Communicative: to listen to and understand directions
Cultural: to learn about tile-making, a traditional Spanish craft
TPR: to have students make an **azulejo**

Related Components

Assessment	Transparencies
Portfolio: p. 39-40	Unit 4: Project
CD ROM	**Video:**
Unit 4: Manos a la obra	Tape/Book
	Unit 4: Seg. 5

Search to frame 1145629

Materials

- an unpainted tile (or piece of white cardboard)
- PBO (or poster) paints
- carbon paper
- a paintbrush with a fine tip
- a design (or photocopy of it)
- a pencil
- adhesive tape

GETTING STARTED

In this exercise, encourage students to use their eyes more than their ears. They should concentrate on the actions and listen only for clues, not for each and every word.
Have students create their designs beforehand. If they wish to keep the originals, they should make photocopies. If possible, show the **azulejo**-making segment of the Unit 4 video.

DISCUSS

Read aloud the introductory text, then ask such comprehension questions as:
¿Dónde hay azulejos en España y América Latina?
¿Qué colores son "muy vivos"?

MANOS A LA OBRA

AZULEJOS ESPAÑOLES

Muchas casas y edificios en España y América Latina están decorados con azulejos. Hay azulejos en las escaleras, en las paredes y en los patios. Muchos tienen diseños geométricos o caligrafía. Otros tienen figuras humanas, plantas y frutas o animales. Todos tienen colores muy vivos.

TE TOCA A TI

Ahora vas a pintar tu propio azulejo. Busca un diseño. Puede ser una fruta, un pájaro, tu nombre o apellido, el número de tu casa o cualquier otra cosa.° Haz tu diseño y escoge tus colores.

228

✔ CULTURE NOTE

Although the Koran prohibits the representation of humans in the decoration of mosques, the rule did not apply to other locations.

Materiales

un azulejo blanco

pintura PBO de colores
vivos para azulejos

papel carbón

un pincel fino°

una fotocopia de tu diseño

un lápiz y cinta adhesiva

Display each of the materials as you or a volunteer read the text aloud. (If you do not wish to use tiles, use white cardboard and poster paints. Students whos don't mind drawing over their designs need not pfotocopy them.)

Act out each of the verbs.

Contrast a thin and a thick brush. Review the names of colors, and ask students to say which colors they want to use.

Using the directions in the book, lead students through the creation of an **azulejo**.

1. Act out the process as you or a volunteer read aloud the instructions.

2. After you have done the activities a few times, invite volunteers to perform them as you read aloud the directions.

3. Do this as TPR with the whole class.

CHECK

Have students perform the tile-making actions as you describe them, but give the instructions in a different order.

PORTFOLIO

Have students include the design and/or **azulejo** in their Portfolio.

1 Pon el papel carbón encima del azulejo. Después, usa cinta adhesiva para pegar° tu diseño y el papel carbón al azulejo.

2 Con el lápiz, calca° tu diseño de la fotocopia. Ahora puedes verlo sobre el azulejo.

3 Con el pincel fino y la pintura PBO, pinta tu diseño sobre el azulejo. Puedes usar varios colores.

4 Deja secar° el azulejo durante 24 horas. Pon el azulejo en el horno a 350°F por 45 minutos. Déjalo enfriar° y... ¡listo!

calca *trace*
cualquier otra cosa
 anything else
deja secar *let dry*

déjalo enfriar *let it cool*
pegar *to stick*
el pincel fino *thin brush*

Para hispanohablantes

Tell the class about **azulejos** you have seen. Where were they and what were the designs like?

229

Objectives
- to expand reading comprehension
- to relate the study of Spanish to other disciplines

Related Components

Activity Book p. 112	Audio Tapes Adelante: 11B
Assessment Portfolio: p. 39-40	Video: Tape/Book Unit 4: Seg. 4

Search to frame 1113806

El Coto de Doñana

About Doñana
The Doñana National Park and wildlife reserve covers 173,000 acres of coastal dunes, wetlands, and uplands. More than 250,000 people visit the park each year. It was named for the wife (**doña Ana**) of a duke who took part in the Spanish Armada.

Possible Answers:
- *El Coto de Doñana está en el sur de Andalucía, muy cerca de África.*
- *Es importante porque allí viven muchas aves y animales en peligro de extinción.*

Other Questions:
¿Qué animales viven en reservas norteamericanas?
(some examples: bison, bald eagles, wolves)
¿Adónde van las aves del Coto de Doñana cuando emigran?
If there are any nature reserve areas in your vicinity, ask about them. *¿Saben dónde hay reservas ecológicas en los Estados Unidos?*
(some examples: Assateague Island, MD; Everglades, FL; Glacier Bay, AL)

 ECOLOGÍA

El Coto° de Doñana

El Coto de Doñana es la reserva ecológica más grande° de España. Está en el sur de Andalucía. Las aves° del norte de Europa paran° allí cuando emigran hacia África. El Coto de Doñana también es muy famoso en todo el mundo por la diversidad de su fauna y su flora.

- ¿Dónde está el Coto de Doñana?
- ¿Por qué es importante?

 TECNOLOGÍA

Un AVE que es un tren

El AVE es uno de los trenes más rápidos° y modernos del mundo. Va de Madrid a Sevilla (más de 300 millas) ¡en sólo dos horas y media! El AVE puede ir a más de 180 millas por hora. El tren tiene un restaurante y también puedes escuchar música y ver películas. Nota: AVE es una sigla:° significa "alta velocidad española".

- ¿Qué es el AVE?
- ¿En cuánto tiempo va de Madrid a Sevilla?
- ¿Qué quiere decir la sigla AVE?

las aves *birds*	**más rápidos** *fastest*
el coto *reserve*	**paran** *stop*
más grande *largest*	**la sigla** *acronym*

230

Un AVE que es un tren

About the AVE
Although the AVE is capable of reaching 186 mph, its average speed is a little over 100 mph. The 212-seat trains depart about seven times a day. There are three classes; the most expensive costs twice as much as the cheapest. In 1992, the year the line went into service, the lowest off-peak fare was about $75.

Answers:
- *El AVE es uno de los trenes más rápidos y modernos del mundo.*
- *El AVE va de Madrid a Sevilla en dos horas y media.*
- *La sigla AVE quiere decir "alta velocidad española".*

Geography Link: The distance between Madrid and Seville is around 300 miles. What is a comparable distance between two cities in the United States? (Example: Los Angeles and San Francisco are 379 miles apart)

IDIOMAS

¡JAQUE MATE!°

En el ajedrez, si ganas° dices *jaque mate*. La expresión *jaque mate* viene del árabe y significa "muerte al jeque".° Los árabes llevaron este juego a España. Desde allí el ajedrez se extendió° por toda Europa y las Américas.

- ¿Qué quiere decir *jaque mate*?
- ¿Quiénes llevaron el ajedrez a España?

LITERATURA

EL POETA DE LOS GITANOS

El poeta español Federico García Lorca nació° en Granada en 1899 y murió° en 1936. Escribió sobre la vida° en Andalucía y la cultura de los gitanos. Uno de sus libros de poemas más famosos es el *Romancero gitano*.

- ¿Sobre qué escribió García Lorca?
- ¿Dónde nació?

jaque mate *checkmate*
"muerte al jeque" *"death to the sheik"*
murió *died*
nació *was born*

si ganas *if you win*
se extendió *spread*
la vida *life*

231

El poeta de los gitanos

About Federico García Lorca
Federico García Lorca is considered one of the world's great poets and playwrights. He acquired an international reputation with plays such as *House of Bernarda Alba* and *Blood Wedding*. Lorca was murdered soon after the outbreak of the Spanish Civil War in 1936.

Possible Answers:
- *Escribió sobre la vida en Andalucía y la cultura de los gitanos.*
- *Nació en Granada.*

Other Questions:
¿Cuál es su libro más popular?
¿En qué lugar de España está Granada?
¿Cuántos años hace que murió Lorca?

¡Jaque mate!

About Chess
The game of chess has been played since ancient times. It came originally from Hindustan, in the north of India. In the sixth century the game was introduced into Persia, then into Arab lands. The Arabs brought chess to Europe through Spain.

Answers:
- *Quiere decir "muerte al jeque".*
- *Los árabes llevaron el ajedrez a España.*

Activity
Distribute 32 black and 32 white 4"x 4" squares. Have students write facts, words, or other information they learned in this *Adelante*. Place cards on the wall to create a giant chess "review board."

▶▶▶ INTERNET LINKS

El Coto de Doñana http://www.unn.ac. uk/~isu8/spain.html
About the AVE http://latoso.cheme. cornell.edu/SpainArchives/Info/ave.info
Chess Fans in Peru E-mail a message to: listasrcp@rcp.net.pe. Do not put a subject in the heading. Write: *subscribe ajedrez* [your address]. Example:*subscribe ajedrez perez@abc.org.us*
Lorca's Poetry http://www.bart.nl/~dtheb /litverde.html

UNIDAD 5 ESTADOS UNIDOS
NUESTRAS COMUNIDADES LATINAS

 In this unit

We're on the move, making lightning visits to the three US cities with the largest Hispanic communities: New York, Miami, and Los Angeles. After we explore the incredibly diverse and far-reaching Hispanic communication media (Chapter 9), a flying shopping trip gives us an idea of what urban Hispanics are buying and selling today (Chapter 10). In New York we concentrate on newspapers and magazines, but a trip to a radio station leads to a radio station in Los Angeles, and watching Hispanic television back in New York catapults us into the biggest Hispanic TV channel in Miami. In Los Angeles we price jewelry and clothing before settling on a tie for Dad.

Outdoor murals are popular in all three Hispanic communities, and before we say our final *hasta luego,* we make a few special stops in both the colorful unit video and the *Adelante* section of the student book. In Los Angeles we look at some of the most outstanding painted walls in the US before joining master muralists Judy Baca and Frank Romero in their studios. Then, in the unit project, we put our heads and hands together and make a world-class mural of our own.

VIDEO LINKS

Text	Video Segment
Unit Overview Unit Opener	**1. Introduction to Los Angeles, Miami, New York** A rapid-fire collage of Hispanic life in three US communities
Chapter 9	**2. Los medios de comunicación** Hispanic media in the US: newspapers, magazines, radio, TV grammar: preterite of verb **ver;** comparative adjectives, direct object pronouns
Chapter 10	**3. ¿Vamos de compras?** shopping words, looking for gifts, asking for prices, paying for purchases grammar: preterite of verb **ir;** demonstrative adjectives **este** and **ese;** indirect object pronouns; the verb **dar**
Adelante	**4. Adelante** Murals in Hispanic communities, and a visit with Los Angeles muralist Frank Romero
Manos a la obra	**5. Manos a la obra** How to make a mural

232A

New York City

Large Scale Hispanic migration to New York City began with Puerto Ricans in the 1940s and '50s. According to the 1990 census, 1,780,000 Hispanics live in the city, almost 25 percent of the total population. Half the Hispanics are Puerto Rican, while Dominicans, the fastest growing group of Spanish-speaking immigrants, make up 22 percent. Each group has gravitated toward specific communities—the Dominicans, for example, to Washington Heights, a neighborhood at the northern tip of Manhattan. The city celebrates its Hispanic heritage by designating official days in honor of the different communities. There is also a museum, El Museo del Barrio, dedicated to the extraordinary diversity of Hispanic art and culture in New York.

Miami

Parts of southern Florida were settled by Spaniards in the 16th century, but Latin Americans did not begin flocking to Miami until World War II. It was a natural point of arrival, close to the southern hemisphere and blessed with a climate familiar to most of the immigrants. Starting in the early 1960s, Cubans arrived and settled in great numbers, most of them fleeing Castro's Communist revolution. As of 1990, 62.5 percent of the city's population was Hispanic. Cubans are still the largest group, followed by Nicaraguans. Other Spanish-speaking residents come from Colombia, Panama, Puerto Rico, and Venezuela. Hispanic ways of life can be experienced firsthand in enclaves such as downtown Miami's Little Havana.

Los Angeles

Mexico dominates Hispanic Los Angeles. Even the name dates from when the city was the capital of Alta California, a Mexican province ceded to the US in 1848. With a Hispanic population of 800,000 (39.9 percent of the total), Los Angeles has the largest Spanish-speaking population in the western hemisphere. The Hispanic presence is evident all year long. You see it in historic buildings such as El Pueblo de Los Angeles and in more recent manifestations such as the Estrada Courts murals in East Los Angeles. You hear it on Spanish-language radio stations such as KALI and KLAX. And you're surrounded by it during Fiesta Broadway, the largest and most spectacular Cinco de Mayo celebration in the US. *¡Arriba Los Angeles!*

And More

New York, Miami, and Los Angeles are the three U.S. cities with the largest Hispanic communities. But there are many other cities with important Hispanic communities, such as San Antonio, Jacksonville, Washington DC, Chicago, Dallas, Las Vegas, Phoenix, San Deigeo, and Seattle.

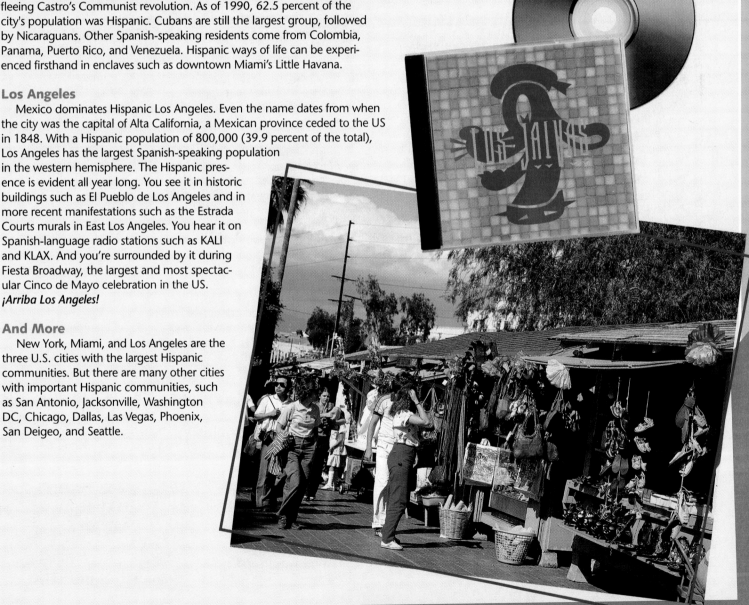

UNIDAD 5 ACTIVIDADES

Mi doble vida

Objective
- to have students identify with the Hispanic experience in the United States

Use
after beginning Unit 5

Materials
- world map
- TRB, Activity Support Page 17, *Mi doble vida—entrevista*

Preparation
- Read aloud the unit introduction to New York, Los Angeles, Miami and other places in the US with large Hispanic populations..

Activity
- On the world map, have students locate Hispanic countries near New York, Los Angeles, and Miami. Talk about where they think most Hispanics in these three cities come from and why.
- Have each student pick one of the cities and team up with someone who chose a different one.
- Hand out copies of the interview sheet. Partners interview each other, role-playing recent Hispanic arrivals to the United States. They base their answers on the excerpts and what they already know.
- The interview answers might begin:—*Me llamo Juan García Sanchez. Tengo 15 años. Soy de Puerto Rico. Vine a Nueva York con mi madre, mis dos hermanas y mi abuela. Vinimos en avión, y vimos la Estatua de la Libertad muy bien desde el avión,* etc.
- Correct the interviews. Have students present them in class and discuss what they've learned.

Variations
- Videotape interviews so students can watch them.
- Post the written interviews around the room and ask everyone to read them.

Flan fabuloso

HANDS ON: COOKING

Objective
- to prepare *flan*, a traditional Hispanic custard pudding

Use
after beginning Unit 5

Ingredients
- 1/2 cup sugar (for caramel sauce)
- 4-5 tbs. water (for caramel sauce)
- 4-5 eggs
- 1 14-oz. can sweetened condensed milk
- 1 14-oz. can whole milk

Supplies
- saucepan
- 8"round mold or 6 individual molds
- blender
- knife and plate

Preparation
Caramel Sauce
- Dissolve sugar with water in a small saucepan.
- Heat mixture on a medium flame until it starts to bubble and turns golden (about 10 minutes).
- Remove sauce from stove immediately and pour into round mold or individual molds. *¡Cuidado!* The caramel sauce is extremely hot.
- Tilt the mold to coat sides and let the caramel cool.

Flan
- Beat eggs in a blender.
- Add sweetened condensed milk.
- Fill empty milk can with whole milk, add to eggs and condensed milk. Blend ingredients well.
- Pour mixture into caramel-coated mold and bake 45-60 minutes at 375°F or microwave 20 minutes on high power.
- Chill *flan,* then run a knife around the edge to loosen from mold.
- Cover mold with a plate and, holding mold and plate carefully, turn over to drop *flan* from mold. Serves 6.

FYI
Enjoyed in all Hispanic communities, this traditional dessert came to the Americas from Spain, where *flan* is still a favorite way to end a meal.

Poesía americana

WRITING CONNECTION

Objectives
- to translate a poem in Spanish into English
- to write a poem in Spanish

Use
after beginning Unit 5

Materials
- TRB Acitivity Support Page 18, *Poesía americana*
Spanish = English/ English = Spanish dictionaries

Activity
- distribute activity suppport page and read "Diez cosas a hacer en el centro" aloud.
- give students ten minutes to translate the poem into English, and then have them discuss the poem. You might begin the discussion by asking how a simple list can tell a story.
- Have students write a list poem of their own, either directly in Spanish or in English first, using dictionaries to translate from English to Spanish as they used them to translate "Diez cosas a hacer en el centro" into English.
- Have students read aloud their translations from the Spanish, their original Spanish poems, and their translations from the English. Ask them to discuss the similarities and differences of the various poems.

Ten Things To Do Downtown
Return books to library
Call Ramona, she's not home
Check out sneaker prices at Superplus
Watch a man feed pigeons
Fell the breeze from their wings when a car backfires
Call Ramona, she's still not there
Buy a container of orange juice and drink the whole thing
Find out when the movie starts
Call Ramona
Run ten blocks to Ramona's house.

Rock chicano

MUSIC CONNECTION

Objective
- to explore Mexican-American contributions to rock and roll music

Use
after beginning Unit 5

Materials
- TRB Activity Support Page 19, *Rock chicano*
- English = Spanish/ Spanish = English dictionaries

Preparation
- Hand out song sheet and have students discuss the lyrics, translating when necessary.
- Share the FYI below, as well as anything else you know about Mexican-American rock and roll. Play tapes if you have them.

Activity
- Divide class into groups of 4 and have each group write a rock song either directly in Spanish, like *"La Bamba"* and *"Oye cómo va,* or in English just before translating it into Spanish. Ask them to follow the models by using rhyme, repetition, and refrains.
- When songs are finished, someone from each group reads their song out loud. Students vote for the two songs they like best.
- Ask the groups to perform their hits—with instruments, if they're available and the songwriters can play them. Everyone else, dance!

OYE COMO VA
Words and Music by
TITO PUENTE

FYI
You can hear a Mexican influence in songs by Bob Dylan, Jimi Hendrix, and other non-Hispanic musicians, but the best Chicano rock and roll is by Mexican Americans: Richie Valens (*"La Bamba,"* "Donna"), Question Mark and the Mysterians ("96 Tears," "I Need Somebody"), Cannibal and the Headhunters ("Land of a Thousand Dances"), Santana ("Black Magic Woman," *"Oye cómo va"*), and Los Lobos (*"La Bamba"* again).

ESTADOS UNIDOS: NUESTRAS COMUNIDADES LATINA

Communicative Objectives

- to talk about the Hispanic influence in three cities in the United States
- to talk about communication and the media
- to talk about shopping

Related Components

Transparencies	Video: Tape/Book
Unit 5	Unit 5: Seg. 1

Search to frame 1170525

GETTING STARTED

Ask students what they associate with each of these cities. Forms of the media—movies, television, newspapers, and records—should be among the things they mention.

Using the Video
Show Segment 1 of the Unit 5 video, an introduction to the three cities.

Using the Transparencies
To help orient students, use the Locator Map Transparency. You may want to use other Unit 5 transparencies at this time.

DISCUSS

Presenting the Cities
For more information about these cities, refer to pages 232A—232D.

Using the Text
English: After students have read the introduction, ask comprehension and critical-thinking questions. For example: Why have cities like Los Angeles, Miami, and New York become centers of Hispanic population?
Spanish: Ask Spanish speakers to share with the class any words or phrases they associate with media, entertainment, and shopping.

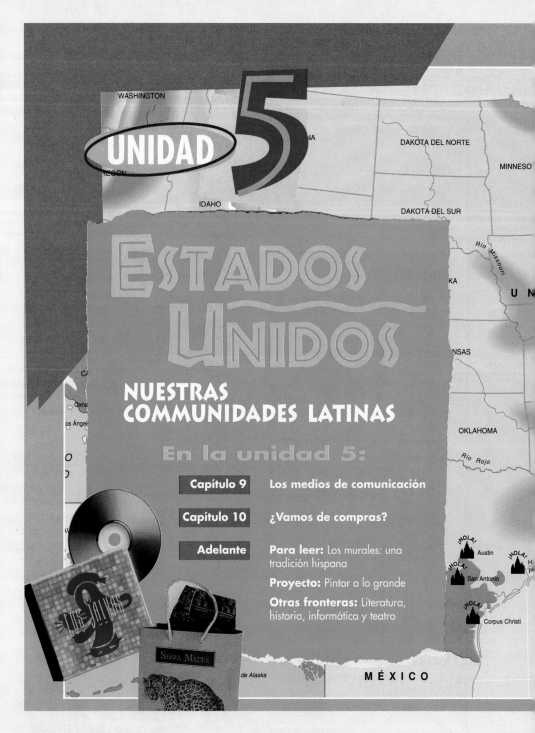

UNIDAD 5

ESTADOS UNIDOS

NUESTRAS COMMUNIDADES LATINAS

En la unidad 5:

Capítulo 9 — Los medios de comunicación

Capítulo 10 — ¿Vamos de compras?

Adelante — **Para leer:** Los murales: una tradición hispana

Proyecto: Pintar a lo grande

Otras fronteras: Literatura, historia, informática y teatro

Unit Components

Activity Book	Audio Book	CD ROM	Transparencies
p. 113-132	Script: p. 73-76; 81-84	Unit 5 Conexiones Chapters 9-10	Unit 5: Chapters 9-10
Assessment Oral Proficiency: p. 29-30 Listening Script: p. 17-18 Chapter Tests: p. 93-104 Portfolio: p. 41-42	Activities: p. 77-80; 85-88 **Audio Tapes** Chapter: 6A, 6B Adelante: 12A, 12B Assessment: 15A, 15B Conexiones: 18A	**Cuaderno** p. 69-84 **Magazine** Juntos en Los Estados Unidos	**Tutor Pages** p. 39-46 **Video: Tape/Book** Unit 5: Segments 1-5

Un festival en la Pequeña Habana, en Miami.

De compras en la calle Olvera, en Los Angeles.

Una celebración en Nueva York.

S panish is spoken in many parts of the U.S. Change the stations on your radio or TV and you're bound to hear Spanish spoken or sung. Look at the stores around you. You may find newspapers or magazines written in Spanish. There are probably Spanish products on your supermarket shelves.

This unit will take you to some Spanish-speaking communities in the United States. You will visit a street fair in a Spanish-speaking neighborhood and do a little shopping . As you walk through the streets of these neighborhoods, you'll see Spanish on billboards, movie theatres, signs in stores, and even on street signs. Spanish is read, spoken, and heard in many U.S. neighborhoods — Spanish is all around you!

Colorful murals are a form of expression in many Spanish-speaking neighborhoods. You will learn about the artists who created them, discover the origins and meaning of this kind of art, and understand why it is such an important part of the culture of Spanish-speaking peoples. Then you and your class will create a mural of your own that will speak for you!

233

INTERDISCIPLINARY CONNECTIONS

To provide other perspectives, assign research projects like these:

Music

Find several non-Hispanic musicians who combine Latin music with their own compositions. Find others who brought their Latin heritage to mainstream music. If possible, bring recordings to class. (Examples of non-Hispanics: David Byrne, rock with latin rhythms; Dizzy Gillespie, jazz with Cuban influence; Hispanics: Los Lobos; Gloria Estefan; Linda Ronstadt; Jon Secada)

Geography

What are the population and the size of Los Angeles, Miami, and New York? In what year and by whom was each founded? (**Los Angeles:** 3,485,557 people; 465 sq. miles; founded by the Spanish governor of California in 1781.
Miami: 358,648 people; 34 sq. miles; a U. S. settler founded a village in 1842.
New York: 7,322,564 people; 301 sq. miles; trading post established by Henry Hudson in 1609.)

✓ CULTURE NOTE

The city of Los Angeles was named for its river, which a Spanish expedition of 1769 had named in honor of *Nuestra Señora la Reina de los Ángeles de Porciúncula.*

 INTERNET LINK

For access to most web sites: http:// www.yahoo.com/Society_and_Culture/ Cultures/Chicano_Latino_American/

	Objetivos page 235	Conversemos pages 236-237	Realidades pages 238-239	Palabras en acción pages 240-241
Comunicación	• To talk about media: television, radio, newspapers, magazines, movies	Discuss watching TV, reading newspapers and magazines	Read text, answer questions, talk about TV and radio programs	Activities 1-8: Read cartoon, make lists; discuss people, things to do, movies and TV programs; make and label collage; write TV ad
	• To talk about programs you like or dislike	Discuss your media and music preferences	Read text, answer questions, talk about TV and radio programs; make and present table	Activities 2-8: Read cartoon, make lists; discuss people, things to do, movies and TV programs; make and label collage; write TV ad
Vocabulario temático	• To know the expressions for TV programs	Talk about different kinds of TV programs	Read text, answer questions, discuss TV programs	Activities 5, 6: Read cartoon, discuss movies and TV programs
	• To know the expressions for types of music	Talk about different types of music		
	• To know the expressions for newspapers, magazines	Talk about different reading materials	Read text, answer questions, discuss newspaper guide to TV and radio	Activities 3, 7: Read cartoon, discuss people; make and label collage
	• To know the expressions for electronic equipment	Talk about using TV set and radio		Activities 1-7: Read cartoon, make lists; discuss people, things to do, movies and TV programs; make and label collage
Estructura	• To talk about what you saw or watched: the preterite of the verb *ver*	Use preterite of *ver* to talk about TV programs watched last week	Read text, answer questions, talk about TV programs watched last week	Activity 5: Read cartoon, discuss movies and TV programs
	• To talk about comparing things: *más* or *menos...que*	Use *más* or *menos...que,* to compare TV programs	Read text, answer questions, compare TV programs	Activity 8: Write TV ad
	• To talk about people or things: direct object pronouns	Use direct object pronouns to discuss music		Activity 5: Read cartoon, discuss movies and TV programs
Cultura	Spanish-language communications media in the U.S.		Miami's *El Nuevo Herald:* the Spanish-language newspaper with the highest circulation in the US	A day in the life of Los Angeles Hispanic community
Integración		Locations, what people like to do	Describing places and things, what people like to do	Locations, ways to travel around the city

Para comunicarnos mejor (1) pages 242-243	Para comunicarnos mejor (2) pages 244-245	Situaciones pages 246-247	Para resolver pages 248-249	Notes
Activities 1, 3: Discuss TV programs seen last night; discuss favorite examples of different media	**Activities 1, 2:** Talk about sections of the newspaper; Have partners discuss where they saw media-related items	**Activities 1-5:** Read text, answer questions; discuss radio; make and present survey; choose programming, make table; write ad		
Activities 3: Discuss different types of music; talk about favorite examples of different media		**Activities 1, 4, 5:** Read text, answer questions; choose programming, make table; write ad	**Pasos 2-4:** Read mail-order ad, make lists; decide what music to order, discuss choices; report decisions	
Activities 1, 3: Discuss TV programs seen last night				
Activity 2: Discuss different types of music		**Activities 1, 4, 5:** Read text, answer questions; choose programming, make table; write ad	**Pasos 2-4:** Read mail-order ad, make lists; decide what music to order, discuss choices; report decisions	
Activity 3: Discuss favorite examples of different media	**Activities 1, 2:** Have partners talk about sections of the newspaper; discuss where they saw media-related items			
	Activity 2: Have partners discuss where they saw media-related items			
Activity 1: Discuss TV programs seen last night	**Activity 2:** Have partners discuss where they saw media-related items			
Activities 2, 3: Discuss different types of music and favorite examples of different media		**Activity 3:** Make and present survey	**Pasos 3, 4:** Read mail-order ad, decide what music to order, discuss choices; report decisions	
	Activity 3: Have partners talk about who they invited to a party	**Activity 2:** Discuss radio stations and programs		
	Reading Spanish-language newspapers		Hispanic musicians in the US	Entérate page 250 MTV Latino
Activities, time of day, days of week	People (family and friends), activities that you do	Ways to travel, time of day, days of week, what to do, places to go	Places in the city, locations	Stating age, favorite activities, places to go

Veo, oigo, leo

MEDIA CONNECTION

Objective
• to explore student media habits, using Chapter 9 *Vocabulario temático*

Use
after *Palabras en acción,* pages 240-241

Materials
• 3" x 5" index cards, one per student

Activity
• Have students jot down what they watched, heard, and read the day before. They should include title, medium, type of program or genre, and time. For example:

A.M. Report	radio	noticiero	1/2 hora
Jane Eyre	libro	novela	2 horas
Action Police	tele	policíaca	1 1/2 horas
Coolio	C.D.	rap	1/2 hora

estudiante	Veo		Oigo		Leo	
	televisión	cines y videos	radio	cintas y C.D.s	libros	revistas y periódicos
Linda	1 ½			1/2	2	
CLASE						

• After filling out cards, students write up their notes in sentences, using at least 10 words from the *Vocabulario temático.* For example: *Mi familia escuchó* A.M. Report *en la radio. El noticiero nos dió las noticias y el tiempo. Todas la mañanas escucho el pronóstico tiempo. Al volver de la escuela leí por dos horas* Jane Eyre, *una novela romántica de Charlotte Bronte, para mi clase de literatura. Vi* Action Police *por una hora y media,* etc.
• Each student presents his/her statistics and adds them to the chart. (See inset.)
• Together, the class totals the amount of time spent on each medium, and makes a pie chart or graph of their media preferences.

¿Qué viste?

GAME

Objective
• to describe people, places, and things, using the preterite of *ver* and direct object pronouns

Use
after ***Para comunicarnos mejor,*** page 244

Materials
• *Juntos,* Chapters 1–9

Preparation
• Select a scorekeeper.
• Divide the class into teams of 9.
• Each team member studies the pictures in a different chapter of *Juntos.*

Activity
• Have students put away all copies of *Juntos.* Pair teams.
• The first player from team A describes a picture from his/her chapter. For example:—***En el capítulo 9 vi una foto de la presentadora Cristina Salgari.*** The team B player who studied the same chapter replaces the direct object with a direct object pronoun:—***Yo la vi también.*** Student A asks:—***¿Qué más viste?*** Student B:—***Vi un cine duplex.*** Student A:—***Yo lo vi también.*** Student B:—***¿Qué más viste?*** Student A:—***Vi a un chico con patines en línea.*** Student B:—***Yo lo vi también.*** Student A:—***¿Qué más viste?,*** etc.
• Each correct sentence is a point for the team. Descriptions cannot be repeated. Players who make mistakes with verbs or direct object pronouns lose their turn to their opponents.
• Play continues until neither player can think of more pictures or until a time limit is up. Then another pair plays, using their chapter's pictures.
• When all players have played, the team with the most points wins.

MUSIC CONNECTION

Objective
• to talk about musical preferences, using Chapter 9 *Vocabulario temático*

MÚSICA LATINA Y MUCHO MÁS

Use
after *Palabras en acción,* pages 240–241

Materials
• CD or audiocassette player

Preparation
• Ask students to bring in tapes or CDs of their favorite kinds of music.

Activity
• Students list their favorite kinds of music on the board. For example: hip-hop, classical, *salsa*, blues, country and western, jazz, *merengue,* etc.
• A volunteer comes to the front and gives clues to his/her favorite music without actually naming it. This student, A, might say:—*Es música moderna.*
• After each clue, students ask questions to identify the music. Student B might ask:—*¿Es música electrónica?*
• Student asks questions until he/she receives a negative response, whereupon another student continues the questioning. For example, student B might go on:—*¿Es música de los Estados Unidos?*—*No.* Another student, C:—*¿Es música del Caribe?*—*Sí.*
• If, after 10 questions, the kind of music hasn't been identified, the volunteer plays his/her tape. And someone might raise a hand to say:—*¡Es Bob Marley! ¡Es reggae!*
• Whoever guesses the music correctly goes next. If no one guesses correctly, student A identifies the music and the next volunteer comes to the front.

Variation
• Repeat the activity with favorite TV programs or books.

Objective
• to compare different kinds of television programs, using *más/menos* (adjective) *que*

Use
after *Para comunicarnos mejor,* page 242

Materials
• 8 3" x 5" index cards

Preparation
• On each card write the name of one of the 8 kinds of television programs listed in the Chapter 9 *Vocabulario temático.*
• On the chalkboard write the comparative adjectives: *más/menos* (adjective) *que.*
• Have students brainstorm adjectives they can use to describe television programs: *interesante, popular, serio, cómico, educativo, entretenido, fantástico, informativo, realista, violento, largo, corto, emocionante, divertido,* etc.

Activity
• Place the cards face down on a desk and have each student, in turn, select 2 of them. For example: John selects a *los anuncios* card and a *los dibujos animados* card. He must use them with a comparative adjective—either one of the adjectives brainstormed, with *más/menos* (adjective) *que.* For example:—*Los anuncios son más cortos que los dibujos animados.*
• The 2 cards are then returned to the pack and the next student picks 2 cards. Sentences cannot be repeated, and play continues until everyone has had a turn.

Variation
• Students compare 5 programs they saw during the past 2 weeks, using comparative adjectives and the preterite of *ver.* For example, Jane says:—*La semana pasada vi un programa sobre África, y vi otro programa sobre los huracanes. El programa sobre África era mucho más entretenido y me gustó mucho más que el programa sobre los huracanes.*

LOS MEDIOS DE COMUNICACIÓN

Introduce the chapter and its theme by asking students to think of examples of American influence in other countries. (Examples they might know: Hollywood films and actors; TV shows like *Melrose Place;* MTV, and rock groups.) Then ask if they can name any media, groups, or people in (not from) other countries that influence our lives in a similar way.

Related Components

Audio Tapes	Conexiones
Conexiones: 18A, Ch. 9	Chapter 9
	Video: Tape/Book
CD ROM	Unit 5: Seg. 2
Chapter 9	

Search to frame 1182512

GETTING STARTED

Ask students to look at the photograph on the student pages. Ask what they think the caption means in English. Then ask critical thinking questions. Some suggestions: *¿Miras los canales de la television hispana? ¿Te gustaría visitar un estudio de televisión?*

Thinking About Language

You can use this opportunity to deal with a potential problem that English-speakers have with direct-object pronouns.

Direct-Object Pronouns

A common problem that English-speakers have when learning to use direct-object pronouns is the tendency always to equate **lo** with *it.* The best way to avoid this may be to run a few simple drills with common phrases before you explain the grammar. For example:

Invitar: Introduce the concept by talking about a party and suggesting well-known people, e.g., *Donald Trump ¿lo invitamos?* Have the class answer with *sí/no lo/la invitamos.* Emphasize male guests to reinforce the **lo** usage.

Conocer: Ask about celebrities, classmates, and made-up names. Have them answer with *sí/no lo/la conozco:*

Q: *Juan, ¿conoces a Gloria Estefan?*
A: *Sí, la conozco.*
Q: *María, ¿conoces a Pepe Panza?*
A: *No, no lo conozco.*

CAPÍTULO 9

LOS MEDIOS DE COMUNICACIÓN

En los estudios de un canal hispano, en Miami.

234

Ver: Ask *Viste a...ayer?* Have them answer with *sí/no lo/la vi.* Vary it with questions in the present tense.

Chapter Components

Activity Book	Audio Book	CD ROM	Transparencies
p. 113-122	Script: p. 73-76	Chapter 9	Chapter 9
Assessment	Activities: p. 77-80	Conexiones	Tutor Pages
Oral Proficiency:	Audio Tapes	Chapter 9	p. 39-42
p. 29	Listening: 6A	Cuaderno	Video: Tape/Book
Listening Script: p. 17	Assessment: 15A	p. 69-76	Unit 5: Seg. 3
Chapter Test:	Ch. 9	Magazine	
p. 93-98	Conexiones: 18A, Ch. 9	Juntos en Los Estados Unidos	

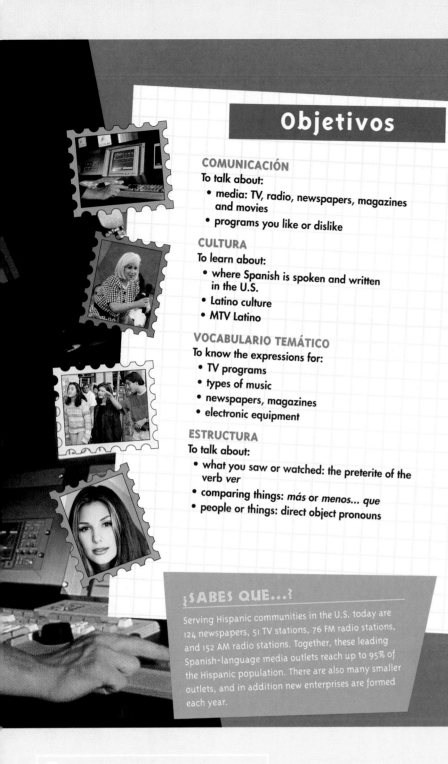

Objetivos

COMUNICACIÓN
To talk about:
- media: TV, radio, newspapers, magazines and movies
- programs you like or dislike

CULTURA
To learn about:
- where Spanish is spoken and written in the U.S.
- Latino culture
- MTV Latino

VOCABULARIO TEMÁTICO
To know the expressions for:
- TV programs
- types of music
- newspapers, magazines
- electronic equipment

ESTRUCTURA
To talk about:
- what you saw or watched: the preterite of the verb *ver*
- comparing things: *más* or *menos... que*
- people or things: direct object pronouns

¿SABES QUE...?
Serving Hispanic communities in the U.S. today are 124 newspapers, 51 TV stations, 76 FM radio stations, and 152 AM radio stations. Together, these leading Spanish-language media outlets reach up to 95% of the Hispanic population. There are also many smaller outlets, and in addition new enterprises are formed each year.

235

ACTIVITIES

Here are some additional activities that you may wish to use as you work through this chapter with your students.

Communication
Encourage after-class activities that may enhance student interest and proficiency. Some ideas:
- watch a news broadcast in Spanish
- browse through the Latin/Spanish section of a music store to learn the names of some of the artists and the titles of their albums

Culture
The written word can only hint at what life is like in other lands. To encourage greater understanding:
- have students report on Americans of Hispanic background working in films, television, music, or news
- show the video that accompanies Unit 5 of this textbook

Vocabulary
To reinforce vocabulary, have students:
- List one channel's programs for an evening and write in Spanish what type of program each is
- use photos and drawings to create a picture dictionary about media

Structure
To reinforce the preterite of **ver** and direct-object pronouns:
- **Game:** Teams ask questions about the types of programs they watch on television. Specific questions should be answered with direct-object pronouns. (*¿Viste el noticiero anoche?/Sí, lo vi.*)

Chicano/LatinoNet http://latino.sscnet. ucla.edu:80/research/research.html

Communicative Objectives

To talk about:
- music and television
- newspapers and magazines

Related Components

Activity Book p. 113	**Cuaderno** p. 69
Audio Book Script: Seg. 1	**Transparencies** Ch.9: Conversemos
Audio Tapes Listening:6A, Seg. 1	

GETTING STARTED

Take a quick poll to see which types of media are the most popular. Ask how students feel their lives would be different without these media.

ACTIVITIES

These activities give students an opportunity to begin communicating with each other and with you, focusing on the theme and objectives of the chapter. The activities can be used as oral class activities, or, if you prefer, you can pair students to achieve more interaction.

¿Qué te gusta ver en la televisión?
Class activity to review the use of **me gusta** and to introduce TV vocabulary. Ask the question in the title, and ask for examples of each type of show. Ask students which programs they like and dislike. Encourage the use of alternative answers.
Have students write five sentences about TV programs they are going to watch.
Example: *Esta noche voy a ver* Melrose Place *en el canal 5.*

¿Qué programa viste anoche?
Class activity to introduce the preterite of **ver** and the use of comparisons. Review the preterite of **-er** verbs in Chapter 7. Present **vi** and **viste** in sentences about TV shows. Expand with variations that include other times and subjects (e.g., *Ayer vi a tres de Uds. en el mall*).

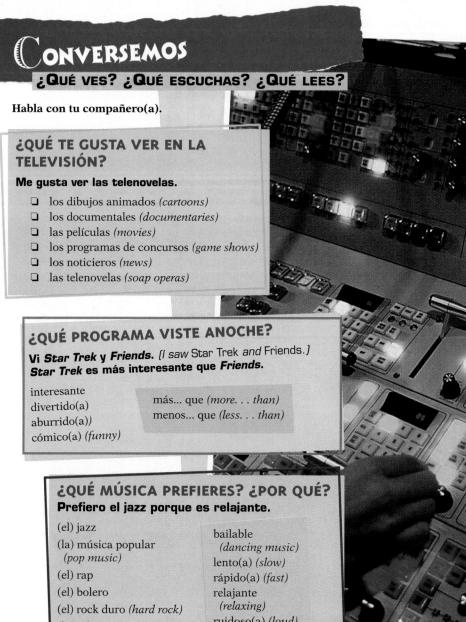

CONVERSEMOS

¿QUÉ VES? ¿QUÉ ESCUCHAS? ¿QUÉ LEES?

Habla con tu compañero(a).

¿QUÉ TE GUSTA VER EN LA TELEVISIÓN?

Me gusta ver las telenovelas.

- ❑ los dibujos animados *(cartoons)*
- ❑ los documentales *(documentaries)*
- ❑ las películas *(movies)*
- ❑ los programas de concursos *(game shows)*
- ❑ los noticieros *(news)*
- ❑ las telenovelas *(soap operas)*

¿QUÉ PROGRAMA VISTE ANOCHE?

Vi *Star Trek* y *Friends*. [*I saw* Star Trek *and* Friends.]
Star Trek es más interesante que *Friends*.

interesante
divertido(a)
aburrido(a))
cómico(a) *(funny)*

más... que *(more. . . than)*
menos... que *(less. . . than)*

¿QUÉ MÚSICA PREFIERES? ¿POR QUÉ?
Prefiero el jazz porque es relajante.

(el) jazz
(la) música popular *(pop music)*
(el) rap
(el) bolero
(el) rock duro *(hard rock)*
(la) salsa
(la) música tex-mex

bailable *(dancing music)*
lento(a) *(slow)*
rápido(a) *(fast)*
relajante *(relaxing)*
ruidoso(a) *(loud)*

236

Demonstrate comparisons with people and objects in the classroom. Examples:
Marta es más alta que Bob.
Este libro es menos interesante que el otro.
Ask the question in the title.

¿Qué música prefieres? ¿Por qué?
Class activity to introduce music vocabulary and adjectives.
Review **escuchar**. Ask the questions in the title. Have students compare these kinds of music. Example: *¿Prefiero el bolero porque es más lento.* Extend this by using unusual adjectives from earlier lessons. Examples: *caliente, dulce, fresca, fría, picante.* Make sure students understand that you are using them in a playful and experimental way.

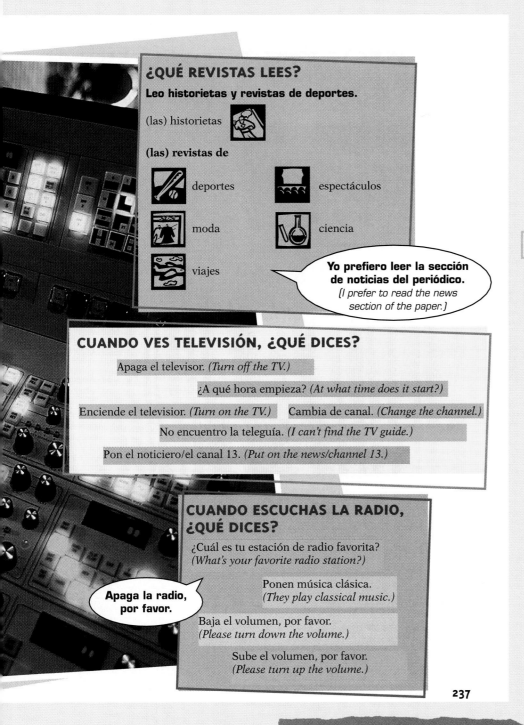

¿QUÉ REVISTAS LEES?

Leo historietas y revistas de deportes.

(las) historietas

(las) revistas de

deportes

espectáculos

moda

ciencia

viajes

> **Yo prefiero leer la sección de noticias del periódico.**
> *(I prefer to read the news section of the paper.)*

CUANDO VES TELEVISIÓN, ¿QUÉ DICES?

Apaga el televisor. *(Turn off the TV.)*

¿A qué hora empieza? *(At what time does it start?)*

Enciende el televisor. *(Turn on the TV.)*   Cambia de canal. *(Change the channel.)*

No encuentro la teleguía. *(I can't find the TV guide.)*

Pon el noticiero/el canal 13. *(Put on the news/channel 13.)*

CUANDO ESCUCHAS LA RADIO, ¿QUÉ DICES?

¿Cuál es tu estación de radio favorita?
(What's your favorite radio station?)

Ponen música clásica.
(They play classical music.)

> **Apaga la radio, por favor.**

Baja el volumen, por favor.
(Please turn down the volume.)

Sube el volumen, por favor.
(Please turn up the volume.)

237

¿Qué revista lees?
Class activity to introduce vocabulary for periodicals. Ask which parts of the paper students prefer.

Cuándo ves televisión, ¿qué dices?
Class activity to introduce useful phrases for talking about TVs and radios. Illustrate **apagar/encender** with the light switch. Ask for cognates for **encender** (*incense* and *incendiary,* both from a Latin root for *fire*).Make questions with the phrases *(¿Cambias mucho de canal? ¿Qué canal te gusta más? Es tarde. ¿Apago el televisor?)*

CHECK

- *¿Qué viste ayer en la televisión?*
- *¿Qué tipo de música te gusta más?*
- *¿Qué tipo de música es más bailable?*
- *¿Qué revistas lees?*

LOG BOOK
Have students make a list of TV programs they watch. Use the vocabulary on these pages to classify and describe them.

REALIDADES

Communicative Objectives
- to talk about TV and radio programs
- to use a radio/TV schedule

Related Components

Activity Book p. 114	Audio Tapes Listening Tape:6A, Seg. 2
Audio Book Script: Seg. 2	Cuaderno p. 70

GETTING STARTED

Ask what this page appears to be. Have any students ever looked at Spanish-language television? What did they watch? What was it like? If no one has watched, ask what students expect they would see.

DISCUSS

Talk about these television personalities. Do any of them look familiar? (Cristina has hosted talk shows in English.) What kind of shows do you think these people do? Ask about these television and radio programs. Suggestions:

El Nuevo Herald
¿Qué sección del periódico es?
¿Saben de qué periódico es?
¿Y de qué ciudad es El Nuevo Herald? (It is in Miami, but there are no clear clues on the page.)

En la televisión
¿Están aquí todos los canales de la televisión? (No, only Spanish channels.)
¿Cuántos canales hay? ¿ Qué son? (Hay siete canales; 23, 33, 41, 47, 51, Olé y Galavisión. The last two are cable channels.)
¿Cómo se llama el programa del canal 41 a las 8:30? (Alondra)
¿Qué tipo de programa es? (telenovela)
¿A qué hora empieza Cristina? *(Empieza a las cuatro de la tarde.)*
¿Cuántas películas hay esta noche? (dos)
¿Qué actor hay en Arriba y abajo? *(Cantinflas)*

En la radio
¿Qué programa hay en Radio Caribe?
¿Cuál programa te gustaría escuchar?
¿Por qué?
¿A quiénes puedes escuchar en los programas de radio?

REALIDADES

PROGRAMACIÓN DE MIAMI

EL NUEVO HERALD

MUY ESPECIAL

◼ EN LA TELEVISIÓN

Canal 23: *Cristina*
4:00 p.m.
Los jóvenes y la televisión, un programa informativo y educativo

Canal 23 : *Sábado Gigante*
7:30 p.m.
Don Francisco, en un entretenido programa de música, concursos y entrevistas con estrellas del cine y los deportes.

Canal 41:
Noticiero Univisión
7:30 p.m.
Patricia Janiot y Jorge Gestoso, con las últimas noticias internacionales.

Canal 51: *Cine Latino*
9:30 p.m.
Arriba y abajo. Comedia con Cantinflas. 2 hrs.

◼ EN LA RADIO

WQBA-FM *(107.5)* **10:00 a.m.**
Por la mañana Lili Estefan en un divertido programa de salsa y música popular.

WSUA-AM *(1260)* **2:00 p.m.**
Radio Caribe Roberto Vengoechea presenta música bailable.

WMEX-AM *(1420)* **6:00 p.m.**
Deportivo Béisbol San Diego – Florida.

PROGRAMAS DE LA NOCHE 7:30-10:30

		7:30	8:30	9:30	10:30
23		*Sábado Gigante*			
33		*Marimar.* Telenovela	*Divertido.* Concursos	*Bienvenido.* Entrevistas	
41		*Noticiero Univisión*	*Alondra.* Telenovela	Fútbol: Perú - Chile	
47		Baloncesto: Miami Heat - San Antonio		*Telenoticias*	
51		*Jorge Porcel.* Entrevistas	*Onda Latina.* Música	Película: *Arriba y abajo*	
OLÉ		*El gato travieso.* Dibujos animados	*Música Moderna*		
GALA VISIÓN		Película: *El viejo*		*La Calle Ocho.* Documental	

Reaching All Students

For Auditory Learners
Tape a Spanish radio program to play for the class. Try to determine what the focus of the program is and write down words that you recognize.

For Kinesthetic Learners
Choose one of these programs and act out what you think happens on the show. Others guess the program's name.

HABLA DE LA PROGRAMACIÓN

A. Di qué programas hay esta noche. ¿En qué canal? ¿A qué hora empiezan?

> *En el canal GALAVISIÓN hay una película. Empieza a las 7:30.*

B. Mira la programación "Muy especial". ¿Qué programas te gustaría ver o escuchar? ¿Por qué? Habla con tu compañero(a).

> — *Me gustaría ver Sábado Gigante. Me gustan los concursos. ¿Y a ti?*
> — *Me gustaría escuchar Radio Caribe. Me gusta la música bailable.*

C. ¿Qué programas de televisión viste la semana pasada? ¿Cuál te gustó más? ¿Por qué?

> *Vi Real World y Los Simpsons. Real World me gustó más. Es un programa más divertido que Los Simpsons.*

¿QUÉ OPINAS?

Haz una lista de cinco tipos de programas de televisión. En grupo, hablen de los programas que ve cada uno(a).

Haz una tabla. Usa el modelo.

PROGRAMAS

	yo	Inés	Jaime	Eva
telenovelas	X			
documentales	X	X		X
películas		X	X	

Presenta los resultados a la clase.

¡SABES QUE...?

Miami's *El Nuevo Herald* has the highest circulation of any Spanish-language newspaper in the United States. This sister publication of the *Miami Herald* offers expanded Latin American news as well as local news of interest to South Florida's large Hispanic population (one million people).

239

Communicative Objective
• To talk about films, TV, music, and newspapers

Related Components

Activity Book p. 115-116	Transparencies Ch. 9: Palabras en acción
Cuaderno p. 71-72	Tutor Page p. 39

GETTING STARTED

Ask students which activities and objects in the drawing they saw earlier in the unit and which are new.

DISCUSS

Comment on and ask questions about what the people in the drawing are doing. For example:
La madre de Ana no puede leer. ¿Por qué?
¿Qué es "El viaje a Isla Verde"?

Para hispanohablantes

Some Spanish speakers in your class may use other expressions than the ones introduced in this chapter. Ask them to share with the class. A few variations:
los anuncios: los comerciales, los avisos, los consejos comerciales, la propaganda
la cinta: el cassette
los dibujos animados: los muñequitos, las caricaturas
enciende: prende
el estéreo: el tocadiscos
las historietas: el tebeo, las tiras cómicas
el noticiero: el informativo
las películas: los films
el rock duro: el rock pesado
la sección de viajes: la sección de turismo
la televisión: el televisor
el tocacintas: el pasacassette
la videocasetera: la grabadora de video

PALABRAS EN ACCIÓN

UN DÍA EN LOS ÁNGELES

Apartamento 2C
las historietas

Superchico es más divertido que Carmen San Pedro.

Sí, Superchico es mejor.

Luis, apaga el televisor. La cena está lista.

el videojuego

Apartamento 1C

la videocasetera

¿Dónde está el control remoto?

el periódico

Periódicos y revistas

la teleguía

Diario de Los Ángeles

el control remoto

Diario de Los Ángeles

Ciencia moderna

1 ¿Qué ves en el dibujo?

Haz una lista de las cosas que ves en cada apartamento. Compara tu lista con las listas de tus compañeros(as).

Apt. 1C: el sofá,
el control remoto ...

2 En español

Haz una lista de todos los lugares donde la gente puede escuchar o leer español. Compara tu lista con las listas de tus compañeros(as).

En el quiosco,...

3 ¿Qué hacen?

Habla con tu compañero(a) sobre lo que hacen las personas del dibujo. Escoge cinco personas.

— *¿Qué hace la chica del apartamento 2F?*
— *Lee una revista de espectáculos y escucha música.*

4 ¿Qué te gustaría hacer?

Haz un diálogo con tu compañero(a) sobre dos lugares del dibujo.

— *¿Quieres ir conmigo al cine?*
— *Sí. ¿Qué película quieres ver?*
— *Me gustaría ver El viaje a Isla Verde.*

For students having difficulty talking about the media or musical styles, you might consider:
• **The tutor page:** Pair the student with a native speaker or a more able student, using the tutor page.
• **Actividades:** see page 234C: *Mi música favorita*

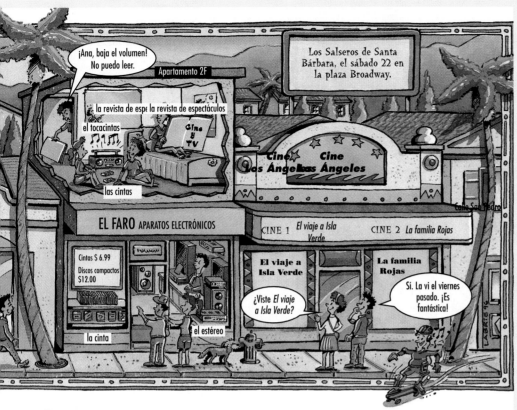

¡Ana, baja el volumen!
No puedo leer.

Apartamento 2F

Los Salseros de Santa
Bárbara, el sábado 22 en
la plaza Broadway.

la revista de espe la revista de espectáculos

el tocacintas

Cine
y
TV

las cintas

Cine☆ Cine
Los Ángeles as Ángeles

Calle San Pedro

EL FARO APARATOS ELECTRÓNICOS

CINE 1 El viaje a Isla
Verde

CINE 2 La familia Rojas

Cintas $ 6.99
Discos compactos
$12.00

El viaje a
Isla Verde

La familia
Rojas

¿Viste El viaje
a Isla Verde?

Sí. La vi el viernes
pasado. ¡Es
fantástica!

la cinta

el estéreo

⑤ ¿Qué viste...?

Habla con tu compañero(a) sobre las
películas y programas de televisión que
vieron esta semana. Haz tres diálogos.

— ¿Viste la película...?
— Claro que la vi. Es fantástica.
— ¿Viste el programa...?
— No, no lo vi.

⑥ ¿Qué te gustaría ver?

Tú y tu amigo(a) ven la televisión. Hagan
un diálogo.

— ¿Qué te gustaría ver?
— Pon el noticiero.
— ¿A qué hora empieza?
— A las 7:00 en el canal 5.

⑦ Collage

Diseña un cartel sobre los medios de
comunicación hispanos. Busca fotos y
dibujos en revistas y periódicos. Escoge
un título para cada dibujo o foto.

⑧ Tú eres el autor

Escribe un anuncio de televisión.

¡Compra Música moderna,
la revista de reggae y rap!
Es divertida. Es informativa.
¡Es fantástica!

241

ACTIVITIES

1. Individual and Group Activity
Make a list of the things you see in each
apartment. Compare lists.
Analysis: Categorize all of the vocabulary
into two columns: one for feminine, one
for masculine.

2. Individual and Group Activity
Make a list of all the places people can listen to or read Spanish. Compare lists.
Extension: Set time aside once a week to
listen to or read something in Spanish.

3. Pair Activity
Choose five people in the drawing and talk
about what each of them is doing.

4. Pair Activity
Choose two places in the drawing and say
what you would like to do there. Make up
a dialog.
Application: Say which of these activities
you would not like to do, and why.

5. Pair Activity
Write three dialogs about the movies or TV
shows you saw this week.
Analysis: List the activities that other pairs
did this week that you did not do.

6. Pair Activity
Write a dialog about what you would like
to watch on TV.
For Auditory Learners: Record dialogs
from the last three activities. Exchange
tapes with other groups and transcribe
them. In groups, compare the transcripts
with the original and correct, if necessary.

7. Hands-On Activity
Homework for individuals or groups. Make
a poster about Hispanic television, music,
and so forth. Use photos and drawings
from magazines and newspapers. Write a
title for each photo or drawing.
For Visual Learners: Display the collages
and describe one to the class. The class
guesses which collage it is.

8. Writing Activity
Write a television commercial in Spanish.
For Kinesthetic Learners: Act out the
commercials for the class.

CHECK

• ¿Qué hacen las personas en el dibujo?
• ¿Qué aparatos electrónicos hay en el
  dibujo?
• Mira el dibujo ¿qué actividad prefieres?

LOG BOOK
Have students write an outline of a TV or
radio Show they would like to create.

Communicative Objectives
- to say what you saw or watched, using the preterite of **ver**
- to compare things, using **más...que**, **menos...que**, and **mejor/peor que**

Related Components

Activity Book p. 117-118	**Audio Tapes** Listening: 6A, Seg. 3
Audio Book Script: Seg. 3 Activities: p. 77	**Cuaderno** p. 73
	Tutor Page p. 40

GETTING STARTED

Ask students to review the preterite tense of **-er** verbs. Compare the preterite and present tenses of **ver**. Ask them to figure out ways in which they can compare one thing to another in Spanish.

Language in Context

Remind students of the expression *mirar la televisión*, "to watch television" (in the *Encuentros*). Point out that **ver** is usually used to mean "to see," but, as in English, it can be used almost interchangeably to refer to looking at television. Review the paradigm.
Review the comparisons and ask a series of choice questions. Examples:
¿Cuál es más divertida, la televisión o la radio? La radio es más divertida que la televisión, ¿no?
Yo creo que una telenovela es menos educativa que un libro. ¿Y tú?
El canal 13 es mejor que el canal 27.

DISCUSS

Review vocabulary with questions and statements that make comparisons and incorporate preterite forms of **ver**:
¿Vieron la televisión esta mañana? ¿Es más interesante o menos interesante que el periódico? ¿Cuál tiene más noticias?
¿Qué programas educativos vio tu familia en el fin de semana?
¿Tomás, no viste al director ayer? El me dijo que te vio en su oficina.
Yo no te vi ayer, ¿tú me viste a mí?

To talk about what you saw or watched, use the preterite of the verb *ver*.

— Anoche vi el noticiero.   Last night I watched the news.
— Nosotros vimos la telenovela.   We watched the soap opera.

Here are the forms of the verb *ver* in the preterite tense.

the preterite of ver (to see, to watch)

yo	vi	nosotros(as)	vimos
tú	viste	vosotros(as)	visteis
usted	vio	ustedes	vieron
él/ella	vio	ellos/ellas	vieron

To make comparisons, use *más* *(more)* or *menos* *(less)* followed by an adjective and *que* *(than).*

Note that the adjective has the same gender and number as the first noun in the comparison.

La salsa es más popular que el reggae.   Salsa is more popular than reggae.

El jazz es menos ruidoso que el rock duro.   Jazz is less noisy than hard rock.

Los dibujos animados son más cómicos que las telenovelas.   Cartoons are funnier than soap operas.

To say "better than" or "worse than," use ***mejor*** *(better)* or ***peor*** *(worse)* followed by que (than).

El rap es mejor/peor que el reggae.

For students having difficulty using **más/menos...que** and **mejor/peor que** to make comparisons, you might consider:
- **The tutor page:** Pair the student with a native speaker or a more able student, using the tutor page.
- **Actividades:** see pages 234C and 234D: *Veo, oigo, leo* and *¿Más o menos qué...?*

1 Anoche en televisión

¿Qué vieron anoche? Pregúntale a tu compañero(a).

—¿Qué vieron ustedes anoche?
—Vimos dibujos animados.

1. ustedes
2. tus compañeros(as)
3. tu amigo(a)
4. tu hermano(a)
5. tus padres
6. ¿y tú?

2 Sobre música

Con tu compañero(a), compara los diferentes tipos de música.

—¿Qué prefieres, la salsa o el rock?
—Prefiero la salsa. Es más relajante que el rock.

1. relajante
2. popular
3. rápido(a)
4. bailable
5. ruidoso(a)
6. lento(a)

Tipos de música
el rap
el reggae
la salsa
la música popular
el rock
el jazz

3 ¿Cuál te gusta más?

Pregúntale a tu compañero(a).

—¿Qué historieta te gusta más, Garfield o Peanuts?
—Me gusta más Garfield. Es más cómica que Peanuts.

• historietas
• telenovelas
• videojuegos
• noticieros
• programas de concursos
• programas de entrevistas

Es...
entretenido(a)
divertido(a)
interesante
popular
emocionante
cómico(a)

243

ACTIVITIES

Students use the preterite of **ver** and comparisons to talk about the media.

1. Pair Activity
What did these people watch last night? Ask your partner.
Possible Answers:
1. See model on student page.
2. ¿Qué vieron tus compañeros anoche?
Ellos vieron los documentales.
3. ¿Qué vio tu amigo anoche?
Mi amigo vio un programa de concursos.
4. ¿Qué vio tu hermano(a) anoche?
Él vio una telenovela.
5. ¿Qué vieron tus padres anoche?
Ellos vieron el noticiero.
6. ¿Qué viste anoche?
Yo vi una película.

2. Pair Activity
Compare different types of music.
Possible Answers:
1. See model on student page.
2. ¿Qué prefieres, el rock o el jazz?
Prefiero el rock. Es más popular que el jazz.
3. ¿Qué prefieres, la salsa o la música popular?
Prefiero la salsa. Es más rápida que la música popular.
4. ¿Qué prefieres, el rap o la salsa?
Prefiero la salsa. El rap es menos bailable que la salsa.
5. ¿Qué prefieres, el rock o la música popular? Prefiero la música popular. Es menos ruidosa que el rock.
6. ¿Qué prefieres, el reggae o el jazz?
Prefiero el reggae. Es menos lento que el jazz.
Analysis: Write six sentences comparing musical groups. Use the adjectives from the list and from previous chapters.

3. Pair Activity
Ask a partner about types of TV shows. Which does he or she prefer? Why? Make comparisons.
Possible Answers:
1. See model on student page.
2. ¿Qué telenovela te gusta más?
Me gusta All My Children. Es más emocionante que General Hospital.
3. ¿Qué videojuego te gusta más?
Me gusta Sega Genesis. Nintendo es menos divertido que Sega Genesis.
4. ¿Qué noticiero te gusta más?
Me gusta el noticiero de Galavisión. Los pronósticos del tiempo son más divertidos que los de Univisión.
5. ¿Qué programa de concursos te gusta más? Me gusta Wheel of Fortune. Es más interesante que Jeopardy.
6. ¿Qué programa de entrevistas te gusta más?
Me gusta Cristina. Es más popular que David Letterman.

CHECK

• ¿Qué programas vio usted anoche en la televisión?
• ¿Viste una telenovela ayer?
• ¿Vieron ustedes una película interesante?
• ¿Cuál te gusta más, el rap o el jazz?

243

Communicative Objective
• to use direct-object pronouns to avoid repeating a noun

Related Components

Activity Book p. 119-120	**Audio Tapes** Listening: 6A, Seg. 4
Audio Book Script: Seg.4 Activities: p. 78	**Cuaderno** p. 74
	Tutor Page p. 41

GETTING STARTED

Ask questions about the realia: where they are from, why they are in Spanish, and so on. Point out the question **¿Lo leíste?** in the subtitle. Ask what it probably means.

Language in Context

You may wish to preface these materials with the suggestions in *Thinking About Language* (page 234).
Write these two sentences on the board: *I read the book.* and *Yo leo el libro.*
Ask if there is another way to express this idea in English. Elicit: *I read it.*
Write *I read it* and *Yo lo leo* on the board. Ask what is different about the sentences. (the position of the pronoun **lo**)
Ask if the personal pronoun **yo** is essential to the Spanish sentence—and why it is not. Then erase **Yo** and capitalize **lo**. Ask if the location of **lo** really makes any difference to the information contained in the sentence. Demonstrate and explain the use of the direct-object pronouns **la, los,** and **las.**

DISCUSS

Review vocabulary with questions that incorporate direct-object pronouns:
Yo no quiero pizza. ¿Quién la quiere?
¿Tienes el libro? ¿Dónde lo tienes?
Necesito la guitarra. ¿Quién la tiene?
¿Tienen los cuadernos?¿Quiénes los tienen?
No necesito este lápiz. ¿Quién lo necesita?
Necesito el reloj. ¿Lo ves?
Me encantó el programa de la televisión sobre las fiestas de México, ¿tú lo viste?

To refer to people and things, use direct object pronouns.

— ¿Leíste el periódico?	Did you read the newspaper?
— Sí, lo leí.	Yes, I read it.

Here are the direct object pronouns for "him," "her," "it," and "them."

direct object pronouns			
lo	him, it	**los**	them (masc.)
la	her, it	**las**	them (fem.)

□ Direct object pronouns have the same gender and number as the nouns they replace. Notice that they are placed before the verb.

— ¿Tienes los discos compactos?	Do you have the CD's?
— Sí, los tengo.	Yes, I have them.
— Vieron a Jay Leno anoche?	Did you watch Jay Leno last night?
— No, no lo vimos.	No, we didn't watch him.
— ¿Leíste las historietas?	Did you read the comics?
— Sí, las leí.	Yes, I read them.
— ¿Invitaste a Raquel?	Did you invite Raquel?
— ¡Claro que la invité!	Of course I invited her!

For students having difficulty using direct-object pronouns, you might consider:
• **The tutor page:** Pair the student with a native speaker or a more able student, using the tutor page.
• **Actividades:** see page 234D: *¿Qué viste?*

1 ¿Qué leíste en el periódico?

¿En qué sección lo leíste? Pregúntale a tu compañero(a).

—*El domingo leí un artículo sobre fútbol.*
—*¿Sí? ¿En qué sección lo leíste?*
—*Lo leí en la sección de deportes.*

1. un artículo sobre fútbol
2. una encuesta sobre los medios de comunicación
3. dos artículos sobre las playas de Miami
4. la programación de televisión
5. un artículo sobre computadoras
6. dos entrevistas con el Presidente

EL PAÍS DEL DOMINGO

ÍNDICE

...y también
La revista
La teleguía
Las historietas
El tiempo

2 ¿Lo viste?

¿Dónde lo viste? Pregúntale a tu compañero(a)

— *No encuentro la teleguía.*
  ¿Tú no la viste?
— *Sí, la vi en la sala.*

1. la teleguía
2. mis cintas
3. mi videojuego
4. la sección de deportes
5. el control remoto
6. los discos compactos de Luis Miguel

En...
la sala
el comedor
tu dormitorio
el sótano
la cocina

3 Invitaciones

Pregúntale a tu compañero(a) a quién invitó a su última fiesta.

— *¿Invitaste a tus vecinos?*
— *Sí, los invité. Son muy divertidos.*
  (No, no los invité.)

1. a tus vecinos
2. a tu mejor amiga
3. a tu profesor(a) de español
4. a tus abuelos
5. a tu novio(a)
6. a tus compañeros(as)

245

ACTIVITIES

Students use direct-object pronouns to talk about reading, seeing, and inviting.

1. Pair Activity
Create a dialog, saying in which section of the paper you saw each article.
Possible Answers:
1. See model on student page.
Note: As the second line does not vary, it has been omitted in these answers.
2. ...una encuesta sobre los medios de comunicación.
Lo leí en la sección de espectáculos.

3. ...dos artículos sobre las playas de Miami.
Los leí en Viajes.
4. ...la programación de televisión.
La leí en las noticas locales.
5. ...un artículo sobre computadores.
Lo leí en la sección de informática.
6. ...dos entrevistas con el Presidente.
Las leí en las noticias internacionales.

2. Pair Activity
Ask your partner where he or she saw each of these objects.
Possible Answers:
1. See model on student page.
2. ...mis cintas. Las viste?
Sí, las vi en el sótano.
3. ...mi video juego. ¿Lo viste?
Sí, lo vi en tu dormitorio.
4. ...la sección de deportes. ¿La viste?
Sí, la vi en la cocina.
5. ...el control remoto? ¿Lo viste?
Sí, lo vi en el comedor.
6. ...los discos compactos de Luis Miguel. ¿Los viste?
Sí, los vi en el garaje.

3. Pair Activity
Ask your partner whom he or she invited to his or her last party.
Possible Answers:
1. See model on student page.
2. ...a tu mejor amiga?
Sí, la invité. ¡Es muy simpática!
3. ...a tu profesor(a) de español?
Sí, lo (la) invité. Es muy inteligente.
4. ...a tus abuelos?
No, no los invité. Son muy viejos.
5. ...a tu novio(a)?
Sí, lo (la) invité. ¡Es muy guapo(a)!
6. ...a tus compañeras?
Sí, las invité. Ellas son muy populares.

CHECK

• ¿Cuáles son tus frutas favoritas? ¿Dónde las compras?
• La tarea es muy importante. ¿La hiciste?
• ¿Leíste la última historieta de Batman?

LOG BOOK
Make four lists of five nouns each that belong under these headings: **lo, la, los,** and **las.**

Para hispanohablantes

Create a simple skit or story in which someone is talking about something and only uses **lo** or **la** to refer to it. Read or perform it for the class to see if they can figure out what is being talked about.

245

Objectives
Communicative: to talk about radio
Cultural: to learn about Hispanic radio

Related Components

Assessment	**Conexiones**
Oral Proficiency:	Chapter 9
p. 29	**Magazine**
Audio Book	Juntos en Los
Script: Seg. 5	Estados Unidos
Activities: p. 79	**Tutor Page**
Audio Tapes	p. 42
Listening: 6A, Seg. 5	
Conexiones: 18A,	
Ch. 9	

GETTING STARTED

At this point, students should be able to correctly use the preterite of **ver**, direct-object pronouns, comparative adjectives, and all of the chapter vocabulary.
Read aloud, and have volunteers read aloud, the texts. Ask critical-thinking and comprehension questions.

APPLY

1. Individual or Class Activity
A. Read the ads and answer the questions.
Possible Answers:
*KLAX pone música ranchera mexicana.
CARACOL pone noticias del día. FM92 pone el sonido joven. Super KQ pone los clásicos de la música Latina. WSUA pone música romántica. WQBA pone música alegre.
Me gustaría escuchar el noticiero sobre Nicaragua y Voces y canciones.
KLAX llegó a ser el número uno de las listas de audiencia en Los Ángeles.*

2. Pair Activity
Talk about your favorite radio station, the programs you listen to, and the times that they are on.
Answers: See model on student page.

3. Group Activity
Take a survey to find the most popular radio station in your group. See the example.
Present your results to the class.
Answers: See model on student page.
For Auditory Learners: Listen to a Spanish-language broadcast for two minutes. Write down any words or phrases you understand. Compare notes.

4. Group Activity
Create programming for your own radio station. Write the programs you will have, their names, what type of music each will play, and what time they will be on.
Answers: See model on student page.
Next, design a chart that shows the programs for a day. Present it to the class.
Evaluation: Rate each other's stations.

5. Homework or Classwork
Write an ad for a Spanish radio station. Use the information on the lefthand page.
Answers: See realia on student page.
Analysis: Compare the ads of two class members. Say which station you think would be more popular and why.

SITUACIONES
LOS RITMOS DE LA RADIO

LOS MEJORES PROGRAMAS DE HOY:

6 a.m. WQBA-FM (107.5) *Mañanas alegres.* Programa de música, noticias, concursos y entrevistas.

9:30 a.m. WSUA-AM (1260) *Voces y canciones.* Música romántica.

1:00 p.m. WSUA-AM (1260) *Mundo del deporte.* Noticiero sobre el mundo del deporte internacional y nacional.

2:00 p.m. WOCN-AM (1450) *La voz.* Noticiero sobre Nicaragua.

TU MUNDO MÚSICA RADIO

Escucha música, entrevistas y noticias del mundo latinoamericano en las estaciones de la Asociación de Radios de Habla Hispanas de Estados Unidos. ¿Quieres información cada minuto? ¿Quieres bailar los ritmos más bailables de nuestra música? ¿Quieres escuchar las mejores transmisiones de fútbol? Estamos contigo todos los días, durante las 24 horas.

PARTICIPAN:

KLAX Música ranchera mexicana a todas horas.

CARACOL Las noticias del día, para gente despierta.

FM92 El sonido más joven de Miami.

Super KQ Los clásicos de la música latina.

UNA ESTACIÓN DE RADIO HISPANA,
NÚMERO UNO EN LOS ÁNGELES

KLAX, una estación de radio hispana, llegó en octubre al número uno de las listas de audiencia de Los Ángeles. La KLAX sólo pone música ranchera mexicana. KLAX es una de las nueve estaciones de radio de Los Ángeles con todas las transmisiones en español. El vicepresidente de la estación, Alfredo Rodríguez, dice que "esta noticia es muy importante para el mercado hispano".

PARA TU REFERENCIA

la audiencia *audience*
durante *during*
la gente despierta *wide awake people*
llegó *reached*
el mundo *world*
las transmisiones *broadcasts*
la voz (pl. voces) *voice*

 Las estaciones de radio hispanas

Lee la programación de radio y contesta las preguntas.

- ¿Qué tipo de música pone cada estación de radio?
- ¿Qué programas de radio te gustaría escuchar?
- ¿Cuál es la noticia importante para el mercado hispano?

246

2 **¿Qué estación escuchas?**

Habla con tu compañero(a) sobre tu estación de radio favorita.
Digan qué programas escuchan y a qué hora.

— *Yo escucho la estación WQBA-FM (107.5).*
— *¿Cuándo la escuchas?*
— *La escucho todos los días.*
— *¿Qué tipo de programas escuchas?*
— *Los noticieros.*
— *¿A qué hora los escuchas?*
— *A las 6:00 de la mañana y a las 10:00 de
la noche.*

 3 **Encuesta**

En grupo, hagan una encuesta para saber cuál es la
estación más popular de su ciudad o pueblo. Anoten los resultados.

Estación	yo	mis compañeros(as)
LSQ -FM		XX
Clásica		XXX
UU3-AM	X	XXXX
LATINA		X

Presenten los resultados a la clase. Comparen una estación con otra.

UU3-AM es más popular que LSQ-FM.

 4 **Tu estación de radio**

En grupo, preparen la programación de una estación de radio.
Piensen qué programas van a tener, los nombres de cada
programa, qué tipo de música van a poner y a qué hora.

*Nuestra estación va a tener un programa de entrevistas.
El nombre del programa va a ser Bienvenidos y va a estar todos
los días a las 12:00 y a las 6:00 de la tarde. También va a tener
un noticiero, Noticias de hoy, a las 10:00 de la mañana y a las
3:00 de la tarde. A las 4:00 de la tarde vamos a tener un
programa de música latina.*

Luego, hagan una tabla con la programación. Preséntenla
a la clase.

5 **Anuncio**

Escribe el anuncio de una estación de radio hispana en tu ciudad. Usa
la información de la página anterior.

247

 CHECK

- *¿Cuándo escuchas la radio?*
- *¿Qué estación escuchas?*
- *¿Te gusta escuchar música clásica o pre-
fieres música popular?*

PORTFOLIO

Have students add art to their radio advertisement or program guide.

Language Note

Like **foto**, **radio** is short for something else.
This is why we say **la radio** to talk about
the medium (**la radiodifusión**) or a trans-
mitter (**la radioemisora**), and call an appliance **el radio** (**el radiorreceptor**).

Para hispanohablantes

Write a short radio ad for your favorite
radio show. Read it to the class.

For students having difficulty talking
about the radio and various types of programming, you might consider:
- **The tutor page:** Pair the student with a
native speaker or a more able student,
using the tutor page.

 **INTERNET LINK**

Links to Latin music pages: http://
www.bart.nl:80/~dtheb/musica.html

Objectives
Communicative: to plan a musical event
Cultural: to learn about Hispanic music

Related Components

Transparencies	Video: Tape/Book
Ch. 9: Para resolver	Unit 5: Seg. 2

GETTING STARTED

Ask students what they consider when they select music for a party. Do they assume that most of their friends like the same records? Why?

APPLY

Form small groups. Each will plan a class function that includes *música latina*.

PASO 1: ¿Qué tipo de fiesta van a organizar?
Decide which type of party you will organize. Use suggestions from the list or develop your own ideas.

PASO 2: ¿Qué tipo de música van a necesitar?
Divide the list of Latin music into two parts: dancing and listening. Decide what type of music you will play and why you chose it.
Possible Answers:
• *Nos gusta Ana Gabriel para escuchar y los Fania All-Stars para bailar.*
• *Vamos a encargar "Selena Live!" por Selena y Los Dinos, "Luna" por Ana Gabriel y "Salsa" por los Fania All-Stars.*
• *Vamos a poner música mexicana y tejana porque es emocionante y bailable.*

Teacher Note: If students are not familiar with the artists and groups listed, have them choose any that seem appealing.

PASO 3: ¿Qué discos van a comprar?
Use the *Música Latina* list to choose:
• your favorite groups and artists
• which discs you will order

PARA RESOLVER

MÚSICA LATINA

En grupos, van a escoger la música para una celebración.

PASO 1 ¿Qué tipo de fiesta van a organizar?
Hablen de la celebración que quieren planear:

• una fiesta de graduación
• un baile de cumpleaños
• una fiesta del Club de Español

PASO 2 ¿Qué tipo de música van a necesitar?
Lean el catálogo de Música Latina y hagan una lista de música bailable y otra de música para escuchar. Decidan qué tipo de música van a poner en la fiesta y por qué la prefieren.

PASO 3 ¿Qué discos van a comprar?
• Escojan los discos de sus grupos y cantantes favoritos.
• Decidan qué discos van a comprar.

PASO 4 Y ahora...
Informen a la clase.

> *Vamos a organizar la fiesta del Club de Español. Vamos a poner música bailable. Vamos a comprar discos de... y de... Son discos de salsa y... La salsa es mejor que... porque...*

PASO 5 Los discos favoritos
¿Cuáles son los discos favoritos de la clase? ¿Qué tipo de música es?

¡SABES QUE...?
The range of international Hispanic performers runs from opera singers to leading-edge pop stars. It moves from rockers like **Los Caifanes** to Latin jazz musicians like Dave Valentin and Paquito D'Rivera; from crooners like Vikki Carr to rappers like Lisa M; from folk singers like the Argentine Mercedes Sosa to Tex-Mex artist Tish Hinojosa.

248

PASO 4: Y ahora...
Tell the class about the event that you have planned.
Answers: See model on student page.
Challenge: Create a graphic organizer for one of the other activities in Paso 1. Use such categories as **música bailable** and some of your own. (Examples: *música aburrida, acuático, cara, lenta, moderna, picante, popular, romántica, triste.*) The music does not have to be Latin.

PASO 5: Los discos favoritos
What are the most popular compact discs? What is the favorite musical style?
• Have a volunteer list compact discs and musical styles on the board as others name them.
• Have another write the numbers for each disc and style as representatives of the groups report on their choices.
• Add up the results.

MÚSICA LATINA Y MUCHO MÁS

10 CDS O CINTAS POR $1.00

MEXICANA Y TEJANA

Ana Gabriel—Luna 472•910
(Sony Latin)

Los Fugitivos—Te conquistaré 486•514
(Rodven)

Bronco—Pura sangre 107•698
(Melody)

Selena y Los Dinos—Selena Live! 461•293
(EMI Latin)

Ana Gabriel—Mi México 432•369
(Sony Discos)

Leonardo Favio—Los mayores éxitos 416•529
(Sony Discos)

Vicente Fernández—Lástima que seas ajena

(Sony Discos) 464•065

Selena—Amor prohibido 477•646
(EMI Latin)

Vicente Fernández—Mientras ustedes... 417•600
(Sony Discos)

Alejandro Fernández—Grandes éxitos a la manera de Alejandro Fernández 486•522
(Sony Discos)

Selena—Mis mejores canciones 481•333
(EMI Latin)

Los Rehenes—Ni el primero, ni el último 117•622
(FonoVisa)

Yndio—16 éxitos de oro 437•632
(EMI Latin)

(Sony Discos) 114•371

Liberación—Para estar contigo 119•040
(FonoVisa)

La Mafia—Ahora y siempre 453•597
(Sony Discos)

Vicente Fernández y Ramón Ayala—Arriba el Norte y arriba el Sur 437•921
(Sony Discos)

Los Yonic's—14 super éxitos 437•640
(EMI Latin)

Vicente Fernández—Recordando a Los Panchos 489•708
(Sony Discos)

Ezequiel Peña—Yo vendo unos ojos verdes 119•057
(FonoVisa)

TROPICAL Y SALSA

Frankie Ruiz—No dudes de mí 116•962
(Rodven)

India—Dicen que soy 106•948
(Sony/SoHo Latin)

Jerry Rivera—Lo nuevo y lo mejor 114•405
(Sony Tropical)

Cachao—Master Sessions, Vol. 1 489•146
(Crescent Moon)

Fania All-Stars—Salsa 484•071
(Fania)

Héctor Lavoe—Hector's Gold 483•941
(Fania)

Frankie Ruiz—Oro salsero 487•686/397•687
(Rodven)

Paquito Guzmán—Oro salsero—20 éxitos 488•650/398•651
(Rodven)

Danny Rivera—Las caras del amor 487•744
(Sony latin)

Oscar D'León—Oro salsero—20 éxitos 488•668/398•669
(Rodven)

Eddie Santiago—Oro salsero 487•694/397•695
(Rodven)

Rubén Blades—Live! 415•026
(Elektra)

Tony Vega—Si me miras a los ojos 487•652
(RMM)

Fania All-Stars—Greatest Hits 484•089
(Fania)

RMM La combinación perfecta Varios artistas 470•888
(RMM)

Orquesta Guayacán—A puro golpe 481•499
(RMM)

Grupo Niche—Un alto en el camino 476•580
(SDI)

POP LATINO

Plácido Domingo—De mi alma latina 103•028
(Angel)

Maná—En vivo 116•723/396•721
(Live)

Gloria Estefan—Hold Me, Thrill Me, Kiss Me 110•486
(Epic)

Gloria Estefan—Éxitos de Gloria Estefan 415•174
(Sony Discos)

Garibaldi—Éxitos de Garibaldi 476•705
(Rodven)

Ricardo Montaner—Éxitos y...algo más 475•491
(Rodven)

The Barrio Boyz—Donde quiera que estés 468•801
(EMI Latin)

ABBA—Oro 466•748
(PolyGram Latino)

Maná—Dónde jugarán los niños 466•532
(WEA Latina)

Leo Dan—Serie de colección. 15 éxitos auténticos 416•545
(Sony Discos)

Los fantasmas del Caribe—Caramelo 465•062
(Rodven)

Luis Miguel—Aries 464•016
(WEA Latina)

Gipsy Kings—Live 499•678
(Elektra/Musician)

Gala—Gregorian Dance 114•298
(PolyGram Latino)

Myriam Hernández—Todo lo mío 444•661
(EMI Latin)

Luis Miguel—Romance 432•518
(WEA Latina)

Ana Gabriel—Silueta 443•366
(Sony Discos)

CHECK

PORTFOLIO

Have students select and research a group or artist from the *Música Latina* list. Have them design a cover sheet that includes a biography of the artist(s) and a description of the music.

(Backgound Other Popular Latin Music Styles)

Bolero: slow, sentimental dance or song

Bossa Nova: melodic, sophisticated listening music created by Antonio Carlos Jobim of Brazil in the 1950s

Chachachá: Cuban dance popular in the 1940s and 50s

Cumbia: dance music from the Atlantic coast of Colombia (and now popular in Mexico)

Llanera: rhythmic, sentimental music from the plains of Colombia, featuring the harp as lead instrument

Mambo: up tempo Latin dance music that originated in Cuba and was developed by New York big bands

Merengue: up tempo dance music from the Dominican Republic

Rumba: Afro-Cuban dance music that highlights vocals and percussion

Salsa: originating from *son*—the African-Spanish fusion music of Oriente Province, Cuba—blended with the Big Band and Puerto Rican music of New York City

Samba: a rhythmic Brazilian dance form developed from African, Brazilian, and European music that gained world popularity in the 1940s

Tango: an Argentinian dance of violent, complex, and sensual movements

Vallenato: country music with a virtuoso accordion lead, from the Atlantic coast of Colombia

(Mexican, Spanish, and Andean music are described in Units 2, 4, and 6.)

Para hispanohablantes

Write a short biography of your favorite singer or group.

▶▶▶INTERNET LINK

Major links to Latin music http://www.bart.nl:80/~dtheb/musica.html

Objectives
Communicative: to talk about music
Cultural: to learn about the influence of Latin music in the United States

Related Components

Audio Tapes Conexiones: 18A, Ch. 9 **Conexiones** Chapter 9	**Magazine** Juntos en Los Estados Unidos

GETTING STARTED

Ask if anyone watches MTV regularly. Have any students watched MTV Latino? What do they think of it?

DISCUSS

Using the Realia
Have volunteers read sections of the MTV Latino page. Ask comprehension and critical-thinking questions. Suggestions:

MTV Latino
¿A qué hispanos les gusta MTV?

Conexión
¿Cómo puedes oír tu voz en MTV?

MTV Clásico
¿Cómo se dice en inglés clásico?
¿Hay libros clásicos? ¿Cuáles?
¿Hay rock clásico? ¿Cuál?
¿Qué videos deben estar en "MTV Clásico"?

MTV Afuera
¿Qué hay esta semana en "MTV Afuera"?
¿En que país está Guadalajara?
¿De dónde son los mariachis?

Semana Rock
¿Cuáles son las noticias en "Semana Rock"?
¿Quién sabe qué son asuntos sociales?

Insomnia
¿Te gustaría ver Insomnia?
¿Por qué?

ENTÉRATE
MTV LATINO

MUSIC TELEVISION®
LATINO

El canal que los jóvenes hispanos prefieren. El 50% de los hispanos en Estados Unidos tiene entre 12 y 34 años. Y ellos escogen MTV Latino.

Conexión
lunes y viernes, de 3:30 a 4:30 p.m.

Llama por teléfono y escoge tu video favorito. Vas a poder oír° tu voz en MTV.

MTV Clásico
lunes y viernes, de 7:00 a 8:00 p.m.

Una retrospectiva de videos clásicos de MTV. Y también, de cortos° clásicos latinos.

MTV Afuera°
lunes y viernes, de 8:00 a 9:00 p.m.

Un viaje por toda América Latina. Esta semana presentamos un viaje a Guadalajara, México, y un vistazo° a la vida de un mariachi.

afuera *abroad*
un vistazo a *a look at*
sin parar *non stop*
los cortos *(movie/video) clips*
los asuntos *issues*
oír *to hear*

250

SEMANA ROCK
lunes y viernes, de 10:00 a 10:30 p.m.

Noticias sobre música, moda, artistas, bandas, conciertos, cine y asuntos° sociales. Esta semana, un informe especial sobre rap.

INSOMNIA
domingo y lunes, de 3:00 a 5:00 a.m.

Dos horas de música sin parar.°

TE TOCA A TI

Lee la programación de *MTV Latino*. Di qué oraciones son ciertas y cuáles son falsas. Corrige las oraciones falsas.

1. Puedes llamar a *Semana Rock* y oír tu voz en *MTV*.
2. *MTV Afuera* presenta viajes a países latinoamericanos.
3. *Insomnia* presenta cinco horas de música sin parar.

CHECK

Te toca a ti
Answers:
1. *Falsa. Tienes que llamar a "Conexión" para oír tu voz en MTV.*
2. *Cierta.*
3. *Falsa. "Insomnia" presenta dos horas de música sin parar.*

PORTFOLIO
Have groups suggest themes and ideas for new MTV Latino shows.

INTERNET LINK
MTV Internacional http://mtv.com:80/ Latino/4.1VjGal.html

VOCABULARIO TEMÁTICO

Por Tele Visión
On television

los anuncios *commercials*
el canal *channel*
los dibujos animados *cartoons*
los documentales
  documentaries
la película *movie*
los programas de concursos
  game shows
el noticiero *news*
las telenovelas *soap operas*

¿Cómo es el programa?
What is the program like?

cómico(a) *funny*
educativo(a) *educational*
entretenido(a) *entertaining*
fantástico(a) *fantastic*
informativo(a) *informative*

Tipos de música
Kinds of music

el bolero *bolero*
el jazz *jazz*
el rap *rap*
el rock duro *hard rock*
la música clásica
  classical music
la música popular *pop music*
la música tex-mex
  tex-mex music

la salsa *salsa*

¿Cómo es la música?
What is the music like?

bailable *dancing music*
lento(a) *slow*
rápido(a) *fast*
relajante *relaxing*
ruidoso(a) *loud*

Los aparatos electrónicos
Electronic appliances

la videocasetera
  video cassette recorder
la cinta *tape cassette*
el estéreo *stereo*
el tocacintas *cassette player*

Para leer
To read

las historietas *comics*
la revista de espectáculos
  entertainment magazine
la revista de moda
  fashion magazine
la sección de noticias
  news section
la teleguía *tv guide*

Expresiones y palabras

¿A qué hora empieza?
  At what time does it start?

Apaga... *Turn off . . .*
Baja el volumen.
  Turn down the volume.
Cambia de canal.
  Change the channel.
Enciende... *Turn on . . .*
más/menos... que
  more/less . . . than
no encuentro... *I can't find . . .*
Pon el canal.../el noticiero.
  put on channel. . . /the news.
poner música...
  to play. . . music
Sube el volumen.
  Turn up the volume.
el cine *movie theater*
el control remoto
  remote control
la estación de radio
  radio station
lo *him, it*
la *her, it*
los/las *them*
los medios de comunicación
  media
mejor (que) *better (than)*
peor (que) *worse (than)*
preferir *to prefer*
ver to see *to watch*

LA CONEXIÓN INGLÉS-ESPAÑOL

In this chapter, you have learned the word ***informativo(a).*** This Spanish term has an English cognate. What is it? Now look at the following words:

positivo(a)   *negativo(a)*
decorativo(a)   *selectivo(a)*
comparativo(a)   *relativo(a)*
activo(a)   *intensivo(a)*

Can you make up a rule that will help you find cognates for all these words?

251

La conexión inglés-español

Possible Rule: If a word ends in **-ivo** or **-iva,** change the final letter to **-e.**

Objectives
- to review vocabulary
- to correctly pronunce words containing two consecutive vowel letters

Related Components

Activity Book Chapter Review: p. 121-122	**Audio Book** Script: Seg. 6 Activities p. 80
Assessment Listening Script: p. 17 Chapter Test: p. 93-98	**Audio Tapes** Listening: 6A, Seg. 6 Assessment: 15A, Ch. 9 **Cuaderno** p. 75-76

Pronunciation: consecutive vowels

A diphthong is the combination of two vowels belonging to the same syllable and is of two types: "rising" (where the oral passage widens), and "falling "(where the oral passage narrows).

- Some examples of "rising diphthongs" are:
"ia" - *cambia, iglesia, genial*
"ie" - *noticiero, empieza, enciende, viento*
"io" - *anuncios, radio, medios, estadio*
"ue" - *suéter, muebles*

- Some examples of "falling diphthongs are:
"ai " (spelled "ay" at end of word) - *bailable, hay*
"ei" (spelled "ey"at end of word) - *seis, rey, reina*
"oi " (spelled "oy" at end of word) - *estoy, soy*
"au" - *auto, autor, jaula*

- The pronunciation of all of these combinations of letters are the automatic result of saying the two vowels as close together as possible so as to form a single sound. Thus the diphthong "ai" in Spanish is pronounced like the English word "eye." If two vowels come together, but it is necessary to treat them as members of separate syllables, a written accent mark is used to indicate this:
maíz, librería

- Spanish also has some tripthongs (the coming together of three vowels) as in *rocíais, averigüéis, buey*

LOG BOOK
Have students write down the English phonetics next to Spanish words they have difficulty pronouncing.

	Objetivos page 253	Conversemos pages 254-255	Realidades pages 256-257	Palabras en acción pages 258-259
Comunicación	• To talk about places to shop and things to buy	Discuss places to shop and things to buy	Read text, answer questions, discuss places to shop and things to buy, conduct group survey and report to class	Activities 1-5, 7, 8: Read cartoon, make lists; describe store; explain what people do; talk about buying; discuss birthday gifts; make collage
	• To talk about store transactions	Discuss different kinds of store transactions		Activity 6: Have partners role-play sales conversation
Vocabulario temático	• To know the expressions for different kinds of stores	Talk about different kinds of stores	Read text, answer questions, discuss different kinds of stores, conduct group survey and report to class	Activities 1, 2, 4, 6: Read cartoon, make list; describe store; talk about buying; role-play sale conversation
	• To know the expressions for products to buy	Talk about different products to buy	Read text, answer questions, discuss different products to buy	Activities 1, 5, 7, 8: Read cartoon, make lists; explain what people do; talk about buying; discuss birthday gifts; make collage
	• To know the expressions for different shopping transactions	Talk about different kinds of shopping transactions		Activity 6: Have partners role-play sales conversation
Estructura	• To talk about where you or someone else went: the preterite of *ir*	Use the preterite of *ir* to discuss stores	Read text, answer questions, talk about where a girl shopped	
	• To talk about specific people or things: demonstrative adjectives	Use demonstrative adjectives to discuss specific things		Activity 6: Have partners role-play sales conversation
	• To talk about giving something to someone: the preterite of *dar* + indirect object pronouns	Use the preterite of *dar* + indirect object pronouns to talk about giving something to someone		
Cultura	Early Spanish settlements in the US		Latin American success stories in the US	Useful terms and tips for going shopping
Integración		Locations, numbers, places to go, what to do	Days of week, time of day, locations, numbers, descriptions of places, what people would like to do	Places to go, descriptions of places, locations, items people have or don't have

¿VAMOS DE COMPRAS?

Para comunicarnos mejor (1) pages 260-261	Para comunicarnos mejor (2) pages 262-263	Situaciones pages 264-265	Para resolver pages 266-267	Notes
Activities 1, 2: Have students talk about where they went, what they bought; discuss shopping	Activity 3: Have partners talk about gifts their grandmother's bought	Activities 1-4: Read text, talk about purchases for block party; discuss newspaper ad; make list, write ad; bring items to class market, bargain with customers	Pasos 1-3: Read catalog, discuss what to buy; write dialog for telephone order	
Activity 3: Have partner's role-play exchanging items		Activity 4: Bring items to class market, bargain with customers	Pasos 3, 4: Read catalog, write dialog for telephone order; write letter to accompany return of purchase and request for exchange	
Activities 1-3: Have students talk about where they went, what they bought; discuss shopping; role-play exchanging items	Activity 3: Have students talk about gifts their grandmother's bought		Pasos 1, 3: Read catalog, discuss what to buy; write dialog for telephone order	
Activities 1-3: Have students talk about where they went, what they bought; discuss shopping; role-play exchanging items	Activities 1-3: Talk about fifteenth birthdays; interview friends about clothing, money, gifts; talk about gifts their grandmothers bought	Activities 1-4: Read text, talk about purchases for block party; discuss newspaper ad; make list, write ad; bring items to class market, bargain with customers	Pasos 1-4: Read catalog, discuss what to buy; write dialog for telephone order; write letter to accompany return of purchase and request for exchange	
Activity 3: Have partners role-play exchanging items		Activity 4: Bring items to class market, bargain with customers	Pasos 3, 4: Read catalog, write dialog for telephone order; write letter to accompany return of purchase and request for exchange	
Use preterite forms of ir. Activities 1, 2: Have studebts talk about where they went, what they bought; discuss shopping		Activity 1: Read text, talk about purchases for block party		
Activity 3: Have partners role-play exchanging items		Activities 1, 4: Read text, talk about purchases for block party; bring items to class market, bargain with customers	Pasos 1, 2: Read catalog, discuss what to buy	
	Use all indirect object pronouns. Activities 1, 2.3: Talk about fifteenth birthdays; interview friends about money	Activity 4: Bring items to class market, bargain with customers		
		Bargain at a block party	Good ideas for gift purchases from a Spanish-language catalog	Entérate page 268 Hispanic populations in the US
Directions, locations, places to go	Describing places, people, favorite activities and places	Locations, what people have to do, days of week, time of day, numbers, addresses	Numbers, locations, describing places	

Equis cero*

GAME

Objective
• to play a tic-tac-toe game, using Chapter 10 *Vocabulario temático*

Use
after *Palabras en acción,* pages 258-259

Preparation
• Draw a large grid, 3 squares by 3 squares, on the board.
• In each of the 9 squares, write one place to make purchases. (See *Vocabulario temático* for list.)

Equis cero

feria	puesto	tiendo de disco
tienda de comestibles	feria ✗	almacón
zapatená	feria	tienda doapardo elecronica

Activity
• Select a scorekeeper to record game winners.
• Choose 2 students to play against each other. One's mark is X; the other's, O. They flip a coin to see who goes first.
• Ask the 2 students:—*¿Dónde quieres ir de compras?* If player X wants to mark the center square (*joyería*), he/she says:—*Quiero ir a la joyería para comprar un anillo para mi madre.* Since *un anillo* can be bought in a *joyería,* the player marks an X in the square.
• Then player O goes, selecting another square and naming an object to purchase there. Objects mentioned in a round cannot be repeated in the next round, but they can be used in subsequent rounds.
• Game continues until a player gets 3 marks in a row.
• The winner picks another student to play with.

Variations
• Use this activity to pair other places/things to do; music/adjectives that describe music; vacation spots/appropriate clothing; scholastic subjects/school rooms or activity areas; sports/where they're played, etc.

* **Equis cero**, literally, XO, or tic-tac-toe

¿Adónde fuiste?

GAME

Objective
• to play a game about vacations and outings, using the preterite of the irregular verb **ir**

Use
after *Para comunicarnos mejor,* page 260

Preparation
• Have students jot down a place they visited on vacation or on an outing, and list 3 things they did there. For example, the student who will be player 1 on team A writes: *Fuimos a California para ver a mis tíos y primos. Fuimos a Disneylandia, hicimos surf en el Océano Pacífico y fuimos a la calle Olvera en Los Angeles para comprar camisetas.*

Activity
• Have students select a scorekeeper and form teams A and B.
• Player 1 from team A comes to the front of the classroom and gives you his/her written notes.
• In row order, teams alternate asking questions to guess the team A player's place and activities. For example, player B1 asks:—*¿Fueron muy lejos?* Player A1:—*Sí, fuimos muy lejos.* Player A2:—*¿Fueron en avión?*—Player A1:—*Sí, fuimos en avión.* Player B2:—*¿Fueron a Europa?* Player A1:—*No, no fuimos a Europa.* Questioning continues until teams have guessed the correct place and activities. Then a player from team B comes to the front.
• Teams receive 1 point for each question that reveals a correct place or activity. The team with the most points wins.

¿Este libro o ese diccionario?

MATH CONNECTION

Objective
- to talk about what to buy, using the singular demonstrative adjectives **este/esta** and **ese/esa** and Chapter 10 *Vocabulario temático*

Use
after *Para comunicarnos mejor,* page 260

Materials
- pictures of things to buy that are listed in the Chapter 10 *Vocabulario temático*
- posterboard
- stick-on notes
- index cards and a paper bag

Preparation
- Have students bring in, glued to posterboard, a picture of something that can be bought in a store and that is listed in the Chapter 10 *Vocabulario temático.* The actual price should be written on a stick-on note, stuck to the back of the picture and folded so it can't be read.
- Each student also writes the price of the item on an index card and places it in the bag.

Activity
- Divide the classroom into front (**este/esta**) and back (**ese/esa**).
- From their seats, students hold up their pictures so players can see them.
- Player A comes to the front and picks a price card from the bag. The player then tries to choose an item or items to match the price on the card, using the demonstrative adjective that indicates whether the item is near (front) or far (back). The item may cost up to $10 less than the card price, but not a penny more. For example, the student has chosen a card with the price $139.95. He/she says:—*Quiero esta pulsera que es $85. Quiero esa billetera de $45.*
- The correct prices are revealed. If player A has not gone over the figure on the card, he/she keeps the item or items pictured. If player A has gone over the price, both price card and picture or pictures stay in the game and player B goes next.
- Play until all the items have been bought.

¿En qué le puedo ayudar?

WRITING CONNECTION

Objective
- to write and perform a skit about shopping, using the verb **dar**, indirect object pronouns **me, te, nos, le, les,** and Chapter 10 *Vocabulario temático*

Use
after *Para comunicarnos mejor,* page 262

Materials
- TRB Activity Support Page 20. *¿En qué le puedo ayudar?*

Activity
- Distribute activity support page.
- Pair students and have them use the activity support page to write 10 lines of dialog for a salesperson and a customer at one of the places mentioned in Chapter 10. Offer suggestions, correct grammar.
- The skit can be funny or serious, use props or not, but it must use the verb **dar** and as many indirect object pronouns as possible. As per the activity support page, the salesperson might start off:—*Buenas tardes, ¿en qué le puedo ayudar?* Customer:—*Buenas. Quiero un regalo de cumpleaños para mi amiga.* Salesperson:—*¿Cuánto dinero quiere Ud. gastar?* Customer—*Pues, hasta $25. ¿Tiene una pulsera bonita o unos aretes?* Salesperson:—*Vamos a ver. ¿Le quiere regalar una de estas pulseras de plata? Le cuesta solo $22.99 y es un regalo muy bonito.*
- Have students rehearse and present their skits.
- Vote on the funniest, most dramatic, most informative, etc. Present the best skits to school groups, parents, and other Spanish classes.

Variations
- Have students tell what they observed in each skit, using **dar** and indirect object pronouns. For example, a student might report: *El dependiente le dio el cambio al cliente.*
- Record skits on video or audio tape. Have students review tapes so they can correct mispronunciations.

¿VAMOS DE COMPRAS?

Introduce the chapter and its theme by asking students to think about where they shop. Do they prefer department stores? Small specialty stores? Giant malls? Has anyone ever shopped for food at a open-air "farmers' market"? Point out that in many Hispanic countries people buy food and other products in open-air markets very much like these.

Related Components

Audio Tapes	Conexiones
Conexiones: 18A, Ch. 10	Chapter 10
	Video: Tape/Book
CD ROM	Unit 5: Seg. 3
Chapter 10	

Search to frame 1234806

GETTING STARTED

Have students look at the photograph. Ask if any of them have been to Los Angeles or know something about the city. Some possible critical thinking questions:
¿Qué hacen estas chicas? ¿Qué miran?

Thinking About Language

You can use this opportunity to talk about irregular verbs with your students.

Irregular Pasts
Students may become discouraged when they are introduced to a past tense as irregular as that of **ir** (as they will be in this chapter). The spelling shifts from **ir** to **voy** to **fui** make this verb seem much too difficult to learn. One way to make this seem less frightening is to remind them that they have learned the same sorts of things in English.
Ask them to imagine that they live in a Spanish-speaking country and are studying English. They have just begun to learn the past tense. They have learned to say *walked, lived, wanted, rented,* and *learned.* Ask what they would expect to be the past tense of these words:
buy, sell, ride, write, draw, go, and *am*

CAPÍTULO 10

¿VAMOS DE COMPRAS?

252

Chapter Components

Assessment	Audio Tapes	Conexiones	Tutor Pages
Oral Proficiency: p. 30	Listening: 6B	Chapter 10	p. 43-46
Listening Script: p. 18	Assessment: 15B Ch. 10	**Cuaderno** p. 77-84	**Video: Tape/Book** Unit 5: Seg. 2
Chapter Test: p. 99-104	Conexiones: 18A, Ch. 10	**Magazine** Juntos en	
Audio Book	**CD ROM**	Los Estados Unidos	
Script: p. 81-84	Chapter 10	**Transparencies**	
Activities: p. 85-88		Chapter 10	

Objetivos

COMUNICACIÓN
To talk about:
- places to shop and things to buy
- store transactions

CULTURA
To learn about:
- Hispanic shopping districts in New York, Miami, San Antonio, and Los Angeles
- areas in the U.S. with Hispanic populations

VOCABULARIO TEMÁTICO
To know the expressions for:
- different kinds of stores
- products to buy
- different shopping transactions

ESTRUCTURA
To talk about:
- where you or someone else went: the preterite of *ir*
- specific people or things: demonstrative adjectives
- giving something to someone: the preterite of *dar* and indirect object pronouns

¿SABES QUE...?

After Christopher Columbus's voyages, Spaniards began to colonize most of Latin America, but they also settled in what today is California, Texas, Arizona and New Mexico. Many states and cities have names derived from Spanish. For instance, Florida means *flowery*, Arizona comes from two Spanish words meaning *arid zone*, Colorado is *red*, Los Angeles means *the angels*, Las Vegas means *fertile lowlands*, and Sacramento is the Spanish word for *sacrament*.

◀ **De compras por la calle Olvera, en Los Ángeles.**

253

Communicative Objectives
• to talk about shopping
• to talk to a salesperson
• to talk about gifts and giving

Related Components

Activity Book p. 123	Cuaderno p. 77
Audio Book Script: Seg. 1	Transparencies Ch.10: Conversemos
Audio Tapes Listening: 6B, Seg. 1	

GETTING STARTED

Have students look at the logos for the first segment and try to figure out what each word or phrase means.

ACTIVITIES

These activities give students an opportunity to begin communicating with each other and with you, focusing on the theme and objectives of the chapter. The activities can be used as oral class activities, or, if you prefer, you can pair students to achieve more interaction.

Generalmente, ¿a qué tiendas vas?
Class activity to introduce shopping vocabulary and review **ir a**. Ask the title question, then begin to vary the questions:
¿Vas a la tienda de discos?
¿Qué compras allí?
¿Cuándo vas al supermercado?
¿Por qué vas?

¿Adónde fuiste de compras?
¿Qué compraste?
Class activity to introduce merchandise vocabulary and review the preterite of **ir**. Read aloud the name of each item and use speech and body language to make sure everyone understands. After each one, ask *¿Dónde compras [queso]?*
Ask the questions in the title. Extend the activity by reviewing vocabulary: *abrigo, traje de baño, protector solar, radio, contestador automático, arroz, helado, cintas, discos compactos, botas, tenis.*
Note that the foods sold in a *bodega* and a *supermercado* are pretty much the same.

CONVERSEMOS
LAS COMPRAS Y TÚ

Habla con tu compañero(a

GENERALMENTE, ¿A QUÉ TIENDAS VAS?

Voy...

al almacén

a la farmacia

a la joyería

a la tienda de aparatos electrónicos

a la tienda de ropa

a la tienda de discos

al supermercado

a la zapatería

¿ADÓNDE FUISTE DE COMPRAS? ¿QUÉ COMPRASTE?

Fui a la farmacia. Compré pasta de dientes.
(I went to the drugstore. I bought toothpaste.)

a la farmacia
(el) maquillaje
(el) jabón
(la) pasta de dientes

al supermercado
(el) queso
(las) verduras
(la) leche

al almacén
una corbata
un cinturón de cuero
una gorra

254

MEETING INDIVIDUAL NEEDS

Reaching All Students

For Auditory Learners
Act as a salesperson and a customer, and record. Exchange with other pairs.

For Visual Learners
Play the game Hangman using this chapter's vocabulary.

For Kinesthetic Learners
Students set up a "store" that sells simple items, then act the roles of salespersons and customers.

¿PARA QUIÉN COMPRASTE UN REGALO?
¿QUÉ LE REGALASTE?

Compré un regalo para mi amiga. Le di un broche.
(I bought a present for my girlfriend. I gave her a pin.)

Para...

mi amigo(a)

mi papá

mi mamá

mi primo(a)

mi novio(a)

Le regalé...

 un broche

 un perfume

 un collar

 un anillo

 un libro

 una pulsera de plata

 una cámara

un reloj

botas tejanas

EN LA TIENDA

¿Qué dice...?

el/la vendedor(a) *(salesperson)*

¿En qué le puedo ayudar?
(May I help you?)

¿Qué desea?
(What would you like?)

¿Tiene el recibo?
(Do you have the receipt?)

Lo siento. Sólo aceptamos dinero
en efectivo. *(Sorry. We only take cash.)*

¿Qué talla usa?
(What size do you wear?)

¿Qué número usa?
(What shoe size do you wear?)

el cliente/la clienta *(customer)*

¿Puedo devolver / cambiar este
anillo / esa pulsera...? *(May I return /
exchange this ring / that
bracelet . . . ?)*

¿Está(n) en rebaja?
(Is it / are they on sale?)

No funciona.
(It doesn't work.)

Es una ganga.
(It's a bargain.)

¿Aceptan tarjetas de crédito / cheques?
(Do you take credit cards / checks?)

Talla mediana.
(Medium size.)

Número seis y medio.
(Size 6½.)

¿Qué precio tiene?
(What's the price?)

255

Class activity to introduce gift-giving
vocabulary. Help students figure out what
the words mean. (**Plata** may require such
questions as: What can jewelry be made
of?) Ask the title questions. Ask where they
bought each gift.

En la tienda

Class activity to introduce shopping
phrases. Have students think of what they
would need to know to buy a shirt in a
Spanish-speaking country. (size, color,
material, etc.)
Act out the exchanges between client and
clerk. Have volunteers work with you or in
pairs to model the exchanges. Have pairs
practice the exchanges.

CHECK

- *¿Qué le regalaste a tu padre para su
  cumpleaños?*
- *¿Adónde fuiste de compras el fin de semana pasado?*
- *¿Qué talla de ropa usas? ¿Y qué número de
  zapatos?*

PORTFOLIO

Suggest that students cut out small store
ads and paste them on sheets of paper.
Under each ad they write in Spanish the
kind of store it is and the names of some of
the items sold there.

Communicative Objectives
- to talk about shopping
- to talk about things done in the past, using the preterite tense and time expressions

Related Components

Activity Book p. 124	**Audio Tapes** Listening Tape: 6B, Seg. 2
Audio Book Script: Seg. 2	**Cuaderno** p. 78

GETTING STARTED

Have students look at the photos and guess what kinds of places these are and what the people are doing.

DISCUSS

Read aloud, or have volunteers read aloud, each paragraph. Talk about these texts and photos. Ask comprehension and critical-thinking questions. Examples:

Introduction
¿Qué es "una ganga"? ¿Algo caro o barato?
Si una pulsera de plata cuesta $5.00, ¿es una ganga?
¿Creen qué es de plata?

En el Harlem hispano
¿Qué compró Ana Luisa?
¿Qué otras cosas puede comprar allí?

En La Pequeña Habana
¿Qué hay en La Pequeña Habana?
¿Qué compró Ana Luisa?
¿Te gustaría comer pasta de guayaba
¿No te gustan los dulces?
La Pequeña Habana también se llama Calle Ocho. ¿Por qué creen que se llama así?
(Es la calle principal del barrio cubano. Hay muchas tiendas y restaurantes hispanos.)

En el vecindario latino de Los Ángeles
¿Qué visitó Ana Luisa?
¿Qué compró allí?
¿Qué más puedes comprar en una joyería?
¿Quiénes tienen joyas aquí?

En la tienda de artesanías mexicanas de San Antonio
¿Qué compró la chica allí?
¿A ustedes les gustan las piñatas?
¿Qué va a hacer con el sarape?

REALIDADES
DE COMPRAS EN ESPAÑOL

DE COMPRAS EN
SAN ANTONIO, LOS ÁNGELES, NUEVA YORK Y MIAMI

CON ANA LUISA REYES

Ir de compras por los vecindarios hispanos es siempre muy divertido. Hay cosas que son una ganga y que no hay en otros lugares. Este artículo cuenta mis aventuras por las comunidades latinas de Miami, Los Ángeles, San Antonio y Nueva York.

En el Harlem hispano de Nueva York, en la calle 116, venden ropa, comida típica del Caribe, cámaras, discos compactos, cintas, libros y mucho más. Allí compré una camiseta con la bandera de Puerto Rico.

En La Pequeña Habana, en Miami, hay bodegas que venden productos típicos cubanos: frijoles negros y frutas tropicales como el mamey y la papaya. Allí compré pasta de guayaba, un dulce delicioso que los cubanos comen con queso blanco.

En las joyerías del vecindario latino de Los Ángeles hay joyas de plata: aretes, collares, broches, anillos... Fui a una joyería en la calle Olvera y compré una pulsera muy bonita.

En esta tienda de artesanías mexicanas de San Antonio compré regalos para toda mi familia. Una piñata para mi hermano, una blusa bordada para mi madre, un cinturón de cuero para mi padre y un sarape para decorar mi cuarto.

256

MEETING INDIVIDUAL NEEDS

Reaching All Students

For Visual Learners
Make a picture dictionary of the vocabulary in this chapter.

For Kinesthetic Learners
Choose a city and act out typical things you imagine would go on there.

For Auditory Learners
One partner says five words from the vocabulary. The other writes them down.

HABLA DEL ARTÍCULO

A. Haz una lista de las tiendas y de las cosas que puedes comprar en cada tienda.

> *En la calle 116, en Nueva York, puedo comprar discos compactos de música latina.*

B. ¿Adónde fue Ana Luisa Reyes?¿Qué vio?

> *Fue a una joyería en Los Ángeles. Vio joyas de plata.*

C. ¿Qué cosas compró? ¿Dónde? Habla con tu compañero(a).

> — *¿Qué compró en Nueva York?*
> — *Una camiseta con la bandera de Puerto Rico.*
> — *¿Dónde la compró?*
> — *En la calle 116, en el Harlem hispano.*

¿QUÉ OPINAS?

¿Adónde y cuándo vas de compras? Pregúntales a tres compañeros(as). Anota los resultados en una tabla.

Tiendas	Rosa	Marina	Alex
de discos	los sábados	a veces	nunca
zapatería			
joyería			
de aparatos electrónicos			
librería			
almacén			

Compara tu tabla con las tablas de otros(as) estudiantes.

¿SABES QUE...?

Many Latin Americans have had successful careers in the U.S. in different fields. In film, actors such as Andy García or Rosie Pérez have become household names. One of Florida's past governors, Robert Martínez, is of Hispanic origin. In music, singers such as Gloria Estefan or Rubén Blades have had hit songs on the Top 100 list.

257

ACTIVITIES

Habla del artículo

Individual and Pair Activities: Comprehension
A. Make a list of the stores and what you can buy at each.
B. Where did Ana Luisa Reyes go? What did she see?
C. Speak with a partner about what she bought and where.
Answers: See models on student page.
Challenge: In pairs, ask each other about the things that Ana Luisa found in each of the cities. Do not refer to your books.

¿Qué opinas?

Group Activity: Taking a Poll
When and where do you go shopping? Ask three classmates, and make a chart of your group's preferences.

Class Activity: Evaluation
List stores on the board as volunteers name them. Write in the numbers for each store as representatives of each group report their polls.
Evaluation: Rank the popularity of the stores. Suggest reasons for the rankings.

CHECK

- *¿Qué lugares visitó Ana Luisa?*
- *¿Qué compró en cada lugar?*
- *¿Qué otros productos venden en los mercados que ella visitó?*
- *¿Hay gangas en nuestra ciudad? ¿Dónde?*

LOG BOOK
Have students list vocabulary they find especially difficult.

Para hispanohablantes

What Hispanic foods or other products does your family buy? Where do you find them?

PALABRAS EN ACCIÓN

Communicative Objectives

To talk about:
- things you can buy
- gifts
- exchanging something you bought

Related Components

Activity Book p. 125-126	Transparencies Ch. 10: Palabras en acción
Cuaderno p. 79-80	Tutor Page p. 43

GETTING STARTED

Ask if anyone has ever gone to or sold things at a street fair or tag sale. What are these like? What do people do?

DISCUSS

Have volunteers read aloud the dialog and act out the activities in the drawing. Ask questions about objects in the drawing (e.g., Is there anything people wear on their feet? What are they called?).

PALABRAS EN ACCIÓN

EN LA FERIA

① ¿Qué ves en el dibujo?

Escoge tres puestos del dibujo. Haz una lista de las cosas que te gustaría comprar en cada uno. Compara tu lista con la lista de tu compañero(a).

En el puesto Todo de cuero: el cinturón,...

② ¿Qué puesto es?

Describe uno de los puestos del dibujo. Tu compañero(a) tiene que adivinar cuál es.

— *Hay un hombre con una gorra. Cerca hay un puesto de ropa.*
— *Es el puesto Música Latina.*

③ ¿Qué hacen?

Escoge cinco personas del dibujo. Explica qué hace cada una.

- *El hombre de la joyería Esmeralda vende joyas.*
- *El cliente de la joyería Esmeralda mira un collar.*

④ ¿Qué compras en la feria?

Habla con tu compañero(a) sobre cuatro cosas que te gustaría comprar. Explica dónde venden cada cosa.

— *Quiero comprar cacahuates.*
— *¿Dónde los venden?*
— *En el puesto Todo rico.*

258

For students having difficulty talking about things you can buy and where to buy them, you might consider:
- **The tutor page:** Pair the student with a native speaker or a more able student, using the tutor page.
- **Actividades:** see page 252C: *Equis cero*

5 ¿Qué le regalaste a...?

Habla con tu compañero(a) de lo que les regalaste a dos personas para su cumpleaños.

Le regalé un collar a mi hermana.
Le regalé un cinturón a mi novio(a).

6 Miniteatro

Escoge un puesto de la feria. Tú eres el cliente/la clienta y tu compañero(a) es el vendedor/la vendedora.

Vendedor(a): *Buenos días, ¿qué desea?*
Cliente(a): *Me gustaría devolver esta camisa. Me queda pequeña.*
Vendedor(a): *¿Tiene el recibo?*
Cliente(a): *Sí, aquí está.*

7 Collage

En grupo, hagan un anuncio de una feria en la calle. Digan dónde y cuándo va a ser. Usen fotos y dibujos de revistas y periódicos. Hagan una lista de las cosas que van a vender.

8 Tú eres el autor

Haz una lista de regalos para cinco personas. Indica para quién es cada regalo.

Una cámara para mi hermano.
Aretes de plata para mi amiga...

259

1. Pair Activity
Choose three of the stands. Make a list of things that you would like to buy at each. Compare lists with a partner.
Analysis: With a partner, take turns naming (or describing) a **puesto** at the fair and naming an object sold there.

2. Pair Activity
Describe one place in the drawing. Your partner has to guess which place it is.

3. Individual or Pair Activity
Choose five people in the drawing. Say what each person is doing.
Analysis: Describe what each of the five people is wearing.

4. Pair Activity
Talk to your partner about four things that you would like to buy. Say where each thing is sold.
Synthesis: Imagine that you went to the fair. Say when you went and talk about three things you bought.

5. Pair Activity
Talk to your partner about what you gave two people for their birthdays.
Extension: Say where you bought the presents.

6. Roleplay Activity
Choose a street fair stand. You and your partner are the customer and salesperson. Create and act out a dialog.
For Kinesthetic Learners: Try to sell your shoes to other classmates. If they don't want to buy, try to exchange the shoes for something they have.

7. Hands-On Activity
Homework or classwork for groups. Make a poster for a street fair. Say where and when it will be held. Use photos and drawings. Make a list of things that you will sell there.
For Auditory Learners: Make a radio ad for the street fair. Perform it for the class.

8. Writing Activity
Make a list of gifts for five people. Say who will receive each gift.

CHECK

- ¿Qué te gustaría comprar en una feria?
- ¿Qué le regalaste a tu mejor amigo para su cumpleaños?
- ¿Qué te gustaría cambiar? ¿Por qué?
- ¿En qué le puedo ayudar?

LOG BOOK
Have students write down what kind of table they would have at a street fair and list some things they would have to sell.

Community Link
Find out if there are any street fairs or outdoor markets in your town that offer Hispanic products. Go there and try speaking Spanish with the vendors.

PARA COMUNICARNOS MEJOR

Communicative Objectives
- to say where you went, using the preterite of **ir**
- to point out people and things, using demonstrative adjectives

Related Components

Activity Book p. 127-128	**Audio Tapes** Listening: 6B, Seg. 3
Audio Book Script: Seg. 3 Activities: p. 85	**Cuaderno** p.81
	Tutor Page p. 44

GETTING STARTED

Language in Context

Preterite Forms of *ir*
Have volunteers read aloud the examples. Review the paradigm.

Demonstrative Adjectives
Point to an object across the room and ask, incorrectly, *What is this object?* Hold up a few pencils and ask: *What are those objects?* Then ask if there was anything unusual about your questions. Encourage discussion of the difference between *this* and *that,* and how they are used for things that are nearby or far away. Also discuss the importance of number when using adjectives with nouns.
Read aloud the texts about demonstrative adjectives, and have volunteers read the examples.

DISCUSS

Review vocabulary and introduce new vocabulary with questions that use demonstrative adjectives and/or preterite forms of **ir.**
¿Qué prefieres, Marta, este anillo o ese broche?
Anoche, yo fui al cine. ¿Adónde fuiste tú?
¿Qué fueron Uds. a comprar en el almacén?
Ese anillo, ¿es de oro o de plata?
¿Compraste la gorra en este puesto o en esa tienda?
¿Dónde es mejor la pasta de guayaba, en este puesto o en esa bodega?
¿Quieres esta foto? ¿O estas fotos?
¿Adónde fue el tiempo?

PARA COMUNICARNOS MEJOR
¿ADÓNDE FUISTE AYER?

To say where you or somebody else went, use the preterite of the verb *ir.*

—*Fui a la joyería.*	I went to the jewelry store.
—*Nosotros fuimos a una zapatería.*	We went to a shoe store.

Here are the forms of *ir* in the preterite tense.

the preterite of ir (to go)

yo	fui	nosotros(as)	fuimos
tú	fuiste	vosotros(as)	fuisteis
usted	fue	ustedes	fueron
él/ella	fue	ellos/ellas	fueron

To point out specific people and things, use demonstrative adjectives.

¿Quieres este anillo?	Do you want this ring?
Esa mujer vende aretes.	That woman sells earrings.

Demonstrative adjectives come before nouns. They have the same gender and number as the nouns they modify.

demonstrative adjectives

singular		plural	
este anillo	*this ring*	**estos** anillos	*these rings*
esta pulsera	*this bracelet*	**estas** pulseras	*these bracelets*
ese perfume	*that perfume*	**esos** perfumes	*those perfumes*
esa gorra	*that cap*	**esas** gorras	*those caps*

260

For students having difficulty using the preterite of **ir,** you might consider:
- **The tutor page:** Pair the student with a native speaker or a more able student, using the tutor page.
- **Actividades:** see page 252C: *¿Adónde fuiste?*

1 De compras

¿Adónde fuiste ayer? ¿Qué compraste? Pregúntale
a tu compañero(a).

— ¿Adónde fuiste ayer?
— Fui a la feria.
— ¿Qué compraste?
— Compré cacahuates y dulces.

Fui...
a la feria
a la farmacia
a la joyería
a la bodega
al almacén
a la tienda de discos

2 En el centro comercial

¿Adónde fueron? Pregúntale a tu compañero(a).

— ¿Adónde fueron tus amigos?
— Fueron a la zapatería El botín. Compraron botas de cuero.

1. tus amigos   4. tu compañero(a) de clase

2. tu amiga   5. tu amiga y tú

3. tus hermanos(as)   6. ¿y tú?

3 ¿En qué le puedo ayudar?

Estás en el almacén y quieres cambiar varios regalos. Tu
compañero(a) es el/la vendedor(a).

— ¿En qué le puedo ayudar?
— Quiero cambiar este collar.
— ¿Le gustan esos broches? Están en rebaja.
— Sí, me gustan. Quiero ese broche de plata.

1. collar/broches
2. aretes/pulseras
3. tocacintas/cámaras
4. maquillaje/perfume
5. zapatos/botas
6. gorra/corbata

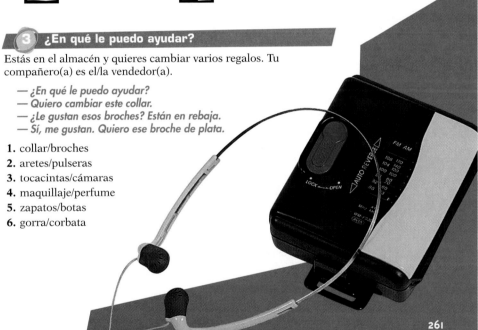

261

Communicative Objectives

- to indicate for whom something is done, using indirect-object pronouns
- to say you gave something to someone, using the preterite of **dar**

Related Components

Activity Book p. 129-130	**Audio Tapes** Listening: 6B, Seg. 4
Audio Book Script: Seg.4 Activities: p. 86	**Cuaderno** p. 82
	Tutor Page p. 45

GETTING STARTED

Ask students to name the objects on this page in Spanish.

Language in Context

Indirect-Object Pronouns

Write two sentences in English, leaving blanks where indirect-object pronouns would go. Example:
I gave __ a book on his birthday.
He gave __ a necklace.
Ask what words probably go in the blank spaces. Then point out that the sentences are about *I* and *he,* and ask why we use *him* and *me* instead of *I* and *he.* Discuss the differences between subject pronouns and indirect-object pronouns.

Preterite Forms of *dar*

Review the text and paradigm. Have volunteers read the sentences aloud.

DISCUSS

Review vocabulary from previous chapters and introduce some of this chapter's new vocabulary with questions that use the preterite of **dar** and indirect-object pronouns.
¿Qué le diste a Ricardo?
¿Quién te compró la camisa?
¿Por qué me compraste un libro?
¿Te invité a mi fiesta?
¿Por qué le dimos a María dos cuadernos?
¿Qué te dieron tu papá y tú mamá?
¿Cuántas aspirinas te di?
Le dimos mucho dinero.

PARA COMUNICARNOS MEJOR

¿QUÉ LE REGALASTE?

To say to whom or for whom something is intended, use indirect object nouns and pronouns.

— *¿Qué le regalaste a tu hermana?*	What present did you give your sister?
— *Le regalé un collar.*	I gave her a necklace.
— *¿Qué te regalaron?*	What present did they give you?
— *Me regalaron una cámara.*	They gave me a camera.

Here are the forms of indirect object pronouns.

indirect object pronouns			
me	to me	**nos**	to us
te	to you (informal)	**os**	to you (pl.)
le	to him, her, it, you (formal)	**les**	to them, you (pl.)

To say that you gave something to someone, use the preterite of *dar (to give)* with an indirect object pronoun.

— *¿Qué le diste a tu hermano?*	What did you give your brother?
— *Le di una bolsa de dulces.*	I gave him a bag of candies.

Here are the forms of the verb **dar** in the preterite tense.

¡OJO!

The verb *dar* in the present tense is conjugated like other *-ar* verbs, except for the *yo* form: *doy.*

doy	**damos**
das	**dais**
da	**dan**

the preterite of dar (to give)			
yo	di	nosotros(as)	dimos
tú	diste	vosotros(as)	disteis
usted	dio	ustedes	dieron
él/ella	dio	ellos/ellas	dieron

For students having difficulty
using the preterite of **dar** and indirect object pronouns, you might consider:

- **The tutor page:** Pair the student with a native speaker or a more able student, using the tutor page.
- **Actividades:** see page 252D: *¿En qué le puedo ayudar?*

1 Regalos

¿Qué le dieron a la quinceañera para su cumpleaños? Pregúntale a tu compañero(a).

— *¿Qué le dio la mamá?*
— *Le dio una pulsera de oro.*

1. la mamá
2. los abuelos
3. el novio
4. el padrino
5. ustedes
6. ¿y tú?

2 Entrevista

Entrevista a tres compañeros(as).

— *¿Quién te compra la ropa?*
— *Mi madre me compra la ropa.*

• ¿Quién te compra la ropa?
• ¿Quién te da dinero cuando sales?
• ¿Quién te regala cintas o discos compactos?
• ¿Quién te escribe cartas?
• ¿Quién te prepara la comida?

3 En el almacén

¿Qué les compró tu abuela? Pregúntale a tu compañero(a).

— *¿Qué les compró tu abuela a tus hermanos?*
— *Les compró gorras.*

1. a tus hermanos
2. a ti
3. a tu papá
4. a tus tíos
5. a ustedes
6. a tu mamá

Regalos
gorras
un cinturón
un perfume
una blusa bordada
camisetas
dulces
maquillaje

263

Students use the preterite of **dar** and indirect-object pronouns to talk about having received something.

1. Pair Activity
What did these people give the birthday girl? Ask and answer questions.
Possible Answers:
1. See model on student page.
2. *¿Qué le dieron los abuelos?*
Le dieron un anillo.
3. *¿Qué le dio el novio?*
Le dio un sombrero tejano.

4. *¿Qué le dio el padrino?*
Le dio una cámara.
5. *¿Qué le dieron ustedes?*
Le dimos unas botas tejanas.
6. *Y tú ¿qué le diste?*
Le di un perfume.

For Visual and Auditory Learners: Act out giving things to classmates. The class must make up sentences about who gave what to whom. Example: *María y Juan le dieron a la profesora dos cuadernos.*

2 Group Activity
Ask three classmates these questions.
Possible Answers:
• See model on student page.
• *Mi padre me da dinero cuando salgo.*
• *Mis amigos me regalan cintas o discos compactos.*
• *Mi hermana me escribe cartas.*
• *Mis abuelos me preparan la comida.*
Application: Think of five things that people have given you, and write sentences about each. For example:
Ayer, mi amiga me dio sus apuntes.

3. Pair Activity
What did your grandmother buy for these people?
Possible Answers:
1. See model on student page.
2. *¿Qué te compró tu abuela?*
Me compró una blusa bordada.
3. *¿Qué le compró tu abuela a tu papá?*
Le compró un reloj.
4. *¿Qué les compró tu abuela a tus tíos?*
Les compró cinturones.
5. *¿Qué les compró tu abuela a ustedes?*
Nos compró dulces muy ricos.
6. *¿Qué le compró tu abuela a tu mamá?*
Le compró dulces y un broche.

CHECK

• *¿Qué le diste a tu mamá para su cumpleaños?*
• *¿Cuándo te compró Chris el libro?*
• *¿Cuánto dinero le dimos?*
• *¿Qué me compraste?*
• *¿Qué le dieron Marta y Manolo a su hijo?*

LOG BOOK
Have students write sentences that say what members of their family bought for each other during the last year.

Para hispanohablantes
Think of songs in Spanish that have the word **dar** in the title or in the chorus. Sing one for the class.

Communicative Objectives

• to talk about buying, exchanging, giving, or returning something

Related Components

Assessment Oral Proficiency: p. 30	**Conexiones** Chapter 10
Audio Book Script: Seg. 5 Activities: p. 87	**Magazine** Juntos en Los Estados Unidos
Audio Tapes Listening: 6B, Seg. 5 Conexiones: 18A, Ch. 10	**Tutor Page** p. 46

GETTING STARTED

Students should now be able to use the preterite forms of **dar** and **ir**, indirect-object pronouns, demonstrative adjectives, and all of the chapter vocabulary.
Have students look at the flyer and the ads. Is everything here for sale? What does **cambio** mean? Elicit *trade* as well as *exchange*. What does **regalo** mean?

APPLY

1. Pair Activity

You and your partner went to a neighborhood fair. Say what you bought and for whom you bought it.
Answers: See model on student page.
Application: Say when you went to the neighborhood fair. What day? What time?

2. Pair Activity

Look at the ads in the newspaper. Talk to your partner about what you would like to buy or exchange.
Answers: See model on student page.
Application: What do you have that you would like to trade? Say why.

3. Individual Activity

Make a list of things you would like to give away, exchange or sell. Write an ad that gives details and prices.
Analysis: Exchange advertisements with your partner and talk about which things you would like from each other's list.

SITUACIONES
¡TODO ES UNA GANGA!

EL SÁBADO 10 DE MAYO

Feria de la Calle 116

DE 9:00 A.M. A 5:00 P.M.

VENDEMOS:

bicicleta	$35
patines número 8½	$15
tocacintas	$10
chaleco de cuero talla mediana	$18
tenis rojos número 8½	$12
aretes y collar de plata	$8
pulseras	$3 cada una
camisetas talla extra grande	$3
cinturones	$3 cada uno
gorras	$1 cada una

Vendo un disco de los Rolling Stones y un libro sobre animales. Sólo $6 cada cosa. Marcos L. 555-7432.

Vendo una colección de broches. Casi nuevos y muy baratos. Mari García 555-5487.

Cambio aretes y pulseras de plata por cintas de música latina. Aurora Zimmer 555-6893.

Regalo dos perros. Busco familia cariñosa y responsable. Mercedes 555-3256.

¡Y muchas cosas más!

(Sólo aceptamos dinero en efectivo.)

PARA TU REFERENCIA

cariñoso(a) *affectionate*
casi *almost*
regatear *to bargain*

264

4. Class Activity

Organize a class fair to give away, trade, or sell things. Remember that you must bargain with one another!
Answers: See model on student page.
Application: Tell someone what you bought, traded, or got at the fair, and who you got it for.
Note: You may prefer to do this activity with words written on index cards instead of real objects.

For students having difficulty using the demonstrative adjectives **este/esta** and **ese/esa** to talk about buying something, you might consider:
• **The tutor page:** Pair the student with a native speaker or a more able student, using the tutor page.
• **Actividades:** see page 252D: *¿Este libro o ese diccionario*

1 En la feria del vecindario

Tú y tu compañero(a) fueron a la feria del vecindario. Digan qué compraron y para quién.

— ¿Fuiste a la feria de la calle 116?
— Sí, allí compré estos tenis rojos.
— Ah, ¡qué chévere!
— Y tú, ¿qué compraste?
— Le compré estos aretes a mi hermana.

2 ¿Compras o cambias?

Mira los anuncios del periódico. Habla con tu compañero(a) sobre qué les gustaría comprar o cambiar.

— Me gustaría cambiar mis cintas de música latina por unas pulseras de plata. ¿Y a ti?
— A mí me gustaría comprar un regalo para mi mamá.
— ¿Por qué no le compras un collar?

3 Tu anuncio

Haz una lista de las cosas que quieres regalar, cambiar o vender. Escribe un anuncio con toda la información. Incluye los precios.

4 En la feria de la clase

Hagan una feria en su clase para regalar, cambiar o vender sus cosas. Recuerden, ¡tienen que regatear!

— ¿Cuánto cuesta ese collar?
— Sólo 99 centavos.
— Lo cambio por este champú.
— Sí, si me das esa tarjeta de béisbol también.
— Muy bien.

265

- ¿Qué te compraste?
- ¿Qué cambiaste?
- ¿Qué te regalaron?
- ¿Qué fue una ganga?
- ¿Fuiste a una feria del vecindario el año pasado? ¿Qué compraste?

LOG BOOK

Have students write about something they were given, who bought it for them, and where that person bought it.

Background

Los Angeles Once a Spanish colony, this megalopolis is still nearly 40 percent Hispanic. Evidence of this influence can be found throughout the city, from the murals in East Los Angeles to the nine Spanish-language radio stations. The city's origins are remembered in the district called *El Pueblo de Los Ángeles* Historic Monument.

Miami This city has come to be considered the commercial capital not just of Florida but of Latin America. Most of the Spanish speakers here were born in Cuba or have parents who were born there. Cuban immigrants arrived in several waves that began in 1959, after a Communist revolution on the island.

New York City The largest city in the United States has the most diverse population of any city in the world. Hispanics account for almost 24 percent of the population, but no single community predominates. (Among the largest groups are Puerto Ricans, Dominicans, and Colombians.)

Para hispanohablantes

Tell the class your favorite places to find interesting things at bargain prices.

Communicative Objectives
- to talk about mail-order shopping
- to talk to a salesperson on the phone
- to explain why you are returning or exchanging something

Related Components

Transparencies	Video: Tape/Book
Ch. 10: Para resolver	Unit 5: Seg. 3

Search to frame 1234806

GETTING STARTED

Have students imagine that they are going to buy something over the phone. What would they have to tell the person who takes their order?

APPLY

Form groups. Explain that each group will buy something from a mail-order house. Make sure they understand what **por correo** means.

PASO 1: ¿Qué les gustaría comprar?
Read the catalog page and say what you would like to buy. Make a copy of the order form and fill it out.
Answers: See model on student page.

PASO 2: ¡Es una ganga!
Buy a present for a friend. Discuss what your friend would like and the price of each item. Decide what to buy.
Answers: See model on student page.
Evaluation: You have $25 to spend on gifts for three friends. Say whom each is for, how much it costs, and why that person will like the gift.

PASO 3: ¿En qué le puedo ayudar?
Write a dialog between a telephone salesperson and a customer. Include:
- what the customer will buy
- if it can be exchanged or returned
- the style, size, color, and price
- the customer's name, address, and phone number
- the total cost (include taxes, and shipping and handling charges)
- whether the customer will pay by check or credit card

PARA RESOLVER
COMPRAS POR TELÉFONO

PASO 1 ¿Qué les gustaría comprar?

Lean la página del catálogo. Digan qué les gustaría comprar.

— ¿Qué te gustaría comprar de este catálogo?
— Me gustaría comprar este anillo o esta gorra.

PASO 2 ¡Es una ganga!

Ahora, van a comprar un regalo para un(a) amigo(a). Piensen qué le gustaría a su amigo(a). Hablen de los precios de cada cosa. Decidan qué van a comprar.

— ¿Qué le gustaría más a Nélida, este anillo o estos aretes?
— El anillo es muy bonito.
— Sí, y sólo cuesta $4.99. ¡Es una ganga!

PASO 3 ¿En qué le puedo ayudar?

Van a hacer una compra por teléfono. Preparen un diálogo entre el/la vendedor(a) y el/la cliente(a). Incluyan:

- qué van a comprar
- si pueden devolver o cambiar el regalo
- el modelo, la talla, el color del regalo y el precio
- su nombre, dirección y número de teléfono
- cuánto es el total de la compra (incluyan los gastos de envío y los impuestos)
- si van a pagar con cheque o con tarjeta de crédito

PASO 4 Un problema

Quieren cambiar el regalo que compraron. En una carta, expliquen por qué. Digan qué quieren ahora.

Les devolvemos el anillo que compramos porque le queda grande a nuestra amiga. Lo queremos cambiar por...

PARA TU REFERENCIA

la fecha de vencimiento *expiration date*
los gastos de envío *shipping charges*
los impuestos *tax*

PASO 4: Un problema
You want to exchange the gift that you bought for a friend. Write a letter in which you explain why you are returning it. Say what you want to exchange it for.
Answers: See model on student page.
Analysis: On the board, write a class letter using the best reasons for not liking the present.

MEETING INDIVIDUAL NEEDS

Reaching All Students

For Auditory Learners
Sell a partner something by telephone. Say what it includes and what it costs. Answer your customer's questions.

For Visual Learners
Prepare a catalog and an order sheet for it. Make copies and have others order merchandise from your catalog.

1 ARETES DE PLATA
Modelos: A, B y C
Precios: A) **$2.99**
B) **$3.99**
C) **$4.99**

2 GORRAS DE
BÉISBOL
Talla única
Modelos: A, B y C
Precio: **$4.99**

3 CINTURONES DE
CUERO
Tallas: pequeña/
mediana/grande
Modelos: A, B y C
Precio: **$29.99**

4 ANILLOS DE
PLATA
Modelos: A, B y C
Precios: A) **$4.99**
B) **$6.99**
C) **$5.99**

La casa del regalo
Doctor Lamia N° 49
Miami, Florida 92304
1-800-555-3147

Nombre _____ Apellido_____

Dirección_____

Ciudad_____ Estado _____ Código Postal _____

Teléfono_____

	Cantidad	Talla	Modelo	Color	Precio	
Cinturón de cuero						
Gorra						
Aretes						
Anillo						

Aceptamos:

❑ cheque ❑ Visa ❑ MasterCard

N° ⬜⬜⬜⬜⬜⬜⬜⬜⬜⬜⬜⬜⬜⬜⬜⬜

Fecha de vencimiento: _____

Total	
Gastos de envío	+ $2.95
Impuestos 8%	
Total	

PORTFOLIO
Students may want to place the completed order form in their portfolios with cut out pictures illustrating each selection.

Shopping Words
brand *la marca*
catalog *el catálogo*
code *el código*
guarantee *la garantía*
mail order *el pedido por correo*
mailorder house *el almacén de ventas por correo*
merchandise *la mercancía*
order *el pedido*
price *el precio*
product *el producto*
to send for *mandar a pedir*
shipping and handling *los gastos de envío*
telephone sales representative *el operador, la operadora*

Para hispanohablantes

Go around the class and ask each group the questions on the order form. Take down their orders.

267

Cultural Objective
• to discuss the growth of the Hispanic population of the United States

Related Components

Audio Tapes	Chapter 10
Conexiones: 18A, Ch. 10	**Magazine**
Conexiones	Juntos en Los Estados Unidos

GETTING STARTED

Have students guess how many people of Hispanic origin live in the United States. What made them think of that number?

DISCUSS

Using the Text

Read aloud the first paragraph and ask comprehension and critical-thinking questions. Examples:
¿Cómo se dice en inglés población?
¿Cuántas personas de origen hispano había en Estados Unidos en 1979?
En 1979 había 14 millones de personas. Ahora hay 26 millones. ¿Cuántos más hay ahora?

Using the Graphs

Read aloud the title question of the first graph. Ask comprehension and critical-thinking questions. Suggestions:
¿Cuántos países hay en este gráfico?
(Hay nueve países, Puerto Rico y "otros países".)
¿Todos los hispanos son mexicanos?
¿Qué porcentaje es mexicano?
¿Qué porcentaje es cubano?
¿Qué países en la gráfica son parte de Centroamérica? (Nicaragua, Guatemala, El Salvador)
¿Qué porcentaje de los hispanos en Estados Unidos es de Centroamérica?
The second graph:
¿En qué estado hay más hispanos?
¿Hay menos hispanos en Nueva York que en Florida?

LA POBLACIÓN° HISPANA

En 1979, había° más o menos 14 millones de personas de origen hispano en Estados Unidos. ¿Sabes que hoy hay más de 26 millones? Eso significa° que de cada diez habitantes° de los Estados Unidos, uno es de origen hispano.

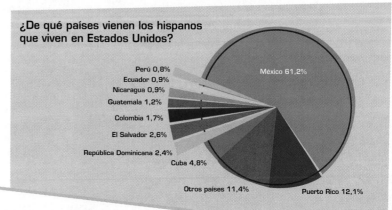

¿De qué países vienen los hispanos que viven en Estados Unidos?

Perú 0,8%
Ecuador 0,9%
Nicaragua 0,9%
Guatemala 1,2%
Colombia 1,7%
El Salvador 2,6%
República Dominicana 2,4%
Cuba 4,8%
México 61,2%
Otros países 11,4%
Puerto Rico 12,1%

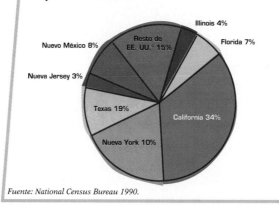

¿En qué partes de Estados Unidos viven los hispanos? ¿Qué porcentaje de la población hispana total hay en cada estado?

Illinois 4%
Nuevo México 8%
Resto de EE. UU.° 15%
Florida 7%
Nueva Jersey 3%
Texas 19%
California 34%
Nueva York 10%

Fuente: National Census Bureau 1990.

EE. UU. *U.S.*
eso significa *that means*
había *there was/were*

los habitantes *inhabitants*
menos de *less than*
la población *population*

268

TE TOCA A TI

Di qué oraciones son ciertas y cuáles son falsas. Corrige las oraciones falsas.

1. Hay menos de° 20 millones de hispanos en Estados Unidos.
2. California es el estado donde hay más personas de origen hispano.
3. Hoy, de cada 10 habitantes de los Estados Unidos, uno es de origen hispano.
4. El 50% de la población hispana en Estados Unidos es de origen mexicano.

CHECK

Te toca a ti
Answers:
1. *Falsa. Hay más de 26 millones.*
2. *Cierta.*
3. *Cierta.*
4. *Falsa. El 61.2% es de origen mexicano.*

Para hispanohablantes

Make a similar graph representing the percentage of Hispanic people in your community.

▶▶▶ **INTERNET LINK**

U.S Census Information Maps http://www.census.gov:80/ftp/pub/geo/www/mapGallery/RHOriginPD-1990.html

VOCABULARIO TEMÁTICO

Las tiendas
Stores

el almacén *department store*
la feria *street fair*
la joyería *jewelry store*
el puesto *booth*
el supermercado *supermarket*
la tienda de discos *record store*
la zapatería *shoe store*

Las compras
Purchases

el anillo *ring*
los aretes *earrings*
la bolsa *bag*
las botas tejanas *cowboy boots*
el broche *pin*
el cinturón *belt*
el collar *necklace*
la corbata *necktie*
los dulces *candies*
la gorra *cap*
las joyas *jewels*
el maquillaje *makeup*
el perfume *perfume*
la pulsera *bracelet*
el reloj *watch, clock*
las sandalias *sandals*

¿De qué es?
What's it made of?

de plata *(made of) silver*
de oro *(made of) gold*
de cuero *(made of) leather*

En la tienda
At the store

¿Aceptan tarjetas de crédito/ cheques? *Do you take credit cards/checks?*
¿En qué le puedo ayudar? *May I help you?*
Es una ganga. *It's a bargain.*
Está en rebaja. *It's on sale.*
Me queda pequeño/grande. *It's too small/big for me.*
No funciona. *It doesn't work.*
¿Qué desea? *What would you like?*
¿Qué precio tiene? *What's the price?*
Sólo aceptamos dinero en efectivo. *We only take cash.*
el(la) vendedor(a) *salesperson*

Expresiones y palabras

bordado(a) *embroidered*
cambiar *to exchange, to change*
el cheque *check*
dar *to give*
devolver *to return (to give back)*

este/esta *this*
estos/estas *these*
ese/esa *that*
esos/esas *those*
le *to him, her, it, you (formal sing.)*
les *to them, you (pl.)*
me/te *to me, you (informal, sing.)*
mediano(a) *medium*
nos/os *to us, you (informal, pl.)*
el número (de zapatos) *(shoe) size*
pagar *to pay*
el recibo *receipt*
regalar *to give a present*
sólo *only*
la talla *clothing size*
la tarjeta de crédito *credit card*
vender *to sell*

Expresiones de las Américas

la bodega *grocery store*
el cacahuate *peanut*
la pasta de guayaba *guava paste*
el sarape *shawl*

LA CONEXIÓN INGLÉS-ESPAÑOL

You know the Spanish word for *bookstore*, **librería**. Look in the *Vocabulario temático* for other Spanish words with the same ending **-ería**. What common meaning do these words have in English? What do you think the words **florería** and **lechería** mean in English?

269

VOCABULARIO TEMÁTICO

Objectives
• to review vocabulary
• to correctly pronounce words containing the double "ll" and "y"

Related Components

Activity Book	Audio Tapes
Chapter Review: p. 131-132	Listening: 6B, Seg. 6
Assessment	Assessment: 15B, Ch. 10
Listening Script: p. 18	**Cuaderno**
Chapter Test: p. 99-104	p. 83-84
Audio Book	
Script: Seg. 6	
Activities p. 88	

Pronunciation: "ll" and "y"

The double "ll" is preferably pronounced like an "l" sound followed by a "y" as in the English expression "call you." In some countries (like Mexico), however, it is pronounced like the "y" in the English word "yes."
collar, anillo, maquillaje, caballo

Since 1994, the "ll" is no longer regarded as a letter of the alphabet, but rather as an occurrence of one "l" following another.

The Spanish letter "y" is pronounced like the "y" in "yes." In some regions, however, there is a tendency to pronounce it with a "zh" sound as in the English word "azure" or the French pronunciation of the "j" in the phrase "Bon Jour."
joyería, ya, yo, Yuto, Yolanda

At the end of a word the letter "y" is pronounced like the Spanish vowel "i."

LOG BOOK
Have students write sentences or tongue-twisters with words that contain **ll** or **y**.

La conexión inglés-español

In English, these words usually mean a place where something is sold. **Florería** means "flower store" and **lechería** means "milk store."
Possible Rule: If a noun ends in **-ería**, cover the ending and see if you recognize or can figure out what the remaining part of the noun means. Examples:

flor-	*flor*	**joy-**	*joya*
lech-	*leche*	**libr-**	*libro*
taqu-	*taco*	**zapat-**	*zapato*

ADELANTE

Objectives

Pre-Reading Strategy: to elicit meaning from photographs and captions

Cultural: to examine the uses of murals

Related Components

CD ROM	Video:
Unit 5: Adelante	**Tape/Book**
Magazine	Unit 5: Seg. 4
Juntos en Los Estados Unidos	

Search to frame 1264612

GETTING STARTED

What is the purpose of murals? Do you think they are just decoration or do they have some other purpose?

Using the Video

Show Segment 4 of the Unit 5 video.

Antes de leer

Have volunteers read aloud the introduction and the captions. Have students make the list suggested in the introduction. Discuss the questions.

Explain what murals are and how they are made, and encourage students to express their opinions about these images and the uses of these murals.

About Murals

Mural is a catch-all word for images on walls (from Latin *muralis*, of a wall). The walls may be indoors or outdoors, and the images may or may not be painted. Frescoes are painted on plastered walls while the plaster is still wet. (Giotto and Michelangelo painted frescos.) Some murals are made of small pieces of stone or glass (mosaic). Others are painted on canvas and glued to walls. (Many of the public-works murals of the Depression were done this way.) Most of the works on these pages were painted on brick or concrete with industrial paints. They will have a short lifespan if not retouched every few years.

ADELANTE

ANTES DE LEER

Los murales son una forma de expresión de las comunidades hispanas de Estados Unidos. La mayoría de los murales están en las ciudades.

¿Hay murales en tu comunidad? ¿Cómo son? ¿Viste alguna vez° un mural? ¿Dónde?

Mira los fotos de las páginas 270-273. Haz una lista de las características que asocias con los murales.

Tony García, alias *Chico*, es un muralista puertorriqueño que vive en Nueva York. Su mural, *Dedicated to the L.E.S.*, celebra la diversidad hispana en el Lower East Side, en Manhattan.

¿viste alguna vez...? did you ever see . . .?

270

Adelante Components

Activity Book	Audio Tapes	Magazine	Video: Tape/Book
p. 133-136	Adelante: 12A, 12B	Juntos en Los	Unit 5: Seg. 4-5
Assessment	**CD ROM**	Estados Unidos	
Portfolio: p. 41-42	Unit 5: Adelante	**Transparencies**	
		Unit 5: Adelante	

◄ Este mural del famoso artista mexicano Diego Rivera se llama *Historia de México*. Rivera tuvo° una gran influencia sobre los muralistas del mundo° hispano.

◄ *Chico* empezó haciendo° murales en las calles y tiendas de Nueva York. Este mural es un homenaje al jazz. Está en Manhattan.

◄ Muchos murales celebran ocasiones especiales. Este mural está en Miami y celebra el Día de la Tierra.°

el mundo *world*
el Día de la Tierra *Earthday*
haciendo *making*
tuvo *had*

271

Using the Photos

Dedicated to the L.E.S.

New York's Lower East Side (L.E.S.) has been the traditional home of immigrants since the 1800s. Much of the population is Hispanic today—so much so that many people call the area by its Hispanic name: *Loisaida* (Lower East Side). Questions:
¿Qué creen que es el L.E.S.?
¿Qué celebra este mural?
¿Quién pintó este mural?
¿De qué país es Chico?
¿Dónde vive?

Diego Rivera

This is part of a huge mural that Rivera painted on the staircase of the National Palace. It depicts Mexico's history from the fall of Tenochtitlán to 1935. This segment focuses on Benito Juárez and the period from 1855 to 1876.
¿En qué es diferente el mural de Rivera del mural de Chico?
Hay más personas. Son personas de la historia. Es más realista, ¿verdad?

Jazz

¿Qué hacen las personas en el mural?
¿Creen que las formas y los colores representan bien al jazz?
¿Qué es un homenaje?

Music Link: What are the instruments? Find their names in Spanish.

Miami

¿Qué formas ves en este mural?
¿Piensas que celebra el Día de la Tierra?
¿Por qué?

Environmental Link: What message do you feel is important to communicate on Earth Day? What images would you use to communicate this message?

Para hispanohablantes

These four murals were done for different reasons. Write a few lines about how you think the murals are different.

▶▶▶ INTERNET LINK

Chicano Murals http://latino.sscnet.ucla.edu:80/murals/Sparc/sparctour.html

Objectives

Cultural: to learn about Hispanic muralists and their work
Reading Strategy: to identify main ideas using photos, titles, and captions

Related Components

Activity Book	Audio Tapes
p. 133	Adelante: 12A

GETTING STARTED

Have students compare the murals in this and the previous lesson. What are their themes? What are their messages?

Background

Altamira is located in the north of Spain near the city of Santander. The cave contains 150 paintings of animals that were done sometime about 14,000 B.C. The artists' reasons for making these paintings are not known. The paintings were discovered in 1875.

Diego Rivera celebrated Mexican workers and peasants with a style of simple forms and strong colors. With José Orozco and David Siquieros, he was a leader of the most important muralist movement of the 20th century, influencing artists from Jackson Pollock to Víctor Ochoa.
Detroit Industry is part of a series of frescoes Rivera painted on the walls of the Detroit Institute of the Arts.

Víctor Ochoa, one of the better muralists of Southern California, became known for his paintings on the Coronado Bay Bridge in his hometown of San Diego. His portrait of Geronimo depicts the Apache leader as a freedom fighter rather than the evil renegade of dime novels.

DEL MUNDO HISPANO

Los murales
Una tradición hispana

Los murales son un medio de comunicación visual típico de la tradición cultural hispana. En Los Ángeles, Miami o Nueva York, donde viven muchos hispanos, puedes ver murales por todas partes.°

Los primeros muralistas fueron° los hombres y mujeres prehistóricos. Ellos pintaron animales y personas en las paredes de

▲ Éste es uno de los dibujos más antiguos del mundo. Está en Altamira, en el norte de España.

las cavernas. Hoy día, algunos murales representan la sociedad o la historia de un país. Otros expresan una protesta popular.

Diego Rivera
México (1886-1957)

El mexicano Diego Rivera es uno de los muralistas más famosos de este siglo.

▲ Este mural, *Detroit Industry* (1932-33) es una de las obras más importantes de Diego Rivera en Estados Unidos. Está en Detroit y representa la industria del automóvil en esa ciudad.

fueron *were*
por todas partes *everywhere*

272

DISCUSS

Suggestions for discussion:

Los murales Una tradición hispana

¿Qué es un medio de comunicación visual?
¿Quiénes fueron los primeros muralistas?
¿Qué pintaron? ¿Dónde?
¿Por qué pinta murales la gente de hoy?
¿Qué representan los murales que pintan?

Archaeology Link: Do you know of other unusual paintings, sculptures, or other works made by people of the past? Use an encyclopedia to find out why they were made.
Examples: the pyramids of the Egyptians, Aztecs, and Maya

▲ Este mural de Ben Valenzuela representa la importancia de la música a lo largo de° la historia. Está en el George Washington Middle School, en Long Beach, California.

Los murales de Rivera ilustran la historia y la cultura de su país.

Rivera hizo varios murales en las paredes de edificios públicos de México. Su idea era crear un arte para todos. Rivera también pintó muchos murales en Estados Unidos. Su influencia sobre los muralistas de este país es muy importante.

Víctor Ochoa
San Diego (1948)

Víctor Ochoa es uno de los muralistas más conocidos° del movimiento de arte chicano° de San Diego. Uno de los murales más famosos

de Ochoa se llama *Gerónimo*, en honor al héroe de los apaches. Está en el Centro Cultural de la Raza, en San Diego.

Murales en las escuelas

En muchas escuelas hay murales hechos° por artistas conocidos o por los estudiantes. Así los jóvenes muestran° su creatividad y expresan sus ideas.

Este mural en la calle Elvira, está en un vecindario hispano de Los Ángeles. ▶

a lo largo de *throughout*
chicano *Mexican-American*
conocidos *known*

hechos *made*
muestran *(they) show*

273

Diego Rivera

¿Quién es Diego Rivera?
¿Qué ilustran los murales de Diego Rivera?
¿Para quién es el arte de Diego Rivera?
¿Dónde hay murales de Diego Rivera?
¿Quién es un muralista de Estados Unidos?

Culture Link: What aspect of your culture would you illustrate in a mural?

Víctor Ochoa

¿Dónde están los murales de Víctor Ochoa?
¿Era hispano Gerónimo?
¿Qué héroe te gustaría pintar en un mural?

Murales en las escuelas
¿Por qué hay murales en las escuelas?
¿Hay murales en tu escuela?
¿En qué lugar de tu escuela te gustaría ver un mural?

Architecture Link: What are murals good for? Do you think all public buildings should have murals inside? Outside?

CHECK

• *¿Qué son los murales?*
• *¿Quiénes pintaron estos murales?*
• *¿Qué muestran estos murales?*

LOG BOOK
Some murals show heroes, some show important events, others show everyday people. Write a paragraph explaining who or what you would choose to make a mural about, and say why.

Para hispanohablantes

Place large pieces of paper on opposite sides of the wall. Describe an image using the *Vocabulario Temático*. (You may want to prepare a small sketch and write down the description beforehand.) Have two volunteers draw the image you described. Which depiction has all the things you mentioned in it?

▶▶▶ INTERNET LINK

Diego Rivera Web Museum http://www. diegorivera.com/
Chicano Mural Tour http://latino.sscnet. ucla.edu:80/murals/Sparc/sparctour.html

These activities can be done as classwork or as homework.

Objectives
Organizing Skills: using lists to organize information
Communication Skills: speaking about preferences and expressing opinions

Related Components

Activity Book p. 134	Assessment Portfolio: p. 41-42

ACTIVITIES

1. Los murales
Individual Activity Use the graphic organizer to arrange information about the murals on the preceding pages.
Note: Make up titles where necessary*.
Possible Answers:

Título
1. *Detroit Industry*
2. *Historia de México*
3. *Dedicated to the L.E.S.*
4. *Jazz**
5. *El día de la tierra**
6. *El animal**
7. *La música**

Artista
1. Diego Rivera   2. Diego Rivera
3. Chico   4. Chico
5. *Anónimo*   6. *Anónimo*
7. Ben Valenzuela

Tema
1. *el trabajo*   2. *la historia*
3. *la gente*   4. *la música*
5. *la tierra*   6. *un animal*
7. *la música*

¿Qué ves?
1. *máquinas, hombres*
2. *hombres, banderas, un edificio*
3. *una mujer bailando*
4. *músicos, guitarra, saxofón, piano*
5. *plantas*
6. *un animal*
7. *músicos, edificios, árboles*

Colores
1. *azul, blanco, verde, gris*
2. *negro, blanco, rojo, amarillo, marrón*
3. *verde, negro, rojo, amarillo, marrón, anaranjado, morado*
4. *amarillo, anaranjado, blanco, verde, rojo, marrón*
5. *rojo, anaranjado, amarillo, morado*

6. *negro, marrón, anaranjado*
7. *azul, verde, rojo, amarillo, marrón, anaranjado, negro, blanco*

2. Sobre los murales
Pair Activity Which mural do you like the most? Which the least? Say why. Talk about what you see there: the colors, landscape, themes, drawings.
Possible Answer:
El mural que más me gusta es el animal prehistórico en la caverna de Altamira. El dibujo y los colores son muy realistas. El tema de los animales es interesante.

3. Compruébalo
Individual Activity Say which sentences are true and which are false.
Answers: **1.** *Falso. Tony García trabaja en Nueva York.* **2.** *Cierto.* **3.** *Falso. Diego Rivera hizo muchos murales en Estados Unidos.* **4.** *Cierto.*

DESPUÉS DE LEER

❶ Los murales
Usa una gráfica para organizar la información sobre los murales. Sigue el modelo.

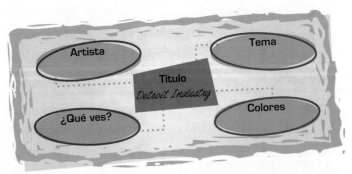

❷ Sobre los murales
Habla con tu compañero(a). ¿Qué mural te gusta más? ¿Qué mural te gusta menos? Di por qué. Incluye:

- los colores
- qué ves
- el paisaje
- los temas
- los dibujos

❸ Compruébalo
Di cuáles de las siguientes oraciones son ciertas y cuáles son falsas.

1. El muralista Tony García trabaja en Puerto Rico.

2. Víctor Ochoa es un artista del movimiento de arte chicano de San Diego.

3. Diego Rivera nunca hizo murales fuera de México.

4. Los dibujos de Altamira son muy antiguos.

274

1. DESCRIBE UN CUADRO

En parejas, hagan una investigación sobre un mural o un cuadro de un artista hispano. Busquen información en libros o enciclopedias. Escriban una pequeña descripción y preséntenla a la clase. Incluyan:

- por qué lo escogieron
- dónde está
- quién es el/la artista
- cómo es y qué colores tiene
- cuándo lo pintó
- qué representa

2. SU TELEGUÍA

En grupos, escriban su página ideal de la teleguía. Incluyan todos los programas que les gustaría ver y una pequeña descripción de cada uno. Pueden inventar sus propios programas.

| 12:00 p.m. | Programa de cocina: Hoy, pastel de chocolate |
| 12:30 p.m. | Dibujos animados: *Los Simpsons* |

3. ESCRIBE UNA POSTAL

La estación de radio WACG-FM tiene un programa de concursos. El premio° es un televisor. Para ganar, tienes que escribir una postal explicando° por qué WACG-FM es tu radio favorita o por qué el Canal 13 es tu canal favorito. La respuesta más original gana el premio.

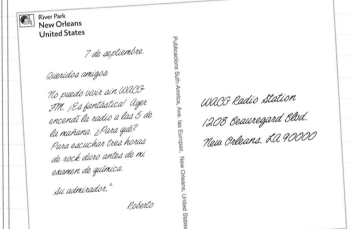

River Park
New Orleans
United States

Publicacions Suth-America, Ave. las Europas, New Orleans, United States

7 de septiembre.

Queridos amigos

No puedo vivir sin WACG-FM. ¡Es fantástica! Ayer encendí la radio a las 5 de la mañana. ¿Para qué? Para escuchar tres horas de rock duro antes de mi examen de química.

Su admirador.°

Roberto

WACG Radio Station
1208 Beauregard Blvd.
New Orleans, LA 90000

el admirador *fan*
explicando *explaining*
el premio *prize*

275

Objectives
- to practice writing
- to use vocabulary from this unit

Related Components

Activity Book	Assessment
p. 135	Portfolio: p.41-42

ACTIVITIES

1. Describe un cuadro
Pair Activity Students will research a mural or painting by a Hispanic artist and write a description to present to the class. Include:
- why you chose it
- who the artist is
- when it was painted
- where it is
- what it is like and what its colors are
- what it represents

2. Su teleguía
Group Activity Students will write their ideal television-guide magazine page. They should include all the programs they would like to see, and add a brief description of each. They can invent their own programs.
Answers: See model on student page

3. Escribe una postal
Individual Activity Write a postcard to WACG-FM to say why it is your favorite radio station (or why Channel 13 is your favorite television station). The most original response will win a prize.
Edit: Exchange cards and edit each other's work. Circle words you think are misspelled. Review with your partner.
Present: Read your final draft aloud to a new partner. The class may want to give a prize for the most original answer.
Answers: See model on student page.

PORTFOLIO
Encourage students to select one of these assignments to add to their portfolios.

Para hispanohablantes

After you finish your own letter, help other students edit.

Objectives

Communicative: to listen to and understand directions
Cultural: to learn about murals
TPR: to have students create their own murals

Related Components

Assessment	Transparencies
Portfolio: p. 41-42	Unit 5: Project
CD ROM	**Video:**
Unit 5: Manos a la obra	**Tape/Book** Unit 5: Seg. 5

Search to frame 1280320

Materials

1. a drawing
2. colored paints
3. paintbrushes
4. a pencil
5. charcoal
6. a short ruler
7. a long ruler or T-square
8. brown wrapping paper
9. see-.through paper
10. adhesive tape

GETTING STARTED

In this exercise, students should use their eyes more than their ears. They should concentrate on what they see and listen only for clues.
You may wish to assign the creation of a suitable drawing as homework.
Before students open their books, try a brief TPR session in which you have them draw a pattern of squares. This will introduce several key words. Show the mural-making segment of the Unit 5 video.

DISCUSS

Talk briefly about the concept of scale vs. size. Murals are usually large, but their subjects may be the same size as they really are. In the mural on these pages, the humans are more or less life-sized, but the bird is a different scale.
Point out that scale is related to both an English word that is spelled the same way but means "to climb up", and to the Spanish word *escalera,* which means staircase.

276

PINTAR A LO GRANDE°

Los murales siempre han sido° un importante medio de comunicación. En los años sesenta, muchos artistas norteamericanos pintaron murales sobre la paz° y los problemas sociales. Estos murales decoran las calles de muchas ciudades de Estados Unidos.

TE TOCA A TI

MATERIALES:

un dibujo

pinturas de colores

pinceles

un lápiz

carboncillo°

una regla corta

una regla larga

papel marrón fuerte

papel transparente°

cinta adhesiva

Ahora tú vas a hacer un mural. Piensa en un tema interesante. Haz un dibujo sobre ese tema en un papel.

Busca una pared. Puede ser una pared interior o exterior. Puede estar en tu escuela o en la calle. **¡No te olvides de pedir permiso!**° Antes de empezar, tienes que limpiar° la pared.

Un mural en una calle de Nueva York. ▶

a lo grande *on a grand scale*
el carboncillo *charcoal*
han sido *(they) have been*
limpiar *to clean*

el papel transparente *see-through paper*
la paz *peace*
pedir permiso *to ask for permission*

276

Pintar a lo grande

Read the texts aloud or have a volunteer read them aloud.
Continue with steps 1-4. Make sure that students understand all the commands. Pay particular attention to *cuadrícula/cuadrado,* and *escoge.* Explain the point of drawing the squares on the transparent paper by drawing a small square with a letter or other design and extending it to a larger one.

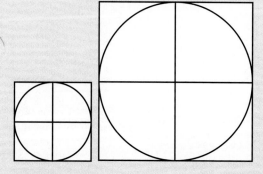

1 Pon el papel transparente sobre tu dibujo. Con la regla corta, cuadricula° el papel transparente. Copia° tu dibujo en el papel transparente. Copia sólo las formas más grandes.

2 Con la regla larga, cuadricula la pared. Haz el mismo° número de cuadrados° que hiciste en el papel transparente. En el papel marrón haz varios cuadrados del mismo tamaño° que los cuadrados de la pared .

3 Escoge una parte de tu dibujo y cópiala en el papel marrón. Usa el mismo número de cuadrados. Corta el dibujo que hiciste en el papel marrón. Pégalo en la pared, sobre el cuadrado correspondiente.° Con el carboncillo, dibújalo en la pared. Haz lo mismo con los otros cuadrados.

4 Pinta las áreas más grandes primero y después las áreas más pequeñas. Y ahora... ¡invita a tus amigos a admirar tu mural!

copia *copy*
correspondiente *corresponding*
cuadrados *squares*
cuadricula *divide into squares*
mismo *same*
tamaño *size*

277

Using the directions in the book, lead students through the creation of a mural. If the space, time, and/or materials for creating a mural are not available, you may wish to use large pieces of wrapping paper.
1. Act out the process as you read aloud the instructions.
2. After you have done this several times, invite volunteers to do it as you read aloud the directions.
3. Do this as TPR with the whole class.

CHECK

Use the commands in other sentences or instructions and have students perform as you say them.

PORTFOLIO
Write the answer to Activity 1 in *Después de leer* using your group's information.

Para hispanohablantes

Pretend you are an art critic writing about one of the murals in the *Adelante*. Write a detailed description for a reader who has never seen it.

Objectives
• to identify main ideas
• to relate the study of Spanish to other disciplines

Related Components

Activity Book p. 136	Audio Tapes Adelante: 12B
Assessment Portfolio: p. 41-42	Video: Tape/Book Unit 5: Seg. 4

Search to frame 1264612

Soñando con otro país

About Dreaming in Cuban
Cristina Garcia was born in Havana in 1958, and grew up in New York City. She has worked as a correspondent for *Time*. Her novel tells the story of several generations of a Cuban family. The grandmother, who supports the revolution, remains in Cuba, while her daughter flees to New York City. The novel presents aspects of Cuban culture in both countries.

Possible Answers:
• *Cristina García cuenta las aventuras de una adolescente en Nueva York.*
Answers will vary.

Activity
Have students skim the reading for the main idea of the passage. Emphasize reading for general ideas. Ask such questions as:
¿Qué hace la protagonista?
¿A qué nos ayuda la novela?
Guide students through a more detailed reading, focusing on unknown words. Have students answer the questions based on their personal experiences.

▶▶▶INTERNET LINKS

Castillo de San Marcos http://www.nps.gov:80/parklists/index/casa.html
Nuyorican Poets Cafe http://www.metrobeat.com:80/nyc/locations/lbo0047.html
Latinolink http://www.latinolink.com:80/lifv1i1.shtml
Chicano/LatinoNet http//latino.sscnet.ucla.edu

LITERATURA
SOÑANDO° CON OTRO PAÍS

Millones de personas en Estados Unidos sueñan° con su país de origen. Éste es el caso de Cristina García, una joven escritora cubano-americana. Cristina escribió su primera novela, *Dreaming in Cuban*, en inglés. En ella, nos cuenta las aventuras de una adolescente en Nueva York, las dificultades con sus padres, y su viaje a Cuba para buscar a su abuela. Es una novela muy divertida sobre dos culturas muy diferentes: la cubana y la estadounidense. Con su libro, Cristina nos ayuda a comprender la experiencia de los inmigrantes en este país.

• ¿Qué cuenta Cristina García en *Dreaming in Cuban*?

• ¿Tienes un amigo o amiga de otro país? ¿De dónde es? ¿Cuál es su experiencia en este país?

HISTORIA
SAN AGUSTÍN, FLORIDA

S¿Sabías que la ciudad más antigua de Estados Unidos está en Florida? Se llama San Agustín, y ya existía° cuando los ingleses llegaron a Virginia. La fundó° el español Pedro Menéndez de Avilés en 1565. Fue la primera° ciudad que los europeos establecieron° en Estados Unidos. Allí está también la fortaleza más antigua del país: el Castillo de San Marcos.

• ¿Cuándo fundaron tu ciudad? ¿Quién la fundó?

• ¿Cuál es el edificio más antiguo de tu ciudad? Según tu opinión, ¿tenemos que conservar los edificios antiguos? ¿Por qué?

278

establecieron *established*	soñando (soñar) *dreaming*
fundó *founded*	sueñan *dream*
primera *first*	ya existía *it already existed*

San Augustín, Florida

About St. Augustine
This fortress-city was strategically located to protect the route of Spanish treasure ships. Sir Francis Drake burned it in 1586, long before the Castillo de San Marcos was built to defend it (1696).
The modern city is very small, with a population in the low thousands, but its history and well-preserved period houses attract tourists year-round.

Possible Answers:
• Answers will vary.
• Answers will vary.

Activity
Have students skim, then do a more extensive reading. Ask:
¿Por qué es importante San Agustín?
¿Quiénes establecieron la ciudad?
¿Qué es el castillo San Marcos?
Follow with an intensive reading, and answer questions about vocabulary.

INFORMÁTICA LATINONET

LatinoNet es la primera red de comunicación por computadoras para la comunidad hispana. Conecta organizaciones, profesionales, académicos y estudiantes de todo el país. Este servicio está a disposición° del público por medio de° America Online. Ofrece información sobre organizaciones, actividades culturales, becas° para estudiantes, oportunidades de empleo° y mucho más.

- ¿Qué es LatinoNet? ¿Qué ofrece?

- ¿Qué información te gustaría obtener de LatinoNet? ¿Por qué?

TEATRO CAFÉ CALIENTE

En 1992 un grupo de artistas chicanos de Los Ángeles fundaron Café Caliente. Según Eddie Ayala, líder de la banda de rock Aztec Radio y director de Café Caliente, el propósito° de Café Caliente "es estimular un ambiente de teatro en la comunidad chicana". Entre los artistas de Café Caliente están Guillermo Gómez-Peña, ganador° del Genius Grant de la Fundación MacArthur, y la actriz Yarelli Arizmendi.

- ¿Quiénes fundaron Café Caliente?

- ¿Cuál es el propósito de Café Caliente?

- En tu opinión, ¿es importante la función de Café Caliente? ¿Por qué?

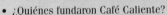

las becas *scholarships*
el empleo *job*
está a disposición *is available*

el ganador *winner*
por medio de *through*
el propósito *purpose*

279

Café Caliente

About Café Caliente
Café Caliente, say its founders, is "an event, not a place." The cafe now offers about ten events a year. Ayala, a Chicano musician, has worked in such groups as Blondie and the Sex Pistols. Mexican-born Gómez Peña is a performance artist who tries to bring together the Latino and Anglo worlds.

Possible Answers:
- *Un grupo de artistas chicanos fundaron Café Caliente.*
- *El propósito es estimular un ambiente de teatro en la comunidad chicana.*
- Answers will vary.

Other Questions
Guide students through the reading in the same way as in the previous activities.
¿De qué grupo de músicos es el director de Café Caliente?
¿Conoces a la actriz Yarelli Arizmendi?

LatinoNet

About LatinoNet
LatinoNet was one of the first efforts to establish a Hispanic presence on the Internet. Other, more extensive, projects have appeared with the growth of the World Wide Web, among them Latinolink and UCLA's Chicano/LatinoNet. Also, the universities and governments of many Spanish-speaking countries have established many new sites.

Possible Answers:
- *Es una red de comunicación por computadora para la comunidad hispana. Ofrece información.*
- Answers will vary.

Activity
Guide students through the reading following the format used earlier. Invite them to share their Internet experiences and to discuss ways in which Internet can be useful for the study of Spanish.

6 PERÚ, ARGENTINA, CHILE: VIAJE AL SUR

✦ In this unit

We fly to South America on a trip that takes us to Peru, Argentina, and Chile. The trip requires a lot of special planning because we're exchange students (Chapter 11), but we couldn't be happier about Peru, the country we choose to be our home away from home (Chapter 12). We've listened to experienced exchange students and studied the literature, but nothing really prepares us for the thrill of getting off the jet in Lima. And from Lima we head for the Andes to explore the mile-high baroque splendor of Cuzco.

During our stay in South America, we visit three mysterious places that are featured in both the unit video and the *Adelante* section of the student book. Our first stop is Chile's Easter Island, where blank-eyed stone monoliths stare out at the surrounding Pacific Ocean. Then we survey the Nazca Lines in southern Peru, white chalk scars that can only be seen from the air. Who put them here, and for whom? From Cuzco, we take a short steep train ride even higher into the Andes, and get off at the Inca empire's holiest city, Machu Picchu, all stone and cloud, and lost to the world at large until rediscovered by archaeologist Hiram Bingham in 1911.

VIDEO LINKS

Text	Video Segment
Unit Overview Unit Opener	**1. Introduction to Peru, Argentina, Chile** A quick tour of three South American countries
Chapter 11	**2. Viajes de intercambio** Getting ready to leave the US as an exchange student: listening to experienced exchange students, asking questions, choosing a country grammar: the verbs **decir** and **pedir**; **tú** commands with irregular verbs
Chapter 12	**3. Bienvenidos a Perú** Sightseeing words, meeting the family you'll stay with, looking around Lima, traveling to Cuzco, visiting the market grammar: the present progressive tense; the verbs **ser** and **estar**; superlatives **más** and **-ísimo**
Adelante	**4. Adelante** Easter Island, the Nazca Lines, Machu Picchu
Manos a la obra	**5. Manos a la obra** How to make a Peruvian-style papier-maché mask

Peru

Situated on the west coast of South America, Peru was once the center of the huge Inca empire that extended into modern-day Bolivia, Chile, and Ecuador. The rulers of this sophisticated civilization were great conquerors and builders of fabulous cities. The Inca empire fell to Spanish conquistador Francisco Pizarro in 1533. After being ruled by Spain for almost 300 years, Peru gained independence in 1824 following a bloody revolution led by Simón Bolívar. Its political history has been checkered by revolts and dictatorships, but Peru is now a constitutional republic with an elected parliament and president. Poverty is high, especially among the Indian population. And devastating earthquakes have exacerbated the difficulties faced by the people of the Land of the Incas.

Chile

Averaging 100 miles in width but a full 2,600 miles long, Chile faces the Pacific Ocean to the west and is bordered by the Andes Mountains to the east. There are deserts, rain forests, fertile farmlands, enormous lakes, and numerous rivers; far to the south, in the harsh Antarctic region, there are snow-covered glaciers, fjords, and islands. Chile achieved independence in 1818 and has had a troubled political history ever since. Salvador Allende, the first Marxist leader to be elected democratically, was overthrown and killed in 1973. There followed almost 15 years of repressive military rule. Now an elected president and parliament lead the country peacefully.

Argentina

The heart of this vast concentration of natural resources is the capital city of Buenos Aires. Called the Paris of South America for its elegance and active cultural life, Buenos Aires was founded in the mid-16th century and early in the 19th century became the first Latin American city to rebel against Spain. Argentina achieved independence in 1816. A key feature of the country's landscape is the Pampas, an enormous grassy plain stretching 300 miles southward from Buenos Aires. Ideal for grazing cattle, the Pampas has made Argentina the beef ranch of South America. Argentina's most controversial leader was Juan Perón (1895-1974). He and his charismatic wife Eva were adored by some and hated by others during the troublesome years after World War II when he ruled the country. Despite political upheavals, Argentina has maintained a romantic image derived from Pampas cowboys and the tango-dancing sophisticates of Buenos Aires.

Los caminos de los Incas

HISTORY CONNECTION

Objective
- to explore the Inca empire's unique network of roads and waterways

Use
after begining Unit 6

Materials
- TRB Activity Support Page 21, *Caminos y ríos del imperio inca* (maps)
- world globe

Preparation
- Share the FYI and anything else you know about Inca transportation and communication.

Activity
- Pass out the maps. Have students use the globe to identify modern-day countries that would have been part of the Inca empire.
- Ask students why they think good roads and navigable rivers were important to the Incas. Would the roads and rivers have become more or less important as the empire expanded? Why?
- Now ask students why they think the roads and rivers were important to the Spaniards. How might South American history have been different if small numbers of armored men on horseback hadn't been able to move quickly?

FYI
Stretching along 2,500 miles of the Andes mountain range, the Inca empire included parts of modern-day Peru, Chile, Ecuador, and Bolivia. This vast empire would have been impossible to rule without innumerable rivers and the 14,000 miles of roads and highways that made possible trade and communication between mountains, jungles, and desert shores. The Inca people navigated the rivers on reed or balsa rafts and, although the wheel was unknown to them, their well-built stone roads were used by runners, litter-carriers, and llama trains. When the Spaniards came with horses, cannons, and carriages, they found waiting a transportation and communication system that suited their plans of conquest perfectly. The Inca empire fell in 1533.

Papas arequipeñas

HANDS ON: COOKING

Objective
- to prepare and eat a spicy potato dish from Arequipa, a city in southern Peru

Use
after begining Unit 6

Ingredients
- 2 lbs. small boiling potatoes (e.g., new potatoes)
- 1/2 cup roasted peanuts
- 2 or 3 jalapeño or serrano peppers, seeded
- 1/2 cup half and half
- salt and pepper
- 1/2 cup grated Muenster cheese
- 3 green onions (including some of the green)
- 6 hard-boiled eggs cut in half
- 1/2 cup black olives
- cilantro

Supplies
- saucepan
- measuring cup
- food processor or blender
- serving dish

Preparation
- Scrub potatoes and boil.
- While potatoes are boiling, combine peanuts, peppers, half and half, salt, pepper, cheese, and onions in a food processor or blender. Purée until sauce is the thickness of mayonnaise.
- When potatoes are tender, drain, cut in half, and arrange cut side down on a warm platter.
- Pour sauce over potatoes.
- Garnish with hard-boiled eggs, olives, and cilantro. Serve at room temperature as an *aperitivo* or *entrada*. Serves 6.

FYI
Potatoes, the world's fourth largest food crop, originated in Peru and have been cultivated there for about 8,000 years. Peruvian *papas* may be round or fingerlike, small as cherries or big as a fist, and either pink, white, blue, yellow, red, brown, or purple. Flavors vary from almost sweet with a hint of cinnamon, to starchy, waxy, nutty, or bitter. Quite a few of these varieties are now available in the United States.

El desierto de Atacama

GEOGRAPHY CONNECTION

Objective
• to explore Chile's Atacama Desert

Use
after begining Unit 6

Materials
• Transparency Unit 6, *El desierto de Atacama*
• overhead projector
• TRB Activity Support Page 22, *El desierto de Atacama* (fact sheet)
• TRB Activity Support Page 23, *El desierto de Atacama* (work sheet)
• posterboard

Preparation
• Have students volunteer any information they already have about Chile's Atacama Desert. Write the information on the chalkboard.

Activity
• Project transparency and read fact sheet.
• Distribute the work sheet and have students fill in the blanks.
• Form two groups. Have each group create a posterboard chart for the facts they've gathered.
• Have a member from each group come to the front, share a fact about the desert, and write it on the chart.
• When there are no more facts to share, display the two charts for reference and review.
• Which group has the most facts? Which group's chart shows the facts most clearly?

Bailamos el tango

HANDS ON: DANCING

Objectives
• to explore the history of the Argentinian tango
• to learn some basic tango steps

Use
after begining Unit 6

Materials
• TRB Activity Support Page 24, *Bailamos el tango* (dance steps)
• TRB Activity Support Page 25, *Huellas del tango* (male footprints)
• TRB Activity Support Page 26, *Huellas del tango* (female footprints)
• CD or audiocassette player

Preparation
• Bring in tango recordings. Share the FYI below.

Activity
• Clear space. Distribute tango steps and footprints.
• Tape footprints to floor in the pattern shown.
• Have a volunteer couple follow the tango instructions without music. Other couples follow.
• Put on a recording and turn up the volume.

FYI
The slow, sensuous tango appeared in Buenos Aires around 1880. By 1915 it was the rage of Paris, London, and Rome. During the 1920s and '30s you could see and hear the tango in almost every bar and club in Buenos Aires. Now the San Thelmo district, with its narrow streets, old buildings, and late-night cafés, is one of the few places where the tango reigns as it did during the heyday of the legendary singer Carlos Gardél.

PERÚ, ARGENTINA, CHILE: VIAJE AL SUR

Objectives
- to introduce Peru, Argentina, and Chile
- to develop cross-cultural awareness

Related Components

Transparencies Unit 6	Video: Tape/Book Unit 6: Seg. 1

Search to frame 1312125

GETTING STARTED

Does anyone know someone who has been an exchange student? What was it like? What kinds of things would students expect to do as exchange students? Why do students study abroad?

Using the Video

Show Segment 1 of the Unit 6 video, an introduction to Peru, Argentina, and Chile.

Using the Transparencies

To help orient students, use the Locator Map Transparency. You may also want to use the other Unit 6 transparencies at this time.

DISCUSS

Presenting Peru, Argentina, and Chile

For more information about these countries, refer to pages 280A—280D.

Using the Text

English: After students read the introduction, ask comprehension and critical-thinking questions. For example:
Which city will we live in and which will we visit?
Have you ever seen photos of the statues on Easter Island? Can you describe them? (There is a photo on page 319.)
Spanish: Have students scan the lefthand page for unfamiliar words.
¿Qué es el Proyecto? Es cuando hacemos algo, como una piñata, ¿no?
¿Qué creen que es **Una máscara?**
¿Qué es arqueología?

UNIDAD 6

PERÚ, ARGENTINA, CHILE:

VIAJE AL SUR
En la unidad 6:

Capítulo 11	Viajes de intercambio
Capítulo 12	Bienvenidos a Perú
Adelante	**Para leer:** Misterios del Sur

Proyecto: Una máscara para ti

Otras fronteras: Idiomas, ecología, informática y geografía

280

Unit Components

Activity Book p. 137-156	Audio Book Script: p. 89-92; 97-100	CD ROM Unit 6	Transparencies Unit 6: Chapters 11-12
Assessment Oral Proficiency: p. 31-32 Listening Script: p.19-20 Chapter Tests: p. 105-116 Portfolio: p. 43-44	Activities: p. 93-96; 101-104 **Audio Tapes** Chapter: 7A, 7B Adelante: 13A, 13B Assessment: 15B Conexiones: 18B	**Conexiones** Chapters 11-12 **Cuaderno** p. 85-100 **Magazine** Juntos en América del Sur	**Tutor Pages** p. 47-54 **Video: Tape/Book** Unit 6: Segments 1-5

La cordillera de los Andes y las ruinas de Machu Picchu, en Perú.

Suppose you could take off for a country where Spanish is the primary language and spend a month, a semester, or even a year living there with a family. Just imagine the advantages of such a trip!

In this unit, you are going to explore student exchange programs to see what you have to do to plan and prepare for a trip to such South American countries as Peru, Chile and Argentina. Then you will fly to Peru, where you will meet your new Peruvian family and visit Cuzco, the ancient capital of the Incan empire. The mysterious ruins of Machu Picchu will be your next stop.

You will explore other centuries-old mysteries of South America as you try to solve the riddle of the pictures drawn in the sands of the Nazca desert. You will also encounter the giant statues of Easter Island, abandoned there hundreds of years ago. An unforgettable experience awaits you! ¡Vamos!

281

INTERDISCIPLINARY CONNECTIONS

To provide other perspectives, assign research projects like these:

Geography

How many countries are there in South America? Make a list and find them on a map. (There are 12: Argentina, Bolivia, Brazil, Chile, Colombia, Ecuador, Guyana, Paraguay, Peru, Suriname, Uruguay, and Venezuela; French Guiana is an overseas department, or province, of France)

Math

How long is Chile? How many times long is it as it is wide? (It is 2,800 miles long and 265 miles at its widest point. It is about 10 times as long as it is wide.)

Geography

Do the three countries in this unit share a common border? (Chile shares borders with Peru and Argentina.) What other countries share borders with them? (Peru: Ecuador, Colombia, Bolivia, and Brazil; Chile: Bolivia; Argentina: Bolivia, Brazil, Paraguay, and Uruguay.)

CULTURE NOTE

Machu Picchu, shown in the photo, is an ancient city perched on a terraced space between two peaks fifty miles northwest of Cuzco. The city was probably a fortress and religious center before the Spaniards arrived, and may have been the final Inca stronghold. Its existence was forgotten until an American, Hiram Bingham, encountered the ruins in 1911. The buildings are made of stone (their thatched roofs disappeared long ago). Perhaps a thousand people lived there.

Argentina, Chile, and Peru:
http://www.cibercentro.com/turismo/

	Objetivos page 283	Conversemos pages 284-285	Realidades pages 286-287	Palabras en acción pages 288-289
Comunicación	• To talk about reasons for participating in a foreign exchange program	Discuss reasons for participating in a foreign exchange program	Read text, make lists, answer questions, discuss reasons to be a foreign exchange student	Activity 2: Read cartoon, have partners discuss places they would like to visit
	• To talk about how to prepare for a trip abroad	Discuss how to prepare for a trip abroad		Activities 1, 3-8: Read cartoon, make list; discuss foreign exchange program; give advice, role-play travel agent and customer; make and label collage; write letter
	• To talk about what to do to participate	Discuss what to do in order to participate in a foreign exchange program	Read text, make lists, answer questions, discuss preparations for foreign exchange program	Activities 1, 3, 5, 7: Read cartoon, make list; discuss foreign exchange program; give advice, make and label collage
Vocabulario temático	• To know the expressions for ways to obtain travel information	Talk about different ways to obtain travel information		Activities 5, 6: Read cartoon, give advice; role-play travel agent and customer
	• To know the expressions for documents needed for travel	Talk about documents needed for travel	Read text, make lists, discuss documents needed for travel	Activities 1, 3, 5, 7: Read cartoon, make list; discuss foreign exchange program; give advice; make and label collage
	• To know the expressions for giving travel advice	Talk about some of the things needed to travel	Read text, make lists, discuss things needed to travel	Activities 1, 4-6, 8: Read cartoon, make list; discuss foreign exchange program; give advice; role-play travel agent and customer; write letter
Estructura	• To talk about what someone says: the verb *decir*		Read text, make lists, conduct survey	
	• To talk about how to ask for something: the verb *pedir*	Use *pedir* to discuss asking people for information	Read text, make lists, conduct survey	Activity 5: Read cartoon, give advice
	• To talk about telling a friend to do something: the irregular *tú* commands	Use the irregular *tú* commands to tell a friend what to take and do on a trip		Activity 5: Read cartoon, give advice to foreign exchange student
Cultura	Exploring South America as an exchange student		Background data and special expressions of Peru, Chile, and Argentina	
Integración		Enjoyable places to go, responsibilities, travel and vacation items	Locations, geographic features, places to go in a city, months of the year, enjoyable things to do	Travel items, enjoyable places to go, clothes items

Para comunicarnos mejor (1) pages 290-291	Para comunicarnos mejor (2) pages 292-293	Situaciones pages 294-295	Para resolver pages 296-297	Notes
Activity 2: Interview classmates, report to class		**Activities 1, 5: Read text, make list; write plans**	**Pasos 1, 4: Read travel brochure, list reasons to visit; make travel brochure**	
Activity 1: Discuss information needed for trip abroad	**Activities 1-3: Give travel advice; discuss preparations for trip abroad; ask for help getting ready for airport**	**Activity 3: Read text, role-play conversation**	**Pasos 2, 4: Read travel brochure, write advice; make travel brochure**	
		Activities 1-5: Read text, make lists; role-play conversation; discuss hobbies and pastimes; write plans	**Pasos 2, 4: Read travel brochure, write advice; make travel brochure**	
	Activity 1: Give travel advice	**Activity 3: Read text, role-play conversation**	**Paso 4: Read travel brochure, make travel brochure**	
		Activities 2, 3: Read text, make list; role-play conversation	**Pasos 2, 4: Read travel brochure, write advice; make travel brochure**	
	Activities 1-3: Give travel advice; discuss preparations for trip abroad; ask for help getting ready for airport	**Activities 1, 3: Read text, make list; role-play conversation**	**Pasos 2, 4: Read travel brochure, write advice; make travel brochure**	
Use all forms of *decir*. Activity 2: Interview classmates, report to class		**Activity 1: Read text, make list**		
Use all forms of *pedir*. Activities 1, 3: Discuss information needed for trip abroad, and what to order in restaurants		**Activities 1-3: Read text, make lists; role-play conversation**		
	Activities 1-3: Give travel advice; discuss preparations for trip abroad; ask for help getting ready for airport	**Activity 3: Read text, role-play conversation**	**Pasos 1-4: Read travel brochure, list reasons to visit; write advice; make travel brochure**	
Delicious foods of South America		**The Andes**	**Skiing in Argentina**	**Entérate page 298 Chilean poet Pablo Neruda**
Travel items, places to go, travel plans	Travel items, responsibilities, restrictions	Geographic features, responsibilities, travel and other items, favorite activities and sports, school courses	Locations, what to do, clothes items, numbers, sports item, activities	School subjects, numbers, dates

Mi pictografía

ART CONNECTION

Objective
- to create pictograms with pictures of items listed in Chapter 11 *Vocabulario temático*

Use
after *Palabras en acción,* pages 288–289

Materials
- magazine and newspaper pictures of items named in Chapter 11
- posterboard

Activity
- Each student brings in 8 pictures of the items named in the Chapter 11 *Vocabulario temático.*
- Students write stories 4 to 6 sentences long, leaving blanks for the words they have pictures for.
- When stories are finished and you have corrected them, have students print them in big letters on posterboard and paste their pictures in the blanks.
- Collect finished pictograms, redistribute, and have students read stories out loud, replacing pictures with Spanish words. For example, a story might begin: *Elena está en el aeropuerto. Ella va a Perú para aprender* (Spanish flag). *En su maleta lleva una* (camera) *para sacar muchas fotos y un* (cassette player). *En el bolso de mano lleva el* (passport). *Está muy* (happy face) *y saca su* (airline ticket).
- Display pictograms.

Variation
- Use this activity to review *Vocabulario temático* from other chapters.

Querida familia

WRITING CONNECTION

Objective
- to write a letter of introduction to a host family in Peru, Chile, or Argentina, using Chapter 11 *Vocabulario temático*

Use
after *Palabras en acción,* pages 288–289

Activity
- Pair students and have them write a letter to a host family in Peru, Chile, or Argentina.
- Ask them to introduce themselves and tell about their likes and dislikes, interests and hobbies, preferences in food, and anything special they want to do while visiting. After furnishing airline information and trip dates, they can ask for more information. For example:
  Querida familia Pérez:

  Me llamo Karen Johnston y tengo 15 años. Ustedes ya saben que voy a pasar con su familia seis semanas. Mis padres dicen que soy muy joven para estar fuera de casa más tiempo.

  Llego el 15 de mayo. Salgo de Nueva York en el vuelo 850 de Lan-Chile. El vuelo llega a las 4 de la tarde. ¿Pueden ir a buscarme al aeropuerto?

  Estudio español desde el sexto grado y me gusta mucho. Es mi clase favorita y siempre saco muy buenas notas. Me interesa mucho visitar Machu Picchu porque hablamos tanto de él en clase.

  Hasta pronto
      Su nueva hija y hermana,
      Karen

  P.D. Todavía no sé si allí es verano o invierno en mayo y junio. ¿Qué tipo de ropa debo llevar?
- Circulate to offer suggestions and check writing.
- Have the writers read their letters aloud and then ask the class questions based on the letters. For example:— *¿Qué quiere ver Karen?—¿A qué país va?—¿Qué no sabe Karen?*
- Display the letters and have students discuss the ones they consider most effective.

Variation
- One partner writes the student's letter and the other writes the host's response.

Lo que digo y lo que pido

Objective
- to distinguish things to say from things to ask for, using the verbs **decir** and **pedir**

Use
after *Para comunicarnos mejor,* page 290

Preparation
- Have students brainstorm places they like to go and list them on the chalkboard.

Activity
- Choose a class recorder to monitor student responses.
- Have each student select one place and tell what they say *(digo)* and what they ask for *(pido)* there. For example: John chooses *restaurante* and says:—*Cuando voy a un restaurante chino, pido arroz con pollo y verduras y digo "La comida es deliciosa."* Sandra chooses *discoteca* and says:—*Cuando voy a la discoteca pido un refresco y digo "¡Vamos a bailar!"*
- Students listen carefully and, for round 2, ask each other questions about what they heard. For example, Janice asks Eddy:—*¿Qué dice Sandra cuando va a la discoteca y qué pide?* Eddy:—*Sandra dice "¡Vamos a bailar!" y pide un refresco.* Students who answer correctly participate in the next round.
- Beside remembering what a classmate said, players in round 3 must add what they would say and ask for in the same place. For example, Starr might say:—*Cuando Sandra va a la discoteca dice "¡Vamos a bailar¡" y pide un refresco. Y cuando yo voy a la discoteca digo "¡Qué calor tengo!" y pido un vaso de agua fría.*
- Students play until they reach the end of the chalkboard list.

"Un vaso de fría, por favor."

¡Hazlo, por favor!

Objective
- to tell people to whom we are close to do things, using irregular affirmative **tú** commands

Use
after *Para comunicarnos mejor,* page 292

Activity
- On the chalkboard, list irregular forms of the verbs you want to practice. For example: **decir—di, ser—sé, hacer—haz, tener—ten, ir—ve, venir—ven, poner—pon, ver—ve, salir—sal.**
- Set the scene for students. For example: "You are at the airport before leaving on a trip to Peru as an exchange student. Here to say goodbye is a family member or friend whom you ask to take care of a few last-minute chores."
- Give students 10 minutes to jot down as many irregular *tú* commands as they can.
- When time is up, go around the room in row order and have each student give you a command to write on the chalkboard.
- Pair students and have them select 3 commands from the chalkboard to pantomime. For example: *1. Pon agua en las plantas de mi cuarto. 2. Ve a la casa de mi amigo Warren. 3. Dile que estoy en Perú.* Give them time to rehearse.
- Each pair has 3 minutes to pantomime out the commands. If they stump the class, they go again after everyone else has played. If the class guesses the commands correctly, the next pair goes. Commands already guessed can't be used again.

Variation
- Practice **tú** commands with verbs studied in earlier chapters.

VIAJES DE INTERCAMBIO

Introduce the chapter and its theme by asking students if they have ever thought about being exchange students. What do they like about the idea? Where would they most like to go? Why?

Related Components

Audio Tapes	Conexiones
Conexiones: 18B, Ch. 11	Chapter 11
	Video: Tape/Book
CD ROM	Unit 6: Seg. 2
Chapter 11	

Search to frame 1321102

 GETTING STARTED

Have students look at the photograph. Ask if they have ever visited the ruins of an ancient civilization. Ask critical thinking and comprehension questions:
Según tu opinión, ¿Por qué visitan estos chicos Machu Picchu?
¿Te gustaria visitar Machu Picchu?

Thinking About Language

You can use this opportunity to encourage your students to think about and discuss the extent and diversity of language.

Languages of Latin America
Students may have the impression that Spanish is the only language spoken in South America. These questions may expand their horizons. Assign the questions as homework or simply ask students to make educated guesses.

- How many European languages besides Spanish are the *official* languages of countries in South America?
  (Portuguese is spoken in Brazil, English in Belize, Dutch in Suriname, and French in Haiti and the department of French Guiana.)
- How many Native American languages are spoken in South America?
  (About 600 have been shown to have existed. Over 100 of them are extinct.)
- How many Native American languages are the *official* languages of countries in Latin America?
  (Spanish-speaking countries with additional official languages: Bolivia, Quechua and Aymara languages; Peru, Quechua language)
- How many languages are spoken in the world today?

Una excursión a las ruinas de Machu Picchu, en Perú.

282

There are somewhere between 3,000 and 5,000 living languages—some spoken by only a few hundred people.

Chapter Components

Activity Book	Audio Book	CD ROM	Transparencies
p. 137-146	Script: p. 89-92	Chapter 11	Chapter 11
Assessment	Activities: p. 93-96	**Conexiones**	**Tutor Pages**
Oral Proficiency: p. 31	**Audio Tapes**	Chapter 11	p. 47-50
Listening Script: p. 19	Listening: 7A	**Cuaderno**	**Video: Tape/Book**
Chapter Test: p. 105-110	Assessment: 15B, Ch. 11	p. 85-92	Unit 6: Seg. 3
	Conexiones: 18B, Ch. 11	**Magazine**	
		Juntos en América del Sur	

Objetivos

COMUNICACIÓN

To talk about:

- reasons for participating in a foreign exchange program
- what to do to participate
- how to prepare for a trip abroad

CULTURA

To learn about:

- exchange programs in Argentina, Chile and Peru
- the Chilean poet Pablo Neruda

VOCABULARIO TEMÁTICO

To know the expressions for:

- ways to obtain travel information
- documents needed for travel
- giving travel advice

ESTRUCTURA

To talk about:

- what someone says: the verb *decir*
- how to ask for something: the verb *pedir*
- telling a friend to do something: the irregular *tú* commands

¿SABES QUE...?

The most effective and fun way to explore the language and culture of other countries may be as an exchange student. Several organizations sponsor exchange programs for high school students in countries such as Chile, Peru, and Argentina. Programs vary in length — from an intensive month of exposure to a year-long experience. But be sure to consult your calendar carefully before applying. Did you know that the regular school year in South America starts in March or April and lasts through December?

283

ACTIVITIES

Here are some additional activities that you may wish to use as you work through this chapter with your students.

Communication

Encourage after-class activities that may enhance student interest and proficiency. Some ideas:

- have students contact an agency that arranges student exchange programs for information on schools in South America
- have them interview local students who have been in exchange programs or foreign students who attend their school

Culture

To promote greater understanding:

- encourage interested students to look into exchange programs
- have students go to a travel agency for information about South America
- show the video that accompanies Unit 6 of this textbook

Vocabulary

To reinforce vocabulary, have students:

- create humorous travel skits
- locate travel brochures or Internet information in Spanish

Structure

To reinforce forms of **decir** and **pedir,** and irregular **tú** commands:

- have students make humorous captions for photos using **decir**
- circles of four or more ask for and order things (the game is more fun if they intentionally mess up orders)
  A: *Me gustaría tomar un helado de vainilla.*
  B: *El señor pide un helado de chocolate.*
  C: *Haz una enchilada de chocolate.*

►►►INTERNET LINK

Quechua Homepage http://www.cs. brandeis.edu/~barry/Quechua.html

Communicative Objectives

- to talk about exchange programs
- to ask for travel information, using the present tense of **pedir**
- to give advice, using irregular **tú** commands

Related Components

Activity Book p. 137	Cuaderno p. 85
Audio Book Script: Seg. 1	Transparencies Ch. 11: Conversemos
Audio Tapes Listening: 7A, Seg. 1	

GETTING STARTED

Ask students what they would like to do or study—in addition to Spanish—if they took part in an exchange program.

ACTIVITIES

These activities give students an opportunity to begin communicating with each other and with you, focusing on the theme and objectives of the chapter. The activities can be used as oral class activities, or, if you prefer, you can pair students to achieve more interaction.

¿Te gustaría ir de intercambio al extranjero? ¿Por qué?
Class activity to review common phrases and introduce vocabulary. Discuss the vocabulary phrases and ask the questions in the title. Have students say why they would like to go. Encourage the use of alternative answers including why they would *not* like to go.

¿A quién le pides información para el viaje?
Class activity to review indirect-object pronouns and introduce **pedir**. Read aloud the question and the example. As you model the other three questions and answers, make sure that everyone knows what these people do.
Possible Questions and Statements:
¿A quién le pides información para los viajes de intercambio?
Le pido información a la representante de la agencia de intercambio.

CONVERSEMOS

LOS VIAJES DE INTERCAMBIO Y TÚ

Habla con tu compañero(a).

¿TE GUSTARÍA IR DE INTERCAMBIO AL EXTRANJERO? ¿POR QUÉ?

Sí, porque me interesa aprender bien otro idioma.

Me gustaría...   Quiero...   Me interesa...

- aprender bien otro idioma
  (to learn another language well)

- conocer otras costumbres
  (to get to know other customs)

- conocer otros jóvenes
  (to meet other young people)

- divertirme *(to have fun)*

¡Me encantaría ir de viaje!
(I would love to go on a trip!)

¿A QUIÉN LE PIDES INFORMACIÓN PARA EL VIAJE?

Le pido información a la agente de viajes.
(I ask the travel agent for information.)

- el/la agente de viajes *(travel agent)*

- el/la representante de la agencia de intercambio
  (exchange program representative)

- el/la representante del consulado
  (consulate representative)

- el/la consejero(a) de mi escuela
  (school counselor)

284

¿A quién le pides información sobre el país donde quieres estudiar?
Le pido información al representante del consulado.
¿De qué consulado es?
Del consulado de Chile.
¿A quién le pides información sobre las materias que tienes que estudiar?
Le pido información a la consejera de mi escuela.
¿Cómo se llama la consejera?
Se llama señora Pardo.

Reaching All Students

For Auditory Learners
Pronounce a word and have students compete to find it on these pages.

For Visual Learners
Make flash cards using the commands in section 4. Partners quiz each other.

For Kinesthetic Learners
Have volunteers take turns acting out the commands.

¿QUÉ TIENES QUE HACER PARA PARTICIPAR EN UN PROGRAMA DE INTERCAMBIO?

Tengo que hacer los trámites.
(I have to do the paperwork.)

❑ llenar la solicitud *(to fill out the application form)*

❑ pedir cartas de recomendación
(to ask for letters of recommendation)

❑ sacar el pasaporte / la visa *(to get a passport / visa)*

❑ hacer los trámites *(to do the paperwork)*

SI UN AMIGO O UNA AMIGA VA DE VIAJE, ¿QUÉ CONSEJOS LE DAS?

Lleva...

 sólo una maleta

 los documentos

 el pasaje

 un bolso de mano

 cheques de viajero

 la cámara

Antes de viajar:

Cambia dinero.
(Exchange money.)

Haz la maleta.
(Pack your suitcase.)

Pon tu nombre en la maleta.
(Put your name on the suitcase.)

Haz la reserva de avión.
(Make your plane reservation.)

Haz el itinerario.
(Plan the itinerary.)

Sal temprano.
(Leave early.)

En el país:

Respeta las costumbres.
(Respect the customs.)

Sé cortés.
(Be courteous.)

285

¿Qué tienes que hacer para participar en un programa de intercambio?
Class activity to review **tener que** and introduce paperwork phrases. First ask students what paperwork they would expect to have to do, then model these sentences. Pick out groups of four students and ask them to volunteer to share the paperwork.
Q: *¿Qué vas a hacer tú?*
A: *Voy a hacer los trámites.*
After a few times, change the rules and ask students to volunteer another student for one of the jobs.
Q: *¿Quién tiene que sacar las visas?*
A: *Jorge tiene que sacar las visas.*
Q: *¿Y qué debe hacer Marta?*
A: *Marta debe hablar con el representante de la agencia de intercambio.*

Si un amigo o una amiga va de viaje, ¿qué consejos le das?
Class activity to introduce irregular **tú** commands and chapter vocabulary. After a volunteer models each phrase, ask in English why this is good advice.
Lead the class through TPR commands and actions using this list.

CHECK

• *¿Quiéres ir de intercambio al extranjero? ¿A qué país?*

• *¿Qué tienes que pedir al representante de una agencia de intercambio para participar en el programa, una solicitud o un pasaporte?*

• *¿Cuál es la cosa más importante que tienes hacer antes de ir de viaje?*

LOG BOOK
Have students write three commands that use the verb **llevar**—and that are not found on this page.

Objectives
Communicative: to use irregular **tú** commands
Cultural: to learn about exchange programs

Related Components

Activity Book p. 138	**Audio Tapes** Listening Tape: 7A, Seg. 2
Audio Book Script: Seg. 2	**Cuaderno** p. 86

GETTING STARTED

Ask students to look at the photos. Which of these places do they think they would they prefer to live in? Why?

DISCUSS

Talk about the photographs and captions, and ask questions. Suggestions:

Descubre un mundo en español
Ask why all these sentences have exclamation marks. Was the writer excited about the program or is there another reason? Elicit the fact that these are commands, not statements, and that commands are often signaled by exclamation marks.

Cuzco (Perú)
¿En qué país está Cuzco?
¿Es cuzco ahora la capital? ¿Y antes? ¿Fue la capital? ¿De qué?
¿Adónde debes ir en Cuzco si prefieres los deportes?
¿Y si te gusta el arte?

Valdivia (Chile)
¿En qué parte de Chile está Valdivia?
¿Qué es lo más interesante de Valdivia?
¿Qué vas a llevar contigo si vas a mochilear? (una mochila)
¿Qué son Aguas Calientes y Puyehue?
¿Qué hay en Puyehue? ¿Cómo es?

Buenos Aires (Argentina)
¿Qué puedes hacer en Buenos Aires?
¿Qué quiere decir "pasear por los bosques"?
¿Qué creen que es Palermo? (un parque)
¿Qué palabra en inglés es como bárbaro?
¿Qué quiere decir bárbaro?
¿Qué otros lugares son bárbaros?

REALIDADES
GUÍA DE INTERCAMBIO ESTUDIANTIL

DESCUBRE UN Mundo EN español

¡Vive con una familia en Perú, Argentina o Chile! ¡Conoce otras culturas! ¡Practica deportes! ¡Haz nuevos amigos! ¡Aprende español!

Programas de intercambio estudiantil en América del Sur

Cuzco (Perú)
Cuzco fue la capital del imperio inca. Si te gusta el arte, visita la Plaza de Armas o los museos. Si prefieres los deportes, ven a navegar por el río Urubamba. También puedes hacer una excursión a las ruinas de Machu Picchu.

Valdivia (Chile)
La naturaleza es lo más interesante de Valdivia, una ciudad de la región de los lagos. Sal a mochilear* por los parques nacionales, como Aguas Calientes o Puyehue, con su gran volcán.

* *Expresión de Chile.*

286

Buenos Aires (Argentina)
¿Te gustaría vivir en una de las grandes ciudades del mundo? Visita Buenos Aires. Allí puedes aprender a jugar al fútbol, visitar museos y exposiciones, o pasear por los bosques de Palermo. ¡Es bárbaro!*

Información importante
La duración del intercambio es de un año. Los programas empiezan en julio, agosto o enero.

Los trámites necesarios para participar en este programa son:
- llenar la solicitud de intercambio
- sacar el pasaporte y la visa
- presentar la autorización de los padres
- presentar tres cartas de recomendación
- presentar un certificado de estudios
- presentar un certificado médico

* *Expresión de Argentina.*

Información importante
¿Cuánto tiempo tienes que estar en el programa de intercambio?
¿En qué mes te gustaría ir?
¿Qué trámites tienes que hacer?

MEETING INDIVIDUAL NEEDS

Reaching All Students

For Auditory Learners
Pairs ask each other about the reading. Write down the questions and answers after each round. Compare them with the work of other pairs.

For Kinesthetic Learners
In pairs, make a list of commands from these pages. Take turns giving and acting out commands based on these.

HABLA DE LA GUÍA

A. Dile a tu compañero(a) qué tiene que hacer para participar en el programa de intercambio.

- *llena la solicitud de intercambio*
- *saca el pasaporte*

B. Haz una lista de todas las cosas que te gustaría hacer en cada lugar.

> *Cuzco: Me gustaría estudiar la cultura del imperio inca.*
> *Valdivia: Me gustaría salir a mochilear por...*
> *Buenos Aires: Me gustaría...*

C. ¿Cuándo te gustaría ir de intercambio? ¿A qué lugar te gustaría ir? ¿Por qué? Habla con tu compañero(a).

> — *¿Cuándo te gustaría ir de intercambio?*
> — *En enero.*
> — *¿Adónde te gustaría ir?*
> — *A Chile, porque quiero ver un volcán. Y a ti, ¿adónde te gustaría ir?*

¿QUÉ OPINAS?

¿Por qué te gustaría participar en un programa de intercambio? Haz una encuesta entre tus compañeros(as). Cada uno(a) puede dar más de una respuesta. Anota las respuestas en una tabla.

ENCUESTA		
Porque quiero...	yo	la clase
aprender bien otro idioma	✓	ЖЖ
divertirme	✓	ЖЖ
conocer otras culturas		///
conocer otras costumbres		//
hacer nuevos amigos		ЖЖ //

Según la encuesta, ¿cuál es la razón principal para participar en un programa de intercambio?

287

Communicative Objectives

To talk about:

- student-exchange programs
- where you would like to go
- what you should bring
- travel advice

Related Components

Activity Book
p. 139-140
Cuaderno
p. 87-88

GETTING STARTED

Has there ever been a student-exchange fair at your school? What kinds of fairs have you had? Are they useful? How?

DISCUSS

Ask which individuals seem to be more interested in studying and which are attracted by other things the countries have to offer.

Imaginen que sólo uno de estos estudiantes va a ir a estudiar a otro país. ¿Cuál de ellos crees que va a ser? ¿Por qué?

Para hispanohablantes

Some Spanish speakers in your class may use other words or expressions. Ask them to share with the class. A few variations:

el bolso de mano: el maletín, el bulto

el certificado de estudios: la transcripción de créditos

el certificado médico: el certificado de salud

la reserva (de avión): las reservaciones

el pasaje: el boleto

los trámites: los requisitos

la visa: el visado

PALABRAS EN ACCIÓN

LA FERIA DE INTERCAMBIO ESTUDIANTIL

1 ¿Qué ves en el dibujo?

¿Qué necesitan las personas del dibujo para ir de intercambio? Haz una lista.

la visa, las cartas de recomendación,...

2 ¿Adónde te gustaría ir?

Mira los carteles de cada país. Habla con tu compañero(a) sobre dos lugares que te gustaría visitar. ¿Qué te gustaría hacer allí?

— *¿Adónde te gustaría ir?*
— *A Argentina, a esquiar en las montañas. ¿Y a ti?*
— *Yo prefiero ir a...*

3 ¿Qué vas a llevar?

Mira la lista del dibujo. ¿Qué necesitas para el viaje? Habla con tu compañero(a).

— *¿Qué vas a llevar?*
— *Una cámara. ¿Y tú?*

4 El programa de intercambio

¿Qué tienes que hacer para participar en un programa de intercambio? Habla con tu compañero(a).

— *Me interesa ir de intercambio. ¿Qué tengo que hacer?*
— *Tienes que sacar el pasaporte.*
— *Ya tengo pasaporte. ¿Qué más necesito?*

288

For students having difficulty talking about exchange programs and travel, or giving travel advice, you might consider:

- **The tutor page:** Pair the student with a native speaker or a more able student, using the tutor page.
- **Actividades:** see page 282C: *Mi pictografía*

289

 Consejos de viaje

Tu amigo(a) va a ir de intercambio al extranjero. Dale tres consejos.

- *Saca la visa.*
- *Llena la solicitud.*
- *Lleva cheques de viajero.*

 Miniteatro

Estás en una agencia de viajes. Tu compañero(a) es el/la agente de viajes. Hagan un diálogo.

Agente: *¿Adónde te gustaría ir?*
Estudiante: *A Chile. ¿Qué documentos necesito?*

 Collage

Diseña un cartel sobre un programa de intercambio. Busca fotos y dibujos en revistas y periódicos. Escribe un título para cada foto. Presenta tu cartel a la clase.

8 Tú eres el autor

Vas a ir de intercambio a vivir con una familia en otro país. Haz una lista de preguntas para ellos.

¿Qué tiempo hace allí?
¿Qué ropa tengo que llevar?

289

1. Individual Activity

Make a list of things these people need to participate in an exchange program.
Application: Make a list of the people they need to speak with before taking part in an exchange program.

2. Pair Activity

Look at the posters. Talk to your partner about two places you would like to visit. What would you like to do there?
Application: Say why you do not want to visit the other place.

3. Pair Activity

Look at the list of things you should remember to take. Talk to your partner about what you need to take on a trip.
Application: Talk about the clothing you need to take.

4. Pair Activity

Talk to your partner about what you have to do in order to participate in a student-exchange program.

5. Pair Activity

Your partner is going to be an exchange student. Give three pieces of advice.

6. Roleplay Activity

You are a client in a travel agency. Your partner is the agent. Write a dialog.
Challenge: Memorize and act out other pairs' dialogs for the class.

7. Hands-On Activity

Homework for individuals or small groups. Design a poster about exchange programs. Use newspaper and magazine pictures, and write captions. Display your poster.
Synthesis: Imagine that you went on one of the exchange programs. Write a diary entry describing one day's activities.

8. Writing Activity

You're going on an exchange program. Write a list of questions for the family you will live with in that country.

CHECK

- *¿Adónde te gustaría ir en un programa de intercambio?*
- *¿Qué necesitas llevar cuando vas de viaje?*
- *¿Qué consejos me das si voy de intercambio al extranjero?*

LOG BOOK

Have students write a sentence about themselves that they would share with people their own age in the country they want to visit.

Communicative Objectives
- to tell what someone says, using **decir**
- to say that someone asks for something, using **pedir**

Related Components

Activity Book p. 141-142	**Audio Tapes** Listening: 7A, Seg. 3
Audio Book Script: Seg. 3 Activities: p. 93	**Cuaderno** p. 89
	Tutor Page p. 48

GETTING STARTED

Have students use *ask for* and *say* in several sentences. Have them contrast these verbs with *ask* and *talk.*

Language in Context

Demonstrate the differences between these four words in Spanish. For example:
*El mesero me **pregunta** qué quiero comer.*
*Yo le **pido** una hamburgesa.*
***Hablo** con una amiga.*
*Le **digo** que voy a salir el sábado.*
Go over the forms of **pedir** and **decir.**

DISCUSS

Review vocabulary from previous chapters and introduce some of this chapter's new vocabulary with questions and statements that incorporate **pedir** and **decir.**
¿Qué pides en el consulado?
¿Qué dicen tus padres en sus cartas?
¿Qué decimos los profesores cuando una persona llega tarde a la clase?
¿Qué dicen tus amigos cuando vas de viaje?
¿Qué pides en la cafetería de la escuela?
Yo digo ¡Buenos días! por la mañana, ¿y tú, qué dices por la mañana?

PARA COMUNICARNOS MEJOR

¿QUÉ DICE? ¿QUÉ TE PIDE?

To tell what someone says, use the verb *decir*. To say that somebody asks for something, use the verb *pedir*.

— ¿Qué dice tu amiga?
— Dice que quiere mi número de teléfono y me pide la dirección.

What does your friend say? She says that she wants my phone number, and she asks me for my address.

Note that ***decir que*** means "to say that . . ."

Juan dice que quiere ir a Chile.

John says that he wants to go to Chile.

In the present tense, the stem of ***decir*** and ***pedir*** changes from *e* to *i* in all forms except ***nosotros(as)*** and ***vosotros(as).***

pedir (i) (to ask for)		decir (i) (to say, to tell)
yo	pido	digo
tú	pides	dices
usted	pide	dice
él/ella	pide	dice
nosotros(as)	pedimos	decimos
vosotros(as)	pedís	decís
ustedes	piden	dicen
ellos/ellas	piden	dicen

For students having difficulty using **decir** and **pedir** to say that someone says or asks for something, you might consider:
- **The tutor page:** Pair the student with a native speaker or a more able student, using the tutor page.
- **Actividades:** see page 282D: *Lo que digo y lo que pido*

Planes de viaje

Tu clase planea un viaje a Perú. Los estudiantes, los padres y los profesores necesitan más información. ¿Qué pide cada uno?

— ¿Qué pide el consejero?
— Pide una lista de hoteles.

1. el/la consejero(a)
2. los estudiantes
3. el/la profesor(a) de español
4. tú y tus compañeros(as)
5. los padres
6. ¿y tú?

¿Qué piden?
información sobre el viaje
itinerarios y mapas
una lista de hoteles
folletos turísticos
un calendario de las fiestas
el precio de los pasajes

2 Entrevista

A. Entrevista a seis compañeros(as). Pregúntales adónde quieren ir de vacaciones este año y por qué. Anota los nombres de cada estudiante y sus respuestas en una tabla.

Nombre	¿Adónde?	¿Por qué?
Esteban	San Juan	las playas son maravillosas
Juana y Daniel	Nueva York	la ciudad es bárbara
María	Denver	las montañas son fabulosas

B. Informa a la clase.

Esteban quiere ir a San Juan. Dice que las playas son maravillosas. Juana y Daniel quieren ir a Nueva York. Dicen que la ciudad es bárbara.

3 Comidas de las Américas

¿Qué piden ustedes? Pregúntales a tus compañeros(as).

— En un restaurante peruano, ¿qué piden?
— Pedimos cebiche. ¿Y ustedes?

1. peruano
2. chileno
3. argentino
4. mexicano
5. italiano

¿SABES QUE...?

South America has a great variety of interesting and delicious foods. The most typical Peruvian dish is *cebiche*, raw fish marinated in lemon juice. It's served with corn and sweet potatoes. Another traditional dish is *sopa a la criolla*, a soup with beef, noodles, milk, and vegetables. In Chile, some of the most popular dishes are *empanadas*, oven-baked turnovers stuffed with ground meat, onions, raisins, and olives, and *humitas*, packets of ground corn. Argentina is famous for its *asados* (barbecues) and *bifes* (beefsteaks).

291

4. ¿Qué piden tú y tus compañeros?
Mis compañeros y yo pedimos itinerarios y mapas.
5. ¿Qué piden los padres?
Los padres piden el precio de los pasajes.
6. ¿Qué pides tú?
Yo pido un calendario de las fiestas.

2. Group Activity
A. Ask six classmates where they would like to vacation this year and why. Write their answers on a chart like this one.
B. Share the results with the class.
Answers: See model on student page.

3. General Activity
Ask your classmates what they order in the restaurants in the list.
Possible Answers:
1. See model on student page.
2. *Pedimos empanadas y humitas.*
3. *Pedimos asados y bifes.*
4. *Pedimos tacos y enchiladas.*
5. *Pedimos pasta.*

CHECK

• ¿Qué piden los profesores todos los días?
• ¿Qué dicen tus profesores cuando no haces la tarea?
• ¿Qué le pides a tu padre?
• ¿Qué pides en tu restaurante favorito?

LOG BOOK
Write sentences about the forms of **decir** and **pedir** that do not follow the rules for **-ir** verbs.

ACTIVITIES

Students use **decir** and **pedir** to say that someone says or asks for something.

1. Individual Activity
Your class is planning a trip to Peru and needs more information. What do the people in the list ask for?
Possible answers:
1. See model on student page.
2. ¿Qué piden los estudiantes?
Los estudiantes piden folletos turísticos.
3. ¿Qué pide la profesora de español?
La profesora de español pide información sobre el viaje.

Communicative Objective
• to tell someone to do something, using irregular **tú** commands

Related Components

Activity Book p. 143-144	**Audio Tapes** Listening: 7A, Seg. 4
Audio Book Script: Seg.4 Activities: p. 94	**Cuaderno** p. 90
	Tutor Page p. 49

GETTING STARTED

Ask what the people in the photo are probably doing and saying.

Language in Context

Ask students to look at the infinitives in the box. What do they have in common? (They are all -**er** or -**ir** verbs.)
Remind them that **tú** commands usually take the same form as the third-person singular, as in:
José pide la visa. and *¡Pide la visa, José!*
Explain that irregular **tú** commands are variations that evolved because people were not comfortable saying the sound that would be "regular."
Explain that when an object pronoun is used with an affirmative command, they are pronounced (and written) as if they were part of the command. Example:
Pon la carta en la mesa. Ponla en la mesa.

DISCUSS

Review vocabulary from previous chapters and introduce some of this chapter's new vocabulary with irregular **tú** commands.
Di tu nombre.
Pon tu nombre en el cuaderno.
Haz la tarea ahora.
Sé bueno con tus compañeros.
Ven aquí.
Sal del salón de clases.
Ve a la pizarra.

PARA COMUNICARNOS MEJOR
¡HAZ LAS MALETAS!

To tell a friend to do something, you can use an informal *(tú)* command.

Some *tú* commands have irregular forms.

Pon todos los regalos en el bolso de mano.	Put all the presents in the handbag.
Sé cortés con tu familia peruana.	Be courteous with your Peruvian family.

Here are some verbs that have an irregular *tú* command form.

irregular informal commands			
decir	**di**	salir	**sal**
hacer	**haz**	ser	**sé**
ir	**ve**	tener	**ten**
poner	**pon**	venir	**ven**

☐ Direct and/or indirect object pronouns must be attached to the end of the affirmative command.

Dime qué documentos necesitas.	Tell me what documents you need.
— *Pon tu nombre en la maleta.*	Put your name on the suitcase.
— *Hazlo tú. Yo no tengo bolígrafo.*	You do it. I don't have a pen.

292

For students having difficulty communicating with irregular **tú** commands, you might consider:
• **The tutor page:** Pair the student with a native speaker or a more able student, using the tutor page.
• **Actividades:** see page 282D: *¡Hazlo, por favor!*

1 Consejos a mi amigo(a) chileno(a)

Un(a) amigo(a) chileno(a) quiere visitar Estados Unidos. Dale cuatro consejos para su viaje.

Ve al consulado de Estados Unidos y pide una visa.

ir	**venir**
al consulado de Estados Unidos	pronto
a la agencia de viajes	en verano
a la agencia de intercambio	para mi cumpleaños

hacer	**poner**
los trámites temprano	tu nombre en la maleta
las maletas dos días antes	los cheques de viajero en
de salir	el bolso de mano

2 ¡Hazlo tú!

Tu compañero(a) y tú planean un viaje al extranjero. ¿Qué va a hacer cada uno(a)?

— *Haz las maletas.*
— *Muy bien. Y tú, sal ahora y compra un diccionario de español.*

- hacer las maletas
- salir y comprar un diccionario de español
- hacer el itinerario
- ir a buscar los pasajes
- poner los documentos en el bolso
- tener los pasaportes contigo

3 Antes de salir

En dos horas vas a salir de viaje y tienes mucho que hacer. Pídele ayuda a tu compañero(a).

— *¿Dónde pongo la cámara?*
— *Ponla en la maleta.*
— *¿Cuándo hago el bolso de mano?*
— *Hazlo ahora.*

¿Cuándo...?
hacer el bolso de mano
hacer las maletas
hacer las reservas

¿Dónde...?
poner la cámara
poner el pasaporte
poner los folletos

293

2. Pair Activity

You and your partner are planning a trip to another country. What is each of you going to do to get ready?

Answers: See model on student page.
—*Haz el itinerario.*
—*Muy bien. Y tú, sal y busca los pasajes.*
—*Pon los documentos en el bolso.*
—*Y tú, ten los pasaportes contigo.*

Application: Use **no debes** to tell your partner what *not* to do or bring.

3. Pair Activity

You are leaving for the airport in two hours and you have a lot to do before that. Create a dialog in which you ask your partner for help.

Answers: See model on student page.
Synthesis: Write a chronological list of commands for a substitute teacher.

CHECK

- *¿Qué es más importante que lo haces antes de ir de viaje?*
- *¿Qué consejos le das a un amigo que quiere ir de viaje?*
- *¿Qué le dices a un amigo cuando le ayudas a hacer la maleta?*
- *¿Qué pides cuando vas a una agencia de viajes?*

LOG BOOK

Have students write several sentences with commands that they feel would be the most useful.

Para hispanohablantes

Write a list of commands that you hear members of your family say often.

ACTIVITIES

Students use irregular **tú** commands to talk about things to do before a trip.

1. Individual Activity

Give four bits of advice to a Chilean friend who wants to visit the United States.

Some Possible Answers:
ir: *Ve a la agencia de viajes y haz la reserva de avión.*
hacer: *Haz las maletas dos días antes de salir y pon tu nombre en las maletas.*
venir: *Ven pronto y sal temprano.*
poner: *Pon los cheques de viajero en el bolso de mano y cambia dinero.*

293

Communicative Objective
• to talk about preparing to participate in an exchange program

Related Components

Assessment	Conexiones
Oral Proficiency: p. 31	Chapter 11
Audio Book	**Magazine**
Script: Seg. 5	Juntos en América del Sur
Activities: p. 95	**Tutor Page**
Audio Tapes	p. 50
Listening: 7A, Seg. 5	
Conexiones: 18B, Ch. 10	

GETTING STARTED

Students should now be able to use **decir**, **pedir**, irregular **tú** commands, and all of the chapter vocabulary.

Ask what types of problems might arise while participating in an exchange program. Do students think they would suffer from homesickness? What would they do if they didn't get along with the family? What if they didn't like the food?

APPLY

1. Individual or Class Activity
Answer the questions about the brochure.
Possible Answers:
• *El folleto dice que Argentina es un país con una naturaleza maravillosa.*
• *El folleto pide nombre y apellido, dirección, teléfono, fecha de nacimiento y el nombre de la madre, del padre o del/de la tutor(a).*
• *Las fechas del programa son del 12 de julio al 16 de agosto.*
• *Los requisitos para participar en el programa son: un año de estudios de español y tener de 16 a 18 años de edad.*
Extension: Play the roles of program interviewer and student while you fill out the personal-information questionnaire.

2. Individual Activity
Make a list of the documents you are required to show in order to participate in the exchange program.
Answers: See model on student page and *certificado médico/el pasaporte/la visa*
Analysis: Say who you have to talk to and where you have to go in order to get the documents.

3. Pair Activity
Make a dialog between a representative of a student-exchange program and a student. Ask:
• what you have to do
• what documents you need
• what other things you need to bring
• where you can get more information
Application: Convince a friend to go with you on an exchange program. Write what you know about the program and what one must do to apply.

4. Pair Activity
To participate in an exchange program, you must answer these questions about your interests and activities:
• What are your favorite activities?
• What would you like to study in the future?
• Do you play any sports? Which?
• Do you like music? Do you sing in a choir? Do you play an instrument?
Application: Write sentences with *Me interesa...* to express what you would like to do in Argentina.

SITUACIONES

FOLLETO DE INTERCAMBIO

ARGENTINA
Programa de intercambio cultural

Argentina es un país con una naturaleza maravillosa. Tiene de todo: montañas, ríos, lagos y una larga costa en el océano Atlántico. También tiene grandes ciudades, como Buenos Aires. ¡Ven al sur! ¡Visita Argentina y conoce a su gente!

Fechas del programa:
Del 12 de julio al 16 de agosto

Requisitos:
• Un año de estudios de español
• Tener de 16 a 18 años de edad

Información escolar:
• Certificado de estudios

Documentos necesarios:
• Autorización de la madre, del padre o del/de la tutor(a)
• Certificado médico
• Pasaporte
• Visa

Información personal:

Nombre y apellido: _____

Dirección: _____

Teléfono: _____

Fecha de nacimiento: _____

Nombre de la madre, del padre o del/de la tutor(a): _____

① ¿Qué dice el folleto?

Contesta las preguntas.
• ¿Qué dice el folleto sobre Argentina?
• ¿Qué información pide el folleto?
• ¿Cuáles son las fechas del programa de intercambio?
• ¿Cuáles son los requisitos para participar en el programa?

PARA TU REFERENCIA
la costa *coast*
la fecha de nacimiento *date of birth*
la naturaleza *nature*
los requisitos *requirements*
el/la tutor(a) *guardian*

294

¿Qué te piden?

Haz una lista de los documentos que te piden para participar en el programa de intercambio cultural. Por ejemplo:

- *autorización de tus padres o de tu tutor(a)*
- *certificado de estudios*

 ¿Qué tienes que llevar?

Haz un diálogo con tu compañero(a) entre un(a) representante del programa de intercambio y un(a) estudiante. Pregunta:

- qué tienes que hacer
- qué documentos necesitas
- qué otras cosas tienes que llevar
- dónde pides más información

4 Me interesa...

Para participar en programas de intercambio tienes que contestar preguntas sobre tus intereses y actividades favoritas. Trabaja con tu compañero(a).

- ¿Cuáles son tus actividades favoritas?
- ¿Qué te gustaría estudiar en el futuro?
- ¿Practicas deportes? ¿Cuáles?
- ¿Te gusta la música? ¿Cantas en un coro? ¿Tocas un instrumento?

5 Vamos a escribir

Vas a participar en un programa de intercambio. Escribe a qué país vas, cuándo vas y con quién vas a vivir.

295

5. Homework or Classwork
You are going to participate in an exchange program. Write what country you are going to, when you will go, and with whom you will live.
Possible Answer:
Voy a participar en un programa de intercambio el año próximo. Voy a visitar Argentina y voy a vivir con la familia Sánchez.
Challenge: Pretend you are a student from Argentina who wants to study in the United States. Write a short letter saying where you would like to study.

CHECK

- *¿Por qué te gustaría ir a un programa de intercambio cultural a Argentina?*
- *¿Qué documentos necesitas para participar en un programa de intercambio?*
- *¿Qué consejos le das a un amigo que quiere participar en un programa de intercambio?*

LOG BOOK
Have students write what they think is the best reason for participating in a student-exchange program.

Para hispanohablantes

In Spanish, create a brochure and an application form for an exchange program in your school for Latin Americans.

Background

You can obtain information on exchange programs from the *Advisory List of International Travel and Exchange Programs* published by the **Council on Standards for International Educational Travel (CSIET)**
Phone: (703) 771-2040
Fax: (703) 771-2046
For information about the program mentioned in the Unit 6 video, contact:
Youth for Understanding International Exchange: 1-800-RU-READY (787-3239)

For students having difficulty communicating about their interests or about exchange programs, you might consider:
- **The tutor page:** Pair the student with a native speaker or a more advanced student, using the tutor page.
- **Actividades:** see page 282C: *Querida familia*

**INTERNET LINK**

Exchange Programs http://agoralang.com:80/study.html

Communicative Objective
• to tell people about a place you think they should visit

Related Components

Transparencies	Video: Tape/Book
Ch. 11: Para resolver	Unit 6: Seg. 3

Search to frame 1321102

GETTING STARTED

Have students estimate how far south Bariloche is by asking: If Bariloche were in *North* America, how far north do you think it would be? As far as Florida? Colorado? Canada? (Colorado—a state known for excellent skiing.)

APPLY

Form groups. Explain that each group will create a brochure about places of interest in your city or state for foreign students.

PASO 1: ¿Adónde?
Note: You may wish to assign places to avoid repetition. Providing tourist materials will make it easier for groups to obtain information. If necessary, extend the scope of the activities to cover well-known places in other states.
Choose a place. Write about what it is like. Include:
• its name and where it is
• why that place is worth visiting
• what you can do there
• where a foreign student could live (with a family, in a hotel, on a farm...)
Extension: Ask other groups about the places they chose. Example: *¿Qué actividades puedes hacer en el lugar?*

PASO 2: Antes del viaje
Make a list of advice for a foreign student who is going to visit this place. Be sure to cover:
• travel documents
• clothes and other necessary items
• sporting equipment
• important telephone numbers
Answers: See model on student page.

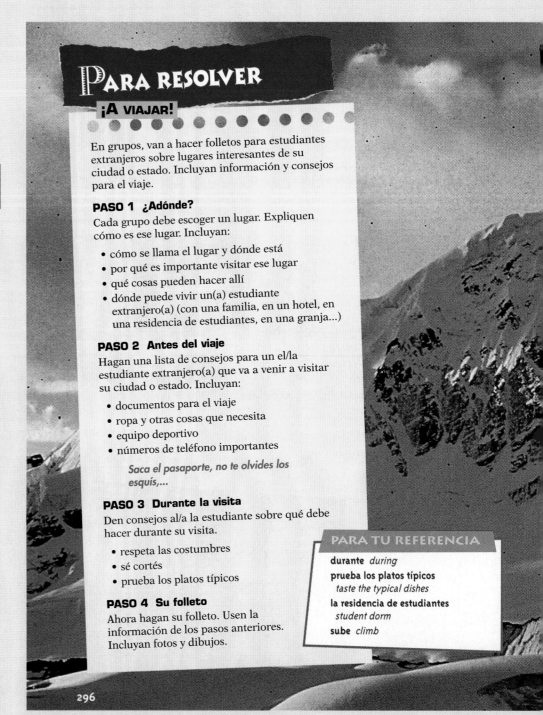

PARA RESOLVER
¡A VIAJAR!

En grupos, van a hacer folletos para estudiantes extranjeros sobre lugares interesantes de su ciudad o estado. Incluyan información y consejos para el viaje.

PASO 1 ¿Adónde?
Cada grupo debe escoger un lugar. Expliquen cómo es ese lugar. Incluyan:
• cómo se llama el lugar y dónde está
• por qué es importante visitar ese lugar
• qué cosas pueden hacer allí
• dónde puede vivir un(a) estudiante extranjero(a) (con una familia, en un hotel, en una residencia de estudiantes, en una granja...)

PASO 2 Antes del viaje
Hagan una lista de consejos para un el/la estudiante extranjero(a) que va a venir a visitar su ciudad o estado. Incluyan:
• documentos para el viaje
• ropa y otras cosas que necesita
• equipo deportivo
• números de teléfono importantes

Saca el pasaporte, no te olvides los esquís,...

PASO 3 Durante la visita
Den consejos al/a la estudiante sobre qué debe hacer durante su visita.
• respeta las costumbres
• sé cortés
• prueba los platos típicos

PASO 4 Su folleto
Ahora hagan su folleto. Usen la información de los pasos anteriores. Incluyan fotos y dibujos.

PARA TU REFERENCIA
durante *during*
prueba los platos típicos
  taste the typical dishes
la residencia de estudiantes
  student dorm
sube *climb*

296

PASO 3: Durante la visita
Give the student advice about what to do during his or her visit. Don't forget:
• respect local customs
• be courteous
• try local foods
Extension: Take turns playing the role of the student and explaining what you were advised to do. Use **decir** and **tener que**. Example:
Los estudiantes dicen que tengo que respetar las costumbres de New York.

PASO 4: Su folleto
Make your brochure. Use information and advice from the previous steps. Include photos and drawings.
Analysis: Compare and contrast brochures. Find three similarities and three differences between your group's brochure and those of other groups.

Bariloche
ARGENTINA

En la sección argentina de los Andes hay un lugar maravilloso: Bariloche.

. Compra el pasaje.
. Cambia dinero.
. Haz la maleta y...

¡VEN A ESQUIAR DE JUNIO A SEPTIEMBRE!

Ven a las montañas más espectaculares de América del Sur. Haz nuevos amigos y visita con ellos el lago Nahuel Huapi. Sube al volcán Tronador. Vive con una familia, en una residencia de estudiantes, en una granja o en un hotel. Prueba los platos típicos de estas montañas. VE A UNA AGENCIA DE VIAJES Y PIDE MÁS INFORMACIÓN.

297

CHECK

PORTFOLIO
Students may wish to include the brochure from *Paso 4* in their portfolios.

Mountain Sports Words

Skiing
Alpine skiing *el esquí alpino*
avalanche *el alud, la avalancha*
chairlift *el telesilla*
cross-country skiing *el esquí a campo traviesa, el esquí de fondo*
downhill *el descenso*
mittens *las manoplas*
parka *el anorak*
ski boots *las botas de esquiar*
ski goggles *las gafas de nieve*
ski lift *el telesquí*
ski lodge *el refugio*
ski resort *la estación de esquí*
ski slope/ski trail *la pista*
ski suit *el mono de esquiar*

Hiking & Mountain Climbing
campfire *la hoguera de campamento*
campsite *la zona de acampar*
cliff (mountain) *el precipicio*
cliff (seaside) *el acantilado*
hiking *el senderismo*
mountain climbing *el alpinismo*
rappeling *el descenso a soga doble*
rock climbing *la escalada*
rope *la cuerda*
tent *la tienda de campaña*
trail *el sendero*

Para hispanohablantes

Conduct an interview with someone from a South American country. Ask questions about the climate, geography, and culture. Report to the class.

✓ CULTURE NOTE

San Carlos de Bariloche is 3 hours by air from Buenos Aires; Bariloche, the resort, is about 10 miles from the town. It offers about 1,600 skiable acres. There are 15 lifts (1 tram, 9 chairs, 5 surface). The top elevation is 6,720 feet; the vertical drop 3,350 feet.

▶▶▶ INTERNET LINK

Information about Skiing http://www.goski.com:80/argent.htm

ENTÉRATE

Cultural Objective
• to learn about the Chilean poet Pablo Neruda

Related Components

Audio Tapes	Magazine
Conexiones: 18B, Ch. 11	Juntos en América del Sur
Conexiones Chapter 11	

GETTING STARTED

Ask students why they think people write poetry. What are some differences between poetry and stories?

DISCUSS

Using the Text

After reading aloud each paragraph, ask some comprehension and critical-thinking questions. Suggestions:
¿Quién fue Pablo Neruda?
¿Qué premio ganó?
¿Qué otras ventajas tiene saber español u otro idioma?
¿En qué año publicó Veinte poemas de amor y una canción desesperada? (*Publicó el libro a los 20 años, en el año 1924.*)
Otros escritores hispanos ganaron el premio Nobel de Literatura. ¿Saben ustedes cómo se llaman?
(Recent winners: Mexican Octavio Paz, 1990; Spaniard Camilo José Cela, 1989; Colombian Gabriel García Márquez, 1982; Spaniard Vicente Alexandre, 1977; Guatemalan Miguel Ángel Asturias, 1967)

CHECK

Te toca a ti
Answers:

1. *Neruda adquirió fama internacional con la obra* Veinte poemas de amor y una canción desesperada.
2. *Los temas de* Canto general *son la historia y la cultura de América Latina.*
3. *El tema de las* Odas elementales *es las cosas de cada día.*

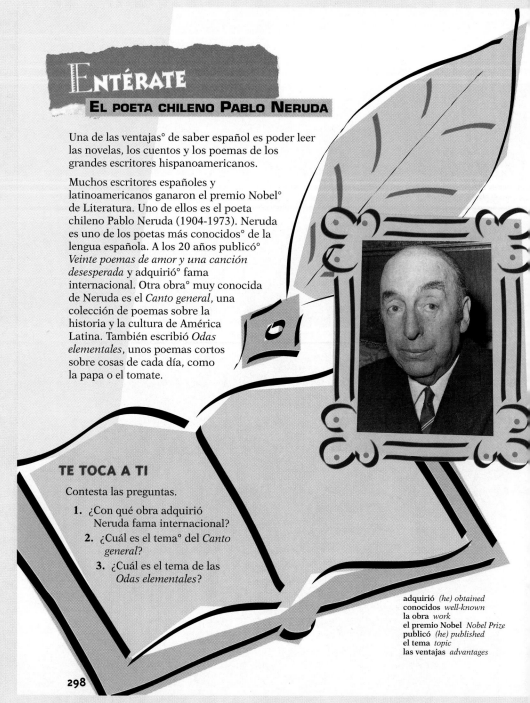

ENTÉRATE

EL POETA CHILENO PABLO NERUDA

Una de las ventajas° de saber español es poder leer las novelas, los cuentos y los poemas de los grandes escritores hispanoamericanos.

Muchos escritores españoles y latinoamericanos ganaron el premio Nobel° de Literatura. Uno de ellos es el poeta chileno Pablo Neruda (1904-1973). Neruda es uno de los poetas más conocidos° de la lengua española. A los 20 años publicó° *Veinte poemas de amor y una canción desesperada* y adquirió° fama internacional. Otra obra° muy conocida de Neruda es el *Canto general*, una colección de poemas sobre la historia y la cultura de América Latina. También escribió *Odas elementales*, unos poemas cortos sobre cosas de cada día, como la papa o el tomate.

TE TOCA A TI

Contesta las preguntas.

1. ¿Con qué obra adquirió Neruda fama internacional?
2. ¿Cuál es el tema° del *Canto general*?
3. ¿Cuál es el tema de las *Odas elementales*?

adquirió *(he) obtained*
conocidos *well-known*
la obra *work*
el premio Nobel *Nobel Prize*
publicó *(he) published*
el tema *topic*
las ventajas *advantages*

298

About Pablo Neruda
His real name was Ricardo Neftalí Reyes Basualto. He borrowed the pen name Neruda from a 19th-century Czech writer. Neruda began a diplomatic career in 1927 and was transferred to Spain in 1934. There he witnessed the Civil War and the rise of Facism in Europe, events that led him to join the Communist Party in 1943. He won the Nobel Prize for literature in 1971.

PORTFOLIO
Find a Pablo Neruda poem in the library and copy it. Underline all the words you recognize, and write down what you think the poet is saying. Read an English translation to confirm your interpretation.

▶▶▶INTERNET LINK
Neruda in Spanish http://www.uchile.cl/historia/neruda.html

VOCABULARIO TEMÁTICO

Razones para viajar al extranjero
Reasons for traveling abroad

aprender bien otro idioma
to learn another language well
conocer otras costumbres
to get to know other customs
conocer a otras culturas
to get to know other cultures
conocer otros jóvenes
to meet other young people
divertirse to have fun
hacer amigos to make friends

Información sobre el viaje
Travel information

la agencia de intercambio
exchange agency
el/la agente de viajes
travel agent
el/la consejero(a) counselor
el consulado consulate
el/la representante de...
representative of . . .

Cosas que necesitas para viajar
Things you need to travel

el bolso de mano handbag
los cheques de viajero
traveler's checks
los documentos documents
el itinerario itinerary
la maleta suitcase
el pasaje (airline) ticket

Documentos para un programa de intercambio
Documents for an exchange program

la autorización de los padres
parents' authorization
las cartas de recomendación
letters of recommendation
el certificado médico
health certificate
el certificado de estudios
school transcript
la visa visa

Consejos para viajar
Travel advice

Cambia dinero.
Exchange money.
Haz el itinerario.
Plan the itinerary.
Haz la maleta.
Pack the suitcase.
Haz la reserva de avión.
Make your plane reservation.
Haz los trámites.
Do the paperwork.
Llena la solicitud.
Fill out the application form.
Pide la visa. Ask for a visa.
Pon tu nombre en la maleta.
Put your name on the suitcase.
Respeta las costumbres (del otro país). Respect the customs
(of the other country).
Saca el pasaporte.
Get the passport.

Sal temprano. Leave early.
Sé cortés. Be courteous.

Expresiones y palabras
ir al extranjero
to go abroad
ir de viaje
to go on a trip
Me encantaría.
I would love to.
Me interesa...
I'm interested in . . .
el avión plane
decir to say
los estudios studies
el folleto brochure
llenar to fill out
la montaña mountain
pedir to ask for
perfectamente perfectly
poner to put
el programa de intercambio estudiantil student exchange
program
venir to come
viajar to travel

Expresiones de Argentina y Chile
¡Es bárbaro(a)!
It's great! (Argentina)
salir a mochilear
to go backpacking (Chile)

LA CONEXIÓN INGLÉS-ESPAÑOL

There are some Spanish words that look similar to English words, but their meanings are completely different. These are called "false cognates." An example of a false cognate is the Spanish word *idioma*. Although it looks like the English word *idiom*, *idioma* really means *language*. Another example is the word *pariente*, which looks like *parent*, but means *relative*.

Can you think of any other false cognates you have learned? Why do you think a false cognate is also referred to as a *"falso amigo"*?

299

La conexión inglés-español

Among the "false cognates" on the student page are **carta, mano,** and **saca.** Be careful with the term *cognate.* It means "related by birth," and some words that appear to be false cognates are not. For example, **divertirse,** "to have fun" or "to amuse oneself," is a cognate of *divert* , "to turn aside." But *divert* has more than one meaning. Can you find another cognate on this page that appears to be false but is not?

Communicative Objectives
- to review vocabulary
- to correctly pronounce words containing the letters "p" and "t"

Related Components

Activity Book	Audio Book
Chapter Review: p. 145-146	Script: Seg. 6 Activities p. 96
Assessment	**Audio Tapes**
Listening Script: p. 19	Listening: 7A, Seg. 6
Chapter Test: p. 105-110	Assessment: 15B, Ch. 11
	Cuaderno p. 91-92

Pronunciation: "p" and "t"

The pronunciation of the letter "p" is different in Spanish and English. The same is true of the letter "t." The main differences are as follows:

- "p" - Have the student tear off a small strip of paper and hold it between the thumb and forefinger in front of the mouth about an inch or two away. Have your student say the English "p" three times and observe the brisk movement of the paper. Then have him/her say the Spanish "p" three times. Since the Spanish "p" is not made with an accompanying puff of air, the paper should not move at all if the letter is being pronounced correctly.

Have the students practice saying the following Spanish words while holding the paper in front of their mouths:
aprender, pasaje, pide, pon, respeta, programa.

- The English "t" and "k" are also accompanied by a puff of air (though less in quantity when compared to the "p"). This puffing (called aspiration) is absent in the Spanish pronunciation of these letters.

- Another difference between the Spanish "t" and the English "t" is that the Spanish "t" is pronounced with the tongue touching the front teeth, whereas the English "t" is pronounced farther back in the mouth.

Practice saying "t" in the following set of words:
agente, itinerario, documentos, montaña, solicitud, certificado, pasaporte, interesa

LOG BOOK
Have students write a poem of their own including some **p** words in it.

	Objetivos page 301	Conversemos pages 302-303	Realidades pages 304-305	Palabras en acción pages 306-307
Comunicación	• To talk about what you and others are doing right now		Read text, answer questions, discuss diary of travel in Peru	Activities 1-4, 8: Read cartoon, make list; discuss what some characters sell, what some feel; write letter
	• To talk about travel highlights	Discuss highlights of travel in Peru	Read text, answer questions, make class list	Activities 1-3, 5-8: Read cartoon, make list; discuss what some characters sell, what to buy; talk about a trip; make poster; write letter
	• To talk about shopping for souvenirs	Discuss shopping for souvenirs in Peru	Read text, answer questions, discuss diary of travel in Peru	Activities 3, 5: Read cartoon, discuss what some characters sell, what to buy
Vocabulario temático	• To know the expressions for geographical features	Talk about some of Peru's geographical features	Read text, answer questions, discuss geographical features of Peru, make class list	Activity 1: Read cartoon, make list of geographical features of Cuzco
	• To know the expressions for souvenirs	Talk about buying souvenirs in Peru	Read text, answer questions, discuss diary of travel in Peru	Activities 3, 5: Read cartoon, discuss what some characters sell, what to buy
	• To know the expressions for descriptions of geographical features	Describe geographical features of Peru	Read text, answer questions, describe geographical feature, make class list	Activities 1, 2, 6-8: Read cartoon, make list; discuss actions; talk about a trip; make poster; write letter
Estructura	• To talk about actions in progress: the present progressive tense		Read text, use present progressive tense to answer questions and to discuss diary of travel in Peru	Activities 2-4, 8: Read cartoon, discuss what some characters sell, what some feel; write letter
	• To talk about qualities of persons, places, or things: the superlative construction	Use the superlative construction to talk about places in Peru	Read text, answer questions, discuss diary of travel in Peru, make class list	Activities 1, 5, 8: Read cartoon, make list; discuss what to buy in Cuzco; write letter
	• To talk about characteristics, location, origin, emotions: uses of the verbs ser and estar	Use estar to talk about emotions and ser to talk about characteristics	Read text, answer questions, discuss diary of travel in Peru, make class list	Activities 3, 4, 8: Read cartoon, discuss what some characters sell, what some feel; write letter
Cultura	The Festival of the Sun in Cuzco			
Integración		Different places, ways to travel, describing feelings, items to buy	Numbers, dates, locations, activities and places	Family and friends, pointing out and describing people and things

Para comunicarnos mejor (1) pages 308-309	Para comunicarnos mejor (2) pages 310-311	Situaciones pages 312-313	Para resolver pages 314-315	Notes
Activity 1: Act out phone call	**Activities 1, 3: Discuss tourists in Cuzco; play *Veo, veo***	**Activity 2: Read map, describe what people are doing**	**Paso 3: Read ads, write imaginary postcard**	
Activity 2: Discuss places in Peru	**Activities 1, 2: Discuss tourists in Cuzco; describe places you've seen**	**Activities 1-4: Read map, find names; talk about what people are doing; write itinerary; write in diary**	**Pasos 1, 3, 4: Read ads, choose place to go; write imaginary postcard; write ad**	
	Activity 1: Discuss tourists in Cuzco	**Activities 2-4: Read map, talk about what people are doing; write itinerary; write in diary**		
Activities 1-3: Act out phone call; discuss places in Peru; talk about your state	**Activities 1, 2: Discuss tourists in Cuzco; describe places you've seen**	**Activities 1, 3, 4: Read map, find names; write itinerary; write in diary**		
	Activity 1: Discuss tourists in Cuzco	**Activities 2-4: Read map, talk about what people are doing; write itinerary; write in diary**		
Activities 1-3: Act out phone call; discuss places in Peru; talk about your state	**Activities 1, 2: Discuss tourists in Cuzco; describe places you've seen**	**Activities 1-4: Read map, find names; describe what people are doing; write itinerary; write in diary**	**Pasos 1-4: Read ads, choose place; list things to do and equipment; write imaginary postcard; write ad**	
Activity 1: Act out phone call	**Activities 1-3: Discuss tourists in Cuzco; describe places you've seen; play *Veo, veo***	**Activity 2: Read map, describe what people are doing**	**Paso 3: Read ads, write imaginary postcard**	
Activities 2, 3: Discuss places in Peru; talk about your state		**Activities 2, 4: Read map, describe what people are doing; write in diary**	**Pasos 3, 4: Read ads, write imaginary postcard; write ad**	
Activities 1-3: Act out phone call; discuss places in Peru; talk about your state	**Activities 1-3: Discuss tourists in Cuzco; describe places you've seen; play *Veo, veo***	**Activities 2, 4: Read map, talk about what people are doing; write in diary**	**Pasos 3, 4: Read ads, write imaginary postcard; write ad**	
			Manco Capac and the foundation of Cuzco	**Entérate page 316 The Andean llama**
Travel or vacation, places, reactions to places or events	Locations, reactions; talking about home; people, places, and events; describing feelings	Numbers, activities, people, places; flora and fauna; locations, directions, what to do; transportation	What to do, where to go, travel and vacations, geography, directions	Animals, numbers, units of measurement, origin

De Lima a Cuzco

WRITING CONNECTION

Objective
- to describe an imaginary trip from Lima to Cuzco, using Chapter 12 *Vocabulario temático*

Use
after *Palabras en acción,* pages 306-307

Materials
- TRB Activity Support Page 27, *De Lima a Cuzco*
- posterboard
- marker

Preparation
- Assign one word or phrase from the Chapter 12 *Vocabulario temático* to each student.

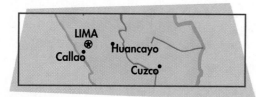

Activity
- Have students work in pairs to write entries for a journal of an imaginary trip from Lima to Cuzco in December (a summer month in Peru). Beside using their 2 words and/or phrases, they should tell how they traveled, what they did when they arrived, and anything else they think pertinent.
- Each helps the other write his/her entry, using as much as possible of the remaining Chapter 12 vocabulary. For example, if a pair is assigned *desierto* and *paisaje,* one of them might write:—*No vimos nada del desierto, porque el desierto está al norte del Perú.* And the other: *Cuando subimos en el avión el paisaje era espectacular. Era impresionante ver los Andes llenos de nieve.*
- Distribute activity support page. Help students correct their entries, and then have them transfer the entries to their diary pages.
- Next, students form teams of 10. Each team chooses a coherent order for their entries, gives them consecutive dates, and returns the individual entries to their authors.
- When the author of the first entry presents it to the class, he/she glues it to the posterboard and underlines all words from the Chapter 12 *Vocabulario temático.*
- After all the entries have been presented, each team counts its underlined words. Who has the most?

¿Qué están haciendo?

ART CONNECTION

Objective
- to describe events as they happen, using the present progressive tense

Use
after *Para comunicarnos mejor,* page 308

Materials
- 4-frame comic strips from newspapers
- envelopes
- 3" x 5" index cards
- glue sticks
- posterboard

Preparation
- Each student brings in a comic strip that shows different actions in each frame.
- Students cut their strips into individual frames and place the frames in an envelope.
- On a card, each student writes what is happening in the frames, using the progressive tense to describe the actions in sequence.
- Students write their names on the backs of the cards and hand them in with the envelopes.

Activity
- Pair students and hand out an envelope to each pair. You keep the cards.
- Pairs have 10 minutes to sequence their story, paste it on paper, and make notes explaining the sequence.
- You select one card and read it twice while students listen carefully. For example:—*1. Hay un hombre caminando por las montañas. 2. El hombre está admirando el paisaje. Hace mucho sol. 3. El hombre está comiendo en el campo. 4. Está lloviendo mucho y el hombre está bajando la montaña rápidamente.*
- The pair with the frames for this story identify it and then describe their picture story to the class to see whether it matches the sequence on the card. If no one responds to the story, read the name on the back of the card and have that student look for the strip in the classroom.
- Have students discuss differences in the two versions of the story, using the progressive tense.
- Play until all envelopes and cards have been used. If there isn't enough time, save them to use later for practice in writing, sequencing, and pantomiming.

El más el menos

GAME

Objective
- to talk about extraordinary facts and world records, using superlatives

Use
after *Para comunicarnos mejor,* page 308

Materials
- world almanacs (at least 4)

Activity
- Divide the class into 4 teams. Give each team at least one almanac. (Even better: each pair of students has an almanac of their own.)
- Decide on several topics to investigate, one at a time: *deportes, geografía, historia, música, arte, cine,* etc.
- Each team has 10 minutes to look up facts and write questions for the other teams. If the topic is *geografía,* the teams look up the answers for questions such as:*¿Cuál es el río más largo del mundo? (El Nilo es el río más largo del mundo). ¿Cuál es el océano más grande del mundo? (El Océano Pacífico es el océano más grande del mundo). ¿Cuál es la zona más seca de América del Sur? (El desierto de Atacama es la zona más seca de América del Sur).*
- Team A asks team B a question, team B asks team C, etc. If B answers A correctly, B receives a point and asks C the next question. If a team answers incorrectly, the question passes to the next team. Teams must know the answers to their own questions, but you should be ready to pronunce Spanish place names.
- When questions in one category are exhausted, the team with the most points chooses the next category.

Variation
- Play another round reviewing the superlatives used by making new sentences with *-ísimo.* For example:—*El Río Nilo es larguísimo.* Then ask students to substitute another word or phrase for which the *-ísimo* superlative would also be appropriate. For example:—*La película Gone With the Wind es larguísima.*

¿Soy o estoy guapa?

ART CONNECTION

Objective
- to play a game about people, places, and things, using the verbs *ser* and *estar*

Use
after *Para comunicarnos mejor,* page 310

Materials
- 3" x 5" index cards

Preparation
- Have students bring in magazine pictures, glued to posterboard, of people, places, and things.
- Divide cards into sets of 6 and write one of the following **ser/estar** phrases on each card: *¿Qué/quién...?, ¿De dónde...?, ¿Dónde...ahora?, ¿Qué...haciendo?, ¿Cómo:...?, ¿Qué hora:...?*
- Make one set of cards for each group of 6 students.

Activity
- Review cards. Then review paradigms of **ser** and **estar.** Remind students to use **ser** with permanent states, **estar** with temporary ones. Write paradigms on chalkboard.
- Form groups of 6 students. Have each group choose a scorekeeper and a playing order.
- Place one picture and set of cards face down on each group's table. Groups play simultaneously.
- Begin play by turning over the picture. If it were Einstein at a chalkboard covered with figures, Player 1 could choose the *¿Qué/quién...?* card and say:—*Es científico o matemático.* Player 2, choosing *¿Qué...haciendo?* says:—*Está hablando de los números.* Player 3, choosing *¿De dónde...?,—Es de Alemania,* etc.
- Circulate to help with vocabulary.
- When everyone has played, shuffle cards, put them face down, and give group a new picture.
- Scorekeepers keep track of points and announce the group winner(s) at the end of the game.

Rules
- If a player can't think of a sentence or uses the wrong verb, another group member can try.
- If no one can use the card, the first student to have tried turns over a new card.

BIENVENIDOS A PERÚ

Introduce the chapter and its theme by asking students what they would do before going to South America. What should they consider when planning a trip? When would be the best time to go, and what should they bring?

Related Components

Audio Tapes	Conexiones
Conexiones: 18B, Ch. 12	Chapter 12
	Video: Tape/Book
CD ROM	Unit 6: Seg. 3
Chapter 12	

Search to frame 1395003

GETTING STARTED

Have students look at the photograph on the page. Possible comprehension and critical thinking questions:
¿Dónde está Cuzco?
¿Por qué era importante el sol para los incas?

Thinking About Language

You can use this opportunity to introduce a way to remember new vocabulary.

Hidden Cognates

The *Conexión inglés-español* features at the end of each chapter draw attention to some of the more obvious cognate clues. Here is a way to make students aware of more subtle clues.
Display these words from this chapter: **desierto, océano, selva.** Ask what they probably mean. Give them this hint: **selva** is not as direct a cognate as the others, but students should know at least one English word related to it.
The English adjective *sylvan,* which they know from *Pennsylvania* ("Penn's Forest") and may have encountered in a play by Shakespeare, has to do with woods. In the context of **desierto** and **océano,** an educated guess might lead to *forest;* the correct word, *jungle,* is not far away.
Remind them that many English words come from Latin. And sometimes, if they take a close look, they may think of a word that will give them a clue—and will make the Spanish word easier to remember.
What English words do these suggest?
Altísimo (suggests *altitude,* height above sea level)
Lana (suggests *lanolin,* which is used in cosmetics and comes from sheep)
Mundo (suggests *mundane,* "of the world, commonplace")
Piedra (suggests *petrified*)

CAPÍTULO 12

BIENVENIDOS A PERÚ

300

Chapter Components

Activity Book p. 147-156	Audio Book Script: p. 97-100	CD ROM Chapter 12	Transparencies Chapter 12
Assessment Oral Proficiency: p. 32 Listening Script: p. 20 Chapter Test: p. 111-116	Activities: p. 101-104 **Audio Tapes** Listening: 7B Assessment: 15B, Ch. 12 Conexiones: 18B, Ch. 12	**Conexiones** Chapter 12 **Cuaderno** p. 93-100 **Magazine** Juntos en América del Sur	**Tutor Pages** p. 51-54 **Video: Tape/Book** Unit 6: Seg. 2

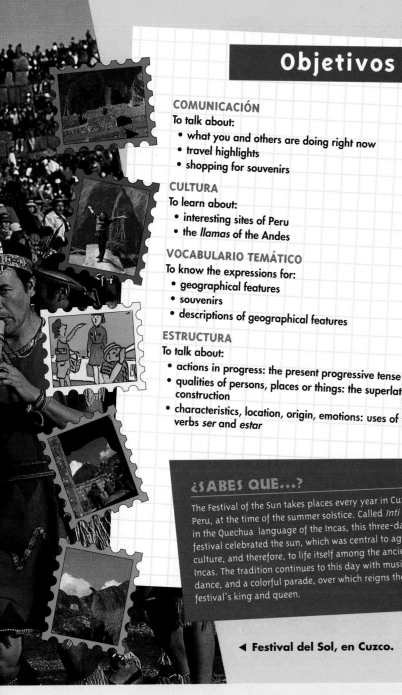

Objetivos

COMUNICACIÓN

To talk about:
- what you and others are doing right now
- travel highlights
- shopping for souvenirs

CULTURA

To learn about:
- interesting sites of Peru
- the *llamas* of the Andes

VOCABULARIO TEMÁTICO

To know the expressions for:
- geographical features
- souvenirs
- descriptions of geographical features

ESTRUCTURA

To talk about:
- actions in progress: the present progressive tense
- qualities of persons, places or things: the superlative construction
- characteristics, location, origin, emotions: uses of the verbs *ser* and *estar*

¿SABES QUE...?

The Festival of the Sun takes places every year in Cuzco, Peru, at the time of the summer solstice. Called *Inti Rami* in the Quechua language of the Incas, this three-day festival celebrated the sun, which was central to agriculture, and therefore, to life itself among the ancient Incas. The tradition continues to this day with music, dance, and a colorful parade, over which reigns the festival's king and queen.

◀ **Festival del Sol, en Cuzco.**

301

ACTIVITIES

Communication

Encourage after-class activities that may enhance student interest and proficiency. Some ideas:
- have students find out more about South America by talking to their history, literature, and geography teachers
- have students collect newspaper articles on South America for one week and post them in class

Culture

The written word can only hint at what life is like in other lands. To encourage greater understanding:
- suggest students look at travel guides for Argentina, Chile, and Peru
- play traditional Andean music in class
- show the video that accompanies Unit 6 of this textbook

Vocabulary

To reinforce vocabulary, have students:
- make and compare lists of the ten most useful words in this chapter
- write sentences about one of the countries in South America
- play Hangman with this chapter's vocabulary

Structure

To reinforce **ser** and **estar**:
- from time to time, ask individuals: *¿Cómo eres y cómo estás? ¿De dónde eres y dónde estás?*

▶▶▶ INTERNET LINK

Peru: Facts http://www.lonelyplanet.com.au:80/dest/sam/peru.htm

Communicative Objectives

- to talk about what students did and where they went
- to talk about means of transportation

Related Components

Activity Book p. 147	Cuaderno p. 93
Audio Book Script: Seg. 1	Transparencies Ch. 12: Conversemos
Audio Tapes Listening: 7B, Seg. 1	

GETTING STARTED

Ask students to identify the objects and activities pictured. Make sure they understand what each image represents.

ACTIVITIES

These activities give students an opportunity to begin communicating with each other and with you, focusing on the theme and objectives of the chapter. The activities can be used as oral class activities, or, if you prefer, you can pair students to achieve more interaction.

Generalmente, ¿cómo estás antes de un viaje?¿Y después?
Class activity to introduce vocabulary. Describe and ask about travel scenarios. Use body language to emphasize the feelings. Example:
Estás en el aeropuerto. Vas a subir al avión. ¿Cómo te sientes? ¿Emocionado? ¿Triste? ¿Cuántos de ustedes están nerviosos?
Extend this by applying it to holidays, tests, and other emotional situations.

¿Adónde fuiste en tu último viaje?¿Qué visitaste?
Class activity to review the preterite and introduce vocabulary. Model the question and answer and ask *¿Qué visitaste en Perú?* Allow invented locations (e.g., *el castillo de Drácula*).
Ask about places students know about. Vary the question structure (e.g., *Cuando visitaste Nueva York, ¿adónde fuiste?*)

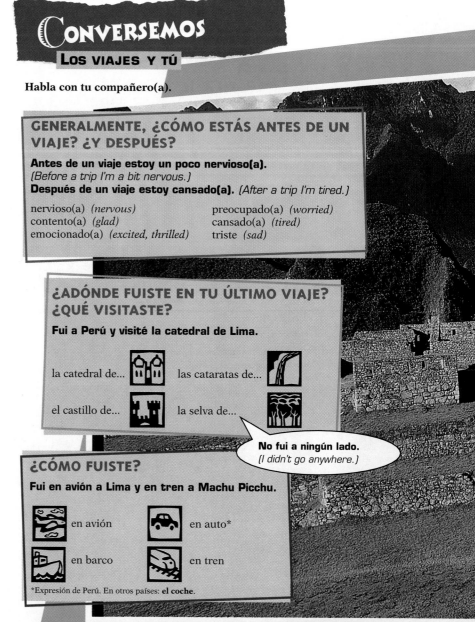

CONVERSEMOS

LOS VIAJES Y TÚ

Habla con tu compañero(a).

GENERALMENTE, ¿CÓMO ESTÁS ANTES DE UN VIAJE? ¿Y DESPUÉS?

Antes de un viaje estoy un poco nervioso(a).
(Before a trip I'm a bit nervous.)
Después de un viaje estoy cansado(a). *(After a trip I'm tired.)*

nervioso(a) *(nervous)*	preocupado(a) *(worried)*
contento(a) *(glad)*	cansado(a) *(tired)*
emocionado(a) *(excited, thrilled)*	triste *(sad)*

¿ADÓNDE FUISTE EN TU ÚLTIMO VIAJE? ¿QUÉ VISITASTE?

Fui a Perú y visité la catedral de Lima.

la catedral de...   las cataratas de...

el castillo de...   la selva de...

No fui a ningún lado.
(I didn't go anywhere.)

¿CÓMO FUISTE?

Fui en avión a Lima y en tren a Machu Picchu.

en avión   en auto*

en barco   en tren

*Expresión de Perú. En otros países: **el coche**.

302

¿Cómo fuiste?
Class activity about transportation. When you ask the title question, refer to specific locations (*¿Cómo fuiste a Disney World?*). Extend with variations, such as:
¿Cómo fuiste a casa ayer, en autobús o en coche?
¿Y cómo fue tu padre al trabajo ayer?
¿Cómo fue Cristóbal Colón a América, en avión o en bicicleta?

MEETING INDIVIDUAL NEEDS

Reaching All Students

For Auditory Learners
The first person says *Yo compré [un tapiz]*, and each person adds an item: *Yo compré [un tapiz y un poncho.]*

For Visual Learners
Students describe travel photos to the class in the style of tour guides.

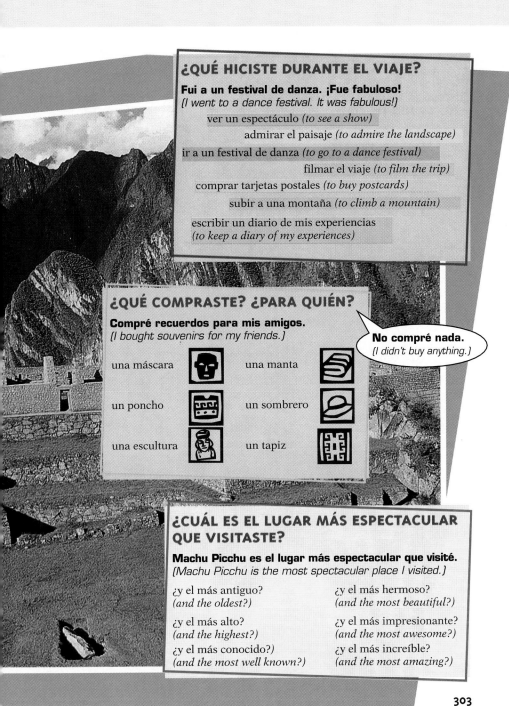

¿QUÉ HICISTE DURANTE EL VIAJE?

Fui a un festival de danza. ¡Fue fabuloso!
(I went to a dance festival. It was fabulous!)

ver un espectáculo *(to see a show)*

admirar el paisaje *(to admire the landscape)*

ir a un festival de danza *(to go to a dance festival)*

filmar el viaje *(to film the trip)*

comprar tarjetas postales *(to buy postcards)*

subir a una montaña *(to climb a mountain)*

escribir un diario de mis experiencias
(to keep a diary of my experiences)

¿QUÉ COMPRASTE? ¿PARA QUIÉN?

Compré recuerdos para mis amigos.
(I bought souvenirs for my friends.)

No compré nada.
(I didn't buy anything.)

una máscara   una manta

un poncho   un sombrero

una escultura   un tapiz

¿CUÁL ES EL LUGAR MÁS ESPECTACULAR QUE VISITASTE?

Machu Picchu es el lugar más espectacular que visité.
(Machu Picchu is the most spectacular place I visited.)

¿y el más antiguo?
(and the oldest?)

¿y el más hermoso?
(and the most beautiful?)

¿y el más alto?
(and the highest?)

¿y el más impresionante?
(and the most awesome?)

¿y el más conocido?
(and the most well known?)

¿y el más increíble?
(and the most amazing?)

303

¿Qué hiciste durante el viaje?

Class activity to talk about things you did on a trip, using preterite forms and new vocabulary. Model the title question and expressions.

Extend this by using questions from the earlier segments. Examples:
¿Estás nervioso cuando subes una montaña?
¿Cómo fuiste al espectáculo?
Provide more examples of the use of **durante** (e.g., *¿Qué hiciste durante el festival de danza?*)

¿Qué compraste? ¿Para quién?

Class activity to review the preterite of **comprar** and introduce vocabulary for shopping. Model the questions and the answer. Then ask these and other questions. Example:
¿Saben ustedes qué recuerdo compré para mi madre?
Extend this by having everyone select a favorite souvenir. Then poll the class:
¿A quiénes les gustó más la máscara?

¿Cuál es el lugar más espectacular que visitaste?

Class activity to introduce the superlative construction. Review **más... que, mejor... que, menos... que, peor... que,** and use **más... que** to introduce **el... más:**
Macchu Pichu es más hermosa que Cuzco.
Macchu Pichu es la ciudad más hermosa que vi en Perú.
Extend this by using other adjectives (e.g., *emocionante, aburrido, interesante*) and stating comparisons in other ways *(Peoria es menos conocida que Chicago. Chicago es la ciudad más conocida en el estado de Illinois.)*.

CHECK

- *¿Adónde fuiste durante tus vacaciones?*
- *¿Cómo fuiste, en coche o en avión?*
- *¿Compraste recuerdos? ¿Qué compraste?*
- *¿Cuál es tu clase más interesante?*

PORTFOLIO

Have students write five or six sentences about *el lugar más espectacular que visité.*

REALIDADES

Communicative Objectives
- to use superlatives to describe something
- to learn about Peru

Related Components

Activity Book p. 148	**Audio Tapes** Listening Tape: 7B, Seg. 2
Audio Book Script: Seg. 2	**Cuaderno** p. 94

GETTING STARTED

Has anyone ever kept a travel diary? What kinds of things did (would) you mention?

DISCUSS

Ask students to look at the dates on the photos and in the diary, and to establish the order in which things happened. Talk about the diary and the photos, and ask questions. Suggestions:

jueves 25 de junio
¿Dónde están y adónde van?
¿De dónde vienen? (Miren la foto del 22.)
Show on a map: *Esa cordillera es larga. Ésta es larguísima.*

domingo 28, Machu Picchu
¿Qué ciudad es increíble?
¿Qué lugar piensas que es impresionante?
¿Qué hace la chica?
Miren, yo también estoy sacando fotos.

miércoles 1 de julio
Escucha: alto, altura.
Si el lago está a 3.865 metros de altura, ¿está altísimo?

viernes 3 de julio
¿Cómo es el Cañón de Colca?
¿Cuál es más profundo, el Gran Cañón del Colorado o el Cañón de Colca?

martes 7 de julio,
¿Qué hay en el desierto de Nazca?
¿Cuántos años tienen los dibujos?

las fotos
¿Quiénes viajaron con Teo?
¿Qué compraron en el mercado de Cuzco?

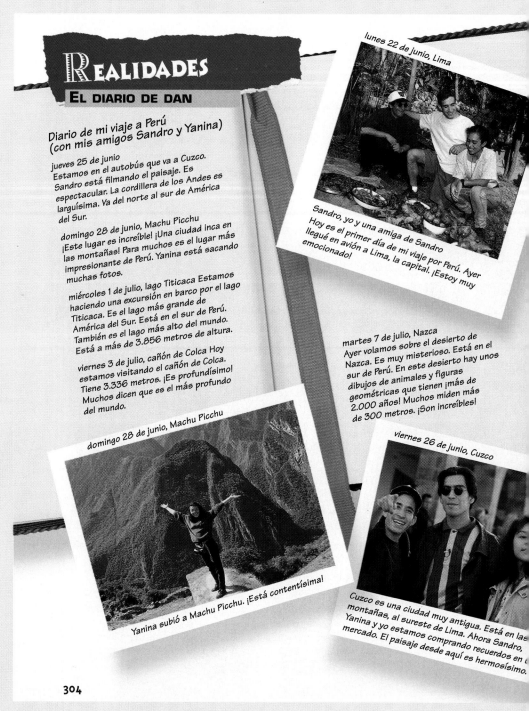

REALIDADES
EL DIARIO DE DAN

Diario de mi viaje a Perú
(con mis amigos Sandro y Yanina)

jueves 25 de junio
Estamos en el autobús que va a Cuzco. Sandro está filmando el paisaje. Es espectacular. La cordillera de los Andes es larguísima. Va del norte al sur de América del Sur.

domingo 28 de junio, Machu Picchu
¡Este lugar es increíble! ¡Una ciudad inca en las montañas! Para muchos es el lugar más impresionante de Perú. Yanina está sacando muchas fotos.

miércoles 1 de julio, lago Titicaca Estamos haciendo una excursión en barco por el lago Titicaca. Es el lago más grande de América del Sur. Está en el sur de Perú. También es el lago más alto del mundo. Está a más de 3.856 metros de altura.

viernes 3 de julio, cañón de Colca Hoy estamos visitando el cañón de Colca. Tiene 3.336 metros. ¡Es profundísimo! Muchos dicen que es el más profundo del mundo.

lunes 22 de junio, Lima
Sandro, yo y una amiga de Sandro Hoy es el primer día de mi viaje por Perú. Ayer llegué en avión a Lima, la capital. ¡Estoy muy emocionado!

martes 7 de julio, Nazca
Ayer volamos sobre el desierto de Nazca. Es muy misterioso. Está en el sur de Perú. En este desierto hay unos dibujos de animales y figuras geométricas que tienen ¡más de 2.000 años! Muchos miden más de 300 metros. ¡Son increíbles!

domingo 28 de junio, Machu Picchu
Yanina subió a Machu Picchu. ¡Está contentísima!

viernes 26 de junio, Cuzco
Cuzco es una ciudad muy antigua. Está en las montañas, al sureste de Lima. Ahora Sandro, Yanina y yo estamos comprando recuerdos en mercado. El paisaje desde aquí es hermosísimo.

304

✓ CULTURE NOTE

The Nazca lines, or geoglyphs, include images as much as 1,000 feet tall and lines as long as 13 miles. They were drawn by removing the darker sediments of the desert soil and exposing lighter surfaces. About 2,000 years old, they owe their preservation to a lack of rain and wind that cleans but has not destroyed them. Most of the figures are undecipherable from the ground, but a few were drawn on hillsides.

HABLA DEL DIARIO DE VIAJE

A. ¿Qué lugar es?

> *un lago altísimo: el lago Titicaca*

- una ciudad muy antigua con un paisaje hermosísimo
- una cordillera larguísima
- el lugar más impresionante de Perú
- un cañón profundísimo
- un desierto muy misterioso

B. Pregúntale a tu compañero(a) qué lugares visitaron Dan y sus amigos, dónde están y cómo son según el diario.

> — ¿Dónde está Cuzco?
> — Está en las montañas, al este de Lima.
> — ¿Cómo es?
> — Es una ciudad muy antigua.

C. Habla con tu compañero(a) sobre lo que Dan y sus amigos hicieron durante su viaje.

> — ¿Qué hicieron en el lago Tititaca?
> — Hicieron una excursión en barco.

¿QUÉ OPINAS?

En grupo, hagan una lista de lugares especiales del mundo que conocen. Digan cómo es cada uno. Anoten las respuestas en la tabla. Usen el modelo.

¿Cuál es el lugar más...?	espectacular	divertido	misterioso	conocido	impresionante	aburrido
El Gran Cañón del Colorado	✓	✓				
Nueva York					✓	
Las cataratas del Niágara						
Los Alpes						
Los Andes						
El desierto del Sahara						

Informen a la clase de los resultados.

Habla del diario de viaje

Pair Activity: Description
A. Which places in Peru are these?
Correct Answers:
- *Cuzco*
- *la cordillera de los Andes*
- *Machu Picchu*
- *el cañón de Colca*
- *el desierto de Nazca*

B. Take turns asking what places Dan and his friends visited, where those places are, and how they are described in his diary.
C. Talk about what Dan and his friends did during their trip.
Answers: See models on student page.
Application: Use the adjectives on these pages to describe a place in your state.

¿Qué opinas?

Group Activity: Taking a Poll
List places you know something about. Choose an adjective to describe each one. Record the group's responses on a chart.
Analysis: Each group reports to the class, and results are combined. The class talks about the final chart.

CHECK

- ¿Donde tú vives, ¿qué lugar es profundísimo? ¿Y qué lugar es hermosísimo? ¿Y famosísimo?
- ¿Cuál de estos lugares en Perú crees que es el más interesante? ¿Por qué?
- ¿Qué te gustaría hacer en uno de los lugares que visitaron los chicos?

305

Para hispanohablantes

Write a paragraph describing a photo of a place that interests you. Read your paragraph to the class.

Communicative Objectives

To talk about:
• souvenirs
• what people are doing
• what things are made of

Related Components

Activity Book p. 149-150	Transparencies Ch. 12: Palabras en acción
Cuaderno p. 95-96	Tutor Page p. 51

GETTING STARTED

Ask if anyone has ever been to a store or market that specializes in souvenirs. How was it similar to the one in the drawing? How was it different?

DISCUSS

Review location expressions with a few questions about the drawing. Examples:
¿Qué ropa hay a la izquierda del dibujo?
¿Qué está vendiendo la persona que está en la mesa, a la derecha del dibujo?

Para hispanohablantes

Some Spanish speakers in your class may use other words or expressions. Ask them to share with the class. A few variations:

la catarata: la cascada, el salto de agua
delgado/a: flaco/a
filmar video: grabar video
la manta: la frisa, la frazada
la máscara: la careta
el paisaje: la vista
de piedra: de roca
la selva: la jungla

PALABRAS EN ACCIÓN

COMPRANDO RECUERDOS

el océano

la costa

Estoy buscando a mi hija. Estoy muy preocupado.

el tapiz

¿Qué está haciendo?

el poncho

el sombrero

Está haciendo una manta de lana. Es hermosísima, ¿no?

¿Qué tal la excursión?

¡Fue una experiencia increíble!

la manta

 1 ¿Qué ves en el dibujo?

Haz una lista de las cosas que ves en el dibujo. Compara tu lista con la lista de tu compañero(a).

una manta de lana,...

2 ¿Qué hace?

Con tu compañero(a), digan qué hacen las personas del dibujo.

Un chico filma las esculturas.
Un hombre busca a su hija.

3 ¿Qué están vendiendo?

Di qué están vendiendo las personas del dibujo.

Un hombre está vendiendo máscaras de madera.
Una mujer está vendiendo mantas de lana.

4 ¿Cómo está?

¿Cómo están las personas del dibujo? Pregúntale a tu compañero(a).

— ¿Cómo está el padre de la chica?
— Está preocupado.

306

For students having difficulty talking about traveling or describing places of interest, you might consider:
• **The tutor page:** Pair the student with a native speaker or a more able student, using the tutor page.
• **Actividades:** see page 300C: *De Lima a Cuzco*

5 Recuerdos del mundo

¿Qué recuerdos te gustaría comprar?
Habla con tu compañero(a).

— ¿Qué recuerdos te gustaría
comprar?
— Me gustaría comprar una escultura
de piedra.

6 Viajes por el mundo

Habla con tu compañero(a) de las cosas
que hiciste durante un viaje.

— Cuando fui a Yellowstone compré
muchas tarjetas postales. ¿Y tú?
— Yo, cuando fui a España, visité la
catedral de Sevilla.

7 Cartel

Haz un cartel para invitar a gente de otros
países a una fiesta tradicional de tu pueblo
o ciudad. Di cuándo es, qué celebran y
dónde la celebran.

8 Tú eres el autor

Estás en Perú, en un viaje de intercambio.
En una carta a tus padres, di qué cosas
estás viendo.

Queridos papá y mamá:

*Les escribo esta carta desde Cuzco.
La cordillera de los Andes es
impresionante. Mañana voy a ir a
la playa. Mi amigo dice que la
costa de Perú es hermosísima.
¡Hasta pronto!*

Ramón

307

1. Pair Activity
Make and compare lists of the things you
see in the drawing.
Application: Say what several objects in
the drawing are made of. For example:
Las mesas son de madera.

2. Pair Activity
Say what each person in the drawing is
doing.
Application: Say what other students in
your class are doing.

3. Individual or Pair Activity
Say what the people in the drawing are
selling.
Challenge: Say what other people in the
drawing are doing. Example:
Unos señores están tocando la guitarra.

4. Pair Activity
Say how you think the people in the
drawing are feeling.

5. Pair Activity
Discuss what you would like to buy in
Cuzco and why.
Application: Describe an object you
bought recently.

6. Roleplay Activity
Talk with a partner about what you did
during a trip.
Application: Ask what your partner's family
members did recently. Example:
¿Qué hicieron tus padres anoche?

7. Hands-On Activity
Make a poster inviting people from other
countries to a traditional festival in your
town or city. Say when it is, what you celebrate, and where.
Analysis: Put up the posters and have
other students say to what celebration they
are going and why.

8. Synthesizing Activity
You are in Peru on an exchange program.
Write a letter to your family about some of
the things you have been seeing.
Synthesis: Write a note telling family mem-
bers what souvenirs you bought for them.
Describe the presents.

CHECK

- *¿Qué están vendiendo las personas en el
dibujo?*
- *¿Qué compraste en tu último viaje?*
- *Describe un lugar que visitaste.*

LOG BOOK
Have students write down any vocabulary
they have difficulty remembering.

Community Link
Go to a crafts fair in your community and
describe what you see.

PARA COMUNICARNOS MEJOR

Communicative Objectives

• to say what is happening right now, using a form of **estar** and the present participle of a verb
• to say that something or someone is outstanding, using **el/la... más**
• to emphasize something, by adding **-ísimo/a** to an adjective

Related Components

Activity Book p. 151-152	**Audio Tapes** Listening: 7B, Seg. 3
Audio Book Script: Seg. 3 Activities: p. 101	**Cuaderno** p. 97
	Tutor Page p. 52

GETTING STARTED

Language in Context

Present Progressive Tense: Have a volunteer pretend to be a private detective walking down a street in Peru and talking into a cellular phone in English. The investigator is describing what he or she is seeing and doing.

Superlatives: Draw three figures, two the same size and one taller, and compare them. Example: *Juan y Tina son altos, pero Claudio es la persona más alta de la clase.* Draw another, much taller figure and add: *Miguel es altísimo.*
Ask how to express these ideas in English.

DISCUSS

Review vocabulary and introduce some of this chapter's vocabulary with questions and statements that use present progressive and superlative constructions.
¿Qué estamos haciendo ahora?
¿Qué están diciendo ustedes?
¿Por qué estás hablando?
¿Cuál es la clase más interesante?
¿Y quién es altísimo?
¿Qué están escribiendo?
¿Qué estoy leyendo?

PARA COMUNICARNOS MEJOR
¿QUÉ ESTÁS HACIENDO EN PERÚ?

To describe an action in progress, use the present progressive tense.

To form the present progressive, use a form of the verb *estar (to be)* followed by a present participle (called *gerundio* in Spanish).

> *Estoy visitando Lima.* I'm visiting Lima.

To form the *gerundio* of regular verbs, replace the *-ar* ending of a verb with *-ando*, and the *-er* and *-ir* endings with *-iendo*.

present progressive			
Verb	**drop**	**add**	
cantar	-ar	-ando	**cantando**
comer	-er	-iendo	**comiendo**
escribir	-ir	-iendo	**escribiendo**

Note that spelling changes occur in the superlative when the last syllable of an adjective starts with **c**, **g**, or ends with **z**:
simpático > **simpatiquísimo**, **largo** > **larguísimo** and **feliz** > **felicísimo**.

To describe a person, place, or thing that stands out from all the rest, use the superlative construction.

To form the superlative, use the definite article, a noun, and *más* followed by an adjective.

> *Cuzco es la ciudad más conocida de Perú.* Cuzco is the best known city in Peru.

□ Another way to form a superlative is to add the ending *-ísimo (-ísima, -ísimos, ísimas)* to the singular form of the adjective. If the adjective ends in a vowel, drop the vowel before adding the superlative ending.

> *La música es popularísima.* The music is very popular.
> *Los Andes son altísimos.* The Andes are extremely high.

308

For students having difficulty using the present progressive or superlative constructions, you might consider:
• **The tutor page:** Pair the student with a native speaker or a more able student, using the tutor page.
• **Actividades:** see pages 300C-300D: *¿Qué están haciendo?* and *El más, el menos*

1 Viajando por Perú

Un(a) amigo(a) está viajando por Perú y te llama por teléfono. Pregúntale qué está haciendo en cada lugar.

> — Hola, hoy estoy en los Andes.
> — ¡Qué bueno! ¿Y qué estás haciendo?
> — Estoy paseando por las montañas.

> En Perú
> pasear por las montañas
> sacar fotos
> visitar la catedral
> navegar
> admirar el paisaje
> ver el Festival del Sol

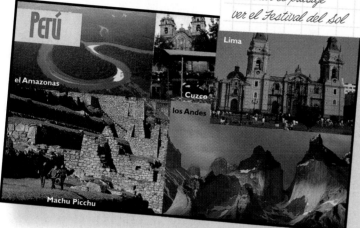

2 ¿Cómo es?

Con tu compañero(a), habla de lugares y otras cosas de Perú.

> — ¿Cómo son los Andes?
> — Son altísimos.

1. los Andes/altos
2. el río Amazonas/largo
3. el lago Titicaca/grande
4. la catedral/interesante
5. la selva/hermosa
6. el cañón de Colca/profundo

3 En tu estado

¿Cuál es el lugar más...? Pregúntale a tu compañero(a).

> — En tu opinión, ¿cuál es el lugar más espectacular del estado?
> — El lago...

1. espectacular
2. conocido
3. alto
4. interesante
5. popular
6. grande

309

PARA COMUNICARNOS MEJOR

Objective
- to learn about the different uses and meanings of **ser** and **estar**

Related Components

Activity Book p. 153-154	**Audio Tapes** Listening: 7B, Seg. 4
Audio Book Script: Seg. 4 Activities: p. 102	**Cuaderno** p. 98
	Tutor Page p. 53

GETTING STARTED

Language in Context

Ask how many different things *I am*...or *It is*...can mean. (Refer to the student edition list of things that **ser** and **estar** are used to express.)

Go over the list, clarifying and giving (and asking for) examples:

El libro es aburrido. Yo estoy aburrido.
El hielo es frío. Mi café está frío.
¿Estás listo? ¿Eres listo?

Discuss advantages and disadvantages of having two words to express what English expresses with one. Make sure students understand that **ser** and **estar** are not synonyms but must always be used in specific situations.

Collaborate with the class in the creation of two brief "stories": one that employs the five uses of **ser** and one that employs the three uses of **estar**. If there is time, try variations on this theme, such as a story in which neither word may be used twice in a row (i.e., you must alternate between **ser** sentences and **estar** sentences).

DISCUSS

Review vocabulary and introduce some of this chapter's vocabulary with questions and statements employing **ser** and **estar**.

¿Quién es tu mejor amigo?
¿Qué es tu mejor amigo?
¿Cómo es tu mejor amigo?
¿Cómo está tu mejor amigo?
¿De dónde es tu mejor amigo?
¿Dónde está tu mejor amigo?
¿Cuándo es su cumpleaños?
¿Qué está haciendo tu mejor amigo?

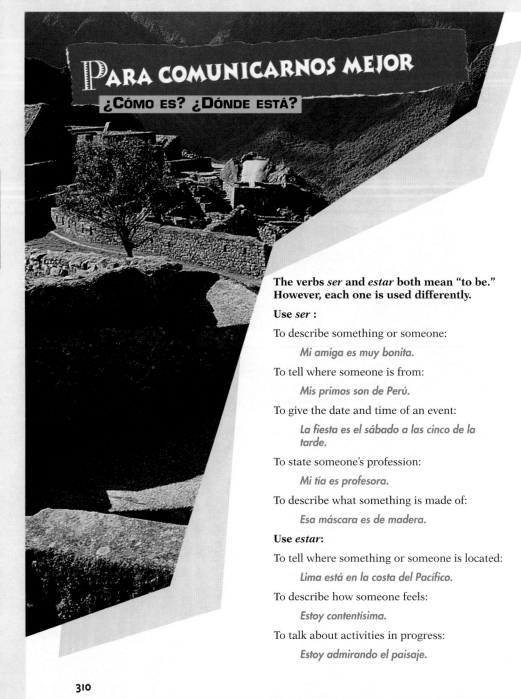

PARA COMUNICARNOS MEJOR
¿CÓMO ES? ¿DÓNDE ESTÁ?

The verbs *ser* and *estar* both mean "to be." However, each one is used differently.

Use *ser* :

To describe something or someone:

> *Mi amiga es muy bonita.*

To tell where someone is from:

> *Mis primos son de Perú.*

To give the date and time of an event:

> *La fiesta es el sábado a las cinco de la tarde.*

To state someone's profession:

> *Mi tía es profesora.*

To describe what something is made of:

> *Esa máscara es de madera.*

Use *estar*:

To tell where something or someone is located:

> *Lima está en la costa del Pacífico.*

To describe how someone feels:

> *Estoy contentísima.*

To talk about activities in progress:

> *Estoy admirando el paisaje.*

310

For students having difficulty with the different uses of **ser** and **estar,** you might consider:
- **The tutor page:** Pair the student with a native speaker or a more able student, using the tutor page.
- **Actividades:** see page 300D: *¿Soy o estoy guapa?*

1 Una visita a Cuzco

Un grupo de turistas está visitando Cuzco. ¿Qué están haciendo? ¿Cómo están?

— *Una mujer está escuchando música de los Andes. Está muy emocionada.*

1. una mujer/escuchar música de los Andes
2. un chico/sacar fotos de un festival de danza
3. dos jóvenes/comprar tapices en el mercado
4. un padre/buscar a su hija
5. dos chicas/pasear por la Plaza de Armas
6. un hombre/subir a una montaña

¿Cómo está(n)?
emocionado(a)
cansado(a)
contento(a)
nervioso(a)
preocupado(a)

2 Centros turísticos

Nombra cinco lugares. Di dónde están y cómo son.

Las cataratas del Niágara están en el estado de Nueva York y son impresionantes.

1. las cataratas de...
2. el desierto de...
3. las montañas de...

4. el lago...
5. el valle...
6. la playa...

3 Veo, veo

¿Sabes jugar al *Veo, veo*? Una persona dice que ve una cosa, pero no dice qué es; sus compañeros(as) le hacen preguntas para adivinar.

— *Veo, veo.*
— *¿Qué ves?*
— *Una cosa.*
— *¿De qué es?*
— *Es de lana.*
— *¿De qué color es?*
— *Es azul.*

Veo, veo
¿De qué color es?
¿De qué es?
¿Cómo es?
¿Dónde está?

¡Es un poncho!

311

Students use the present progressive to say what people are doing, **estar** to say how someone feels or where something is, and **ser** to describe someone/thing.

1. Individual or Pair Activity
Some tourists are visiting Cuzco. What are they doing and how do they feel?
Possible Answers:
1. See model on student page.
2. *Un chico está sacando fotos de un festival de danza. Está contentísimo.*
3. *Dos jóvenes están comprando tapices en el mercado. Están muy nerviosos.*
4. *Un padre está buscando a su hija. Está muy preocupado.*
5. *Dos chicas están paseando por la Plaza de Armas. Están muy contentas.*
6. *Un señor está subiendo una montaña. Está cansadísimo.*

2. Individual or Pair Activity
Name five places you have visited. Say where they are and describe them.
Possible Answers:
1. See model on student page.
2. *El desierto de Nazca está en Perú y es espectacular.*
3. *Las montañas Rocosas están en Colorado. Son impresionantísimas.*
4. *El lago Superior está en Minnesota y es muy frío.*
5. *El valle del río Colorado está en Arizona y es el paisaje más impresionante del país.*
6. *La playa Ipanema está en Río de Janeiro y es hermosísima.*

3. General Activity
Can you play *Veo, veo*? One person says "I see something," but doesn't say what it is. The others have five questions to guess what it is. (See model on student page.)

- *¿Cómo eres?*
- *¿Dónde está Perú?*
- *¿Qué es tu madre?*
- *¿Cómo estás hoy?*
- *¿De dónde es tu padre?*
- *¿Qué está haciendo Carlos?*

PORTFOLIO
Write a story that includes all the uses of **ser** and **estar**. (See the suggestion in *Language in Context.*)

TALLER DE ESCRITORES

Objectives
- to develop writing skills
- to integrate the grammar and vocabulary for this unit

Related Components

Activity Book	Assessment
p. 143-144	Portfolio: p. 38

◻ ACTIVITIES

1. ¿Una vida solitaria?
Homework:
Individual activity to review chapter vocabulary and the future tense.

2. Las escuelas del futuro
Homework:
Individual activity to review chapter vocabulary, vocabulary from previous levels, the future tense, and possibly the subjunctive after conjunctions such as para que.

3. Libros y predicciones
Homework: Individual activity to review vocabulary, the future tense, and possibly the subjunctive after conjunctions such as cuando.

4. Tu microcuento:
Homework: Individual activity to review a variety of lexical and grammatical items.

SITUACIONES
VIAJES LA AVENTURA

LOS ANDES A CABALLO

PASA CINCO DÍAS VIAJANDO A CABALLO, DE ARGENTINA A CHILE, DURMIENDO AL AIRE LIBRE, ADMIRANDO PAISAJES ESPECTACULARES, VIENDO VOLAR AL CÓNDOR, EL AVE VOLADORA MÁS GRANDE DEL MUNDO, Y CONOCIENDO ESTA LARGUÍSIMA CORDILLERA.

HAY DOS ITINERARIOS POSIBLES:
- POR EL RÍO GRANDE Y CAMPANARIO
- POR EL RÍO ATUEL

EL PRIMERO ES MÁS FÁCIL. EL SEGUNDO LLEGA A ALTURAS MÁS ALTAS, HASTA LOS 4.000 METROS.

LA SELVA DEL AMAZONAS EN BOTE

PASA UNA SEMANA EN EL PARQUE NACIONAL DE MANU, VIAJANDO EN BOTE, ACAMPANDO EN LAS ORILLAS DEL RÍO DE LAS SERPIENTES Y VISITANDO ESTA HERMOSÍSIMA RESERVA NATURAL PERUANA. LA FLORA Y LA FAUNA SON IMPRESIONANTES: HAY MÁS DE 1.000 ESPECIES DE PÁJAROS, 200 ESPECIES DE MAMÍFEROS Y MÁS DE 15.000 ESPECIES DE PLANTAS. EN MANU TAMBIÉN PUEDES VISITAR RUINAS ARQUEOLÓGICAS.

312

How do you keep in touch with friends or relatives back home: mail, e-mail, phone, or fax? In your opinion, what are the advantages and disadvantages of each medium?

A viajar

Haz una lista de las actividades que puedes hacer en los viajes de los anuncios.

Los Andes a caballo: dormir al aire libre,...
La selva del Amazonas en bote: viajar en bote,...

 Viajes increíbles

Pregúntale a tu compañero(a) si alguna vez hizo un viaje similar a los viajes de los anuncios.

— *¿Viajaste alguna vez a un lugar espectacular?*
— *Sí, viajé a las montañas de Colorado.*
— *¿Cómo son?*
— *Son altísimas. El paisaje es increíble...*

 Lugares hermosísimos

Con tu compañero(a), habla de un lugar hermosísimo que te gustaría visitar. Di dónde está y describe cómo es el lugar.

— *Me gustaría visitar las cataratas del Niágara.*
— *¿Dónde están?*
— *En el norte del estado de Nueva York, cerca de Buffalo.*
— *¿Cómo son?*
— *Son las cataratas más grandes de América del Norte y son altísimas. Y a ti, ¿qué lugar te gustaría visitar?*

 Entrevista

Entrevista a un(a) compañero(a). Pregúntale cuál fue el peor viaje que hizo y por qué. Informa a la clase.

Juan hizo un viaje al valle del Hudson. No hizo excursiones por el valle porque llovió muchísimo. Fue el peor viaje de su vida.

 Una postal

Estás visitando Perú. Escríbele una postal a tu amigo(a). Dile dónde estás, qué lugares estás visitando, cómo son esos lugares y qué estás haciendo.

Querido Esteban:
Te estoy escribiendo desde Perú. Ayer visité Lima, la capital. Es hermosísima. Estoy practicando muchísimo español y estoy conociendo gente simpatiquísima. Mañana voy a ir a Machu Picchu.
Hasta pronto,

Carlos

PARA TU REFERENCIA

a caballo *by horse*
acampando *camping*
el alojamiento *accomodation*
el ave voladora *flying bird*
el bote *boat*
durmiendo *sleeping*
el segundo *the second one*

313

3. Pair Activity
Talk about a very beautiful place you would like to visit. Say where it is and describe it.
Answers: See model on student page.
Extension: One partner says something, and the other says it in a stronger way:
A: *Es tarde.*
B: *¡No es tarde, es tardísimo!*

4. Pair Activity
Interview your partner about the worst trip he or she has taken, and what made it so. (If you never had an unpleasant trip, make one up.) Tell the class what you found out about your partner's trip.
Answers: See model on student page.
Extension: Exaggerate the description in the example. Use **más** and **-ísimo/a.**

5. Homework or Classwork
You're visiting Peru. Write a postcard to a friend, saying where you are, what places you're visiting, what they are like, and what you are doing.
Answers: See model on student page.
Challenge: Imagine that you are in Hollywood. Describe what famous people you see and say what they are doing when you see them.

CHECK

• *¿Qué hay de interesante en la selva del Amazonas?*
• *¿Qué están haciendo los caballos en la foto?*
• *¿Dónde está el Parque Nacional de Manu?*
• *¿Cómo es tu compañera?*
• *¿Cómo es tu película favorita?*

LOG BOOK
Have students write a description of a person using **ser, estar,** the present progressive, and at least one superlative.

Para hispanohablantes

Make riddles using descriptions of class members and have the class guess who they are. Write them down and make copies to distribute to the class.

Objectives
Communicative: to describe geographic characteristics of a country
Cultural: to learn about a country in South America

Related Components

Transparencies	Video: Tape/Book
Ch. 12: Para resolver	Unit 6: Seg. 3

Search to frame 1395003

GETTING STARTED

Ask students to volunteer anything they know about South America. Has anybody in the class lived in South America? What images come to mind when South America is mentioned?

APPLY

Divide the class into groups. Each group will research one of these countries:

Argentina	Ecuador
Bolivia	Paraguay
Chile	Uruguay
Colombia	Venezuela

PASO 1: Los países
Select a country and describe where it is located in relation to other countries. **Note:** Make sure that each group selects a different country. Do not allow Peru. Because students will probably not be able to find Spanish sources, allow them to use the English names.
Answers: See model on student page.
Application: Write a slightly inaccurate statement about where your country is located. Trade statements with another group and correct what they wrote.

PASO 2: La investigación
Find out about the country you chose. Write a paragraph about the capital of that country and five places of special geographic interest in that country. Describe each place.
Answers: See model on student page.
Class Activity: One member of each group reads the group's paragraph to the class while another member points to the places on a map.

PASO 3: Las actividades
Make a list of activities that people can do in that country.
Answers: See model on student page.
Synthesis: Imagine that you are in that country. Write a postcard to a friend or family member from each of the five places described in the paragraph from Step 2, saying what you are doing and seeing there.

PASO 4: La información
Make a map of the country. Draw logos for the places and the activities you chose. Write the name of each place. Use the map on page 315 as a model.

PASO 5: Intercambios
Show and explain your map to the class.

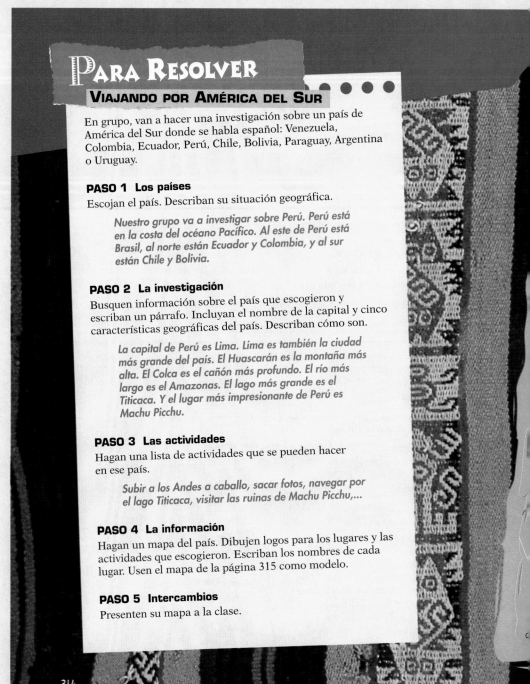

PARA RESOLVER
VIAJANDO POR AMÉRICA DEL SUR

En grupo, van a hacer una investigación sobre un país de América del Sur donde se habla español: Venezuela, Colombia, Ecuador, Perú, Chile, Bolivia, Paraguay, Argentina o Uruguay.

PASO 1 Los países
Escojan el país. Describan su situación geográfica.

> *Nuestro grupo va a investigar sobre Perú. Perú está en la costa del océano Pacífico. Al este de Perú está Brasil, al norte están Ecuador y Colombia, y al sur están Chile y Bolivia.*

PASO 2 La investigación
Busquen información sobre el país que escogieron y escriban un párrafo. Incluyan el nombre de la capital y cinco características geográficas del país. Describan cómo son.

> *La capital de Perú es Lima. Lima es también la ciudad más grande del país. El Huascarán es la montaña más alta. El Colca es el cañón más profundo. El río más largo es el Amazonas. El lago más grande es el Titicaca. Y el lugar más impresionante de Perú es Machu Picchu.*

PASO 3 Las actividades
Hagan una lista de actividades que se pueden hacer en ese país.

> *Subir a los Andes a caballo, sacar fotos, navegar por el lago Titicaca, visitar las ruinas de Machu Picchu,...*

PASO 4 La información
Hagan un mapa del país. Dibujen logos para los lugares y las actividades que escogieron. Escriban los nombres de cada lugar. Usen el mapa de la página 315 como modelo.

PASO 5 Intercambios
Presenten su mapa a la clase.

314

Mar Caribe

OCÉANO ATLÁNTICO

Barranquilla

Caracas

PANAMÁ

VENEZUELA

Bogotá

COLOMBIA

Georgetown
Paramaribo

Salto del
Ángel

GUYANA

SURINAM

Cayena

GUAYANA FRANCESA (Fr.)

Quito

Río Orinoco

ECUADOR

Río Amazonas

Ecuador

PERÚ

gos
or)

CORDILLERA DE LOS ANDES

Machu
Picchu

BRASIL

Lima

Cuzco

Lago
Titicaca

La Paz

BOLIVIA

Brasília

N

Sucre

PARAGUAY

co de Capricornio

CHILE

San Miguel
de Tucumán

Asunción

Cataratas
del Iguazú

Río de Janeiro

São Paulo

ANO

Aconcagua
(6959 m)

Río Paraná

ÍFICO

Valparaíso

Córdoba

Santiago

ARGENTINA

URUGUAY

Montevideo

OCÉANO
ATLÁNTICO

Concepción

Buenos
Aires

Río de la Plata

ica del Sur

nacional

Estrecho de
Magallanes

Islas Malvinas
(R.U.)

300

600 kilómetros

300

Cabo de Hornos

Tierra
del Fuego

¿SABES QUE...?

According to legend, Manco Capac, the first Inca, emerged from the waters of Lake Titicaca and was sent by the Sun God, Inti, to civilize the people of the earth. Manco Capac used a golden staff, given to him by Inti, to find the right place to settle. At the spot where the staff sank into the ground, he created Cuzco, the capital of the Inca empire. Cuzco is a Quechua word that means "belly button of the world." To the Incas, the belly button is the source and center of energy.

315

MEETING INDIVIDUAL NEEDS

Reaching All Students

For Visual Learners
Draw cartoons of your group in your country. Write captions in which you say what you are doing.

For Kinesthetic Learners
One person mimes the actions and reactions of a traveler as another narrates: *José está andando en los Andes. José está pensando "¡Estas montañas son altísimas!"*

CHECK

LOG BOOK
Write a summary of your research notes.

Background
Suggestions for the Lists
Capitals and geographic location are indicated on the map.

Argentina
Aconcagua, *montaña más alta, sacar fotos;* **Iguazu,** *cataratas más altas, visitar;* **Buenos Aires,** *ciudad más grande, hacer compras*

Bolivia
La Paz, *la ciudad más grande y la capital más alta, visitar la ciudad;* **Nevado Samaja,** *la montaña más alta, sacar fotos;* **Cerca de Fortaleza,** *el lugar más bajo, visitar;* **Lago Titicaca,** *el lago más alto, navegar*

Chile
Atacama, *un desierto, visitar;* **la isla de Pascua,** *lugar misterioso, sacar fotos;* **Llanquihue,** *lago muy grande, navegar;* **Torres del Paine,** *parque nacional, visitar*

Colombia
Cristobal Colón, *montaña más alta, subir a la montaña;* **Nevado del Ruiz,** *un volcán, visitar el volcán;* **Río Amazonas,** *el río más largo de las Américas, sacar fotos de los animales*

Ecuador
Volcán Chimborazo, *un volcán, subir al volcán,* **Islas Galápagos,** *islas con animales muy interesantes, sacar fotos;* **el Ecuador,** *una línea imaginaria, acampar*

Paraguay
Río Paraguay, *un río, navegar;* **Ruinas de los Jesuitas,** *misiones antiguas, ver artesanías;* **Ypacaraí e Ypoá,** *los lagos más grandes de Paraguay, navegar*

Uruguay
Mirador Nacional, *la montaña más alta de Uruguay, ver el paisaje;* **Embalse del Río Negro,** *un río, nadar;* **Río Uruguay,** *el río más importante, navegar*

Venezuela
Lago Maracaibo, *el lago más grande de América del Sur;* **Caracas,** *ciudad importante, visitar museos;* **El salto del Ángel,** *la catarata más alta del mundo, acampar*

Objectives

Communicative: to describe an animal
Cultural: to learn about the llama, an important animal in the Andes

Related Components

Audio Tapes	Conexiones
Conexiones: 18B, Ch. 12	Chapter 12
	Magazine
	Juntos en América del Sur

GETTING STARTED

Ask if anyone has ever seen a llama. What do students know about this animal?

DISCUSS

Using the Text

Ask some comprehension and critical-thinking questions. Suggestions:
¿Dónde viven las llamas?
¿De dónde son los camellos?
¿Cuáles son los primos de la llama?
¿De qué colores tienen el pelo?

Using Context Clues

Miren la foto de la llama. ¿Saben cómo se llama la llama? La llama se llama Lana.
Ask if anyone had any problems understanding what you said. Why?
Elicit the idea that some words are spelled and/or sound the same but have different meanings. Ask for examples of English homonyms, such as *pale* and *pail*. Do we confuse these? How do context clues help us tell which meaning is the right one? How do we know that the word **llama** on this page—and in the sentence above— refers to the animal and not the phrase *is called?* (Some things: the photo, the article **la** in front of the word, the names of similar animals, the description)
Why does Spanish have these two words that look and sound alike? (The animal is native to Peru and was named before the Spanish arrived.)

ENTÉRATE
LAS LLAMAS DE LOS ANDES

La llama es el animal más típico de los Andes. Es de la familia de los camellos.° Otros "camellos de los Andes" son la alpaca, la vicuña y el guanaco. Como el camello, todos tienen el cuello° muy largo. La llama es la más grande. Mide aproximadamente 1 metro 80 centímetros. Generalmente tiene el pelo blanco, pero también hay llamas negras y marrones.

La función de las llamas en Perú y otros países de los Andes es muy importante. Son animales de carga° que pueden llevar hasta 45 kilos. Están muy bien adaptadas al terreno montañoso° de los Andes. La lana de la llama sirve para° hacer tapices, telas° y tejidos.°

TE TOCA A TI

Completa las oraciones.

1. La llama es de la familia de...
2. Tres parientes de la llama son...
3. La llama mide...
4. La llama puede llevar hasta 45 kilos. Es un animal de...
5. La lana de la llama sirve para...

los animales de carga *pack animals*
los camellos *camels*
el cuello *neck*
sirve para *is used to*
las telas *fabrics*
los tejidos *woven goods*
el terreno montañoso *mountainous terrain*

316

CHECK

Te toca a ti
Answers:

1. ...los camellos.
2. ...la alpaca, la vicuña y el guanaco.
3. ...aproximademente 1 metro 80 centímetros.
4. ...carga.
5. ...hacer tapices, telas y tejidos.

Para hispanohablantes

Have you or anyone in your family ever owned an animal as unusual as a llama? Tell the class about it.

▶▶▶ INTERNET LINK

LlamaWeb http://www.webcom.com/ ~degraham/New.html

VOCABULARIO TEMÁTICO

¿Cómo viajas?
How do you travel?

en avión *by plane*
en barco *by boat*
en tren *by train*

La geografía de un país
The geography of a country

el cañón *canyon*
las cataratas *falls*
la cordillera *mountain range*
la costa *coast*
el desierto *desert*
la selva *rain forest*
el océano *ocean*
el valle *valley*

Lugares para visitar
Places to visit

el castillo *castle*
la catedral *cathedral*
la fortaleza *fortress*

Actividades turísticas
Travel related activities

admirar *to admire*
escribir un diario
 to keep a diary
filmar *to film*
subir a *to climb (a mountain)*

¿Cómo es el paisaje?
What is the landscape like?

altísimo(a) *extremely high*
alto(a) *high*

conocido(a) *well known*
espectacular *spectacular*
hermosísimo(a)
 exceptionally beautiful
hermoso(a) *beautiful*
impresionante *awesome*
increíble *amazing*
larguísimo(a) *extremely long*
misterioso *mysterious*
profundísimo *extremely deep*
profundo *deep*

Las artesanías y los recuerdos
Crafts and souvenirs

la escultura *sculpture*
la manta *blanket*
la máscara *mask*
el poncho *poncho*
el sombrero *hat*
el tapiz *tapestry*

¿De qué es?
What is it made of?

de lana *made of wool*
de madera *made of wood*
de piedra *made of stone*

¿Cómo estás?
How do you feel?

cansado(a) *tired*
contento(a) *glad*
emocionado(a) *excited, moved*
nervioso(a) *nervous*
preocupado(a) *worried*
triste *sad*

¿Cuánto mide?
How tall is it?

el centímetro *centimeter*
el metro *meter*
mide... *it measures . . .; he/she is . . . (feet/meters) tall*
miden *they measure . . . they are . . . (feet/meters) tall*
el pie *(measurement) foot*

Expresiones y palabras

el/la más alto(a) *the highest*
el/la más grande *the largest*
el/la/los/las más... *the most . . .*
No fui a ningún lado.
 I didn't go anywhere.
de altura *in height*
buscar *to look for*
el espectáculo *show*
la experiencia *experience*
el festival de danza
 dance festival
la guía turística *travel guide*
el mundo *world*
el paisaje *landscape*

Expresiones de Perú

el auto *car*
mi pata *my friend*

LA CONEXIÓN INGLÉS-ESPAÑOL

You know the meaning of the Spanish words *delicioso, famoso*, and *fabuloso*. What connection do you see between the endings of these words and their English cognates?

Look in the *Vocabulario temático*. Are there words that show the same pattern? What rule can you make up to find the English cognates of words like these?

317

La conexión inglés-español

The **-oso** endings of **delicioso, famoso,** and **fabuloso** are the equivalent of the **-ous** endings of their English cognates. In the *Vocabulario,* **misterioso** (mysterious) and **nervioso** (nervous) fit this pattern, although English drops the **i** in **nervioso**. Not all Spanish words that end in **-oso** have English cognates (e.g., **hermoso** and **peligroso**), and not all cognates end in **-ous** (e.g., *talentoso* and *lluvioso*).

Communicative Objectives
• to review vocabulary
• to correctly pronounce words containing the letter "k" and "w"

Related Components

Activity Book	Audio Tapes
Chapter Review: p. 155-156	Listening: 7B, Seg. 6 Assessment: 15B, Ch. 12
Assessment Listening Script: p. 20 Chapter Test: p. 111-116	**Cuaderno** p. 99-100
Audio Book Script: Seg. 6 Activities p. 104	

Pronunciation: "k" and "w"

The letters "k" and "w" are rarely used in Spanish and appear only in words of foreign origin like *kilómetro, kilograma, Kansas, William,* and *Wichita*. The sound of the English letter "k" as in Karl is typically represented as a "hard" "c" before "r," "l," "a," "o," or "u" as in the words *increíble, cliente, catedral, barco,* and *espectáculo*. Before the Spanish letters "e" and "i" the "k" sound is spelled "qu" as in the words *que, quien, aquí*.

The "w" sound of English is typically represented in Spanish as a rising diphthong with the letter "u" as the first vowel as in *fui, fué, agua, averiguo*. If the letter "u" is preceded by the letter "g" or "q" and is followed by an "e" or "i," it must have a dieresis to produce a "w" sound, as in the word *vergüenza*.

Note also that in some regions of the Spanish speaking world a hard "g" sound is heard (but not written) at the beginning of words starting with a "w" sound as in *huevo* and *huerta*, which are often heard as "gwaybo" and "gwerta."

ADELANTE

Objectives

Pre-Reading Strategy: to elicit meaning from photographs and captions

Cultural: to learn about pre-Columbian civilizations

Related Components

CD ROM	**Video:**
Unit 6: Adelante	**Tape/Book**
Magazine	Unit 6: Seg. 4
Juntos en América del Sur	

Search to frame 1441128

GETTING STARTED

Ask students to name some of the world's most impressive places built by people. How old are they? Where are they?

Using the Video

Show Segment 4 of the Unit 6 video, an introduction to Easter Island, Machu Picchu, and Nazca.

Antes de leer

Have students look at the photos and ask what they think the section will be about. Read aloud the introduction. Ask a few comprehension questions. For example:
¿Dónde están estos lugares?
¿Qué tipo de misterio es Machu Picchu?
¿Desde dónde puedes ver los dibujos de Nazca?
Ask students to locate the first cognate on these pages, starting from the upper-left corner (**antes,** cognate of *anterior*). Continue asking for the next cognate until you are sure that everyone understands the task. (You may wish to limit this to the present two pages, which contain many cognates.)

Mysteries of the South

There are ancient architectural structures in South America that date from many centuries ago. To this day, they stand as testimony to the knowledge and accomplishments of the civilizations that built them. Some of the best known of these places are Machu Picchu and the lines of Nazca in Peru, and the Moais in Isla de Pascua, Chile.

ADELANTE

ANTES DE LEER

En América del Sur puedes encontrar tres de los enigmas más grandes de la historia: en Perú, la increíble ciudad inca de Machu Picchu y las líneas° del desierto de Nazca; en Chile, las gigantes° esculturas moais de la Isla de Pascua.°

Lee el texto de las páginas 318–321. ¿Qué palabras no comprendes? ¿Puedes adivinar su significado? ¿Son cognados? Haz una lista de todos los cognados que ves.

Estas antiguas ruinas están en las montañas, cerca de Cuzco.

gigantes *giant*
la Isla de Pascua *Easter Island*
las líneas *lines*

318

Adelante Components

Activity Book	Audio Tapes	Magazine	Video: Tape/Book
p. 157-160	Adelante: 13A, 13B	Juntos en América del Sur	Unit 6: Seg. 4-5
Assessment	**CD ROM**		
Portfolio: p. 43-44	Unit 6: Adelante	**Transparencies**	
		Unit 6: Adelante	

◄ Machu Picchu es un gran misterio arquitectónico.° ¿Cómo cortaron° y montaron° los incas estas piedras sin tener hierro° ni cemento?

◄ Los dibujos de Nazca son tan grandes que sólo se pueden ver° desde un avión. ¿Son mensajes? ¿Para quién?

◄ Las famosas estatuas moais están en la Isla de Pascua, en el Pacífico. ¿Qué representan?

arquitectónico *architectural*   montaron *they assembled*
cortaron *they cut*   se pueden ver *they can be seen*
el hierro *iron*

319

Using the Photos

Machu Picchu

Machu Picchu is a city made almost completely of stone. (The roofs were thatched.) The stones were cut with such incredible precision that it was possible to join them without mortar. We do not know exactly how the stones were cut.

Nazca

Nazca is an ancient city in southern Peru known for its skillful weaving and dyeing, and polychrome pottery. The term Nazca also refers to a culture that existed during the period from 200 B.C. to 600 A.D. For information on the Nazca lines, see the "Background" section on page 320.

Isla de Pascua (Easter Island)

These statues, most of which are male, probably represent either gods or chiefs. They were carved from soft volcanic rock in one location and moved to sites all around the island. Their average height is about 20 feet.

Information for Travelers

Tours to Machu Picchu are available in any Peruvian travel agency. Most people take a one-day round-trip from Cuzco.
There are flights to Isla de Pascua from Santiago, Chile.

Para hispanohablantes

Choose one of the mysteries on this page and write a paragraph explaining why and how you think it was made.

Objectives

Cultural: to learn about ancient cultures
Reading Strategy: to elicit meaning from context

Related Components

Activity Book p. 157	Audio Tapes Adelante: 13A

GETTING STARTED

Ask students about the oldest buildings and statues in their city and why they were built. Would ancient civilizations have other reasons for building the places and things shown here?

Background

Machu Picchu, which means "Ancient Peak," was probably built in the 1400s and abandoned less than a hundred years later. Its existence was known to people of the Urubamba Valley, but the rest of the world was unaware of it until a Yale professor named Hiram Bingham arrived there in July 1911.

Easter Island was probably populated before A.D. 500, either by Native Americans or by Polynesians from the Marquesas. The unusual name was given by a Dutch explorer who reached the island on Easter Sunday, 1722.

The Nazca lines, or geoglyphs, include images as much as 1,000 feet tall and lines as long as 12 miles. They were drawn by removing the darker sediments of the desert soil and exposing lighter surfaces. About 2,000 years old, they owe their preservation to a lack of rain and wind that cleans but has not destroyed them. Most of the figures are undecipherable from the ground, but a few were drawn on hillsides.

DEL MUNDO HISPANO

MISTERIOS
DEL SUR

Machu Picchu

Hace más de 700 años,° los incas construyeron° Machu Picchu. A más de 7.000 pies de altura, hicieron calles, casas, acueductos, palacios, templos y áreas para cultivar. ¿No es increíble?

▲ En 1911 una expedición de la Universidad de Yale encontró° las ruinas de la ciudad de Machu Picchu.

abandonaron *(they) abandoned*
algunos *some*
consacradas *consecrated*
construyeron *(they) built*
cultivar *to cultivate*

320

Nadie° sabe por qué los incas construyeron la ciudad de Machu Picchu en las montañas. ¿Quiénes vivían° allí? ¿Cómo la construyeron? ¿Cuándo y por qué la abandonaron?° Hay muchas teorías, pero los expertos de todo el mundo todavía tienen muchas dudas.

Una teoría dice que Machu Picchu era° un santuario.° Algunos° piensan que Machu Picchu era la ciudad de las *mamacunas*, muchachas consagradas° a adorar al sol.

La Isla de Pascua

En la Isla de Pascua, a más de 2.300 millas de la costa de Chile, hay unas estatuas de piedra gigantes. Se llaman *moais*. Muchos moais pesan más de 80 toneladas° y miden 68 pies.

Los moais son altísimos. Muchos son tan altos como un edificio de cuatro pisos.° ▶

de cuatro pisos *four-story high*
encontró *found*
era *was*
Hace más de 700 años *More than 700 years ago*

Según varios expertos, los moais tienen más de 1.600 años. Son un gran misterio: ¿quiénes los hicieron? ¿Por qué? ¿Cómo hicieron estas estatuas gigantes?

Las líneas de Nazca

Las líneas de Nazca son unos dibujos grandísimos que están en el desierto de Nazca, en el sur de Perú.

nadie *nobody*
el santuario *sanctuary*
las toneladas *tons*
vivían *(they) lived*

DISCUSS

Suggestions for discussion:

Machu Picchu

¿Qué era Machu Picchu?
¿Qué hay en Machu Picchu?
¿Cuándo construyeron Machu Picchu?
¿Conoces otro lugar como Machu Picchu?
¿Cuál es una teoría sobre Machu Picchu?
¿Cuándo construyeron Machu Picchu?
¿Qué eran las mamacunas?

La isla de Pascua

¿Dónde está la isla de Pascua?
¿Qué hay en la isla?
¿Cómo son los moais?
¿Cuántos años tienen los moais?
¿Por qué son un misterio los moais?

Science Link: Easter Island is thousands of miles from land. How do you think the original inhabitants of the island got there? Where is it likely that they came from?

Representan animales y figuras geométricas. Muchos dibujos miden más de 1.000 pies. Sólo puedes verlos desde un avión.

Según los expertos, tienen más de 2.000 años. ¡Y todavía podemos verlos!

Hay varias teorías sobre el significado de estos dibujos. Según una teoría, las líneas de Nazca eran regalos de los nativos para los dioses.° Otra teoría dice que son un calendario astronómico. ¿Qué piensas tú?

▲ **Las líneas de Nazca se vieron° por primera vez desde un avión en 1939.**

los dioses *gods*
se vieron *were seen*

321

Las líneas de Nazca

¿Qué son las líneas de Nazca?
¿Dónde están?
¿Qué representan las líneas?
¿Son pequeñas o grandes?
¿Son antiguas o modernas?
¿Cómo puedes ver las líneas?
¿Cuántos años tienen las líneas de Nazca?
¿Qué piensan los científicos?

Art Link: Was the airplane necessary for people to figure out what—if anything—the Nazca lines represented? How else could people have discovered what these drawings looked like?

Thinking About Culture

What Is a Mystery?
Ask why we speak of these structures as mysteries. Is it because they served some purpose that the people who built them did not understand? Or is it because those purposes have been forgotten, and we are the ones who do not understand?

What Is a Discovery?
People often speak of Machu Picchu as having been "discovered" by Hiram Bingham of Yale, yet the people who lived in that valley knew that the city existed. Ask students if there is a better word than *discovery*. How does this situation compare to Columbus's "discovery" of America?

CHECK

¿Quiénes construyeron Machu Picchu?
¿Qué son los moais?
¿Dónde están las líneas de Nazca?

LOG BOOK
Have students write down two things they learned about each of the places in these pages.

These activities can be done as classwork or as homework.

Objectives
Organizing Skills: using lists and tables to organize information
Communication Skills: writing sentences

Related Components

Activity Book p. 158	Assessment Portfolio: p. 43-44

ACTIVITIES

1. Palabras similares
Individual Activity Look at the list of cognates you started making on page 318. Make a table like this one and put the cognates in categories.
Possible Answers
(examples from pp. 318-19)

Sustantivos	Verbos	Adjetivos
América	*adivinar*	*antiguo*
cemento	*montaron*	*arquitectónico*
cognado	*representan*	*famosas*
desierto		*gigantes*
estatuas		*grandes*
isla		
líneas		
misterio		
montañas		

2. Sobre los misterios del Sur
Individual Activity Use the information in the *Adelante* to complete the table.
Possible Answers:

Isla de Pascua
¿Dónde? *una isla en el Océano Pacífico*
País *Chile*
¿Qué hay? *estatuas de piedra (moais)*
¿Qué más? *pesan más de 80 toneladas y miden 68 pies*

Machu Picchu
¿Dónde? *en los Andes*
País *Perú*
¿Qué hay? *acueductos, palacios y templos*
¿Qué más? *más de 7.000 pies de altura*

Líneas de Nazca
¿Dónde? *en el desierto*
País *Perú*
¿Qué hay? *dibujos grandísimos*
¿Qué más? *tienen más de 2.000 años*

DESPUÉS DE LEER

① Palabras similares

Mira tu lista de cognados. Completa la tabla según las categorías.

Sustantivos°	Verbos	Adjetivos
enigma	abandonaron	astronómico

② Sobre los misterios del Sur

Completa la tabla según el texto de las páginas anteriores.

	¿Dónde? (lugar geográfico)	País	¿Qué hay?	¿Qué más?
Isla de Pascua	una isla en...			
Machu Picchu				más de 7.000 pies de altura
Líneas de Nazca		Perú		

③ Un misterio

Escoge uno de los lugares misteriosos de América del Sur. Escribe tres oraciones sobre el lugar.

> *La Isla de Pascua está en el océano Pacífico. Allí hay... Una teoría dice que...*

④ Completa las oraciones

1. En el desierto de Nazca...
2. Los moais son...
3. A más de 7.000 pies de altura...
4. Las líneas de Nazca son...

los sustantivos *nouns*

---

3. Un misterio
Individual Activity Use the information from the table to write three sentences about one of the three "mysteries of South America."
Answers: See model on student page.

4. Completa las oraciones
Individual Activity Complete the sentences.
Possible Answers:
1. ...hay dibujos muy grandes.
2. ...estatuas de piedra gigantes.
3. ...los incas construyeron Machu Picchu.
4. ...unos dibujos grandísimos.

TALLER DE ESCRITORES

1. OTRO MISTERIO

Con tu compañero(a), investiguen otro misterio del mundo. Escriban seis oraciones sobre ese misterio. Incluyan:

- dónde está
- por qué es un misterio
- qué dicen los expertos

2. INTERCAMBIO ELECTRÓNICO

Con tu compañero(a), hagan una lista de cuatro preguntas. Pidan información sobre uno de los lugares del texto "Misterios del Sur". Usen el correo electrónico para mandar sus preguntas.

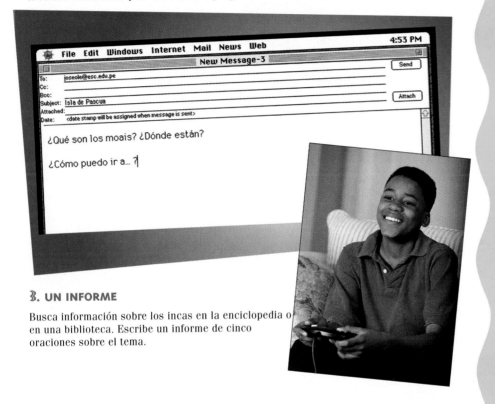

3. UN INFORME

Busca información sobre los incas en la enciclopedia o en una biblioteca. Escribe un informe de cinco oraciones sobre el tema.

323

Objectives
- to practice writing
- to use vocabulary from this unit

Related Components

Activity Book p. 159	Assessment Portfolio: p.43-44

ACTIVITIES

1. Otro misterio
Pair Activity Students will research another of the world's mysteries and write six sentences about it, including:
- where it is
- why it is a mystery
- what the experts say

(**Ideas:** Stonehenge, the Serpent Mound in Ohio, the cave paintings of Altamira)
You may prefer to allow students to invent and describe a mystery.

2. Intercambio electrónico
Pair Activity Students will prepare four questions about one of the places in *Misterios del Sur* for an e-mail message.
Note: If specific addresses and willing correspondents are unavailable, e-mail is not really an option. Instead, have students write their questions and exchange with a pair who worked on a different topic.

3. Un informe
Students research information on the Incas, then write a report of five sentences on the subject. To expand, let pairs of students continue working on their reports together.
Edit: Students exchange reports and edit each other's work. Have them work together to prepare final drafts.
Present: Students read their final drafts aloud to the class.

PORTFOLIO
Encourage students to select one of these assignments to add to their portfolios.

Objectives

Communicative: to listen to and understand directions
Cultural: to learn about mask-making, a tradition of Peru
TPR: to have students make masks

Related Components

Assessment	Transparencies
Portfolio: p. 43-44	Unit 6: Project
CD ROM	**Video:**
Unit 6: Manos a la obra	Tape/Book
	Unit 6: Seg. 5

Search to frame 1480400

Materials

- newspaper
- flour cooked in water
- powdered chalk
- paints and brushes
- sandpaper

GETTING STARTED

In this exercise, encourage students to use their eyes more than their ears. Rather than try to understand every word, they should concentrate on the actions and listen only for clues.

Before students open their books, try a brief TPR session showing students the commands *drain, mix, cover,* and *sand.* This will introduce several of the key words in the mask-making segment of the video.

DISCUSS

Read aloud the introductory text, then ask a few either/or comprehension questions, such as:

¿Qué debo hacer primero, poner el papel en agua o mezclar el papel con harina molida?
¿Debo poner la masa encima del molde o dentro del molde?

Read the text again, and ask comprehension questions after each sentence.

MANOS A LA OBRA

UNA MÁSCARA PARA TI

Usar las máscaras es una costumbre muy popular en fiestas y celebraciones de todo el mundo. En Perú, el arte de hacer máscaras es una tradición muy antigua. Según esta tradición, una máscara es un objeto mágico.

TE TOCA A TI

Aquí tienes los pasos para hacer una máscara. Primero tienes que decidir qué tipo de máscara quieres hacer. ¿Un animal? ¿Un monstruo?° ¿Un personaje mitológico?°

Para hacer una máscara necesitas un molde.° Usa una máscara de plástico.°

Máscara de oro en las excavaciones de Sipán, Perú.

escurre *drain*
la masa *dough*
el molde *mold*
el monstruo *monster*
el personaje mitológico *character from mythology*
el plástico *plastic*

1 Pon el papel de periódico en agua. Tiene que estar allí durante seis horas.

2 Escurre° el papel. Con la harina cocida, la tiza molida y el papel haz una masa.°

324

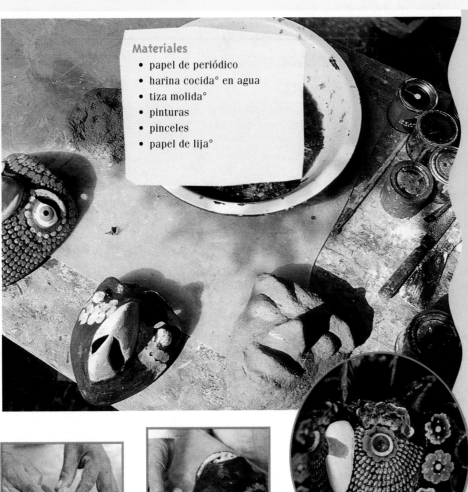

Materiales

- papel de periódico
- harina cocida° en agua
- tiza molida°
- pinturas
- pinceles
- papel de lija°

3 Cubre° el molde con la mesa. Haz una capa° no muy fina.° Pon la máscara al sol.

4 Lija° la máscara antes de pintarla y decorarla. ¡Y ya está! Ya puedes usar tu máscara.

la capa *coat*
cubre *cover*
fina *thin*
la harina cocida *cooked flour*
lija *smooth*
el papel de lija *sandpaper*
la tiza molida *powdered chalk*

325

Objectives
- to expand reading comprehension
- to relate the study of Spanish to other disciplines

Related Components

Activity Book p. 160	**Audio Tapes** Adelante: 13B
Assessment Portfolio: p. 43-44	**Video: Tape/Book** Unit 6: Seg. 4

Search to frame 1441128

El idioma de los Incas

About Quechua
In pre-Columbian times, *Quechua,* or *Runasimi,* was the official language of the Inca empire (many languages were spoken by the peoples subjugated by the Incas). It is the indigenous language of a large portion of the South American highlands.

Answers:
- *Hablan quechua en Perú y Bolivia.*
- *Más de ocho millones de personas hablan quechua.*

Activity
Can you name other languages native to the Americas? Where are those languages spoken? How have Native Americans preserved their languages? (Today many Native American peoples actively preserve their languages by using them for everyday speech, in ceremonies, and on written documents. Among the many examples of Native Americans with living native languages are the Navajo and Hopi in the southwestern United States, the Cherokee in Oklahoma and other locations, the Iroquois in the northeastern United States and Canada, the Inuit in Alaska and northern Canada, the *Guaraní* in Paraguay, and the *Zapotec* in Mexico.)

▶▶▶ **INTERNET LINKS**

Quechua http://metro.turnpike.net/D/dbran/runasimi.html
The Tofo Project http://drylands.nasm.edu:1995/camanchaca.html

326

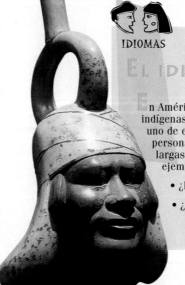

IDIOMAS

EL IDIOMA DE LOS INCAS

En América del Sur y América del Norte hay grandes grupos de indígenas que conservan sus idiomas nativos. El **quechua** es uno de estos idiomas. Lo hablan° más de ocho millones de personas en Perú y Bolivia. Las palabras quechuas son muy largas y no son similares al español. En quechua, por ejemplo, *Tahuantinsuyo* es el nombre del imperio inca.

- ¿Dónde hablan quechua?
- ¿Cuántas personas hablan quechua?

ECOLOGÍA

COSECHA° DE NUBES

El Tofo es una montaña de Chile de más de 2.600 pies de altura. Allí, un equipo de investigadores° chilenos está desarrollando° un proyecto para llevar agua a lugares donde la necesitan. El nombre que los investigadores dan a este proyecto es "Cosecha de nubes".

El proyecto consiste en poner unas redes de plástico en una montaña muy alta. Cuando las nubes entran en contacto° con las redes, forman gotas° de agua. Después, el agua va al pueblo por una tubería.°

Según los investigadores, es posible que otros proyectos similares lleven° agua a lugares en más de 22 países de América Latina y de África.

- ¿Qué es El Tofo y en qué país está?
- ¿Cómo llaman los investigadores al proyecto El Tofo?
- ¿En qué consiste el proyecto?

la cosecha *harvest*	**Lo hablan** *It is spoken by*	**las redes** *nets*
desarrollando *developing*	**los investigadores**	**la tubería** *set of pipes*
entran en contacto *get in touch*	*researchers*	
forman gotas *(they) form drops*	**lleven** *(they) bring*	

326

Cosecha de nubes

About the Tofo Project
The nets are supported by posts, like a fence. The fine mesh provides places for the fog to condense. The system uses simple, inexpensive materials; care and management are simple enough for local people to manage; and the cost is a quarter of what it would be to truck water in from outside.

Possible Answers:
- *El Tofo es una montaña en Chile.*
- *Le llaman "cosecha de nubes".*
- *Consiste en poner redes de plástico en una montaña alta. Cuando las nubes entran en contacto con las redes, forman agua, que después va al pueblo por una tubería.*

Math Link: At El Tofo, one 40- by 13- foot fog trap produces 45 gallons of water a day. How many gallons could each of Chuchungo's 350 residents have if there are 50 fog traps? (About 6.5 gallons)

INFORMÁTICA

EL QUIPU

Los incas inventaron el **quipu**, un sistema muy preciso para guardar° información y datos. El quipu consiste en cuerdas,° largas y cortas, de diferentes colores. Las cuerdas tienen nudos° que representan los números 1, 10, 100, etc. Según el tamaño, color y posición de los nudos los incas podían° leer y recordar° datos y eventos importantes.

• ¿Qué es el quipu?

• ¿Quiénes inventaron el quipu?

• ¿En qué consiste?

GEOGRAFÍA

LAS CATARATAS DEL IGUAZÚ

En la selva que está entre Argentina y Brasil, están las cataratas más espectaculares de toda América del Sur: las cataratas del Iguazú. El nombre de las cataratas viene del **guaraní** y significa "grandes aguas". El guaraní es el idioma nativo de Paraguay, de la parte suroeste de Brasil y del noroeste de Argentina.

• ¿Dónde están las cataratas del Iguazú?

• ¿Qué significa "Iguazú" en guaraní?

• ¿Dónde hablan guaraní?

las cuerdas *ropes*
se extienden *they are stretched*
guardar *to keep*

los nudos *knots*
podían *(they) could*
recordar *to remember*

327

Las cataratas del Iguazú

About the waterfalls

The Iguazú falls are taller than Niagara and twice as wide. The horseshoe-shaped falls are part of the border between Brazil and Argentina. The red tint of the waters is due to the sandstone riverbeds.

Possible Answers:

• *Las cataratas de Iguazú están en la selva entre Argentina y Brazil.*

• *Iguazú quiere decir "grandes aguas" en guaraní.*

• *Hablan guaraní en Paraguay, en el suroeste de Brasil y el noreste de Argentina.*

Social Studies Link: Many of the older cities in our country are located near waterfalls. Why do you think this is so? (Waterfalls provided power for mills and electricity. Rivers provided inexpensive transportation.)

El quipu

About the Quipu

The Incas used *quipus* to record census data and historical information, and to send messages across their empire. The quipu consists of a long main string that is held horizontally. Several strings hang from it. The color, length, position, and the way in which knots were made were elements of this system of recording information. The name comes from a *Quechua* word that means "knot."

Possible Answers:

• *El quipu es un sistema para guardar información.*

• *Los incas inventaron el quipu.*

• *El quipu tiene cuerdas largas y cortas de diferentes colores, con nudos.*

Other Questions:

Why did the Incas use such a complicated system? (They did not have a written language.)

Can you think of any other forms of writing that do not use an alphabet? (There are numerous hieroglyphic systems, the best-known of which are the ancient Egyptian and the Mayan. Braille uses six raised dots in various combinations. Musical notation might also be considered a form of writing. Note that Greek, Arabic, and similar systems do use alphabets.)

Verbos

In level one, you learn to communicate using the present tense, the preterite, and the imperative forms for *tú*. You also learn the present progressive tense, which uses a present tense form of *estar* with a present participle.

In the following charts, the verbs are listed in categories: regular, irregular, stem–changing, reflexive, and verbs with spelling changes. You will also find a chart for *gustar*.

Within each chart, the verbs are listed according to their infinitive forms (*comprar, comer, compartir*). This is the form in which verbs appear in a dictionary or a glossary. You will find a few extras, such as imperative or preterite forms that you haven't yet seen for certain verbs. You will probably find them very helpful as you begin to communicate in Spanish. Refer to these pages often.

Regular Verbs

Infinitive Present Participle	Indicative		Imperative
	Present	Preterite	
-ar verbs			
comprar	compro	compré	
comprando	compras	compraste	compra
	compra	compró	
	compramos	compramos	
	compráis	comprasteis	
	compran	compraron	
-er verbs			
comer	como	comí	
comiendo	comes	comiste	come
	come	comió	
	comemos	comimos	
	coméis	comisteis	
	comen	comieron	
-ir verbs			
compartir	comparto	compartí	
compartiendo	compartes	compartiste	comparte
	comparte	compartió	
	compartimos	compartimos	
	compartís	compartisteis	
	comparten	compartieron	

Irregular Verbs

Infinitive Present Participle	Indicative		Imperative
	Present	Preterite	
dar	doy	di	
dando	das	diste	da
	da	dio	
	damos	dimos	
	dais	disteis	
	dan	dieron	
decir	digo	dije	
diciendo	dices	dijiste	di
	dice	dijo	
	decimos	dijimos	
	decís	dijisteis	
	dicen	dijeron	
estar	estoy	estuve	
estando	estás	estuviste	está
	está	estuvo	
	estamos	estuvimos	
	estáis	estuvisteis	
	están	estuvieron	
hacer	hago	hice	
haciendo	haces	hiciste	haz
	hace	hizo	
	hacemos	hicimos	
	hacéis	hicisteis	
	hacen	hicieron	
ir	voy	fui	
yendo	vas	fuiste	ve
	va	fue	
	vamos	fuimos	
	vais	fuisteis	
	van	fueron	

Infinitive Present Participle	Indicative		Imperative
	Present	Preterite	
saber	sé	supe	
sabiendo	sabes	supiste	sabe
	sabe	supo	
	sabemos	supimos	
	sabéis	supisteis	
	saben	supieron	
salir	salgo	salí	
saliendo	sales	saliste	sal
	sale	salió	
	salimos	salimos	
	salís	salisteis	
	salen	salieron	
ser	soy	fui	
siendo	eres	fuiste	sé
	es	fue	
	somos	fuimos	
	sois	fuisteis	
	son	fueron	
tener	tengo	tuve	
teniendo	tienes	tuviste	ten
	tiene	tuvo	
	tenemos	tuvimos	
	tenéis	tuvisteis	
	tienen	tuvieron	
ver	veo	vi	
viendo	ves	viste	ve
	ve	vio	
	vemos	vimos	
	veis	visteis	

Stem–Changing Verbs

Infinitive Present Participle	Indicative		Imperative
	Present	Preterite	
jugar (u > ue) jugando	juego juegas juega jugamos jugáis juegan	jugué jugaste jugó jugamos jugasteis jugaron	juega
pedir (e > i) pidiendo	pido pides pide pedimos pedís piden	pedí pediste pidió pedimos pedisteis pidieron	pide
poder (o > ue) pudiendo	puedo puedes puede podemos podéis pueden	pude pudiste pudo pudimos pudisteis pudieron	puede
querer (e > ie) queriendo	quiero quieres quiere queremos queréis quieren	quise quisiste quiso quisimos quisisteis quisieron	quiere

330

Verbs with Spelling Changes

Infinitive Present Participle	Indicative		Imperative
	Present	Preterite	
conocer (c > zc)	conozco	conocí	
conociendo	conoces	conociste	conoce
	conoce	conoció	
	conocemos	conocimos	
	conocéis	conocisteis	
	conocen	conocieron	
empezar (z > c)	empiezo	empecé	
empezando	empiezas	empezaste	empieza
	empieza	empezó	
	empezamos	empezamos	
	empezáis	empezasteis	
	empiezan	empezaron	
leer (e > y)	leo	leí	
leyendo	lees	leíste	lee
	lee	leyó	
	leemos	leímos	
	leéis	leísteis	
	leen	leyeron	
sacar (c > qu)	saco	saqué	
sacando	sacas	sacaste	saca
	saca	sacó	
	sacamos	sacamos	
	sacáis	sacasteis	
	sacan	sacaron	

Reflexive Verbs

Infinitive Present Participle	Indicative		Imperative
	Present	Preterite	
lavarse	me lavo	me lavé	
lavándose	te lavas	te lavaste	lávate
	se lava	se lavó	
	nos lavamos	nos lavamos	
	os laváis	os lavasteis	
	se lavan	se lavaron	
	se lavan	se lavaron	
ponerse	me pongo	me puse	
poniéndose	te pones	te pusiste	ponte
	se pone	se puso	
	nos ponemos	nos pusimos	
	os ponéis	os pusisteis	
	se ponen	se pusieron	
	se ponen	se pusieron	

Gustar: Present Tense

Infinitive Present Participle	If one thing is liked:	If more than one thing is liked:
gustar gustando	me te le nos os les } gusta	me te le nos os les } gustan

GLOSARIO ESPAÑOL–INGLÉS

A

a *at to*
abajo *downstairs, below*
el abrigo *coat*
abril *April*
abrir *to open*
la abuela *grandmother*
el abuelo *grandfather*
los abuelos *grandparents*
aburrido(a) *boring*
el aceite *oil*
aceptar *to accept*
aceptar tarjetas de crédito/cheques *to take credit cards/checks*
acomodar *to hold*
la actividad *activity*
acuático(a) *aquatic*
adaptado(a) *adapted*
adiós *good bye*
admirar *to admire*
¿adónde...? *where . . . ?*
la aduana *customs*
el aeropuerto *airport*
las afueras *suburbs*
la agencia *agency*
agencia de intercambio *exchange agency*
el/la agente de viajes *travel agent*
agosto *August*
el agua mineral *mineral water*
el aguacate *avocado*
el águila (las águilas) *eagle*
ahora *now*
el aire *air*
al aire libre *outdoors*

el ajedrez *chess*
al (a+el=al) *to the*
al extranjero *abroad*
al lado de *next to*
el alemán (language) *German*
las aletas *fins*
la alfombra *rug*
el álgebra *algebra*
¿Algo más? *Anything else?*
allí *there, over there*
el almacén *department store*
el almuerzo *lunch*
alquilar *to rent*
el alquiler *rental*
el altar *altar*
alto(a) *tall*
la altura *height*
amarillo(a) *yellow*
la América del Sur *South America*
el/la amigo(a) *friend*
anaranjado(a) *orange*
el anfibio *amphibian*
el anillo *ring*
el animal *animal*
animal de carga *pack animal*
el aniversario *anniversary*
aniversario de boda *wedding anniversary*
anoche *last night*
antes (de) *before*
antiguo(a) *ancient*
antillano(a) *Antillean*
el anuncio *commercial*
el año *year*
apagar *to turn off*
el aparato electrónico *electronic appliance*
aparcar *to park*

el apellido *last name*

aprender *to learn*
aproximadamente *approximately*
el apunte *note*
aquí *here*
el árbol *tree*
el arco *arch*
la arena *sand*
los aretes *earrings*
el armario *locker*
arquitectónico(a) *architectural*
arriba *upstairs*
el arroz *rice*
el arte *art*
las artesanías *arts and crafts*
ascender (e>ie) *to ascend*
el artículo *article*
el asunto *issue*
atar *to tie*
la atención *attention*
el/la atleta *athlete*
el atletismo *track and field*
el atún *tuna*
la audiencia *audience*
el auto (Perú) *car*
el autobús *bus*
en autobús *by bus*
la autorización *authorization, permission*
el ave (las aves) *bird*
la avenida *avenue*
la aventura *adventure*
el avión *plane*
en avión *by plane*
¡Ay, bendito! (Puerto Rico) *Oh, no!*
ayer *yesterday*
ayudar *to help*
el azúcar *sugar*
azul *blue*
el azulejo *tile*

B

bailable (for) dancing
bailar to dance
el baile dance
  baile de salón ballroom dancing
bajar to go down
  bajar el volumen to turn down the volume
bajo(a) short
el baloncesto basketball
la banda band
la bandera flag
bañarse to take a bath
  la bañera bathtub
barato(a) inexpensive
la barbacoa barbecue
bárbaro(a) (Argentina) great, terrific
el barco boat
  en barco by boat
bastante enough
  bastante bien quite well
el batido milkshake
beber to drink
la bebida beverage
el béisbol baseball
bello(a) beautiful
la biblioteca library
bien good, well, fine
bienvenido(a) welcome
la biología biology
el bistec steak
blanco(a) white
la blusa blouse
la boda wedding
la bodega grocery store
el bolero bolero
el boleto ticket
el bolígrafo pen
la bolsa bag
el bolso de mano handbag
bonito(a) pretty
bordado(a) embroidered

el/la borinqueño(a) a person from Puerto Rico
el borrador eraser
el bosque woods
las botas boots
  botas tejanas cowboy boots
el bote a motor motorboat
el broche pin
bucear to scuba dive
el buceo scuba diving
¡Buen provecho! Enjoy your meal!
bueno(a) good
  ¡Buenos días! Good morning!
  ¡Buenas tardes! Good afternoon!
  ¡Buenas noches! Good evening!, Good night!
buscar to look for

C

el caballero gentleman
el caballo horse
el cacahuate peanut
cada each
  cada vez más more and more
el café coffee
la cafetería cafeteria
la calculadora calculator
el calendario calendar
caliente hot, warm
la calle street
el calor heat
la cama bed
la cámara camera
cambiar to change
  cambiar el canal to change the channel
  cambiar dinero to exchange money
el cambio exchange
el camello camel

caminar to walk
camino de las misiones mission trail
el camión (Mexico) bus, (generally truck)
la camisa shirt
la camiseta T-shirt
el campanario bell tower
el campo countryside
el canal channel
  canal de televisión T.V. channel
la cancha court
la canción song
el/la cantante singer
cantar to sing
  cantar en el coro to sing in the choir
la caña cane
la capital capital
el capítulo chapter
la caravana trailer
cariñoso(a) affectionate
la carne meat
caro(a) expensive
la carpeta folder, binder
la carrera major, career
la carta card, letter
  carta de recomendación letter of recommendation
el cartel poster
la casa house
  en casa at home
la cascada falls, waterfall
casi almost
castaño brown (hair)
el castillo castle
la catarata waterfall
la catedral cathedral
la celebración celebration
celebrar to celebrate
el cementerio cemetery
la cena dinner
el centímetro centimeter
el centro downtown

centro comercial *shopping center*

cepillarse los dientes *to brush one's teeth*

el cepillo de dientes *toothbrush*

cerca *nearby*

cerca de *near*

el cereal *cereal*

cerrar (e>ie) *to close*

el certificado *certificate*

certificado médico *medical/health certificate*

certificado de estudios *school transcript*

el chaleco *vest*

el chaleco salvavidas *life jacket*

el champú *shampoo*

el chapulín (Mexico) *grasshopper*

la chaqueta *jacket*

el/la chavo(a) (Mexico) *guy, girl*

el cheque *check*

cheque de viajero *traveler's check*

¡chévere! (Puerto Rico) *great!*

chicano(a) *Mexican-American*

el/la chico(a) *boy/girl*

los chicos *young people*

el chile *chili pepper*

la chiringa (Puerto Rico) *kite*

el chocolate *chocolate*

la cima *summit*

el cine *the movies, movie theater*

la cinta *adhesive tape, tape cassette*

el cinturón *belt*

el circuito *trail*

la ciudad *city*

la ciudadela *citadel*

¡Claro que sí! *Of course!*

la clase *classroom, class*

el/la cliente(a) *client*

el coche *car*

en coche *by car*

la cocina *kitchen*

cocinar *to cook*

el código postal *zip code*

la cola *tail*

colgar (o>ue) *to hang*

el collar *necklace*

el colono *colonist*

el color *color*

el comedor *dining room*

comer *to eat*

la comida *food, meal*

comida rápida *fast food*

¿Cómo...? *How . . . ?*

¿Cómo está(s)? *How are you?*

¿Cómo se dice... en español? *How do you say . . . in Spanish?*

¿Cómo te llamas? *What's your name?*

la cómoda *chest of drawers*

cómodo(a) *comfortable*

compartir *to share*

competir (e>i) *to compete*

la composición *composition*

la compra *purchase*

comprar *to buy*

comprender *to understand*

la computadora *computer*

la comunidad *communitiy*

con *with*

el concierto *concert*

el concurso *contest, game*

el conjunto *building complex*

conmigo *with me*

conocer *to know, to be familiar with*

conocido(a) *known,*

well-known

el/la consejero(a) *counselor*

el consejo *advice*

conservar *to conserve*

el consulado *consulate*

contar (o>ue) *to relate, to tell (a story)*

el contestador automático *answering machine*

contestar *to answer*

contigo *with you*

el control remoto *remote control*

conversemos *let's talk*

el corazón *heart*

la corbata *necktie*

la cordillera *mountain range*

el correo *post office*

por correo *by mail*

cortar *to cut*

cortés *courteous*

el cortijo *farm*

corto(a) *short*

la cosa *thing*

la cosecha *harvest*

la costa *coast*

costar (o>ue) *to cost*

la costumbre *custom*

el coto *natural reserve*

la cotorra *parrot*

crear *to create*

creer *to believe*

cruzar *to cross*

el cuaderno *notebook*

el cuadro *painting*

cuál *what, which*

cualquier *any*

cualquier otra cosa *anything else*

¿cuándo? *when?*

¿cuánto? *how much?*

¿Cuánto cuesta(n)? *How much does it/ do they cost?*

¿Cuánto es? *How much*

¿Cuántos(as)? *How many*

¿cuántas veces

por...? *how many times per . . . ?*

¿Cuántos años tiene(s)? *How old are you?*

el cuarto de baño *bathroom*

cubano(a) *Cuban*

la cuchara *spoon*

el cuchillo *knife*

el cuento *short story*

la cuerda *rope, string*

el cuero *leather*

la cultura *culture*

el cumpleaños *birthday*

D

la dama *lady*

dar *to give*

de *of, from*

¿De qué color es...? *What color is . . . ?*

¿De qué es? *What is it made of?*

debajo de *under*

debes(n) *you should*

no debes(n) *(+ infinitive) you shouldn't*

decir (e>ie) *to say*

la decoración *decoration*

decorar *to decorate*

dedicar *to dedicate*

defenderse (e>ie) *to defend oneself*

dejar *to leave behind*

del (de+el=del) *of the, from the*

delante de *in front of*

delicioso(a) *delicious*

dentro *inside*

el deporte *sport*

deporte acuático *water sport*

la derecha *right*

a la derecha de *to the right of*

a la derecha *to/on your right*

dobla a la derecha

turn right

derecho(a) *straight*

el desayuno *breakfast*

descansar *to rest*

desde *from*

desear *to desire, to wish*

el desierto *desert*

despacio *slow*

después *after, later*

el detalle *detail*

detrás de *behind the*

devolver (o>ue) *to return*

el día *day*

día del santo *Saint's Day*

el diario *newspaper*

dibujar *to draw*

el dibujo *drawing*

los dibujos animados *cartoons*

el diccionario *dictionary*

diciembre *December*

el diente *tooth*

difícil *difficult*

el dinero en efectivo *cash*

la dirección *address*

el/la director(a) de escuela *school principal*

el disco compacto *compact disc*

la discoteca *discotheque*

divertido(a) *funny, amusing*

divertirse (e>ie) *to have fun*

doblar *to turn, to fold*

el documental *documentary*

el documento *document*

el dólar *dollar*

el domingo *Sunday*

¿Dónde? *Where?*

¿de dónde? *from where?*

el dormitorio *bedroom*

ducharse *to take a shower*

el dulce *candy*

dulce *sweet*

durante *during*

E

e *and*

la edad *age*

Edad Media *Middle Ages*

el edificio de apartamentos *apartment building*

la educación *education*

educación física *physical education*

educativo(a) *educational*

el *the*

el más... *the most . . . (the . . . -est)*

él *he, it, him*

la electricidad *electricity*

el/la electricista *electrician*

ella *she, it, her*

ellos/ellas *they, them*

emocionante *exciting*

empezar (e>ie) *to begin*

el empleo *job*

en *in, on*

Encantado(a) *Nice to meet you*

encender (e>ie) *to turn on*

la enchilada *enchilada*

encima de *on top of*

encontrarse (o>ue) *to meet*

enero *January*

enfermo(a) *ill*

la ensalada *salad*

enseñar *to teach*

entérate *find out*

la entrada *entrance, entrance ticket*

entre *between*

el entrenamiento *training*

entretenido(a) *entertaining*

la entrevista *interview*

la época *time, period*

el equipo *team*
esa/ese/eso *that*
esas/esos *those*
escribir *to write*
el/la escritor(a) *writer*
el escritorio *desk*
escuchar *to listen*
la escuela *school*
la escultura *sculpture*
el esnórquel *snorkel*
el español *Spanish language*
en español *in Spanish*
especial *special*
espectacular *spectacular*
el espectáculo *show*
el espejo *mirror*
el esqueleto *skeleton*
el esquí *ski*
esquiar *to ski*
esta/este/esto *this*
la estación *station (as in the radio station or metro station) season*
el estadio *stadium*
el estante *shelf*
estar *to be*
estas/estos *these*
la estatua *statue*
el este *east*
el estéreo *stereo*
el estilo *style*
estilo de vida *lifestyle*
la estrella *star*
el/la estudiante *student*
estudiar *to study*
los estudios *studies*
la estufa *stove*
el examen (los exámenes) *exams*
la excursión *excursion, field trip*
la excusa *excuse*
el éxito *success*
la experiencia *experience*
el experimento *experiment*
explicar *to explain*
la exposición *exhibition*

exposición de arte *art exhibition*
extraescolar *extracurricular*

F

la fábrica *factory*
fabuloso(a) *fabulous*
fácil *easy*
la falda *skirt*
la familia *family*
famoso(a) *famous*
fantástico(a) *fantastic*
la farmacia *pharmacy*
fatal *awful*
favorito(a) *favorite*
febrero *February*
la fecha *date*
fecha de nacimiento *date of birth*
fecha de vencimiento *expiration date*
felicidades *congratulations*
¡Feliz cumpleaños! *Happy birthday!*
feo(a) *ugly*
la feria *fair, street fair*
el festival de danza *dance festival*
el fichero *card catalogue*
la fiesta *party*
filmar *to make a film or a video*
el fin *end*
Fin de Año *New Year's Eve*
fin de la semana *weekend*
la finca *farm*
fino(a) *thin, fine*
el flan *custard pie*
la flor *flower*
el folleto *brochure*
folleto turístico *travel brochure*
la fórmula *formula*
la fortaleza *fortress*
la foto *photo*
el francés *French*

language
el fregadero *sink*
fresco(a) *fresh, cool*
el frijol *bean*
frío(a) *cold*
el frisbi *Frisbee*
la frontera *border*
la fruta *fruit*
la fuente *fountain*
fuera *outside*
fuera de *outside of*
la fuerza *strength*
funcionar *to work*
el fútbol *soccer*
el fútbol americano *football*

G

la galleta *cookie*
ganar *to win*
la ganga *bargain*
el garaje *garage*
la gasolinera *gas station*
los gastos de envío *shipping and handling charges*
el gato *cat*
generalmente *usually*
genial *cool, nice, pleasant*
la gente *people*
la geografía *geography*
la geometría *geometry*
el/la gigante *giant*
el gimnasio *gym*
gitano(a) *gypsy*
el globo *balloon*
la gorra *cap*
el gorro *hat*
la gota *drop*
grabar *to record*
gracias *thank you*
el grado *degree*
la graduación *graduation*
la gráfica de barras *bar graph*
grande *large, big*
la granja *farm*
gratis *free*
gris *grey*

el **guacamole** (Mexico) *guacamole*

el **guajolote** (Mexico) *turkey*

el **guante** *glove*

guapo(a) *good looking*

guardar *to keep*

el/la **guía** *guide*

la **guitarra** *guitar*

gustar (+ infinitive) *to like to do something*

gustar (+ noun) *to like*

(See page 332 for summary.)

H

había *there was/were*

hablar *to speak, to talk*

hablar por teléfono *to talk on the phone*

hace (with weather expressions)

hace buen tiempo *the weather is nice*

hace calor *it's hot*

hace fresco *it's cool*

hace frío *it's cold*

hace mal tiempo *the weather is bad*

hace sol *it's sunny*

hace viento *it's windy*

hacer *to do, to make*

hacer amigos *to make friends*

hacer esquí acuático *to water ski*

hacer jet esquí *to jet ski*

hacer la maleta *to pack the suitcase*

hacer la reserva de avión *to make plane reservations*

hacer los trámites *to do the paperwork*

hacer parasailing *to parasail*

hacer surf *to surf*

hacer tabla a vela *to windsurf*

hacer un picnic *to have a picnic*

hacer una barbacoa *to have a barbecue*

hacer una fiesta *to have a party*

el **hambre** *hunger*

la **hamburguesa** *hamburger*

la **harina** *flour*

hasta *until, up to*

Hasta luego. *See you later.*

Hasta mañana. *See you tomorrow.*

hay *there is/there are*

hecho *made*

el **helado** *ice cream*

el **helecho** *fern*

la **hermana** *sister*

el **hermano** *brother*

los **hermanos** *brothers and sisters or brothers*

hermoso(a) *beautiful*

el **hielo** *ice*

el **hierro** *iron*

la **hija** *daughter*

el **hijo** *son*

los **hijos** *children or sons*

hispano(a) *Hispanic*

la **historia** *history*

histórico(a) *historical*

las **historietas** *comics*

¡Hola! *Hi!, ¡Hello!*

el **hombre** *man*

honrar *to honor*

la **hora** *time*

¿A qué hora? *At what time?*

¿Qué hora es? *What time is it?*

el **horario** *schedule*

horrible *awful*

la **hospitalidad** *hospitality*

el **hotel** *hotel*

hoy *today*

el **huevo** *egg*

el **huracán** *hurricane*

I

ibérico(a) *Iberian*

la **idea** *idea*

ideal *ideal*

el **idioma** *language*

la **iglesia** *church*

el **imperio** *empire*

el **impermeable** *raincoat*

impresionante *impressive*

el **impuesto** *tax*

incluir *to include*

increíble *amazing*

la **información** *information*

la **informática** *computer science*

informativo(a) *informative*

el **informe** *report*

el **inglés** *English language*

el **inodoro** *toilet*

inteligente *intelligent*

el **intercambio** *exchange*

interesante *interesting*

la **inundación** (las **inundaciones**) *flood*

el **invierno** *winter*

la **invitación** (las **invitaciones**) *invitation*

el/la **invitado(a)** *guest*

invitar *to invite*

ir *to go*

la **isla** *island*

el **italiano** *Italian language*

el **itinerario** *itinerary*

la **izquierda** *left*

a la izquierda de *to the left of*

J

el **jabón** *soap*

el **jardín** *garden*

el **jardinero** *outfielder*

el **jazz** *jazz*

338

el jonrón *home run*
joven *young*
el/la joven *young person*
los jóvenes *youths*
la joya *jewel*
la joyería *jewelry store*
judío(a) *Jewish*
el jueves *Thursday*
jugar (u>ue) *to play*
 jugar a las paletas *to play paddleball*
 jugar al ajedrez *to play chess*
 jugar al baloncesto *to play basketball*
 jugar al béisbol *to play baseball*
 jugar al frisbi *to play Frisbee*
 jugar al fútbol *to play soccer*
 jugar al fútbol americano *to play football*
 jugar al voleibol *to play volleyball*
 jugar al tenis *to play tennis*
 jugar con la arena *to play in the sand*
 jugar con la nieve *to play in the snow*
 jugar con videojuegos *to play videogames*
el juguete *toy*
el jugo *juice*
julio *July*
junio *June*
junto a *by, next to*
juntos *together*

K

el kilo *kilo*

L

la *the, it, her*
el laberinto *maze*
el laboratorio *laboratory*
el lado *side*

al lado de *next to*
el lago *lake*
la lámpara *lamp*
la lana *wool*
lanzar *to throw*
el lápiz (los lápices) *pencil*
largo(a) *long*
 a lo largo de *along*
las *the, them*
latino(a) *Latin*
el laúd *lute*
el lavaplatos *dishwasher*
lavar *to wash*
 lavarse el pelo *to wash one's hair*
le *to/for him, her, it, you (singular)*
la leche *milk*
la lechuga *lettuce*
leer *to read*
lejos *far away*
 lejos de *far from*
lenta(o) *slow*
los lentes de bucear *diving mask*
los lentes de sol *sunglasses*
les *to/for them, you (plural)*
levantar la mano *to raise a hand*
la leyenda *legend*
la libra *pound*
la librería *bookstore*
el libro *book*
la lija *sandpaper*
la lima *lime*
la limonada *lemonade*
limpiar *to clean*
el lince *lynx*
la línea *line*
la lista *list*
listo(a) *ready*
la literatura *literature*
llamar *to call*
 llamar por teléfono *to call on the telephone*
 llamarse *to be named*
la llegada *arrival*

llegar *to arrive*
llenar *to fill out*
llevar *to carry, to wear*
llover (o>ue) *to rain*
llueve *it rains, it's raining*
 Llueve a cántaros *It's raining cats and dogs*
la lluvia *rain*
 lluvia torrencial *torrential rain*
lo *that, which, it, him*
 lo más *the most*
 Lo siento *I'm sorry*
el lobo *wolf*
los *the, them*
luego *then*
el lugar *place*
 en cualquier lugar *anywhere*
el lujo *luxury*
la luna *moon*
el lunes *Monday*

M

la madera *wood*
la madre *mother*
la madrina *godmother*
el maíz *corn*
la maleta *suitcase*
mal *bad, terrible*
malo(a) *bad*
la mamá *mom*
el mamey *an apricot-like fruit*
el mamífero *mammal*
mandar *to send*
manejar *to drive*
la mano *hand*
la manta *blanket*
la mantequilla *butter*
la manzana *apple*
mañana *tomorrow*
la mañana *morning*
 de la mañana *in the morning*
 por la mañana *in the morning*
el mapa *map*
el maquillaje *makeup*

la **máquina** *machine*
el **mar** *sea*
la **maravilla** *wonder*
el **marisco** *shellfish*
marrón *brown*
el **martes** *Tuesday*
marzo *March*
más *more*
  más...que
    more ... than
  más de... (with a
    number) *more
    than ...*
la **masa** *dough*
la **máscara** *mask*
la **mascota** *pet*
las **matemáticas**
    mathematics
la **materia** *subject*
mayo *May*
la **mayoría** *mostly*
me *to/for me/myself*
el/la **mecánico(a)**
    mechanic
mediano(a) *medium*
el **medio ambiente**
    environment
el **medio de**
    comunicación *media*
medir (e>i) *to
    measure*
mejor...que *better
    ... than*
el **melón** *melon*
menos *less*
  menos de *less than*
    (with a number)
  menos... que *less ...
    than*
el **mensaje** *message*
el **menú** *menu*
el **mercado** *market*
la **merienda** *snack*
el **mes** *month*
  mes pasado *last
    month*
la **mesa** *table*
  mesa de noche
    night table
el/la **mesero(a)**
    waiter/waitress
el **metro** *meter*

el **metro** *subway*
  en metro *on the
    subway, by subway*
la **mezcla** *mixture*
la **mezquita** *mosque*
mi(s) *my*
mí *me*
el **microscopio**
    microscope
el **miembro** *member*
el **miércoles** *Wednesday*
la **migración**
    immigration
la **milla** *mile*
mirar *to watch, to see*
el/la **misionero(a)**
    missionary
el/la **mismo(a)** *same*
la **mochila** *backpack*
la **moda** *style*
  de moda *in style*
moderno(a) *modern*
mojar *to dampen, to
    soak*
molestar *to disturb*
el **momento** *moment*
la **montaña** *mountain*
montar *to ride, to
    mount*
  montar a caballo *to
    ride a horse*
  montar en bicicleta
    to ride a bike
el **monte** *hill*
morado(a) *purple*
mostrar (o>ue) *to
    show*
la **moto** *motorbike*
mover (o>ue) *to
    move*
mucho(a) *a lot*
Mucho gusto *Nice to
    meet you*
muchos(as) *many*
el **mueble** *furniture*
el **muerto** *dead*
la **mujer** *woman*
el **mundo** *world*
el **museo** *museum*
la **música** *music*
  música popular *pop
    music*

música tejana *Texan
    (country) music*
el/la **musulmán/
    musulmana** *Moslem*
muy *very*

N

nació *he/she was born*
nada *nothing*
  de nada *you're
    welcome*
  nada especial
    nothing special
nadar *to swim*
la **naranja** *orange*
la **natación** *swimming*
la **naturaleza** *nature*
la **navegación** *sailing*
navegar *to sail*
la **Navidad** *Christmas*
necesitar *to need*
negro(a) *black*
nevar (e>ie) *to snow*
la **nieve** *snow*
ningún *none*
el/la **niño(a)** *child*
  los niños *children*
el **nivel** *level*
no *no*
  ¿no? *isn't it?/is it?*
  No debes(n) *You
    shouldn't*
  No te olvides de
    Don't forget ...
la **noche** *evening, night*
  **de la noche, por la
    noche** *in the evening,
    at night*
el **nombre** *name*
el **norte** *north*
nos *to/for us/ourselves*
  nos vemos *see you,
    goodbye*
nosotros(as) *we, us*
la **nota** *grade*
el **noticiero** *newscast*
la **novela** *novel*
noviembre *November*
el/la **novio(a)** *boyfriend/
    girlfriend*

la **nube** *cloud*
   nublado(a) *cloudy*
el **nudo** *knot*
   nuestro(a) *our*
   nuevo(a) *new*
el **número** *number*
   **número de
   zapato** *shoe size*
   **número de
   teléfono** *telephone
   number*
   nunca *never*

o *or*
los **objetivos** *objectives*
   obligatorio(a)
   mandatory
la **obra** *work*
   obras de arte *art
   works*
   obras de teatro
   theater plays
la **ocasión** *occasion*
   octubre *October*
   ocupar *to occupy*
el **oeste** *west*
la **oficina** *office*
   oficina de cambio
   exchange office
   **oficina del
   director** *principal's
   office*
el **oficio** *trade*
   ofrecer *to offer*
   oír *to hear*
la **ola** *wave*
la **oración** *sentence*
el **oro** *gold*
   os *yourselves
   (informal, pl.)*
   oscuro(a) *dark*
el **otoño** *fall, autumn*
   otro/otra *other,
   another*
   ¡Oye! *Listen!*

P

el **padre** *father*
los **padres** *parents*

el **padrino** *godfather*
   ¡padrísimo(a)!
   (Mexico) great!
la **página** *page*
   **¿En qué página
   está?** *On what page
   is it?*
el **país** *country*
el **paisaje** *landscape*
el **pájaro** *bird*
   palabras en acción
   words in action
el **palacio** *palace*
la **paleta** *paddle*
el **pan** *bread*
los **pantalones (el
   pantalón)** *pants*
la **papa** *potato*
el **papá** *dad*
el **papalote** *(Mexico)
   kite*
las **papas fritas** *French
   fries*
el **papel** *paper*
   para *for, to*
   **para comunicarnos
   mejor** *for better
   communication*
   para resolver *to
   figure it out, to resolve*
el **paracaídas** *parachute*
la **parada** *stop*
el **paraguas** *umbrella*
   parar *to stop*
   parecer *to seem*
la **pared** *wall*
el/la **pariente(a)** *relative*
el **parque** *park*
   **el parque de
   diversiones**
   amusement park
el **partido** *(sports) game*
el **pasaje** *airline ticket*
el **pasaporte** *passport*
   pasar *to spend, to pass*
   pasar aventuras *to
   have adventures*
la **Pascua** *Easter*
   pasear (por) *to stroll*
   pasear en bote *to
   take a boat ride*
el **pasillo** *hallway*

la **pasta de dientes**
   toothpaste
la **pasta de guava** *guava
   paste*
el **pastel** *cake*
el/la **pata** *(Perú) friend*
el **patinaje** *rollerblading*
   patinar *to skate*
   patinar sobre hielo
   to ice-skate
el **patio** *courtyard*
la **paz** *peace*
   paz mundial *world
   peace*
   pedir (e>i) *to ask for*
   pegar *to glue*
   peinarse *to comb
   one's hair*
el **peine** *comb*
la **película** *movie, film*
el **peligro** *danger*
   en peligro de *in
   danger of*
   peligroso(a)
   dangerous
   pelirrojo(a)
   red-headed
el **pelo** *hair*
la **pelota** *ball*
la **península** *peninsula*
   peor... que *worse . . .
   than*
   pequeño(a) *little,
   small*
   perder (e>ie) *to lose*
   ¡Perdón! *Excuse me!*
   perfectamente
   perfectly
el **perfume** *perfume*
el **periódico** *newspaper*
el **periodismo**
   journalism
   pero *but*
el **perro** *dog*
la **persona** *person*
el **personaje** *character*
   pesar *to weigh*
el **pescado** *fish*
el/la **pescador(a)**
   fisherman, woman
la **peseta** *Spain's
   currency unit*

el peso *Mexican currency unit*
el pez (los peces) *fish*
el piano *piano*
picante *spicy*
el picnic *picnic*
el pico *(mountain) peak*
el pie *foot*
  a pie *on foot, walking*
la piedra *stone*
la piel *skin*
la pintura *painting*
la piña *pineapple*
la piñata *pinata*
la pirámide *pyramid*
la piscina *swimming pool*
el piso *floor*
la pizarra *chalkboard*
la pizza *pizza*
la planta *plant*
la plata *silver*
el plátano *banana*
el plato *plate*
  plato del día *daily special*
  plato principal *main course*
la playa *beach*
la plaza *square*
poco(a) *few*
poder (o>ue) *to be able, can*
el poema *poem*
el pollo *chicken*
el poncho *poncho*
poner *to put, to place*
  poner música *to play music*
  ponerse *to wear, to put on*
póngase de pie *stand up*
popular *popular*
por *by, for*
  por favor *please*
  por medio de *through*
  ¿Por qué? *Why?*
  por supuesto *of course*

porque *because*
el postre *dessert*
practicar *to play, to practice*
  practicar deportes *to play sports*
preferir (e>ie) *to prefer*
la pregunta *question*
el premio Nobel *Nobel Prize*
prepararse *to get ready*
prestar atención *to pay attention*
la primavera *spring*
la primera comunión *first communion*
el/la primero(a) *first*
el/la primo(a) *cousin*
probar (o>ue) *to taste*
la probabilidad *probability*
el problema *problem*
el/la profesor(a) *teacher*
profundo(a) *deep*
el programa *program*
  programa de intercambio *exchange program*
  programa de intercambio estudantil *student exchange program*
el promedio *average*
  promedio de calificaciones *grade point average*
el pronóstico del tiempo *weather forecast*
pronto *soon*
el propósito *purpose*
el protector solar *sunscreen*
publicar *to publish*
el pueblo *town, village*
la puerta *door*
el puesto *booth*
la pulgada *inch*
la pulsera *bracelet*
el punto *(in a game)*

point
el punto de interés *sights*

que *that*
¿Qué? *What?*
  ¡Qué lástima! *What a shame!*
  ¡Qué rollo! (Spain) *What a drag!*
  ¿Qué tal? *How are you doing?*
quedarse *to stay*
querer (e>ie) *to want*
querido(a) *dear*
el queso *cheese*
¿Quién? *Who?*
la química *chemistry*
la quinceañera *sweet sixteen*
el quiosco *newsstand*

la radio *radio, radio station*
la rama *branch*
la rana *frog*
el rancho *ranch*
el rap *rap*
rápido(a) *fast*
el ratón *mouse*
la raza *race*
la razón *reason*
  realidades *from real life*
la rebaja *sale*
  en rebaja *on sale*
el recibo *receipt*
la recomendación *recommendation*
  ¿Recuerdas? *Do you remember?*
el recuerdo *souvenir*
los recuerdos *memories*
la red *net*
el refresco *soft drink*
el refrigerador *refrigerator*

342

regalar *to give a present*
el regalo *gift, present*
la regata *regatta*
el reggae *reggae*
la región *region*
regresar *to return*
regular *so-so*
relajante *relaxing*
relleno(a) *filled*
el reloj *watch, clock*
remar *to row*
el remo *oar*
la reparación *repair*
el/la representante *representative*
el requisito *requirement*
la reserva, *reservation*
la residencia de estudiantes *student dorms*
respetar *to respect*
el restaurante *restaurant*
restaurante de comida rápida *fast food restaurant*
reunirse *to meet*
la revista *magazine*
revista de espectáculos *entertainment magazine*
revista de moda *fashion magazine*
el rey *king*
rico(a) *good, tasty*
el río *river*
el rock duro *hard rock*
rojo(a) *red*
romper *to break*
la ropa *clothing*
el ropero *closet*
rubio(a) *blonde*
la rueda *wheel*
ruidoso(a) *noisy*
la ruina *ruin*

S

el sábado *Saturday*

saber *to know how*
el sabor *flavor*
sacar *to take, to get*
sacar el pasaporte *to get your passport*
sacar fotos *to take pictures*
sacar una buena/ mala nota *to get a good/bad grade*
la sal *salt*
la sala *living room*
la sala de video *video arcade*
la salida *exit*
salida de emergencia *emergency exit*
salir *to go out*
salir a mochilear *(Chile) to go backpacking, to go trekking*
salir temprano *to go out early*
el salón de actos *auditorium*
la salsa *salsa*
la salud *health*
saludar *to greet*
el/la salvavidas *lifeguard*
la sandalia *sandal*
el sándwich *sandwich*
el sarape *shawl*
se *to/for him/her/it/ them, himself, herself, themselves*
se extendió *it spread*
se fundó *it was founded*
secarse *to dry off*
la sección de noticias *news section*
la sed *thirst*
seguir (e>i) *to follow, to continue*
según *according to*
seleccionar *to choose*
la selva *rain forest*
la semana *week*
semana pasada *last week*

semanal *weekly*
el sendero *path*
sensacional *sensational*
sentarse (e>ie) *to sit down*
la señal *signal, street sign*
el señor *Mr.*
la señora *Mrs.*
señoras *ladies*
la señorita *Ms.*
septiembre *September*
ser *to be*
el servicio *restroom*
la servilleta *napkin*
la sevillana *typical dance from Seville*
siempre *always*
el siglo *century*
significar *to mean*
la silla *chair*
el sillón *armchair*
la similitud *similarity*
simpático(a) *nice*
sin *without*
la sinagoga *synagogue*
la situación *situation*
sobre *about, concerning*
sobre todo *above all*
¡Socorro! *Help!*
el sofá *sofa*
el sol *sun*
solamente *only*
la solicitud *application*
solo/sola *alone*
sólo *only*
el sombrero *hat*
sombrero tejano *cowboy hat*
la sombrilla *beach umbrella*
el sonido alto/bajo *high/low pitch*
soñando *dreaming*
la sopa *soup*
la sorpresa *surprise*
el sótano *basement*
su(s) *your (formal), his, her, their*

343

subir *to climb*
la suerte *luck*
el suéter *sweater*
el supermercado *supermarket*
el sur *south*

T

la tabla a vela *sailboard*
  tabla de surf *wind surfing board*
el taco *taco*
  tal vez *perhaps, maybe*
la talla *clothing size*
  talla única *one size*
  también *also, too*
el tambor *drum*
  tampoco *neither*
el tanque de oxígeno *oxygen tank*
la tapa *cover*
el tapiz *tapestry*
  los tapices *tapestries*
la taquería *taco shop*
  tarde *late*
la tarde *afternoon, evening*
  de la tarde, por la tarde *in the afternoon, in the evening*
la tarea *homework*
la tarjeta *greeting card*
  tarjeta de crédito *credit card*
  tarjeta postal *postcard*
el taxi *cab, taxi*
  taxi acuático *ferry*
  en taxi *by taxi*
la taza *cup*
el té *tea*
  te *to/for you; yourself*
el teatro *theater*
el techo *ceiling*
  tejano(a) *from Texas*
la tela *cloth*
el teléfono *telephone*
la teleguía *tv guide*
la telenovela *soap opera*

la televisión *television*
el televisor *television set*
el tema *theme*
la temperatura *temperature*
  temperatura máxima/mínima *high/low temperature*
el templo *temple*
  temprano(a) *early*
  ¡Ten cuidado! *Be careful!*
el tenedor *fork*
  tener *to have*
  tener cuidado *to be careful*
  tener ganas *to feel like . . .*
  tener hambre/sed *to be hungry/thirsty*
  tener miedo *to be afraid*
  tener que *(+ infinitive of another verb) to have to do something*
los tenis *sneakers*
la terraza *terrace*
el terreno montañoso(a) *mountainous terrain*
  ti *you*
el/los tianguis (Mexico) *street market*
el tiempo *weather, time*
la tienda *store, shop*
  tienda de aparatos electrónicos *electronic appliance store*
  tienda de comestibles *grocery store*
  tienda de discos *record store*
la tía *aunt*
el tío *uncle*
  típico(a) *typical*
el tipo *type*
el título *title*
la tiza *chalk*
la toalla *towel*
el tocacintas *cassette player*
tocar (un instrumento musical) *to play (a musical instrument)*
  todavía *still*
  todo(a) *all*
  todos los días *everyday*
tomar *to drink*
  tomar el sol *to sunbathe*
el tomate *tomato*
la tonelada *ton*
la tormenta *storm*
la torre *tower*
la tortilla *tortilla*
la tortuga *turtle*
  trabajar *to work*
el trabajo *work*
  traer *to bring*
el traje de baño *bathing suit*
el trámite *paperwork*
la transmisión *broadcast*
  transparente *transparent*
el tren *train*
  en tren *by train*
  tropical *tropical*
  tú *you*
  tu(s) *your*
el tubo de ensayo *test tube*
el/la tutor(a) *guardian*

U

el/la último(a) *latest, last*
  un/una *a, an, one*
  unos/unas *some*
  usar *to use*
  usted *you* (sing., formal)
  ustedes *you* (pl., formal)

V

  Va a llover/nevar *It's*

going to rain/snow

Va a volver pronto *He/she/it will return soon*

la vainilla *vanilla*

¡Vale! (Spain) *O.K.!*

el valle *valley*

los vaqueros *jeans*

variable *variable*

el vaso *glass*

el vecindario *neighborhood*

el/la vecino(a) *neighbor*

vegetariano(a) *vegeterian*

la vela *candle*

el velero *sail boat*

el/la vendedor(a) *salesperson*

vender *to sell*

venir (e>ie) *to come*

la venta *sale*

la ventaja *advantage*

la ventana *window*

ver *to see*

el verano *summer*

¿verdad? *isn't it/is it?*

verde *green*

la verdura *vegetable*

el vestido *dress*

la vez (las veces) *time, occasion*

  a veces *sometimes*

viajar *to travel*

la victoria *victory*

la videocasetera *video cassette recorder*

el videojuego *videogame*

viejo(a) *old*

el viento *wind*

el viernes *Friday*

la visa *visa*

visitar *to visit*

la vista *view*

  a la vista (de) *in view (of)*

  vista panorámica *panoramic view*

el vistazo *look*

vivir *to live*

el vocabulario *vocabulary*

volar (o>ue) *to fly*

el volcán *volcano*

el voleibol *volleyball*

el volumen *volume*

vosotros(as) *(plural, familiar) you*

la voz (las voces) *voice*

Y

y *and*

ya *already*

ya existía *it already existed*

yo *I*

el yogur *yogurt*

Z

la zapatería *shoe store*

el zapato *shoe*

la zona *zone*

  zona arqueológica *archaeological zone*

346

GLOSARIO INGLÉS-ESPAÑOL

A

a *un, una*
abroad *al extranjero*
to accept *aceptar*
activity *la actividad*
ad *el anuncio*
  classified ad *el anuncio clasificado*
address *la dirección*
to admire *admirar*
adventure *la aventura*
advice *el consejo*
after *después (de)*
afternoon *la tarde*
  good afternoon *buenas tardes*
  in the afternoon *de la tarde, por la tarde*
agency *la agencia*
airport *el aeropuerto*
algebra *el álgebra*
alone *solo(a)*
also *también*
always *siempre*
amazing *increíble*
amusing *divertido(a)*
ancient *antiguo(a)*
another *otro(a)*
to answer *contestar*
answering machine *el contestador automático*
anything else? *¿algo más?*
apartment *el apartamento*
  apartment building *el edificio de apartamentos*
apple *la manzana*
  appliance, electronic *el aparato electrónico*
application *la solicitud*
appointment *la cita*
April *abril*

aquatic *acuático(a)*
armchair *el sillón*
to arrive *llegar*
art *el arte*
  arts and crafts *las artesanías*
to ask for *pedir*
auditorium *el salón de actos*
August *agosto*
aunt *la tía*
autumn *el otoño*
avenue *la avenida*
avocado *el aguacate*
awesome *impresionante*
awful *horrible, fatal*

B

backpack *la mochila*
bag *la bolsa*
ball *la pelota*
balloon *el globo*
banana *el plátano*
barbecue *la barbacoa*
  to have a barbecue *hacer una barbacoa*
bargain *la ganga*
baseball *el béisbol*
  to play baseball *jugar al béisbol*
basement *el sótano*
basketball *el baloncesto*
  to play basketball *jugar al baloncesto*
to bathe *bañarse*
bathing suit *el traje de baño*
bathroom *el cuarto de baño*
bathtub *la bañera*
to be *ser, estar*
  to be hungry *tener hambre*
  to be thirsty *tener sed*
beach *la playa*

  at the beach *en la playa*
beans *los frijoles*
beautiful *hermoso(a)*
because *porque*
bed *la cama*
bedroom *el dormitorio, (Mexico) la recámara*
before *antes de*
to begin *empezar*
behind *detrás de*
below *abajo, debajo*
belt *el cinturón*
better than . . . *mejor que...*
between *entre*
beverage *la bebida*
binder *la carpeta*
biology *la biología*
bird *el pájaro*
birthday *el cumpleaños*
  Happy Birthday! *¡Feliz cumpleaños!*
black *negro(a)*
blackboard *la pizarra*
blanket *la manta*
blonde *rubio(a)*
blouse *la blusa*
blue *azul*
boat *el barco, el bote*
  motorboat *el bote a motor*
  by boat *en bote*
  to take a boat ride *pasear en bote*
book *el libro*
bookstore *la librería*
booth *el puesto*
boots *las botas*
boring *aburrido(a)*
  How boring! *¡Qué aburrido(a)!*
boy *el niño, el chico*
boyfriend *el novio*
bracelet *la pulsera*
bread *el pan*
to break *romper*
breakfast *el desayuno*

347

brochure *el folleto*
brother *el hermano*
brown *marrón*
to **brush one's teeth** *cepillarse los dientes*
bus *el autobús, el camión*
 by bus *en autobús*
but *pero*
butter *la mantequilla*
to **buy** *comprar*

C

cab *el taxi*
cake *el pastel*
calculator *la calculadora*
calendar *el calendario*
to **call (on the telephone)** *llamar por teléfono*
camera *la cámara*
can (to be able to) *poder*
candle *la vela*
candy *el dulce*
cap *la gorra*
capital (city) *la capital*
car *el coche, el carro*
 by car *en coche*
card catalogue *el fichero*
 greeting card *tarjeta*
careful (to be careful) *tener cuidado*
to **carry** *llevar*
cartoons *los dibujos animados*
cash *el dinero en efectivo*
cassette player *el tocacintas*
cat *el gato*
cathedral *la catedral*
celebrate *celebrar*
celebration *la celebración*
centimeter *el centímetro*
cereal *el cereal*
chair *la silla*
chalk *la tiza*
change *el cambio*
to **change** *cambiar*
 to **change the channel**
  cambiar el canal
channel *el canal*
chapter *el capítulo*
check *el cheque*
 traveler's checks *los cheques de viajero*
cheese *el queso*
chemistry *la química*
chess *el ajedrez*
 to play chess *jugar al ajedrez*
chest of drawers *la cómoda*
chicken *el pollo*
choir *el coro*
to **choose** *seleccionar, escoger*
church *la iglesia*
city *la ciudad*
class *la clase*
classroom *el salón de clase*
to **climb** *subir, escalar*
 to climb a mountain *escalar una montaña*
clock *el reloj*
closet *el ropero*
clothing *la ropa*
clothing size *la talla*
cloud *la nube*
 it's cloudy *está nublado*
coast *la costa*
coat *el abrigo*
coffee *el café*
cold *frío(a)*
 it's cold (weather) *hace frío*
colors *los colores*
comb *el peine*
 to comb one's hair *peinarse*
comics *las historietas*
commercial *el anuncio*
compact disc *el disco compacto*
composition *la composición*
computer *la computadora*
 computer science *la informática*
concert *el concierto*

Congratulations! *¡Felicidades!*
consulate *el consulado*
contests *los concursos*
to **continue** *seguir*
to **cook** *cocinar*
cookie *la galleta*
cool *fresco(a)*
 it's cool *hace fresco*
counselor *el/la consejero(a)*
country *el país*
countryside *el campo*
courteous *cortés*
courtyard *el patio*
cousin *el primo, la prima*
credit card *la tarjeta de crédito*
culture *la cultura*
cup *la taza*
custard pie *el flan*
custom *la costumbre*
customs *la aduana*

D

dance *el baile*
to **dance** *bailar*
dangerous *peligroso(a)*
date *la fecha*
daughter *la hija*
day *el día*
December *diciembre*
to **decorate** *decorar*
degree *el grado*
delicious *delicioso(a), rico(a)*
department store *el almacén*
desert *el desierto*
desk *el escritorio*
dessert *el postre*
dictionary *el diccionario*
difficult *difícil*
dining room *el comedor*
dinner *la cena*
discotheque *la discoteca*
dishwasher *el lavaplatos*

348

to **dive** *bucear*
diving mask *el lente de bucear*
to **do** *hacer*
document *el documento*
documentary *el documental*
dog *el perro*
dollar *el dólar*
door *la puerta*
downstairs *abajo*
downtown *el centro*
drawing *el dibujo*
dress *el vestido*
drink *la bebida*
to **drink** *tomar, beber*
to **dry off** *secarse*

E

early *temprano*
earrings *los aretes*
east *el este*
easy *fácil*
to **eat** *comer*
educational *educativo(a)*
egg *huevo*
embroidered *bordado(a)*
emergency exit *la salida de emergencia*
English (language) *el inglés*
Enjoy your meal! *¡Buen provecho!*
enough *bastante*
entertaining *entretenido(a)*
entertainment *el espectáculo*
equipment *el equipo*
eraser *el borrador*
evening *la noche*
  good evening *buenas noches*
  in the evening *por la noche, de la noche*
everyday *todos los días*
everything *todo(a)*
exam *el examen*
to **exchange** *cambiar*

to exchange money *cambiar dinero*
  exchange program *el programa de intercambio*
exciting *emocionante*
excursion *la excursión*
excuse *excusa*
exhibition *la exposición*
exit *la salida*
expensive *caro(a)*
experience *la experiencia*
experiment *el experimento*

F

fabulous *fabuloso(a)*
family *la familia*
famous *famoso(a)*
fantastic *fantástico(a)*
far *lejos*
far from *lejos de*
farm *la granja*
fashion *la moda*
  to be in fashion *estar de moda*
fast *rápido(a)*
father *el padre*
favorite *favorito(a)*
February *febrero*
few *poco(a)*
film *la película*
to **find** *encontrar*
fine *bien*
fins (swimming) *las aletas*
first *el primero/la primera*
fish *el pescado, el pez*
flower *la flor*
to **fly** *volar*
folder *la carpeta*
to **follow** *seguir*
food *la comida*
fast food *la comida rápida*
foot *el pie*
  on foot *a pie*
football *el fútbol americano*
for *para, por*
fork *el tenedor*
fort *el fuerte*

fortress *la fortaleza*
fountain *la fuente*
French (language) *el francés*
French fries *las papas fritas*
fresh *fresco(a)*
Friday *el viernes*
friend *el amigo, la amiga*
frisbee *el frisbi*
  to play frisbee *jugar al frisbi*
from (location) *de,* (time) *desde*
from . . . to *del... al*
fruit *la fruta*
fun *divertido(a)*
  to have fun *divertirse*
furniture *los muebles*

G

game (sports) *el partido*
  game *el juego*
game show *el programa de concursos*
garage *el garaje*
garden *el jardín*
gas station *la gasolinera*
gentleman *caballero*
geography *la geografía*
geometry *la geometría*
gift *el regalo*
girl *la niña, la chica, la muchacha*
to **give** *dar*
  to give a present *regalar*
glass (drinking) *el vaso*
gloves *los guantes*
to **go** *ir*
  to go on a trip *ir de viaje*
  to go shopping *ir de compras*
godfather *el padrino*
godmother *la madrina*
gold *de oro*
good *bueno(a)*

It's so good! *¡Ay, qué rico(a)!*

goodbye *adiós, nos vemos, hasta luego*

grade (for a course in school) *la nota*

to get a good/bad grade *sacar una buena/mala nota*

graduation *la graduación*

grandfather *el abuelo*

grandmother *la abuela*

grandparents *los abuelos*

Great! (expression) *¡Qué bueno! ¡Qué bien!*, (Puerto Rican expression) *¡Qué chévere!*, (Mexican expression) *¡padrísimo!*

green *verde*

greeting card *la tarjeta*

grey *gris*

grocery store *la tienda de comestibles, la bodega*

guest *el/la invitado(a)*

guide *el/la guía*

guitar *la guitarra*

gym *el gimnasio*

H

hair *el pelo*

hallway *el pasillo*

hamburger *la hamburguesa*

hand *la mano*

handbag *el bolso de mano*

handsome *guapo(a)*

hat *el gorro, el sombrero*

to **have** *tener*

to have (to do something) *tener que* (plus infinitive)

health certificate *el certificado médico*

Hello! *¡Hola!*

Help! *¡Socorro!*

to **help** *ayudar*

here *aquí*

Hi! *¡Hola!*

history *la historia*

homework *la tarea*

hot (temperature) *caliente*, (spicy) *picante*, (weather) *calor*

hour *la hora*

house *la casa*

how *cómo*

How are you? (familiar) *¿Cómo estás?*, (formal) *¿Cómo está?*

How's it going? *¿Cómo va?*

How much does it (do they) cost? *¿Cuánto cuesta(n)?*

How old are you? (familiar) *¿Cuántos años tienes?*, (formal) *¿Cuántos años tiene?*

hurricane *el huracán*

I

ice *el hielo*

ice cream *el helado*

idea *la idea*

What a great idea! *¡Qué buena idea!*

ill *enfermo(a)*

in *en*

in front of *delante de*

inch *la pulgada*

inexpensive *barato(a)*

information *la información*

informative *informativo(a)*

inside *dentro de*

intelligent *inteligente*

interesting *interesante*

interview *la entrevista*

invitation *la invitación*

to **invite** *invitar*

itinerary *el itinerario*

J

jacket *la chaqueta*

life jacket *el salvavidas*

January *enero*

jeans *los vaqueros*

to **jet ski** *hacer jet esquí*

jewel *la joya*

jewelry store *la joyería*

juice *el jugo*

July *julio*

June *junio*

K

kind *el tipo*

kitchen *la cocina*

kite *la chiringa, la cometa*

knife *el cuchillo*

to **know** *conocer*

known (well-known) *conocido(a)*

to **know how** *saber*

L

laboratory *el laboratorio*

lady *la dama*

lake *el lago*

lamp *la lámpara*

landscape *el paisaje*

language *el idioma, la lengua*

large *grande*

last *pasado(a)*

last (the) *el pasado, el último/la última*

late *tarde*

later *más tarde*

See you later! *¡Hasta luego!*

to **learn (to do something)** *aprender a*

to **leave** *dejar, salir*

to leave a message *dejar un mensaje*

left *la izquierda*

on the left of *a la izquierda de*
to the left *a la izquierda*
turn left *dobla a la izquierda*
lemonade *la limonada*
less . . . than *menos... que*
Let's go! *¡Vamos!*
letter *la carta*
lettuce *la lechuga*
library *la biblioteca*
lifeguard (person) *el/la salvavidas*
to like *gustar*
to listen *escuchar*
literature *la literatura*
little *poco*
 a little *un poco*
to live *vivir*
living room *la sala*
locker *el armario*
long *largo(a)*
to look (at) *mirar*
to look for *buscar*
luck *la suerte*
 What bad luck! *¡Qué mala suerte!*
 What luck! *¡Qué suerte!*
lunch *el almuerzo*

M

magazine *la revista*
to make *hacer*
makeup *el maquillaje*
man *hombre, señor*
many *muchos(as)*
map *el mapa*
March *marzo*
market *el mercado,* (Mexican word) *el/los tianguis*
mask *la máscara*
May *mayo*
meal *la comida*
meat *la carne*
media *los medios de comunicación*

medicine *el medicamento*
medium *mediano(a)*
to meet *encontrarse, conocer a alguien*
message *el mensaje*
meter *el metro*
microscope *el microscopio*
milk *la leche*
milkshake *el batido*
mineral water *el agua mineral*
mirror *el espejo*
modern *moderno(a)*
mole *el mole*
Monday *el lunes*
monthly *mensual*
more *más*
 more . . . than *más... que*
morning *la mañana*
 good morning *buenos días*
 in the morning *de/por la mañana*
mother *la madre*
motorbike *la moto*
mountain *la montaña*
mountain range *la cordillera*
mouse *el ratón*
movie *la película*
 movie theater *el cine*
Miss *Señorita*
Mr. *Señor*
Mrs. *Señora*
museum *el museo*
music *la música*

N

name *el nombre*
 last name *el apellido*
 my name is . . . *me llamo...*
 What's your name? (formal) *¿Cómo se llama?,* (familiar) *¿Cómo te llamas?*

napkin *la servilleta*
near *cerca de*
nearby *cerca*
necklace *el collar*
necktie *la corbata*
to need *necesitar*
neighbor *el vecino, la vecina*
neighborhood *el vecindario*
neither *tampoco*
net *la red*
never *nunca*
new *nuevo(a)*
news *las noticias*
 news section *la sección de noticias*
newscast *el noticiero*
newspaper *el periódico, el diario*
newsstand *el quiosco*
next to *al lado de*
nice (person) *simpático(a)*
 Nice to meet you *Encantado(a), Mucho gusto*
night *la noche*
 good night *buenas noches*
 in the night, at night *de la noche, por la noche*
 last night *anoche*
noisy *ruidoso(a)*
north *el norte*
not yet *todavía no*
notebook *el cuaderno*
notes *los apuntes*
nothing *nada*
 nothing special *nada especial*
novel *la novela*
November *noviembre*
now *ahora, en este momento*
number *el número*

O

oar *el remo*
occasion *la ocasión*
October *octubre*
of *de*
  Of course! *¡Claro que sí!*
office *la oficina*
O.K. (expression of Spain)
    ¡Vale!
old *viejo(a)*
on top of *encima de*
once *una vez*
only *sólo(a), solamente*
to **open** *abrir*
orange (color)
    anaranjado(a),
    (fruit) *la naranja*
to **order** *pedir*
other *otro(a)*
outdoors *al aire libre*
outside of *fuera de*

P

paddle *la paleta*
  to play paddleball
    jugar a las paletas
page *la página*
palace *el palacio*
pants *los pantalones*
paper *el papel*
paperwork *los trámites*
parachute *el paracaídas*
to **parasail** *hacer*
    parasailing
parents *los padres*
  parents permission
    autorización de los padres
park *el parque*
to **participate** *participar*
party *la fiesta*
  to have a party *hacer*
    una fiesta
passport *el pasaporte*
patio *el patio*
peanut *el cacahuate*
pen *el bolígrafo*

pencil *el lápiz*
perfectly *perfectamente*
perfume *el perfume*
perhaps *tal vez*
permission
  la autorización
pet *la mascota*
pharmacy *la farmacia*
photo *la foto*
photocopy *la fotocopia*
physical education
  la educación física
picnic *el picnic*
  to have a picnic
    hacer un picnic
pin *el broche*
pineapple *la piña*
place *el lugar*
plane *el avión*
  by plane *en avión*
plan *el plan*
plant *la planta*
plate *el plato*
to **play** *jugar*
  to play sports (in general)
    practicar deportes
  to play an instrument
    tocar un instrumento
  to play piano *tocar el*
    piano
  to play the guitaar *tocar*
    la guitarra
plaza *la plaza*
please *por favor*
pleasure *el gusto*
poem *el poema*
pop music *la música*
  popular
popular *popular*
post office *el correo*
postcard *la tarjeta postal*
poster *el cartel*
potato *la papa*
pound *la libra*
to **practice** *practicar*
to **prefer** *preferir*
pretty *bonito(a)*
principal (main) *principal*
  (of a school) *el/la*
  director(a) de escuela

problem *el problema*
product *el producto*
program *el programa*
  programming (TV)
    la programación
purple *morado(a)*

Q

quite *bastante*

R

radio *la radio*
rain *la lluvia*
to **rain** *llover*
rain forest *la selva*
raincoat *el impermeable*
ranch *el rancho, la finca*
rather *bastante*
to **read** *leer*
ready *listo(a)*
to get ready *prepararse*
realistic *realista*
receipt *el recibo*
recommendation *la*
  recomendación
red *rojo(a)*
refrigerator *el refrigerador*
relaxing *relajante*
remote control *el*
  control remoto
to **rent** *alquilar*
report *el informe*
representative *el/la*
  representante
reservation *la*
  reservación, la reserva
to **respect** *respetar*
restaurant *el restaurante*
restroom *el servicio*
to **return** *volver*
rice *el arroz*
right *la derecha*
  on the right of *a la*
    derecha de
  to the right *a la derecha*

turn right *dobla a la derecha*
right? *¿verdad?*
ring *el anillo*
river *el río*
romantic *romántico(a)*
to row *remar*
rug *la alfombra*

S

to sail *navegar*
sail boat *el velero*
salad *la ensalada*
sale *la rebaja*
 on sale *en rebaja*
salesperson *el/la vendedor(a)*
salsa *la salsa*
sand *la arena*
sandwich *el sándwich*
Saturday *el sábado*
schedule *el horario*
school *la escuela*
sculpture *la escultura*
sea *el mar*
season *la estación*
section *la sección*
semester *el semestre*
September *septiembre*
to set *poner*
 to set the table *poner la mesa*
shampoo *el champú*
to share *compartir*
shelves *los estantes*
shirt *la camisa*
 t-shirt *la camiseta*
shoe store *la zapatería*
shoes *los zapatos*
shopping center *el centro comercial*
short *bajo(a), corto(a)*
show *el espectáculo*
to shower *ducharse*
sign, signal *la señal*
silver *de plata*
to sing *cantar*

sink *el fregadero*
sister *la hermana*
size (clothes) *la talla*
to skate *patinar*
 to ice skate *patinar sobre hielo*
ski *el esquí*
to ski *esquiar*
to skin-dive *bucear*
skirt *la falda*
slow *lento(a)*
sneakers *los tenis*
snorkel *el esnórquel*
snow *la nieve*
to snow *nevar*
soap *el jabón*
soap opera *la telenovela*
soccer *el fútbol*
 to play soccer *jugar al fútbol*
soda *el refresco*
sofa *el sofá*
soft *suave*
sometimes *a veces*
son *el hijo*
soon *pronto*
sorry (I'm sorry) *lo siento*
soup *la sopa*
south *el sur*
souvenir *el recuerdo*
Spanish (language) *el español*
special *especial*
spectacular *espectacular*
to spend *pasar*
 to spend money *gastar dinero*
 to spend time *pasar el tiempo*
spicy *picante*
spoon *la cuchara*
sports *los deportes*
spring *la primavera*
stadium *el estadio*
station *la estación*
to stay (at home) *quedarse (en casa)*
steak *el bistec*
stereo *el estéreo*
still *todavía*

stone *la piedra*
stop *la parada*
 bus stop *la parada de autobús*
store *la tienda*
storm *la tormenta*
story *el cuento*
stovetop *la estufa*
straight *derecho(a)*
street *la calle*
street fair *la feria*
student *el/la estudiante*
 student exchange agency *la agencia de intercambio*
studies *los estudios*
to study *estudiar*
suburbs *las afueras*
subway *el metro*
 by subway *en metro*
suitcase *la maleta*
summer *el verano*
sun *el sol*
 it's sunny *hace sol*
to sunbathe *tomar el sol*
Sunday *el domingo*
sunglasses *los lentes de sol*
sunscreen *el protector solar*
supermarket *el supermercado*
to surf *hacer surf*
surfboard *la tabla de surf*
sweater *el suéter*
sweet *dulce*
to swim *nadar*
swimming pool *la piscina*

T

table *la mesa*
table cloth *la manta*
taco *el taco*
taco shop *la taquería*
to take *tomar*
 to take a bath *bañarse*
 to take a shower *ducharse*

353

to take a walk *pasear (por)*

to take pictures *sacar fotos*

to **talk** *hablar*

to **talk on the phone** *hablar por teléfono*

talk show *el programa de entrevistas*

tall *alto(a)*

tape cassette *la cinta*

tapestry *el tapiz*

taxi *el taxi*

taxi stand *la parada de taxis*

by taxi *en taxi*

tea *el té*

teacher *el/la profesor(a)*

team *el equipo*

telephone *el teléfono*

television *la televisión*

television set *el televisor*

temperature *la temperatura*

maximum temperature *la temperatura máxima*

minimum temperature *la temperatura mínima*

test tube *el tubo de ensayo*

thank you *gracias*

that *ese/esa/eso*

the *el/la/los/las*

theater (movies) *el cine*, (plays, events) *el teatro*

then *luego*

there (over there) *allí*

there is, there are *hay*

these *estos/estas*

thing *la cosa*

this *este/esta/esto*

those *esos/esas, aquellos/aquellas*

Thursday *el jueves*

ticket *el boleto*

airline ticket *el pasaje*

theater ticket *la entrada*

time *la hora*

at what time *a qué hora*

one time *una vez*

toilet *el inodoro*

tomato *el tomate*

tomorrow *mañana*

see you tomorrow *hasta mañana*

tooth *el diente*

toothbrush *el cepillo de dientes*

toothpaste *la pasta de dientes*

towel *la toalla*

town square *la plaza*

train *el tren*

by train *en tren*

to **travel** *viajar*

travel agent *el/la agente de viajes*

travel brochure *el folleto turístico*

tree *el árbol*

trip *el viaje, la excursión*

Tuesday *el martes*

tuna *el atún*

to **turn up (the volume)** *subir (el volumen)*

turn down (the volume) *bajar (el volumen)*

turtle *la tortuga*

tv program guide *la teleguía*

typical *típico(a)*

U

umbrella *el paraguas*

beach umbrella *la sombrilla*

uncle *el tío*

under *debajo de*

underneath, below *debajo*

to **understand** *comprender*

up to *hasta*

upstairs *arriba*

usually *generalmente*

V

valley *el valle*

vanilla *la vainilla*

vegetables *las verduras*

very *muy*

vest (under jacket) *el chaleco*

video cassette recorder *la videocasetera*

video game *el videojuego*

view *la vista*

panoramic view *la vista panorámica*

violent *violento(a)*

to **visit** *visitar*

vocabulary *el vocabulario*

volleyball *el voleibol*

to play volleyball *jugar al voleibol*

volume *el volumen*

to turn up/down the volume *subir/bajar el volumen*

W

waiter, waitress *el/la mesero(a)*

wall *la pared*

to **walk** *caminar*

to **want** *querer*

to **wash one's hair** *lavarse el pelo*

watch *el reloj*

to **watch** *mirar, ver*

to **water-ski** *hacer esquí acuático*

wave *la ola*

weather *el tiempo*

weather forecast *el pronóstico del tiempo*

the weather is nice/bad *hace buen/mal tiempo*

What is the weather like? *¿Qué tiempo hace?*

wedding *la boda*

wedding anniversary
  el aniversario de boda
Wednesday *el miércoles*
week *la semana*
  last week *la semana
  pasada*
weekend *el fin de
  semana*
to **weigh** *pesar*
welcome *bienvenido(a)*
  you're welcome *de nada*
well *bien*
west *el oeste*
What a drag! *¡Qué rollo!*
What a shame!
  ¡Qué lástima!
when *cuando*
when? *¿cuándo?*
where? *¿adónde?, ¿dónde?*
  where are you from?
  ¿de dónde eres?
  where are you going?
  ¿adónde vas?
  where is it? *¿dónde está?*
white *blanco(a)*
Who? *¿Quién?*
Why? *¿Por qué?*
to **win** (a game) *ganar
  (el partido)*
wind *el viento*
  it's windy *hace viento*
to **windsurf** *hacer tabla a
  vela*
windsurfing board *la tabla
  a vela*
winter *el invierno*
with *con*
  with me *conmigo*
  with you (familiar)
  contigo, (formal) *con
  usted*
woman *la señora, la mujer*
wood *la madera*
wool *la lana*
work *el trabajo*
to **work** *funcionar*
worse *peor*
  worse than . . . *peor que...*
to **write** *escribir*

Y

year *el año*
yellow *amarillo(a)*
yesterday *ayer*
yogurt *el yogur*
young *joven*

Z

zip code *el código postal*

355

ÍNDICE

Note: unless otherwise specified, verbs are in the present tense.
For irregular verbs, see the infinitive form.

A

a: use of **a** after **conocer** preceding a noun referring to a person 100
al (**a** + **el**) 50, 164

adjectives
  agreement with nouns 20, 98
  comparison of adjectives with **más/menos...que** 242
  demonstrative adjectives **este, estos, esta(s), ese, esos, esa(s)** 260
  plural formation 20, 98
  possessive adjectives
    mi, tu, su 15, 118
    mis, tus, sus 21, 118
    nuestro(a, os, as) 118
    su(s) to mean it 118
  superlative constructions 308

agreement
  adjectives with nouns 20, 98
  definite articles with nouns 5
  indefinite articles with nouns 19
  muchos(as) 29
  pocos(as) 29

possessive adjectives
  mi(s), tu(s), su(s) 21, 118
  su(s) to mean *their* 118
  nuestro(s), nuestra(s) 118
alphabet (Spanish) 38

articles
  definite (**el, la, los, las**) 5
  indefinite (**un, una**) 19

C

commands
  informal (**tú**) commands for regular verbs (affirmative commands) 166
  informal (**tú**) commands for irregular verbs 292
  no debes + the infinitive of another verb 166
  tener que 166
conocer all forms 100

D

dar (present and preterite) 262
de used to show origin 11
(no) debes 166
decir 290
del (**de** + **el**) 116
demonstrative adjectives **este, estos, esta(s), ese, esos, esa(s)** 260
demostrative pronouns **ésta, éste** 19

E

estar
  estoy, estás, está 9
  all forms 116
  present progressive 308
  estar contrasted with **ser** 310

G

gender
  adjectives (agreement with nouns) 20, 98
  articles (agreement with nouns) 5
  nouns 5

gustar
  gusta with **me, te, le** + infinitive of another verb 17, 68
  gusta with **no** 16, 68
  gusta(n) with **me, te, le** + noun 68
  use of **a mí, a ti, a usted, a él, a ella** or **a** + name of a person for emphasis or clarity 68
  gusta with **nos, les** + infinitive of another verb 164
  use of **a ustedes, a ellos, a ellas** or **a** + name of a person for emphasis or clarity 164

H

hacer present tense 100, preterite 196
hay 28

I

interrogatives
  adónde 50; **cómo** 7; **cuál** 7; **de qué** 29; **dónde** 4; **cuándo** 23; **cuánto(s)** 12, 18, 19, 31; **por qué; qué** 7
ir
  present tense (with **a** plus name of place and with **a** plus infinitive) 50
  preterite 260
  question (**¿adónde?**) with **ir** 50

CREDITS

Contributing Writers
Pilar Álamo, Luisa N. Alfonso, Adrián Collado, Eva Gasteazoro, Ron Horning, Saskia Gorospe-Rombouts, Stephen McGroarty, Daniel Montoya, Nela Navarro-LaPointe, Mariana Pavetto, Candy Rodó, Isabel Sampedro, Jeff Segall, Tanya Torres, Pedro Valiente, Walter Vega

Contributing Editors
Inés Greenberger
José Luis Benavides, Raquel Díez, Claudia DoCampo, Richard deFuria, Eva Garriga, Andrea Heiss, Elvira Ortiz, Margaret Maujenest, Sharon Montoya, Andrés Palomino, Timothy Patrick, Mercedes Roffé, Vincent Smith, Marta Vengoechea

Design/Production
Design: **Rhea Banker,**
Chuck Yuen, Sandra Schmitt
Production Management: Helen Breen,
Jo Ann Hauck
Electronic Production: Gwen Waldron,
Lynne Torrey
Photo Research: Rory Maxwell, Elisa Frohlich,
Omni-Photo Communications

Editorial and Design Development
Curriculum Concepts, New York

Text Credits
Grateful acknowledgment is made to the following for permission to reprint copyrighted material:
El Museo del Barrio; Logo and information concerning membership and cultural mission of El Museo del Barrio, New York City used with permission.
MTV Latino, Inc.; MTV Latino and program titles:

Conexión™, MTV Clásico™, MTV Afuera™, Semana Rock™, and Insomnia™ are used by permission. © 1995 MTV Networks. MTV Networks, a division of Viacom International Inc. All Rights Reserved.
The Miami Herald Publishing Company; Copy and titles from El Nuevo Herald pages. Reprinted with permission of The Miami Herald.
Note: Every effort has been made to locate the copyright owner of material printed in this book. Omissions brought to our attention will be corrected in subsequent printings.

Art Credits
044 Nancy Doniger; 048 Manuel King; 062 Nancy Doniger; 062 Mike Quon; 067 Jennifer Bolten; 083 Janine Cabossel; 084 Barbara Samanovich; 086-087 Janine Cabossel; 092 Nancy Doniger; 096 Fanny Berry; 101 Barbara Samanovich; 110 Nancy Doniger; 110 Mike Quon; 114 Manuel King; 118 Teresa Berasi; 134-135 Janine Cabossel; 140 Nancy Doniger; 140 Mike Quon; 144 Darius Detwiler; 149 Scott MacNeil; 152 Scott MacNeil; 158 Nancy Doniger; 162 George Thompson; 165 Nancy Doniger; 182-183 Janine Cabossel; 192 Tim Eagon; 206 Nancy Doniger; 206 Mike Quon; 210 Philip Scheuer; 215 Philip Scheuer; 230-231 Janine Cabossel; 237 Nancy Doniger; 243 Loretta Gomez; 254 Nancy Doniger; 258 Ann Stanley; 261 Nancy Doniger; 262-263 Rita Lascaro; 278-279 Janine Cabossel; 284 Nancy Doniger; 302 Nancy Doniger; 306 Fanny Berry; 311 Nancy Doniger; 326-327 Janine Cabossel
Encuentros Art Chris Reed
Maps by Monotype Composition Company, Inc.

Photo credits
xxx bottom center Robert Frerck/Odyssey/Chicago; xxx bottom left Robert Frerck/Woodfin Camp and Associates, Inc.; xxx bottom right Henry Cordero; xxx top Robert Frerck/Odyssey/Chicago; xxx-xxxi Superstock; xxxi bottom left Vera Lentz; xxxi bottom right Daniel Aubry/Odyssey/Chicago; xxxi center Anna Elias; xxxi top Robert Frerck/Odyssey/Chicago; 000cover bottom left J.H.(Pete) Carmichael/The Image Bank; 000cover bottom right George Holton/Photo Researchers, Inc.; 000cover center left Ira Block/The Image Bank; 000cover center right Henry Cordero; 000cover top Michal Heron; 001 Johnny Stockshooter/International Stock; 002 Rocio Escobar; 003 Anna Elias; 006 Anna Elias; 007 Cristina Salvador; 010 bottom Anna Elias; 010 center left Giuliano du Portu; 010 center right Anna Elias; 010 top left Anna Elias; 010 top right Colin Fisher; 011 left Giuliano du Portu; 011 right Anna Elias; 012 bottom left Giuliano du Portu; 012 bottom left center Christine Galida; 012 bottom right Cristina Salvador; 012 bottom right center Cristina Salvador; 012 top Giuliano du Portu; 013 Anna Elias; 014 Colin Fisher; 033 Colin Fisher; 040 bottom left Stephen Ogilvy; 040 center bottom Stephen Ogilvy; 040-041 Robert Frerck/Odyssey; 042-043 Colin Fisher; 043 bottom Colin Fisher; 043 center Henry Cordero; 043 top Michal Heron; 044-045 Michal Heron; 046 left Henry Cordero; 046 right Henry Cordero; 046-047 bottom Michal Heron; 046-47 top Henry Cordero; 047 bottom Henry Cordero; 047 top Michal Heron; 052 bottom Colin Fisher; 052 top Henry Cordero; 053 Rob Gage/FPG International; 055 bottom Colin Fisher; 056 Michal Heron; 058 Lou Bopp; 058 Henry Cordero; 058 bottom Colin Fisher; 058 center Colin Fisher; 058 top Colin Fisher; 059 Dennie Cody/FPG International; 060-061 Colin Fisher; 061 bottom Colin Fisher; 061 bottom center Colin Fisher; 061 center Michal Heron; 061 top Christine Galida; 061 top center Henry Cordero; 062-063 Christine Galida; 064 bottom Michal Heron; 064 center Henry Cordero; 064 left Henry Cordero; 064 top right Henry Cordero; 065 Colin Fisher; 068 Michal Heron; 071 bottom Bob Daemmrich; 071 top Colin Fisher; 073 1995

358

Photodisc, Inc.; 076 left Colin Fisher; 076 right Colin Fisher; 076-077 Henry Cordero; 078 Henry Cordero; 078-079 Doug Bryant; 079 bottom Colin Fisher; 079 center Colin Fisher; 079 top Michal Lustbader/Photo Researchers, Inc.; 080 bottom Henry Cordero; 080 top Michal Heron; 081 top left Michal Heron; 081 top right Tim Davis/Photo Researchers, Inc.; 081bottom Colin Fisher; 083 Mexican Government Tourism Office; 085 bottom left Colin Fisher; 085 bottom right Colin Fisher; 085 top left Colin Fisher; 085 top right Colin Fisher; 086 bottom left Courtesty of Elena Climent; 086 top left Robert Frerck/Odyssey/Chicago; 087 bottom right Joel Rogers/Tony Stone Images; 087 top right Henry Cordero; 088 left 1995 PhotoDisc, Inc.; 088 right Michael Friedman; 088-089 David Muench; 090-091 Robert Frerck/Odyssey/Chicago; 091 bottom Robert Frerck/Odyssey/Chicago; 091 bottom center Henry Cordero; 091 center Lou Bopp; 091 top Henry Cordero; 091 top Henry Cordero; 091 top center Henry Cordero; 091 top center Henry Cordero; 092-093 Henry Cordero; 094 bottom Courtesy of Gloria Mendez; 094 bottom center Christine Galida; 094 center Personal Collection; 094 top Courtesty of Pilar Alamo; 094 top center Henry Cordero; 095 Arthur Tilley/FPG International; 098 Lou Bopp; 099 Stephen Simpson; 100 1995 PhotoDisc, Inc.; 101 bottom 1995 PhotoDisc, Inc.; 101 top 1995 PhotoDisc, Inc.; 102 Henry Cordero; 102 Shelley Rotner; 102 Shelley Rotner; 106 left Jack Parsons/Omni-Photo Communications, Inc.; 106 right Robert Frerck/Odyssey/Chicago; 108-109 Henry Cordero; 109 bottom center Reagan Bradshaw; 109 top Shelley Rotner; 109 top center Christine Galida; 110-111 Shelley Rotner; 116 Christine Galida; 119 Reagan Bradshaw; 122 left Stephen Ogilvy; 122 right 1995 PhotoDisc, Inc.; 122-123 1995 PhotoDisc, Inc.; 124 bottom Christine Galida; 124 top Robert Reiff/FPG International; 126-127 Al Rendon/Southwest Images; 127 bottom Superstock; 127 center Arista Texas; 127 top Henry Cordero; 128 left Clark Evans; 128 right San Antonio Convention & Visitors Bureau; 129 bottom Clark Evans; 129 bottom center Superstock; 129 center Clark Evans; 129 top John P. Endress/The Stock Market; 129 top center Henry Cordero; 131 bottom Ken Karp; 131 top 1995 PhotoDisc, Inc.; 132 Henry Cordero; 133 bottom center Henry Cordero; 133 bottom left Henry Cordero; 133 bottom right Henry Cordero; 133 top center Henry Cordero; 133 top left Henry Cordero; 133 top right Henry Cordero; 134 Thomas Dimock/The Stock Market; 134-135 Christine Galida; 135 bottom Lowell Wolff; 135 top Bruce Hands/Stock Boston; 136-137 Robert Frerck/Odyssey/Chicago; 137 left Lou Bopp; 137 right Lou Bopp; 138-139 Bill Romerhaus/North Shore Photography; 139 bottom Henry Cordero; 139 center Markus Boesch/Allsport; 139 top Ulli Seer/Tony Stone Images; 139 top center Mitchel Layton/Duomo; 140-141 Tony Stone Images; 142 bottom left David Madison/Tony Stone Images; 142 bottom right Steve Lucas/International Stock Photo; 142 center Ulli Seer/Tony Stone Images; 142 top left James Andrew Bareham/Tony Stone Images; 142 top right Sunstar/Leo de Wys Inc.; 143 Bachmann/PhotoEdit; 146 Suzanne Vlamis/International Stock Photo; 149 1995 PhotoDisc, Inc.; 150 Paul Barton/The Stock Market; 151 Markus Boesch/Allsport; 152 Lou Bopp; 154 left Michael Ponzini/Focus on Sports; 154 right Mitchel Layton/Duomo; 155 left Henry Cordero; 155 right Henry Cordero; 156-157 Chris Huxley/Leo de Wys Inc.; 157 top Harvey Lloyd/The Stock Market; 158-159 Harvey Lloyd/The Stock Market; 160 Henry Cordero; 164 Paco Elvira; 165 Anna Elias; 166 David Young-Wolff/PhotoEdit; 167 Grace Davies/Omni-Photo Communications, Inc.; 168 Thomas R. Fletcher/Stock Boston; 170-171 Comstock; 171 Farrell Grehan/Photo Researchers, Inc.; 172 Henry Cordeo; 174 Frans Lanting/Photo Researchers, Inc.; 174-175 Thomas R. Fletcher/Stock Boston; 175 bottom Raymond A. Mendez/Animals Animals; 175 center Fenton Furrer; 175 top center J. C. Carton/Bruce Coleman Inc.; 175 top right Suzanne Murphy-Larronde/DDB Stock Photos; 176 bottom Wolfgang Kaehler; 176 center Fenton Furrer; 176 top Suzanne Murphy-Larronde/DDB Stock Photo; 176-177 John Mitchell/Photo Researchers Inc.; 177 Wolfgang Kaehler; 179 Arthur Tilley/FPG; 180 bottom center Stephen Ogilvy; 180 bottom left Stephen Ogilvy; 180 bottom right Stephen Ogilvy; 180 top Bob Daemmrich/Stock Boston; 181 bottom center Stephen Ogilvy; 181 bottom left Stephen Ogilvy; 181 bottom right Stephen Ogilvy; 181 center Stephen Ogilvy; 181 top Bill Galley/Stock Boston; 182 Courtesy of Nancy Hoffman Gallery; 182-183 Douglas Faulkner/Photo Researchers, Inc.; 183 bottom David Young-Wolff/PhotoEdit; 183 top Dr. Seth Shostak/Science Photo Library/Photo Researchers, Inc.; 184 left Anna Elias; 184 right Stephen Ogilvy; 184-185 Oliver Benn/Tony Stone Images; 186-187 Anna Elias; 187 bottom Anna Elias; 187 center Anna Elias; 187 top Anna Elias; 187 top center Paco Elvira; 188-189 Joseph Razzo; 190 bottom left Anna Elias; 190 bottom right Anna Elias; 190 center left Anna Elias; 190 center left Anna Elias; 190 center right Anna Elias; 190 top left Anna Elias; 190 top right Courau/Explorer/Photo Researchers, Inc.; 194 Anna Elias; 196 Anna Elias; 199 Jim Cummins/FPG International; 200 Anna Elias; 201 Anna Elias; 201 bottom left Anna Elias; 201 bottom right Anna Elias; 201 top left Anna Elias; 201 top right Anna Elias; 202 Anna Elias; 204-205 Paco Elvira; 205 center Anna Elias; 205 top Anna Elias; 205 top center Paco Elvira; 206-207 Anna Elias; 212-213 Paco Elvira; 213 Jim Cummins/FPG International; 214 Anna Elias; 217 Anna Elias; 218 bottom M. Zapke/Image Pool Andalusia; 218 top Anna Elias; 218-219 Anna Elias; 218-219 bottom Robert Frerck/Odyssey/Chicago; 219 bottom Anna Elias; 219 top Adam Woolfitt/International Stock Photo; 220 David Simson/Stock Boston; 222-223 Romilly Lockyer/The Image Bank; 223 bottom Anna Elias;